PRENTICE HALL

Earth Science

Prentice Hall

Earth Science

Charles R. Coble

Dean of School of Education
East Carolina University
Greenville, North Carolina

Dale R. Rice

Department of Curriculum and Teaching
Auburn University
Auburn University, Alabama

Kenneth J. Walla

Science Coordinator
Lamar Consolidated School District
Rosenberg, Texas

Elaine G. Murray

Earth Science Consultant
Missoula, Montana

Prentice Hall
Englewood Cliffs, New Jersey
Needham, Massachusetts

Prentice Hall Earth Science Program

Student Text and Annotated Teacher's Edition

Laboratory Manual with Annotated Teacher's Edition

Teacher's Resource Book

Test Bank with Software and DIAL-A-TEST™ Service

Earth Science Critical Thinking Skills Transparencies

Earth Science Courseware

Other programs in this series

Prentice Hall Life Science © 1991

Prentice Hall Physical Science © 1991

Prentice Hall Earth Science presents science as a process that involves research, experimentation, and the development of theories that can hold great explanatory and predictive powers. This approach reflects the challenges and intellectual rewards available to students in the ever-changing discipline of science.

Photo credits begin on p. 632

The photograph on the cover shows the sun rising over Monument Valley Tribal Park in Arizona. (Tom Till)

SECOND EDITION

ISBN 0-13-713835-0

10 9 8 7 6 5 4 3 2

Prentice Hall
A Division of Simon & Schuster
Englewood Cliffs, New Jersey 07632

Earth Science Reviewers

John K. Bennett
Science Specialist
State Department of Tennessee
Cookeville, Tennessee

Steven Carlson
Earth Science Instructor
Estacada Junior High
Estacada, Oregon

Edward A. Dalton
President
National Energy Foundation
Salt Lake City, Utah

John Leo Davis
Science Instructor
Monroe Central School
Parker City, Indiana

Linda Grant
National Science Consultant
Bedford, Texas

David LaHart
Senior Instructor
Florida Solar Energy Center
Cape Canaveral, Florida

Edee Wiziecki
Science Instructor
Columbia Middle School
Champaign, Illinois

David Batch
Director
Abrams Planetarium
East Lansing, Michigan

Reading Consultant

Patricia N. Schwab
Director of Undergraduate Advisement and Lecturer
University of South Carolina
Columbia, South Carolina

Contents

UNIT ONE Exploring the Universe **2–119**

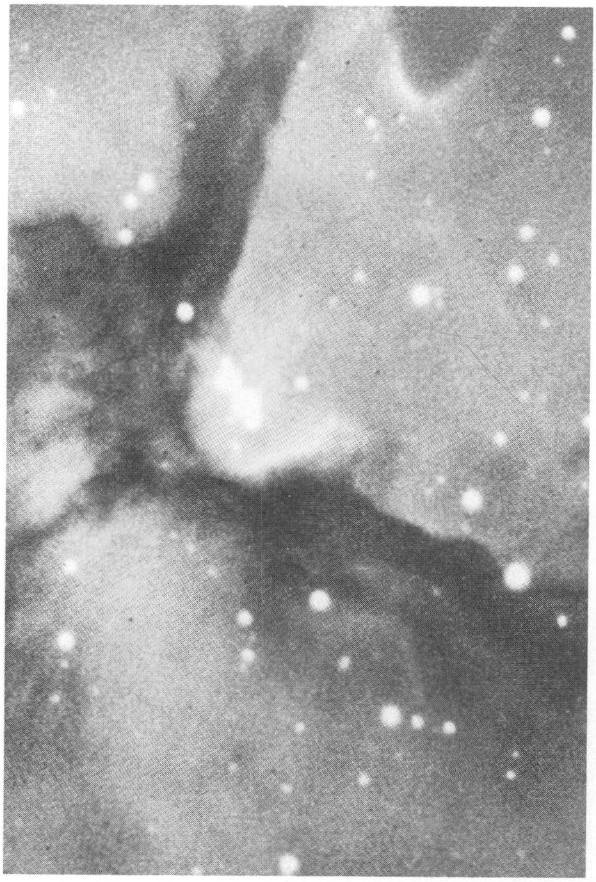

UNIT FOUR The Changing Earth: Surface Activity 320-437

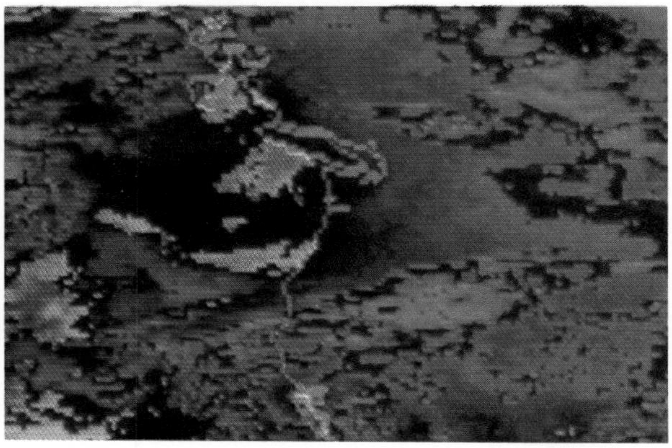

UNIT FIVE The Changing Earth: Subsurface Activity 438–501

UNIT SIX History of the Earth 502–545

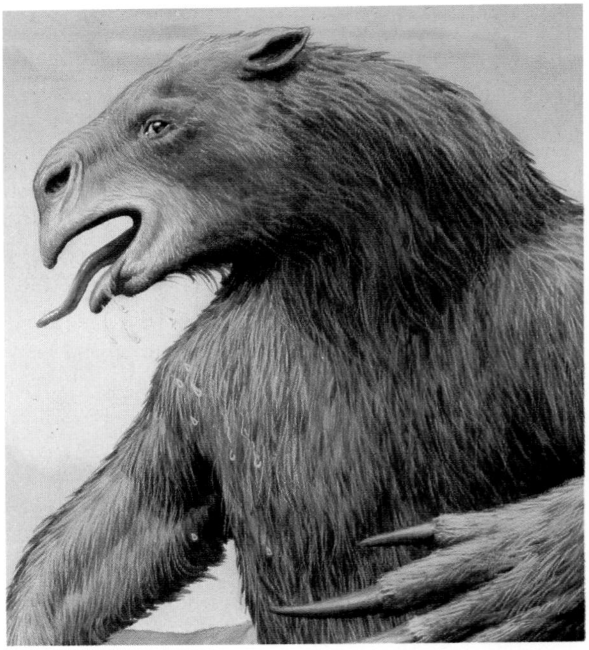

UNIT SEVEN New Directions in Earth Science 546–593

Reference Section 594

UNIT ONE

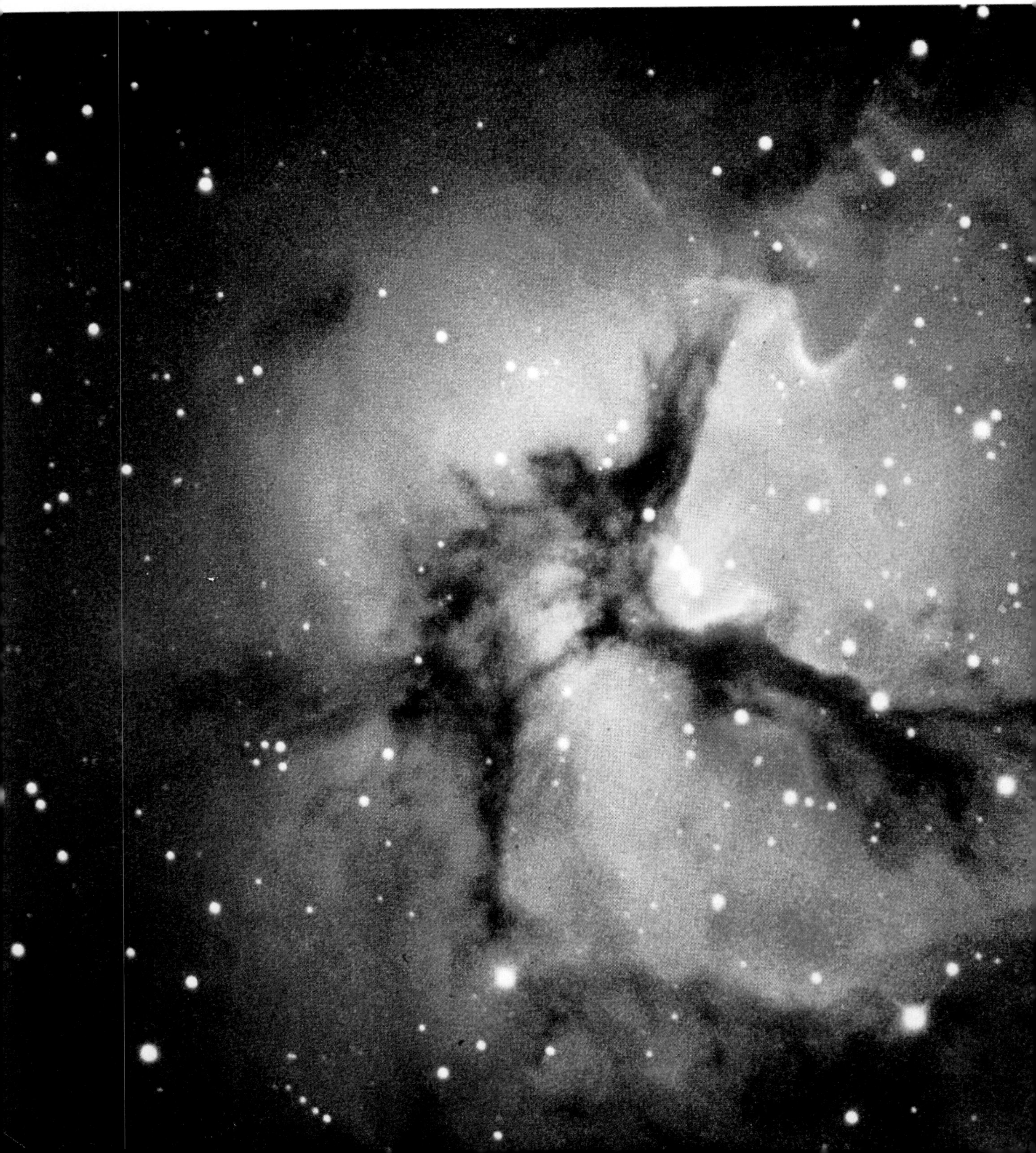

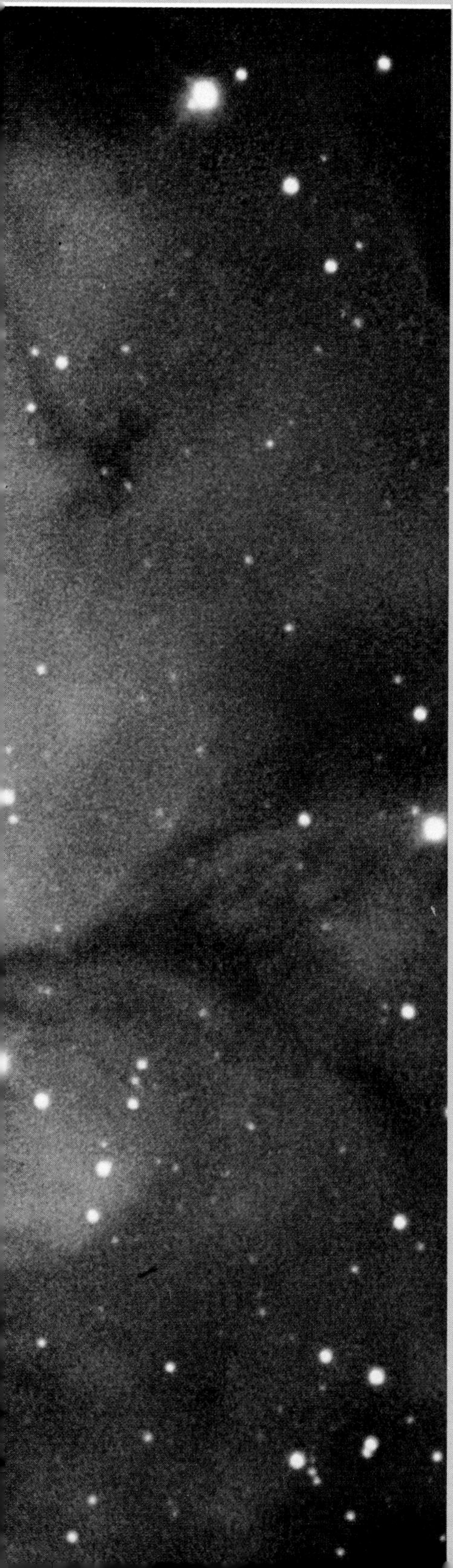

Exploring the Universe

Set aglow by fiery stars within the core, the gases of the Trifid Nebula sweep out into the blackness of space. The red cloud balloons out to a size almost unimaginable. It could gobble up thousands and thousands of solar systems. But it is so far away from the earth that people can enjoy its beauty without fearing it will engulf them. Although about 5000 light-years, or 50,000 trillion kilometers, from the earth, the dazzling cloud is one of the earth's neighbors in space. It is part of the earth's starry neighborhood, the Milky Way Galaxy. The Trifid Nebula is a mysterious object. Equally mysterious are the objects in the solar system—the stars, the sun, the planets, the planets' moons, meteors, asteroids, and the earth itself. In the pages that follow, you will explore these and other objects in space and perhaps begin to unravel some of their mysteries.

CHAPTERS

The Trifid Nebula is a huge mass of glowing gas and stars. It contains many young stars that generate a great deal of heat and light. The red portions of the nebula are mainly glowing hydrogen gas. The blue regions contain mostly dust particles that reflect the light from the stars in the nebula.

Exploring Earth Science

1

CHAPTER SECTIONS

CHAPTER OBJECTIVES

After completing this chapter, you will be able to

1–1 Explain the steps you can use to investigate a scientific question or problem.

1–2 Identify the units of measurement in the metric system.

1–3 Describe some of the tools used by earth scientists.

1–4 List the important safety rules you must follow in the science laboratory.

Did you hear the weather report on the radio this morning? Have you ever found a fossil and wondered how it was formed? Have you ever wondered why the moon appears to change its shape? If you have done any of these things, you have had a brief encounter with earth science.

Earth scientists study the earth and its characteristics. They investigate the far reaches of space, the depths of the oceans, and the interior of the earth. For example, an earth scientist might explain the formation of the unusual structures called pinnacles, found in only one place on the earth—a desert near the west coast of Australia. You can see these pinnacles in the photograph on the opposite page.

The earth scientist would soon discover that the pinnacles in the Australian desert were formed from substances left behind in the shells and skeletons of sea creatures. Millions of years ago, long after water no longer covered this part of Australia, sand dunes were blown over the pinnacles. Only a few hundred years ago, the shifting sand dunes slid away and revealed these strange structures. The pinnacles are another bit of evidence that the Australian desert was once a part of the ocean floor.

Rocky pinnacles on the Perth desert in Australia

Section Objective

To identify the steps in the scientific method

1–1 What Is Science?

The word *science* comes from the Latin word *scire,* which means "to know." Science involves a constant search for information about the universe in which you live. The universe around you and inside of you is a collection of countless mysteries. It is the job of scientists to solve these mysteries. And like any good detective, a scientist uses special methods to find truths about nature.

These truths are called facts. An example of a fact is that the sun is a source of light and heat. But science is more than a list of facts. Jules Henri Poincaré, a famous nineteenth-century French scientist, put it this way: "Science is built up with facts, as a house is with stones. But a collection of facts is no more a science than a heap of stones is a house."

Scientists go beyond simply discovering facts. They tie the facts together in an orderly way. Sometimes they solve a problem by piecing together facts that seem unrelated. Scientists also observe the world around them. They come up with ideas to explain what they see. And they perform experiments to test their ideas. After a study of facts, observations, and experiments, scientists may develop a **theory.** A theory is the most logical explanation for events that happen in nature.

Figure 1–1 *It is a fact that energy from the sun heats the earth. A theory would explain why some parts of the earth absorb more heat energy than others.*

A scientific theory must be able to be tested. If it is tested again and again and still found useful, the theory is kept. If further observations or experiments disprove it, the theory is changed or rejected. A theory is a valuable scientific tool because it helps explain past events and predict future events.

Scientists may use the term **law** when a theory or explanation for events has been tested many times and is generally accepted as true. But even scientific laws can be changed as a result of further observations and experiments. This points out the spirit at the heart of science: Always allow questions to be asked and new scientific explanations to be considered.

Sharpen Your Skills

Changing Theories

Write a 200-word essay explaining how new evidence can cause a change in an existing theory. Use the following words in your essay:

scientific method
control
variable
hypothesis
experimenting
data
measurement
conclusion

Scientific Methods

Scientists investigate problems every day. Sometimes they take many years to solve a problem. Sometimes the problem remains unsolved.

When scientists try to solve a problem, they usually search for an answer in an orderly and systematic manner. This systematic approach to problem solving is called the **scientific method.** The basic steps of any scientific method are shown in Figure 1–2. These steps need not be followed in any particular order, even though some orders make more sense than others. The following example shows how an earth scientist might use the scientific method to solve a problem.

Figure 1–2 *The steps in the scientific method usually proceed in this order.*

STEPS IN A SCIENTIFIC METHOD

1. Stating the problem
2. Gathering information on the problem
3. Forming a hypothesis
4. Experimenting
5. Recording and analyzing data
6. Stating a conclusion

Stating the Problem

Perhaps you have stepped into a lake or ocean during the winter. If so, you probably noticed that the temperature of the water was lower than it was during the summer. You may have even questioned why this was so. If you have wondered about such things, you have taken the first step toward recognizing a scientific problem.

Before investigating any problem, scientists must develop a clear statement defining the problem. In this example, the earth scientist might state the problem the following way: What factor causes the temperature of the water to be lower during the winter than during the summer?

Figure 1–3 *At sunset on a summer day, a great blue heron stands near the water's edge. The water is warmer than it was during the winter. What caused the change in temperature?*

Gathering Information on the Problem

The earth scientist might begin to solve the problem by gathering information. The scientist would first find out how conditions during the winter when the water is cooler differ from conditions during the summer when the water is warmer. The information might include the position of the sun during the winter and the summer.

Forming a Hypothesis

After gathering information, the earth scientist would then suggest a possible solution to the problem. A proposed solution to a scientific problem is called a **hypothesis** (high-PAHTH-uh-sihs). A hypothesis almost always follows the gathering of information about a problem. But sometimes a hypothesis is a sudden idea that springs from a new and original way of looking at a problem.

One hypothesis the earth scientist might consider as a solution to the problem is the following: The water is cooler during the winter than during the summer because the sun, the earth's source of heat, is farther from the earth during the winter. But the scientist would soon discover that the sun is actually closer to the earth during the winter.

Now the earth scientist would consider the situation again and arrive at a new hypothesis: The water is cooler during the winter than during the summer because the position of the sun is different during the two seasons. Position, in this case, means more than distance from the earth. It also involves the angle at which the sun's rays strike the earth.

Experimenting

Scientists must find evidence that either supports a hypothesis or does not support it. That is, they must test a hypothesis to show whether or not it is correct. Such testing is usually done by performing one or more experiments.

Scientists perform experiments according to specific rules. By following these rules, they can be confident that the evidence they uncover will clearly support or not support a hypothesis. To test the hypothesis that the angle of the sun's rays affects the temperature of the water, the earth scientist would have to design an appropriate experiment. Let's see how this might actually be done.

First the earth scientist would place a measured amount of water into a container. The scientist would then place a thermometer into the water, just below the surface. Then the scientist would place a heat source above the container. Because the heat source requires an electric current, the scientist would take care to make sure that none of the electric wires comes in contact with the water. The heat source takes the place of the sun in the experiment. Since the scientist is testing the effect of the angle of the sun's rays during the winter, the heat source would be angled exactly as the sun is in relation to the earth during the winter. In this experimental setup, then, the angle of the heat source is the **variable.** A variable in any experiment is the one factor that is being tested.

In any experiment, scientists ideally test only one variable at a time. In this way, they can be fairly certain that the results of the experiment are caused by one and only one factor. To avoid the possibility of hidden, unknown variables, scientists run a **control** experiment. The control experiment setup is exactly like the experimental setup except the control experiment does not contain the variable.

In the control experiment for this example, the earth scientist would make sure that the setup is exactly the same as the experimental setup except for the angle of the heat source's rays. A container

Sharpen Your Skills

Observing Rock Samples

To be useful, one person's observations must give meaningful information to another person.

1. Obtain four rocks of about the same size.

2. Place a small piece of masking tape on each rock and number each 1 through 4.

3. On a sheet of paper, write down as many observations as you can about each rock next to its number.

4. Rewrite your observations, without numbers, on another sheet of paper. Give this sheet of paper and the rocks to a classmate.

5. Ask your classmate to match the observations to the rocks. Did your classmate make correct matches? Why or why not?

Figure 1–4 *What is the variable in this experiment?*

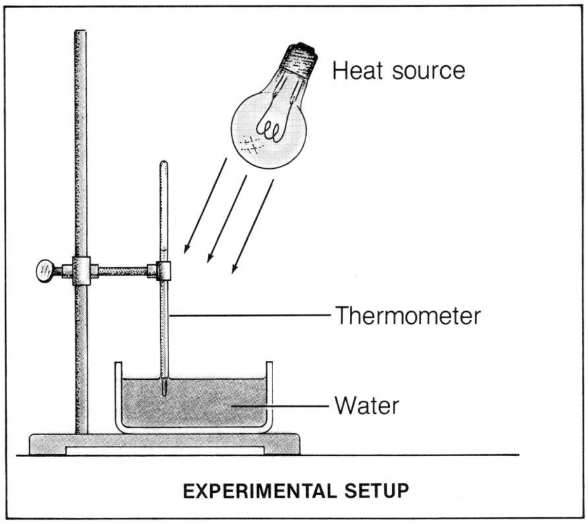

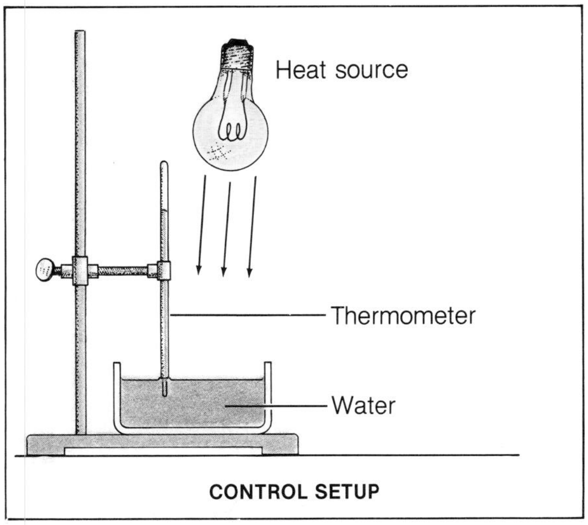

would be filled with the same amount of water. A thermometer would again be placed just below the surface of the water. The heat source would be placed at the exact same height above the container. But this time, the heat source would not be angled. It would be placed directly over the container. In this way, the earth scientist could be sure that the results of the experimental setup were due to the variable, the angle of the heat source's rays, and not to a hidden factor.

Recording and Analyzing Data

In any experiment, scientists must observe the experiment and write down important information. Recorded observations and measurements are called **data.**

In the earth science experiment, the data would include the time intervals at which the containers were observed and the temperature of the water in both containers at each interval. The earth scientist would record these observations for both the experimental setup and the control setup. The scientist might record the data for both setups in tables such as the following:

Figure 1–5 *Scientists often record their observations in data tables. What are the time intervals in these data tables?*

Heat Source at Angle *(experimental setup)*

Time (min)	0	15	30	45	60	75	90	105	120	135	150
Temperature (°C)	20.0	20.5	21.0	21.5	22.0	23.0	23.5	24.0	25.0	26.5	27.5

Heat Source Directly Above *(control setup)*

Time (min)	0	15	30	45	60	75	90	105	120	135	150
Temperature (°C)	20.0	21.0	22.0	23.0	24.0	26.0	27.0	28.5	30.0	30.5	31.0

To visually compare the data, the scientist would construct a graph on which to plot the data. Since the data tables contain two types of measurements, the graph would have two axes. See Figure 1–6.

The horizontal axis of the graph would stand for the time measurements in the data tables. Time

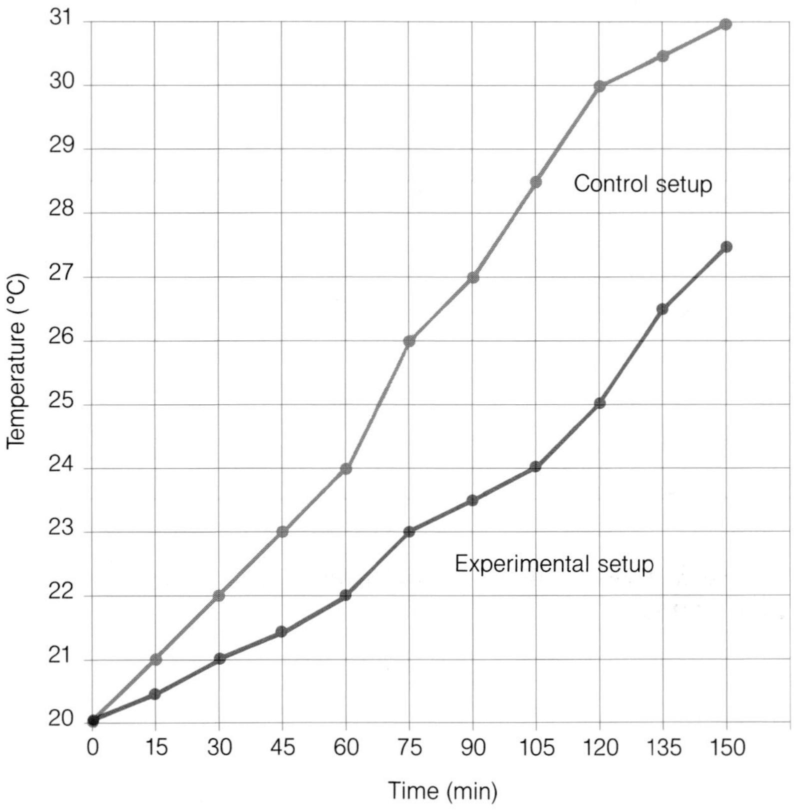

Figure 1–6 *The information in a data table can be placed on a graph. What conclusion can you draw from this graph about the rate of temperature change?*

measurements were made every 15 minutes. So the horizontal axis would be marked with intervals of 15 minutes. The space between equal intervals would have to be equal. For example, the space between 15 minutes and 30 minutes would be the same as between 30 minutes and 45 minutes.

The vertical axis of the graph would stand for the temperature measurements in the data tables. The lowest temperature reached in the experiment was 20°C and the highest was 31°C. So the vertical axis would begin at 20°C and end at 31°C. Each interval of temperature would have to be equal to every other interval.

After the axes of the graph were set up, the earth scientist would first graph the data from the experimental setup. Each pair of data points from the data table would be plotted. At 0 minutes, the temperature was 20°C. So the scientist would place a dot where 0 minutes and 20°C intersected—in the lower left corner of the graph. The next pair of data points was 15 minutes and 20.5°C. So the scientist would lightly draw a vertical line from the 15-minute interval of the horizontal axis and then a

Sharpen Your Skills

Graphing Temperatures

1. Over a ten-day period, read the weather section of a newspaper.

2. Each day, record in a chart the day's date and the high and low temperatures for your town.

3. If the newspaper gives the temperature in degrees Fahrenheit, convert the temperature to degrees Celsius using the formula

$$°C = 5/9 \times (°F - 32)$$

4. After ten days, plot your data in a graph. Use the vertical axis for temperature and the horizontal axis for day. Use red pencil for daily high temperatures and blue pencil for daily low temperatures.

5. Draw lines connecting the points for both the daily highs and lows.

Based on your graph, write a short essay describing the temperature patterns you observed.

Sharpen Your Skills

Testing a Hypothesis

Perform the following experiment to test the hypothesis that fresh water freezes at a higher temperature than salt water.

1. Fill two small, identical containers with equal amounts of tap water. Into only one container, add a tablespoon of salt and stir until all the salt dissolves.

2. Without spilling any water, place the two containers side by side in the freezer.

3. Every 5 minutes check both containers. Record your observations. Stop when the water in one of the containers is frozen.

What is the variable in this experiment? What is the control? What are the data? Why did you use identical containers? What conclusions have you reached about the effect of salt on the freezing point of water?

Eric Gordon

horizontal line from the 20.5°C interval of the vertical axis. The scientist would then place a dot at the place where the two lines intersected. This dot would represent the data points 15 minutes and 20.5°C. The scientist would plot the rest of the data pairs from the data table in this manner.

When all the data pairs were plotted, the scientist would draw a line through all the dots. This line would represent the graph of the experimental setup data. Then the scientist would graph all the data pairs from the control setup. Figure 1–6 shows what the two lines would look like. After analyzing the lines on the graph, the scientist would quickly determine that the temperature of the water rose more slowly in the experimental setup than it did in the control setup.

Stating a Conclusion

The results from a single experiment are not enough to reach a conclusion. Scientists must run an experiment over and over again before they can consider the data accurate.

The earth scientist would repeat the experiment many times before coming to a conclusion. After running the experiment many times and getting the same results, the scientist would come to the conclusion that the angle of the heat source's rays does indeed affect the temperature of the water. The scientist would further conclude that the temperature of the water rises higher when the sun's rays strike the water at a direct angle than when they strike the water at an indirect angle.

Branches of Earth Science

Earth science is one major branch of science. It deals with the study of the earth, its history, its changes, and its place in the universe. As scientific knowledge has expanded, the major branches of science have become more specialized. Earth science can be divided into several specialized branches.

One branch of earth science is **geology** (jee-AHL-uh-jee). Geology is the study of the earth's origin, history, and structure. Another branch of earth science is **meteorology** (mee-tee-uh-RAHL-uh-jee).

Figure 1–7 *There are many branches of earth science. Which of these photographs represents an area of study in geology? In oceanography? In meteorology?*

Meteorology is the study of the earth's atmosphere, weather, and climate. A third branch of earth science is **oceanography** (oh-shuh-NAHG-ruh-fee). Oceanography is the study of the earth's oceans, including their physical features, life forms, and natural resources. Another branch of earth science is **astronomy** (uh-STRAHN-uh-mee). Astronomy is the study of the position, composition, size, and other characteristics of the planets, stars, and other objects in space.

As with any branch of science, earth science has many special terms that may be unfamiliar to you. The chart in Figure 1–8 on page 14 gives the meanings of many common science prefixes and suffixes. Learning the meanings of these prefixes and suffixes will make learning new science terms easier. And knowing the meaning of science terms will increase your understanding of earth science. Suppose, for example, you see the term *isotherm* on a weather map. From the chart, you know that the prefix *iso-* means equal and the suffix *-therm* means heat. So you can quickly determine that isotherms are lines that connect areas of equal heat, or equal temperature.

Sharpen Your Skills

Branches of Earth Science

Read carefully the description of the various branches of earth science. Then look around and list some of the objects and events in the world around you. Decide which branch of earth science would study each of the objects and events you selected. Summarize your conclusions in a chart.

Prefix	Meaning	Prefix	Meaning	Suffix	Meaning
anti-	reverse	**in-**	inside	**-cline**	incline
astro-	of a star	**inter-**	between	**-graphy**	description of
atmo-	vapor	**iso-**	equal	**-logy**	science of
bathy-	depth	**litho-**	stone	**-meter**	having to do with measuring
chromo-	color	**meteor-**	things in the air	**-nomy**	systemized knowledge of
chrono-	time	**micro-**	small	**-oid**	resembling
con-	together	**petro-**	rock	**-scope**	instrument for seeing
de-	undo	**proto-**	primitive	**-sphere**	round
dia-	away from	**seismo-**	earthquake	**-therm**	heat
epi-	over	**strato-**	covering	**-verge**	turn
ex-	out	**sub-**	under		
geo-	earth	**tele-**	to a distance		
hemi-	half	**trans-**	across		
hydro-	water				

Figure 1–8 *Learning the meanings of prefixes and suffixes, such as those shown in this table, will make it easier for you to learn new science terms. According to this table, what does the word chronometer mean?*

SECTION REVIEW

1. Identify the steps in the scientific method.
2. What are the four main branches of earth science?
3. Using Figure 1–8, determine what the terms "seismology" and "petrology" mean.
4. If you were to measure the length of a shadow cast by a flagpole, what variables would affect your measurement?

Section Objective

To identify standard metric units

1–2 Scientific Measurements

Experimenting is an important step of any scientific method. Most experiments, of course, involve some form of measuring. **Experimental measurements must not only be reliable and accurate but also be easily communicated to others.** So a system of measurement with standard units must be used. Otherwise scientists around the world would not be able to compare and analyze data.

COMMONLY USED METRIC UNITS

Length

Length is the distance from one point to another.
A meter is slightly longer than a yard.
1 meter (m) = 100 centimeters (cm)
1 meter = 1000 millimeters (mm)
1 meter = 1,000,000 micrometers (μm)
1 meter = 1,000,000,000 nanometers (nm)
1 meter = 10,000,000,000 angstroms (Å)
1000 meters = 1 kilometer (km)

Mass

Mass is the amount of matter in an object.
A gram has a mass equal to about one paper clip.
1 kilogram (kg) = 1000 grams (g)
1 gram = 1000 milligrams (mg)
1000 kilograms = 1 metric ton (t)

Volume

Volume is the amount of space an object takes up.
A liter is slightly larger than a quart.
1 liter (L) = 1000 milliliters (mL) or 1000 cubic centimeters (cm^3)

Temperature

Temperature is the measure of hotness or coldness in degrees Celsius (°C).
0 °C = freezing point of water
100 °C = boiling point of water

Figure 1–9 *The metric system is easy to use because it is based on units of ten. How many centimeters are there in 10 meters?*

The system used today by all scientists is called the **metric system.** The metric system is a decimal system. That is, it is based on the number ten and multiples of ten, such as 100 and 1000. Some frequently used metric units and their abbreviations are listed in Figure 1–9. Each unit in the metric system is ten times larger or ten times smaller than the next smaller or larger unit. So calculations with metric units are very easy.

Length

The **meter** is the basic unit of length in the metric system. A meter is equal to about 39.4 inches. A scientist might measure the length of the block you live on in meters. But sometimes scientists need to measure distances much longer than your block. To measure longer distances, the kilometer may be used. The prefix *kilo-* means 1000. As you might have guessed, there are 1000 meters in a kilometer. A kilometer is about the length of 12 city blocks.

Meters are divided into smaller units of measurement called centimeters. The prefix *centi-* means one-hundredth. So there are 100 centimeters in a meter. Meters may be divided into units even smaller than a centimeter. One of these units is the

Sharpen Your Skills

Prefixes and Suffixes

Use the prefixes and suffixes given in Figure 1–8 on page 14 to form words that match the following definitions. Use at least one prefix and one suffix to form each word or phrase.

- instrument for seeing small objects
- instrument for seeing distant objects
- one-half of a planet
- study of water
- study of the earth
- method of measuring distant events

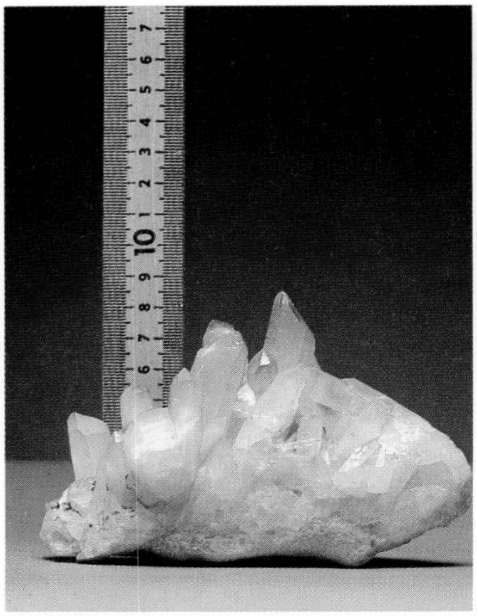

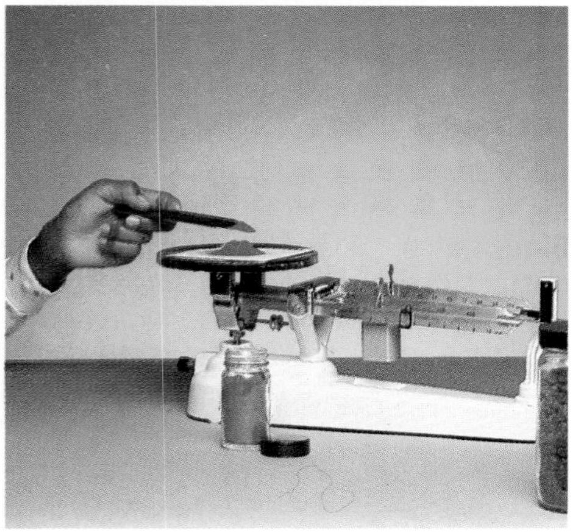

Figure 1–10 *Scientists use many tools to study their world. A ruler (left) is used to measure length. A graduated cylinder (center) is used to measure the volume of liquids. A Celsius thermometer (right) is used to measure temperature. A triple-beam balance (bottom left) is used to measure mass.*

millimeter. The prefix *milli-* means one-thousandth. So there are 1000 millimeters in a meter. How many millimeters are there in a kilometer?

On the earth, meters and kilometers are very useful units of measurement. But in space, distances are often too far to be measured in kilometers. So astronomers often use a unit of distance called the **light-year.** A light-year is the distance light travels in one year. Since light travels at a rate of about 300,000 kilometers per second, a light-year is about 9.5 trillion kilometers. You can think of a light-year as a "ruler made of light." But keep in mind that a light-year measures distance, not time.

A light-year may seem like an enormous distance. But in space, a light-year is not very far at all. The closest star system to the earth, besides the earth's sun, is over 4 light-years away. It takes the light from that star system over four years to reach the earth. Yet even that distance seems very short when compared to the distance of the farthest known star systems. The light from the most distant stars may take more than 12 billion light-years to reach the earth. Unbelievable as it may seem, the light from those distant stars began its journey toward the earth long before the earth had even been formed.

Volume

Volume is a measure of the amount of space occupied by an object. The **liter** is the basic unit of volume in the metric system. A liter is a little larger than a quart. Liters can be divided into smaller units. To measure small volumes, scientists use the milliliter or cubic centimeter. One liter contains 1000 milliliters or 1000 cubic centimeters. Milliliters are used to measure the volume of liquids. Cubic centimeters measure the volume of solids or liquids.

Mass and Weight

The **kilogram** is the basic unit of mass in the metric system. **Mass** is the amount of matter in an object. For example, there is more matter in a truck than in a toy wagon. So a truck has more mass than a toy wagon. To measure small units of mass, scientists use the gram. One kilogram is equal to 1000 grams.

When you think of an object's mass, you probably think about how much that object weighs. But mass is not at all the same as **weight.** Weight is a measure of the attraction between objects caused by **gravity.** Gravity is a force of attraction between objects. All objects exert a force of gravity on each other. The strength of this gravitational attraction depends on the masses of the objects and their distance from one another.

You live on the earth. The gravitational force of your body attracts the earth toward you. But you have a very small mass compared to the earth. So the force of attraction you exert on the earth is very small. On the other hand, the earth has a very large mass. It exerts a large force of gravity on you, pulling you toward the earth. Your weight on the earth, then, is a measure of how much the earth's force of gravity pulls you down toward the earth's surface. Gravity becomes smaller as the distance between objects increases. So you weigh less on the top of a mountain than on a ship at sea. If you were on a spaceship circling the earth, your weight would be so small that you would be "weightless."

You can see that weight can change. It is not constant. Your weight on the earth's moon, for

Sharpen Your Skills

Does Air Have Mass and Weight?

1. Blow up two balloons to an equal size.

2. Tape or tie each balloon to one end of a meterstick.

3. Attach a string to the center of the meterstick. Hold the string so that the balloons are balanced. If the balloons are of equal size, the meterstick will be horizontal to the floor.

4. Carefully burst one of the balloons with a pin. What happens?

How does the result of this experiment prove that air has both mass and weight?

Eric Gordon

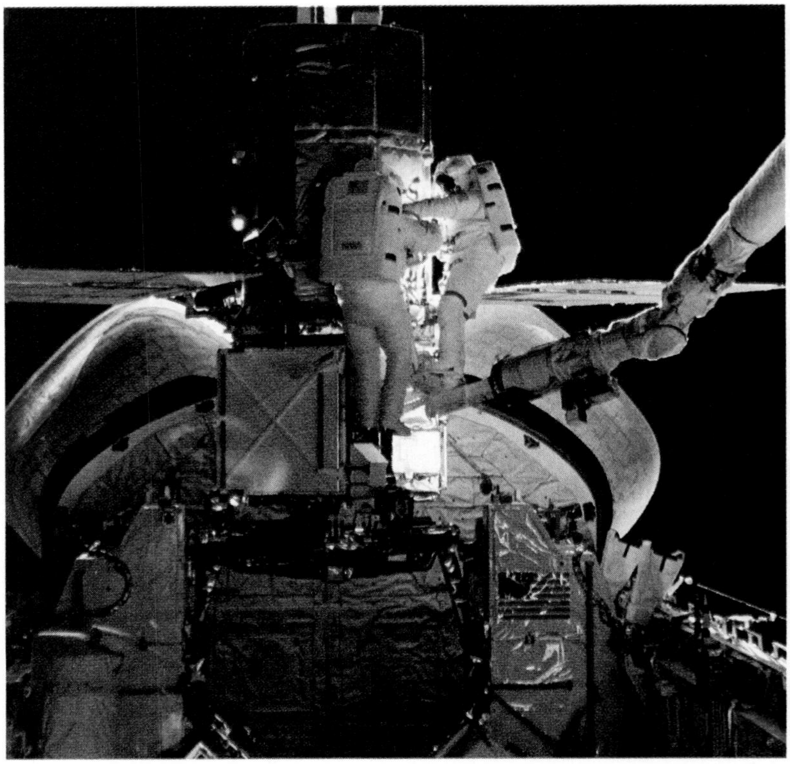

Figure 1–11 *On the earth, these astronauts would never have been able to lift this heavy satellite. But they were able to lift it with ease while floating above the Space Shuttle in orbit around the earth. Can you explain why?*

example, is only about one-sixth of what it would be on the earth. This is because the force of gravity on the moon is only about one-sixth of that on the earth. But whether you were on the earth or the moon, your mass would stay the same. Mass, then, is a constant.

DENSITY Scientists often find it useful to determine how much mass is contained in a given volume. The relationship between mass and volume is called **density.** Density, then, is the mass per unit volume of a particular substance. The relationship between density, mass, and volume can be shown as:

$$\textbf{density} = \frac{\textbf{mass}}{\textbf{volume}}$$

For example, suppose a 1-centimeter cube taken from the planet Mars has a mass of 3.96 grams. The average density of Mars would be:

$$\textbf{density} = \frac{\textbf{3.96 g (mass)}}{\textbf{1 cm}^3\textbf{ (volume)}} = \textbf{3.96 g/cm}^3$$

Sharpen Your Skills

Measuring With the Metric System

Using only metric units, make the following measurements of yourself and your surroundings. List your results in a chart.

- indoor temperature
- outdoor temperature
- your height
- your waist
- distance around your block
- distance to your school
- volume of water you drink in one day

Temperature

The basic unit of temperature in the metric system is the degree **Celsius** (SEHL-see-uhs). The Celsius temperature scale is based on the freezing and boiling points of water. At sea level, pure water freezes at 0°C and boils at 100°C. So each degree Celsius is equal to one-hundredth of the difference between the freezing and boiling points of water. Normal room temperature is about 21°C.

Figure 1–12 *Steam rises out of a hot spring at Yellowstone National Park. What instrument would you use to measure the temperature of the hot spring?*

SECTION REVIEW

1. What are the basic units of length, volume, and mass in the metric system?
2. What is a light-year?
3. How would your mass and weight on Earth differ on a planet with half the gravitational pull of Earth?

CAREER

Oceanographer

HELP WANTED: OCEANOGRAPHER
To collect and analyze data from the ocean floor. An advanced degree in oceanography or geology is required. Strong mathematics background and foreign language skills are helpful.

From the hot, cramped cabin of a tiny underwater craft, three scientists peer into the cold, murky water. In 15 minutes, the craft descends nearly 3000 meters below the ocean's surface. These **oceanographers** are traveling to the mysterious depths of the ocean to photograph the ocean floor and to collect rock samples.

Some oceanographers study the ocean floor. Others study the ways that ocean water moves. Oceanographers also study the substances in ocean water. The information gathered by oceanographers may be used to find oil or mineral deposits, to manage water pollution, or to help underwater crafts navigate. Scientists may also use the information to learn more about the earth's past and possibly its future.

An oceanographer may work for a university, a private institution, the government, oil companies, or other industries. If you would like to find out more about this field, write to International Oceanographic Foundation, 3979 Rickenbacker Causeway, Virginia Key, Miami, FL 33149.

1–3 Tools of an Earth Scientist

Section Objective

To describe tools of an earth scientist

Figure 1–13 *Scientists use a wide variety of tools to gather information. This meteorologist is observing weather patterns with the help of computer-generated images along a section of the northeast coast of the United States.*

Scientists use many different kinds of tools to explore the world around them. The tools may be complicated or simple. A scientist may use a computer to store, retrieve, and analyze large amounts of data. At another time, the same scientist may use paper and pencil to solve a problem. Tools, alone, cannot do the work of a scientist. But they are very important in the advancement of science.

Earth scientists use many special tools to learn about the earth and space. For example, meteorologists use a tool called an anemometer to measure wind speed. They also use a very complicated tool called a weather satellite, which orbits the earth and takes photos that are used to predict weather conditions. Geologists use an instrument called a microscope to magnify objects that are too small to be seen by the human eye alone. The use of a microscope helps geologists study the tiny particles that make up rocks.

Sometimes great discoveries are not made until new tools are invented. For example, the moons of Jupiter did not become visible until the telescope was invented. The same tool also showed that Venus seemed to change its shape as time passed. These discoveries not only added knowledge about space but also caused many scientists to modify ideas that had been accepted for thousands of years.

Astronomers use a variety of tools to study the universe. You will now read about some of these important instruments.

Optical Telescopes

Astronomers use optical (AHP-tih-kuhl) telescopes to study planets, stars, and other objects in space. The two main kinds of optical telescopes are **refracting telescopes** and **reflecting telescopes.**

In a refracting telescope, a series of lenses is used to focus light from the stars. The larger the lenses used, the greater the light-gathering power of the telescope. For example, the large lens of the refracting telescope at Yerkes Observatory in Wisconsin has a diameter of about 101.6 centimeters

(40 inches). This gives the telescope 40,000 times the light-gathering power of the human eye.

Reflecting telescopes use a series of mirrors instead of lenses to gather light from the stars. With such telescopes, astronomers can observe objects many billions of light-years from the earth.

MULTIPLE MIRROR TELESCOPES Recently a new kind of optical telescope has been developed. This telescope, called the Multiple Mirror Telescope, uses many small mirrors rather than one large mirror. The Multiple Mirror Telescope built atop Mount Hopkins in Arizona contains six "72-inch" mirrors. Multiple Mirror Telescopes help lessen the enormous cost of constructing large-mirrored telescopes.

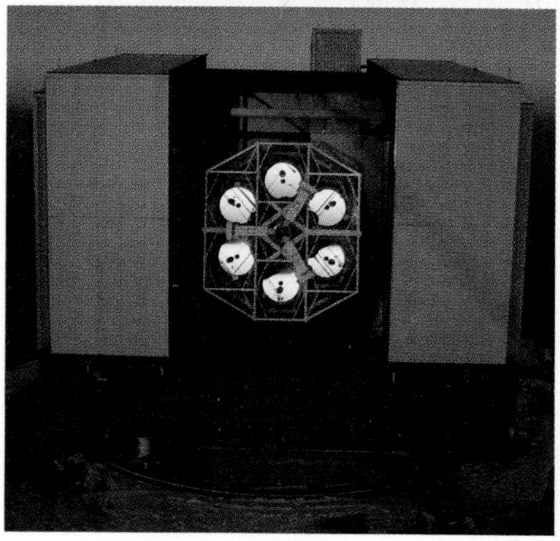

Figure 1–14 *The Hale Telescope at Mount Palomar in California (top) uses one large mirror. The Multiple Mirror Telescope atop Mount Hopkins in Arizona (bottom) uses six mirrors. What kind of telescope are these?*

Infrared Telescopes

Optical telescopes detect visible light given off by stars. Light is a form of energy. But stars give off many forms of energy besides visible light. So astronomers have built telescopes that can detect these "invisible" forms of energy.

For the most part, only stars give off visible light in space. But just about all objects give off infrared energy. Another term for infrared energy is heat energy. In January 1983, the Infrared Astronomy Satellite, or IRAS, was launched into space. IRAS was designed to detect infrared energy given off by

Figure 1–15 *The Large Magellanic Cloud is an enormous collection of stars some 200,000 light-years from the earth. At the left is a view of this cloud as seen through an optical telescope. At the right is the same cloud as seen through the IRAS infrared telescope.*

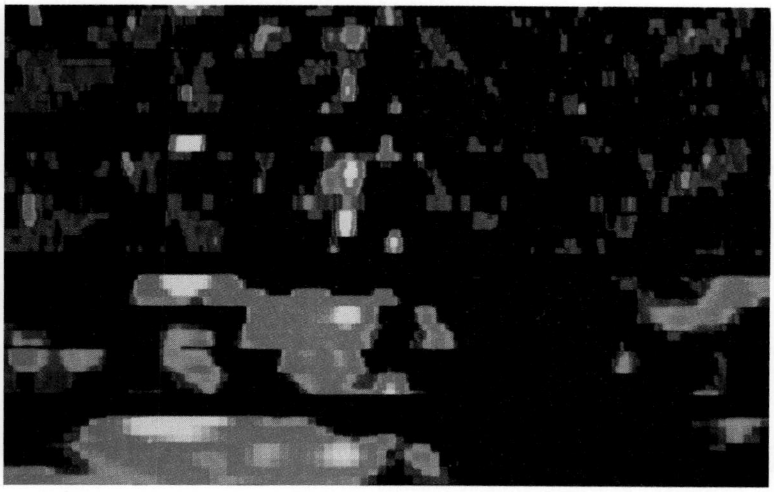

> **Sharpen Your Skills**
>
> *A New Comet*
>
> A new comet with an unusual triple name was discovered by the IRAS telescope. Using books and other reference materials in the library, find out the name of the new comet and the secret of its unusual name.

stars and other objects. Through the IRAS telescope, scientists have detected "newborn" stars too dim to be seen with optical telescopes.

X-ray Telescopes

Almost all stars give off X-rays, another form of energy. But X-rays from space cannot be detected on the earth because the earth's atmosphere blocks them out. In 1970, this problem was solved. A satellite known as *Uhuru* was sent into orbit above the earth's atmosphere. *Uhuru* can detect X-rays coming from objects in space. In fact, *Uhuru* provided astronomers with their first clear glimpse of X-ray sources in the sky. By using such X-ray telescopes, astronomers can study what happens to a star as it dies.

Radio Telescopes

Scientists first detected radio waves from space over 50 years ago. Radio waves are another form of invisible radiation given off by stars, groups of stars, and clouds of dust and gas in space. Since that discovery, astronomers have constructed many radio telescopes to study radio waves from space. Radio waves are not blocked by the earth's atmosphere. So radio telescopes are built on the earth and do not have to be sent into space.

The main part of a radio telescope is shaped like a huge dish. The curved metal dish collects radio waves and then focuses the waves toward an antenna. The signal is then fed from the antenna to a computer. The computer processes the information and converts it into an image.

In the desert of New Mexico, there is a group of 27 radio telescopes known as the Very Large Array, or VLA. The VLA is very useful because it combines the radio-wave detecting power of a group of radio telescopes. With the VLA, astronomers can get a clearer picture of many objects in space than with a single radio telescope. See Figure 1–16.

You can now see that early astronomers were at a great disadvantage. With only simple telescopes, they were not able to discover all the different kinds of radiation that reach the earth from space. Modern astronomers can choose from a variety of

Figure 1–16 *These dish-shaped radio telescopes are among the 27 radio telescopes in the Very Large Array in New Mexico (left). The Arecibo radio telescope in Puerto Rico (right) is one of the world's largest radio telescopes.*

telescopic tools. Science, it seems, needs more than keen minds. It needs the kinds of data that very often only special tools can provide.

SECTION REVIEW

1. What are two tools used by meteorologists? What is one tool used by geologists? Explain the purpose of each tool.
2. What is the difference between refracting and reflecting telescopes?
3. Explain why the gathering of new scientific knowledge is often related to the scientific equipment available at the time.

1–4 Science Safety in the Laboratory

Section Objective

To learn laboratory safety rules

The scientific laboratory is a place of adventure and discovery. Some of the most important events in scientific history have happened in laboratories. The antibiotic powers of penicillin were discovered by a scientist in a laboratory. The plastics used today for clothing and other products were first made by scientists in a laboratory. The list is endless.

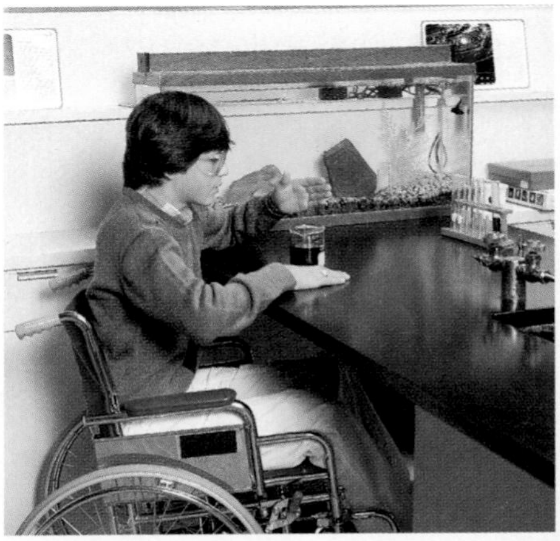

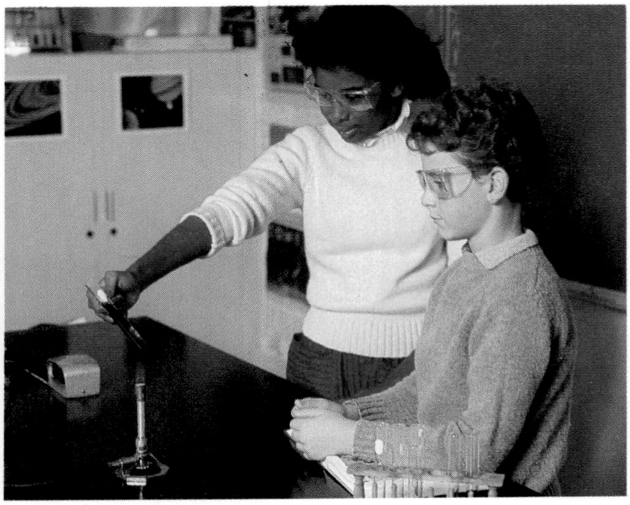

Figure 1–17 *These photographs show some important laboratory safety rules. Always wear safety goggles when working with fire (right). Never directly inhale the fumes from a beaker (top). Pour acids and bases over a sink (bottom).*

To better understand the facts and concepts you will read about in this text, you too may work in the laboratory this year. And the laboratory might just turn out to be an exciting experience for you as well. It should be if you follow instructions and are as careful as a scientist would be.

Perhaps the first thing a scientist learns is that working in the laboratory can produce unexpected results. For example, two chemicals never before mixed might explode. Scientists understand that such events can happen. And they take as many precautions as possible to protect themselves and their fellow workers.

All of the work you will do in the laboratory this year will involve experiments that have been done over and over again. When done properly, they are not only interesting—sometimes even fascinating—but also perfectly safe. But when done improperly, accidents can occur. How can you avoid such problems? The answer is simple. **First and foremost, always follow your teacher's directions or the directions in your textbook exactly as stated.** Never try anything on your own without asking your teacher first. And when you are not sure what you should do, ask first. As you work on your laboratory investigations, you will see safety precaution symbols next to the procedure for the investigation. To learn the meaning of these safety symbols, see Figure 1–18 on page 25.

A detailed list of safety procedures is located in Appendix C on page 599 of this book. Before you enter the laboratory for the first time, make sure that you read each rule carefully. Then read the rules a second time. Make sure that you understand

SAFETY PRECAUTION SYMBOLS

Glassware Safety 

1. Whenever you see this symbol, you will know that you are working with glassware that can easily be broken. Take particular care to handle such glassware safely. And never use broken glassware.
2. Never heat glassware that is not thoroughly dry. Never pick up any glassware unless you are sure it is not hot. If it is hot, use heat-resistant gloves.
3. Always clean glassware thoroughly before putting it away.

Fire Safety 

1. Whenever you see this symbol, you will know that you are working with fire. Never use any source of fire without wearing safety goggles.
2. Never heat anything—particularly chemicals—unless instructed to do so.
3. Never heat anything in a closed container.
4. Never reach across a flame.
5. Always use a clamp, tongs, or heat-resistant gloves to handle hot objects.
6. Always maintain a clean work area, particularly when using a flame.

Heat Safety 

Whenever you see this symbol, you will know that you should put on heat-resistant gloves to avoid burning your hands.

Chemical Safety 

1. Whenever you see this symbol, you will know that you are working with chemicals that could be hazardous.
2. Never smell any chemical directly from its container. Always use your hand to waft some of the odors from the top of the container toward your nose—and only when instructed to do so.
3. Never mix chemicals unless instructed to do so.
4. Never touch or taste any chemical unless instructed to do so.
5. Keep all lids closed when chemicals are not in use. Dispose of all chemicals as instructed by your teacher.
6. Immediately rinse with water any chemicals, particularly acids, off your skin and clothes. Then notify your teacher.

Eye and Face Safety 

1. Whenever you see this symbol, you will know that you are performing an experiment in which you must take precautions to protect your eyes and face by wearing safety goggles.
2. Always point away from you and others a test tube or bottle that is being heated. Chemicals can splash or boil out of the heated test tube.
3. Always wear safety goggles when you see this symbol.

Sharp Instrument Safety 

1. Whenever you see this symbol, you will know that you are working with a sharp instrument.
2. Always use single-edged razors; double-edged razors are too dangerous.
3. Handle any sharp instrument with extreme care. Never cut any material toward you; always cut away from you.
4. Notify your teacher immediately if you are cut in the lab.

Electrical Safety 

1. Whenever you see this symbol, you will know that you are using electricity in the laboratory.
2. Never use long extension cords to plug in an electrical device. Do not plug too many different appliances into one socket or you may overload the socket and cause a fire.
3. Never touch an electrical appliance or outlet with wet hands.

Figure 1–18 *This chart shows the safety precaution symbols you will often find next to Procedure in the laboratory investigations at the end of each chapter. Which symbol would you expect to see when the investigation calls for the use of a Bunsen burner?*

each rule. If you do not, ask your teacher to explain any rules you are unsure of. You may even want to suggest further rules that apply to your classroom.

SECTION REVIEW

1. Why is the laboratory an important part of scientific research?
2. What is the most important general rule to remember when working in the laboratory?
3. What precautions would you take in performing the following experiment safely: Heat a test tube of water over a Bunsen burner until it boils.

1 LABORATORY INVESTIGATION

Building a Telescope

Problem

How does a telescope work?

Materials *(per group)*

Meterstick
2 lens holders
2 convex lenses or magnifying glasses of different sizes
Unlined index card (to be used as a screen)
Card holder

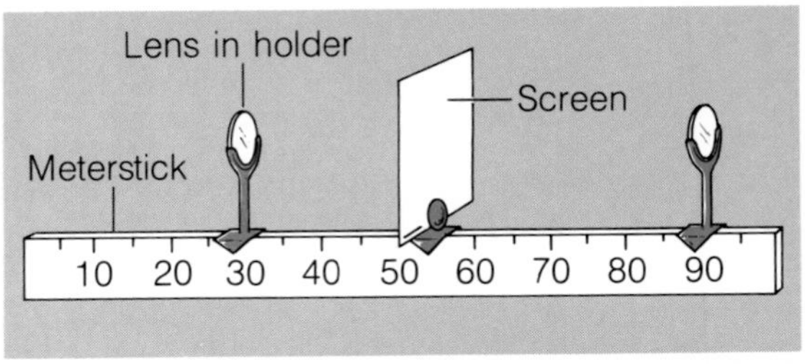

Procedure

1. Put the two lenses in the lens holders and place them on the meterstick as shown in the diagram. Put the card in its holder and locate it on the meterstick between the two lenses.
2. Aim one end of the meterstick at a window or an electric light about 3 to 10 meters away. Light given off or reflected by an object will pass through the lens and form an image of the object on the screen. Carefully slide the lens nearer to the light source back and forth until a clear, sharp image of the light source is formed on the card.
3. The distance between the center of the lens and the sharp image is called the focal length of the lens. Measure the distance between the image and the lens facing the light source to obtain the focal length of that lens. Record your measurement.
4. Turn the other end of the meterstick toward the light source. Without disturbing the screen or the first lens, determine the focal length of the second lens.
5. Point the end of the meterstick that has the lens with the longer focal length toward a distant object. Without changing the positions of the lenses, take the screen out of its holder and look at the distant object through both lenses. You may have to adjust the lenses slightly to focus the image. You have constructed a telescope.

Observations

1. What was the focal length of the first lens? What was the focal length of the second lens?
2. How does the image seen through the lens with the shorter focal length differ from the image seen through the lens with the longer focal length?
3. How does the image of an object seen through the lens with the longer focal length appear different from the object itself?

Conclusions

1. What type of telescope have you constructed? Explain your answer.
2. In a telescope, the lens with the shorter focal length is called the eyepiece. The lens with the longer focal length is called the objective. You can calculate the magnifying power of your telescope by using the following formula:

$$\text{magnifying power} = \frac{\text{focal length of objective}}{\text{focal length of eyepiece}}$$

   Using the formula, calculate the magnifying power of your telescope.
3. What is the relationship between a telescope's magnifying power and the ratio between the focal lengths of the objective and the eyepiece?

CHAPTER REVIEW

SUMMARY

1–1 What Is Science?

❑ The scientific method is a process scientists use to solve problems about nature.

❑ The basic steps of the scientific method are stating the problem, gathering information, forming a hypothesis, experimenting, observing and recording information, and stating a conclusion.

❑ In any experiment, scientists can test only one variable at a time. To avoid the possibility of hidden, unknown variables affecting conclusions, scientists run a control experiment.

❑ The results from a single experiment are not enough to reach a conclusion. Scientists must run an experiment over and over again before they can consider the data accurate.

❑ Four of the main branches of earth science are astronomy, meteorology, geology, and oceanography.

1–2 Scientific Measurements

❑ Experimental measurements must not only be reliable and accurate but also be easily communicated to others.

❑ The meter is the basic unit of length in the metric system.

❑ A light-year is the distance light travels in one year.

❑ The liter is the basic unit of volume in the metric system.

❑ The kilogram is the basic unit of mass in the metric system.

❑ Mass is a measure of the amount of matter in an object. Weight is a measure of the force of attraction between objects caused by gravity.

❑ Density is the measurement of how much mass is contained in a given volume of an object.

❑ The Celsius temperature scale has 100 degrees between the freezing and boiling points of water.

1–3 Tools of an Earth Scientist

❑ Scientists use many different kinds of tools to explore the world around them.

❑ Earth scientists use such tools as anemometers, weather satellites, and microscopes to gather data.

❑ The types of telescopes used by astronomers are refracting, reflecting, infrared, X-ray, and radio telescopes.

1–4 Science Safety in the Laboratory

❑ Whenever working in the laboratory, you should take all necessary safety precautions and use safety equipment when applicable.

❑ Always follow your teacher's instructions or instructions in your textbook exactly as stated.

VOCABULARY

Define each term in a complete sentence.

astronomy
Celsius
control
data
density
geology
gravity
hypothesis
kilogram
law
light-year
liter
mass
meteorology
meter
metric system
oceanography
reflecting telescope
refracting telescope
scientific method
theory
variable
weight

CONTENT REVIEW: MULTIPLE CHOICE

Choose the letter of the answer that best completes each sentence.

1. An orderly, systematic approach to a problem is called the
a. investigation b. scientific method
c. experiment d. conclusion

2. A proposed solution to a scientific problem is called a
a. conclusion b. control c. hypothesis d. theory

3. In any experiment, the one factor being tested is called the
a. control b. data c. variable d. hypothesis

4. The branch of earth science that deals with the earth's history and structure is called
a. geology b. oceanography
c. astronomy d. meteorology

5. The meter is the basic unit of
a. volume b. temperature c. density d. length

6. Very long distances in space are measured in
a. kilograms b. liters c. centimeters d. light-years

7. The basic unit of mass is called the
a. meter b. kilogram c. cubic centimeter d. gram

8. The basic unit of volume is called the
a. gram b. kilogram c. liter d. degree Celsius

9. Optical telescopes detect
a. X-rays b. infrared rays
c. visible light d. radio waves

10. The symbol of a hand next to a laboratory procedure means
a. do not touch broken glassware
b. cover eyes with your hand
c. use heat resistant gloves
d. wear safety goggles

CONTENT REVIEW: COMPLETION

Fill in the word or words that best complete each sentence.

1. Scientists develop a (an) ______________ after careful study of facts, observations, and experiments.

2. A proposed solution to a problem based on information is called a (an) __________.

3. The part of an experiment that contains the variable is called the ______________.

4. ______________ are recorded observations and measurements.

5. The study of weather is part of the branch of earth science called ______________.

6. The ______________ is the system of measurement used by scientists.

7. A (An) ______________ contains 1000 equal units called cubic centimeters.

8. The mass of an object divided by its volume is the object's ______________.

9. Telescopes that use a series of lenses are called ______________ telescopes.

10. ______________ detects X-rays blocked by the earth's atmosphere.

CONTENT REVIEW: TRUE OR FALSE

Determine whether each statement is true or false. If it is true, write "true." If it is false, change the underlined word or words to make the statement true.

1. Any experiment must have two variables to be accurate.
2. The control experiment does not include a variable.
3. The prefix *kilo-* means one hundred.
4. Meters are used to measure volume.
5. The unit of density is g/cm^3.
6. The degree Fahrenheit is the basic unit of temperature in the metric system.
7. Astronomers study the skies with different kinds of microscopes.
8. A series of mirrors is used in reflecting telescopes.
9. To protect your eyes when working with fire or chemicals, always make sure you wear safety goggles.
10. The symbol of a flask means you will be working with a sharp instrument.

CONCEPT REVIEW: SKILL BUILDING

Use the skills you have developed in the chapter to complete each activity.

1. **Designing an experiment** Outline an experiment to test the hypothesis that the angle of the sun's rays does affect the temperature of land on the earth. Make sure that you indicate both your control and experimental setups. State clearly what variable you are testing.
2. **Following safety rules** Explain the potential danger involved in each of the following situations. Describe the safety precautions that should be used to avoid injury to you or your classmates.
   a. pushing a rubber stopper far down into a test tube
   b. pouring acid into a beaker while sitting at your lab table
   c. tasting a white powder to see if it is salty
   d. heating a stoppered test tube of water
   e. deciding on your own to mix two chemicals together
3. **Making metric conversions** Convert the following metric units as indicated.

   4 km = __ m = __ mm
   2 mL = __ cm^3 = __ L
   50 cm = __ mm = __ m
   200 kg = __ g = __ mg
   5000 mg = __ g = __ kg
4. **Making English to metric conversions** Convert the following English units to metric units. You can use the metric conversion chart in Appendix A on page 596:

   2 pounds = __ g
   20 ounces = __ mg
   3 quarts = __ L
   6000 miles = __ km
   10 miles = __ m
   1 mile = __ cm

CONCEPT REVIEW: ESSAY

Discuss each of the following in a brief paragraph.

1. Describe the steps in the scientific method.
2. To investigate a problem why might you go to a library? To a laboratory?
3. Compare refracting and reflecting telescopes.
4. Why must an experiment contain only one variable?
5. Explain why mass is a constant, but weight can change.

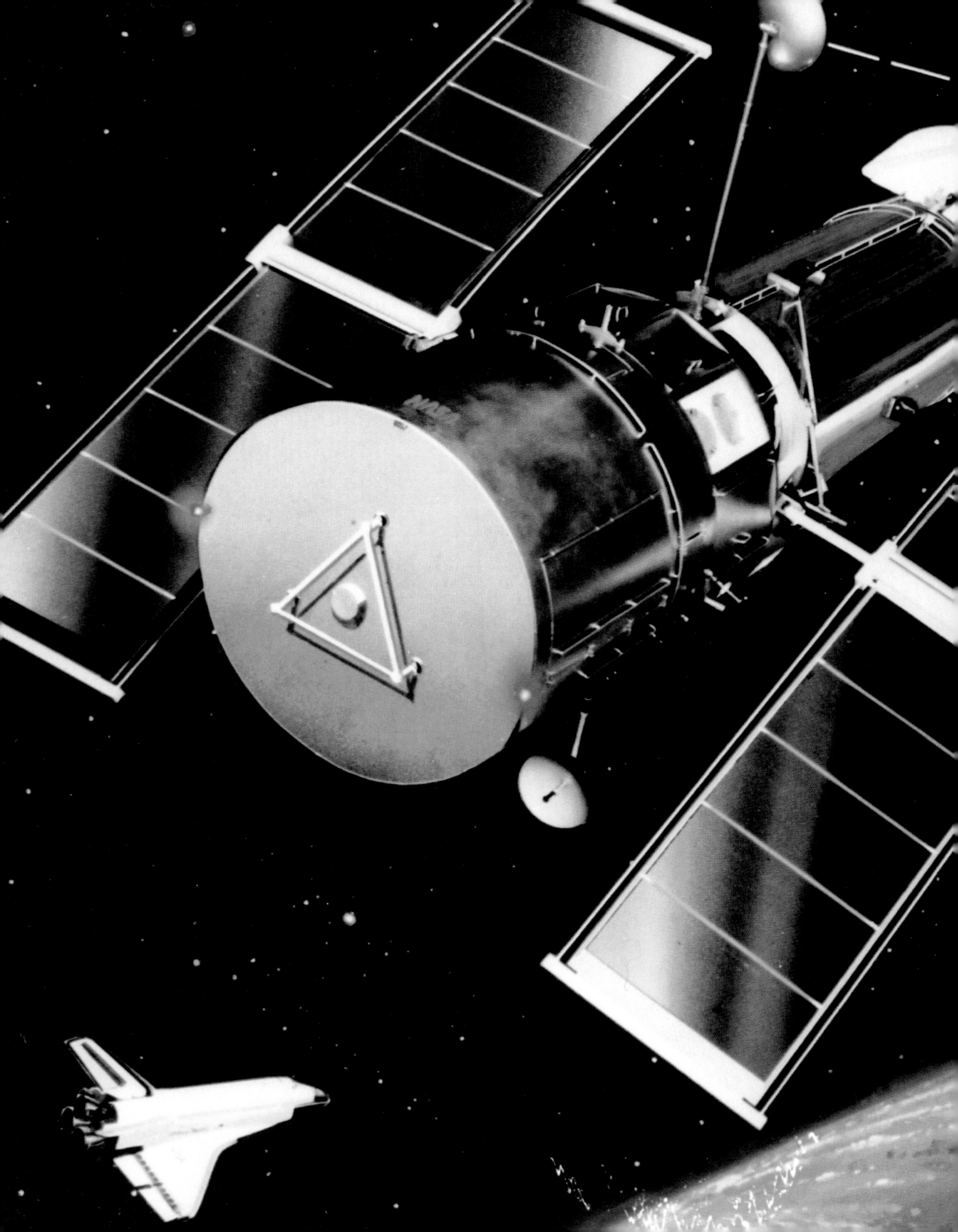

Stars and Galaxies 2

CHAPTER SECTIONS

CHAPTER OBJECTIVES

After completing this chapter, you will be able to

2–1 Explain the theories of the formation of the universe.
2–1 Explain how red shift is used to determine the movements of stars.
2–2 Describe the groups into which stars are classified.
2–2 Identify several major constellations.
2–3 Describe the characteristics of different types of stars.
2–4 Trace the life cycle of a star.

Have you ever tried to imagine just how big outer space is? The distances between objects in space are so great that they are almost impossible to imagine. If you could travel in a spaceship at the speed of light—300,000 kilometers per second—it would take you over four years to reach the closest star other than the sun. The light of some of the stars you see in the night sky left many of these stars thousands of years ago.

Like you, astronomers look up into the night sky and wonder about the nature of stars. They use powerful telescopes to study stars. Yet even the most powerful telescopes on the earth cannot detect every object in space. The illustration on the opposite page shows the Space Telescope, an instrument that will enable astronomers to "see" farther into space than they now can with any telescope on the earth's surface.

The Space Telescope can gather light from stars too distant or too dim to be studied clearly from the earth. Images of these stars will be sent from the Space Telescope to a satellite orbiting the earth. The satellite will then relay information about each image to computers on the earth. The computers can recreate the image. In this way, astronomers hope to gain more information about the universe. In fact, many astronomers believe that the Space Telescope may provide a glimpse of the very edge of the universe!

The Space Telescope will gather information on distant stars without the distorting effect of the earth's atmosphere.

Section Objective

To relate the big bang theory to the formation of the universe

2–1 Formation of the Universe

Astronomers use various telescopes to study stars. Optical telescopes detect visible light from stars. Radio telescopes detect radio waves emitted by stars. X-ray telescopes detect X-rays. And infrared telescopes study infrared radiation from stars. These telescopes are important tools of astronomers.

Telescopes are not the only tools of astronomers. An equally important tool is the **spectroscope.** The light given off by stars usually contains a mixture of several different colors of light. A spectroscope can break up the light from a distant star into its characteristic colors.

When light enters a spectroscope, the light is first focused into a beam by a lens. The beam of light then passes through a **prism.** A prism separates light into its different colors. The band of colors formed when light passes through a prism is called a **spectrum.** See Figure 2–2. The kind of spectrum produced by the light from a star tells astronomers a great deal about that star.

Figure 2–1 *This photograph shows only a small portion of the many billions of stars in the universe.*

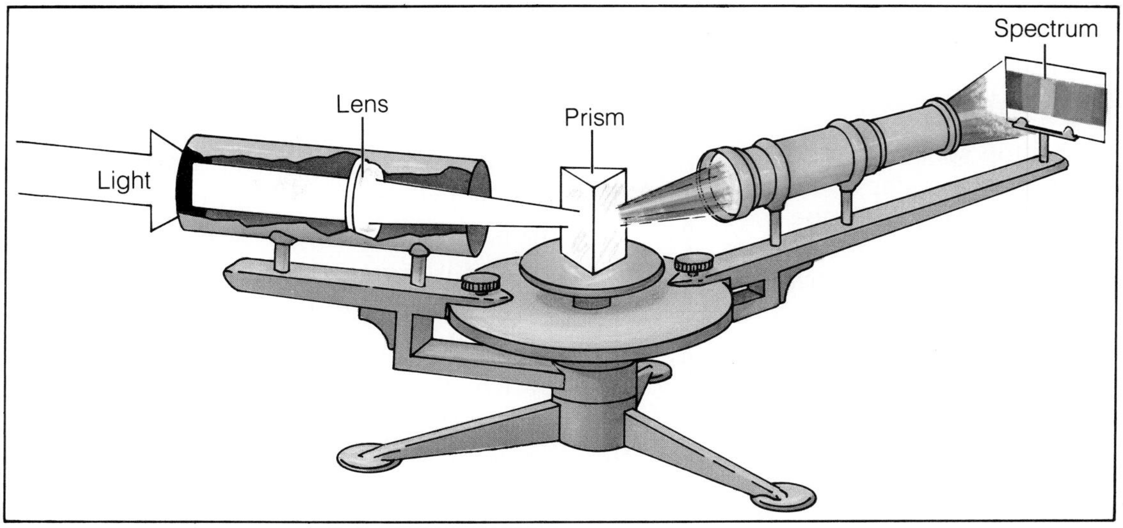

Figure 2–2 *In a spectroscope, light passes through a prism and is broken into a band of colors called a spectrum. What is the order of the colors in the spectrum?*

Stars on the Move

Every single object in the universe is on the move. The moon, for example, moves around the earth. The earth, in turn, travels around the sun. The sun moves about the center of the **galaxy** it is located within. A galaxy is a huge collection of stars. A typical galaxy may contain hundreds of billions of stars, all moving around the center of the galaxy.

Astronomers suggest that there may be as many as 100 billion major galaxies. And each galaxy has billions of stars. Like all the other objects in space, each and every galaxy is on the move. By using a spectroscope, astronomers can determine whether a particular galaxy is moving toward the earth or away from the earth.

Figure 2–3 *Each galaxy in this cluster of galaxies contains several hundred billion or more stars. About how many galaxies are there in the universe?*

The Red Shift

Light travels from stars as light waves. You read that a spectroscope breaks up light into a spectrum. This happens because each color of light has a different wavelength. When light strikes the prism in a spectroscope, the prism bends the light according to the wavelength of each color. Some wavelengths are bent more than others by the prism. So the white light that enters the prism comes out as a band of colors. Each color has a different wavelength.

Suppose a star is rapidly approaching the earth. The light waves from the star will be compressed,

Sharpen Your Skills

Red or Blue Shift?

The top spectrum represents that of a star not moving toward or away from the earth. The bottom two spectra show what would happen if the star were moving with respect to the earth.

1. Compare the bottom two spectra with the top spectum.

2. Determine which spectrum is of a star moving toward the earth and which is of a star moving away.

3. How can your answer to step 2 be explained in terms of red shift and blue shift?

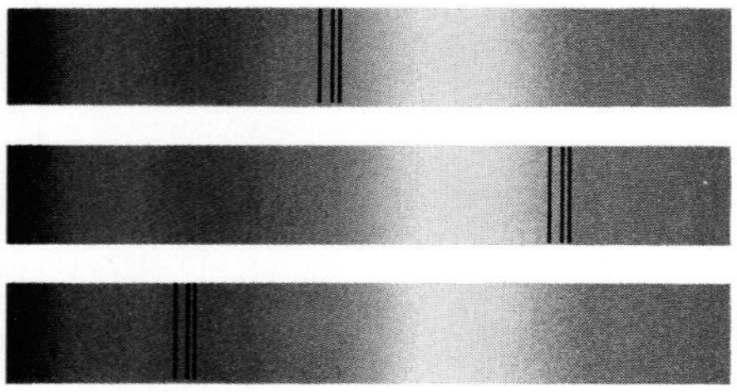

or pushed together. In fact, wavelengths from an approaching star often appear shorter than they really are. Shorter wavelengths of light are characteristic of blue and violet light. So the entire spectrum of an approaching star appears to be shifted slightly toward the blue end of the spectrum. This shifting is called the **blue shift.**

If a star is moving away from the earth, the light waves will be slightly expanded. The wavelengths of the light will appear longer than they really are. Longer wavelengths of light are characteristic of the red end of the spectrum. So the spectrum of a star moving away from the earth appears to be shifted slightly toward the red end. This is called the **red shift.** Astronomers know that the more the spectrum of light is shifted toward the blue or red end of the spectrum, the faster the star is moving toward or away from the earth.

The apparent change in the wavelengths of light that occurs when an object is moving toward or away from the earth is called the **Doppler effect.** You have probably "heard" another kind of Doppler effect right here on the earth. If you are in a car at a railroad crossing when a train is approaching, the sound of the train's whistle will become high-pitched. The sound of the whistle will become low-pitched as the train passes by and moves away from

Figure 2–4 *As the train approaches the crossing (top), sound waves are crowded together and reach the listener's ears with a high pitch. As the train leaves the crossing (bottom), sound waves are farther apart and have a lower pitch. What effect is this?*

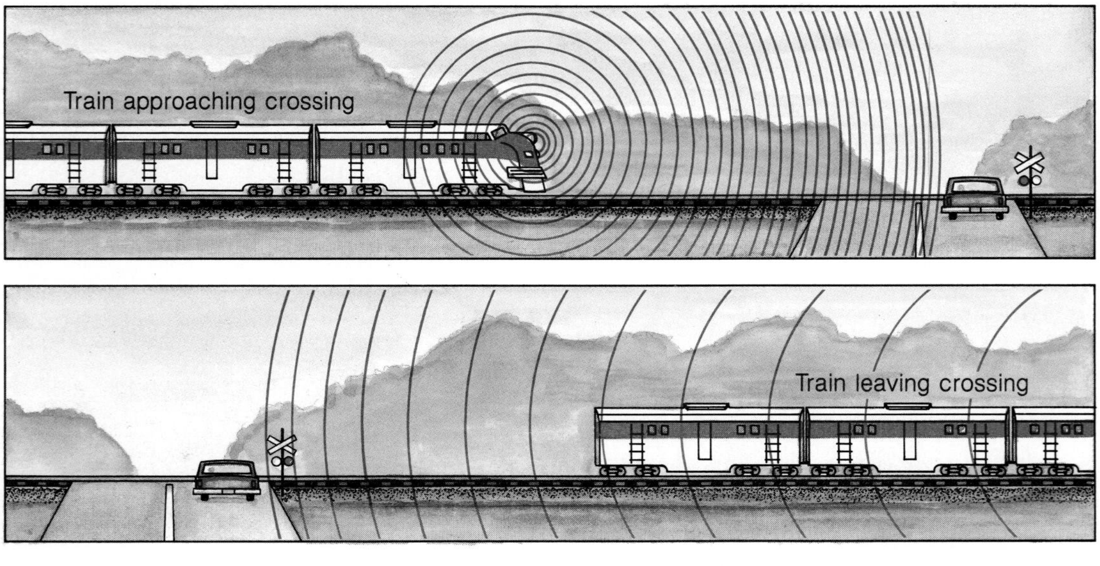

you. In this example, the Doppler effect involves sound waves. But the same principle applies to light waves moving toward or away from the earth.

When astronomers first used the spectroscope to study the light from stars in distant galaxies, they had a big surprise. None of the light from distant galaxies showed a blue shift. That is, none of the galaxies were moving toward the earth. Instead the light from every distant galaxy showed a red shift. Every galaxy in the universe seemed to be moving away from the earth.

After examining the red shifts of distant galaxies, astronomers concluded that the universe is expanding. Galaxies near the edge of the universe are racing away from the center of the universe at tremendous speeds. Galaxies closer to the center are also moving outward, but at slower speeds. What can account for an expanding universe?

The Big Bang Theory

Astronomers believe the expanding universe is the result of an enormous and powerful explosion called the big bang. The **big bang theory** may explain how the universe formed. **The big bang theory states that the universe began to expand with the explosion of concentrated matter and energy and has been expanding ever since.** According to the theory, all of the matter and energy in the universe was then concentrated into a single place. This place, of course, was hot and dense. Then some 15 to 20 billion years ago, an explosion—the big bang—shot the concentrated matter and energy in all directions. The fastest moving matter traveled farthest away. Energy, too, began moving away from the area of the big bang.

If the big bang theory is correct, the energy left from the big bang will be evenly spread out throughout the universe. This energy is known as **background radiation.** And indeed scientists have discovered that the background radiation in the entire universe is almost the same everywhere. This constant background radiation is one observation that supports the big bang theory.

After the initial big bang, the force of **gravity** began to affect the matter racing outward in every

Sharpen Your Skills

Model of an Expanding Universe

1. Cut out small circles from sticky labels. The circles will be the galaxies in your model.

2. Slowly blow up a balloon. Stop as soon as the balloon appears round. Hold the end of the balloon to keep the air from escaping.

3. Have a classmate place the galaxies in various places on the balloon. The balloon now represents the universe and its galaxies.

4. Blow up the balloon until it is completely inflated. As you do, observe what happens to the galaxies.

Do the galaxies get any bigger as the universe expands? What relationship can you find between the speed of the galaxies moving apart and their initial distance from one another?

Figure 2–5 *What does this drawing of several galaxies illustrate?*

direction. Gravity is a force of attraction between objects. All objects have a gravitational attraction for other objects. The more massive the object is, the stronger its gravitational attraction is. This force of gravity began to pull matter into clumps.

At some time, the clumps formed huge clusters of matter. These clumps became the galaxies of the universe. But even as the galaxies were forming, the matter inside the galaxies continued to race away from the area where the big bang had occurred. And this is just what astronomers have discovered. All of the galaxies are speeding away from the center of the universe.

An Open Universe

Most astronomers feel that the big bang theory leads to two possible futures for the universe. Perhaps the galaxies will continue racing outward. In this case, the universe will continue to expand. Such a universe is called an open, eternal universe. But eternal does not mean "forever" when it comes to the universe. In an open universe, the stars will eventually die off as the last of their energy is released. So the future of an open universe is one in which there will be nothing left. An open universe leads to total emptiness. But even if the universe is open, its end will not occur for billions of years.

Figure 2–6 *This quasar is some 12 billion light-years from the earth. How long does it take the quasar's light to reach the earth?*

A Closed Universe

Astronomers do not feel that the universe is an open universe. They suspect that the gravitational attraction between the galaxies will one day cause their movement away from each other to slow down. The expansion of the universe will finally come to a halt. Then gravity will begin to pull the galaxies back toward the center of the universe. When this happens, every galaxy will begin to show a blue shift in its spectrum. Recall that a blue shift means that the galaxy is moving toward the earth.

As the galaxies race back toward the center of the universe, the matter and energy in the universe will again come closer and closer to a central area. After many billions of years, all of the matter and energy will once again be packed into a small area. This area may be no bigger than the period at the end of this sentence. Then another big bang will occur. The formation of a universe will begin all over again. A universe that periodically expands and then contracts back on itself is called a closed universe. In a closed universe, a big bang may occur once every 80 to 100 billion years.

Quasars

If the universe is expanding, then objects near the very edge of the universe are the oldest objects in the universe. Put another way, these objects took longer to reach their present position than objects closer to the center of the universe. The most distant known objects in the universe are 12 billion light-years from the earth. They are called **quasars** (KWAY-zahrz). The word *quasar* stands for *quasi-stellar radio sources.* The prefix *quasi-* means "something like." The word *stellar* means "star." So a quasar is a starlike object that gives off radio waves.

Quasars are among the most studied, and the most mysterious, objects in the universe. They give off mainly radio waves and X-rays. The mystery of quasars is the tremendous amount of energy they give off. Although they seem too small to be galaxies, they give off more energy than 100 or more galaxies combined!

If the big bang theory is correct, then quasars at the very edge of the universe were among the first objects formed after the big bang. In fact, scientists now believe that quasars may represent the earliest stages in the formation of a galaxy. So when scientists observe quasars, they are observing the very edge and the very beginning of the universe. Keep in mind that the light from a quasar 12 billion light-years from the earth has traveled over 12 billion years to reach the earth. Astronomers observing quasars are, in a sense, looking back into time.

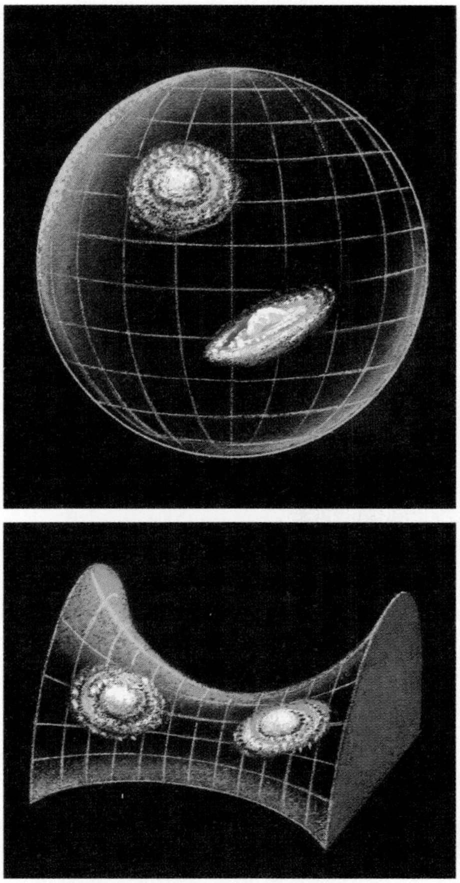

Figure 2–7 *A closed universe will eventually contract. Scientists picture a closed universe as similar to the surface of a ball (top). An open universe will expand until all of the stars die off. Scientists picture an open universe in the shape of a saddle (bottom).*

SECTION REVIEW

1. What happens to the spectrum of a star moving toward the earth? Away from the earth?
2. What two pieces of information provide evidence of the big bang?
3. Name the primary force involved in the formation of galaxies after the big bang.

Section Objective

To classify stars into groups

2–2 Star Groups

When you look up at the sky on a clear night, you can see hundreds of stars. If you use binoculars or a telescope, you will see thousands of other stars. Almost all of the stars you can see, including the sun, are part of a large system of stars called the **Milky Way Galaxy.** The sun, the earth, and the other eight planets are part of the Milky Way.

Until 1924, astronomers believed that the universe was made up of only the Milky Way and the unknown space beyond. In the 1920s, Edwin Hubble and other astronomers used a new telescope at the Mount Wilson Observatory in California. Hubble aimed the telescope at faint patches of light in the sky. When he examined photographs made through the telescope, he discovered that the patches of light were made up of tiny dots of light. Hubble hypothesized that these were other galaxies outside the Milky Way.

Galaxies, which contain various star groups, are the major features of the universe. They are very large, and there are many of them. But they contain only about 1 percent of the matter in the universe. The remaining 99 percent of the matter in the uni-

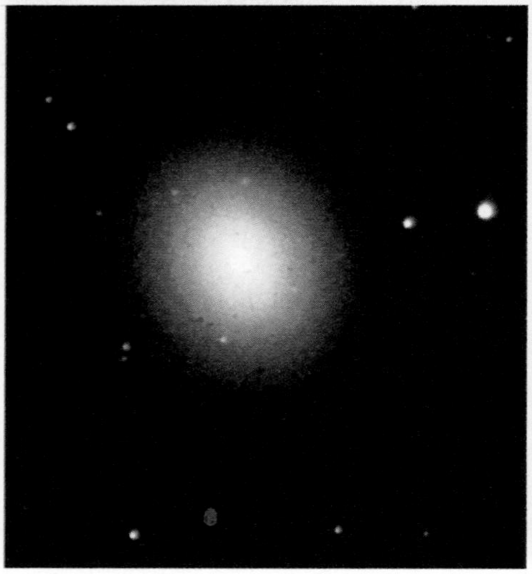

Figure 2–8 *There are three main types of galaxies: spiral galaxies (right), elliptical galaxies (bottom left), and irregular galaxies (top left). What kind of galaxy is the Milky Way?*

CAREER — *Astronomer*

HELP WANTED: ASTRONOMER Position includes research and teaching duties. PhD plus considerable knowledge of mathematics, physics, computers, or engineering required.

There are millions of objects in space, including stars, planets, moons, and comets. Only a small number of these objects are visible from the earth. The study of these objects is one of the oldest sciences, and one of the most exciting. Recent scientific developments have greatly increased our ability to explore and understand outer space.

People who study outer space are called **astronomers.** Most astronomers do research or teach. Some astronomers work in space museums called planetariums. Some study the planets in the solar system. Others are trying to find life elsewhere in the universe.

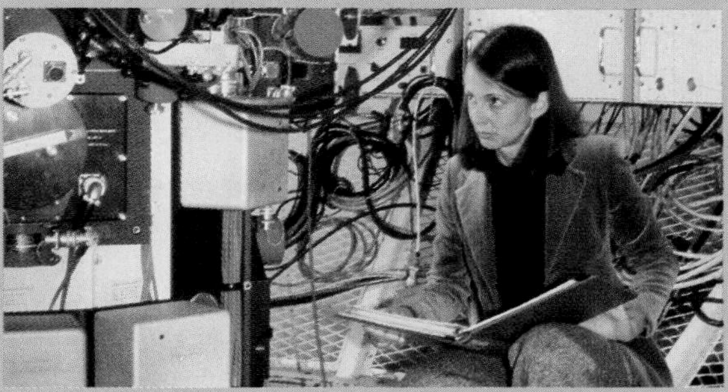

Astronomers use telescopes, computers, and other instruments. They develop and use mathematical equations to explain the behavior of stars and other bodies in space.

People who work in this field are curious and enjoy doing research. They attend college and graduate school and gain a good understanding of science and mathematics. To learn more about this exciting field, write to the American Astronomical Society, Sharp Laboratory, University of Delaware, Newark, DE 19711.

verse is in "empty" space. This matter consists of dust and gases generally not visible. Scientists are able to detect the dust and gases with radio telescopes and other special instruments.

Types of Galaxies

As astronomers examined the many photographs of galaxies, they discovered that galaxies have different shapes. There are three main types of galaxies: elliptical, spiral, and irregular.

Galaxies that vary in shape from nearly spherical, or round, to flat disks are called **elliptical** (ih-LIHP-tih-kuhl) **galaxies.** These galaxies contain very little dust and gas. The stars in elliptical galaxies are generally older than those in other types of galaxies.

Another type of galaxy has a center made up of a thick mass of material and has flattened arms that spiral around the center. This type is called a **spiral galaxy.** The Milky Way Galaxy and the nearby Andromeda Galaxy are spirals.

The third type of galaxy does not have the orderly shape of either the elliptical or the spiral

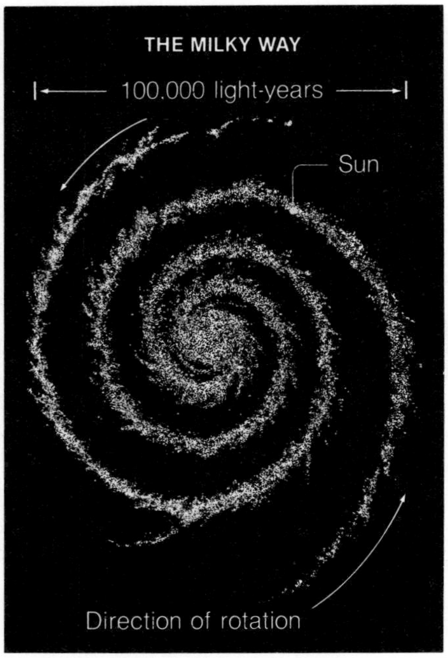

Figure 2–9 *This drawing shows the Milky Way Galaxy and its spiral arms. In what direction does the Milky Way Galaxy rotate?*

galaxy. These galaxies are called **irregular galaxies.** Irregular galaxies have no definite shape. The Large and Small Magellanic Clouds are irregular galaxies. They are the closest galaxies to the Milky Way. Several hundred irregular galaxies have been observed by astronomers. But they are much less common than the other types of galaxies.

The Milky Way Galaxy

All of the stars you can observe with the unaided eye are within the Milky Way Galaxy. The Milky Way Galaxy is a spiral galaxy containing about 100 to 200 billion stars. It also contains many gas and dust clouds called **nebulae** (NEHB-yuh-lee). Nebulae prevent direct observation of many stars in the galaxy. They block out the light of these stars. Most nebulae cannot be seen. But some nebulae can be seen through a telescope because they reflect the light from nearby stars.

Scientists estimate the Milky Way Galaxy to be about 100,000 light-years in diameter and about 15,000 light-years thick. See Figure 2–9. So even at the speed of light, it would take 100,000 years to travel across the Milky Way! The sun and its system of nine planets are located in an outer spiral arm of the Milky Way Galaxy. They are about 30,000 light-years from the center of the galaxy.

As you read, the Milky Way Galaxy is not standing still. It is rotating about its center. If you could view the galaxy from above, you would see that it spins in a counterclockwise direction. It takes the

Figure 2–10 *This edge-on drawing of the Milky Way was made by plotting the locations of over 7000 known stars.*

Figure 2–11 *The Pleiades is an open cluster of stars (left). The Hercules cluster of stars is a globular cluster (right).*

sun and planets approximately 200 million years to move around the center of the galaxy.

Star Clusters

Galaxies such as the Milky Way are the largest groups of stars in the universe. Within an individual galaxy, however, there are many smaller groups of stars. Many stars are found in clusters.

There are two types of star clusters in the Milky Way Galaxy. There are **open clusters** such as the Pleiades. And there are **globular** (GLAHB-yuh-luhr) **clusters** such as the cluster in the constellation Hercules, shown in Figure 2–11. Globular clusters are arranged in a spherical, or round, shape. They may contain more than 100,000 stars. Open clusters are less organized clusters of hundreds of stars.

Star clusters appear to the unaided eye as one star or a faint, white cloud. Why do you think that you cannot see the individual stars in a cluster?

Multiple Star Systems

Star clusters contain hundreds to hundreds of thousands of stars. But stars are often found in much smaller groups. Because the sun is a single star system, astronomers believed for many years that most stars form individual star systems. Today astronomers know that most stars are actually found in pairs called **binary stars.**

Figure 2–12 *This photograph shows Sirius, the Dog Star, and its companion. What kind of star system is this?*

In a binary star system, two stars revolve around each other. Sometimes one of the stars is much brighter than the companion star. When the dim star passes in front of the bright star, the light from the bright star fades. This is because the light from the bright star is blocked out by the dim star. Such star pairs are called **eclipsing binaries.**

Perhaps the most famous eclipsing binary is Algol. Every 69 hours, Algol dims to about one-third its normal brightness as the bright star is blocked by the dim companion star. Algol was named by Arab shepherds who first noticed its mysterious "winking" on and off. Fearing this strange star, they named it Algol, meaning "the ghoul." Without telescopes, the Arab shepherds had no way of knowing that Algol is an eclipsing binary.

Binary star systems are very common. But some star systems contain three or more stars. They are multiple star systems. You may already know that a star called Alpha Centauri is the closest star to the earth after the sun. Alpha Centauri is about 4.3 light-years from the earth. When viewed with the eye alone, Alpha Centauri appears to be a single speck in the sky. But Alpha Centauri is really a triple star system. In fact, one star in the system—Proxima Centauri—is the closest to the earth.

Figure 2–13 *In 1935, a star in the constellation Hercules erupted in a rare nova. A month later, the same star, shown by the arrows, had returned to normal and become dim again.*

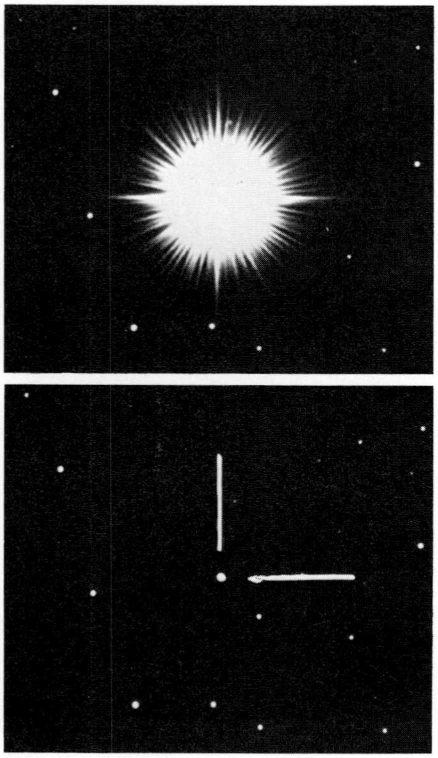

Novas

On rare occasions, astronomers have observed a star that suddenly becomes up to 100 times brighter in just a few days. Soon after it brightens, the star slowly becomes dimmer. This event is called a **nova.** Astronomers now believe that a nova occurs in a binary star system. Gases from one of the stars occasionally strike the surface of the companion star. The result is a nuclear explosion. A tremendous amount of heat, light, and gases bursts into space. This explosion is the nova.

Constellations: Star Groups That Form Patterns

People in ancient times were fascinated by the stars. Nomads, shepherds, and scholars gazed at the stars and wondered about the size, shape, and meaning of the universe. They noticed that there were groups of stars that remained together. They named these patterns of stars after animals, gods, and heroes. These star patterns are **constellations** (kahn-stuh-LAY-shuhnz). What constellations do you know of?

When viewed from the earth, constellation patterns have changed very little over thousands of years. Today 88 different constellations are recognized by astronomers.

One of the most well-known constellations is the Big Bear. The seven stars in the back end and tail of the Big Bear form the Big Dipper. The Big Dipper can be seen in the northern sky. Two bright stars in the cup of the Big Dipper are known as the pointers. They point to **Polaris** (poh-LAR-ihs), or the North Star. See Figure 2–14. The North Star is the last star in the handle of the Little Dipper. The Little Dipper is part of the Little Bear constellation.

On clear winter nights, you can see the large constellation Orion, the Hunter. There are two bright stars in this constellation: Betelgeuse (BEET-uhl-jooz) and Rigel (RIGH-juhl). Nearby are other constellations: Gemini; Canis Major, or the

Sharpen Your Skills

Designing Constellations

1. Choose the star chart in Appendix D that shows the night sky for the current season.

2. Trace on a sheet of paper the outline of the chart, Polaris, and two constellations near the edge of the chart.

3. Take your star chart outside after dark. Locate Polaris and the two constellations.

4. Use the brighter stars to make your own patterns of animals, objects, etc. Draw the new "constellations" on your chart using Polaris and the two constellations as reference points. Referring to the original chart, label as many of the stars as possible.

Figure 2–14 *These are some of the constellations you can see in the night sky. What do the pointer stars point to?*

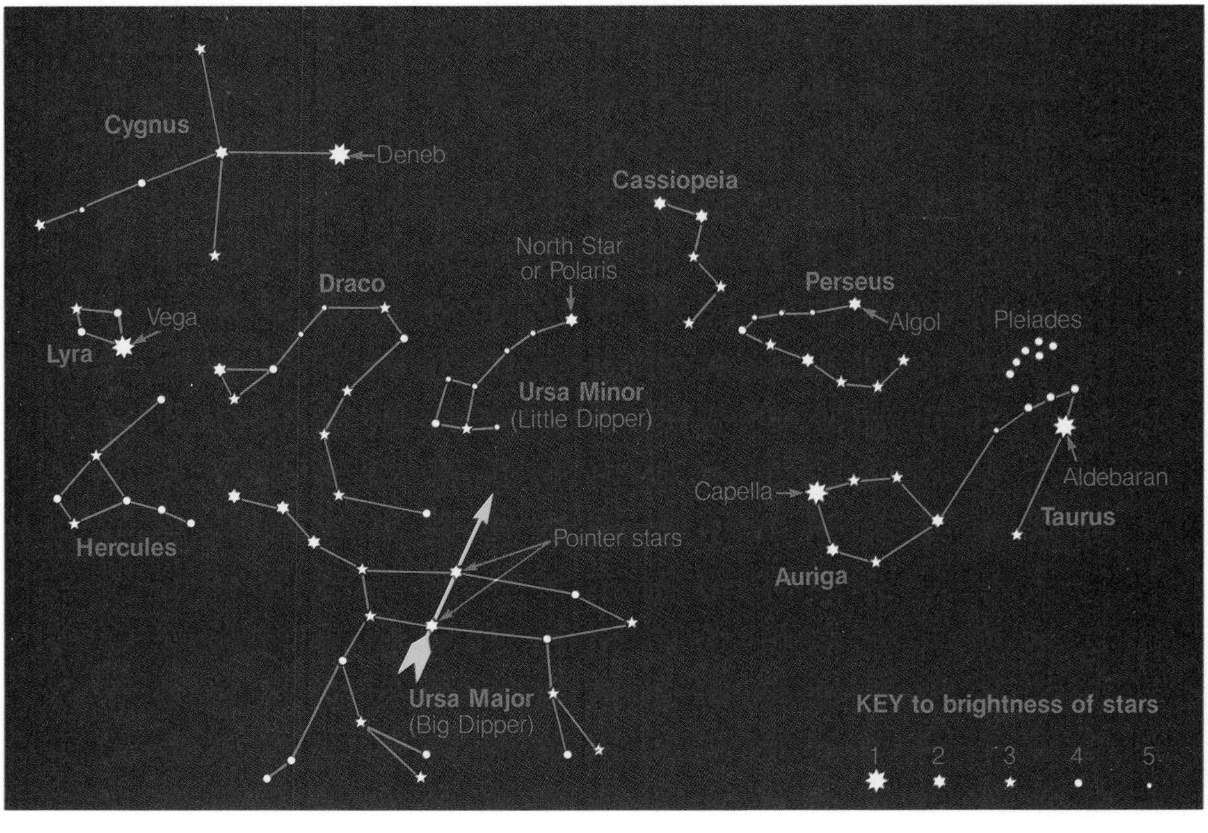

Big Dog; and Canis Minor, or the Little Dog. Some of the summer constellations that are easy to recognize are Scorpius, Leo, and Virgo.

SECTION REVIEW

1. What is the difference between open star clusters and globular star clusters?
2. What is a binary star system?
3. What is an eclipsing binary?

Section Objective

To compare the size, composition, temperature, color, mass, and brightness of stars

2–3 Characteristics of Stars

There may be more than 200 billion billion stars in the universe. In general, the forces that affect the formation, life, and eventual death of all these stars are the same. Yet stars vary in a great many ways. **Stars vary in size, composition, temperature, color, mass, and brightness.**

Astronomers cannot study every star in the sky. There are simply too many. But they can examine the stars closest to the earth. The knowledge they gain from studying these stars can then be applied to other stars too distant to examine in such detail.

Sharpen Your Skills

Using Star Charts

1. Turn to the star charts in Appendix D.

2. Take the star chart outside on a starry night. Make sure you hold the star chart in the proper position for the time and date you are observing the night sky.

3. Make a drawing of what you see.

4. In about one month, repeat this activity.

How many constellations can you find in your first drawing? In your second drawing? Are there any changes in your new drawing? If so, can you explain them?

Sizes of Stars

From the earth, most stars in the sky look like tiny points of light. But they really vary greatly in size. So you cannot judge the size of stars by simply looking at them in the sky.

Astronomers have grouped stars into five main types by size. See Figure 2–15. The vast majority of stars you can see in the night sky are medium-sized stars. The diameter of medium-sized stars ranges from about one-tenth the diameter of the sun to about ten times the diameter of the sun. The sun has a diameter of about 1,392,000 kilometers, which is about 109 times the diameter of the earth.

Stars with a diameter 10 to 100 times that of the sun are **giant stars.** But even giant stars are not the largest of the known stars. Some stars are **supergiant stars.** The diameter of supergiants may be up to 1000 times the diameter of the sun. For a better idea of this size, consider this: If the supergiant star

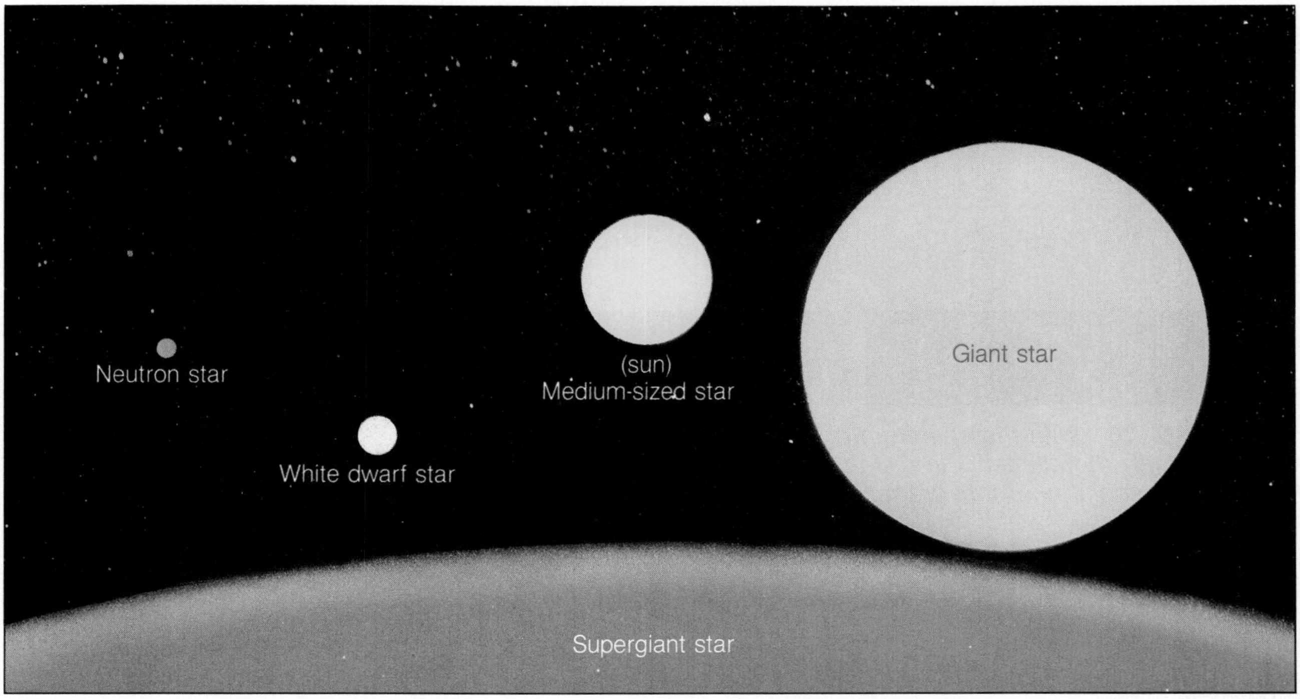

Figure 2–15 *Stars are found in a variety of sizes, from tiny neutron stars to monstrous supergiants.*

Antares replaced the sun, it would extend well beyond the planet Mars. What would happen to the earth if a supergiant star replaced the sun?

Many stars are smaller than the sun, which is a medium-sized star. Some stars, such as one called Van Maanen's star, are called **white dwarfs.** Van Maanen's star has a diameter of about 7380 kilometers, which is little more than one-half the diameter of the earth. The smallest stars are called **neutron stars.** Neutron stars are much smaller than the earth and have a diameter of about 16 kilometers.

Composition of Stars

Astronomers cannot take a bit of a star and test it to see what it is made of. But they can determine the composition of stars, even stars many light-years from the earth. To determine the composition of a star, astronomers use the spectroscope.

How can a spectroscope show what a star is made of? Let's begin with the simple example of ordinary table salt. Table salt, or sodium chloride, is made of the elements sodium and chlorine. If table salt is placed in a flame, the flame will burn bright yellow. The yellow flame is caused by the burning of the sodium in salt. A yellow flame, then, is a characteristic of burning sodium.

Suppose the yellow light from the flame is passed through a spectroscope. No matter how many times this is done, two thin lines will always appear in the spectrum in the same place. See Figure 2–16. In fact, no other element will produce the same two lines as sodium. In a way, these two lines are the "fingerprint" of the element sodium.

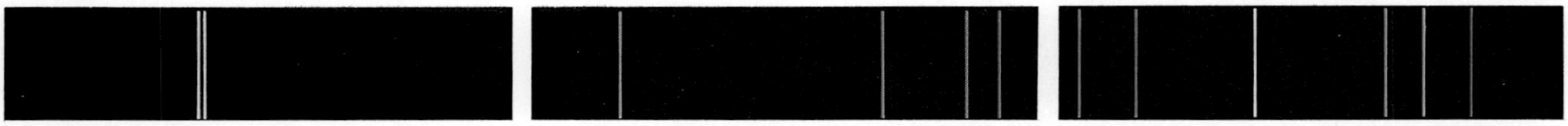

Figure 2–16 *With the spectrum produced by a spectroscope, scientists can identify the elements in distant stars. These spectra are of the elements sodium (left), hydrogen (center), and helium (right).*

Other elements also produce a characteristic set of lines when they are burned and the light given off is passed through a spectroscope. So every known element has a fingerprint. By passing the light from a star through a spectroscope, astronomers can determine exactly what elements are in that star.

By using the spectroscope, astronomers have found that almost all stars have the same general chemical makeup. The most common element in stars is hydrogen. Hydrogen is the lightest element. It makes up 60 to 80 percent of the total mass of a star. The second lightest element is helium. Helium is also the second most common element in a typical star. The combination of hydrogen and helium makes up about 96 to 99 percent of a star's mass. All other elements in a star total little more than 4 percent of the star's mass. These other elements include oxygen, neon, carbon, and nitrogen.

Figure 2–17 *What does the bright red color of the metal indicate to you?*

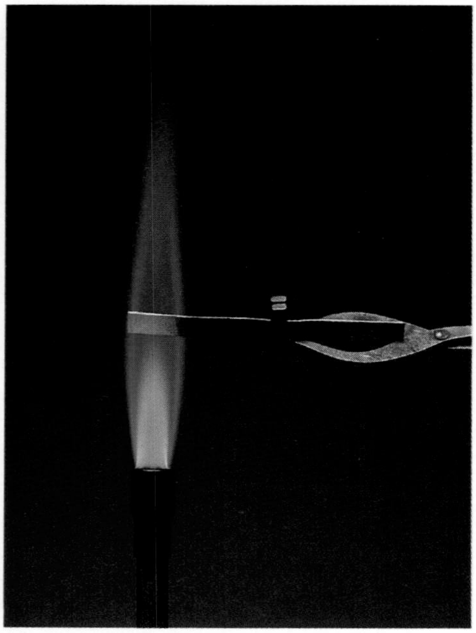

Surface Temperature of Stars

Suppose you place a piece of metal in a hot flame. As the metal heats up, it will begin to change color. Soon it may turn bright red. The color of the heated metal indicates just how hot the metal is. In the same way, the color of the light from a star provides information about the surface temperature of that star.

The sun is a yellow star. But stars come in many other colors. By studying the color of a star, astronomers can determine its surface temperature. Keep in mind that the surface temperature of a star is much lower than the temperature in the star's core. For example, the sun has a surface temperature of about 6000°C. Yet the temperature of the sun's core can reach 15,000,000°C.

Using color as their guide, astronomers have determined that the surface temperature of the hottest stars is about 50,000°C. Such stars shine with a blue-white light. Red stars, which are among the coolest stars, have a surface temperature of about 3000°C. Most other stars have temperatures between these two extremes. See Figure 2–18.

Brightness of Stars

Some stars are brighter than others. The brightness of a star depends on its temperature, size, and distance from the earth. The measure of a star's brightness is called its **magnitude** (MAG-nuh-tood). First magnitude stars are very bright. Second magnitude stars are dimmer. The larger the magnitude number is, the dimmer the star is. The dimmest stars visible to the unaided eye on a clear night are sixth magnitude stars. These stars are about 100 times dimmer than first magnitude stars.

Astronomers refer to two different magnitudes for stars. A star's brightness as it appears from the earth is its **apparent magnitude.** The magnitude scale is based on apparent brightness. Astronomers can also determine the **absolute magnitude** of a star. The absolute magnitude of a star is the actual amount of light it gives off. Stars that have the same absolute magnitude often have different apparent magnitudes. These stars have different apparent magnitudes because they are different distances from the earth. Why do you think two stars with the same apparent magnitude might have different absolute magnitudes?

Most stars have a constant brightness. But some stars do not have a constant brightness. The brightness of these stars varies from time to time. Such stars are called **variable stars.** A special class of variable stars changes in both brightness and size. Such stars are called pulsating variable stars. Polaris, located in the Little Dipper, is a pulsating variable star. It changes from bright to dim and back to bright in a four-day cycle. Sometimes astronomers

Figure 2–18 *The color of a star can help astronomers determine its surface temperature. What color are the hottest stars?*

STAR COLORS AND SURFACE TEMPERATURES

Color	Average Surface Temperature (°C)	Examples
Blue or blue-white	35,000	NGC-5882 Zeta Oridani Spica Algol
White	10,000	Sirius Vega
Yellow	6000	Procyon Sun Alpha Centauri A
Red-orange	5000	Alpha Centauri B
Red	3000	Proxima Centauri Barnard's star

refer to pulsating variable stars as **cepheid** (SEHF-ee-ihd) **variables.** They use this term because the very first pulsating variable star discovered is in a group of stars called Cepheus.

Sharpen Your Skills

Comparing Absolute Magnitude With Apparent Magnitude

1. Obtain two flashlights that are of the same size and bulb wattage.

2. On a dark night, have two classmates hold the flashlights about 10 m away from you. Since the flashlights have the same wattage, they should appear equally bright.

3. Have one classmate move about 20 m farther away. Observe the brightness of each flashlight again.

Has the absolute magnitude changed? Has the apparent magnitude changed? What is the difference between absolute magnitude and apparent magnitude?

The Hertzsprung–Russell Diagram

Early in the twentieth century, two astronomers, Ejnar Hertzsprung and Henry Russell, found a relationship between the absolute magnitude and the temperature of stars. They discovered that as the absolute magnitude of stars increases, the temperature also usually increases. The relationship between the absolute magnitude and the temperature of stars is shown in Figure 2–19. You can see a definite pattern. This pattern forms the **Hertzsprung–Russell (H–R) diagram.**

On the Hertzsprung–Russell diagram, the surface temperature of stars is plotted along the horizontal axis. The absolute magnitude, or actual brightness, of stars is plotted along the vertical axis. If you study Figure 2–19, you will see that most stars fall in an area from the upper left corner to the lower right corner. This area is called the main sequence. The stars within this area are called **main-sequence stars.**

Main-sequence stars make up over 90 percent of the stars in the sky. The hottest main-sequence stars shine with a blue or blue-white light and are located in the upper left corner of the H–R diagram. Cool, dim main-sequence stars appear in the lower right corner.

The other 10 percent of the stars in the H–R diagram were once main-sequence stars. But as these stars aged, they changed. Today they are no longer main-sequence stars. In the area above the main sequence are giant stars and supergiant stars. In the area below the main sequence are tiny white dwarfs.

Distance to Stars

Astronomers use various methods to measure the distance from the earth to stars. One method of measuring the distance to stars is **parallax**

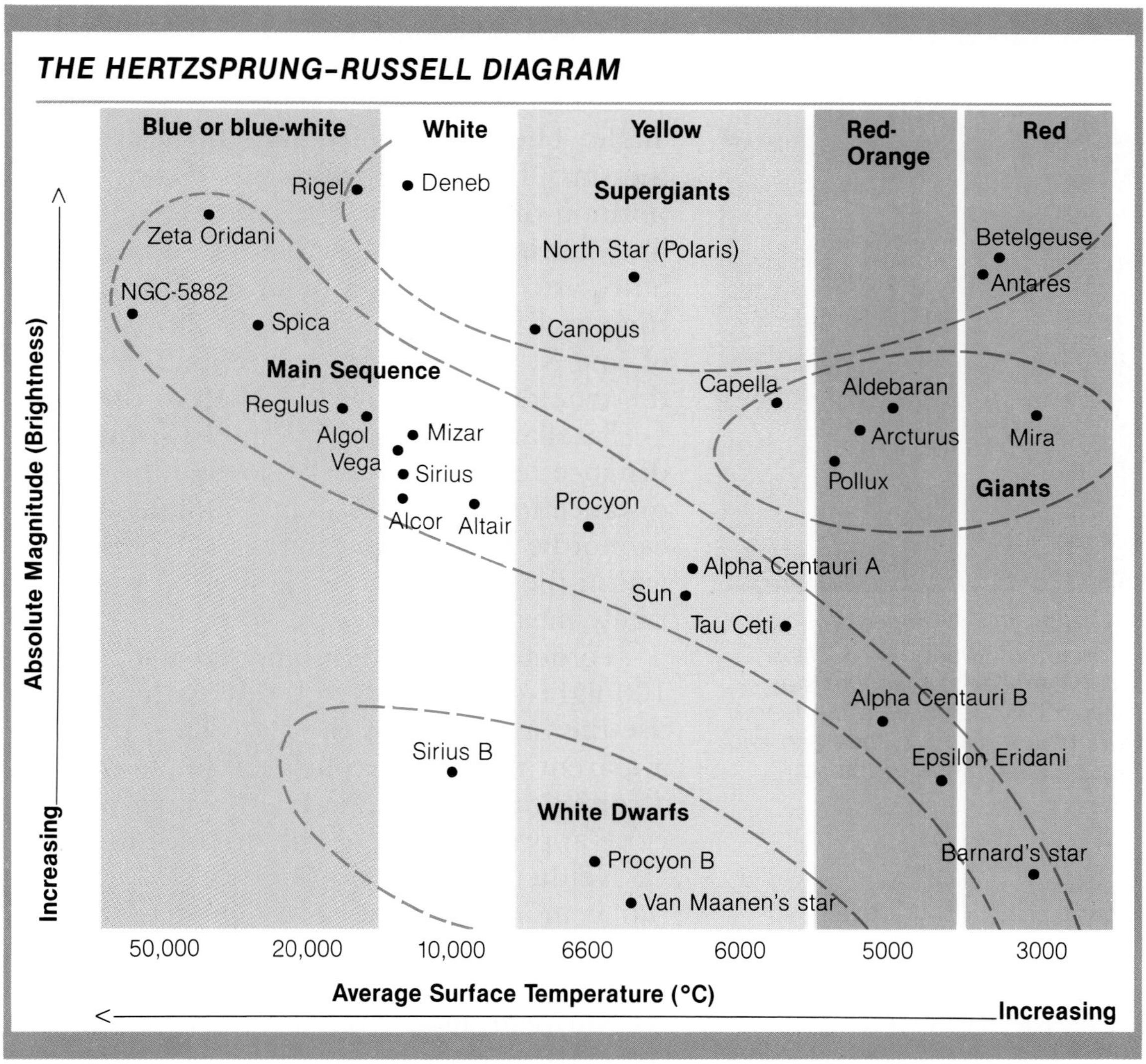

Figure 2–19 *The Hertzsprung–Russell diagram shows that, for most stars, as the absolute magnitude increases, the surface temperature also increases. For main-sequence stars, what is the relationship between temperature and brightness?*

(PAR-uh-laks). Parallax refers to the apparent change in the position of a star in the sky. This apparent change in position is not due to the movement of the star. Instead it is due to the change in the *earth's* position as the earth moves around the sun. The star stays in the same place.

In Figure 2–20 on page 50, you can see how parallax is used to determine the distance to a star. First the apparent position of the star in June and in December is noted. A line is then drawn between the earth's position in these months and the center of the sun. This straight line will become the base of a triangle. The length of this base line is known to astronomers because it has already been carefully measured.

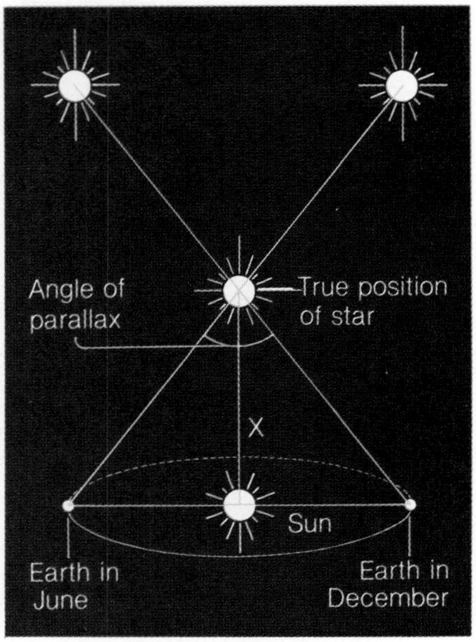

Figure 2–20 *Scientists can use an apparent change in position called parallax to measure star distance. By calculating the length of the line marked X, they can find the actual distance to the star.*

Next a diagonal line is drawn from each end of the base line to the apparent position of the star in June and in December. These three lines form a triangle. The tip of the triangle is the true position of the star. Then a vertical line is drawn from the true position of the star to the base of the triangle. This line, labeled X, is the actual distance to the star. Since astronomers can determine the angles within the parallax triangle, they can calculate the length of line X. In this way, they can accurately measure the true distance from the earth to the star.

Parallax is a reliable method for measuring the distance to stars relatively close to the earth. The distance to stars more than 100 light-years away cannot be found using parallax. Why? The angles within the parallax triangle are too small to be accurately measured.

To determine the distance to a star more than 100 light-years away from the earth, astronomers use the brightness of the star. They plug the star's apparent magnitude and its absolute magnitude into a complicated formula. The formula provides a close approximation of the distance to that star.

Neither brightness nor parallax will work when a star is more than 7 million light-years from the earth. To determine the distance to the most distant stars, astronomers once again use the spectroscope. As you read, light from a star moving away from the earth has a red shift in its spectrum. Astronomers measure the amount of red shift in a star's spectrum and use some very complex formulas to calculate how far from the earth a star is located.

Why Stars Shine

You have learned how light from a star can be used to determine its composition, temperature, and distance. But what exactly causes a star to shine? To answer this question, you must look deep into the core of the star.

Within the core of a star, gravitational forces are very strong. In fact, gravity pulls together the atoms of hydrogen gas in the core so tightly that they become fused together. This process is called **nuclear fusion.** During nuclear fusion, hydrogen atoms are fused to form helium atoms. Nuclear fusion, then, allows a star to produce a new element by combining other elements.

The sun changes about 600 billion kilograms of hydrogen into 595.8 billion kilograms of helium every second! As you can see from these numbers, during this fusion process 4.2 billion kilograms of the original mass of the hydrogen seem to be lost every second. The missing mass has been changed to energy. Most of the mass is changed into heat and light. And that is why a star shines. Of course, not all of the light from nuclear fusion is visible light. Some of it may be infrared rays, ultraviolet rays, radio waves, and X-rays.

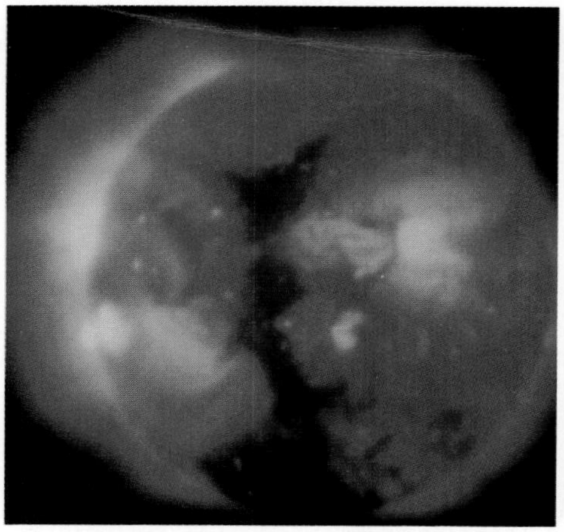

Figure 2–21 *The sun is a dynamic star. What process produces the heat and light the sun gives off?*

SECTION REVIEW

1. How do astronomers determine the surface temperature of a star?
2. What is the difference between apparent magnitude and absolute magnitude?
3. Why are observations of a star made six months apart when using parallax to measure its distance from the earth?

2–4 Life and Death of Stars

Section Objective

To relate the original mass of a star to its life cycle

Astronomers agree that stars change over time. The stars you see, including the sun, did not always look the way they do today. These stars will continue to change. Changes may take place over a few million years, or perhaps several billion years. Astronomers refer to these changes in a star as the life cycle of a star.

Some stars have existed almost since the origin of the universe. Other stars, such as the sun, have come from the matter created by the first stars. From their studies of stars, astronomers have charted the life cycle of a star from its "birth" to its "death." According to the present theory of star formation, the many different kinds of stars in the sky represent the various stages of the life cycle of a star.

Protostars

You read that galaxies contain huge clouds of dust and gases called nebulae. The most current theory of star formation states that new stars are born from the gases in a nebula. Over time, some of the hydrogen gas in a nebula is clumped together by gravity. The hydrogen atoms form a spinning cloud of gas within the nebula. Over millions of years, more and more hydrogen gas is pulled into the spinning cloud. Collisions between hydrogen atoms become more frequent. These collisions cause the hydrogen gas to heat up.

When the temperature within the spinning cloud reaches about 15,000,000°C, nuclear fusion begins. The great heat given off during nuclear fusion causes a new star, or **protostar,** to form. As a result of nuclear fusion, the protostar soon begins to shine and give off heat and light.

Medium-Sized Stars

Once a protostar forms, its life cycle is fixed. Everything that will happen to that star has already been determined. **The main factor that shapes the**

Figure 2–22 *New stars are forming right now in this giant cloud of dust and gas called a nebula. The sun formed in such a nebula about 5 billion years ago.*

life and eventual death of the star is how much mass it began with.

For the first few billion years, the new star continues to shine as its hydrogen is changed into helium by nuclear fusion in the star's core. But eventually most of the star's original supply of hydrogen is used up. By this time, most of the star's core has been changed to helium. Then the helium core begins to shrink. As it shrinks, the core heats up. The outer shell of the star is still composed mainly of hydrogen. The energy released by the heating of the helium core causes the outer hydrogen shell to expand greatly. As the outer shell expands, it cools and its color reddens. At this point, the star is a red giant. It is red because cooler stars shine red. And it is a giant because the star's outer shell has expanded greatly from its original size.

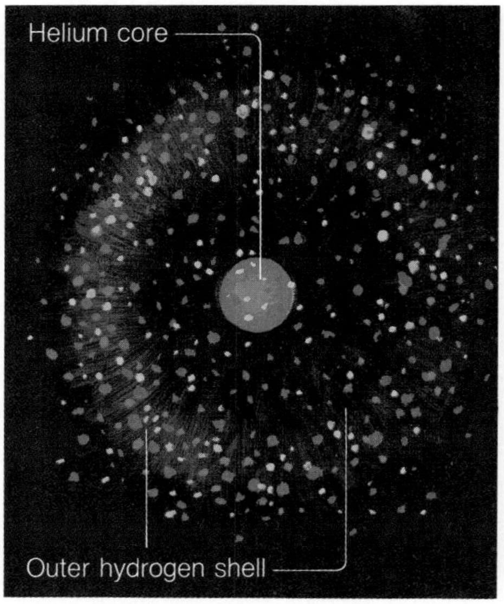

Figure 2–23 *This illustration shows a red giant star. What does the red color of the outer shell indicate?*

As the red giant ages, it continues to "burn" the hydrogen gas in its shell. The temperature within the helium core continues to get hotter and hotter, too. At about 200,000,000°C, the helium atoms in the core fuse together to form carbon atoms. Around this time, the last of the hydrogen gas surrounding the red giant begins to drift away. This drifting gas forms a ring around the central core of the star. This ring is called a planetary nebula. See Figure 2–24.

Figure 2–24 *This ring nebula, or planetary nebula, is all that is left of the gases that once surrounded a red giant star.*

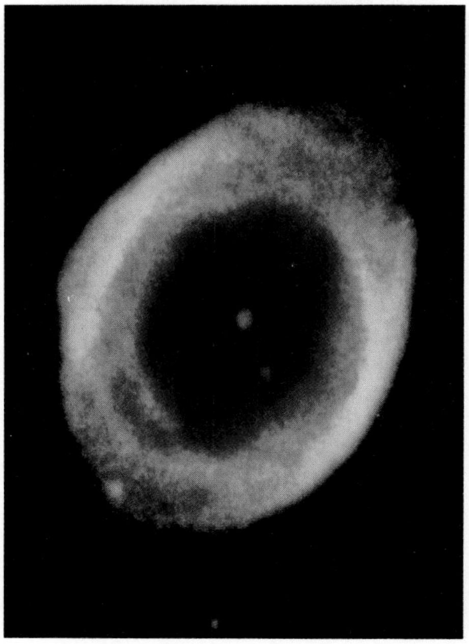

At some point in the red giant's life, the last of the helium atoms in its core is fused into carbon atoms. The star begins to die. Without nuclear fusion taking place in its core, the star slowly cools and fades. Finally gravity causes the last of the star's matter to collapse inward. The matter is squeezed so tightly that the star becomes a tiny white dwarf.

White Dwarfs

The matter squeezed into a white dwarf is extremely dense. In fact, a single teaspoon of matter in a white dwarf may have a mass of several tons. But a white dwarf is not a dead star. It still shines with a cool, white light.

At some point, the last of the white dwarf's energy is gone. It becomes a dead star. The length of time it takes a medium-sized star to become a white dwarf and die depends on the mass of the star

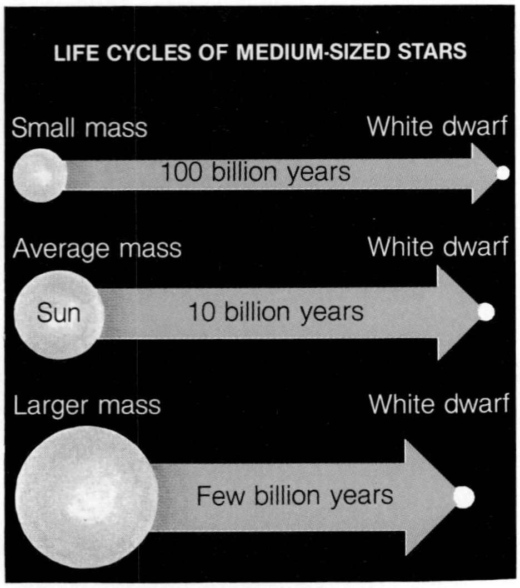

Figure 2–25 *Medium-sized stars all end up as white dwarfs. What is the relationship between mass and the time it takes a medium-sized star to become a white dwarf?*

when it first formed. It will take about 10 billion years for a medium-sized star such as the sun to pass from formation to death. A smaller medium-sized star may take as long as 100 billion years. But a large medium-sized star may die within only a few billion years. As you can see, the smaller the starting mass of a star is, the longer it will live.

Massive Stars

The life cycle of a massive star is quite different from that of a medium-sized star. At formation, massive stars usually have at least six times as much mass as the sun. Massive stars start off like medium-sized stars. They continue on the same life-cycle path until they become red giants. Unlike medium-sized stars, massive stars do not follow the path from red giant to white dwarf. They take a much different path.

Recall that a red giant becomes a white dwarf when all of the helium in its core has turned to carbon. In a massive star, gravity continues to pull together the carbon atoms in the core. When the core is squeezed so tightly that the heat given off reaches about 600,000,000°C, the carbon atoms begin to fuse together to form new elements such as oxygen and nitrogen. The core of the massive star is so hot that fusion continues until the heavy element iron forms. But not even the tremendous heat of the massive star can cause iron atoms to fuse together.

Supernovas

By the time most of the nuclear fusion in a massive star stops, the central core is mainly iron. Although the process is not well understood, the iron atoms begin to absorb energy rather than release energy. Soon this energy is released as the star breaks apart in a tremendous explosion called a **supernova.** A supernova can light the sky for weeks and appear as bright as a million suns.

During a supernova explosion, the heat in a star can reach temperatures up to 100,000,000,000°C! At these very high temperatures, iron atoms within the core fuse together to form new elements. These

Sharpen Your Skills

Predicting the Sun's Fate

The sun is a medium-sized star about 5 billion years old. Using the information in this chapter, predict the future of the sun from the present to its eventual "death." See if you can determine at what point the fate of the earth will be affected by the sun's life cycle.

newly formed elements, along with most of the star's remaining gases, explode into space. The resulting cloud of dust and gases forms a new nebula. The gases in this new nebula contain many elements formed during the supernova. At some point, new stars may form within the new nebula.

Most astronomers agree that the nebula from which the sun and its planets formed was the result of a gigantic supernova many billions of years ago. Why do you think astronomers feel that the sun could not have formed in a nebula of only hydrogen and helium gases?

The most famous supernova ever recorded was observed by Chinese astronomers in 1054. The supernova lit the day sky for 23 days and could be seen at night for over 600 days. Today the remains of this supernova can be seen in the sky as the Crab Nebula. See Figure 2–26. One day, perhaps, new stars will form within the Crab Nebula, and the cycle will begin all over again.

Sharpen Your Skills

A Wondrous Journey

Write a story describing the wondrous sights you would see if you could take a journey from one end of the Milky Way to the other. In your story, use at least five words from the vocabulary list on page 59.

Figure 2–26 *The Crab Nebula formed from the supernova explosion of a dying star.*

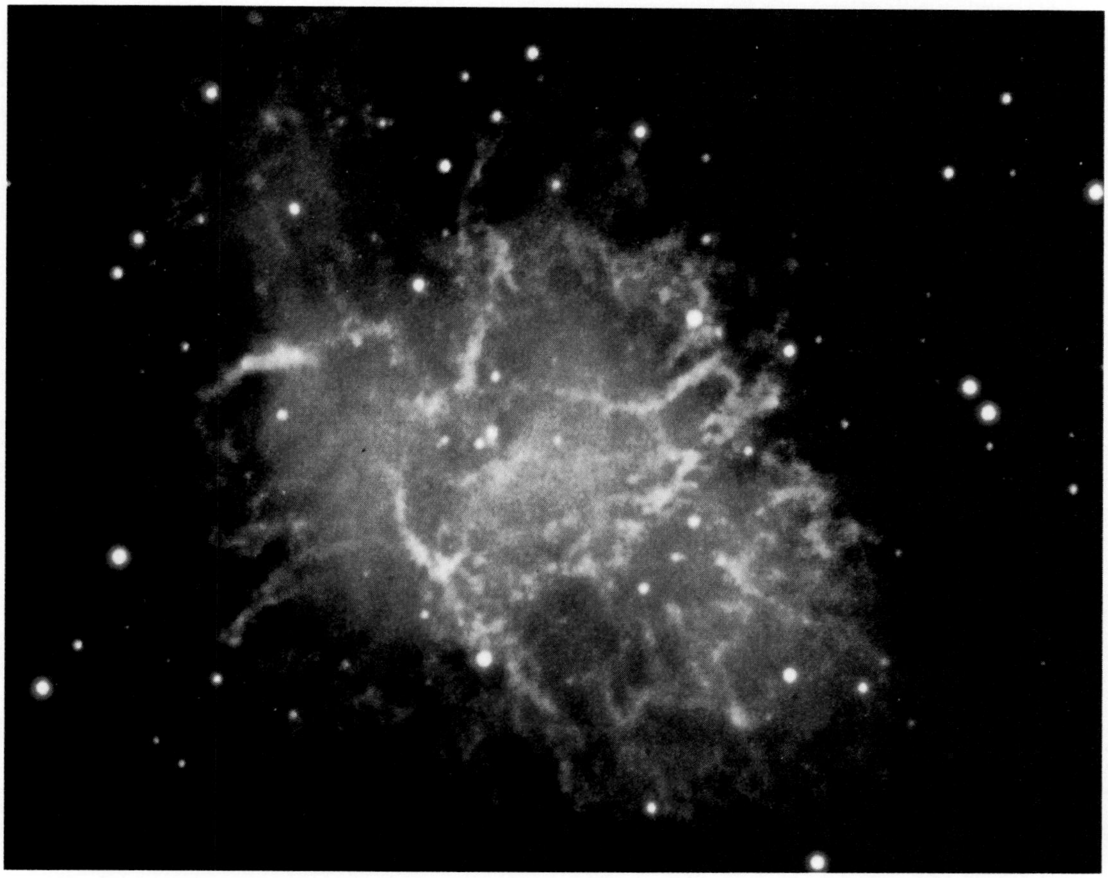

Neutron Stars

What happens to the remains of the core of a star that has undergone a supernova? Again the fate of the core depends on the starting mass of the star. A star that began 6 to 30 times as massive as the sun will end up as a neutron star after a supernova. A neutron star is about as massive as the sun but is often less than 16 kilometers in diameter. Such a star is extremely dense. A teaspoon of neutron star matter would have a mass of about 100 million tons!

Neutron stars spin very rapidly. As a neutron star spins, it gives off energy in the form of radio waves. Usually the radio waves are given off as pulses of energy. Astronomers can detect these pulses of radio waves if the pulses are directed toward the earth. Neutron stars that give off pulses of radio waves are called **pulsars.** So the end result of a supernova may be a pulsar. And in fact, astronomers have found a pulsar at the center of the Crab Nebula. The neutron star in the Crab Nebula pulses at a rate of about 30 times per second.

Black Holes

Suppose a star begins with a mass 30 times or more the mass of the sun. The star will undergo a supernova. But this supermassive star will not form a neutron star. Its fate is even more unusual.

The core left behind after the supernova of a supermassive star is unbelievably dense. It is so

Figure 2–27 *The fate of a star depends on the star's mass when it first formed. The sun is a low-mass star that will one day become a white dwarf and finally a dead black dwarf.*

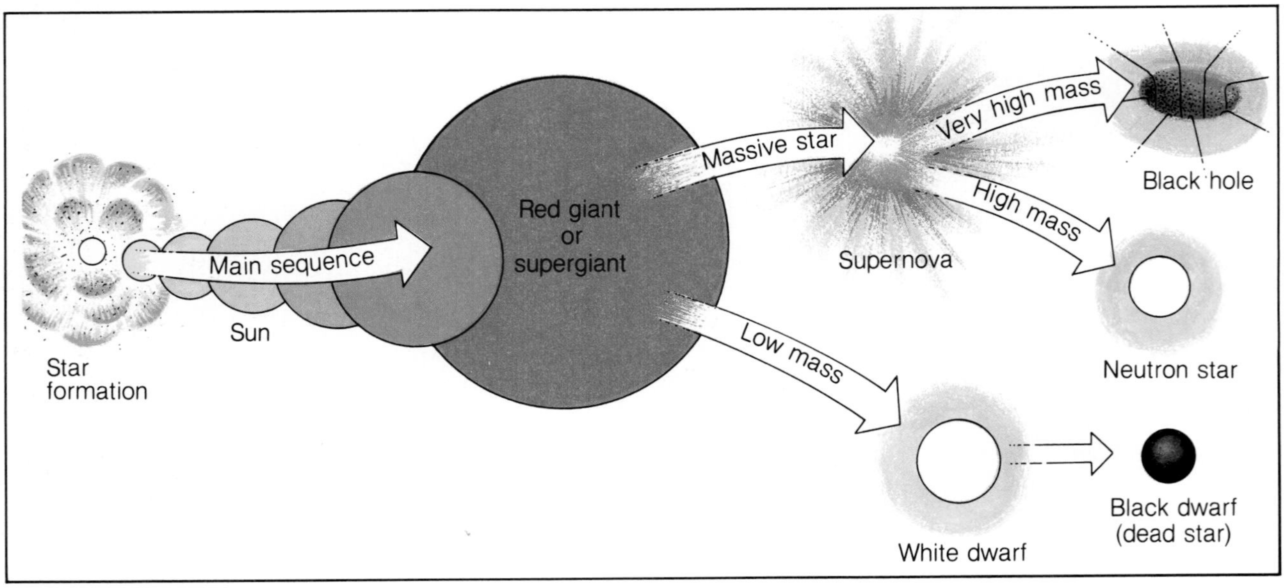

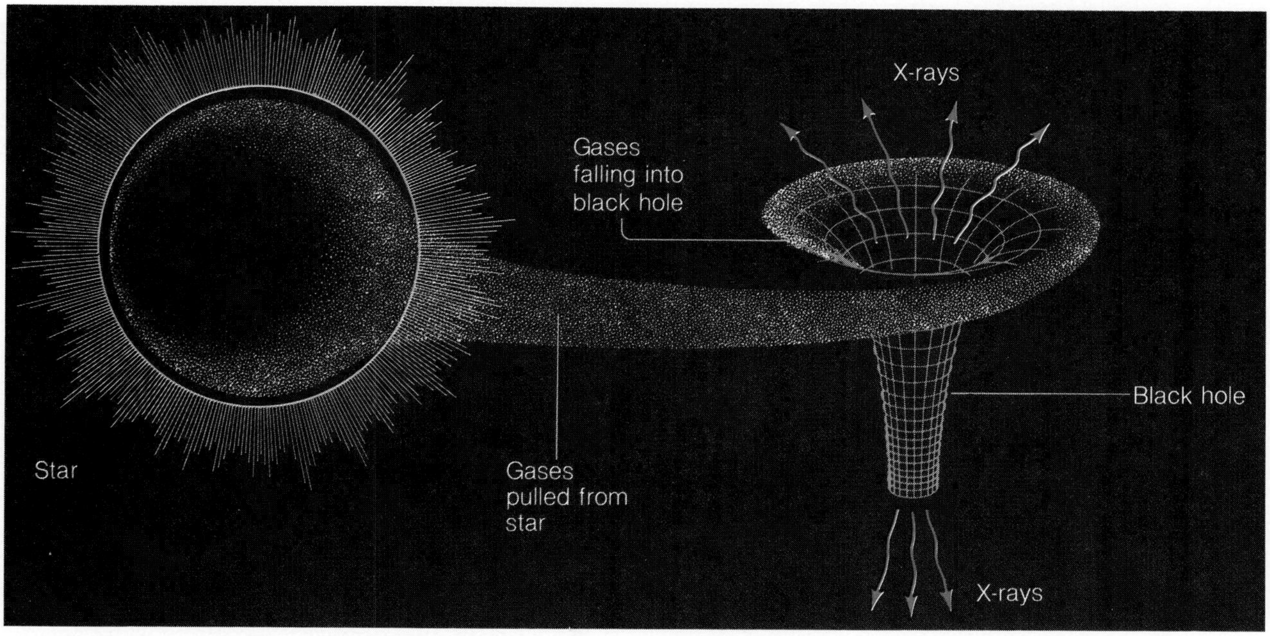

Figure 2–28 *Some black holes have a companion star. Gases from the companion star are pulled into the black hole. When this occurs, the black hole releases a huge burst of X-rays.*

dense, in fact, that it is actually swallowed up by its own gravity. The gravity is so great that nothing, not even passing light, can escape it. The core has become a **black hole.** A black hole, then, is the remains of a supermassive star after a supernova. Black holes have been described as "cosmic vacuum cleaners" because they swallow any nearby matter or energy.

If black holes do not allow even light to escape, how can astronomers find them? Actually, it is very difficult to detect black holes. But some black holes have a companion star. When the gases from the companion star are pulled into a black hole, the gases are heated. Before the gases are sucked into the black hole and lost forever, they may give off some X-rays. So scientists can detect black holes by the X-rays given off when matter falls into the black holes. See Figure 2–28.

Figure 2–29 *This photograph of the center of the Milky Way Galaxy was taken with the IRAS infrared telescope. Scientists now believe that there is a black hole in the center of the Milky Way.*

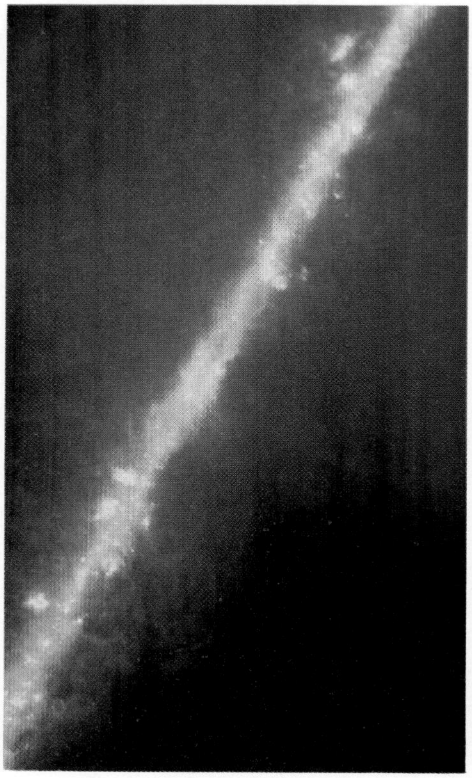

SECTION REVIEW

1. What factor determines the life cycle of a star?
2. What is the next stage in the sun's life cycle?
3. A scientist observes a pulsar in the center of a large nebula. What can the scientist infer about the pulsar's life cycle?

2 LABORATORY INVESTIGATION

Using a Flame Test to Identify Substances

Problem

How can substances be identified by using a flame test?

Materials *(per group)*

Stainless steel teaspoon
Bunsen burner
Safety goggles
Heat-resistant gloves
1 unmarked bottle each of sodium chloride, potassium chloride, and lithium chloride

Procedure

1. Put on the safety goggles.
2. Carefully light the Bunsen burner. **CAUTION:** *If you are not sure how to light a Bunsen burner safely, have your teacher show you the correct procedure.*
3. Put on the heat-resistant gloves.
4. Place the tip of the clean teaspoon in water. Then dip the tip of the spoon into one of the unmarked powders. Make sure that some of the powder sticks to the wet tip.
5. Hold the tip of the spoon in the flame of the Bunsen burner until most of the powder has burned. Observe the color of the flame.
6. Place the tip of the spoon in water again to clean it. Dry the spoon thoroughly to make sure no powder is left on the spoon.
7. Wet the tip of the spoon again. Then dip the tip into the second unmarked powder.
8. Hold the tip of the spoon in the flame until most of the powder has burned. Observe the color of the flame.
9. Clean the spoon again. Wet the tip of the spoon a third time. Dip the tip of the spoon into the third unmarked powder.
10. Hold the tip of the spoon in the flame until most of the powder has burned. Observe the color of the flame.

Observations

1. Record the color of the three flames in a chart similar to the one below.
2. Sodium chloride burns with a yellow flame. Potassium chloride burns with a purple flame. And lithium chloride burns with a red flame. Using this information, determine the identity of each of the unmarked powders. Record the names of the substances in the chart.

Flame Test	Color of Flame	Name of Substance
Powder 1		
Powder 2		
Powder 3		

Conclusions

1. Why is it important to make sure the spoon is thoroughly cleaned before each flame test? Try the investigation without cleaning the spoon to test your answer.
2. Relate this investigation to the way astronomers study a star's composition.

CHAPTER REVIEW

SUMMARY

2–1 Formation of the Universe

❑ A spectroscope breaks up the light from a star into its characteristic colors.

❑ Every distant galaxy shows a red shift in its spectrum. This indicates that the universe is expanding.

❑ Most astronomers agree that the universe began with the big bang, which sent matter and energy exploding off in every direction.

2–2 Star Groups

❑ The three main types of galaxies are elliptical, spiral, and irregular galaxies.

❑ The constellations are groups of stars in which ancient peoples saw imaginary figures.

2–3 Characteristics of Stars

❑ Stars range in size from huge supergiants to tiny neutron stars.

❑ The spectroscope provides evidence about the composition of stars.

❑ A star's brightness as observed from the earth is its apparent magnitude. A star's true brightness is its absolute magnitude.

❑ The Hertzsprung–Russell diagram shows the relationship between a star's absolute magnitude and its temperature.

❑ Nuclear fusion in a star's core causes some mass to change to heat and light.

2–4 Life and Death of Stars

❑ Most astronomers agree that stars are born within nebulae, or huge clouds of dust and gases.

❑ The main factor that shapes the life cycle of a star is the star's starting mass.

❑ Medium-sized stars pass through a red-giant stage before they become white dwarfs and die.

❑ The core of the star left behind after the supernova may become a neutron star or a black hole, depending on the star's starting mass.

VOCABULARY

Define each term in a complete sentence.

absolute magnitude
apparent magnitude
background radiation
big bang theory
binary star
black hole
blue shift
cepheid variable
constellation
Doppler effect
eclipsing binary
elliptical galaxy
galaxy
giant star
globular cluster
gravity
Hertzsprung–Russell diagram
irregular galaxy
magnitude
main-sequence star
Milky Way Galaxy
nebula
neutron star
nova
nuclear fusion
open cluster
parallax
Polaris
prism
protostar
pulsar
quasar
red shift
spectroscope
spectrum
spiral galaxy
supergiant star
supernova
variable star
white dwarf

CONTENT REVIEW: MULTIPLE CHOICE

Choose the letter of the answer that best completes each sentence.

1. Light can be broken up into its different colors by a (an)
a. optical telescope b. flame test c. spectroscope d. parallax

2. The most distant objects in the universe are called
a. neutron stars b. quasars c. pulsars d. irregular galaxies

3. The shape of galaxies such as the Milky Way is
a. elliptical b. irregular c. globular d. spiral

4. The most common element in an average star is
a. helium b. nitrogen c. hydrogen d. carbon

5. The color of a star is an indicator of its
a. size b. inner temperature
c. composition d. surface temperature

6. On the Hertzsprung–Russell diagram, most stars are
a. supergiants b. main-sequence c. giants d. white dwarfs

7. The distance to stars less than 100 light-years from the earth is measured through (a)
a. spectroscope b. red shift c. parallax d. brightness

8. During nuclear fusion, hydrogen atoms are fused into
a. carbon atoms b. iron atoms
c. nitrogen atoms d. helium atoms

9. The main factor that shapes the life cycle of a star is its
a. mass b. color c. composition d. absolute magnitude

10. Supermassive stars end up as
a. main-sequence stars b. neutron stars
c. black holes d. white dwarfs

CONTENT REVIEW: COMPLETION

Fill in the word or words that best complete each sentence.

1. Within a spectroscope, a (an) ________ breaks up light into its colors.

2. A (An) ________ in a star's spectrum indicates that the star is moving toward the earth.

3. ________ is the force of attraction between objects.

4. The Pleiades are an example of a (an) ________.

5. One example of a (an) ________ is Algol.

6. ________ is the second most common element in most stars.

7. A star's brightness as it appears from the earth is called its ________.

8. The ________ the starting mass of a star, the longer it will live.

9. During a (an) ________, the heat in a star can reach temperatures up to 100,000,000,000°C.

10. Stars that spin rapidly and give off radio waves are called ________.

CONTENT REVIEW: TRUE OR FALSE

Determine whether each statement is true or false. If it is true, write "true." If it is false, change the underlined word or words to make the statement true.

1. A red shift in a star's spectrum indicates that the star is moving toward the earth.

2. In an open universe, all the galaxies will eventually move back to the center of the universe.

3. The sun is in the Andromeda Galaxy.

4. The actual amount of light given off by a star is its absolute magnitude.

5. Stars that change in brightness are called variable stars.

6. Most of the core of a red giant is made of hydrogen.

7. White dwarfs are superdense stars with an iron core.

8. Astronomers believe that a white dwarf is spinning rapidly in the center of the Crab Nebula.

9. Heavy elements are produced in a star during a nova explosion.

10. Neutron stars swallow matter like a cosmic vacuum cleaner.

CONCEPT REVIEW: SKILL BUILDING

Use the skills you have developed in the chapter to complete each activity.

1. Interpreting diagrams Examine the spectral lines, or fingerprints, of the elements hydrogen, helium, sodium, and calcium. Compare them with the spectral lines in the spectra labeled X, Y, and Z. Determine which elements produced the spectral lines in spectra X, Y, and Z.

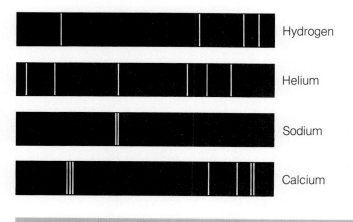

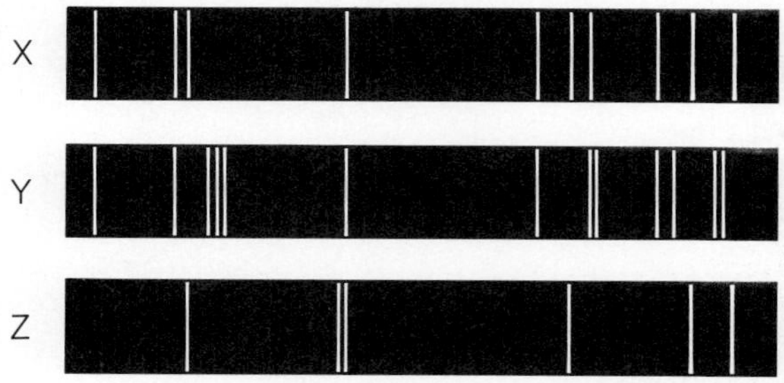

CONCEPT REVIEW: ESSAY

Discuss each of the following in a brief paragraph.

1. When you look at the light from distant stars, you are really looking back in time. Explain what this statement means.

2. Discuss the different ways astronomers use the light from stars to learn more about stars.

3. What information does the Hertzsprung–Russell diagram illustrate?

4. Compare the life cycle of a medium-sized star with that of a massive star.

The Solar System 3

CHAPTER SECTIONS

3–1 Formation of the Solar System
3–2 A Special Star: The Sun
3–3 Motion of the Planets
3–4 Features of the Planets
3–5 Meteoroids, Comets, and Asteroids

CHAPTER OBJECTIVES

After completing this chapter, you will be able to

3–1 Discuss the nebular theory of the formation of the solar system.

3–2 Describe the sun's major characteristics.

3–3 Discuss the motion of objects in the solar system.

3–4 Identify some of the major characteristics of the planets.

3–5 Describe some of the characteristics of meteoroids, comets, and asteroids.

People have looked up at the sky and observed the stars for thousands of years. Long before they built cities or developed a written language, people used the stars to guide them in traveling and in planting their crops. It was not long before people realized that although the stars moved across the sky at night, they stayed in the same position relative to one another.

But people also observed that certain "stars" wandered among the other stars. These peculiar objects did not stay in the same position relative to the other stars. These objects are now called planets. The word *planet* comes from the Greek word *planetes,* meaning "wanderer."

Ever since the planets were first discovered, people have dreamed of visiting them. Most thought that it would never be possible. But beginning in the early 1960s, spacecraft from the earth began to explore planets such as Venus and Mars. Finally, in late July 1976, a small spacecraft, *Viking 1,* landed on Mars. Soon after, *Viking 2* landed on Mars. Together the ships sent back pictures and information about the Martian surface.

What kind of information did the Viking spacecraft send back to the earth? Did they discover life on Mars? After you have read this chapter, you will know the answers to these questions and many more. For today spacecraft have explored almost all of the planets that travel around the sun.

Viking 2 *landed on Mars in a field of red boulders.*

Section Objective

To apply the nebular theory to the formation of the solar system

3–1 Formation of the Solar System

The earth and the other eight planets that travel around the sun make up the **solar system.** The solar system also includes all of the other objects that travel around the sun.

Astronomers have evidence that the solar system is about 5 billion years old. Many explanations have been proposed to account for how the solar system was formed. But today almost all astronomers believe in the **nebular theory. The nebular theory states that the solar system began as a huge cloud of dust and gas called a nebula, which later condensed to form the sun and its nine planets.**

The Sun Forms First

According to the nebular theory, about 5 billion years ago a nebula occupied the region of space in which the solar system is now located. The nebula contained mostly hydrogen and helium gases.

In Chapter 2, you learned that some stars break apart in an enormous explosion called a supernova. The nebula in which the solar system formed would probably still be here today if a supernova in a nearby star had not disrupted the nebula. During the supernova, many elements were formed. These elements spread throughout the nebula. They were the seeds of the elements that would one day make up the matter in the planets in the solar system. At

Figure 3–1 *According to the nebular theory, shock waves from a supernova disrupted a nearby nebula. The nebula began to rotate, and gravity pulled more and more matter into a central disk. That central disk became the sun. Clumps of gas and dust formed around the central disk. They would form the planets and other objects in the solar system.*

the same time, shock waves from the supernova also spread throughout the nebula. These shock waves began the processes that led to the solar system.

In reaction to the passing shock waves, the gases in the nebula began to contract inward. The nebula began to shrink. As it shrank, it began to spin more and more rapidly. In time, the spinning nebula flattened into a huge disk almost 10 billion kilometers in diameter. Near the center, a **protosun,** or newborn sun, began to take shape. As the gases in the nebula continued to collapse inward, the mass, density, and temperature of the protosun increased.

When the density and temperature of the protosun reached a certain level, gravitational forces caused hydrogen atoms to fuse into helium atoms. This nuclear fusion released tremendous amounts of heat and light. The protosun had become a star.

Sharpen Your Skills

A Planetarium Visit

If possible, plan a trip to a nearby planetarium. The planetarium will probably have a dramatic representation of the solar system. Pay particular attention to the planets you might be able to see from your home. Make a note of when they are visible in your area. On a starry night, see if you can find the planets you observed in the planetarium.

Formation of the Planets

Gases and other matter surrounding the newly formed sun continued to spin around the sun. As they did, some of the gases and matter began to clump together. Small clumps became larger and larger clumps. The largest clumps became **protoplanets,** or planets in their early stages.

Protoplanets near the sun became so hot that most of their lightweight gases, such as hydrogen and helium, boiled away. All that remained of the inner protoplanets were clumps of metals and rocky material. Today these inner planets are known as Mercury, Venus, Earth, and Mars.

The gases in the protoplanets farther from the sun did not boil away. These outer protoplanets kept their lightweight gases and grew to enormous sizes. Today these "gas giants" are known as Jupiter, Saturn, Uranus, and Neptune.

As the newly formed planets began to cool, smaller clumps of matter formed around them. These smaller clumps became moons, or **satellites.** Astronomers believe that one of the satellites near Neptune may have broken away from that planet. This satellite became the farthest known planet in our solar system—Pluto. This theory explains why Pluto is similar in composition to many of the icy moons surrounding the outer planets.

Figure 3–2 *This illustration shows the relative sizes of the planets in the solar system. Which planet is the largest?*

Objects other than planets and moons were also forming in the solar system. Between Mars and Jupiter, small clumps of matter formed **asteroids** (AS-tuh-roidz). These rocklike objects are now found in a region of space between Mars and Jupiter called the **asteroid belt.** Farther out in space, near the very edge of the solar system, other clumps of icy matter formed a huge cloud. Today astronomers believe that this cloud may be the home of comets.

SECTION REVIEW

1. If the solar system formed from a nebula that contained mostly hydrogen and helium, why are there so many different elements on the earth?
2. Why is Pluto so different from the other outer planets?
3. How does the nebular theory account for the differences between the inner and outer planets?

3–2 A Special Star: The Sun

Section Objective

To compare the four main layers of the sun

There are billions of stars in the Milky Way Galaxy. The sun is not much different from the vast majority of stars. But to us, it is a very special star. Located some 150 million kilometers from the earth, the sun is the main source of energy for living things. Without the sun, there would be no life on the earth.

Layers of the Sun

The sun is a ball-shaped object made of very hot gases. It is an average star in terms of size, temperature, and mass. It measures 1.35 million kilometers in diameter. If the sun were hollow, over 1 million earths could fit inside it! Although the sun's volume is more than 1 million times greater than that of the earth, its density is only one-quarter that of the earth. Why do you think the earth is more dense than the sun?

Since the sun is made of only gases, there are no clear boundaries within it. But four main layers can be distinguished. **Three layers make up the sun's atmosphere and one layer makes up its interior.**

Figure 3–3 *The corona of the sun becomes visible during a total solar eclipse. What object in space blocks out the rest of the sun during a solar eclipse, as viewed from the earth?*

CORONA The outermost layer of the sun's atmosphere is called the **corona** (kuh-ROH-nuh). Gas particles in the corona can reach temperatures up to 1,700,000°C. But if a spacecraft could pass through the corona and be shielded from the rest of the sun's heat, the temperature of the spacecraft would barely rise! The reason for this is simple. The gas particles in the corona are spread so far apart that

Figure 3–4 *The three main parts of the sun's atmosphere are the corona, the chromosphere, and the photosphere. What is the hottest part of the sun?*

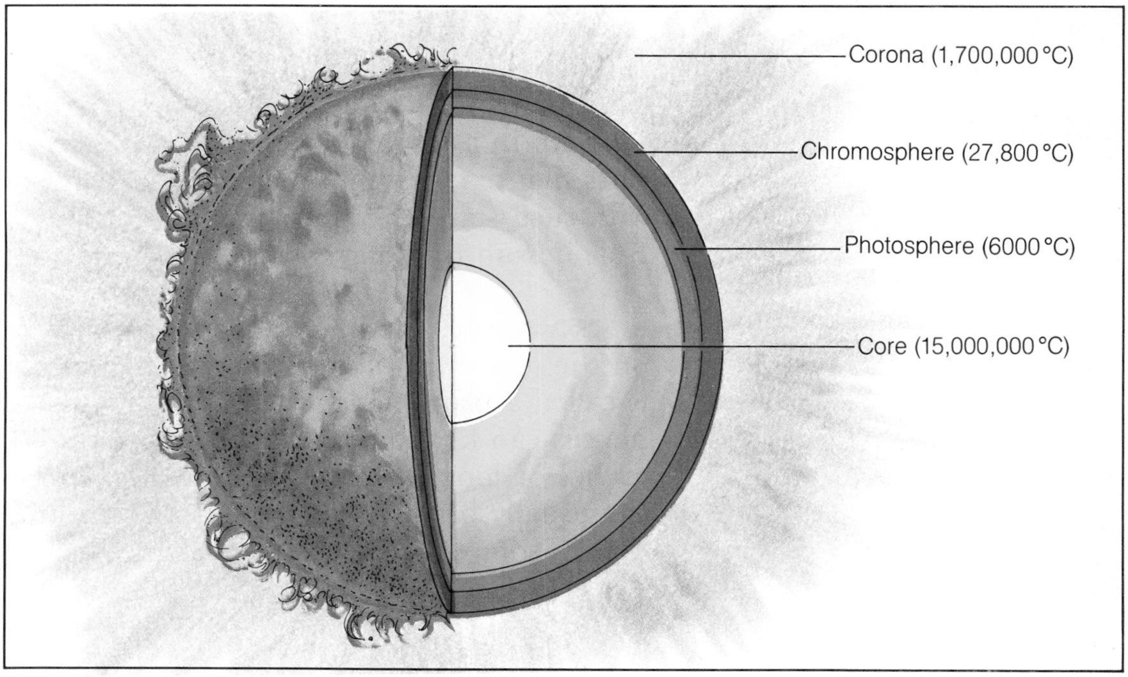

> **Sharpen Your Skills**
>
> *Prefixes and Suffixes*
>
> You can often figure out what a scientific word means if you understand its parts. The words *photosphere* and *chromosphere* are good examples.
>
> Look up the meaning of the prefixes *photo* and *chromo.* Look up the meaning of the suffix *sphere.* Explain why scientists use the words *photosphere* and *chromosphere* as names for two layers of the sun.

not enough particles would strike the spacecraft at any one time to cause a rise in temperature.

CHROMOSPHERE Beneath the corona is the middle layer of the sun's atmosphere, the **chromosphere** (KROH-muh-sfir). The chromosphere is several thousand kilometers thick. But sometimes gases in the chromosphere suddenly flare up and stream into space as far as 16,000 kilometers. Temperatures in the chromosphere average 27,800°C.

PHOTOSPHERE The innermost layer of the sun's atmosphere is called the **photosphere.** The photosphere is about 550 kilometers thick and is often referred to as the surface of the sun. Temperatures in the photosphere usually do not exceed 6000°C.

CORE You may have noticed that temperatures decrease greatly from the corona through the photosphere. But the temperature begins to rise again in the interior of the sun. The interior of the sun includes all of the sun except the three layers of the atmosphere. At the edge of the sun's interior, near the photosphere, temperatures may reach 1,000,000°C. But in the center of the sun, called the **core,** temperatures may reach 15,000,000°C! It is here in the sun's core that hydrogen atoms are fused into helium atoms, releasing the sun's energy as heat and light.

Figure 3–5 *A huge solar prominence rises out of the sun like a twisted sheet of gas. What is a solar prominence?*

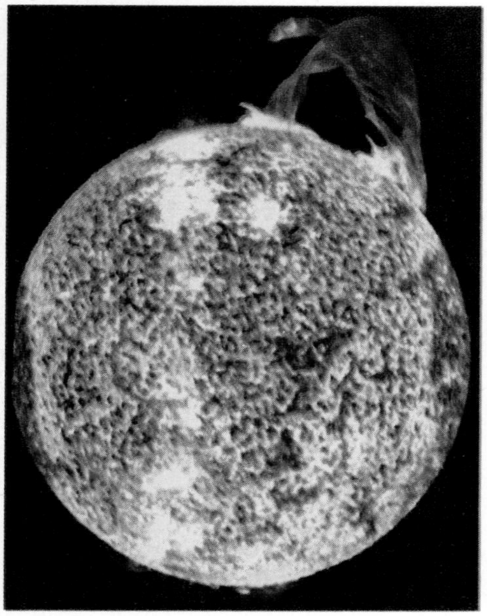

Activity on the Sun

In Chapter 2, you read about stars that suddenly flare up in a bright nova. And you also read about stars that explode in a huge supernova. Compared with such stars, the sun may not seem very active. But the sun does have some active features.

PROMINENCES Many kinds of violent storms occur on the sun from time to time. One such solar storm is called a **prominence** (PRAHM-uh-nuhns). Prominences can be seen from the earth as huge bright arches or loops of gas. These twisted loops of hot gas usually originate in the chromosphere. Prominences sometimes bend backward and shower the gases back onto the sun. Other prominences erupt from the chromosphere to heights of a million kilometers or more above the sun's surface. During a solar prominence, gases and energy are sent into space.

SOLAR FLARES Another kind of storm on the sun shows up as bright bursts of light on the sun's surface. These bursts of light are called a **solar flare.** A solar flare usually does not last more than an hour. But during that time, the temperature of the solar-flare region can be twice that of the rest of the sun's surface. Huge amounts of energy are released into space during a solar flare.

SOLAR WIND The sun's corona releases a continuous stream of high-energy particles into space. This stream of particles is called the **solar wind.** The solar wind is constantly sent out by the sun. But its intensity may increase during a solar flare. An increase in the solar wind can affect radio and telephone communications on the earth.

SUNSPOTS When astronomers observe the sun, they sometimes see dark areas on the sun's surface. These dark areas are called **sunspots.** Sunspots appear dark because they are cooler than the rest of the sun's surface.

Sunspots are storms in the lower atmosphere of the sun. They may be as small as 16 kilometers in diameter or as large as 160,000 kilometers in diameter. The number of sunspots that appear on the sun at any one time is always changing. But periods of very active sunspot activity seem to occur every 10 to 11 years. This activity has interfered with communication systems on the earth.

Astronomers have observed that sunspots move across the sun's surface. This movement indicates that the gases in the sun spin, or rotate. The sun rotates on its **axis.** The axis is an imaginary vertical line through the center of the sun. Gases around the middle of the sun appear to rotate on the axis once every 25 days. But not all parts of the sun rotate at the same speed. Some parts of the sun take longer to rotate than others. What do you think accounts for this?

Sharpen Your Skills

Observing Sunspots

1. Using one side of a pair of binoculars (put masking tape over the other side), focus the image of the sun on a piece of clean, unlined, white paper. **CAUTION:** *Do not look at the sun.* The sun's rays can do permanent damage to your eyes! The paper should be held 20 to 30 cm from the eyepiece of the binoculars.

2. Look for large sunspots, which will appear as dark spots on the image of the sun's disk. Can you detect a change in the position of the sunspots over time?

3. Make diagrams of your observations and compare your findings with those of your classmates.

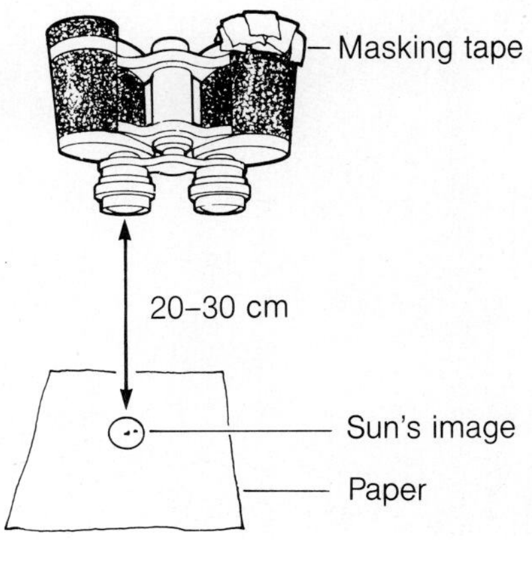

SECTION REVIEW

1. List the four main layers of the sun and compare their temperatures.
2. How have astronomers determined that the sun rotates on its axis?
3. Explain the difference between the solar wind and winds on the earth.

Section Objective

To compare planetary revolution and rotation

3–3 Motion of the Planets

All of the planets in the solar system revolve around the sun and also rotate on their axes. The path a planet takes around the sun is called its **orbit.** An orbit is the path one object in space takes while traveling around another object.

Elliptical Orbits

Early astronomers assumed that planets orbit the sun in perfect circles. But today astronomers know that planets follow an **elliptical orbit.** An elliptical orbit is shaped more like an oval than a circle. You can think of an elliptical orbit as being egg-shaped.

Figure 3–6 *All of the planets revolve around the sun. Note that at some points the orbit of Neptune falls outside that of Pluto. In fact, from 1979 to the year 1999, Neptune will be farther from the sun than Pluto. What is the shape of each planet's orbit?*

Astronomers also know that each planet travels in a counterclockwise elliptical orbit around the sun. Naturally the planets closest to the sun travel the shortest distance. They complete one orbit around the sun in the shortest amount of time. The more distant planets travel a longer distance. So they take a longer time to complete one orbit around the sun. Which planet takes the longest time to complete one orbit around the sun?

Period of Revolution

Another way to say a planet orbits the sun is to say it revolves around the sun. The time it takes a planet to make one revolution around the sun is called its **period of revolution.** A planet's period of revolution is called a year on that planet. For example, Mercury takes about 88 earth-days to revolve once around the sun. So a year on Mercury is about 88 earth-days long. Pluto takes about 248 earth-years to revolve around the sun. So a year on Pluto is about 248 earth-years long.

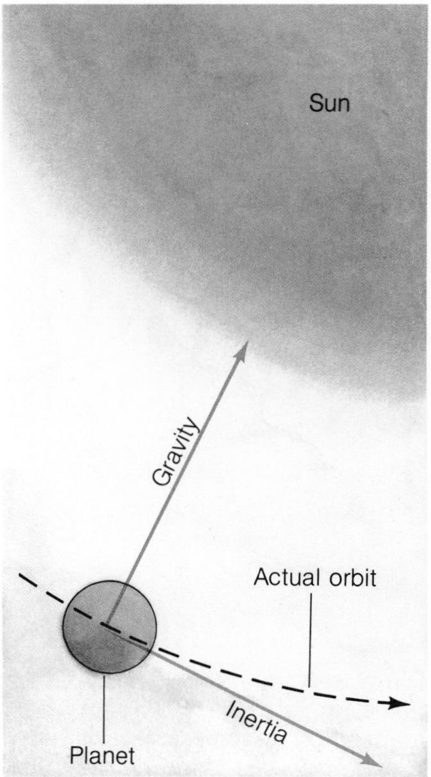

Figure 3–7 *Inertia makes a planet tend to travel in a straight line (blue arrow). But gravity pulls the planet toward the sun (red arrow). What is the effect of the combined action of inertia and gravity?*

Inertia and Gravity

In the seventeenth century, the English scientist Sir Isaac Newton developed the **law of inertia.** The law of inertia states that an object's motion will not change unless that object is acted on by an outside force. According to the law of inertia, a moving object will not change speed or direction unless an outside force causes a change in its motion.

Newton hypothesized that planets, like all other objects, should move in a straight line unless some force causes them to change their motion. But if planets did move in a straight line, they would sail off into space, never to be seen again. Newton knew that some force must be acting on the planets, tugging them into elliptical orbits. That force, he reasoned, is the sun's gravitational pull. So a planet's motion around the sun is the result of two factors. One factor, inertia, causes the planet to move in a straight line. The other factor, gravity, pulls the planet toward the sun. When these two factors combine, a planet moves in an elliptical orbit.

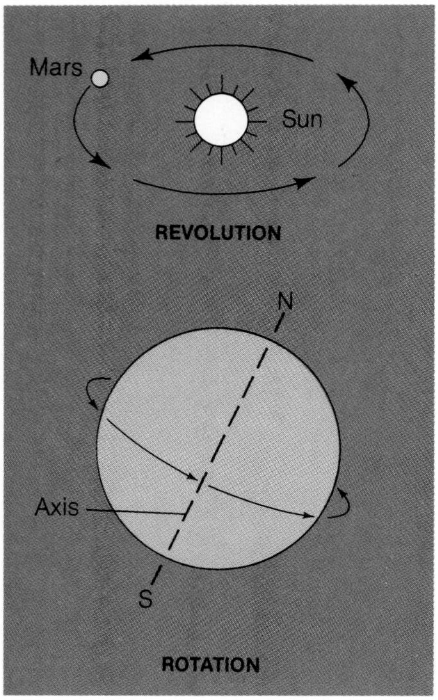

Figure 3–8 *Mars, like all planets, rotates on its axis while it revolves around the sun. The time it takes to rotate once is called its day. What is the time it takes to make one revolution called?*

Period of Rotation

In addition to orbiting the sun, planets spin, or rotate, on their axes. The time it takes a planet to make one rotation on its axis is called its **period of rotation.** Rotation and revolution, then, are the two kinds of planetary motion.

The earth takes about 24 hours to rotate once on its axis. Does that number seem familiar to you? There are 24 hours in an earth-day. So the time it takes a planet to go through one period of rotation is called a day on that planet.

Mercury, the planet closest to the sun, takes almost 59 earth-days to rotate once on its axis. So a day on Mercury is almost 59 earth-days long. Pluto, the most distant planet, takes just over 6 earth-days to rotate once on its axis. So a day on Pluto is a little more than 6 earth-days long.

SECTION REVIEW

1. Describe the shape of an elliptical orbit.
2. What two factors combine to cause planets to travel in elliptical orbits?
3. What are the two kinds of planetary motion?

CAREER — *Solar Engineer*

HELP WANTED: SOLAR ENGINEER Exciting new position designing complex systems for obtaining solar energy for industrial use. Engineering degree required. Only innovative, environmentally aware persons need apply.

For thousands of years, ancient civilizations had only the sun's heat to warm them. Then these people discovered how to control fire. Later, coal, oil, and other fuels were discovered and used to heat homes and other buildings. In this century, much of the earth's fuel resources have been used up. Once again, people are looking to the sun's heat as a source of energy.

People who develop ways to collect and use solar energy are called **solar engineers.** Solar engineers design systems to collect the sun's energy and use it to heat and cool buildings. Other systems they design change solar energy into electrical energy. Solar engineers try to develop systems that are more efficient and less expensive.

Solar engineering is a new and growing field. It offers many challenges to people who enjoy putting scientific knowledge to work.

You can learn more about solar engineering by writing to a college of engineering in your state or to the Solar Energy Research Institute, 1617 Cole Boulevard, Golden, CO 80401.

3–4 Features of the Planets

Section Objective

To identify the special characteristics of the planets in the solar system

Astronomers have studied the planets for many years. But it was not until recently that spacecraft were sent to examine the planets in detail. **The nine planets of the solar system have a very wide variety of surface and atmospheric features.** The most recent data from spacecraft and observations on the earth are shown in Figure 3–10 on pages 74–75.

Mercury

Mercury is so close to the blinding light of the sun that it is very difficult to study this planet from the earth. But in 1974, the spacecraft *Mariner 10* flew past Mercury. *Mariner 10* provided the first close-up view of this barren world.

Mariner 10 found a heavily crater-covered world. The craters were scooped out billions of years ago by the impact of pieces of material striking the surface of the planet. Mercury has almost no atmosphere. So it has no weather. Since there is no rain, snow, or wind to help wear down the craters and carry away the soil particles, the craters are the same as when they were created. As a result, the surface of Mercury has changed very little for the past few billion years.

Photographs from *Mariner 10* also revealed long, steep cliffs on Mercury. Some of the cliffs cut across the planet for hundreds of kilometers. There are also vast plains. These plains were probably formed by lava flowing from volcanoes that erupted billions of years ago. Today there is no evidence of active volcanoes on Mercury.

Mercury rotates on its axis very slowly. It takes Mercury about 59 earth-days to complete one period of rotation. Because of its long period of rotation and its closeness to the sun, the daylight side of Mercury has plenty of time to heat up. And the nighttime side of Mercury has plenty of time to cool off. As a result, temperatures on the daylight side of Mercury can reach 427°C, while temperatures on the nighttime side can fall to −170°C. So Mercury is one of the hottest planets and one of the coldest planets—all at the same time!

Figure 3–9 *This photograph of crater-covered Mercury was taken by* Mariner 10. *The craters were scooped out of the surface billions of years ago. Why have they remained unchanged over all that time?*

THE SOLAR SYSTEM

Name	Average Distance From Sun *(millions of km)*	Diameter *(km)*	Period of Revolution in Earth-time		Period of Rotation		Number of Moons
			Days	*Years*	*Days*	*Hours*	
Mercury	58	4880	88	—	58	16	0
Venus	108	12,104	225	—	243 Retrograde	—	0
Earth	150	12,756	365	—	—	24	1
Mars	228	6794	—	1.88	—	24.5 (about)	2
Jupiter	778	142,700	—	11.86	—	10 (about)	16
Saturn	1427	120,000	—	29.46	—	10.5 (about)	23?
Uranus	2869	50,800	—	84.01	— Retrograde	16.8 (about)	15
Neptune	4486	48,600	—	164.8	—	16	8
Pluto	5890	4000	—	247.7	6	9.5	1

Figure 3–10 *This chart shows the most current information known about the planets. Which planets show retrograde motion?*

Venus

Venus and the earth are sometimes called "sister planets" because their sizes, masses, and densities are about the same. But other characteristics make these planets different.

The earth's atmosphere is made mostly of nitrogen and oxygen. The Venusian atmosphere is made mostly of carbon dioxide. The atmospheric pressure on Venus is almost 91 times that on the earth. The large amount of carbon dioxide in its thick atmosphere is responsible for this enormous atmospheric pressure.

Temperature Extremes (°C) High	Low	Orbital Velocity (km/sec)	Atmosphere	Main Characteristics
427	−170	47.8	Hydrogen, helium, sodium	Rocky, cratered surface; steep cliffs; extremely thin atmosphere
480	−33	35.0	Carbon dioxide	Thick cloud cover, greenhouse effect, vast plains, high mountains
58	−90	29.8	Nitrogen, oxygen	Liquid water, life
−31	−130	24.2	Carbon dioxide, nitrogen, argon, oxygen, water vapor	Polar icecaps, pink sky, rust-colored surface, dominant volcanoes, surface channels
29,700	−95	13.1	Hydrogen, helium, methane, ammonia	Great red spot, thin ring, huge magnetosphere, rocky core surrounded by liquid-hydrogen ocean
?	−180	9.7	Hydrogen, helium, methane, ammonia	Many rings and ringlets, Titan only moon with substantial atmosphere
?	−350	6.8	Hydrogen, helium, methane	Rotates on side, 11 dark mostly narrow rings of methane ice, worldwide ocean of superheated water
?	−220	5.4	Hydrogen, helium, methane	Unusual satellite rotation, 4 rings, great dark spot, rocky core surrounded by slush of water and frozen methane
?	−230	4.7	Methane	Smallest planet, possibly a double planet

The surface of the earth is covered with clouds made of water vapor. The surface of Venus is constantly covered with thick clouds made mostly of sulfuric acid. Water is abundant on the earth's surface. Venus has only very small traces of water vapor.

The highest surface temperature of the earth is about 58°C. The surface temperature of Venus is higher, about 480°C. This high temperature is partly due to the clouds covering Venus. These clouds create a **greenhouse effect.** The clouds trap the heat from the sun beneath them. The trapped heat causes the planet's high temperatures.

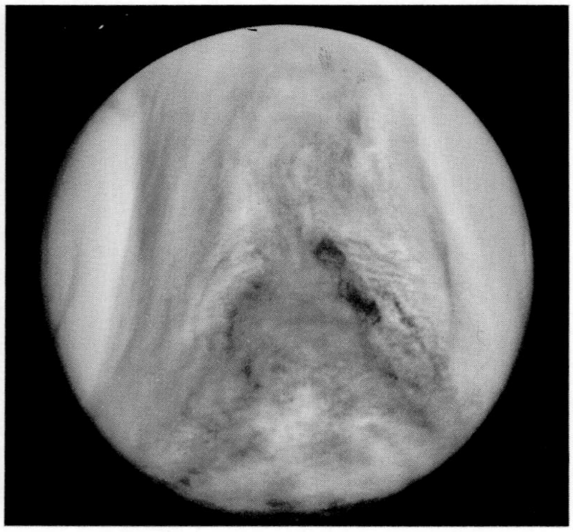

Figure 3–11 *Venus is constantly covered by thick clouds (right). What are the clouds mainly made of? Radar on a spacecraft orbiting Venus was able to penetrate the thick cloud cover to provide this computer-generated map of the Venusian surface (left). The circle on the top is the unfinished portion of the computer picture.*

Because of its thick cloud cover, the surface of Venus cannot be studied from the earth. But in 1975, the Soviet spacecraft *Venera 9* and *Venera 10* landed on Venus. The spacecraft were not able to withstand the harsh conditions. They were able to function for only a few hours before they failed. Yet in that short amount of time, the spacecraft were able to send back important pictures of the Venusian surface. More recently, the United States spacecraft *Pioneer Venus Orbiter* was placed in orbit around Venus. Radar instruments were able to penetrate the thick cloud cover and mapped much of the Venusian surface.

Data from these and other spacecraft have provided a fairly good picture of the conditions on Venus. They revealed many craters on its surface, as well as vast plains and tall mountains. There is some evidence that volcanoes once erupted on Venus. In fact, these volcanoes are probably the source of the carbon dioxide in the thick Venusian atmosphere. Another surface feature is a giant "crack" much deeper and longer than the earth's Grand Canyon.

Perhaps the most interesting data sent back from spacecraft indicate that Venus once had huge oceans. The remains of coastlines and sea beds are quite clear. What happened to the oceans on Venus? Millions, perhaps billions, of years ago, the oceans evaporated as a result of the great heat of the Venusian atmosphere. Gases were released as the water evaporated. These gases escaped into space.

Suppose you could stand on Venus and survive. And further suppose you could see through the thick clouds. What you would see would be quite

Sharpen Your Skills

Inertia

All objects, including planets, have inertia. Inertia is the tendency of an unmoving object to remain in place or of a moving object to continue moving in a straight line. You can observe inertia using a toy truck and a rubber band.

1. First, attach the rubber band to the front of the truck. Then fill the truck with small rocks or any heavy material.

2. Pull on the rubber band until the truck starts to move. Make a note of how much the rubber band must stretch to get the truck moving.

3. Continue pulling the truck with the rubber band. Does the rubber band stretch more or less once the truck is moving? Explain.

unusual. Unlike on the earth, the sun rises in the west on Venus and sets in the east. Venus rotates on its axis from east to west. This "backward" rotation is called **retrograde motion.** Retrograde motion causes the sun to appear to rise in the west and set in the east.

There is another unusual aspect of the rotation of Venus. It takes about 243 earth-days for Venus to complete one period of rotation. So a day on Venus is about 243 earth-days long. But it only takes Venus about 224 earth-days to revolve once around the sun. On Venus, then, a day is actually longer than a year!

The earth is the third planet from the sun. You will study the earth in detail in Chapter 4.

Mars

You read earlier that in 1976 two Viking spacecraft landed on Mars, the fourth planet from the sun. The Viking spacecraft took many pictures of the Martian surface. These pictures revealed a rocky surface with many craters. But the spacecraft were designed to do more than take photographs.

One of the most important tasks of the Viking spacecraft was to analyze Martian soil. To do so, a robot arm scooped up some of the soil and placed the soil in the on-board laboratory. Tests revealed that the Martian soil is similar to the earth's soil in many ways. But there are differences. For centuries, Mars has been known as the red planet. Soil tests

Sharpen Your Skills

Graphing the Sizes of the Planets

1. On a sheet of graph paper, draw a set of axes. Along the horizontal axis place nine marks an equal distance apart. Label each with the name of the planets in order from closest to the sun to farthest from the sun.

2. The vertical axis is for the planets' diameters in kilometers.

3. Plot the diameter of each planet on the graph.

What pattern in the sizes of the planets is evident? If you wanted to plot the size of the sun, how many times larger would your graph have to be?

Figure 3–12 *You can see the thin Martian atmosphere over the horizon in this photograph taken by* Viking 1. *What gives the surface of Mars its reddish color?*

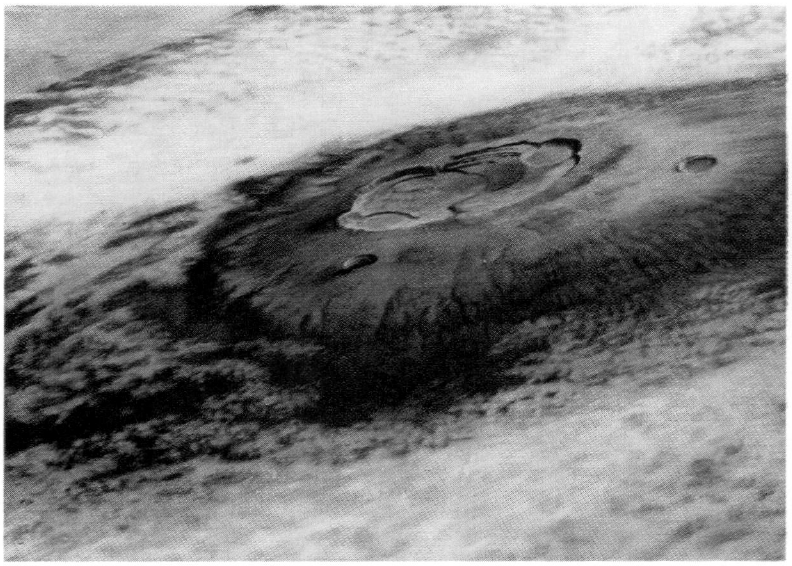

Figure 3–13 *The dead volcano* Olympus Mons *on Mars is the largest volcano ever discovered.*

Eric Gordon

Sharpen Your Skills

United States Spacecraft

The United States has launched a number of spacecraft to investigate the planets in the solar system. The following chart includes many of them. Using reference sources at the library, look up each mission and write a report on when it was launched and when it arrived at its destination. Also include information each mission uncovered. Find out whether any future missions have been planned by NASA.

Spacecraft	Destination
Mariners 2 and 5	Venus
Mariners 4, 6, 7, and 9	Mars
Mariner 10	Venus Mercury
Pioneer 10	Jupiter
Pioneer 11	Jupiter Saturn
Vikings 1 and 2	Mars
Voyager 1	Jupiter Saturn
Voyager 2	Jupiter Saturn Uranus Neptune

showed why this is so. Martian soil is coated with a reddish compound called iron oxide. Perhaps you know iron oxide by its more common name—rust!

Viking spacecraft also tested the soil for signs of life. Although the tests did not reveal any signs of life or life processes, the data did not rule out the possibility that life might exist on Mars.

The Viking spacecraft and observations from the earth aided in the discovery of many other features of Mars. Mars appears to be a planet that has had a very active past. For example, four huge volcanoes are located on Mars. These volcanoes are dormant, or inactive. But large plains covered with lava indicate that the volcanoes were once very active. The largest volcano on Mars is *Olympus Mons. Olympus Mons* is wider across its base than the island of Hawaii and almost three times as tall as Mount Everest. In fact, *Olympus Mons* is the largest known volcano in the solar system.

Astronomers now believe that when the Martian volcanoes were active, they poured out both lava and steam. As the steam cooled, it fell as rain. Rushing rivers may have once crossed the Martian surface, gouging out channels that wander across Mars. Today there is no liquid water on Mars. But frozen water can be found in the northern icecap. Frozen water may also be located under the soil of Mars.

The northern icecap of Mars is made mostly of frozen water, which never melts. But the southern icecap is made mostly of frozen carbon dioxide.

Much of this icecap melts during the Martian summer. But do not be misled by the word *summer.* Since Mars has a very thin atmosphere made mostly of carbon dioxide, it does not retain much heat from the sun. So even during the summer, temperatures on Mars are well below 0°C. That, of course, is why water on Mars stays frozen all year round.

Another interesting feature of Mars is an enormous canyon called *Valles Marineris.* The canyon is 240 kilometers wide at one point and 6.5 kilometers deep. If this canyon were on the earth, it would stretch from California to New York.

Although the atmosphere of Mars is very thin, winds are common. Windstorms sweep across the surface at speeds of up to 200 kilometers per hour. These storms stir up so much dust that the sky may turn a dark pink.

Mars has two moons, or satellites, which orbit the planet. These rocky, crater-covered moons are called Phobos and Deimos. They are much smaller than the earth's moon. The maximum diameter of Phobos is only 25 kilometers. The diameter of Deimos is only 15 kilometers.

Sharpen Your Skills

Galileo Galilei

In 1610, Galileo Galilei first discovered the large moons of Jupiter with a homemade telescope. He published his report in a pamphlet called "The Starry Messenger." Use the library and other sources to write a report about this famous astronomer. Find out which moons are now known as the Galilean satellites. See if you can discover what other information Galileo included in his pamphlet.

Jupiter

Jupiter, the fifth planet from the sun, is by far the largest planet. In fact, Jupiter contains twice the mass of all the other planets combined.

Jupiter is the first of the "gas giants." From the earth, all that can be seen of Jupiter's atmosphere

Figure 3–14 Voyager 1 *detected a thin ring circling Jupiter. The ring in this photograph has been added by an artist. Can you find the giant red spot on Jupiter?*

Sharpen Your Skills

Comparing Diameters

Jupiter, the largest planet, has a diameter of about 142,700 km. Pluto, the smallest planet, has a diameter of about 4000 km. How many times larger than Pluto is Jupiter? That is, how many Plutos lined up in a row will reach across Jupiter's diameter?

is its thick cloud cover. These clouds, which appear as bands of color, are made mostly of hydrogen and helium. Other gases, such as ammonia and methane, are also found in Jupiter's atmosphere.

The clouds covering Jupiter are very active. Huge storms swirl across the surface of the atmosphere. These storms can be observed because the colored bands of the clouds are twisted and turned by the strong winds. Perhaps the most well-known feature of Jupiter's cloud cover is a giant red spot 3 times the size of the earth. This red spot, which is probably a hurricanelike storm, has been observed for more than 300 years. If it is a storm, it is the longest-lasting storm ever observed in the solar system.

Unlike the other planets you have read about, Jupiter probably has only a small solid core. Instead the clouds become thicker and denser as they get closer to the center of the planet. As their density increases, the clouds probably change into a giant ocean of liquid hydrogen.

Because of the thick cloud cover, the atmospheric pressure on Jupiter is enormous. In fact, the pressure near the center of the planet is so great that the liquid-hydrogen ocean probably changes into a form of liquid hydrogen that acts like a metal. This liquid metallic layer may surround a rocky core about the size of the earth. The liquid metallic layer is probably the main cause of Jupiter's gigantic magnetic field. The magnetic field, called the **magnetosphere,** stretches for millions of kilometers beyond the planet. Jupiter's magnetosphere is the largest single structure in the solar system.

Jupiter is unusual in other ways. For example, it gives off more heat than it receives from the sun. Although temperatures are very cold near the tops of the clouds, the temperature near the core may rise to about 30,000°C.

In 1979, two Voyager spacecraft flew past Jupiter. These spacecraft took many thousands of pictures. From these photographs, astronomers discovered a thin ring circling Jupiter. They also discovered gigantic bolts of lightning in the atmosphere and mysterious shimmering sheets of light in the sky. In a few years, the United States will send the *Galileo Jupiter Probe* into Jupiter's atmosphere.

Figure 3–15 *Shown here is an artist's conception of the* Galileo Jupiter Probe. *The probe will enter Jupiter's atmosphere and send back information to the earth.*

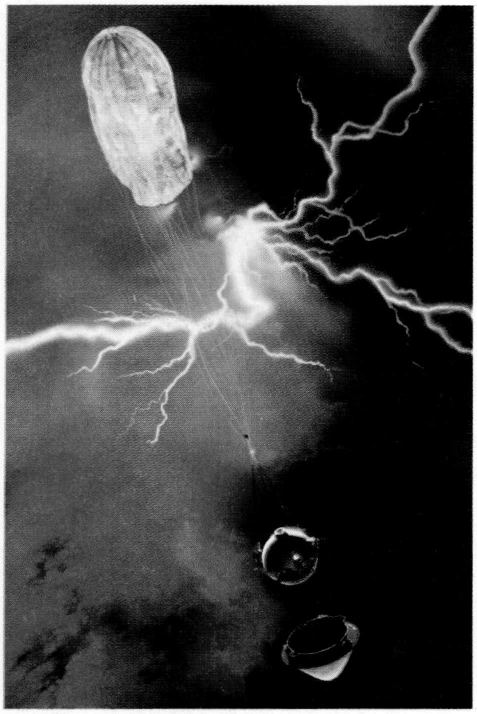

The probe will provide more information about what is happening beneath the thick cloud cover.

In 1610, the scientist Galileo Galilei observed four moons orbiting Jupiter. Today these moons are known as the Galilean satellites. And although at least 16 moons have now been found orbiting Jupiter, the four largest and most interesting are the moons discovered by Galileo over 300 years ago.

IO The innermost of Jupiter's large moons is Io. Io appears to be painted in brilliant orange, yellow, and red colors. These colors are the result of the high sulfur content on Io's surface. Io is the only known object in the solar system besides the earth that has active volcanoes. These volcanoes constantly cover Io's surface with new layers of sulfur and other materials.

EUROPA Beyond Io is the moon Europa. Europa is very different from Io. It is an ice-covered world. Its surface is so smooth that it has been described as a giant billiard ball. Although no active volcanoes have been discovered on Europa, there is some evidence that they may exist. But these volcanoes would be very different from those on the earth. They would spew out mostly water and ice.

GANYMEDE Beyond Europa is Ganymede, Jupiter's largest moon. In fact, Ganymede is the largest moon in the solar system. It is even larger than the planet Mercury. One-half of Ganymede is covered by rock. The other half is covered by ice.

CALLISTO Beyond Ganymede is Callisto. Callisto has many more craters than any other object in the solar system. Astronomers believe that it took billions of years of impact of objects from outer space to form so many craters. So the surface of Callisto probably looks much as it did billions of years ago.

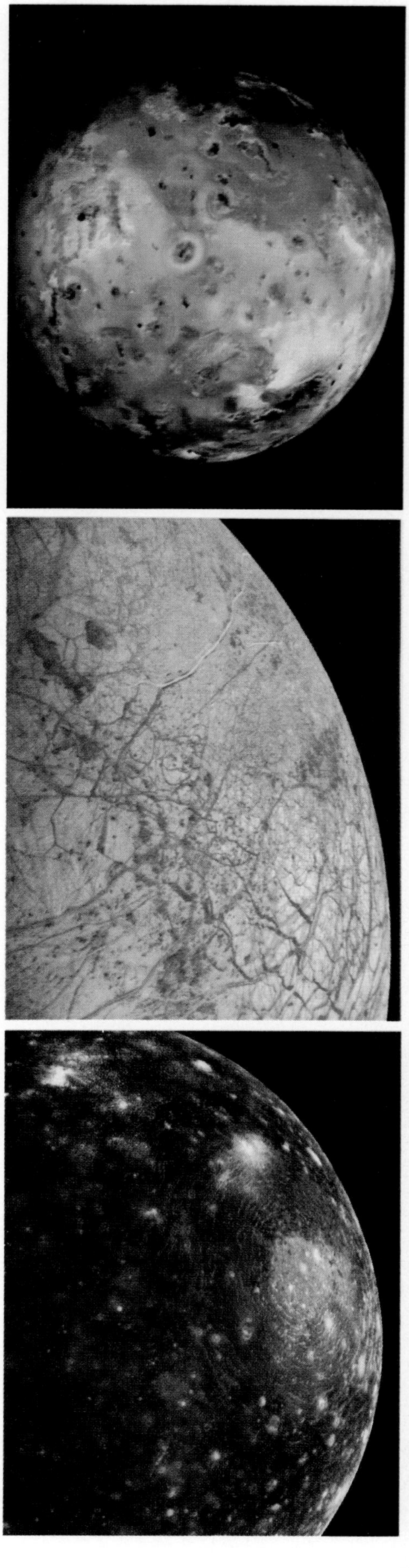

Figure 3–16 *These photographs of Jupiter's inner moons were taken by* Voyager 2. *Io (top) is the only known object other than the earth to have active volcanoes. Europa (center) shows tan streaks that may be shallow valleys. The bright spot near the edge of Callisto (bottom) is a crater billions of years old.*

Figure 3–17 *Here you see an artist's idea of how Voyager appeared as it passed by Saturn and made its way toward the very edge of the solar system and beyond.*

Saturn

Beyond Jupiter lies the sixth planet, Saturn. In many ways, Saturn is similar to Jupiter. It is a "gas giant" with colored bands in its cloud cover. Saturn even has a reddish orange oval spot similar to Jupiter's red spot. Like Jupiter, Saturn gives off more heat than it receives from the sun. And it also has a huge magnetosphere.

Saturn rotates on its axis once every 10 hours or so. This rapid rotation causes the planet to flatten out at its poles and bulge in the middle. Jupiter also rotates rapidly and flattens out at its poles. The rapid rotation of Saturn's cloud cover causes winds in the atmosphere to reach a speed of up to 1800 kilometers per hour. These winds are faster than those in Jupiter's atmosphere. But like Jupiter's clouds, Saturn's clouds are made mostly of hydrogen and helium. Beneath its cloud cover, Saturn may be very similar to Jupiter in structure.

One unusual feature of Saturn is its very low density. In fact, Saturn is the least dense planet in the solar system. If all of the planets could be placed in a giant ocean, Saturn would be the only one to float.

Perhaps Saturn's most beautiful feature is its ring system. Saturn's rings were first discovered by Gali-

Figure 3–18 *Saturn's ring system may well be the most beautiful sight in the solar system. What makes up Saturn's rings?*

leo some 300 years ago. But it was not until the Voyager spacecraft sent back pictures of the ring system that astronomers learned how complex these rings actually are.

Saturn has at least seven major rings. The rings are made of particles of water ice ranging in size from .001 millimeter to almost 100 kilometers. In addition to its seven major rings, Saturn has tens of thousands of tiny ringlets that weave in and out of the major rings. The last of Saturn's rings extends almost 300,000 kilometers away from the planet.

Saturn has more moons than any other planet. At least 17, and possibly 23, moons have been discovered. The most interesting of Saturn's moons is

Figure 3–19 *In this composite photograph, Saturn is surrounded by six of its many moons. The large moon in front is Dione. The other moons (clockwise) are Enceladus, Rhea, Titan, Mimas, and Tethys.*

Figure 3–20 *This illustration shows the relative distances (not sizes) of the planets from the sun. The closest planet, Mercury, averages about 58 million kilometers from the sun. The farthest planet, Pluto, averages about 5900 million kilometers from the sun.*

Titan. Titan is the second largest moon in the solar system. It is the only moon that has its own atmosphere. Titan's atmosphere contains mostly nitrogen. It has smaller amounts of methane, hydrogen cyanide, carbon monoxide, and carbon dioxide. Many of these gases are deadly to life on the earth. But it is interesting to note that before life formed, the earth had an atmosphere very similar to that of Titan. The combination of the gases on Titan gives it an orange haze.

Uranus

Uranus, the seventh planet, is almost twice as far from the sun as Saturn. Uranus is also a "gas giant." Uranus is covered with a thick atmosphere made of hydrogen, helium, and methane. The clouds of Uranus do not have colored bands. Instead they are greenish blue. The clouds are made mostly of methane and hydrogen. Temperatures at the top of the clouds may dip to as low as −350°C.

Data from the *Voyager 2* in January 1986 provide strong evidence that Uranus is covered by an ocean of superheated water that may have formed from melted comets. Because of the extreme pressure from an atmosphere 11,000 kilometers thick, the water does not boil. This worldwide ocean is about 8000 kilometers deep and encloses a rocky, molten core about the size of the earth.

The axis on which Uranus rotates is quite unusual. Unlike the axis of any other planet, the axis of Uranus is tilted at an angle of about 90°. So Uranus seems to be tipped completely on its side. Uranus has 11 known rings. But unlike the rings of Saturn, these rings are dark and probably made of methane ice. Because of the tilt of the axis of Uranus, the rings circle the planet from top to bottom.

Uranus has 15 moons, ranging in diameter from 32 to 1625 kilometers.

Figure 3–21 *This illustration shows the various layers of Uranus. What is the outer atmosphere made of?*

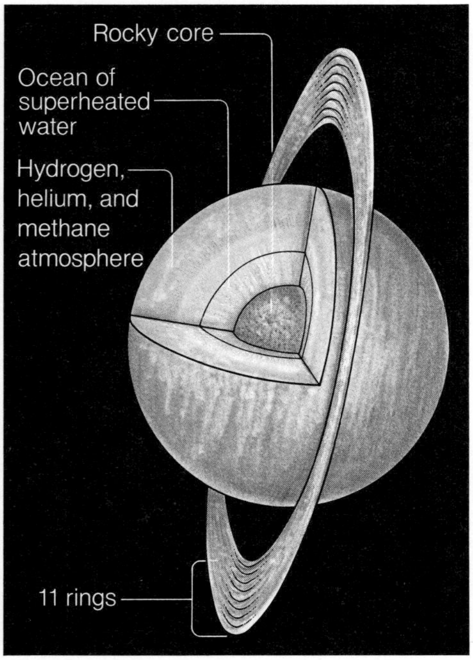

Neptune

Neptune is the eighth planet in the solar system. In many ways, Neptune is a "twin" of Uranus. It is about the same size and has about the same mass as Uranus. And it also glows with a greenish blue color. Neptune has a thick atmosphere made mostly of hydrogen and helium. The atmosphere also contains clouds of methane.

Neptune's surface may be covered by a semi-frozen slush of water and methane, which surrounds a rocky core. Four thin rings circle Neptune. Unlike the methane rings of Uranus, Neptune's rings appear to be made up of dust particles, much like the rings of Saturn. Eight moons have been observed orbiting Neptune.

One of the moons, Triton, is among the largest moons in the solar system. Triton is an icy moon covered with frozen methane. Triton is an unusual moon because it rotates on its axis in an opposite direction from Neptune's direction of rotation. This fact has led some astronomers to conclude that Triton is not an original moon of Neptune. Instead it may be an object captured by Neptune's gravity.

Pluto

Pluto, the ninth planet in the solar system, is little more than a moon-sized object. It is thought to be made mostly of frozen methane and ice. Observations indicate that some of the methane on the daylight side of Pluto evaporates and forms a thin, pink atmosphere. If true, Pluto is the only planet to have an atmosphere on the side facing the sun and none on the side facing away from the sun.

In 1978, a moon was discovered orbiting Pluto. This moon, called Charon, is about one-half the size of Pluto. Because these two objects are so close in size, many astronomers consider Pluto and Charon to be a double planet system.

Sharpen Your Skills

Ellipses

The orbits of the planets about the sun form ellipses. Every ellipse has two fixed points called foci (singular: focus). In any planetary orbit, one of the foci is the sun. Determine whether the distance between the two foci affects the shape of the ellipse.

1. Stick two thumbtacks into a sheet of stiff paper. The tacks should be about 10 centimeters apart. Wind a 30-centimeter piece of string around the thumbtacks and tie the ends together as shown in the diagram. Use a sharp pencil to trace an ellipse, keeping the string tight at all times.

2. Repeat the same procedure, but this time place the thumbtacks about 5 centimeters apart. Compare the two ellipses you have drawn.

3. Predict what shape you will draw if you remove one thumbtack. Then try it.

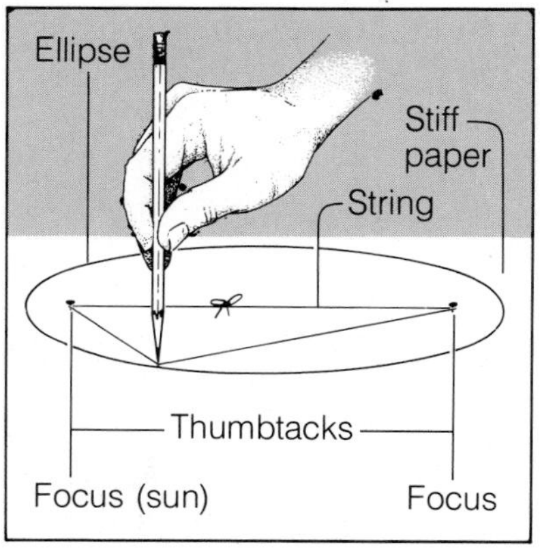

Figure 3–22 *If you could stand on Pluto, the sun would appear as a distant speck of light in the sky. Charon, Pluto's large moon, looms over the horizon. Why are Pluto and Charon sometimes considered a double planet system?*

SECTION REVIEW

1. Which planet is thought to have lost its oceans because of the greenhouse effect?
2. What compound in the Martian soil gives the soil its red color?
3. Which planet's rings are mostly ice particles?
4. Explain why Venus is hotter than Mercury even though Mercury is closer to the sun.

3–5 Meteoroids, Comets, and Asteroids

Section Objective

To classify meteoroids, comets, and asteroids

Meteoroids, comets, and asteroids are minor objects in the solar system. They are much less massive than the planets and most of their moons.

Meteoroids

You have probably seen a "shooting star" on a clear night. The streak of light you saw is caused by a **meteoroid** (MEET-ee-uh-roid) entering the earth's atmosphere. Meteoroids are solid, rocklike objects that revolve around the sun. The friction between a meteoroid and the atmosphere causes the meteoroid to glow and be seen in the night sky. The bright trail or streak of light made of hot gases is called a **meteor** (MEET-ee-uhr).

At different times during the year, the number of meteors you can see increases from the normal rate of 6 or more per hour to 60 or more per hour. These events are called meteor showers.

Most meteoroids burn up while passing through the earth's atmosphere. But some meteoroids are large enough to survive the passage. The stony material that strikes the earth is called a **meteorite.** A few large meteorites have produced great craters on the earth. The most famous is the Barringer meteorite crater in Arizona, shown in Figure 3–23. It is 1.2 kilometers wide. Scientists estimate that the meteorite that caused this crater fell to the earth within the last 20,000 years.

Scientists have examined meteorites and have determined that there are three types of meteoroids. They are grouped according to the material found in them. One type of meteoroid, the iron meteoroid, is made of iron and nickel. Another type, the stony meteoroid, is made of sandlike minerals. The third type, the stony-iron meteoroid, is a combination of these two types. The stony-iron meteoroid is the rarest type of meteoroid. Under what conditions would you expect to best see meteors in the sky?

Sharpen Your Skills

Observing Meteor Showers

Listed below are some of the earth's annual meteor showers and the best dates for viewing them.

Using reference materials in the library, find the sky locations to best observe the meteors. Then try to observe meteors during several clear nights.

Name	Best date
Quadrantids	Jan. 4
Lyrids	Apr. 22
Eta Aquarids	May 5
Orionids	Oct. 21
Taurids	Nov. 8
Geminids	Dec. 14

Figure 3–23 *The Barringer crater, in Arizona, is 1.2 kilometers wide. What caused this huge crater?*

Comets

While reading about the formation of the solar system, you learned that an icy cloud near the edge of the solar system is the home of **comets.** This cloud is known as the Oort cloud because its existence was suggested by Dutch astronomer Jan Oort.

The Oort cloud is located some 15 trillion kilometers from the sun. According to the most current theories, a chunk of icy material from the cloud is occasionally tugged out of the cloud by the gravitational pull of a passing star. This chunk of ice, dust, and gas—called a comet—is then sent speeding toward the sun. For most of its trip toward the sun, the mountain-sized chunk of icy material travels unnoticed. But as it gets closer to the sun, it grows warmer. Some of the ice, dust, and gas in the chunk gets hot enough to form a cloud around the comet's icy core.

Figure 3–24 *Why does the tail of a comet always point away from the sun?*

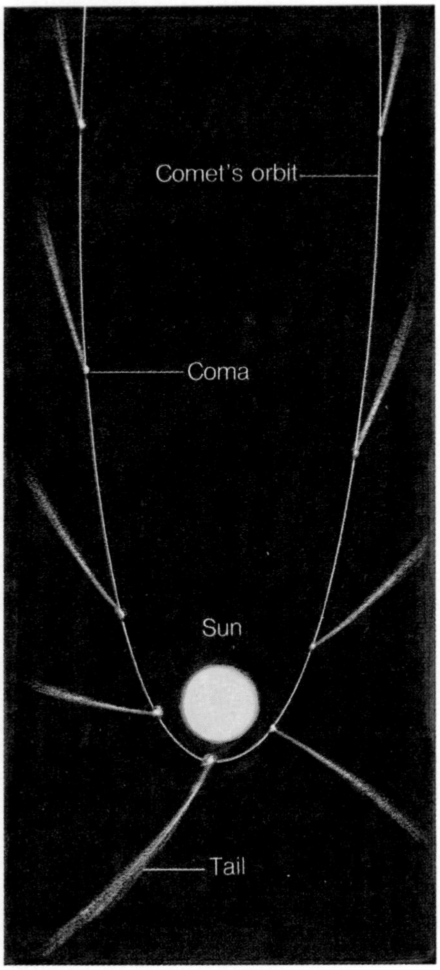

The icy core of the comet is referred to as its nucleus. The cloud of dust and gas surrounding the nucleus is called the **coma.** The nucleus and coma together form the comet's head. As the comet approaches the sun, the head gets warmer and larger. In time, the head may become as large as a few million kilometers.

As the comet approaches the sun, solar wind blows the coma of the head into a long tail. So the tail of the comet always streams away from the sun. In time, the comet will probably travel around the sun and return to the outer edge of the solar system. But some comets crash directly into the sun.

There are about 100,000 comets in the solar system. Most comets orbit the sun over long periods of time. These long-period comets may take many thousands of years to complete one trip around the sun. Other comets are short-period comets. These comets return to the sun every few years.

Halley's Comet

The most famous short-period comet is Halley's comet, named for the English astronomer Edmund Halley. Halley's comet returns to the sun every 76 to 79 years. Its most recent visit to the earth was in 1986. In 1984 and 1985, five space probes were launched from the earth to meet Halley's comet and study its properties.

Between March 6 and 13, 1986, the five probes traveled past Halley's nucleus. The Soviet *Vega 1* probe showed that the dust-covered nucleus is not round and that the coma contains not only fine dust particles but also flying chunks of rock the size of boulders. The Soviet *Vega 2* confirmed that the nucleus is solid. Japan's *Suisei* probe showed that the huge hydrogen coma appears to brighten and darken in a cycle of 53 hours. This observation seems to confirm that the nucleus rotates about once every two days. *Sakigake,* the other Japanese probe, detected waves similar to lightning. The European Space Agency's *Giotto* probe traveled the closest to the comet and showed that the nucleus is black and about 15 kilometers long and at least 4 kilometers wide.

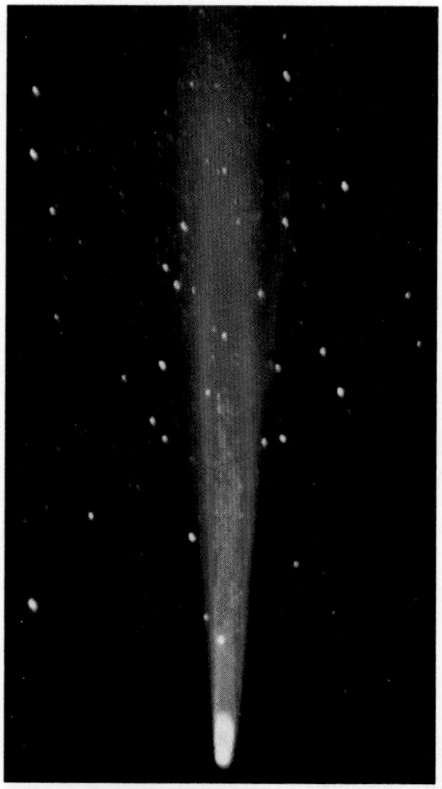

Figure 3–25 *This photograph of Halley's comet was taken in 1910 (top). The colors were added later by a computer. Ancient Babylonians recorded a sighting of what is now called Halley's comet in 164 B.C. on this clay tablet (bottom).*

Asteroids

As you read earlier, there is a large gap between the orbits of Mars and Jupiter. Many scientists believe that a planet should exist in this space. Instead asteroids are found there. This area is known as the asteroid belt. Asteroids are chunks of rock or fragments of planetlike material of varying sizes floating in space. The largest known asteroid is Ceres. It has a diameter of 1,000 kilometers. Most of the other asteroids are only about 1 kilometer in diameter. Astronomers believe that the asteroids in the asteroid belt may be material that never formed into a planet because Jupiter's strong gravity kept the asteroids from coming together.

Not all of the asteroids in the solar system are found within the asteroid belt. A few large asteroids pass near the earth from time to time. Scientists believe that some of the craters on the moon and on the inner planets were probably caused by asteroids colliding with these objects.

SECTION REVIEW

1. What is the word for a meteoroid that strikes the earth?
2. Why does a comet's tail always stream away from the sun?

3 LABORATORY INVESTIGATION

Relative Distances of the Planets

Problem

How can a scale model of the solar system be used to increase your understanding of the planets' relative distances from the sun?

Materials *(per group)*

Spool of string
Meterstick
9 cardboard tags with strings attached
Pencil

Planet	Distance from sun *(km)*	Scale distance from sun *(cm)*
Mercury		
Venus		
Earth		
Mars		
Jupiter		
Saturn		
Uranus		
Neptune		
Pluto		

Procedure

1. Work outdoors or in a large open room like a gym.
2. Write the name of each planet on a separate tag.
3. Use the chart on pages 74–75 to find the distance of each planet from the sun. Record the data in a chart similar to the one shown here.
4. Using a scale of 1 million km = 1 mm, convert the distances to centimeters and record your answers in the chart.
5. The end of the spool of string represents the sun's position. Measure out the scale distance of Mercury from the sun along the string. Tie the tag marked "Mercury" at that point. Repeat this step for each of the other eight planets.
6. Cut the string just past the point at which the "Pluto" tag is tied. Have someone hold each end of the string so that the relative distances of all the planets can be observed.

Observations

1. Are distances between planets greater between the inner or outer planets?
2. Which two consecutive planets are closest? Farthest?

Conclusions

1. If you were to make scale models of each planet would you use the same scale you used to convert the distances between the planets? Explain your answer.
2. Is there an "empty region" along the string that looks as if it should have a planet there? What is actually found in this region in space?
3. Relate the planets' distances from the sun to their compositions.

CHAPTER REVIEW

SUMMARY

3–1 Formation of the Solar System

❑ The solar system began in a huge cloud of dust and gas called a nebula.

❑ According to the nebular theory of solar system formation, the nebula was disrupted by the shock waves of a nearby supernova.

❑ A protosun formed near the center of the nebula. Smaller clumps of gas and dust formed protoplanets around the protosun.

3–2 A Special Star: The Sun

❑ The four main layers of the sun are the corona, the chromosphere, the photosphere, and the sun's core.

❑ Solar storms on the sun include prominences, solar flares, and sunspots.

3–3 Motion of the Planets

❑ A planet's period of revolution is the time it takes that planet to make one complete revolution around the sun, or a year on that planet.

❑ A planet's period of rotation is the time it takes that planet to make one complete rotation on its axis, or a day on that planet.

3–4 Features of the Planets

❑ Mercury is a crater-covered world with high temperatures on its daylight side and low temperatures on its nighttime side.

❑ Venus is a cloud-covered world with high temperatures. The greenhouse effect is the main cause of its high temperatures.

❑ Mars is coated with iron oxide, or rust, which gives the planet its reddish color.

❑ Water on Mars is frozen in the northern icecap or just below the surface of the soil.

❑ The clouds of Jupiter, which make up most of its atmosphere, are made mostly of hydrogen and helium.

❑ Jupiter's core is probably a rocky solid surrounded by a layer of liquid metallic hydrogen.

❑ Jupiter has 16 moons. The four most interesting moons are the Galilean satellites called Io, Europa, Ganymede, and Callisto.

❑ Saturn is similar in appearance and composition to Jupiter.

❑ Saturn's spectacular rings are made mostly of water ice.

❑ Uranus is a cloud-covered world with an atmosphere made mostly of hydrogen, helium, and methane.

❑ The axis of Uranus is tilted at an angle of almost 90°.

❑ Uranus has 15 known moons and 11 known rings. The rings are probably made mostly of methane ice.

❑ Neptune is probably similar to Uranus in appearance and composition.

❑ Neptune has four known rings and eight known moons.

❑ Pluto is a moon-sized, ice-covered world.

3–5 Meteoroids, Comets, and Asteroids

❑ The trail of hot gases from a burning meteoroid is called a meteor. If a part of a meteoroid strikes the earth, it is called a meteorite.

❑ As a comet approaches the sun, some of the ice, dust, and gas heat up and form a cloud around the comet's nucleus.

❑ The cloud of dust and gas surrounding a comet's nucleus is called the coma. The coma and nucleus make up the head of a comet.

❑ Solar wind blows the coma into a long tail, which always streams away from the sun.

❑ Long-period comets return to the sun every few thousand years or more. Short-period comets return to the sun more frequently.

❑ Asteroids are chunks of rock or fragments of planetlike material.

VOCABULARY

Define each term in a complete sentence.

asteroid
asteroid belt
axis
chromosphere
coma
comet
core
corona
elliptical orbit
greenhouse effect
law of inertia
magnetosphere
meteor
meteorite
meteoroid
nebular theory
orbit
period of revolution
period of rotation
photosphere
prominence
protoplanet
protosun
retrograde motion
satellite
solar flare
solar system
solar wind
sunspot

CONTENT REVIEW: MULTIPLE CHOICE

Choose the letter of the answer that best completes each sentence.

1. The outer "gas giants" do not include
a. Jupiter b. Pluto c. Saturn d. Uranus

2. The innermost layer of the sun's atmosphere is called the
a. corona b. core c. photosphere d. chromosphere

3. Bright bursts of light on the sun's surface are solar storms called
a. sunspots b. prominences c. solar flares d. solar windstorms

4. The time it takes a planet to make one complete trip around the sun is called its
a. period of rotation b. day c. period of revolution d. axis

5. A planet with sulfuric acid in its clouds is
a. Venus b. Jupiter c. Mars d. Uranus

6. A planet with retrograde motion is
a. Jupiter b. Mercury c. Pluto d. Venus

7. The innermost of Jupiter's large moons is
a. Europa b. Io c. Callisto d. Ganymede

8. A moon that rotates in an opposite direction from its planet's rotation is
a. Phobos b. Titan c. Triton d. Europa

9. The Oort cloud is the home of
a. asteroids b. Pluto c. comets d. meteoroids

10. Rocklike objects in the region of space between the orbits of Mars and Jupiter are called
a. comets b. protoplanets c. meteorites d. asteroids

CONTENT REVIEW: COMPLETION

Fill in the word or words that best complete each sentence.

1. The solar system began in a cloud of dust and gas called a (an) ________________.

2. The ________________ is the outermost layer of the sun's atmosphere.

3. An ______________ describes the path a planet takes around the sun.
4. The two factors that affect the shape of the path a planet takes around the sun are ______________ and ______________.
5. The process by which heat is trapped beneath the thick clouds of Venus is called the ______________.
6. The southern icecap of Mars contains mostly frozen ______________.
7. ______________ and ______________ are the two main gases in the atmosphere of Jupiter.
8. ______________ is the planet with the most moons.
9. The planet that is little more than a moon-sized object is ______________.
10. The cloud of dust and gas surrounding the nucleus of a comet is called the ______________.

CONTENT REVIEW: TRUE OR FALSE

Determine whether each statement is true or false. If it is true, write "true." If it is false, change the underlined word or words to make the statement true.

1. Because of the tremendous heat of the sun, the outer planets were unable to retain their lightweight gases.
2. Pluto may be an escaped moon of Uranus.
3. The corona is the hottest layer of the sun.
4. All planets orbit the sun in a clockwise direction.
5. The time it takes a planet to spin once on its axis is called its period of rotation.
6. Callisto is the most active moon of Jupiter.
7. The largest magnetosphere in the solar system is produced by Saturn.
8. Uranus is unusual because it rotates on its side.
9. A meteor is the streak of light produced when a small object shoots through the atmosphere.
10. Long-period comets return to the sun every few years.

CONCEPT REVIEW: SKILL BUILDING

Use the skills you have developed in the chapter to complete each activity.

1. **Making graphs** Using the chart on pages 74–75, draw a graph that plots the high and low temperatures on each planet. What conclusions can you draw?
2. **Relating cause and effect** Explain the following observations: a. The surface temperature of Venus is 480°C. b. Mercury's surface has not changed much over the past few million years. c. Mars' southern icecap melts during the summer but its northern icecap does not melt at all. d. Jupiter gives off more heat than it receives from the sun. e. The water covering Uranus does not boil, even at temperatures well above 100°C. f. Pluto may have an atmosphere on only one side.
3. **Applying concepts** Explain why planetary orbits are elliptical.

CONCEPT REVIEW: ESSAY

Discuss each of the following in a brief paragraph.

1. How do sunspots indicate to astronomers that the sun rotates?
2. Describe the two kinds of planetary motion.

The Earth and Moon 4

CHAPTER SECTIONS

CHAPTER OBJECTIVES

After completing this chapter, you will be able to

4–1 Describe some of the major features of the earth.

4–2 Explain the causes of day and night and the seasons.

4–3 Describe the major features of the moon.

4–4 Identify the interactions that occur between the earth, the moon, and the sun.

The first dramatic step into space was taken on October 4, 1957. On that historic day, a Soviet rocket boosted *Sputnik 1* into orbit above the earth. *Sputnik 1* was the earth's first artificial satellite.

The unexpected launching of *Sputnik 1* thrust the United States into the "great space race." Scientists throughout the country began preparations for an American entry into space.

On January 31, 1958, the first American satellite, *Explorer 1,* was launched into space. *Explorer 1* was carried into space by a rocket launched from the Kennedy Space Center in Cape Canaveral, Florida. A short time later, *Explorer 3* was sent into orbit around the earth.

The task of the Explorer satellites was to study cosmic rays. Cosmic rays are a form of energy that strikes the earth from outer space. But soon after they were launched, the Explorer satellites made an unexpected discovery. The satellites found two doughnut-shaped regions of charged particles between 2000 and 20,000 kilometers above the earth's surface. No one had expected to find anything like these two regions. In honor of James Van Allen, the scientist who led the Explorer team, the two regions were named the Van Allen radiation belts.

When you have finished reading this chapter, you will know a great deal more about the Van Allen radiation belts. For now, keep one thing in mind. If it were not for these belts, you would not be reading this chapter—or any other chapter. Without the Van Allen radiation belts, life would not exist on the earth!

Explorer 1, *the first American satellite, orbited the earth in 1958.*

Section Objective

To identify various features of the earth

Figure 4–1 *How much greater is the earth's circumference than its diameter?*

FACTS ABOUT THE EARTH
Average distance from sun About 150,000,000 kilometers
Diameter through equator 12,756.32 kilometers
Circumference around equator 40,075.16 kilometers
Surface area Land area, about 148,300,000 square kilometers, or about 30 percent of total surface area; water area, about 361,800,000 square kilometers, or about 70 percent of total surface area
Rotation period 23 hours, 56 minutes, 4.09 seconds
Revolution period around sun 365 days, 6 hours, 9 minutes, 9.54 seconds
Temperature Highest, 58°C at Al Aziziyah, Libya; lowest, −90°C at Vostok in Antarctica; average surface temperature, 14°C
Highest and lowest land features Highest, Mount Everest, 8848 meters above sea level; lowest, shore of Dead Sea, 396 meters below sea level
Ocean depths Deepest, Mariana Trench in Pacific Ocean southwest of Guam, 11,033 meters below surface; average ocean depth, 3795 meters

4–1 The Planet Earth

Space technology has come a long way since *Explorer 1* was sent into space in 1958. Today scientists have more to rely on than observations made by satellites orbiting the earth. People, too, have viewed the earth from space. In fact, by 1987 more than 130 United States astronauts and Soviet cosmonauts will have had the opportunity to study the earth during space flights.

Photographs taken from space show that the earth is a very beautiful planet. It is covered with blue oceans and waterways, green jungles, brown deserts, and continuously changing cloud patterns.

The Earth's Statistics

The diameter of the earth is about 12,756 kilometers. When compared to the planet Jupiter, which has a diameter of 142,700 kilometers, the earth may not seem to be a very large planet. But the earth is the largest of the inner planets in the solar system. The diameter of Mars, for example, is only about one-half the diameter of the earth.

The earth's circumference, or the distance around the earth, is about 40,075 kilometers at the **equator.** The equator is an imaginary line around the earth that divides the earth into halves, called **hemispheres.** These hemispheres are called the Northern Hemisphere and the Southern Hemisphere. Which hemisphere do you live in?

Features of the Earth

The three main features of the earth are the ground you walk on, the water you drink, and the air you breathe. The ground is a part of the earth's rocky crust, which includes the continents and other landmasses. Of course, the rocks, minerals, soil, and sand on these landmasses are also part of the crust.

The thickness of the crust varies from place to place. Beneath the oceans, the crust may be only 8 kilometers thick. Beneath the continents, the crust may be 32 kilometers thick.

About 70 percent of the earth's surface is covered by water. This water is called the **hydrosphere.**

Figure 4–2 *These unusual rock formations in Arches National Park, Utah, are part of the earth's crust.*

The hydrosphere includes the earth's oceans, rivers and streams, ponds and lakes, seas and bays, and any other bodies of water. Some of the hydrosphere is frozen in the polar icecaps at the North and South poles, as well as in icebergs and glaciers.

About 97 percent of the hydrosphere is salt water. The most common salt in salt water is sodium chloride, or table salt. You might think that the remaining 3 percent of the hydrosphere is fresh water that can be used for drinking. But you would be wrong. Almost 85 percent of the fresh water on the earth is trapped as ice in places like the polar icecaps. With such a small amount of fresh water available for drinking, why does the earth not run out of fresh water?

The oxygen you breathe is part of the earth's **atmosphere.** About 78 percent of the atmosphere is nitrogen. About 21 percent is oxygen. The rest is made up of gases such as argon, carbon dioxide, water vapor, hydrogen, helium, neon, krypton, xenon, and methane. See Figure 4–3.

Figure 4–3 *This graph shows the percentages of the various gases in the atmosphere. How much of the atmosphere do nitrogen and oxygen make up?*

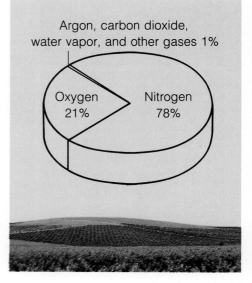

SECTION REVIEW

1. What is the equator? Into what two parts does the equator divide the earth?
2. What percentage of the hydrosphere is fresh water? What percentage of the fresh water is available for drinking?

Section Objective

To relate night and day to the earth's rotation and seasons to the earth's revolution

4–2 The Earth in Space

The earth is the third planet from the sun in the solar system. Like all other planets, the earth revolves around the sun in an elliptical orbit. And like the other planets, the earth rotates on its axis as it travels around the sun. **These two factors—the earth's revolution and rotation—affect both night and day and seasons on the earth.**

Night and Day

It takes the earth about 24 hours to rotate once on its axis. The earth's axis is an imaginary line from the North Pole through the center of the earth to the South Pole. The time the earth takes to complete one rotation is called a day. So a day on the earth is about 24 hours long.

As the earth rotates, part of it faces the sun and is bathed in sunlight. The rest of the earth is in darkness. As the earth continues to rotate, the part that faced the sun soon faces away from the sun. And the part that was in darkness is bathed in sunlight. So the rotation of the earth causes day and night once every 24 hours.

As seen from above the North Pole, the earth rotates in a counterclockwise direction, or from west to east, at a speed of about 1600 kilometers per hour. So the sun appears to come up, or "rise," in the east as the earth turns toward it. It appears to

Figure 4–4 *This five-photo sunrise-to-sunset sequence was taken by a satellite orbiting the earth above South America. What causes day and night on the earth?*

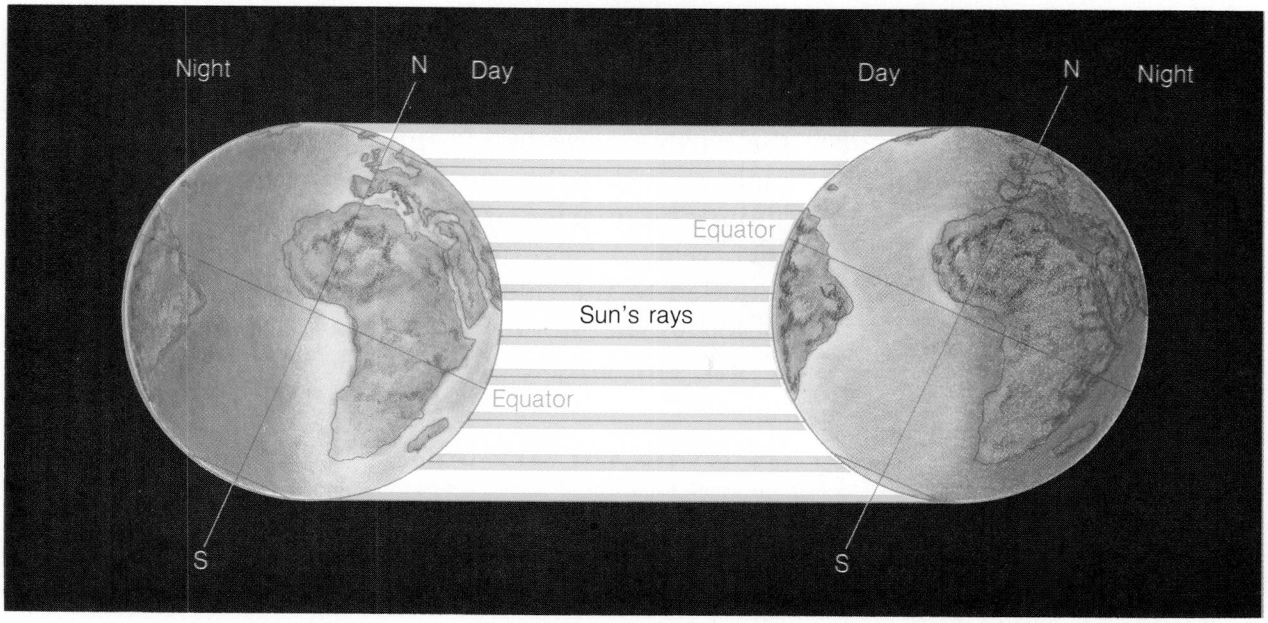

Figure 4–5 *Because of the tilt of the earth's axis, the length of day and night is not constant. At the beginning of summer in the Northern Hemisphere (left), the Arctic is always in daylight and the Antarctic is always dark. What happens at the beginning of winter (right)?*

go down, or "set," in the west as the earth turns away from it.

You may have noticed that throughout the year the length of day and night changes. This happens because the earth's axis is not straight up and down. If the earth's axis were straight up and down, all parts of the earth would have 12 hours of daylight and 12 hours of nighttime every day of the year. Instead the earth's axis is tilted at an angle of 23½°.

Because the axis is slightly tilted, when the North Pole is leaning toward the sun, the South Pole is leaning away from the sun. And when the South Pole is leaning toward the sun, the North Pole is leaning away from the sun. As a result, the number of daylight hours in the Northern and Southern hemispheres is not constant. The hemisphere that leans toward the sun has long days and short nights. The hemisphere that leans away from the sun has short days and long nights. At this moment, is the Northern Hemisphere leaning toward or away from the sun?

A Year in Space

It takes the earth about 365.26 days to complete one revolution, or one complete trip, around the sun. The time the earth takes to make one complete revolution around the sun is called a year. How many times does the earth rotate in one year?

Sharpen Your Skills

The Earth on the Move

The earth travels about 30 km/sec as it orbits the sun. How many kilometers does the earth travel in a minute? In an hour? In a day? In a year?

Sharpen Your Skills

Temperature, Daylight, and the Seasons

1. Keep a log of the high and low temperatures for each day in the school year.
2. Also record when the sun rises and sets each day.
3. Calculate the length of daylight in hours and minutes for each day.

What happens to the high and low temperatures and the length of days as the year progresses from season to season? What relationship do you find between the amount of daylight and the temperature? Explain your observations.

You do not have to look at a calendar to know that there are only 365 days in a calendar year. But the earth rotates 365.26 times in the time it takes to make one complete revolution around the sun. So about one-quarter of a day is left off the calendar each year. As a result, every four years an extra day is added to the calendar year. This extra day is added to the month of February. Do you know what a year with an extra day is called?

Seasons on the Earth

Most people live in a part of the world that has four distinct seasons: winter, spring, summer, and autumn. These different seasons are caused by the tilt of the earth's axis.

As the earth revolves around the sun, the axis is tilted away from the sun for part of the year and toward the sun for part of the year. When the Northern Hemisphere is tilted toward the sun, that half of the earth has summer. At the same time, the Southern Hemisphere is tilted away from the sun and has winter. See Figure 4–6. It is interesting to notice that when the Northern Hemisphere is tilted toward the sun during its summer, the earth is actually farthest away from the sun in its elliptical orbit. The same is true for the Southern Hemisphere dur-

Figure 4–6 *When the North Pole is tilted toward the sun, the Northern Hemisphere receives more sunlight. It is summer. When the North Pole is tilted away from the sun, the Northern Hemisphere receives less sunlight. It is winter. Is the same true for the South Pole and the Southern Hemisphere?*

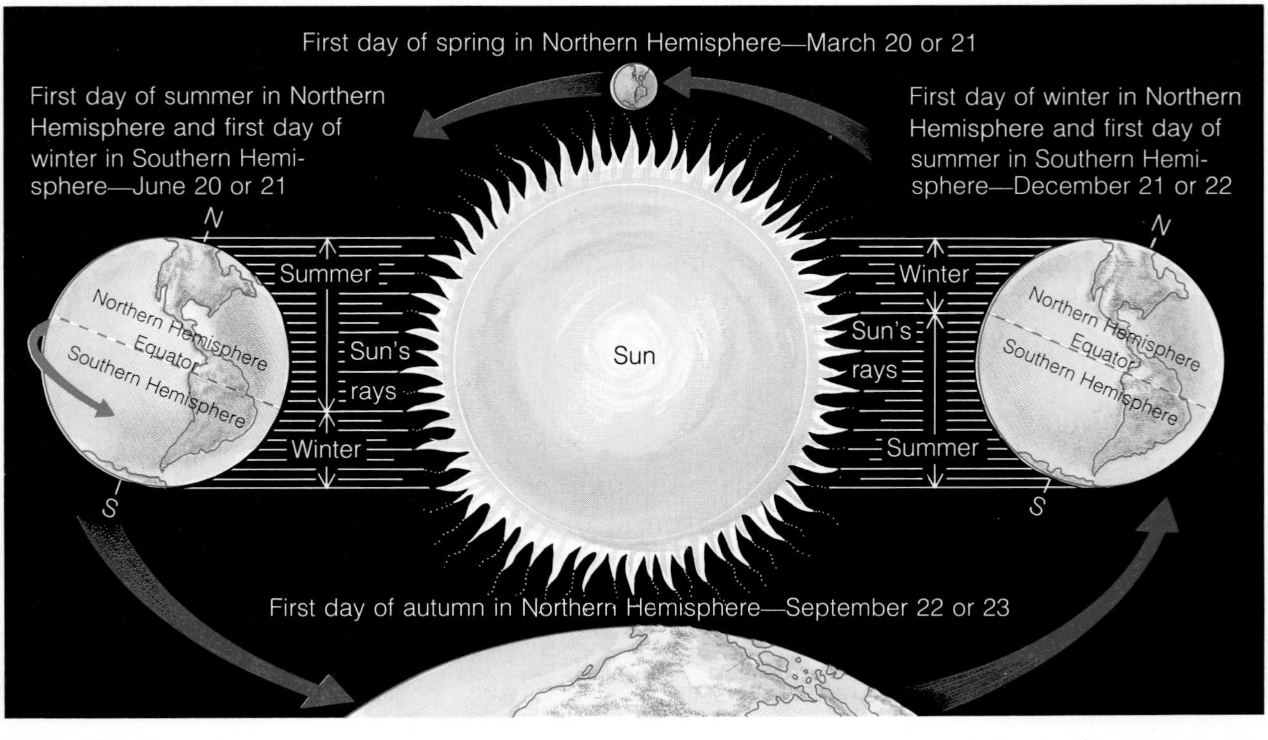

ing its summer. How is the earth tilted when the Southern Hemisphere has winter?

The hemisphere of the earth that is tilted toward the sun receives rays that are more direct. Recall that this hemisphere also has longer days. The combination of more direct rays and longer days causes the earth's surface, its oceans, and its atmosphere to receive more heat in that hemisphere. The result is the summer season.

Summer begins in the Northern Hemisphere on June 20 or 21. This is when the North Pole is tilted its full 23½° toward the sun. The Northern Hemisphere has its longest day at this time, while the Southern Hemisphere has its shortest day. This time of the year is known as the **summer solstice** (SAHL-stihs). The word *solstice* comes from two Latin words meaning "sunstop" and refers to the time when the sun seems to stop moving higher in the sky each day.

After June 21, the sun seems to move lower and lower in the sky until December 21 or 22, when the **winter solstice** occurs. At this time, the North Pole is tilted its full 23½° away from the sun. The shortest day of the year occurs in the Northern Hemisphere, and the longest day occurs in the Southern Hemisphere on the winter solstice.

Twice a year, neither the North Pole nor the South Pole is tilted toward the sun. This occurs in spring and autumn. On the days this happens, day and night are of equal length all over the world. These times are known as **equinoxes** (EE-kwuh-naks-uhz). The word *equinox* means "equal night." In the Northern Hemisphere, spring begins on the **vernal equinox,** March 20 or 21. The North Pole begins its six months of daylight. Autumn begins on the **autumnal equinox,** September 22 or 23. The North Pole begins six months of nighttime. What season begins in the Southern Hemisphere when spring begins in the Northern Hemisphere?

Figure 4–7 *These photographs were taken on the same day in the Northern and Southern hemispheres. It is winter in Aspen, Colorado (bottom). But it is summer at this sheep ranch in Chile (top). On this day, is the North Pole tilted toward or away from the sun?*

The Earth as a Magnet in Space

In Figure 4–8 on page 102, you can see the pattern that forms when iron filings are sprinkled over a plate of glass that covers a magnet. The pattern of iron filings reveals the invisible lines of force formed by the two ends of the magnet.

The earth, much like a magnet, produces similar lines of force. In fact, you might think of the earth as having a giant bar magnet passing from one pole to the other through its center. Where does the earth's magnetism come from? The answer is not clear, but the earth's magnetism is probably the result of the rotation of the earth's inner core. The earth's inner core is a solid made up mainly of iron and nickel.

The earth's magnetism forms a magnetic field around the earth similar to the magnetic field around a bar magnet. This magnetic field is called the **magnetosphere.** The magnetosphere begins at an altitude of about 1000 kilometers and extends to an altitude of 64,000 kilometers on the side of the earth facing toward the sun. But on the side of the earth facing away from the sun, the magnetosphere extends in a tail millions of kilometers long.

On the side of the earth facing away from the sun, the magnetosphere is blown into a long tail by the solar wind. The solar wind is a stream of high-energy particles blown off the sun. The solar wind constantly reshapes the magnetosphere as the earth rotates on its axis.

You can see in Figure 4–8 that the magnetic North and South poles are not in the exact same place as the geographic North and South poles. The geographic poles are at each end of the earth's tilted axis. But the magnetic poles are at the ends of the magnetic field produced by the earth's magnetism.

Earlier you read about the discovery of the **Van Allen radiation belts.** These two doughnut-shaped

Sharpen Your Skills

Lines of Force

You can observe magnetic lines of force for yourself.

1. Place a thin sheet of glass or plastic over a bar magnet.
2. Sprinkle iron filings over the covered magnet.
3. Gently shake the glass or plastic sheet back and forth until a clear pattern of lines of force form.
4. Draw the pattern of lines of force that you observe.

How do the lines of force you observed compare with those in Figure 4–8? Predict how the lines of force would change if you placed another magnet under the glass. Try it.

Figure 4–8 *The earth acts like a giant bar magnet (right) whose lines of force produce the same pattern as a small bar magnet (left).*

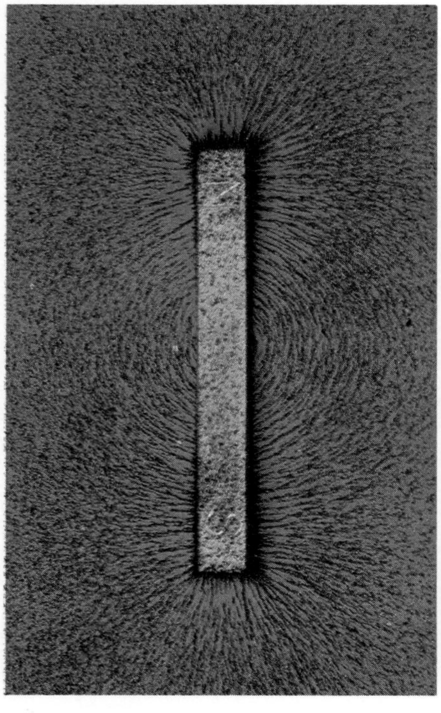

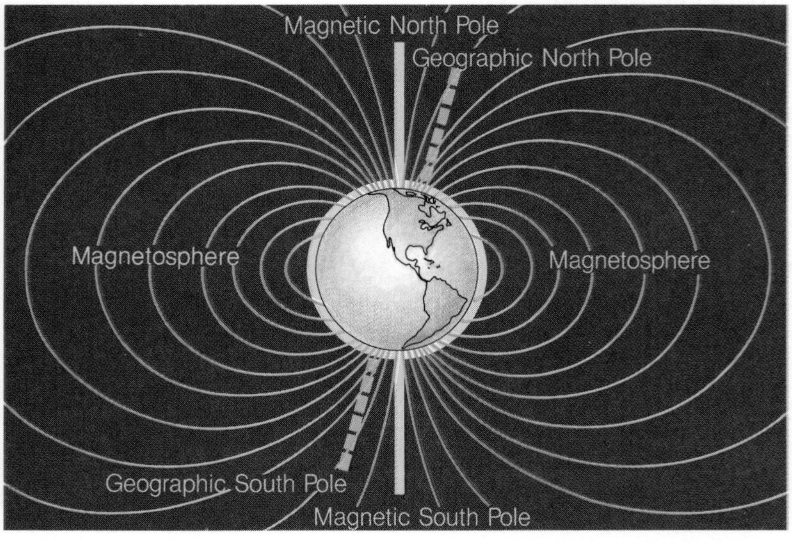

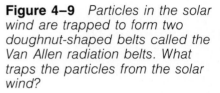

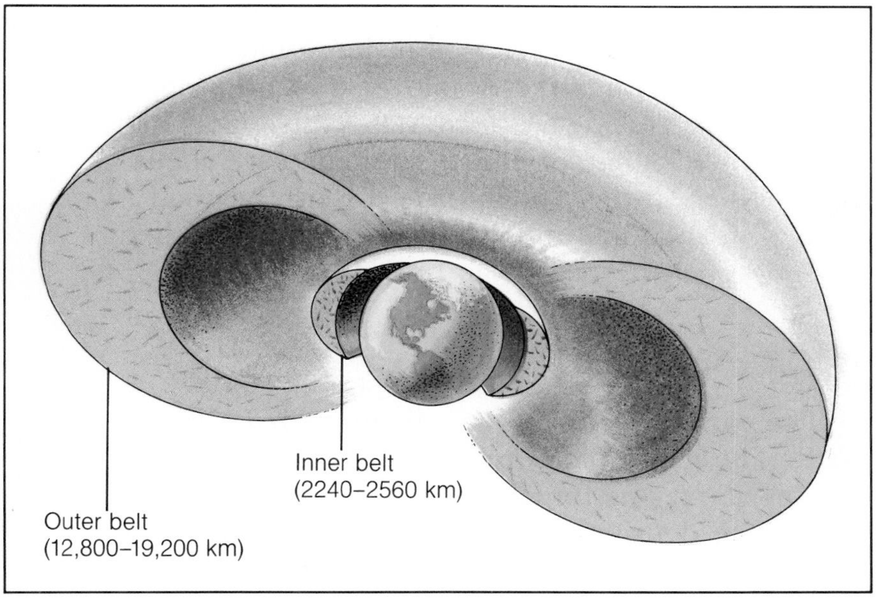

Figure 4–9 *Particles in the solar wind are trapped to form two doughnut-shaped belts called the Van Allen radiation belts. What traps the particles from the solar wind?*

belts are produced by the magnetosphere as it traps some of the particles from the solar wind. The outer belt contains mostly electrons, or negatively charged particles. The inner belt contains mainly protons, or positively charged particles.

The Van Allen radiation belts trap deadly radiation given off by the sun. If the two belts did not trap most of this deadly radiation, life on the earth as it is today would not be possible. The sun's radiation would kill any life forms that developed.

SECTION REVIEW

1. What causes day and night on the earth?
2. How does the tilt of the earth contribute to the occurrence of the seasons?
3. What is the magnetosphere?

4–3 The Earth's Moon

Section Objective

To describe the features and movements of the moon

On July 20, 1969, people took their first steps on the moon. But the effort to put a person on the moon had begun years earlier in 1961. At that time, the National Aeronautics and Space Administration, or NASA, began the Apollo project. The purpose of the Apollo project was to find a way to travel safely to the moon and back.

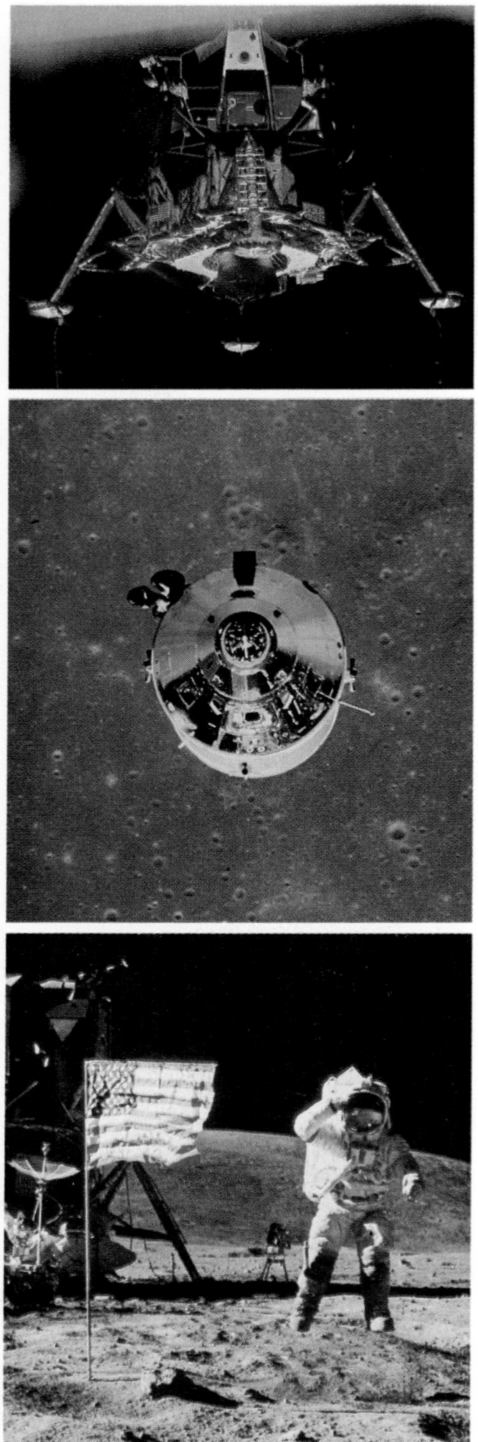

Figure 4–10 *Conquering the moon was a complex mission. Here you see the* Lunar Lander *approaching the moon (top). The shot of the* Apollo Command Module *(center), which remained in orbit during the mission, was taken from the* Lunar Lander *soon after it separated from the* Command Module. *Hours later, the astronauts walked on the moon (bottom).*

The first astronaut to step on the moon's dusty surface was Neil Armstrong. But he would not be the last. By the time the Apollo moon-landing project ended in 1972, 12 United States astronauts had explored the moon. Scientists learned more about the moon from the Apollo project than they had learned in the thousands of years they had studied the moon before the Apollo project.

Moon Statistics

The earth's moon is very different from the earth. The moon measures 3476 kilometers in diameter, or about one-fourth the diameter of the earth. Its average density is much less than the earth's average density. The gravity of the moon also differs from that of the earth. The moon's gravity is only one-sixth that of the earth. So things weigh less on the moon. To find out how much you would weigh on the moon, divide your weight by six. What would your weight be on the moon?

Today scientists know that the average distance to the moon is 384,403 kilometers. How? Among the objects left on the moon by Apollo astronauts was a small mirror. Scientists bounced a laser beam of light from the earth off the small mirror. They then measured the time it took the beam to reflect back to the earth. Since they knew the speed of light, they could judge the distance to the moon accurately.

Astronauts also left instruments on the moon to measure moonquakes. Moonquake instruments have measured up to 3000 moonquakes per year. From the moonquake data, scientists now know that the moon's outer crust is thicker than the earth's. The outer crust of the moon is about 60 kilometers thick on the side of the moon facing the earth and about 100 kilometers thick on the far side of the moon.

Apollo astronauts also brought back samples of moon rocks. The oldest moon rocks are about 4.6 billion years old, which is about the same age as the earth. So it seems likely that the moon and the earth formed at about the same time. A small amount of magnetism in the moon rocks indicates that the inner core of the moon may be made up of iron.

CAREER

Space Engineer

HELP WANTED: SPACE ENGINEER To work on spacecraft development. Must have a Masters degree. Experience in designing satellite systems and strong computer background required.

The people who design spacecraft are **space engineers.** They also plan and develop the vehicles' flight systems for navigation and communication. Some space engineers develop the scientific instruments that are installed in the spacecraft. Other space engineers develop ways to test the craft for safety. The designs may be changed many times. Only when the test results are satisfactory does actual production of a spacecraft begin.

People who like to build things and who find the study of space fascinating might want to work in this field. To do so, they go to college and study engineering, physics, and mathematics for many years. Most space engineers work for the government or for spacecraft manufacturers. Some space engineers teach and do research at universities.

To learn more about a career in space engineering, write to the Johnson Space Center, National Aeronautics and Space Administration, Houston, TX 77058.

Features of the Moon

In 1609, Galileo became the first person to look at the moon through a telescope. He saw light areas and dark areas. The light areas he saw are mountains. They are called **highlands.** Some of the mountain highlands on the moon reach 8000 meters above the surrounding plains. Galileo also saw dark, broad, smooth lowland areas on the moon. He called them **maria** (MAHR-ee-uh). *Maria* is the Latin word for "seas."

Figure 4–11 *The surface of the moon has changed very little since Galileo studied it in 1609.*

Although the term *maria* seems to indicate that there is water on the moon, moon rocks brought back by astronauts show no traces of water. So scientists believe that there never was any water on the moon. The moon is a dry, airless, and very barren place. Noonday temperatures may rise to 127°C. During the long night and in the shadows, surface temperatures may drop to −173°C. Also, since there is no atmosphere, there is no weather on the moon.

Among the most striking features of the moon are its many craters. One of the largest craters on the moon is called Copernicus. It is approximately

Figure 4–12 *Meteorites have been crashing into the moon for billions of years and have carved out many craters. This large crater is over 80 kilometers wide.*

Figure 4–13 *The valley snaking across the moon in this photograph is called a rille. How do scientists believe this rille formed?*

91 kilometers in diameter. Scientists believe that most of the craters were caused by meteorites.

A few of the craters seem to be the remains of volcanic activity. In fact, the maria are filled with hardened rock that may have flowed into the lowland areas as lava billions of years ago. Other evidence that the moon once had active volcanoes can be seen in the long valleys, or **rilles.** Since there was no water to carve the rilles, they were probably dug out of the moon's surface by running lava.

Movements of the Moon

The moon revolves around the earth in an elliptical orbit. At **perigee** (PEHR-uh-jee), the point of its orbit closest to the earth, the moon is about 350,000 kilometers from the earth. At **apogee** (AP-uh-jee), the point of its orbit farthest from the earth, it is about 400,000 kilometers away.

The moon seems to move west across the sky. This apparent movement is caused by the earth's rotation. Actually the moon is moving east when viewed against the background of stars. You can prove this by observing the moon when it is at the western limit of a cluster of stars. If you observe the moon for several hours, its movement east can be seen as it passes in front of each star.

It takes the earth almost 24 hours to rotate once on its axis. It takes the moon much longer. The moon rotates once on its axis every 27⅓ days. This is the same amount of time that it takes the moon to revolve once around the earth. Because the moon's periods of rotation and revolution are the same, a day on the moon is just as long as a year on the moon! As a result, one side of the moon always faces toward the earth. For many years, scientists could observe only this side of the **lunar,** or moon's, surface. But satellites and astronauts have now photographed the entire lunar surface.

SECTION REVIEW

1. What are the highlands? What are maria?
2. What may have formed the moon's rilles?
3. Why is the distance between the earth and the moon given as an average?

4–4 The Moon, the Earth, and the Sun

Section Objective

To relate the motions of the moon, the earth, and the sun to the moon's phases and to eclipses

Gravitational attraction keeps the moon in orbit around the earth and the earth in orbit around the sun. **The related motions of the sun, moon, and earth result in the changing appearance of the moon as seen from the earth and the occasional blocking of the sun's light.**

Phases of the Moon

The moon does not produce its own light. It reflects light from the sun. As the moon orbits the earth, more or less of the moon's surface appears lighted to a viewer on the earth. This makes the moon look as if it had different shapes at different times of the month. The seemingly different shapes of the moon are called phases of the moon. The moon goes through all of its phases every 29½ days.

When the moon passes between the earth and the sun, the side that faces the earth is in darkness. The moon is not visible in the sky. This phase is called the **new moon.** Sometimes you can see some of the dark area because of earthshine. Earthshine is sunlight reflected off the earth onto the moon.

As the moon continues to move in its orbit around the earth, a part of the lighted side of the moon becomes visible. This is called the **waxing-crescent** (KREHS-uhnt) phase. The moon is said to be waxing when its lighted area appears to grow larger. When the lighted area appears to grow smaller, the moon is said to be waning.

About one week after the new-moon phase, the moon has traveled one-fourth of the way around the earth. At this time, one-half of the moon appears lighted. This phase is the first-quarter phase. As the days pass, more of the lighted area can be seen during the **waxing-gibbous** (GIHB-uhs) phase.

About two weeks after the new moon, the entire lighted side of the moon is visible in the sky. This phase is called the **full moon.** The earth is then somewhere between the moon and the sun. The moon takes another two weeks to pass through the **waning-gibbous** phase, last-quarter phase,

Figure 4–14 *How much greater is the moon's circumference than its diameter? How does this ratio compare with the ratio of the earth's circumference to its diameter?*

FACTS ABOUT THE MOON
Average distance from earth 384,403 kilometers
Diameter About 3476 kilometers (about ¼ earth's diameter)
Circumference About 10,927 kilometers
Surface area About 37,943,000 square kilometers
Rotation period 27 days, 7 hours, 43 minutes
Revolution period around earth 29 days, 12 hours, 44 minutes
Length of day and night About 14 earth-days each
Surface gravity About $\frac{1}{6}$ earth's gravity
Mass $\frac{1}{81}$ earth's mass
Volume $\frac{1}{50}$ earth's volume

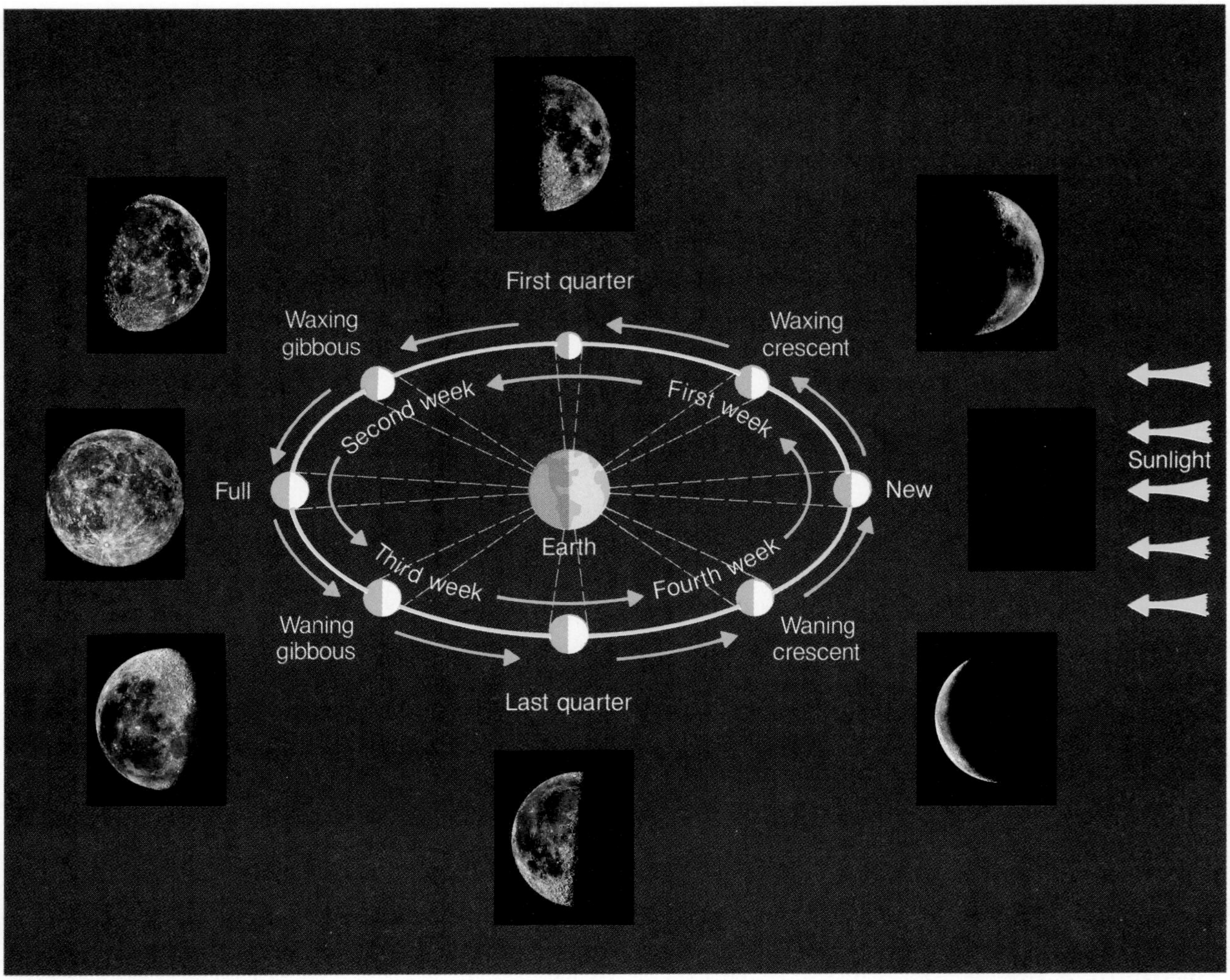

Figure 4–15 *The eight phases of the moon you see from the earth depend on where the moon is in relation to the sun and the earth. How many days does it take for the moon to pass through all eight phases?*

waning-crescent phase, and back to the new moon. The phases of the moon then start all over again. What phase of the moon was visible last night?

Eclipses

As the moon revolves around the earth and the earth and moon revolve around the sun, they block out some of the sun's light. The shadows that result are long cone-shaped areas that extend thousands of kilometers into space. Sometimes the moon moves into the earth's shadow. Other times the moon casts a shadow onto the earth.

The shadows have two parts. There is a small, completely dark, inner area called the **umbra** (UHM-bruh). And there is a larger outer area called the **penumbra** (pih-NUHM-bruh), where light is only partly blocked out.

An **eclipse** (ee-KLIHPS) of the moon, called a **lunar eclipse,** occurs when the moon passes through the earth's shadow. Lunar eclipses can only happen when the earth is directly between the sun and the moon, as shown in the lower part of Figure 4–16. During what phase of the moon do you think lunar eclipses occur?

When the moon passes through the umbra of the earth's shadow, you can see a **total eclipse** of the moon. The moon takes on a dark copper color. Because of the moon's slightly tilted orbit, total eclipses are rare. But the moon frequently passes through the penumbra of the earth's shadow. This causes a partial eclipse, in which the moon's reflected light is dimmed. This event is hardly noticeable, if at all.

A **solar eclipse,** or eclipse of the sun, occurs when the moon is directly between the sun and the earth, as shown in the upper part of Figure 4–16.

Figure 4–16 *During a solar eclipse, the moon passes between the sun and the earth. During a lunar eclipse, the earth passes between the sun and the moon. When does a total eclipse of the moon occur?*

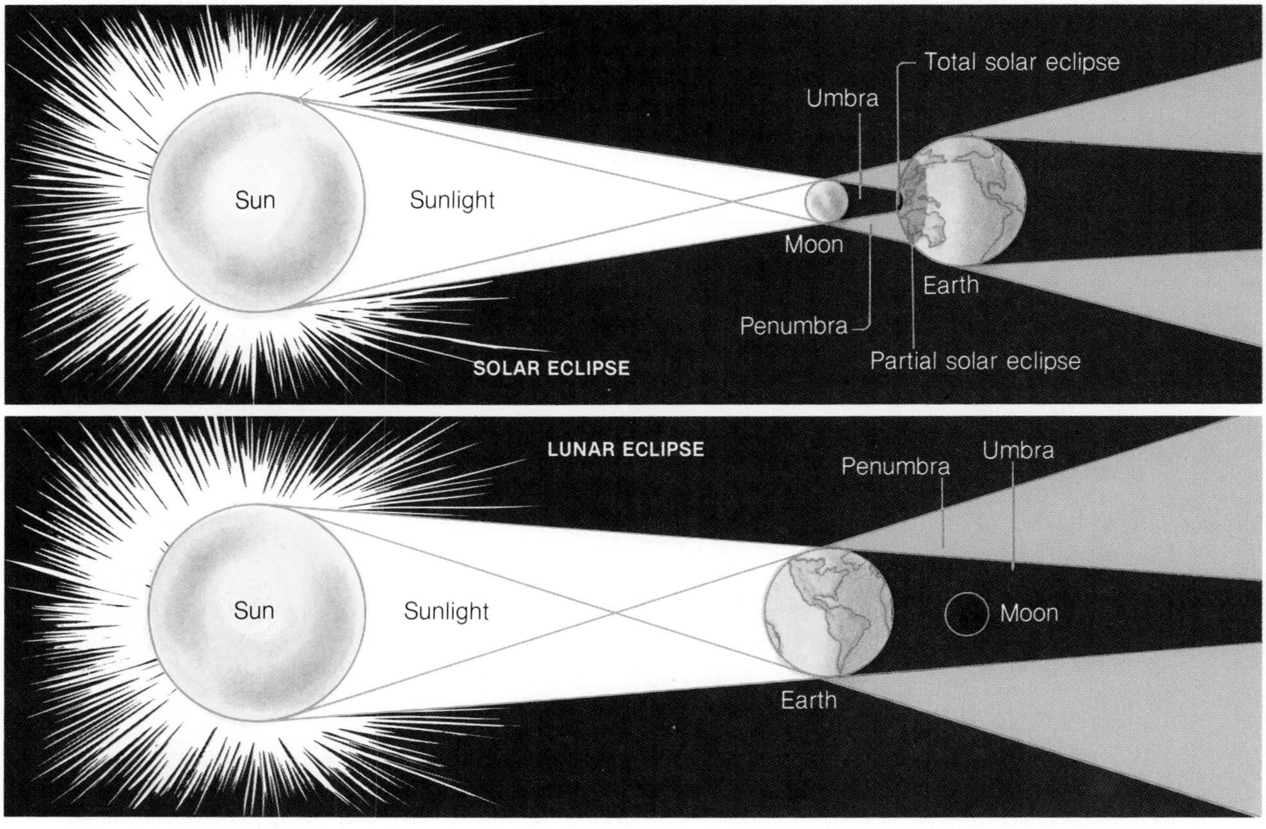

The moon blocks out the sun and casts its shadow onto part of the earth. But people in only a small area of the earth see a total eclipse. People in other areas see a partial eclipse, and some see no eclipse at all. During what phase of the moon do solar eclipses occur?

> **Sharpen Your Skills**
>
> *Moon Observation*
>
> The best time to observe the moon is on the second or third day after the first-quarter phase. At this time, the moon is in a good position in the evening sky. Many of the surface features are clearly visible because the moon is not reflecting full light toward the earth. Details are easier to see.
>
> **1.** Using a pair of binoculars or a small telescope and a labeled photograph of the moon, locate some of the most prominent surface features of the moon.
>
> **2.** Make a list of the features you were able to identify.

Tides

Because the moon is close to the earth, there are interactions between the earth and the moon. One visible interaction is the effect of the gravitational pull of the earth on the moon. As a result of this pull, the side of the moon that faces the earth has a distinct bulge. But the moon also exerts a gravitational pull on the earth. This results in the rise and fall of the ocean level as the moon moves in its orbit around the earth.

If you have ever been to the ocean for a day, you probably noticed that the level of water along the shoreline did not stay the same. For about six hours, the ocean rises on the beach. Then, for the next six hours, the ocean level falls. The rise and fall of the oceans are called **tides.** Tides are caused by the moon's gravitational pull on the earth.

Figure 4–17 *The pull of the moon's gravity causes tides. During a 12-hour period, Los Angeles moves from a high tide (left) to a low tide (center) to another high tide (right). At the same time, the moon moves in its orbit. As a result, the tides occur slightly later each day.*

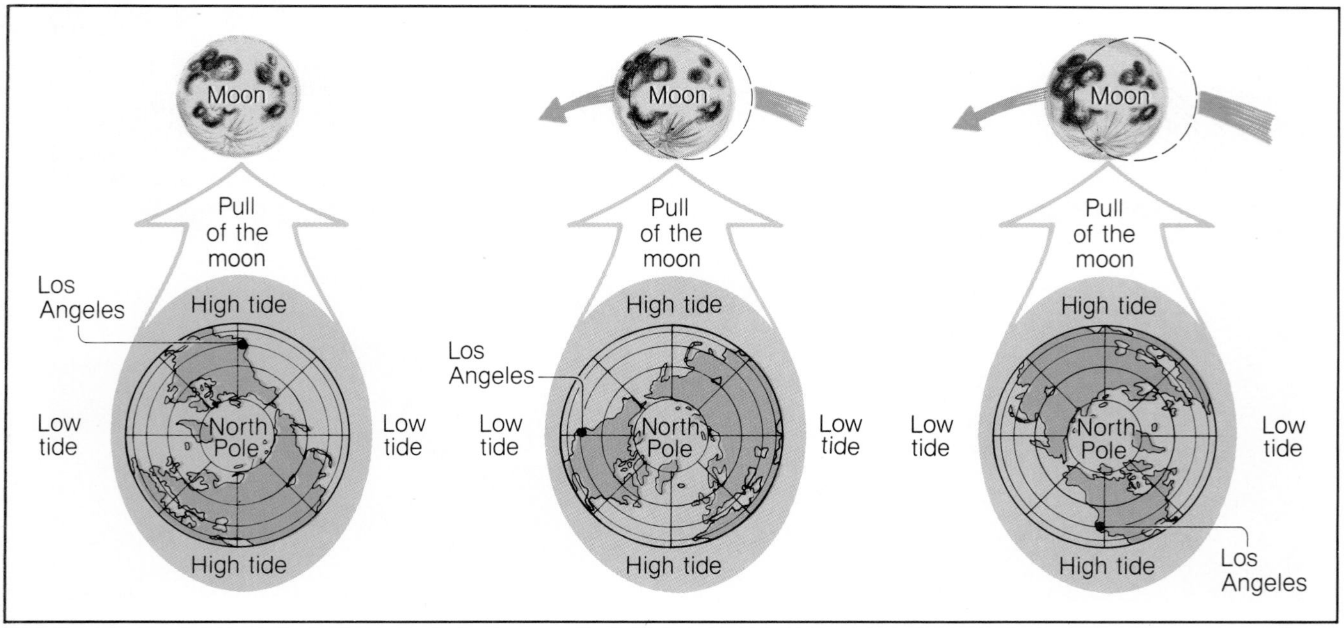

As the moon's gravity pulls on the earth, it creates a slight bulge in the solid parts but causes a larger bulging of the oceans because they are liquid. The oceans bulge in two places. The ocean bulge on the side facing the moon is called the direct tide. There is also a bulge in the ocean on the opposite side of the earth, called the opposite tide. Both bulges are called **high tides.** High tides occur on the side of the earth facing the moon and on the opposite side.

At the same time the high tides occur, **low tides** occur between the two bulges. Because the earth rotates on its axis every 24 hours, the moon's gravitational pull affects different parts of the earth at different times. So there are two high tides and two low tides every 24 hours. But since the moon rises about 50 minutes later every day, the high and low tides are also 50 minutes later each day.

It is interesting to note that when the moon is at its full- and new-moon phases, the earth has higher high tides and lower low tides than at other times. These higher tides are called **spring tides.** They occur when the sun and the moon line up with the earth. The increased effect of the sun's gravity on the earth causes the ocean bulges to become larger.

Similarly, during its first- and last-quarter phases, the moon's gravitational pull on the oceans is partially canceled out by the sun's gravitational pull. This results in lower high tides and higher low tides than normal, called **neap tides.**

The varying distance between the earth and the moon as the moon moves in its orbit also affects the tides. The closer the moon is to the earth, the greater the pull of gravity. If the moon is at perigee during a new or full moon, very high tides and very low tides will occur. These tides can be predicted in advance. So persons living in coastal areas can be warned of possible flooding due to very high tides.

Figure 4–18 *At high tide, Mont-St-Michel in France is surrounded by water (top). A few hours later, at low tide, the island is surrounded by a sandy beach (bottom).*

SECTION REVIEW

1. When would you be able to see a lunar eclipse? A solar eclipse?
2. How does the moon affect tides on the earth?
3. Why does a lunar eclipse occur either two weeks before or two weeks after a total solar eclipse?

4 LABORATORY INVESTIGATION

Using Shadow Patterns to Determine the Apparent Motion of the Sun

Problem

How can the sun's apparent motion in the sky be determined by observing changes in shadow patterns?

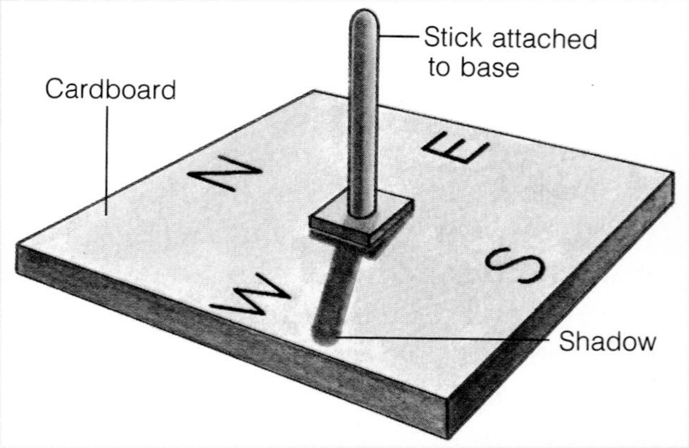

Materials *(per student)*

Sheet of paper
Compass
Wide-tip felt pen
Piece of cardboard (25 cm × 25 cm)
Wooden stick attached upright to a base

Procedure

1. Place the stick attached to a base in the middle of the piece of cardboard. Trace the base on the cardboard so that you will be able to put it in the same place on the cardboard each time you make an observation.
2. Find a sunny area on flat ground to place the stick and cardboard.
3. Using the compass, locate north, south, east, and west. Write the appropriate directions near the edges of the cardboard.
4. With the felt pen, trace the shadow of the stick. Write the time of day along the line. Measure the length of the shadow. Determine in which direction the shadow is pointing. Determine where the sun is located in the sky. **CAUTION:** *Do not look directly at the sun!* Record the information in a chart like the one below.
5. Repeat step 4 five times throughout the day. Be sure you include morning, noon, and afternoon observations.

Observations

1. In which direction does the sun appear to move across the sky?
2. In which direction do the shadows move?
3. At what time of day is the shadow the longest? The shortest?

Conclusions

1. Why does the length of the stick's shadow change throughout the day?
2. What actually causes the sun's apparent motion across the sky?
3. Explain how it is possible to tell time using a sundial.

Time of Day	Shadow Length	Direction of Shadow	Location of Sun

CHAPTER REVIEW

SUMMARY

4–1 The Planet Earth

❑ The diameter of the earth is about 12,756 kilometers. The earth's circumference is about 40,075 kilometers.

❑ The equator is an imaginary line around the earth that divides the earth into the Northern and Southern hemispheres.

❑ The earth's rocky landmasses are part of the crust.

❑ Parts of the earth covered by water make up the hydrosphere.

❑ An envelope of gases surrounding the earth makes up the atmosphere.

4–2 The Earth in Space

❑ The earth's rotation causes day and night once every 24 hours.

❑ Because of the tilt of the earth's axis at an angle of 23½°, the length of day and night on the earth varies during the course of a year.

❑ The earth revolves around the sun once every 365.26 days, or once a year.

❑ The tilt of the earth's axis is the main cause of the seasons.

❑ The magnetosphere is the magnetic field formed by the earth's magnetism.

❑ The Van Allen radiation belts trap deadly radiation from the sun.

4–3 The Earth's Moon

❑ Data from moonquakes indicate that the moon's crust is thicker than the earth's crust.

❑ Highland mountain ranges, broad lowland areas called maria, and craters are among the major features of the moon's surface.

❑ Moon rocks indicate that there has never been any water on the moon. The moon has no atmosphere and thus no weather.

4–4 The Moon, the Earth, and the Sun

❑ Every 29½ days, the moon passes through all its phases.

❑ A lunar eclipse occurs when the moon passes through the earth's shadow.

❑ A solar eclipse occurs when the moon is directly between the earth and the sun.

❑ Tides on the earth are due, in part, to the gravitational pull of the moon on the earth.

VOCABULARY

Define each term in a complete sentence.

apogee
atmosphere
autumnal equinox
eclipse
equator
equinox
full moon
hemisphere
highlands
high tide
hydrosphere
low tide
lunar
lunar eclipse
magnetosphere
maria
neap tide
new moon
penumbra
perigee
rille
solar eclipse
spring tide
summer solstice
tide
total eclipse
umbra
Van Allen radiation belt
vernal equinox
waning-crescent
waning-gibbous
waxing-crescent
waxing-gibbous
winter solstice

CONTENT REVIEW: MULTIPLE CHOICE

Choose the letter of the answer that best completes each sentence.

1. An imaginary line that divides the earth into hemispheres is called the
a. axis b. North Pole c. equator d. umbra

2. Oceans, lakes, and streams are part of the earth's
a. crust b. penumbra c. landmasses d. hydrosphere

3. The most common gas in the atmosphere is
a. oxygen b. nitrogen c. carbon dioxide d. argon

4. When it is summer in the Northern Hemisphere, in the Southern Hemisphere it is
a. spring b. summer c. autumn d. winter

5. In the Northern Hemisphere, the longest day occurs on the
a. winter solstice b. vernal equinox
c. summer solstice d. autumnal equinox

6. The average distance between the earth and the moon is approximately
a. 3800 km b. 380,000 km c. 38,000 km d. 3,800,000 km

7. On the moon, smooth lowland areas are called
a. maria b. rilles c. highlands d. craters

8. The phase of the moon that follows the waning-crescent phase is called the
a. full moon b. new moon
c. waxing-crescent phase d. last quarter

9. In an eclipse, the small, completely dark, inner area of shadow is called
a. the penumbra b. the umbra c. the corona d. none of these

10. The relatively low high tides that occur when the moon is in first- and last-quarter phases are called
a. neap tides b. spring tides c. direct tides d. opposite tides

CONTENT REVIEW: COMPLETION

Fill in the word or words that best complete each sentence.

1. The earth's ______________ is about 40,075 kilometers at the equator.

2. About ______________ of the hydrosphere is salt water.

3. It takes the earth about 24 hours to ______________ on its axis.

4. The hemisphere that is leaning toward the sun has ______________ days and ______________ nights.

5. A (An) ______________ occurs when day and night are of equal length all over the world.

6. The ______________ are two doughnut-shaped regions produced by the earth's magnetosphere as it traps particles from the solar wind.

7. Long valleys, or rilles, on the moon provide evidence that the moon once had ______________.

8. The moon is closest to the earth at ______________.

9. A (An) ______________ occurs when the moon passes through the umbra of the earth's shadow.

10. High tides that are lower than normal are called ______________.

CONTENT REVIEW: TRUE OR FALSE

Determine whether each statement is true or false. If it is true, write "true." If it is false, change the underlined word or words to make the statement true.

1. The diameter of the earth is 12,756 miles.
2. Almost 85 percent of the fresh water on earth is trapped in ice.
3. As seen from the North Pole, the earth rotates in a clockwise direction.
4. The longest day of the year in the Northern Hemisphere occurs during the summer solstice.
5. The earth's core is made up mainly of iron and copper.
6. Scientists believe that there was never any water on the moon.
7. The moon rotates on its axis once every 24 hours.
8. The moon is not visible in the sky during the full-moon phase.
9. An eclipse of the moon is called a lunar eclipse.
10. Tides that are higher than usual are high tides.

CONCEPT REVIEW: SKILL BUILDING

Use the skills you have developed in the chapter to complete each activity.

1. **Making calculations** The human body needs about 2.5 liters of water each day to live. How much fresh water does a person need in a year to live?

   On the average, people use another 260 liters of fresh water every day for washing, cooking, and other daily activities. How much fresh water does the average person use in a year for such daily activities?
2. **Making charts** Make a chart comparing the earth and the moon in terms of size, gravity, temperature, atmosphere, and rotation period. Add any other comparisons to the chart that you can think of.

   Now add the same kind of information about the other planets to your chart. Which planet has features most similar to the earth?
3. **Applying concepts** Lunar eclipses occur during a full-moon phase. The moon goes through its full-moon phase each month. Yet lunar eclipses are fairly rare. Why is there not a lunar eclipse every month? Hint: You may want to use models to help arrive at your answer.
4. **Identifying relationships** The moon seems to move westward across the sky. But when viewed against the background of stars, it appears to move eastward. Explain why this is so.

CONCEPT REVIEW: ESSAY

Discuss each of the following in a brief paragraph.

1. Describe how living conditions on the earth might change if the earth's axis were straight up and down instead of tilted.
2. Describe the season you are experiencing today in terms of the earth's position in space in relation to the sun.
3. Explain why only one side of the moon always faces toward the earth while the other side always faces away from the earth.
4. What are the similarities and differences in the features of the earth and moon?

Adventures in Science

Ian K. Shelton Discovers an EXPLODING STAR

The time: 170,000 years ago. Much of North America is covered by huge sheets of ice. Herds of woolly mammoths and other unusual creatures roam the land. From time to time, the ancestors of modern humans gaze up at the stars twinkling in the night sky. Although these human ancestors have no way of knowing, in a galaxy 170,000 light years away a giant star is exploding.

The time: February 24, 1987. Ian K. Shelton, a young Canadian scientist prepares to spend another long night at the Cerro Tololo Inter-American Observatory in Chile, South America. Shelton assumes it will be another quiet night. But little does he know that light produced when that giant star exploded more than 170,000 years ago will finally reach the earth this night!

Shelton has been studying photographs of a small galaxy called the Large Magellanic Cloud. By early morning, he is ready to call it a night. "I had decided," he recalls, "that enough was enough. It was time to go to

On February 24, 1987, Ian K. Shelton observed the supernova pictured in the background. Photographs taken three years before show the star that became Supernova Shelton (inset).

bed." Yet before going to sleep, Shelton decided to develop one last photograph.

As he studied the last photograph, Shelton realized there was something most unusual in the picture. A bright spot could be seen. Photographs taken of the same area on previous nights had not shown this bright spot. "I was sure there was some flaw on the photograph," he recalled. But then he did something astronomers rarely do. He went outside and looked up at the area of the sky he had just photographed. And without the telescope, or even a pair of binoculars, Shelton saw the same bright spot in the Large Magellanic Cloud. He knew right away that this was something new and unusual.

Shelton could hardly believe what he was seeing. "For more than three hours," he explained later, "I tried several logical explanations. It took me a long time to actually accept that what I had just seen was a supernova."

Supernovas are the last stage in the life of certain giant stars. As the star dies it begins to contract. Then, in its last moments of life, the star explodes and sends matter and energy blasting through the universe.

During a supernova, a star reaches temperatures of billions of degrees Celsius. At those temperatures, atoms in the star fuse and new elements are produced. The light produced by a supernova is brighter than the light produced by a million normal stars. It was that bright light Shelton observed in 1987, after the light had traveled for 170,000 years toward the earth.

Shelton immediately sent telegrams to astronomers all over the world. Observatories in other parts of the world soon confirmed Shelton's discovery. "It's like Christmas," remarked astronomer Stan Woosley from the University of California. This was the first supernova close to the earth that modern astronomers had ever had a chance to study.

Why, you might wonder, is the discovery of a new supernova so important? Many astronomers believe that supernovas cause the birth of new stars. So, by studying supernovas, astronomers can learn a great deal about the life cycles of stars. Also, the elements a supernova produces shower nearby areas of space. In fact, most of the elements on the earth probably formed some 6 billion years ago during a supernova. "The calcium in our bones, the iron in hemoglobin and the oxygen we all breathe came from explosions like this one," says astronomer Woosley.

For Ian K. Shelton, the discovery of an exploding star would change his life. A few weeks after the discovery, the new supernova was officially named Supernova Shelton. Shelton knows he owes some of the credit for the discovery to modern technology. "We couldn't conduct modern astronomy without these wonderful instruments," he has said. "But without the romance, most of us would never have been attracted to this wonderful science in the first place. Just look at that beautiful supernova up there. Isn't that enough to make you glad you're alive?"

Issues in Science

Exploring Space: Passengers on Board?

What do you think of when someone mentions space exploration? Many people would probably describe the feelings they had when they saw astronauts walking on the surface of the moon for the first time. Other people are likely to recall the shock and sadness they felt when they learned of the explosion of the Space Shuttle *Challenger.*

When space exploration is discussed, most people talk about the successes and failures of missions that carried astronauts on board. Yet space probes without astronauts have accomplished a great deal. Such probes have traveled billions of kilometers into unknown space. They have photographed the surfaces of other planets and explored the strange atmospheres and rings that exist around Jupiter and Uranus. On these trips, probes have sent back to Earth millions of photographs as well as vast amounts of other data. In this way, the space program has greatly broadened human understanding of the universe.

Since the Space Shuttle *Challenger* tragedy, many people are asking, Is the astronaut program necessary? Couldn't we learn as much, and in greater safety, with

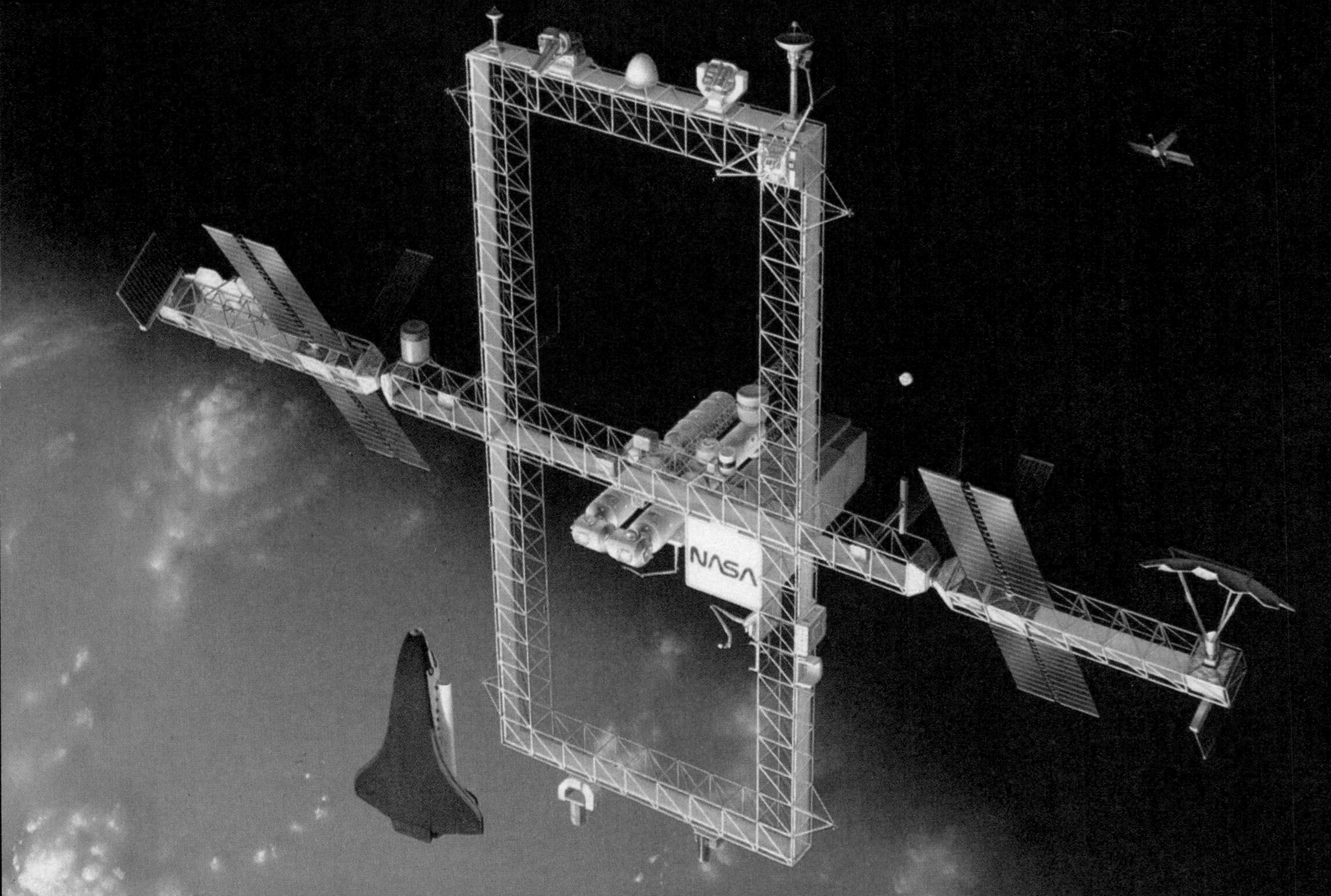

space probes that do not carry humans into space? These people feel that we should depend upon probes that do not carry astronauts for much of our knowledge of space. But many other people feel that the presence of astronauts has added another dimension to our space program.

For many years, the space program relied solely on robot probes. For example, before people landed on the moon the robot craft *Surveyor* explored the moon's surface. Another robot craft, *Voyager 2*, is traveling to the edge of our solar system, examining distant planets on its voyage. This probe, which was launched August 20, 1977, will not fly past Neptune until September 1989. This trip will take twelve years! The factors of distance, time, and safety make a voyage such as this impossible for astronauts.

Even before the *Challenger* disaster, space scientist James A. Van Allen said, "Most national goals are better realized by robot spacecraft." Several other scientists argue that anything an astronaut can do, a space robot can do better.

Many other scientists disagree. They admit that robot spacecraft have made important observations and have sent back vast amounts of data about the planets, moons, asteroids, and comets. But they argue that there is more to space exploration than scientific observations. Dr. Peter Banks of Stanford University says that there are many important medical and biological experiments in space that must be conducted by humans.

Other scientists argue that humans are vital to space exploration because they are able to react quickly to unexpected situations or to evaluate unusual data in space. They feel that robots do not have the vision or sense of touch that humans do. In this view, human senses as well as the ability to reason may be essential for the success of many space experiments.

A number of space scientists now say that both kinds of space missions are linked, so that one cannot go forward without the other. For example, many of the United States planned missions rely on the Space Shuttle and its crew to carry cargo and supplies into space. In space, the crew of the Space Shuttle will retrieve and repair orbiting satellites. Eventually, Space Shuttles will carry passengers to and from space stations.

Many people agree that there can be no turning back from the exploration of the universe. But should people continue to explore space "in person"? Is it true that placing astronauts in space satisfies a human need to explore that no machine can imitate? Or should space exploration be conducted only by robots, computers, and other sophisticated machines?

On September 3, 1976, *Viking 2* landed on the boulder-strewn Utopian Plain of Mars. This robot device tested the Martian soil for evidence of living organisms and radioed its findings back to Earth. On this particular spot, it found no evidence of life.

A shuttle prepares to dock at an orbiting platform in this artist's

UNIT TWO

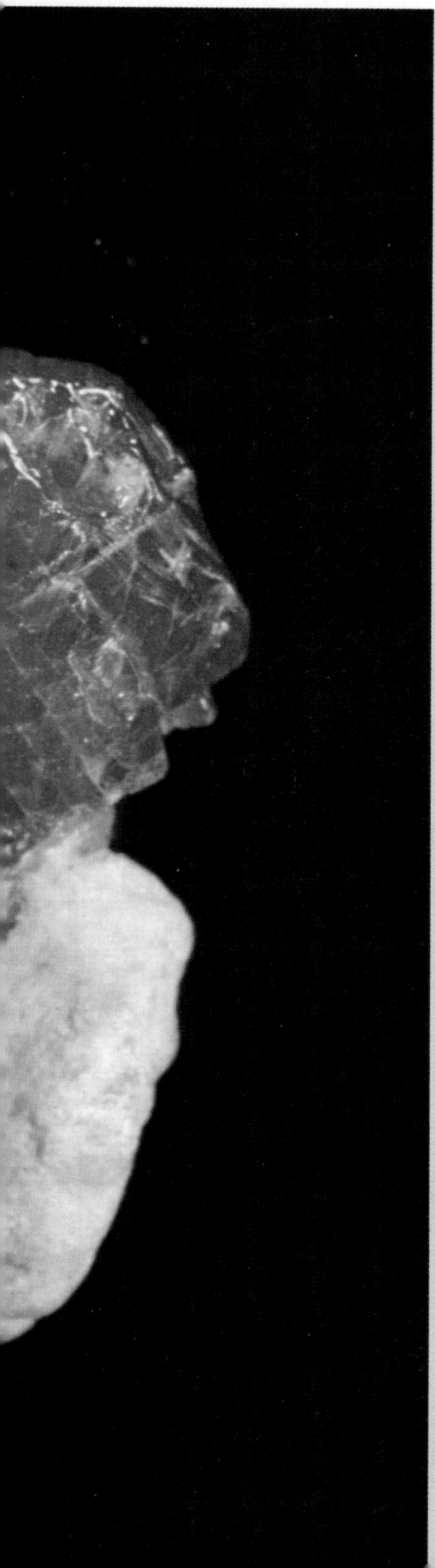

Composition of the Earth

Would you wear a piece of rusty aluminum around your neck? You probably would not. And if the rusty aluminum were impure, you would be even less likely to accept the offer. Would you wear a glistening red ruby around your neck? Few people would turn down this offer. Yet it is the very same as the first offer.

A ruby is nothing more than aluminum rust contaminated with bits of other substances. What changes aluminum rust from a colorless, inexpensive mineral to a colorful, expensive gem? The answer is forces within the earth itself. Tremendous heat and enormous pressure melt and crush rocks. In the process, aluminum rust turns into rubies. As you read the chapters in this unit, you will find out about the materials that make up the earth and the astounding changes they constantly undergo.

CHAPTERS

Tremendous heat and pressure within the earth produce the mineral that makes up rubies, one of the most expensive types of gems on the earth.

The Nature of Matter 5

CHAPTER SECTIONS

5–1 Properties of Matter
5–2 Phases of Matter
5–3 Structure of Matter
5–4 Forms of Matter
5–5 Formation of Compounds

CHAPTER OBJECTIVES

After completing this chapter, you will be able to

5–1 Describe some physical properties of matter.

5–2 Identify the phases of matter.

5–3 Describe the structure of atoms and molecules.

5–4 Compare and contrast elements, compounds, and mixtures.

5–5 Explain how atoms combine to form compounds.

Stop what you are doing for a moment and look around you. You probably see a wide variety of objects. You see a book, a desk, paper, and pencils. Look out the window. You probably see trees, grass, and other buildings. Perhaps you see rocks, clouds, and puddles of water—maybe even mountains, waterfalls, and streams. And although you cannot actually see the air, you know that it is there because you are breathing it or you are feeling it if a gentle breeze is blowing.

Take a look at the photograph on the opposite page. The photograph was taken during a winter freeze in Yellowstone National Park. How would you describe the various objects in the photograph? What characteristics do the objects share? How are the objects different?

The world around you is filled with many different objects. These objects have many unique characteristics such as color, texture, shape, and odor. But do you think that all the millions of objects in nature could be made basically of the same thing? Read on and you will soon be able to answer this question.

A winter scene in Yellowstone National Park shows nature's diversity.

Section Objective

To identify the properties of matter

5–1 Properties of Matter

A bird, a rock, water, air, and a tree are very different from one another. Yet in one very important way, they are the same. All these things are made up of **matter.** Matter is what the world is made up of. All materials consist of matter.

Since all objects are made up of matter, you may wonder what makes one object different from another. To answer this question, you must know about the qualities, or characteristics, that describe an object. Such qualities are called properties.

Every kind of matter has its own properties. The properties belong to that matter just as the color of your eyes belongs to you. Sometimes you can see a property. You can see the color green in grass. Sometimes you can feel a property. Oil has such a special feel that slippery things are described as "oily." Sometimes you can taste a property. Nothing else tastes quite like salt. Color, odor, taste, shape, and texture are examples of properties of matter.

Some properties of matter cannot be observed quite so easily. It is often necessary to test for these

Figure 5–1 *All objects are made of matter. Many of the various forms of matter can be seen in this photograph of the Florida Everglades. Can you identify at least four examples of matter?*

properties to determine what kind of matter the substance is. Properties that can be determined without changing the substance into a new kind of substance are called **physical properties.**

During a test of physical properties, the substance may be changed in some way. But it does not become a new kind of substance. For example, you might break an object into smaller pieces. But each piece will keep the properties of the larger piece. Or you might heat the substance to determine the temperature at which it melts. But even after it melts, it is still the same substance.

Changes that do not produce a new kind of substance are called **physical changes.** During a physical change, the physical properties of a substance are altered, but the substance remains the same kind of matter. Later in this chapter, you will read about another type of change in which new kinds of substances are formed.

Figure 5–2 *During a physical change, the physical properties of a substance are altered. But the substance remains the same kind of matter. The paper floating in the air during this parade has been cut into smaller pieces. But it is still paper. And the melting ice cream is still ice cream.*

Mass

One of the most important physical properties of matter is that it has **mass.** Mass is the amount of matter in an object. Mass is measured in units called grams (g) and kilograms (kg). One kilogram is equal to 1000 grams. To determine the mass of an object, you would use a balance.

Volume

Another important property of matter is that it has **volume.** Volume is the amount of space an object takes up. Volume is expressed in units called liters (L), milliliters (mL), and cubic centimeters (cm^3). One cubic centimeter is the volume occupied by a cube that measures 1 centimeter on each side. One cubic centimeter is equivalent to 1 milliliter.

Using the two physical properties of mass and volume, you can now define matter in a different way. **Matter is anything that has mass and volume.**

Density

The properties of mass and volume can be used to determine another important property of matter. This property is called **density.** Density is the

DENSITIES OF SOME COMMON SUBSTANCES	
Substance	**Density** *(g/cm^3)*
Air	0.0013
Gasoline	0.7
Wood (oak)	0.85
Water (ice)	0.92
Water (liquid)	1.0
Aluminum	2.7
Steel	7.8
Silver	10.5
Lead	11.3
Gold	19.3

Figure 5–3 *This table shows the densities of some common substances. Which substance has the greatest density? Which substance is about 2½ times denser than water?*

amount of matter in a given amount of a substance, or the mass per unit volume of a substance. A piece of lead has more mass than a piece of aluminum *of the same size.* Lead has a higher density than aluminum. All matter has density. The density of a specific kind of matter is a property that helps to identify it and distinguish it from other kinds of matter.

Since density is mass per unit volume, the following formula can be used to find the density of an object:

$$\textbf{density} = \frac{\textbf{mass}}{\textbf{volume}}$$

Mass is usually expressed in grams, and volume in milliliters or cubic centimeters. So density is expressed in grams per milliliter (g/mL) or grams per cubic centimeter (g/cm^3). Suppose 10 g of a substance has a volume of 5 cm^3. What is the density of this substance?

$$\text{density} = \frac{\text{mass}}{\text{volume}}$$

$$\text{d} = \frac{10 \text{ g}}{5 \text{ cm}^3} = \frac{2 \text{ g}}{\text{cm}^3}$$

The density of lead is 11.3 g/cm^3. The density of aluminum is 2.7 g/cm^3. So lead has a density that is more than four times the density of aluminum. The density of water is 1 g/cm^3. Wood floats in

Figure 5–4 *The density of an object, not the size, determines whether the object will float or sink in water. This large ocean liner (left) has an overall density less than 1 g/mL, so it floats in water. The density of the rock (right) is greater than 1 g/mL, so it sinks.*

water because its density, 0.8 g/cm^3, is less than the density of water. What will happen to a piece of lead and a piece of aluminum if they are put in water?

Scientists often compare the density of an object to a standard density. This standard density is the density of water. The comparison, or ratio, of the mass of a substance to the mass of an equal volume of water is called **specific gravity.** The specific gravity of water is 1. The specific gravity of aluminum is 2.7. You will notice that there are no units for specific gravity. It is simply a number. This is because the units cancel out when the densities of the two substances are compared. Specific gravity is an important measurement in the identification of minerals. You will learn more about it in Chapter 6.

In addition to the physical properties you have just read about, there are several other important ones that help identify matter. The ability of a substance to reflect light and to resist being scratched by other substances are two important physical properties. The melting point and boiling point of a substance are two other physical properties.

Figure 5–5 *The Pennzoil Building in Houston, Texas, illustrates another physical property of matter. The glass windows of the building are transparent. They allow light to pass through. The steel is opaque. It absorbs light. So no light passes through.*

SECTION REVIEW

1. What are three important physical properties of matter?
2. What is matter?
3. What is density? What is the formula for finding density? What is specific gravity?
4. The density of silver is 10.5 g/cm^3. What is the mass of a cube of silver with a volume of 4.6 cm^3?

5–2 Phases of Matter

Section Objective

To classify the phases of matter

On the earth, matter can exist in four phases, or states. **The phases of matter are solid, liquid, gas, and plasma.** A **solid** has a definite shape and volume. A pencil, a rock, a cube of sugar, and a diamond are examples of solids. They all have a definite shape and occupy a definite amount of space. What other examples of solids can you name?

A **liquid** has a definite volume but does not have a definite shape. A liquid takes the shape of its

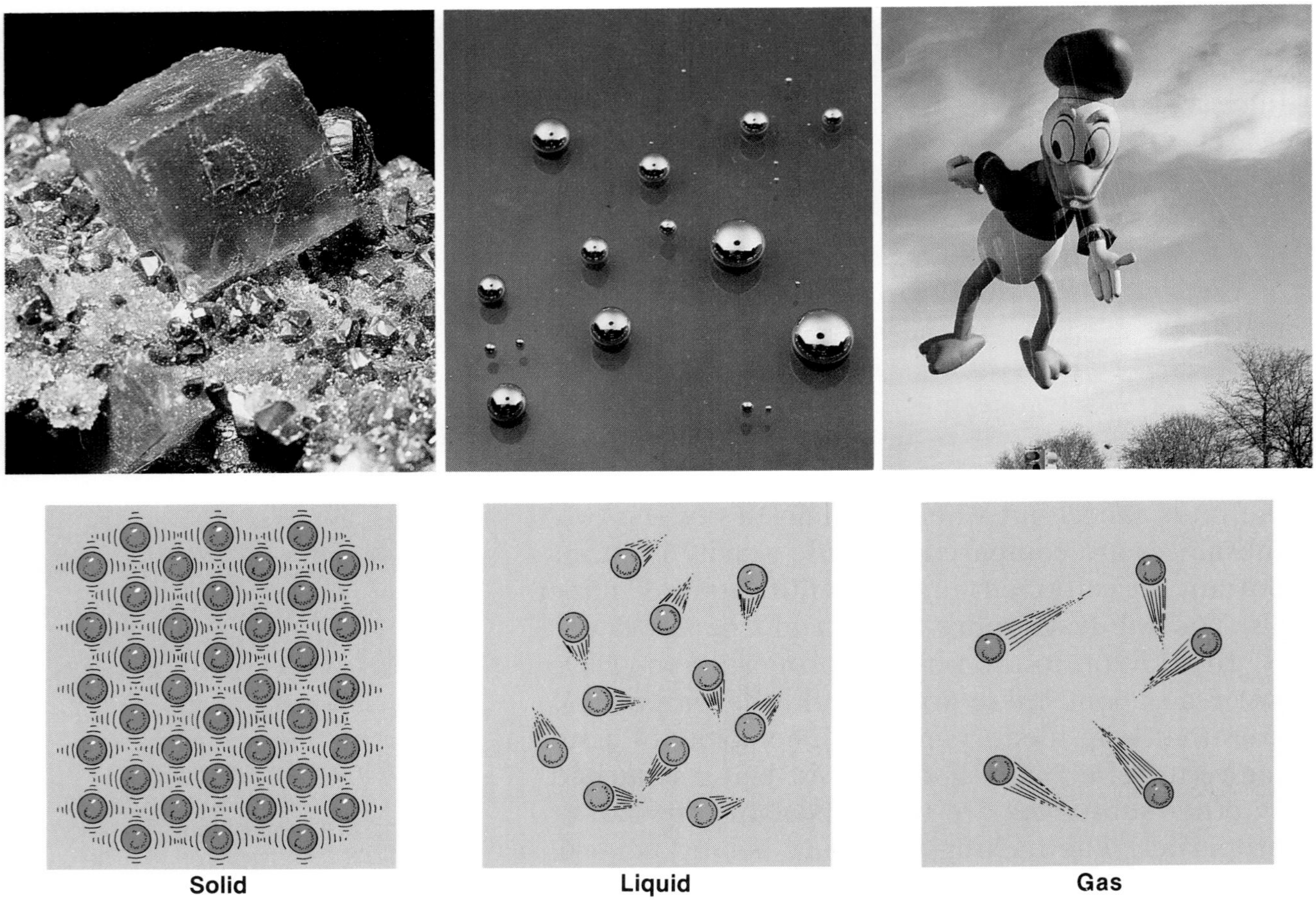

Figure 5–6 *The three most common phases of matter are solid, liquid, and gas. The purple fluorite crystals growing on crystals of galena are solids (left). Mercury is a liquid (center). The helium giving this Donald Duck balloon its shape is a gas (right). The arrangement and movement of particles vary in each phase of matter.*

Figure 5–7 *These eruptions on the sun are examples of the high-energy plasma phase of matter. Where else might plasma be found?*

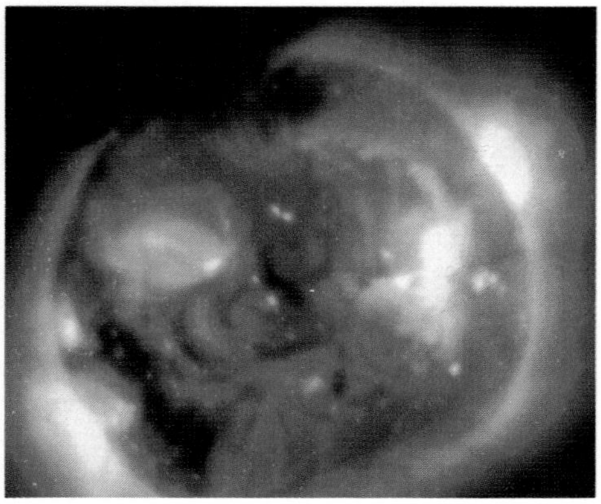

container. So liquid water in a square container is square, and that same liquid water in a round container is round. But in either container, the volume of the liquid water does not get larger or smaller. The volume is constant.

A **gas** does not have a definite volume or a definite shape. A gas fills all the space in a container, regardless of the size or the shape of the container.

The fourth phase of matter is **plasma.** Because matter in the plasma phase is very high in energy, it is dangerous to living things. Plasma is not found naturally on the earth. It is common in stars such as the sun.

To understand the phases of matter, you must know something about **molecules** (MAHL-uh-kyoolz). The different substances that exist are made up of small particles. A molecule is the smallest part of any substance that still has all of the properties of that substance.

The behavior of solids, liquids, and gases can now be explained in terms of the arrangement and movement of molecules. The molecules in a solid are packed closely together in a definite pattern. The molecules cannot move far out of their places. So solids keep their shape.

The molecules in a liquid are close together but are free to move. So a liquid takes the shape of its container. Water poured from a glass to a cup first takes the shape of the glass and then the cup.

The molecules in a gas move about freely. They fill all the available space in a container. You may have noticed, for example, that the gas from an open bottle of ammonia will quickly spread throughout a room. Also, the molecules in a gas are spread very far apart. Because there is a lot of empty space between molecules, the volume of a gas can easily be changed. For example, the volume changes when a gas is forced into a smaller container or released into a larger one. Oxygen, methane, and hydrogen are gases. The helium that makes balloons rise is also a gas. What other gases can you name?

Matter can be changed from one phase to another by adding or taking away heat. If heat is added to a solid, the solid will turn into a liquid. The solid will melt. If heat is taken away from the liquid, the liquid will change back into a solid. The liquid will freeze. If heat is added to a liquid, the liquid will change into a gas, or evaporate. If heat is taken away, the gas will turn back into a liquid, or condense. Water provides good examples of phase changes because it exists naturally and in large amounts in all three phases. The most common phase of water is liquid. It changes into a gas, or water vapor, when it is heated. It turns into a solid, or ice, when it is frozen.

SECTION REVIEW

1. Classify the following examples of matter into their correct phases: nitrogen, water, pencil, rock, soda, oxygen, high-energy substance in stars.
2. Describe the arrangement and movement of molecules in a solid, a liquid, and a gas.
3. What phase change occurs when heat is added to a solid? A liquid? When heat is taken away from a gas? A liquid?

Sharpen Your Skills

Measuring Ammonia Gas Movement

1. Position four or five classmates 1 m apart in a line from the front to the back of the room.

2. Then open a bottle of ammonia about 1 m from the first person in line.

3. Have your classmates raise their hand when they first notice the smell of ammonia gas from the opened bottle.

4. Determine how long it takes the ammonia gas to fill the room.

Figure 5–8 *Ice changes to a liquid and then to water vapor when heat is applied. What are these two processes called?*

Section Objective

To describe the modern model of the atom

5–3 Structure of Matter

You just learned that all substances are made up of smaller particles called molecules. But the story does not end there. All molecules are made up of even smaller particles called **atoms.** Atoms are the basic building blocks of matter. And just as blocks can be put together in many different ways to make many different buildings, so atoms can be joined to form different kinds of matter.

The idea that matter is made up of indivisible particles called atoms is not new. More than 20 centuries ago, some Greek philosophers suggested this idea. In fact, the word *atom* comes from the Greek word *atomos,* meaning "indivisible." In the early nineteenth century, the English scientist John Dalton also proposed that atoms exist. He called his theory the atomic theory.

Dalton's atomic theory stated that atoms are the basic building blocks of all chemical substances. Dalton also believed that an atom is so small that it cannot be seen. Like the Greeks, he thought that an atom is the tiniest form of a substance and that it cannot be broken down any further. Dalton would be quite surprised to learn that scientists have so far identified about 200 different kinds of tinier particles inside the atom!

Figure 5–9 *Physicists learn about subatomic particles by studying their tracks. In specially designed machines called accelerators, atomic particles are made to collide at enormous speeds. When they collide, they leave tracks that can be recorded on film and studied.*

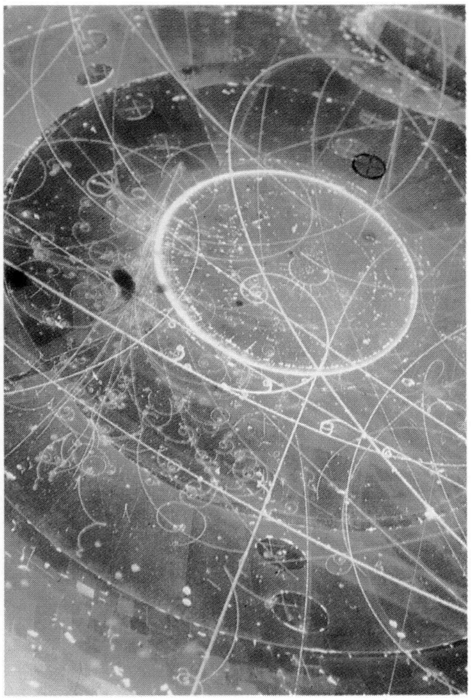

Subatomic Particles

Atoms are made up of even smaller particles called subatomic particles. You may already know the names of three of the particles that make up atoms. **Protons** are particles that carry a positive electric charge. **Neutrons** are particles that have no electric charge. Together these two kinds of particles make up the **nucleus** (NOO-klee-uhs), the center of the atom. The nucleus is surrounded by **electrons.** Electrons are particles that have a negative electric charge. In a neutral, or uncharged, atom, the number of electrons (negatively charged particles) is equal to the number of protons (positively charged particles).

Because of an atom's very small size, scientists have no exact picture of its structure. However, models of atoms have been constructed. Models picture or represent things that cannot be observed directly. Models help people understand the basic structure and behavior of atoms.

According to the modern atomic model, protons and neutrons are found in the nucleus, and electrons are found outside the nucleus. Electrons are found in a region called the electron cloud. This **electron cloud** represents the space in which electrons are *likely* to be found. However, the exact location of an electron cannot be known. Only the probability, or likelihood, of finding an electron at a particular place in an atom can be determined.

Within the electron cloud, electrons are arranged in **energy levels.** Electrons with the lowest energy are found in the energy level closest to the nucleus. Electrons with higher energy are found in energy levels farther from the nucleus. In other words, the location of an electron in a particular energy level within the electron cloud depends on how much energy the electron has.

Each energy level can hold only a certain number of electrons. The first energy level, the energy level closest to the nucleus, can hold at most 2 electrons. The second and third energy levels can each hold 8 electrons. See Figure 5–10.

Sharpen Your Skills

Atomic Models

Before the modern atomic model was developed, many other models of the atom had been proposed. Although not all aspects of these models were correct, many important discoveries were made. Using reference material, write a report about one of the following scientists and his contribution to the understanding of the atom.

Niels Bohr
James Chadwick
Democritus
Ernest Rutherford
J. J. Thomson

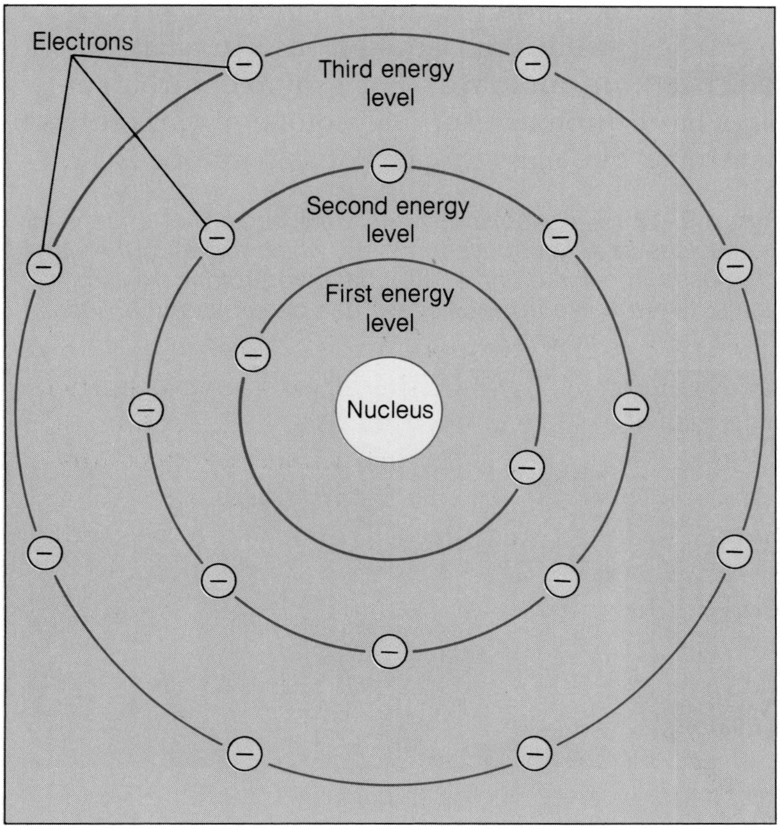

Figure 5–10 *Each energy level within the electron cloud of an atom can hold only a certain number of electrons. How many electrons are there in the first, second, and third energy levels shown here?*

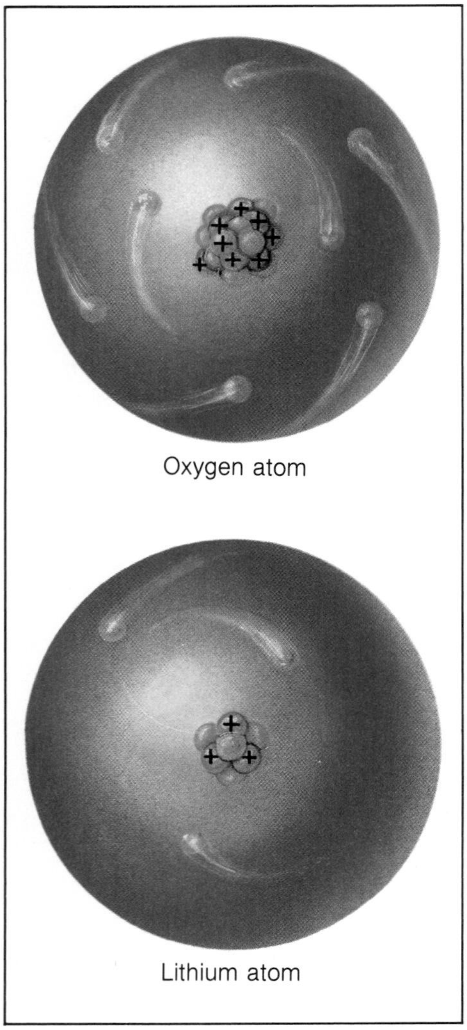

Figure 5–11 *In this diagram, you can see atomic models of oxygen and lithium. What two particles are found in the nucleus? In the region outside the nucleus?*

Each atom has an **atomic number** that identifies it. The atomic number is the number of protons in the nucleus of an atom of a substance. The atomic number of hydrogen is 1. All hydrogen atoms—and only hydrogen atoms—have 1 proton in the nucleus. The atomic number of oxygen is 8. Lead has an atomic number of 82. Aluminum has an atomic number of 13. What is the atomic number of the lithium atom shown in Figure 5–11?

Every element also has a **mass number.** The mass number is the total number of protons and neutrons in an atom. A lithium atom with 3 protons and 4 neutrons has a mass number of 7. The mass number of an oxygen atom that has 8 protons and 8 neutrons is 16. Atomic numbers and mass numbers for several elements are listed in Figure 5–13. What is the mass number of iron? Of chlorine?

Isotopes

The number of protons in every atom of a substance is always the same. But it is possible for the number of neutrons in the atoms of a substance to vary. When the number of neutrons varies, the mass of the atom varies.

Atoms that have the same number of protons but different numbers of neutrons are called **isotopes** (IGH-suh-tohps). For example, carbon always has 6 protons. But one isotope of carbon has 6 neutrons. The mass number of this isotope is 12.

Figure 5–12 *The atomic number is the number of protons in the nucleus of an atom. Neon atoms, which make up the gas often used in colored lights (left), have 10 protons. Helium atoms, which make up a colorless gas often used in balloons (right), have 2 protons.*

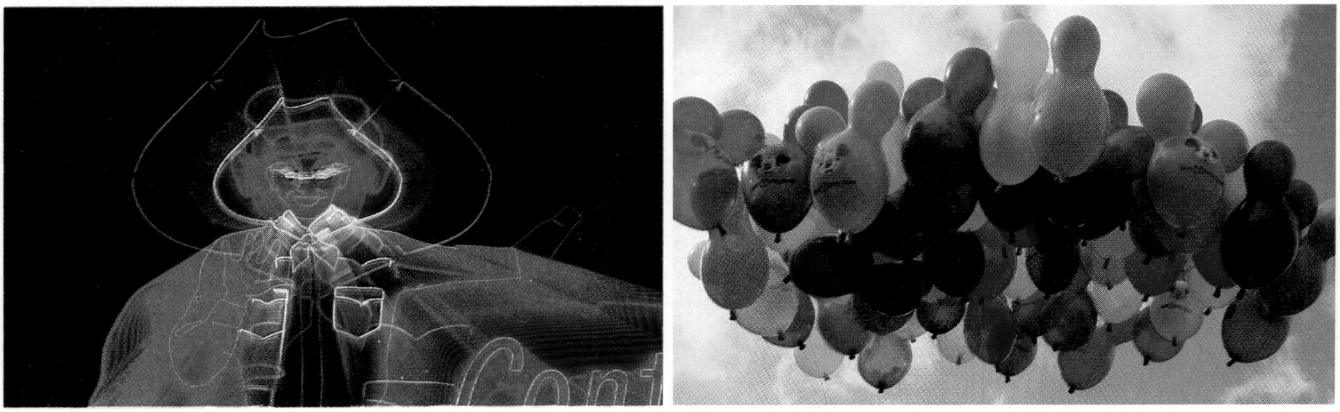

COMMON ELEMENTS

Name	Atomic Number	Mass Number	Name	Atomic Number	Mass Number
Hydrogen	1	1	**Chlorine**	17	35
Helium	2	4	**Calcium**	20	40
Carbon	6	12	**Iron**	26	56
Nitrogen	7	14	**Copper**	29	64
Oxygen	8	16	**Zinc**	30	65
Fluorine	9	19	**Silver**	47	108
Sodium	11	23	**Gold**	79	197
Aluminum	13	27	**Mercury**	80	201
Sulfur	16	32	**Lead**	82	207

Figure 5–13 *The atomic number and mass number of some common elements are listed in this table. Which element has the most protons? The fewest?*

Another isotope of carbon has 8 neutrons. So the mass number of this isotope is 14.

Many substances that exist in nature have isotopes. There are three isotopes of hydrogen. All have 1 proton, but the number of neutrons can be 0, 1, or 2. So the mass number of hydrogen can be 1, 2, or 3, as shown in Figure 5–14. Oxygen is another substance that has isotopes. One isotope of oxygen has 8 protons and 7 neutrons. What is its atomic number? What is its mass number?

Figure 5–14 *The three isotopes of hydrogen are shown here. Notice that the number of protons remains the same. Only the number of neutrons changes. What is the atomic number of each isotope?*

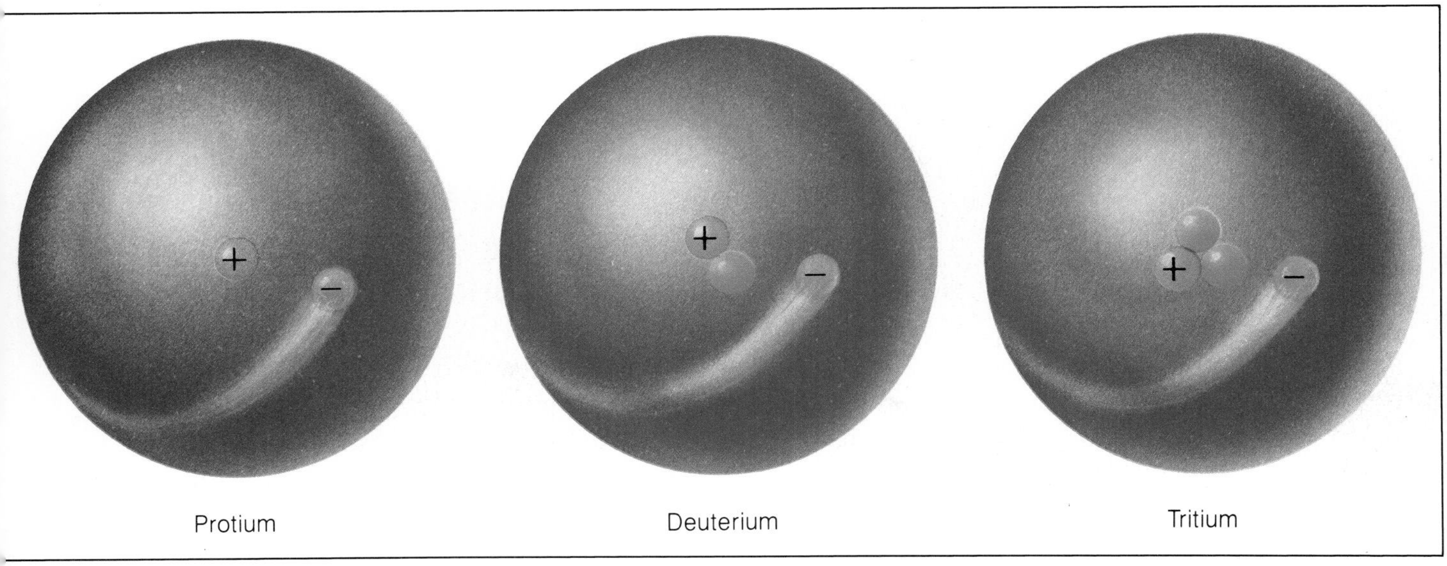

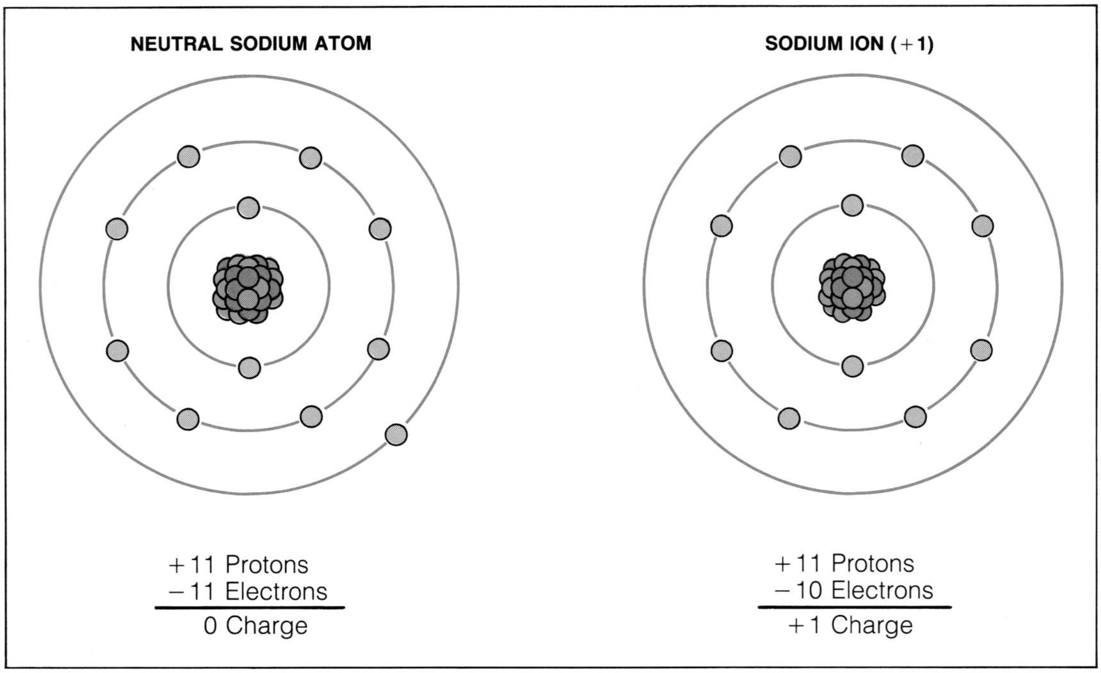

Figure 5–15 *When a neutral atom loses an electron, it becomes a positive ion. The neutral sodium atom has a charge of 0. The sodium ion has a charge of +1.*

Ions

An atom can lose one or more of its electrons, or it can gain one or more electrons. When an atom loses or gains electrons, it is no longer neutral. It has either a positive or a negative charge. Charged atoms are called **ions** (IGH-uhnz). An atom that has lost one electron is a positive ion. It has a charge of +1. An atom that has gained one electron is a negative ion. It has a charge of −1. What is the charge on an atom that has lost two electrons?

SECTION REVIEW

1. Describe the modern atomic model.
2. What is atomic number? Mass number?
3. What is a positive ion? A negative ion?

Section Objective

To compare elements, compounds, and mixtures

5–4 Forms of Matter

All matter can be classified into three forms: elements, compounds, and mixtures. An **element** is a substance that cannot be separated into simpler substances by ordinary chemical means. At present, scientists have identified 109 elements. Most of these occur naturally. But some are made in the laboratory. The elements differ from one another in appearance and properties.

Each element has a name and a chemical symbol made up of one or two letters. Some of the symbols are the same as the first letter of the name of the element. For example, the symbol for oxygen is O, for hydrogen H, for carbon C, and for sulfur S. When the names of two elements begin with the same letter, a second letter is needed to prevent confusion. The symbol for helium is He, for chlorine Cl, and for silicon Si. The symbols for some elements come from the Latin names for the elements. For example, the symbol for iron (Fe) comes from the Latin word *ferrum,* and the symbol for sodium (Na) from the word *natrium.* The symbol for gold (Au) comes from the word *aurum.* Symbols are used as shorthand to represent the names of the elements.

The smallest part of an element is an atom. It is possible to have a single atom of an element such as gold, aluminum, or iron. Atoms can be combined to produce molecules. In the molecules that make up an element, all of the atoms are of the same kind. For example, a sulfur molecule is made up of eight sulfur atoms.

Molecules can also be made up of different kinds of atoms. The different atoms can be put together in many ways to form all of the materials that make up matter. A **compound** is any combination of two or more different kinds of atoms. Water is a compound. It is made up of oxygen and hydrogen atoms linked together. Salt is another compound. It is made up of sodium and chlorine atoms. Some compounds are made up of several elements. Clay is

Figure 5–16 *A chlorine molecule is made of two atoms of chlorine. A molecule of water is made of two hydrogen atoms and one oxygen atom linked together. Which molecule is an element? Which is a compound?*

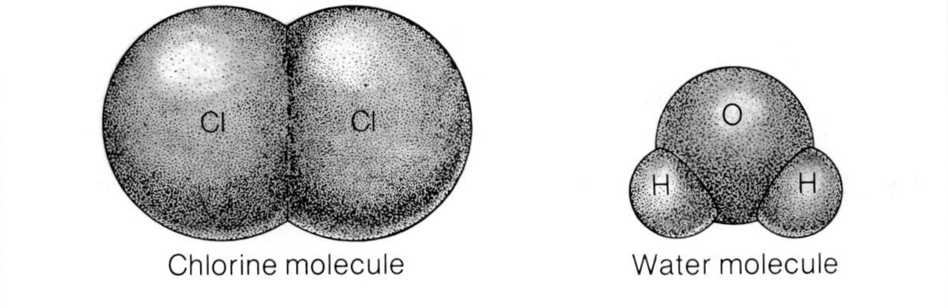

Figure 5–17 *The names and symbols of some common elements are listed in this table. What is the symbol for aluminum? For calcium?*

COMMON ELEMENTS

Name	Symbol
Aluminum	Al
Calcium	Ca
Carbon	C
Chlorine	Cl
Copper	Cu
Fluorine	F
Gold	Au
Helium	He
Hydrogen	H
Iron	Fe
Lead	Pb
Magnesium	Mg
Nitrogen	N
Oxygen	O
Potassium	K
Silicon	Si
Silver	Ag
Sodium	Na
Sulfur	S

Sharpen Your Skills

Collecting Elements

1. From around your home, collect several items made of common elements such as iron, copper, aluminum, or silver.
2. See what items you can find that are made of less common elements.
3. Make a display of the elements you collect. Label each one with its name and chemical symbol.

made up of aluminum, magnesium, silicon, oxygen, and hydrogen. What compounds can you name?

Just as chemical symbols represent elements, a kind of shorthand is used to represent compounds. The symbols for the elements that make up a compound are combined to make a chemical formula (FOR-myoo-luh) for the compound. For example, the chemical formula for salt is NaCl. The compound is made up of the elements sodium and chlorine. The chemical formula for hydrogen chloride is HCl. What elements make up this compound?

When a molecule contains more than one atom of the same element, the number of atoms is written as a small number to the lower right of the symbol. This number is called a subscript. The formula for water is H_2O. According to this formula, every molecule of water is made up of 2 atoms of hydrogen and 1 atom of oxygen. Calcium carbonate is a naturally occurring substance you will learn more about in the next chapter. Its formula is $CaCO_3$. What elements and how many atoms of each are there in this compound?

Some forms of matter are neither elements nor compounds. Instead they are two or more substances mixed together. Such substances are called

CAREER — *Chemist*

HELP WANTED: CHEMIST To design and test chemical substances for plastics manufacturer. Bachelor's degree in chemistry with some experience necessary.

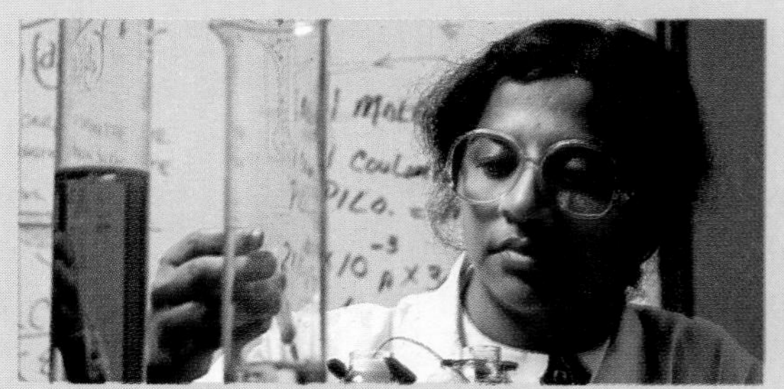

Many of the things you use every day are the products of the work done by **chemists.** Chemists are scientists who study the makeup and properties of substances. They also investigate how substances react with one another. These scientists develop new drugs, dyes, paints, plastics, cosmetics, and fertilizers. They produce fabrics that are nonflammable, stain-resistant, and wrinkle-free.

When chemists develop a new product, they must know the kind and amount of ingredients needed to make that product. Then the chemists must test the product to make sure that it meets company and government standards.

Chemists often study specialized fields in chemistry. For example, some chemists might examine moon rocks to determine their makeup. Other chemists, called geochemists, study the makeup of the earth's crust and the chemical changes that take place within it.

Many colleges have programs designed for people who want to become chemists. People who work in this field have a good imagination and are keen observers. They enjoy working with scientific equipment and doing experiments.

To learn more about this interesting career, write to the American Chemical Society, 1155 16th Street, NW, Washington, DC 20036.

Figure 5–18 *The various kinds of matter can be classified into three forms: elements, compounds, and mixtures. The bars of bullion (left) are made of the element gold. The mineral formation in the Carlsbad Caverns of New Mexico (center) is made of the compound calcium carbonate. And the super burger (right) is a dazzling mixture of substances.*

mixtures. A mixture is two or more substances physically combined. Soil, sea water, and air are examples of mixtures. Soil contains several substances, such as bits of clay, sand, and rocks. Air is a gaseous mixture of mostly nitrogen, oxygen, and water vapor. What is the mixture sea water made up of?

Sharpen Your Skills

Chemical Formulas

What elements and how many atoms of each are there in the following compounds:

$C_{12}H_{22}O_{11}$
Na_2SO_4
$CaCl_2$
KCl
H_2O

SECTION REVIEW

1. What is the difference between an element, a compound, and a mixture?
2. What is a chemical symbol?
3. What is a chemical formula?
4. A blue solid is heated. It gives off a colorless gas and leaves behind a white solid. Is the blue solid an element, a compound, or a mixture? Explain your answer.

5–5 Formation of Compounds

Section Objective

To relate atomic structure to chemical changes

By losing, gaining, or sharing electrons, atoms can combine to form compounds. Sodium can easily lose its outermost electron and combine with an element that can easily gain an electron. Chlorine can

Sharpen Your Skills

Changes in Matter

Write a 250-word essay describing the differences between a physical change and a chemical change. Use the following vocabulary words in your essay:

property	element
matter	compound
mass	atom
volume	electron
density	

easily gain a single electron. So a sodium atom and a chlorine atom can join together to form the compound sodium chloride. Chlorine can also share electrons, as can hydrogen. A hydrogen atom and a chlorine atom join together to form hydrogen chloride. In the compound hydrogen chloride, electrons are shared. See Figure 5–19.

Sodium chloride is a compound. A compound has properties different from the properties of the elements that make it up. A compound is a new substance. The element sodium is a highly active substance that must be stored in oil. It can combine explosively with the water. Chlorine is a yellow-green poisonous gas. It can dissolve in water to form a bleaching liquid. When sodium and chlorine are chemically combined, they form a harmless white compound with a tasty flavor! You probably use this compound—sodium chloride, or table salt—to flavor your food.

When sodium and chlorine combine to form sodium chloride, a **chemical change** takes place. A new substance with new and different properties is formed. The changes that substances undergo when they turn into other substances are called chemical changes. And the properties of matter that describe

Figure 5–19 *One atom of hydrogen and one atom of chlorine share an electron to form the compound hydrogen chloride.*

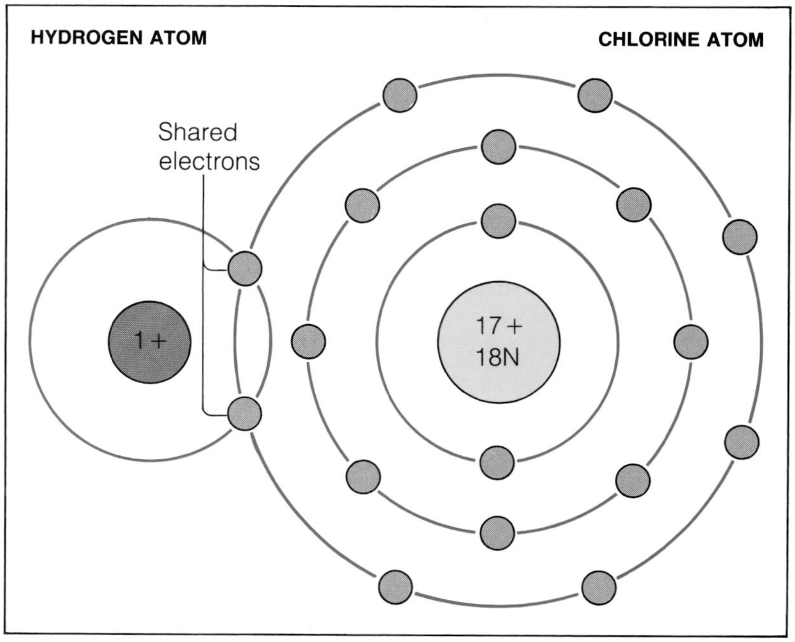

Figure 5–20 *This beautiful fireworks display is produced by a chemical change in which substances such as magnesium, phosphorus, and sulfur combine very rapidly with oxygen. Rusting is also a chemical change in which iron combines slowly with oxygen.*

how substances change into other new substances are called **chemical properties.**

Chemical changes take place when complex substances are broken down into simpler ones. For example, the compound hydrogen chloride can be broken down into the elements hydrogen and chlorine. The compound water can be broken down into the elements hydrogen and oxygen. Chemical changes also take place when new compounds are formed. For example, iron rusts when it is in contact with water and oxygen. The rust that forms is a new compound, iron oxide. It is made up of the elements iron and oxygen. You can see the effects of rusting in Figure 5–20.

Sharpen Your Skills

Chemical and Physical Changes

Many changes are going on around you all the time. Go outdoors and make a list of the changes you see taking place. Do the same in your house. Then indicate whether these changes are chemical or physical. Explain each answer.

SECTION REVIEW

1. How do atoms combine to form compounds?
2. What is a chemical change?
3. Give an example of a chemical change.

5 LABORATORY INVESTIGATION

Finding the Density of Objects

Problem

How can the density of water, a block of wood, a block of plastic, and a block of metal be determined?

Materials *(per group)*

Small block of wood
Small block of metal
Small block of plastic
100 mL water
100-mL graduated cylinder
Metric ruler
Balance with weights

Procedure

1. Using the balance, find the mass in grams of the blocks of wood, metal, and plastic. Record your results in a chart similar to the one on this page.
2. Again using the balance, find the mass of the empty graduated cylinder. Take the cylinder off the balance and fill it with 100 mL of water. Determine the mass of the filled cylinder. Subtract the mass of the empty cylinder from the mass of the filled cylinder to find the mass of the water.
3. One mL of water is equivalent to 1 cm^3 of water. So 100 mL of water has a volume of 100 cm^3. Record this information in your chart.
4. The volume of a solid rectangle is found by multiplying the length times the width times the height of the rectangle. Use the metric ruler to obtain these measurements for the blocks of wood, metal, and plastic. Then calculate the volume of each solid. Record this information in your chart.
5. Find the density of the water, wood, metal, and plastic by dividing the mass by the volume. The formula is:

$$\text{density} = \frac{\text{mass in grams}}{\text{volume in cubic centimeters}}$$

Observations

Which of the objects you tested—wood, metal, and plastic—will float in water?

Conclusions

1. What can you conclude about the relationship of an object's density and its ability to float?
2. If an object has a mass of 54 g and a volume of 20 cm^3, will the object float in water? Explain your answer.
3. If you cut the wood block in half, what would be the density of each piece? Explain your answer.
4. Design a way to find the volume of a solid that has an irregular shape.

Substance	Mass	Volume	Density
Wood			
Metal			
Plastic			
Water			

CHAPTER REVIEW

SUMMARY

5–1 Properties of Matter

❑ All materials consist of matter. Every kind of matter has its own properties.

❑ During a physical change, the physical properties of a substance are altered, but the substance remains the same kind of matter.

❑ Mass is the amount of matter in an object.

❑ Volume is the amount of space an object takes up.

❑ Density is the mass per unit volume of a substance.

5–2 Phases of Matter

❑ Matter exists in four phases: solid, liquid, gas, and plasma.

❑ A solid has a definite shape and volume.

❑ A liquid has a definite volume but does not have a definite shape.

❑ A gas does not have a definite volume or a definite shape.

❑ A molecule is the smallest part of any substance that still has all of the properties of that substance.

❑ Matter can be changed from one phase to another by adding or taking away heat.

5–3 Structure of Matter

❑ Atoms are the building blocks of matter.

❑ Protons and neutrons are found in the nucleus. Electrons are arranged in energy levels in the electron cloud.

❑ The atomic number is the number of protons in the nucleus of an atom of a substance.

❑ The mass number is the total number of protons and neutrons in an atom.

❑ Isotopes have the same number of protons but different numbers of neutrons.

❑ Charged atoms, called ions, have either gained or lost electrons.

5–4 Forms of Matter

❑ An element is a substance that cannot be separated into simpler substances by ordinary chemical means.

❑ The smallest part of an element is an atom.

❑ A compound is any combination of two or more different kinds of atoms.

❑ A mixture is two or more substances physically combined.

5–5 Formation of Compounds

❑ By losing, gaining, or sharing electrons, atoms can combine to form compounds.

❑ The changes that substances undergo when they turn into other substances are called chemical changes.

VOCABULARY

Define each term in a complete sentence.

atom
atomic number
chemical change
chemical property
compound
density
electron
electron cloud
element
energy level
gas
ion
isotope
liquid
mass
mass number
matter
mixture
molecule
neutron
nucleus
physical change
physical property
plasma
proton
solid
specific gravity
volume

CONTENT REVIEW: MULTIPLE CHOICE

Choose the letter of the answer that best completes each sentence.

1. Changes that do not produce a new kind of substance are called
a. chemical changes   b. property changes
c. physical changes   d. matter changes

2. The amount of matter in an object is called its
a. volume   b. mass   c. specific gravity   d. phase

3. The formula for density is
a. volume/mass   b. volume × mass
c. mass/volume   d. mass/specific gravity

4. The phase in which matter has a definite volume but not a definite shape is called the
a. solid phase   b. liquid phase   c. gas phase   d. plasma phase

5. The center of the atom is called the
a. nucleus   b. neutron   c. isotope   d. proton

6. The total number of protons and neutrons in an atom is called the
a. atomic number   b. isotope number
c. mass number   d. electron number

7. The number of protons in every atom of a particular substance is
a. always the same   b. the same as the number of neutrons
c. always changing   d. one less than the number of neutrons

8. Charged atoms are called
a. electrons   b. ions   c. isotopes   d. elements

9. A substance that cannot be separated into simpler substances by ordinary chemical means is called a (an)
a. compound   b. molecule   c. element   d. isotope

10. Two or more substances physically combined are called a (an)
a. element   b. mixture   c. compound   d. physical change

CONTENT REVIEW: COMPLETION

Fill in the word or words that best complete each sentence.

1. Changes that do not produce a new kind of substance are called ______________.

2. The amount of matter in an object is called its ______________.

3. The amount of space an object takes up is called its ______________.

4. Mass per unit volume is called ______________.

5. Matter can be changed from one phase to another by adding or taking away ______________.

6. An electron is located in a particular ______________ according to the amount of energy it has.

7. Atoms that have the same number of protons but different numbers of neutrons are called ______________.

8. A combination of two or more different kinds of atoms is called a (an) ______________.

9. The number of atoms in a molecule of H_2SO_4 is ______________.

10. When a substance with new and different properties is being formed, the change is called a (an) ______________.

CONTENT REVIEW: TRUE OR FALSE

Determine whether each statement is true or false. If it is true, write "true." If it is false, change the underlined word or words to make the statement true.

1. Mass is measured in units called milliliters and cubic centimeters.
2. The ratio of the mass of a substance to the mass of an equal volume of water is called specific gravity.
3. The phase of matter that is very high in energy and dangerous to living things is called plasma.
4. The basic building blocks of matter are called molecules.
5. The positively charged subatomic particle is called the neutron.
6. The space outside the nucleus in which electrons are likely to be found is called the electron cloud.
7. An element with 8 protons, 8 electrons, and 8 neutrons has an atomic number of 24.
8. An atom that has lost an electron is called a negative ion.
9. Two or more substances physically combined are called a mixture.
10. Properties of matter that describe how substances change into other new substances are called physical properties.

CONCEPT REVIEW: SKILL BUILDING

Use the skills you have developed in the chapter to complete each activity.

1. **Making diagrams** Show how a bromine atom combines with a potassium atom to form the compound potassium bromide.
2. **Applying concepts** Use your knowledge of physical and chemical changes to identify each of the following changes: boiling water, burning coal, exploding TNT, baking bread, tarnishing silver, melting butter, digesting dinner.
3. **Relating concepts** Five hundred milliliters of water is heated to its boiling point, 100°C. The heating is continued for five more minutes until only 250 milliliters remain. The temperature of the water is still 100°C. How do you account for the "missing" 250 milliliters of water? Explain why additional heating produced no change in temperature.
4. **Classifying substances** Identify the following substances using the term compound, mixture, or element.

   a. Orange soda b. Sugar c. Bread d. Snow e. Ice cream f. Mercury g. Water
5. **Applying observations** List eight properties of your shoes. Is each a physical or chemical property?

CONCEPT REVIEW: ESSAY

Discuss each of the following in a brief paragraph.

1. Compare the four phases of matter.
2. What are some ways in which the physical or chemical state of matter can be changed?
3. How can physical properties be used to identify substances?
4. How are atomic numbers and mass numbers used to describe atoms?

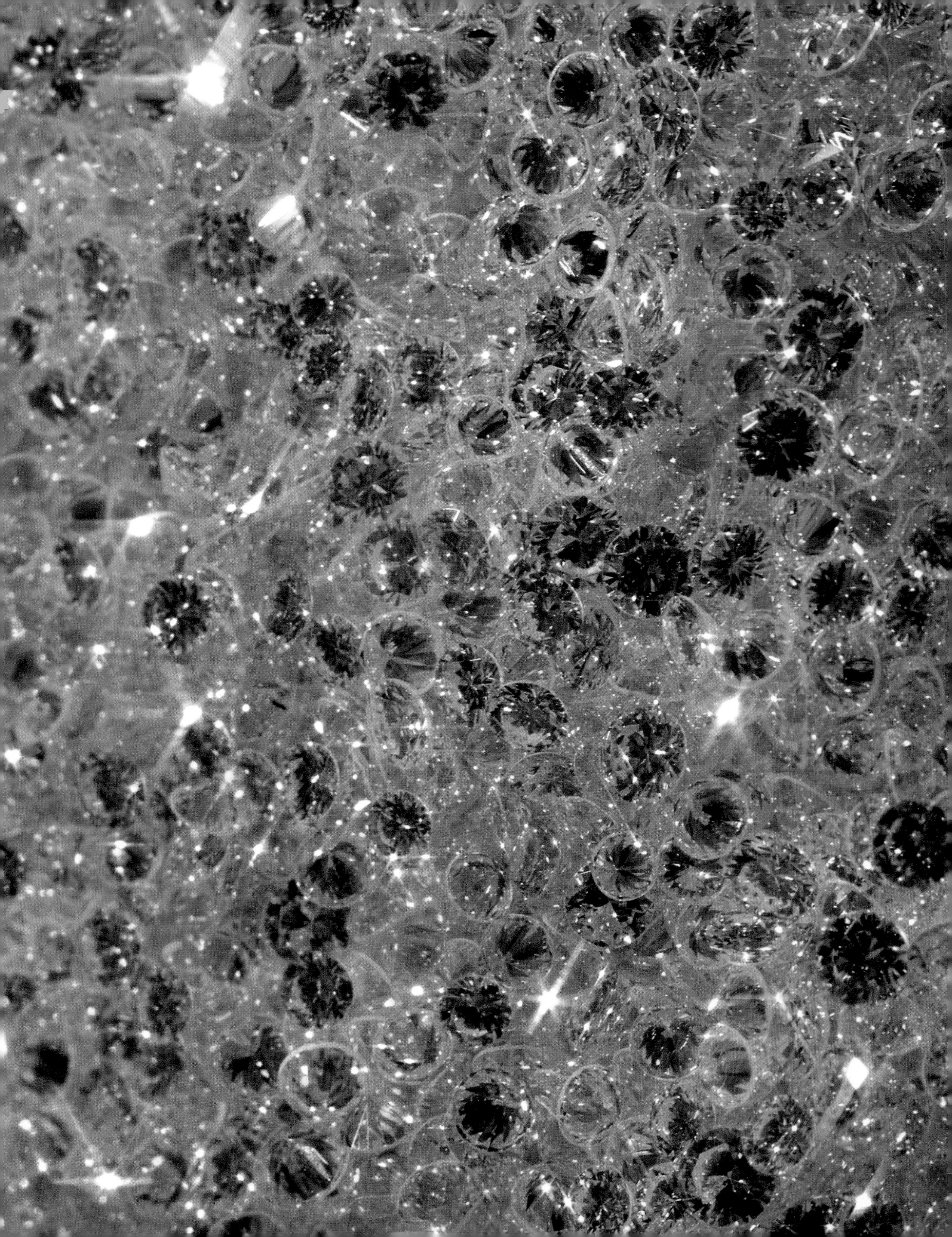

Minerals

6

CHAPTER SECTIONS

CHAPTER OBJECTIVES

After completing this chapter, you will be able to

6–1 Define the term mineral.

6–1 Describe the properties of minerals.

6–2 Identify minerals by their physical properties.

6–3 Describe some uses of minerals.

Throughout history, diamonds have been prized as a symbol of great wealth and power. Many of the world's largest diamonds decorate the crowns and jewelry of royalty. Take, for example, the Orloff diamond—if you can find it!

The story goes that this diamond was once in the eye of an idol in a Buddhist shrine in India. In the 1700s the diamond was stolen by a French soldier, who sold it to a British sea captain. After many thefts and some violent crimes, including murder, the diamond found its way to Russia. It was bought by Count Gregory Orloff from an Armenian merchant for about four million dollars. The Count gave it to Catherine II, Empress of Russia. Later, the diamond disappeared during the Russian Revolution.

Other diamonds also have disappeared before their owners' eyes—not through magic, but through ignorance. Early diamond hunters in South America thought they had a simple test for diamonds. They knew that diamonds are the hardest natural substance known. When the hunters found a stone that looked like a diamond, they hit it with a hammer. Usually, the stone shattered into bits and pieces. To the hunters, the shattering just proved the object was worthless. Actually, the stone may have been a diamond.

What the hunters did not know was that diamonds are brittle. Tap a diamond with a knife edge at exactly the right angle and it breaks cleanly and beautifully along an absolutely straight line. Tap it at the wrong angle and the diamond shatters. Why do diamonds and other precious stones behave in this way? The answer is just a part of the fascinating story of minerals.

Diamonds are among the most precious minerals on the earth.

Section Objective

To describe the five special properties of a mineral

6–1 What Is a Mineral?

The substance you just read about—diamond—is a mineral. A **mineral** is a naturally occurring substance formed in the earth. A mineral may be made of a single element, such as copper, gold, or sulfur. Or a mineral may be made of two or more elements chemically combined to form a compound. For example, the mineral halite is the compound sodium chloride, which is made of the elements sodium and chlorine.

In order for a substance to be called a mineral, it must have five special properties. The first property of a mineral is that it is an **inorganic** substance. Inorganic substances are not formed from living things or the remains of living things. Calcite, a compound made of calcium, carbon, and oxygen, is a mineral. It is formed underground from water containing these dissolved elements. Coal and oil, although found underground, are not minerals because they are formed from decayed plant and animal life.

Figure 6–1 *Chalk (top), aragonite (center), and pearl (bottom) are all made of calcium carbonate or limestone. But only aragonite is a mineral. Why?*

The second property of a mineral is that it occurs naturally in the earth. Steel and cement are manufactured substances. So they are not minerals. But gold, silver, and asbestos, all of which occur naturally, are minerals.

The third property of a mineral is that it is always a solid. The minerals you just read about—halite, calcite, gold, silver, and asbestos—are solids.

The fourth property of a mineral is that, whether it is made of a single element or a compound, it has a definite chemical composition. The mineral silver is made of only silver atoms. The mineral quartz is made entirely of a compound formed from the elements silicon and oxygen. So even though a sample of quartz may contain billions of atoms, its atoms can only be silicon and oxygen joined in a definite way.

The fifth property of a mineral is that its atoms are arranged in a definite pattern repeated over and over again. This repeating pattern of atoms forms a solid called a **crystal.** A crystal has flat sides, or faces, that meet in sharp edges and corners. All minerals have a characteristic crystal shape.

Figure 6–2 *Crystals are found in many different shapes, such as six-sided cubes of fluorite (top right), radiating crystals of wavellite (top left), and needlelike structures of croccolite (bottom). Some minerals form crystals that have such characteristic shapes that you can easily identify the mineral.*

You will learn more about the types of crystals in Section 6–2.

There are more than 2000 different kinds of minerals. Some minerals are very common and are easy to find. Other minerals are rare and very valuable. Certain minerals are very useful. Some are extremely colorful and attractive. But all minerals have the five special properties you just read about. Using these five properties, you can now define a mineral in a more scientific way. **A mineral is a naturally occurring, inorganic solid that has a definite chemical composition and crystal shape.**

Formation of Minerals

Almost all minerals come from the material deep inside the earth. This material is hot liquid rock called **magma.** When magma cools, mineral crystals are formed. How magma cools and where it cools determine the size of the mineral crystals.

When magma cools slowly beneath the earth's crust, large crystals form. Sometimes the crystals are very large. For example, beryl crystals 82 meters long and 8 meters in diameter have been found in Maine. Quartz crystals with masses of thousands of kilograms have been found in Brazil. But crystals as large as these are very rare.

Figure 6–3 *Minerals such as calcite (bottom) are very common and easy to find. But minerals such as realgar (top) are relatively rare.*

Figure 6–4 *These beryl crystals formed as magma cooled slowly beneath the earth's surface (left). What is the relative size of crystals formed this way? The black, glassy mineral obsidian formed from magma that cooled so quickly at the earth's surface that crystals did not form at all (right).*

When magma cools rapidly beneath the earth's crust, small crystals form. Sometimes the magma reaches the surface of the earth and cools so quickly that crystals do not form at all. The black, glassy mineral in Figure 6–4 is obsidian. Obsidian comes from volcanoes and does not form crystals. In this respect, obsidian is an exception to the definition of a mineral. But obsidian is still considered a mineral because it has the other properties of minerals.

Crystals may also form from a mineral dissolved in a liquid. When the liquid evaporates, or changes to a gas, it leaves behind the mineral as crystals. The size of the crystals depends on the speed of evaporation. If evaporation is slow, larger crystals will form. The mineral calcite forms in this way.

A rock called a geode (JEE-ohd) has a hollow interior lined with mineral crystals. This hollow interior was once filled with liquid containing dissolved minerals. When the liquid evaporated, crystals were formed from the dissolved minerals left behind. Most geodes contain quartz crystals.

Figure 6–5 *A geode is a rock whose hollow interior is lined with mineral crystals. What mineral crystals do most geodes contain?*

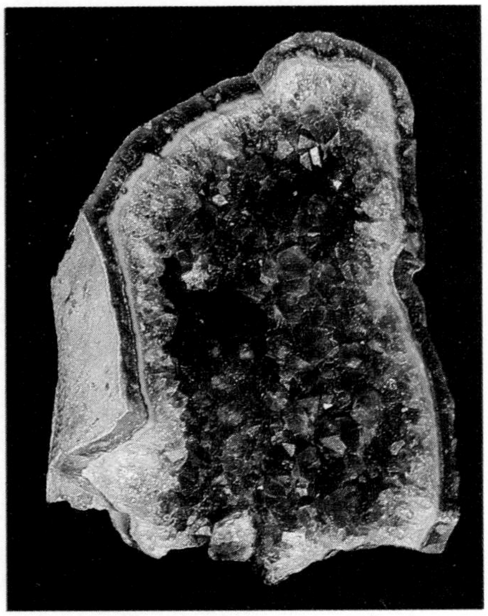

Composition of Minerals

You learned that many minerals are formed from magma, the hot liquid rock beneath the earth's surface. Magma contains large amounts of the elements oxygen and silicon. In fact, these two elements make up almost 75 percent of the earth's crust. Other elements found in large amounts in the earth's crust are aluminum, iron, calcium, sodium, potassium, and magnesium. See Figure 6–6. Since these eight elements are the most abundant elements in the earth's crust, most common minerals are made of combinations of these elements.

More than 2000 different minerals have been identified by scientists. But only about 100 of these are common minerals formed from the eight elements most abundant in the earth's crust. Of these 100 common minerals, fewer than 20 are found *everywhere* in the earth's crust. These minerals make up almost all the rocks in the crust. Scientists call these minerals rock-forming minerals. Quartz, calcite, gypsum, and hematite are examples of rock-forming minerals.

Scientists group minerals according to their chemical composition. Figure 6–7 lists the main mineral groups, the elements that make them up, and examples of each group. The largest groups of minerals are the silicates and carbonates.

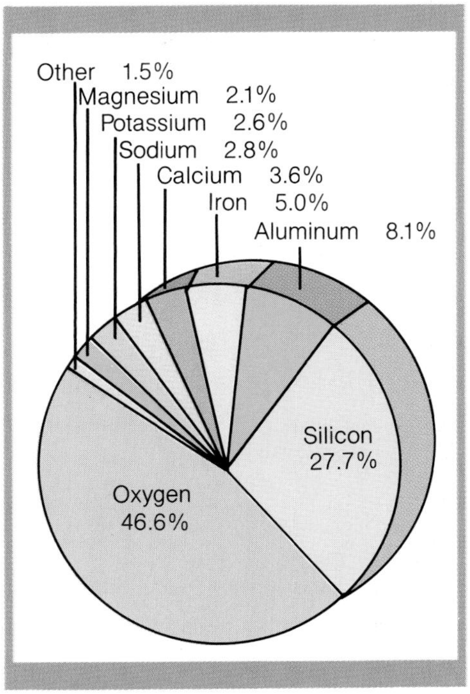

Figure 6–6 *Eight elements make up more than 98 percent of the earth's crust. Which element accounts for nearly 50 percent?*

Figure 6–7 *Minerals are grouped according to their composition. The main mineral groups, their composition, and examples are listed here. Which group contains metals, silicon, and oxygen?*

MAIN MINERAL GROUPS

Group	Composition	Examples
Elements	Uncombined elements Combined atoms	Copper, gold, sulfur
Silicates	Metals, silicon, oxygen	Quartz, feldspar, micas, garnet, beryl, talc
Carbonates	Metals, carbon, oxygen	Calcite, dolomite, siderite
Oxides	Metals, oxygen	Hematite, bauxite
Sulfides	Sulfur, metals	Galena, pyrite, chalcopyrite
Sulfates	Metals, sulfur, oxygen	Gypsum, barite, anhydrite
Halides	Metals, chlorine, fluorine, iodine, or bromine	Halite, fluorite

SECTION REVIEW

1. What five special properties make a substance a mineral?
2. What determines the size of mineral crystals?
3. What elements make up most common minerals?

To identify minerals according to their physical properties

6–2 Identifying Minerals

There are more than 2000 different kinds of minerals. Many of them look alike. So it is not an easy task to tell one mineral from another. In fact, it is usually difficult to identify a mineral just by looking at it. For example, the three minerals in Figure 6–8 all look like gold. Yet only one actually is gold.

Minerals have certain physical properties that can be used to identify them. You can see some of these properties just by looking at a mineral. Other properties can be observed only by testing a mineral. By learning how to recognize the properties of minerals, you will be able to identify many common minerals around you.

Color

The color of a mineral is an easily observed physical property. But color can be used to identify only those few minerals that always have their own characteristic color. The mineral malachite is always

Figure 6–8 *Chalcopyrite is a copper-bearing mineral that looks like gold (top right). Gold is arranged in various formations on this quartz rock (left). These nuggets of pyrite are called "fool's gold" (bottom right).*

green. The mineral azurite is always blue. No other minerals look quite the same as these.

Many minerals, however, come in a variety of colors. The mineral quartz is usually colorless. But it may be purple, yellow, or pink. You would not want to rely on color alone to identify such minerals.

Color is not always a reliable way to identify minerals for another reason. The color of most minerals changes. For example, minerals such as silver and copper turn color when they tarnish. Tarnish forms when the surface of a mineral reacts chemically with oxygen in the air. Rain, heat, cold, and pollution can also change the color of a mineral.

Figure 6–9 *Although the color of a mineral is an easily observed physical property, it is not always a reliable way to identify the mineral. Here you see the mineral quartz in three different varieties: citrine quartz (top right), smoky quartz (top left), and amethyst (bottom). Note that each variety has a characteristic color.*

Luster

The **luster** of a mineral describes the way a mineral reflects light from its surface. Certain minerals reflect light the way highly polished metal does. Such minerals, which include silver, copper, gold, and graphite, have a metallic luster. The mineral in Figure 6–10 has a metallic luster.

Minerals that do not reflect much light often appear dull. Such minerals have a nonmetallic luster. Their appearance is often described as glassy, pearly, silky, greasy, or brilliant. Quartz and tourmaline have a glassy luster. They appear transparent or partly transparent. Mica has a pearly luster. Malachite has a silky luster. Serpentine looks as if it

Figure 6–10 *These crystals of pyrite have a metallic luster. How would you describe this luster?*

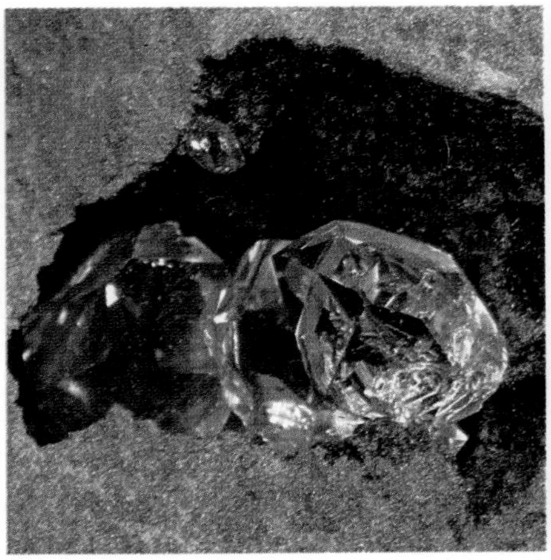

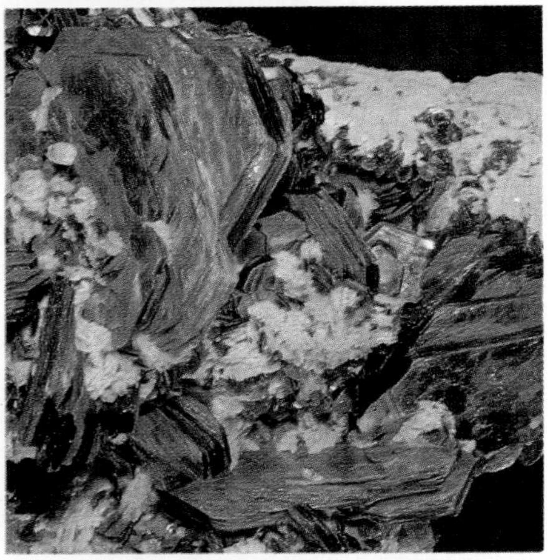

Figure 6–11 *Some minerals have a nonmetallic luster. Tourmaline has a glassy luster (top left). Diamond has a brilliant luster (top center). Malachite is described as having a silky luster (top right), while mica has a pearly luster (center). Serpentine looks as if it is covered by a thin layer of oil. It has a greasy luster (bottom).*

is covered with a thin layer of oil. It has a greasy luster. Diamond has a brilliant luster. As the rays of light are reflected from diamond, they break up into sparkles and flashes of color. Examples of the different lusters are shown in Figure 6–11.

Hardness

The ability of a mineral to resist being scratched is known as its **hardness.** Hardness is one of the most useful properties for identifying minerals. Friedrich Mohs, a German mineralogist, worked out a scale of hardness for minerals. He used ten common minerals and arranged them in order of increasing hardness. The number 1 is assigned to the softest mineral, talc. Diamond, the hardest of the ten minerals, is given the number 10. Each mineral will scratch any mineral with a lower number and will be scratched by any mineral with a higher number. Figure 6–12 shows the minerals of the Mohs hardness scale with their assigned numbers.

To determine the hardness of an unknown mineral, the mineral is rubbed against the surface of each mineral in the hardness scale. If the unknown mineral is scratched by the known mineral, it is softer than the known mineral. If the unknown mineral scratches the known mineral, it is harder

Figure 6–12 *The Mohs hardness scale is a list of ten minerals that represent different degrees of hardness. Each mineral on the scale is harder than the minerals it scratches and softer than the minerals that scratch it. Which mineral is the hardest? The softest?*

MOHS HARDNESS SCALE	
Mineral	**Hardness**
Talc	1
Gypsum	2
Calcite	3
Fluorite	4
Apatite	5
Feldspar	6
Quartz	7
Topaz	8
Corundum	9
Diamond	10

than that mineral. If two minerals do not scratch each other, they have the same hardness.

Suppose that you have a mineral sample that is scratched by fluorite, number 4, but not by calcite, number 3. The sample, however, scratches gypsum, number 2. Using the Mohs scale, what mineral could your sample be made of? You are right if you say calcite or any mineral that has a hardness of 3.

It is not always possible to have the minerals of the Mohs hardness scale with you. In such cases, a field scale is convenient to use. Although a field scale is not as exact as the Mohs scale, the materials it uses are easily obtained. Figure 6–13 shows a field hardness scale.

Figure 6–13 *A field hardness scale can be used when the minerals from the Mohs scale are not available. What mineral sample could be scratched by a penny but not by a fingernail?*

FIELD HARDNESS SCALE	
Hardness	**Common Tests**
1	Easily scratched with fingernail
2	Scratched by fingernail (2.5)
3	Scratched by a penny (3)
4	Scratched easily by a knife, but will not scratch glass
5	Difficult to scratch with a knife; barely scratches glass (5.5)
6	Scratched by a steel file (6.5); easily scratches glass
7	Scratches a steel file and glass

Sharpen Your Skills

Mineral Hardness

1. Obtain five different mineral samples, a penny, a penknife, a piece of glass, and a steel file.

2. Test the minerals to find their hardness according to the scale in Figure 6–13. Most minerals will probably fall between 3 and 7 on the scale.

3. Inside a shallow box, draw a chart listing the minerals by name in order of increasing hardness. Attach the minerals to the chart next to their names.

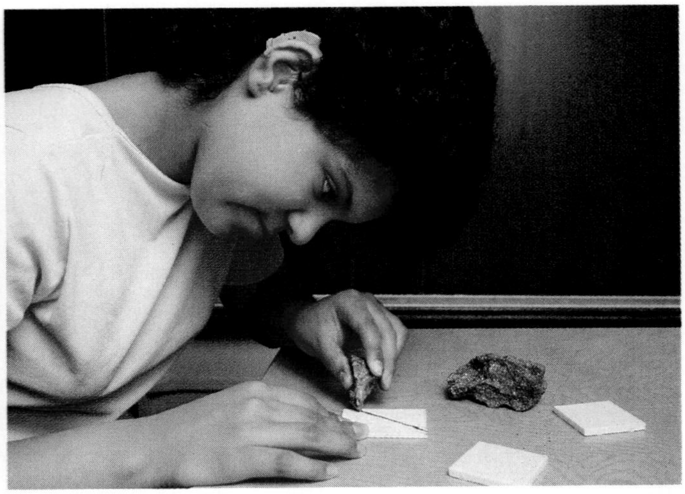

Figure 6–14 *Talc is a mineral that leaves a white streak (left). Graphite is a mineral that leaves a gray-black shiny streak (right). Graphite mixed with clay is the "lead" used in pencils.*

Streak

The color of the powder left by a mineral when it is rubbed against a hard, rough surface is called its **streak.** Streak color can be an excellent clue to identifying minerals that have a characteristic streak color and are fairly soft. Even though the color of a mineral may vary, its streak is always the same. Yet this streak color is often different from the color of the mineral itself. See Figure 6–14.

Streak color is determined by rubbing the mineral sample across a piece of unglazed porcelain. The back of a piece of bathroom tile or a streak plate is good to use. A streak plate has a hardness slightly less than 7. So a streak test is useful only with minerals whose hardness is less than 7. Harder minerals do not leave a streak.

Many minerals have white or colorless streaks. Talc, gypsum, and quartz are examples. Streak is not a useful physical property in identifying minerals such as these. Some other physical property must be used.

Sharpen Your Skills

Rock-Forming Minerals

Only a small number of minerals make up most of the rocks on the earth's surface. These are called the rock-forming minerals.

1. Collect between five and ten different rocks from your neighborhood.

2. Use a rock and mineral field guide to identify the minerals that make up each rock you found.

3. Attach an index card to each rock, label the rock, and list the minerals that you were able to identify in that rock.

Density

Every mineral has a property called density. Density is the amount of matter in a given space. Density can also be expressed as mass per unit volume. The density of a mineral is always the same, no matter what the size of the sample is. Because each mineral has a characteristic density, one mineral can easily be compared with any other mineral.

You can compare the densities of two minerals of about the same size by picking them up and hefting them. The denser mineral feels heavier. This method works well for minerals with very different densities. But scientists need a more exact way of comparing densities. So they use the specific gravity of a mineral.

Specific gravity is the ratio, or comparison, of the density of a mineral to the density of water. In other words, specific gravity tells how many times heavier a certain volume of a mineral is than the same volume of water.

Here is an example. The specific gravity of pyrite, a mineral containing iron and sulfur, is 5.02. This means that a volume of 1 cubic centimeter of pyrite is about five times heavier than a volume of 1 cubic centimeter of water. If the specific gravity of calcite is 2.7, is it denser than water? Than pyrite?

Sharpen Your Skills

Sink or Float

The density of mercury is 13.5 g/cm^3. The density of water is 1.0 g/cm^3. Using the density values given, determine whether each of the following objects will sink or float in mercury and in water:

aluminum	2.7 g/cm^3
lead	11.3 g/cm^3
silver	10.5 g/cm^3
steel	7.8 g/cm^3
platinum	21.4 g/cm^3
oak wood	0.85 g/cm^3
water (ice)	0.90 g/cm^3

Crystal Shape

Most minerals form crystals, or solids that have a definite geometric shape. The shape of a crystal results from the way the atoms or molecules of a

CAREER *Gem Cutter*

HELP WANTED: GEM CUTTER Technical school coursework in gem cutting and jewelry making required. High school graduate preferred. Experience helpful but on-the-job training available.

Among the most valuable treasures obtained from the earth are gems. These hard, beautiful stones include diamonds, rubies, and emeralds. However, rough gems do not look very much like the stones used in jewelry. To become sparkling gems they must be cut and polished. This work is done by **gem cutters.**

Gem cutting requires a great deal of patience and concentration. It also requires a great deal of skill. If a gem cutter makes a mistake, a stone that could have had a value of hundreds of thousands of dollars may suddenly be worthless.

People who want to become gem cutters begin as apprentices. They learn their trade through on-the-job training. At first, apprentices only cut inexpensive stones. As they become more skillful, they work on more valuable stones.

You can learn more about gem cutting by writing to the Gemological Institute of America, 1660 Stewart Street, Santa Monica, CA 90400.

mineral come together as the mineral is forming. Each mineral has its own pattern of atoms or molecules. So each mineral has its own crystal shape.

There are six basic shapes of crystals, or crystal systems. Each shape has a number of faces, or flat surfaces, that meet at certain angles to form sharp edges and corners. Figure 6–15 shows the six crystal

Figure 6–15 *Garnet, corundum, sulfur, crocoite, anatase, and kyanite illustrate the six basic crystal systems. To which system do the fluorite crystals in Figure 6–2 belong?*

CRYSTAL SYSTEMS

System Name	Crystal Shape	Example	
Cubic	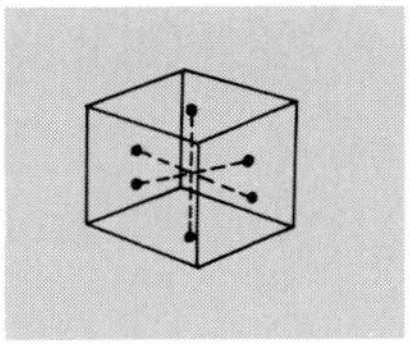		Garnet
Hexagonal	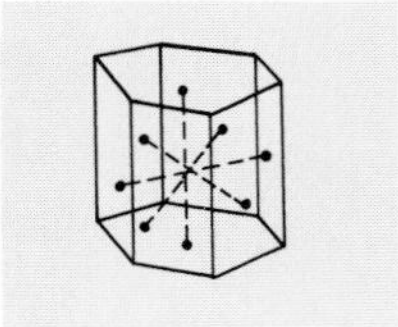		Corundum
Orthorhombic	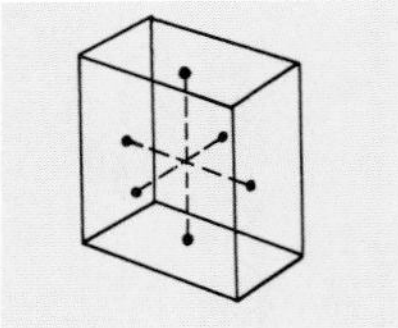		Sulfur
Monoclinic	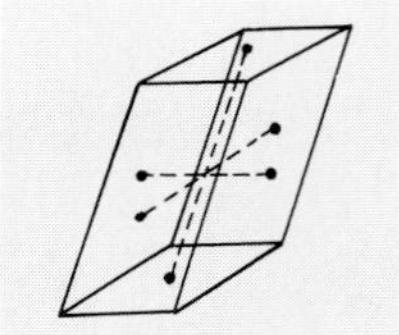		Crocoite
Tetragonal	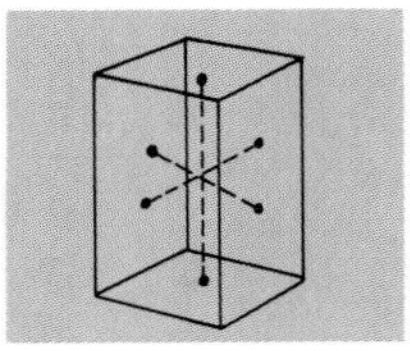		Anatase
Triclinic	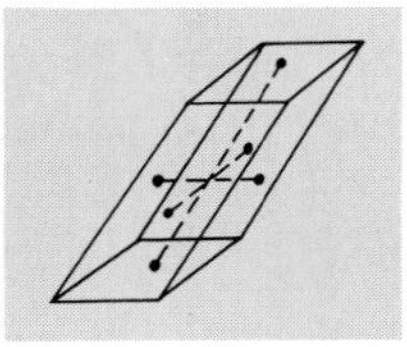	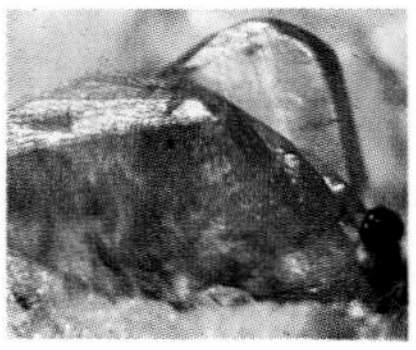	Kyanite

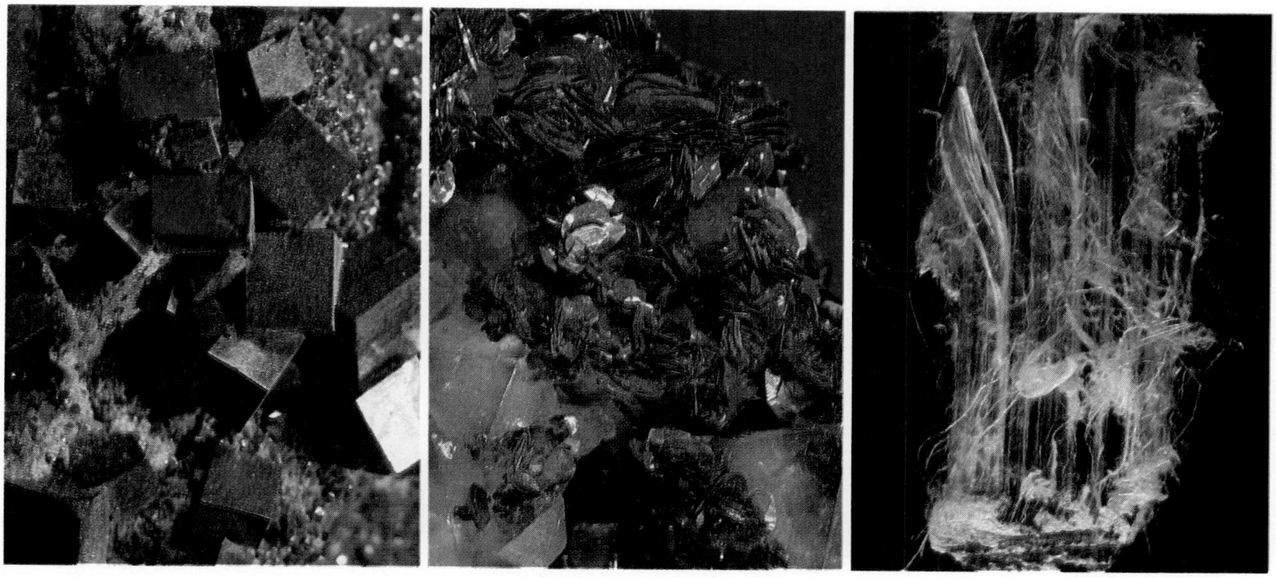

Figure 6–16 *Many minerals break into different shapes. Galena cleaves into cubes (left). Hematite cleaves into thin sheets (center). Asbestos fractures into fibers (right).*

systems and examples of each. You are probably familiar with the mineral halite, or table salt. The sodium and chlorine atoms that form halite crystals are arranged in the shape of a cube. Magnetite and garnet are also cubic crystals.

Cleavage and Fracture

The way a mineral breaks is called **cleavage** or **fracture.** When a mineral breaks along smooth, definite surfaces, cleavage occurs. Cleavage is a characteristic property of a mineral. Halite, for example, always cleaves in three directions. It breaks into small cubes. Mica cleaves along one surface, making layer after layer of very thin sheets.

When a mineral breaks unevenly, fracture occurs. The fracture surfaces are usually rough or jagged. Like cleavage, fracture is a property that helps identify a mineral. For example, quartz has a fracture that looks like a piece of broken glass. Asbestos fractures into fibers.

Special Properties

Some minerals can be identified by special properties. Magnetite, a mineral made of iron and oxygen, is naturally magnetic. Fluorite, made of calcium

Sharpen Your Skills

Crystal-System Models

1. With some straws, construct the six basic crystal systems. Use Figure 6–15 to help you.

2. Label the straw model of each system with a note card.

CHARACTERISTICS OF COMMON MINERALS

Mineral	Color	Luster/ Hardness	Specific Gravity/ Cleavage or Fracture	Uses
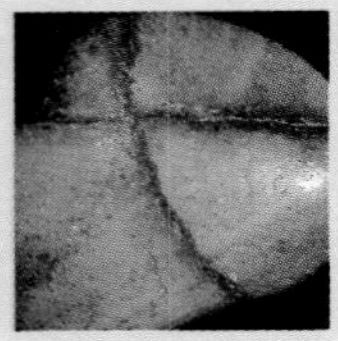 **Jade**	White or green or greyish green	Glassy to silky 6.5–7	3.3–3.5 Fracture	To make jewelry, vases, and figurines
 **Calcite**	White or colorless	Glassy 3	2.71 Perfect cleavage or fracture	In medicine and toothpaste; also found in marble and limestone, which are used as building material
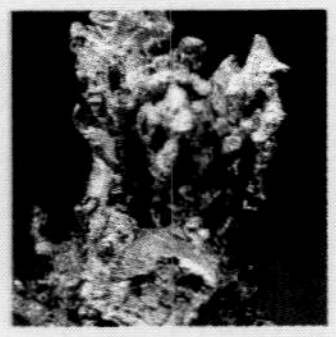 **Graphite**	Black to iron grey	Metallic 1	2.1 Perfect cleavage	In pencils and as a lubricant in machinery, clocks, and locks
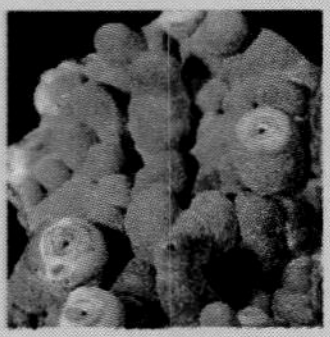 **Malachite**	Bright green	Silky 3.5–4	4 Perfect to fair cleavage or fracture	In jewelry and for table tops
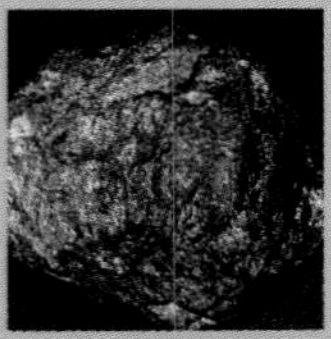 **Silver**	Silver white	Metallic 3	10.5 Fracture	In electrical equipment, photographic chemicals, and jewelry

Figure 6–17 *This table gives characteristics of some common minerals. Which mineral is almost 11 times denser than water? Which mineral is easily scratched with a fingernail?*

and fluorine, glows when put under ultraviolet light. Halite, common table salt, has a special taste. Sulfur has a distinct smell. Calcite fizzes when hydrochloric acid is added to it. And jade has a bell-like ring when tapped.

SECTION REVIEW

1. Describe the two types of mineral luster.
2. What is a mineral's streak?
3. What is a mineral's cleavage?
4. What physical properties can be used to identify a mineral?

6–3 Uses of Minerals

Section Objective

To relate mineral properties to their uses

Throughout history, people have used minerals. At first, minerals were used just as they came from the earth. Later, people learned to combine and process the earth's minerals. **Today many of the earth's minerals are used to meet the everyday needs of people.** Minerals are raw materials for a wide variety of products from dyes to dishes and from table salt to televisions.

Ores

Minerals from which metals and nonmetals can be removed in usable amounts are called **ores.** **Metals** are elements that have certain special properties. Metals have shiny surfaces and are able to conduct electricity and heat. Metals also have the property of **malleability** (mal-ee-uh-BIHL-uh-tee). Malleability is the ability of a substance to be hammered into thin sheets without breaking. Another property of metals is **ductility** (duhk-TIHL-uh-tee). Ductility is the ability of a substance to be pulled into thin strands without breaking. Iron, lead, aluminum, copper, silver, and gold are metals.

Most metals are found combined with other substances, or impurities, in ores. After the ores are removed from the earth by mining, the metals must be removed from the ores. During a process called smelting, the ore is heated in such a way that the metal can be separated from it. For example, iron can be obtained from the ores limonite and hematite. Lead can be processed from the ore galena. And aluminum comes from the ore bauxite.

Metals are very useful. Probably the most useful metal is iron, which is used in making steel. Lead is a metal used in pipes. Copper is a metal used in

Sharpen Your Skills

Mineral Deposits

1. From the library, find a map of the world. Draw or trace the map on a piece of paper. Label Africa, Asia, Europe, North America, South America, Australia, and Antarctica.

2. Find out where uranium, sulfur, aluminum, iron, halite, and gold deposits are located.

3. Using a symbol to represent each mineral, show the locations of these deposits on the map.

4. Make a key by writing the name of each mineral next to its symbol. Make your map colorful and descriptive.

Figure 6–18 *The mineral aluminum can be obtained from the ore bauxite.*

pipes, pennies, and electrical wire. Aluminum is a metal used in the production of cans, foil, lightweight motors, and airplanes. Silver and gold are metals used in fillings for teeth. Silver and gold are also used in decorative objects such as jewelry.

Nonmetals are minerals that are not shiny, are poor conductors of electricity and heat, and are not malleable or ductile. Sulfur, asbestos, and halite are nonmetals.

Some nonmetals are removed from the earth in usable form. Other nonmetals must be processed to separate them from the ores in which they are found. For example, halite can be found in large deposits in usable form. But asbestos must be separated from other minerals, such as serpentine.

Nonmetals are also useful. Sulfur is one of the most useful nonmetals. It is used to make matches, medicines, and fertilizers. It is also used in iron and steel production.

Gems

Some minerals are called **gems.** Gems are rare minerals. They are also beautiful and durable, or lasting. Not very many minerals have all of these qualities. The rarest and most valuable gems are called precious stones. Diamonds and emeralds are precious stones. Other gems are called semiprecious stones. Semiprecious stones are not as rare or valuable as precious stones. Amethysts, zircons, garnets, turquoises, and opals are semiprecious stones. They are all beautiful and durable. But they are more common than precious stones.

Sharpen Your Skills

Diamonds

From the library, gather information about diamonds. In a written report, answer the following questions:

1. Why are diamonds valuable?
2. In what countries are diamonds found?
3. How are diamonds cut to make jewels?
4. What are the major uses of diamonds?
5. How are synthetic diamonds made? What are they used for?

SOME CHARACTERISTICS OF GEMS

	Uncut	Cut	Color
Amethyst		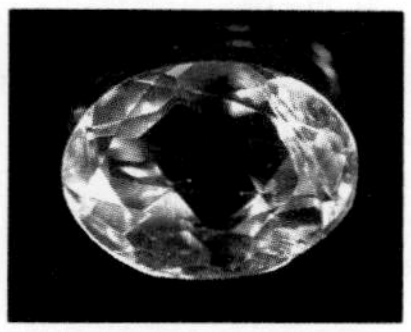	Purple, blue-violet
Aquamarine		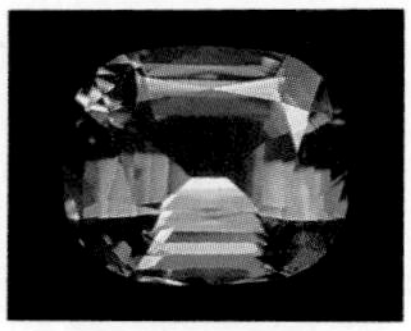	Blue-green, pale blue
Diamond			Yellow, brown, green, blue, violet, black, colorless
Emerald			Green
Ruby		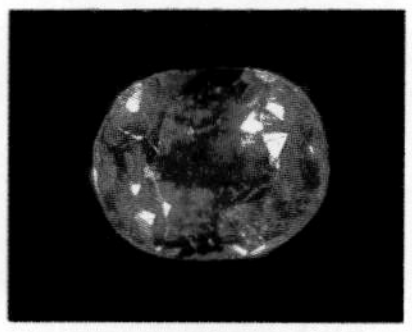	Red, blue-red
Topaz	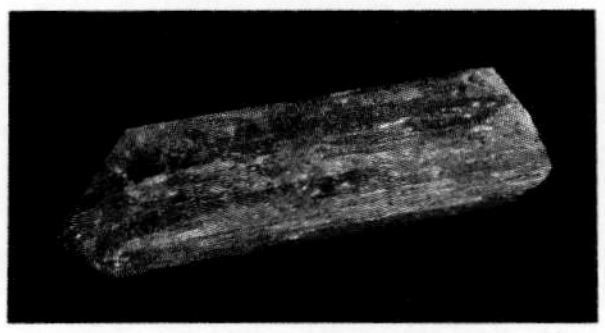		Yellow, brown, pale blue, pink, red, white
Tourmaline			Black, brown, pink, red, green, blue, colorless

Figure 6–19 *Very few minerals have the qualities that make them gems: beauty, rarity, and durability. Some gems in their uncut and cut forms are shown here.*

SECTION REVIEW

1. What is an ore?
2. What is malleability? Ductility?
3. What is a gem?
4. What are two common uses of minerals?

6 LABORATORY INVESTIGATION

Identifying Physical Properties of Minerals

Problem

Can minerals be identified using specific physical properties?

Materials *(per group)*

Streak plate
Paper towels
8 minerals: pyrite, galena, hematite, quartz, talc, graphite, hornblende, halite

Procedure

1. Draw a chart similar to the one on this page. Record the name of each mineral in your chart.
2. Examine each mineral and record its color.
3. Examine each mineral again. This time record its luster.
4. Rub each mineral across the streak plate. Observe the color of the streak. Be sure to wipe the streak plate clean before you test the next mineral. Record the color of each mineral's streak. Some minerals will scratch the streak plate. If a mineral scratches the plate, write "no streak" in the appropriate place in your chart.
5. Observe the mineral carefully. Are there any visible breaks in the sample? If so, record whether the break is a fracture or cleavage.

Observations

1. Which minerals have similar colors?
2. Which minerals have a metallic luster? A nonmetallic luster?
3. Which minerals have a streak unlike the color of the mineral?

Conclusions

1. Which physical property is the least helpful in identifying minerals?
2. Which physical property is the most helpful in identifying minerals?
3. Which physical properties are more helpful than others in identifying minerals?
4. What property or properties can you use to distinguish galena from graphite? Halite from talc?
5. Compare your observations with the data in the Mineral Identification Charts in Appendix E on pages 605–607.

Mineral	Color	Luster	Streak	Cleavage/ fracture

CHAPTER REVIEW

SUMMARY

6–1 What Is a Mineral?

❑ A mineral is a naturally occurring, inorganic solid that has a definite chemical composition and crystal shape.

❑ Almost all minerals come from magma, the hot liquid rock deep inside the earth. The rate of cooling of magma determines the size of the mineral crystals.

❑ When magma cools slowly beneath the earth's crust, large crystals form. When magma cools rapidly beneath the earth's crust, small crystals form.

❑ Crystals also form when a mineral that is dissolved in a liquid is left behind as the liquid evaporates.

❑ A geode is a rock with a hollow interior lined with mineral crystals.

❑ Most common minerals are made up of oxygen, silicon, aluminum, iron, calcium, sodium, potassium, and magnesium.

❑ Scientists group minerals according to their chemical composition.

6–2 Identifying Minerals

❑ The following physical properties are used to identify minerals: color, luster, hardness, streak, density, crystal shape, and cleavage and fracture.

❑ The luster of a mineral describes the way a mineral reflects light from its surface. Minerals have a metallic or nonmetallic luster.

❑ The ability of a mineral to resist being scratched is known as its hardness.

❑ The color of the powder left by a mineral when it is rubbed against a hard, rough surface is called its streak.

❑ Specific gravity is the ratio of the density of a mineral to the density of water.

❑ The shape of a crystal results from the way the atoms or molecules of a mineral come together as the mineral is forming.

❑ There are six basic shapes of crystals, or crystal systems.

❑ The way a mineral breaks is called cleavage or fracture.

6–3 Uses of Minerals

❑ Ores are minerals from which metals and nonmetals can be removed in usable amounts.

❑ The ability of a substance to be hammered into thin sheets without breaking is called malleability.

❑ The ability of a substance to be pulled into thin strands without breaking is called ductility.

❑ Metals and nonmetals are elements that have properties useful to people.

❑ Gems are rare minerals that are beautiful and durable.

VOCABULARY

Define each term in a complete sentence.

cleavage	**gem**	**magma**	**nonmetal**
crystal	**hardness**	**malleability**	**ore**
ductility	**inorganic**	**metal**	**streak**
fracture	**luster**	**mineral**	

CONTENT REVIEW: MULTIPLE CHOICE

Choose the letter of the answer that best completes each sentence.

1. Minerals are
a. solid b. found in the earth c. inorganic d. all of these

2. Hot liquid rock deep inside the earth is called
a. magma b. plasma c. plastic d. mantle

3. A rock that has a hollow interior lined with mineral crystals is called a (an)
a. ore b. gem c. geode d. nonmetal

4. The two most common elements in the earth's crust are
a. oxygen and silicon b. oxygen and nitrogen
c. sodium and iron d. aluminum and magnesium

5. The ability of a mineral to resist scratching is called
a. ductility b. malleability c. hardness d. durability

6. The softest mineral is
a. fluorite b. talc c. diamond d. calcite

7. The mass per unit volume of a mineral is called its
a. ductility b. malleability c. streak d. density

8. The breaking of a mineral along smooth, definite surfaces is called
a. cleavage b. fracture c. splintering d. none of these

9. The ability of a substance to be hammered into thin sheets is called
a. ductility b. malleability c. hardness d. durability

10. Elements that have shiny surfaces and are able to conduct electricity and heat are called
a. metals b. nonmetals c. ores d. geodes

CONTENT REVIEW: COMPLETION

Fill in the word or words that best complete each sentence.

1. A solid in which the atoms are arranged in a definite and repeating pattern is called a (an) ______________.

2. Hot liquid rock beneath the earth's surface is called ______________.

3. When magma cools slowly beneath the earth's crust, the size of the crystals formed is ______________.

4. Minerals that reflect light the way highly polished metal does have a (an) ______________ luster.

5. A commonly used scale that rates the hardness of minerals from 1 to 10 is called the ______________.

6. The color of the powder left by a mineral when it is rubbed against a hard surface is called its ______________.

7. The ratio of the mass of a mineral to the mass of an equal volume of water is called ______________.

8. Minerals from which metals and nonmetals can be removed in usable amounts are called ______________.

9. The ability of a substance to be pulled into thin strands without breaking is called ______________.

10. Gems such as diamonds and emeralds are called ______________.

CONTENT REVIEW: TRUE OR FALSE

Determine whether each statement is true or false. If it is true, write "true." If it is false, change the underlined word or words to make the statement true.

1. Substances not formed from living things or the remains of living things are called organic.
2. The repeating pattern of atoms in a solid forms a crystal.
3. Hot liquid rock is called plasma.
4. A mineral that comes from volcanoes and does not form crystals is obsidian.
5. The chemical properties of minerals are used to identify them.
6. The hardness of a mineral describes how the mineral reflects light from its surface.
7. The specific gravity of a mineral is a comparison of the density of the mineral with the density of water.
8. When a mineral breaks along smooth, definite surfaces, fracture occurs.
9. Minerals from which metals and nonmetals can be removed in usable amounts are called ores.
10. Minerals that are rare, beautiful, and durable are called nonmetals.

CONCEPT REVIEW: SKILL BUILDING

Use the skills you have developed in the chapter to complete each activity.

1. **Classifying** Across the top of a piece of paper, print the numbers 1 to 20. On the next line, separate the numbers into odd and even. Separate the odd numbers into one-digit and two-digit numbers. Do the same with the even numbers.

   Look carefully at the numbers you have written. Some numbers are made from only straight lines. Other numbers are made from only curved lines. Still others are made from both straight and curved lines. Classify each number in the one-digit and two-digit groups according to the following three headings: straight lines, curved lines, straight and curved lines.

   Explain how classification systems are useful in relating similar things.
2. **Applying concepts** Explain the following statement: You can determine the identity of a mineral by showing what it cannot be. Use specific properties of a mineral in your explanation.
3. **Drawing a conclusion** Charcoal, graphite, and diamonds are all made of carbon. Yet they are not considered types of the same mineral. Rubies, sapphires, and corundum are all made of aluminum oxide. They are considered types of the same mineral. Explain why this is so.

CONCEPT REVIEW: ESSAY

Discuss each of the following in a brief paragraph.

1. You are given two minerals that look exactly alike. One sample is gold. The other is pyrite. What tests might you use to tell the two minerals apart?
2. Why is specific gravity more useful than heft in describing the density of a mineral?
3. Which properties of a mineral can be tested without damaging the sample?
4. Describe what your life would be like without minerals.
5. Most minerals cannot be identified simply by their color. Explain.

Rocks

7

CHAPTER SECTIONS

7–1 Introduction to Rocks
7–2 Igneous Rocks
7–3 Sedimentary Rocks
7–4 Metamorphic Rocks

CHAPTER OBJECTIVES

After completing this chapter, you will be able to

7–1 Relate igneous, sedimentary, and metamorphic rocks to the rock cycle.

7–2 Describe the characteristics of igneous rocks.

7–2 Compare various types of igneous rock formations.

7–3 Classify various types of sedimentary rocks.

7–4 Define metamorphism.

7–4 List several types of metamorphic rocks.

Rocks are probably a familiar sight to you. You see them all around you in various shapes, sizes, and colors. But have you ever thought about what rocks are and about the many ways rocks are useful to people?

Prehistoric people used small pieces of rocks to make tools and weapons. Out of large rock formations, these people fashioned their homes. Since then, people have continued to use rocks for building.

Between 2700 and 2200 B.C., the early Egyptians removed blocks of rock from the earth to build temples and pyramids. The pyramids are some of the most famous rock structures ever built. In fact, they are one of the Seven Wonders of the World. Each of the millions of blocks had to be cut and shaped with small hand tools. Other civilizations used rocks to construct aqueducts, bridges, roads, buildings, and statues.

Today rocks are removed from stone quarries through the use of machines, tools, and explosives. And more advanced methods are used to cut and shape them. But rocks are still important to people for a variety of reasons. One important reason is that each rock has its own history. This history is full of action and change. As you read this chapter, you will learn what rocks are, how they are formed and changed over the centuries, and how they are important to you.

The Egyptian pyramid at Giza, built from millions of rocks, rises majestically behind another famous rock structure, the great Sphinx.

Section Objective

To classify rocks by their process of formation

7–1 Introduction to Rocks

There are many different types of rocks on the earth. Rocks are naturally occurring solid materials made of one or more minerals. Most of these minerals are composed of various combinations of eight elements. These elements are oxygen, silicon, aluminum, iron, calcium, sodium, potassium, and magnesium. They are the most abundant elements on the earth. Most rock-forming minerals are composed of these elements.

Scientists who study rocks and their mineral composition are called **petrologists** (pih-TRAHL-uh-jihsts). Petrologists have grouped rocks into three main types. **The general classification of rocks is based on the way the rocks were formed.**

Figure 7–1 *Devil's Postpile National Monument is a spectacular example of igneous rocks (bottom left). Layers of sedimentary rocks formed over millions of years are visible in the Grand Canyon (top). Changes in existing rocks produced these beds of metamorphic rocks (bottom right).*

Types of Rocks

One type of rock is formed from magma. Remember that magma is hot liquid rock that contains dissolved gases. Magma is formed deep in the lower part of the earth's crust and in the upper part of the mantle. Temperatures at these depths, about 60 to 200 kilometers beneath the earth's surface, are near 1400°C. Magma moves upward through the crust. It often rises to the earth's surface and flows out during volcanic eruptions. When magma cools and hardens, it forms **igneous** (IHG-nee-uhs) **rocks.** Igneous rocks are sometimes referred to as "fire-formed" rocks. In fact, the word *igneous* comes from the Latin word *igni,* meaning "coming from fire."

But there is no actual fire involved in the formation of igneous rocks. Tremendous heat produces magma, and the subsequent cooling and hardening of the magma produce igneous rocks.

Another type of rock is formed from **sediments** (SEHD-uh-muhnts). Sediments are small pieces of rocks, shells, or the remains of plants and animals that have been carried along and deposited by wind, water, and ice. Over millions of years, sediments have settled to the bottom of the ocean. Here the sediments have been pressed and cemented together to form **sedimentary** (sehd-uh-MEHN-tuhr-ee) **rocks.**

The third type of rock is formed as a result of changes that occur in existing rocks. Tremendous heat, great pressure, and chemical reactions change existing rocks into new rocks. These new rocks are called **metamorphic** (meht-uh-MOR-fihk) **rocks.** Using these descriptions, can you name some igneous, sedimentary, and metamorphic rocks?

The Rock Cycle

All igneous rocks on the earth began deep within the earth as magma. Some of the magma cooled and hardened beneath the earth's surface. Some of it reached the surface and cooled. Igneous rocks beneath or on the earth's surface are constantly subjected to physical and chemical conditions that change them. As a result of these changes, sedimentary rocks, metamorphic rocks, or new igneous rocks are formed. The continuous changing of rocks from one type to another is called the **rock cycle.** See Figure 7–2 on page 170.

For example, sediments are formed from the breaking down of igneous, sedimentary, and metamorphic rocks on the earth's surface. The sediments are then deposited in layers. In time, these layers of sediments form sedimentary rocks. When these rocks are broken down, they form sediments again.

Some igneous and sedimentary rocks are buried deep beneath the earth's surface. Great pressure and tremendous heat change these rocks into new rocks containing different minerals. These are metamorphic rocks. When metamorphic rocks are exposed at the earth's surface, they, too, will be broken down into sediments.

Sharpen Your Skills

Quarries

Many rocks are taken from the earth in large, solid blocks or in smaller pieces. Places from which large amounts of rocks are excavated are called quarries. Write a report about quarrying stone. In your report, include the answers to the following questions:

1. Where are some stone quarries in the United States?
2. What types of rocks are usually taken from quarries?
3. How are rocks removed from quarries?

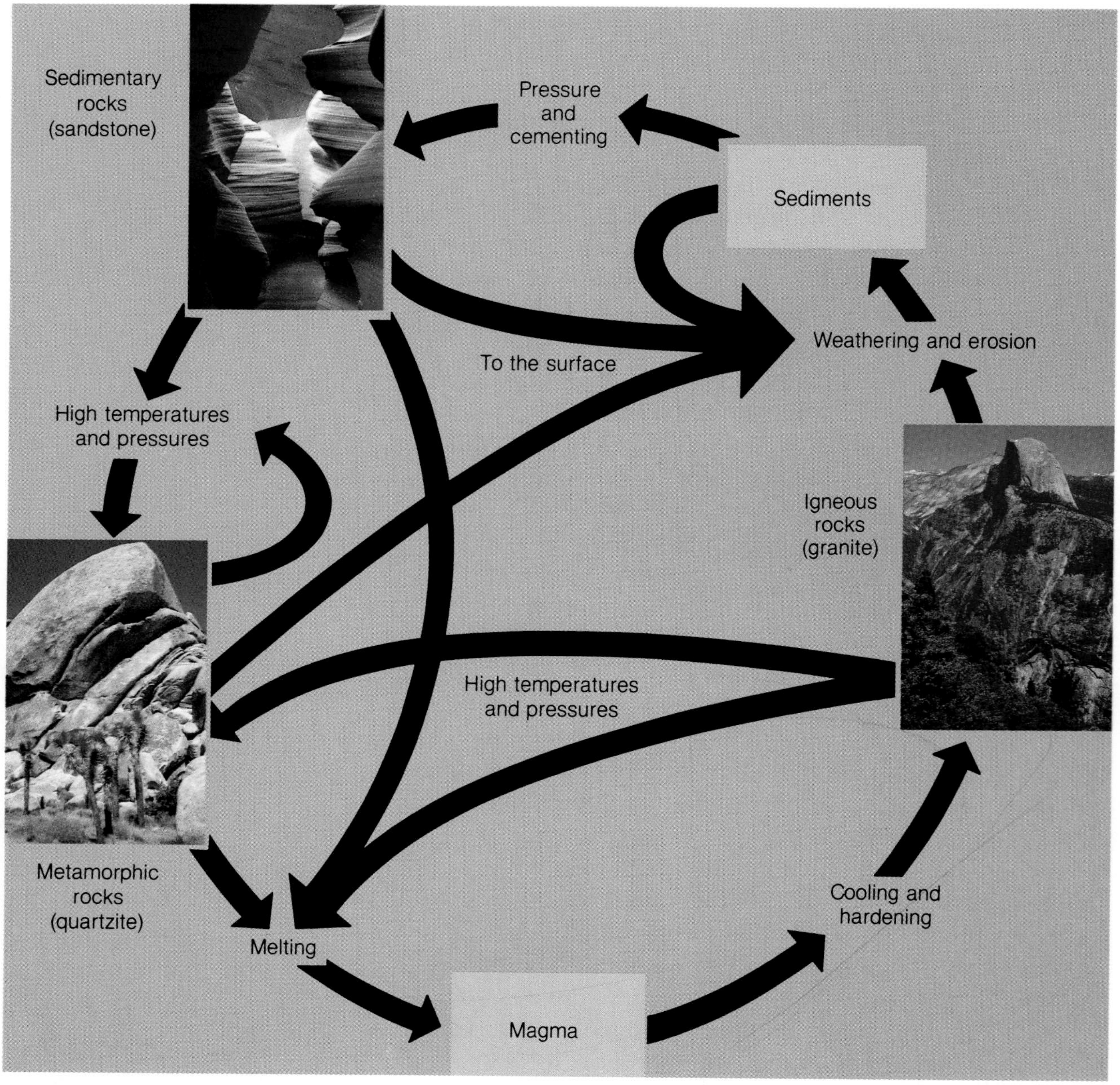

Figure 7–2 *This diagram of the rock cycle shows the many ways that rocks are changed. What changes sedimentary rocks to metamorphic rocks? How does magma form igneous rocks?*

Igneous, sedimentary, and metamorphic rocks may be buried so deep that great pressure and tremendous heat cause them to melt. Magma is formed. The magma rises and cools, forming igneous rocks. The rock cycle goes on and on. And although matter from the earth's crust is changed from one form to another, none of it is lost.

SECTION REVIEW

1. What are the three main types of rocks?
2. How are igneous rocks formed?
3. What is the rock cycle?

7–2 Igneous Rocks

Section Objective

To classify igneous rocks by texture and composition

There are two types of igneous rocks. These types are based on where magma cools and hardens to form the rocks. Igneous rocks formed deep within the earth are called **intrusive** (ihn-TROO-sihv) **rocks.** When magma reaches the surface, it is called lava. Lava is the liquid rock that pours out of volcanoes. Igneous rocks formed from lava at the earth's surface are called **extrusive** (ihk-STROOS-ihv) **rocks.** In what parts of the world would you be likely to find extrusive igneous rocks?

Igneous rocks form when the minerals in magma crystallize, or harden. So igneous rocks consist of tightly interlocking crystals that have a definite size and chemical composition. The size of the crystals in an igneous rock is called its texture. **Texture and chemical composition are the properties used to classify igneous rocks.**

The texture of an igneous rock depends on the time it takes the rock to harden. This time is called the rock's cooling rate. In general, the slower the cooling rate is, the larger the crystals will be. So intrusive rocks, which cool and harden slowly beneath the earth's surface, have large crystals. Igneous rocks made of large crystals are called coarse grained. Granite is an example of a coarse-grained igneous rock.

It is not uncommon for magma to cool extremely slowly. Some trapped magma takes nearly 100 years to cool only a few degrees. As a result, rocks may take thousands of years to form!

If the cooling rate is fast, small crystals will form. So extrusive rocks, which cool quickly at the earth's

Figure 7–3 *Granite, one of the most common coarse-grained igneous rocks, makes up these domes in Yosemite National Park, California (bottom left). These cliffs at Cape Horn, Washington, are made of basalt, the most common fine-grained igneous rock (bottom right). This obsidian dome is an example of an extrusive igneous rock that cools rapidly at the earth's surface (top).*

Figure 7–4 *These six minerals in various combinations make up most igneous rocks. Reading from left to right at the top are quartz, feldspar, and mica. At the bottom are olivine, amphibole, and pyroxene. Based on its color, what minerals is granite rich in? What minerals is basalt rich in?*

surface, have small crystals. Igneous rocks made of small crystals are called fine grained. Basalt is the most common fine-grained igneous rock. Sometimes magma that reaches the surface cools so quickly that crystals do not form. Obsidian, or volcanic glass, is a rock that cools quickly and does not form crystals.

The color of an igneous rock is often a good clue to its composition. Most igneous rocks are made of various combinations of six minerals. These minerals are quartz, feldspar, pyroxene, amphibole, olivine, and mica. See Figure 7–4. Light-colored igneous rocks, such as granite, are rich in quartz and feldspar. Dark-colored igneous rocks, such as basalt, are rich in pyroxene and olivine.

Common Igneous Rocks

One of the most common coarse-grained igneous rocks is granite. The continental crust of the earth is made of granite. Granite is composed mostly of the minerals quartz and feldspar. These minerals are light colored. So granite is light colored. But some granite has dark-colored minerals in it, usually dark mica and hornblende, a type of amphibole.

Other coarse-grained igneous rocks are not as common as granite. Diorite is a light-colored, coarse-grained igneous rock made of feldspars. Gabbro is a dark-colored, coarse-grained igneous rock. Gabbro is dark colored because it has no quartz in it. Peridotite is a very rare coarse-grained igneous rock made of the dark minerals pyroxene and olivine.

Sharpen Your Skills

Helpful Prefixes

Using a dictionary, look up the meanings of the prefixes *in-* and *ex-*. Explain how each prefix helps you to remember the difference between intrusive and extrusive rocks.

Figure 7–5 *Igneous rocks are often formed from hot molten lava that erupts from a volcano (left). Shiprock in New Mexico is the remains of the basaltic inner core of a volcano (right).*

The most common fine-grained igneous rock is basalt. Basalt is made of very small mineral grains that cannot be seen without a microscope. Basalt has the same mineral composition as gabbro. So basalt is a dark-colored igneous rock. Basalt can be found beneath all of the ocean floors. Many volcanic islands, such as Hawaii, Japan, and the Philippines in the Pacific Ocean, are made of basalt. Iceland and the Canary Islands in the Atlantic Ocean are also made of basalt. Two other fine-grained igneous rocks are rhyolite and andesite.

Some rocks begin to cool deep within the earth. So the resulting crystals grow large. Then suddenly the magma is carried up near the earth's surface. Here it cools rapidly, forming small crystals. The result is an igneous rock with large crystals surrounded by small crystals. An igneous rock whose cooling rate has changed and thus has two or more different-sized crystals is called a **porphyry** (POR-fuhr-ee). If the magma is carried to the earth's surface, cooling will occur very rapidly. The porphyry will contain large crystals surrounded by obsidian. Can you explain why obsidian forms?

Sometimes fine-grained igneous rocks form so quickly that gas is trapped in them. Scoria and pumice are formed this way. Scoria (SKOR-ee-uh) has a mineral composition similar to that of basalt, but it is more than 50 percent holes! Pumice (PUHM-ihs) is

Figure 7–6 *The igneous rock porphyry has large crystals surrounded by small crystals (top). The igneous rock scoria cools so quickly that gas is trapped in it, producing hundreds of holes (bottom).*

Figure 7–7 *This table shows the characteristics of some common igneous rocks. Which dark-colored rock cools quickly at the earth's surface? Which light-colored rock contains no crystals?*

IGNEOUS ROCKS

	Intrusive *Coarse grained*	**Extrusive** *Fine grained*
Light colored	Granite Diorite	Rhyolite Andesite Pumice
Dark colored	Gabbro Peridotite	Basalt Obsidian

a natural glass with many holes. It cools so quickly that no visible crystals are formed. Often pumice is so light that it floats in water.

Igneous Rock Formations

Magma does not always flow out onto the earth's surface. Sometimes it flows upward into cracks in rocks or spreads out between rock layers beneath the earth's surface. There it hardens, forming irregular formations of intrusive rock. These formations, called **intrusions,** harden into many different shapes depending on the magma's position when it cools. Intrusions are classified according to their size and their relationship to the older rocks surrounding them. See Figure 7–8.

Figure 7–8 *The different types of intrusive rock formations are shown in this diagram. How are batholiths and dikes different from laccoliths and sills?*

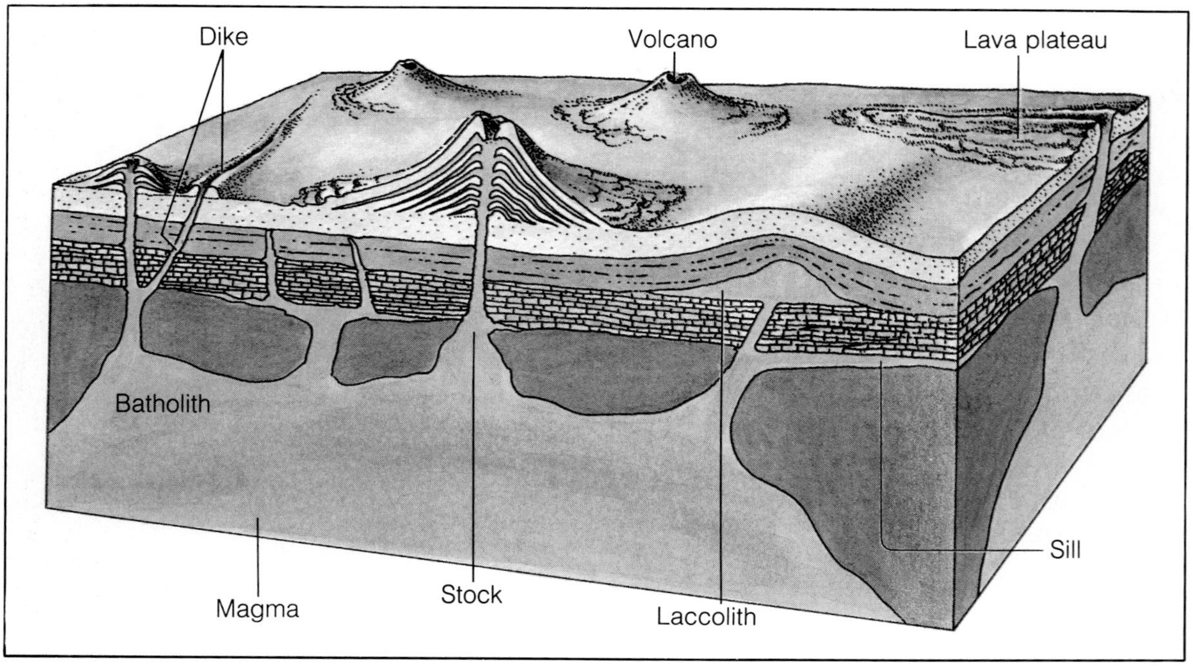

CAREER

Stonemason

HELP WANTED: STONEMASON For apprenticeship position. No experience needed. Learn how to read blueprints and work with different kinds of stone in outdoor settings.

People who work with stone are called **stonemasons.** Stonemasons cut stones, set them in place, align them, and smooth the surfaces. This work requires a great deal of skill and years of experience.

People who wish to learn stonemasonry usually begin as apprentices, or helpers. Apprentices learn as they work. At the same time, they take classes in subjects such as blueprint reading and layout work. They learn about different types of stone and the uses for each type.

Two closely related trades are bricklaying and marble setting. People in these trades complete the same apprenticeship as stonemasons. Bricklayers build walls, fireplaces, and other structures with brick and masonry materials such as cinder block. Marble setters install marble floors and walls.

To learn more about this career, write to the Associated General Contractors of America, Inc., 1957 E Street, NW, Washington, DC 20006.

An intrusive rock formation whose exposed surface is more than 100 square kilometers in area is called a **batholith** (BATH-uh-lihth). A batholith is a huge, irregularly shaped intrusion that extends deep into the earth's crust. Scientists estimate that batholiths extend between 10 and 30 kilometers into the crust. If an intrusion similar to a batholith has an exposed area less than 100 square kilometers, it is called a **stock.**

As you can see from Figure 7–8, batholiths form deep beneath the earth's surface. How do they become exposed? Sometimes movements of the earth push batholiths above the earth's surface. As the overlying rocks are worn away, the batholiths are exposed, looking like large, steep hills.

Most batholiths are granite formations. They form the cores of many of the world's great mountain systems. More than 40,000 square kilometers of the Sierra Nevada range in California is covered by batholiths.

Sometimes magma pushes its way between layers of sedimentary rocks. The magma pushes the overlying rocks up into an arch. The floor of the arch is flat and is parallel to the sedimentary rock layer it

Sharpen Your Skills

Batholith or Stock

Suppose an intrusion has an exposed surface 8 kilometers long and 6 kilometers wide. What is its surface area? Would this intrusion be a batholith or a stock?

Figure 7–9 *A laccolith, such as this one located on the Oregon Trail in central Wyoming, is an intrusive rock formation (left). A sill is another intrusive rock formation. This sill has intruded between sedimentary rock layers in Big Bend National Park, Texas (right). How do you think intrusions become exposed?*

rests on. This domelike intrusion of igneous rock is called a **laccolith** (LAK-uh-lihth).

Magma that pushes its way between layers of sedimentary rocks but does not cause the overlying rocks to arch forms a **sill.** A sill is a sheetlike mass of igneous rock. The Palisades rock formation along the Hudson River bordering New York and New Jersey is a good example of a sill. It is 80 kilometers long and 305 meters thick. You can see another example of a sill in Figure 7–9.

A **dike** is a narrow, flat formation of igneous rock formed in vertical cracks in the existing rocks. A dike is made of hardened magma that has cut across other rock layers.

Sometimes magma flows to the earth's surface to become lava. The lava hardens to form igneous rock formations called **extrusions.** Lava may spread out over a flat area and harden into sheets. The sheets often build up, forming an extrusion called a **lava plateau.** The Columbia Plateau in the northwestern United States is a lava plateau.

Sharpen Your Skills

Model Intrusion

Using papier-mâché, tempera paint, markers, a hardwood base, and any other materials necessary, make a model of an igneous rock intrusion. Use Figure 7–8 to help you make your model.

SECTION REVIEW

1. What are intrusive igneous rocks? Extrusive igneous rocks?
2. How are coarse-grained and fine-grained igneous rocks formed?
3. What are some common igneous rocks?
4. What are some igneous rock intrusions? Extrusions?

7–3 Sedimentary Rocks

Section Objective

To classify sedimentary rocks

The rocks in the limestone cliffs in Figure 7–10 appear to be stacked very neatly, almost like pancakes. One layer is piled on top of another. The layers are almost as straight as if they had been drawn using a ruler. Layered rocks such as these are called sedimentary rocks.

Seventy-five percent of the rocks on the earth's surface are sedimentary rocks. Mud, sand, and gravel are some of the sediments that make up these rocks. Mud is made of tiny fragments of clay minerals. Sand is made of somewhat larger grains of quartz and other minerals. Gravel is made of even larger pieces of broken rocks. Other sediments are formed from the shells of dead sea creatures. When these creatures die, their remains settle to the sea floor. Still other sediments are formed when water evaporates and leaves behind mineral deposits.

Sediments are moved by wind and water. The faster wind and water move, the larger the particles they can carry with them. Flooded rivers move very fast. They can carry even large boulders. Sand and gravel are moved on and off beaches during major storms, such as hurricanes. Dry sand is piled on beaches during windstorms.

Slow-moving wind and water can carry only small grains. A fast-moving river that slows down

Figure 7–10 *These cliff layers in New Zealand, which look like piles of pancakes, are sedimentary rocks. What main characteristic of sedimentary rocks can be seen in these cliffs?*

Sharpen Your Skills

Sedimentation

1. In a 500-mL jar, put one layer each of garden soil, potting soil, coarse-grained sand, fine-grained sand, coarse gravel, and fine gravel. Each layer should be 2 cm deep.

2. Add enough water to fill the jar three-fourths full. Cap the jar and shake vigorously for two to three minutes.

3. Carefully observe the various sediments as they settle out of the water. Which sediments settle out first? Which sediments settle out last?

4. After all of the sediments have settled out, record in a chart the order in which they settled.

Write a short paragraph explaining your observations. What can you tell about the way layers are formed in sedimentary rocks?

will usually deposit the larger particles it is carrying. Mountain streams often leave gravel deposits when they reach flat ground. Why do you think a mountain stream leaves these sediments on flat ground?

Some sediments are carried into lakes and oceans. Sediments carried out into deep water settle slowly to the bottom. They make the water appear muddy and brown. The smallest grains, such as clay particles, can remain suspended in standing water for a long time. These particles take the longest time to settle to the bottom. Any movement of the water will move these particles. How can you tell if water has been still for a long time?

Over millions of years, mud, sand, gravel, bones, and shells settle to the sea floor as sediments. The sediments pile up in layers many hundreds of meters thick. Lower layers are pressed together more and more tightly under the weight of the layers above. The pressure on the lower sediments changes them into rocks. This process is called **compaction** (kuhm-PAK-shuhn). Some sediments are joined together, or cemented, by minerals dissolved in water. This process is called **cementation** (see-mehn-TAY-shuhn). The result of these processes is the formation of layers of sedimentary rocks called **strata** (STRAYT-uh). The major characteristic of all sedimentary rocks is that they form layers.

Figure 7–11 *Fossils, which are the remains or traces of past plant and animal life preserved in rock, are often found in sedimentary rocks. Can you identify this fossil?*

Sedimentary rocks are usually formed in water. Most of the earth has been covered by water at some time in the past. Seventy percent of the earth is covered by water now. So sedimentary rocks are common all over the world. Sedimentary rocks are often rich in fossils. Fossils are the remains or traces of past plant and animal life that have been preserved in rock. Why do you think sedimentary rocks contain many more fossils than igneous rocks do?

Sedimentary rocks are classified according to their composition and texture, or grain size. These properties provide clues to where the sediments came from and how the rocks were formed. Sedimentary rocks are grouped into three main types.

Sharpen Your Skills

A Rock Walk

Write a 500-word essay describing a walk through a rocky area. Make sure you use the following terms: igneous rock, sedimentary rock, metamorphic rock.

Clastic Rocks

One type of sedimentary rock is clastic (KLAS-tihk) rock. Clastic rocks are formed from broken pieces, or fragments, of rocks. Clastic sedimentary rocks are classified according to the size and shape of the fragments in them.

Some clastic rocks are made of rounded pebbles and other rocks of different sizes cemented together by clay, mud, and sand. These rocks are called conglomerates (kuhn-GLAHM-uhr-ihts). Conglomerates form where rivers slow down enough to deposit large pieces of rock. And they form where waves break apart rocks on cliffs and deposit the fragments. The pieces of rock are rounded by the water before they are deposited. Conglomerates are not as common as rocks made of smaller pieces because moving water tends to break large pieces into smaller pieces. You can see from Figure 7–12 why conglomerates were once called "puddingstones."

The clastic rock called breccia (BREHCH-ee-uh) is similar to conglomerate. But its fragments are sharp and angular rather than rounded. The fragments have not been carried far enough by water to have their edges rounded.

Clastic rocks made of small, sand-sized grains are called sandstones. Sandstones are very common rocks. They are formed from the sand on beaches, in riverbeds, and in sand dunes. In sandstones, the sand grains are cemented together by minerals. The minerals harden in the small spaces, or pores, between the grains.

Figure 7–12 *Sedimentary rocks called conglomerates are made of rock particles of different sizes, as well as sand and mud.*

Figure 7–13 *The unusual sandstone formations in Bryce Canyon, Utah, were formed from cliffs made of layers of red sedimentary rocks. The red color is caused by traces of iron.*

Sandstones are usually made of the mineral quartz. Other minerals, such as zircon, garnet, and rutile, are found in sandstones. But they occur in very small amounts. Sandstone is very resistant to wear and decay. It is used as a building stone.

Sandstones can be formed from windblown sand in deserts. The Sahara, Gobi, and Arabian deserts have large sandstone formations that were once sand dunes. Sandstones also form on the beaches of the Mid-Atlantic Coast and the Texas Gulf Coast. How do you think sand dunes change to rock?

Figure 7–14 *This large deposit of shale is made of small particles of clay and mud that have hardened into layers.*

Clastic rocks formed from small particles of clay minerals are called mudrocks. Mudrocks are formed when clay particles are carried by water or wind. When the water or wind stops moving, the clay particles are deposited. Clay particles are flat and can be easily pressed together. Shale is an example of a mudrock. Most shale can be split into flat pieces.

Shale forms in quiet waters such as swamps and bogs. Here the small particles of clay and mud settle and get pressed together. Shale often contains mica flakes, which give the rock surface a smooth, slippery feel.

Another type of mudrock is siltstone. Siltstone is similar to sandstone, but it has much smaller grains. Siltstone contains large quantities of clay.

Organic Rocks

Another type of sedimentary rock is organic rock. Organic rocks are formed either directly or indirectly from material that was once living. Limestones are organic rocks. Limestones are made mostly of calcium carbonate, also known as calcite.

Many animals, such as clams and oysters, grow shells made of calcium carbonate. When the animals die, their shells sink to the ocean floor. At some point, these shells form limestones. Sometimes an entire large shell is found in a limestone rock. But most of the time, the ocean breaks these shells into smaller fragments.

Some simple plants that live in the ocean grow very small crystals of calcium carbonate and form tiny shells. When these plants die, they fall to the ocean floor. The crystals and the plant remains become part of the mud at the bottom of the ocean. Animals such as sea worms eat this mud to get at the plant remains. The crystals are passed out of their bodies as pellets. These pellets are the size of grains of sand and are very common in limestones.

Sometimes many animals with calcium carbonate shells live together. They cement their shells together and over time form large structures called reefs. Corals build limestone reefs off the coast of Florida and around many of the Caribbean and Pacific islands. Oysters build limestone reefs along the Texas Gulf Coast.

Chalk is another organic sedimentary rock. It is a type of limestone composed of small pieces of animal shells and crystals of calcium carbonate that have been pressed together. Unlike other limestones, chalk is soft. Many large chalk deposits were formed millions of years ago.

Coal is another rock that is formed from the remains of living things. It is made from plants such as ferns that lived millions of years ago. When these plants died, their remains began to build up in swamps. As more and more layers of decaying plants built up, pressure changed the layers on the

Sharpen Your Skills

Coral Conversions

The largest coral reef is the Great Barrier Reef, which parallels the northeastern coast of Australia for a distance of about 2000 kilometers. How many meters long is the Coral Reef? How many centimeters? Compare this distance to the distance across the United States, which is 4517 km from east to west.

Figure 7–15 *Coquina is a limestone that contains remains of once-living things. What remains of living things can you find?*

Figure 7–16 *As the water in Mono Lake, California, evaporates, it leaves behind large evaporite formations. Why do you think there is a high concentration of minerals in the lake?*

bottom into coal. The layers above these may be only partly changed into coal. These layers are called peat.

Chemical Rocks

A third type of sedimentary rock is chemical rock. Chemical rocks are formed by chemical means that do not involve any living organisms.

Some chemical rocks are formed when water evaporates and leaves behind mineral deposits. The rocks formed this way are called **evaporites** (ih-VAP-uh-rights). Rock salt and gypsum are evaporites. Large deposits of rock salt and deposits of gypsum can be found in New York, Michigan, and Kansas. Often thick layers of rock salt and gypsum are deposited between layers of shale and limestone.

Some limestone rocks are formed directly from ocean water rather than by living organisms. Chemical changes in ocean water cause grains of calcium carbonate to form. They begin as small grains and get larger as thin layers of calcium carbonate are added from the ocean water. So these limestones are chemical rocks rather than organic rocks.

Sharpen Your Skills

Famous Rock Formations

Using reference materials in the library, look up the following rock formations:

Giant's Causeway
Stone Mountain
Rock of Gibraltar
Garden of the Gods

Write a brief report about each rock formation. Include the answers to the following questions:

1. Where is the rock formation located?
2. What type of rock is the formation composed of?
3. How was the rock formation made?

Sedimentary Rock Structures

Sedimentary rocks have certain features that help to identify them. For example, many sedimentary rocks have visible layers. Even after the sediments that formed the rocks have hardened, the different

Figure 7–17 *Sedimentary rocks are often identified by the features they contain, such as fossils (left), ripple marks (center), and mud cracks (right).*

layers can still be seen. Also, sedimentary rocks often contain fossils.

Ripple marks and mud cracks are other common features of sedimentary rocks. Ripple marks, which look like small waves in the rocks, are formed by water or wind currents moving over loose sediments. Mud cracks are formed on the surface of wet mud as it dries. If ripple marks and mud cracks remain intact as they get buried under new layers of sediments, they may be preserved in the rocks.

Figure 7–18 *This table shows the characteristics of some common sedimentary rocks. Which clastic rock is made of very fine grains of mostly quartz with some clay? Which chemical rock is made of cubic crystals of halite?*

SEDIMENTARY ROCKS

Rock	Texture	Composition
Clastic		
Conglomerate	round pebbles	pebbles, cobbles, boulders cemented by sand and clay
Breccia	angular fragments	
Sandstone	sand-sized grains	quartz
Siltstone	very fine grains	mostly quartz, some clay
Shale	microscopic grains and flakes	mostly clay, some mica
Organic		
Limestone	coarse to microscopic crystals	calcite from animal remains
Chalk	seashells	calcite
Chemical		
Rock salt	cubic crystals	halite
Gypsum	microscopic to coarse crystals	gypsum

SECTION REVIEW

1. How are sedimentary rocks formed?
2. What are the three types of sedimentary rocks?
3. What features help to identify sedimentary rocks?

Section Objective

To relate metamorphism to its effects on rock

7–4 Metamorphic Rocks

Rocks that have been changed from an existing type of rock into a new type are called metamorphic rocks. Metamorphic rocks can be formed from igneous rocks, sedimentary rocks, and other metamorphic rocks. Most metamorphic rocks are formed deep beneath the earth's surface.

The Metamorphic Process

When already existing rocks are buried deep within the earth, tremendous heat, great pressure, and chemical reactions cause them to change into different rocks with different textures and structures. The changing of one type of rock into another as a result of tremendous heat, great pressure, and chemical reactions is called **metamorphism** (meht-uh-MOR-fihz-uhm).

Figure 7–19 *Heat, pressure, and chemical reactions change existing igneous, sedimentary, and metamorphic rocks into metamorphic rocks with different textures and structures. What is this process called?*

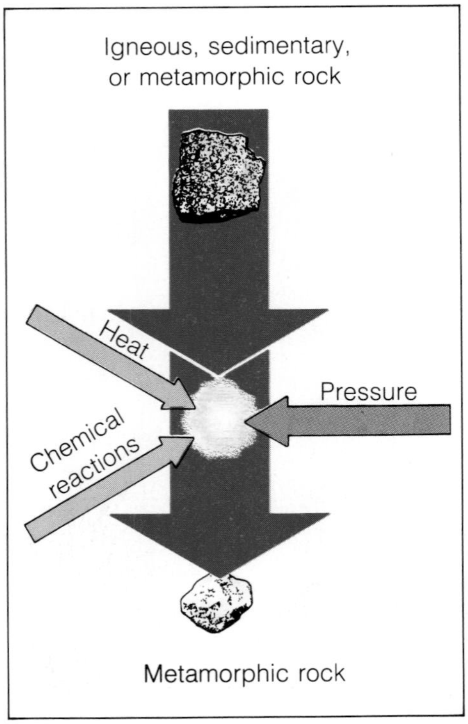

Metamorphic rocks begin to form at depths of 12 to 16 kilometers beneath the earth's surface and at temperatures of 100°C to 200°C. They continue to form at temperatures up to 800°C. Between 100°C and 800°C, the heat makes the rock soft enough for the minerals within it to undergo change. The mineral crystals may change their size or shape. Or they may separate into layers. The great pressure these rocks are under tends to squeeze the mineral crystals together, forming minerals that are denser. Chemical reactions involving the minerals may also occur. As a result, major changes in the rock's composition take place.

The amount of heat, pressure, and chemical reactions varies during metamorphism. Because of this, the degree of metamorphism also varies. If the change in a rock is slight, the original rock can be identified in the new rock. If the change in a rock is great, it may be difficult to tell what the original rock was. The characteristics of the original rock also affect the degree of metamorphism. For example, fine-grained rocks are more easily changed than coarse-grained rocks.

Types of Metamorphism

There are two basic types of metamorphism. The first type is called **contact metamorphism.** Contact metamorphism occurs when rocks are heated by contact with magma or lava. So the effects of contact metamorphism are usually seen only along the edges of igneous rock formations. Existing rocks are changed by the heat, chemicals, and gases released by magma. Sometimes contact metamorphism occurs on the earth's surface as lava flows over the rocks.

The second type of metamorphism is called **regional metamorphism.** Regional metamorphism occurs over large areas when rocks buried deep beneath the earth's surface are changed by increases in temperature and pressure.

Types of Metamorphic Rocks

There are two basic textures of metamorphic rock. Metamorphic rocks with a **foliated** (FOH-lee-ay-tuhd) texture have mineral crystals arranged in parallel layers, or bands. These rocks tend to break along these bands.

Sharpen Your Skills

Too Hot to Handle

Metamorphic rocks form at temperatures as high as 800°C. How many times greater than the boiling point of water, which is 100°C, is this?

Figure 7–20 *The sedimentary rock shale can be changed by heat and pressure into the metamorphic rock slate. What type of texture does slate have?*

Figure 7–21 *The igneous rock granite can be changed by heat and pressure into the metamorphic rock gneiss. How can you tell that gneiss is foliated?*

Foliated rocks form when the mineral crystals in the original rock recrystallize or flatten under pressure. Foliation also takes place when minerals of different densities separate into different layers. In fact, this separation gives many foliated rocks their series of alternating dark and light bands.

A common fine-grained metamorphic rock with a foliated texture is slate. Slate is made from clay or from the sedimentary rock shale. Slate is used today to make flagstones for paths. It was once used to make chalkboards. Because slate is black, these chalkboards were called blackboards. Today chalkboards are not made of slate.

A common medium- to coarse-grained metamorphic rock with a foliated texture is schist (SHIHST).

Figure 7–22 *The sedimentary rock sandstone can be changed by heat and pressure into the metamorphic rock quartzite. What differences can you see between the two rocks?*

METAMORPHIC ROCKS

Rock	Texture	Rock Origin
Foliated		
Slate	fine (microscopic)	shale—sedimentary rock
Schist	medium to coarse	slate—metamorphic rock basalt—igneous rock granite—igneous rock
Gneiss	coarse	granite—igneous rock
Unfoliated		
Quartzite	medium	sandstone—sedimentary rock
Marble	coarse	limestone—sedimentary rock

Figure 7–23 *This table shows the characteristics of some common metamorphic rocks. Which unfoliated rock is formed from limestone? From what rocks does schist form?*

The minerals in schist are visible to the unaided eye. They appear to overlap. Mica is a mineral often found in schist. Schists can form from a number of different rocks, including granite, basalt, and slate.

A common coarse-grained metamorphic rock is gneiss (NIGHS). Gneiss is made from the igneous rock granite and is usually the result of regional metamorphism. The dark and light minerals in gneiss are arranged in alternating bands.

Metamorphic rocks with an **unfoliated** texture do not have bands of crystals and do not break in layers. Two metamorphic rocks with unfoliated textures are quartzite (KWORT-sight) and marble. Quartzite is formed from sandstone, a sedimentary rock made mostly of quartz. During metamorphism, quartz grains change in size and shape. Marble is formed from limestone. Grains of limestone also change in size and shape during metamorphism.

SECTION REVIEW

1. Under what conditions do metamorphic rocks form?
2. What is the difference between contact metamorphism and regional metamorphism?
3. Suppose you find a metamorphic rock that breaks in layers. Predict how this rock formed.

Sharpen Your Skills

Rock Samples

1. Start a rock collection. To obtain a good sampling, try to collect rocks from several different locations. Note where you found each specimen.
2. Bring your rock collection to class. Using reference materials, identify each rock.
3. Tape each rock to a labeled note card or label the rock directly. Indicate the type of rock, its name, and the location in which it was found.
4. Organize your rock specimens according to the various classifications you have learned about in this chapter.

7 LABORATORY INVESTIGATION

Compaction of Clay

Problem

What effect does time have on the compaction of clay?

Materials *(per group)*

500-mL jar with a lid
Grease pencil
Metric ruler
Water
Small block of modeling clay
Salt

Procedure

1. Add 350 mL of water to the jar. Break the clay into small pieces and put the pieces in the jar.
2. Cover the jar and shake the mixture. Observe how long it takes for the clay to mix with the water. Record this observation on your data sheet.
3. Place the jar on a flat surface. Let the clay settle out of the water until you can see a line where the clear water and the clay meet. This is the clay-water interface. If the clay takes a long time to settle, add some salt to speed the settling of the clay.
4. When the clay has settled out, mark the clay-water interface on the jar with a grease pencil. Measure the height of the settled clay to the nearest millimeter. Record this value on your data sheet.
5. Tilt the jar once. Observe what happens at the clay-water interface.
6. Let the jar stand overnight. After 24 hours, mark the clay-water interface. Measure the height of the clay. Record your results.

Observations

1. When the jar was tilted, did any clay mix with the water?
2. After 24 hours, what happened to the height of the clay?

Conclusions

1. What effect does time have on the compaction of clay? Predict what you would observe if you measured the clay compaction after 1 week.
2. Suppose you had shaken the jar one time. Would most of the clay have mixed with the water? How hard would you have had to shake the jar to get all of the clay to mix with the water?
3. How does this investigation relate to the compaction of sediments and the formation of sedimentary rocks?

CHAPTER REVIEW

SUMMARY

7–1 Introduction to Rocks

- Rocks are naturally occurring solid materials made of one or more minerals.
- Igneous rocks are formed when magma cools and hardens.
- Sedimentary rocks are small pieces of rocks, shells, or the remains of plants and animals pressed and cemented together.
- Tremendous heat, great pressure, and chemical reactions change existing rocks into metamorphic rocks.
- The continuous changing of rocks from one type to another is called the rock cycle.

7–2 Igneous Rocks

- Igneous rocks formed deep in the earth are called intrusive rocks. They have large crystals.
- Igneous rocks formed from lava at the earth's surface are called extrusive rocks. They have small crystals.
- Igneous rocks are classified by texture and chemical composition.
- Intrusions are rock formations formed when magma flows upward into cracks in rocks or spreads out between rock layers beneath the earth's surface. Intrusions include batholiths, laccoliths, sills, dikes, and stocks.
- Extrusions are formed when lava flows onto the earth's surface and hardens. A lava plateau is an example of an extrusion.

7–3 Sedimentary Rocks

- Seventy-five percent of the rocks on the earth's surface are sedimentary rocks.
- All sedimentary rocks form layers.
- The three types of sedimentary rocks are clastic rocks, organic rocks, and chemical rocks.

7–4 Metamorphic Rocks

- Rocks that have been changed from an existing type of rock into a new type of rock are called metamorphic rocks.
- The changing of one type of rock into another type as a result of tremendous heat, great pressure, and chemical reactions is called metamorphism.
- Metamorphic rocks have two basic textures: foliated and unfoliated.

VOCABULARY

Define each term in a complete sentence.

batholith
cementation
compaction
contact metamorphism
dike
evaporite
extrusion
extrusive rock
foliated
igneous rock
intrusion
intrusive rock
laccolith
lava plateau
metamorphic rock
metamorphism
petrologist
porphyry
regional metamorphism
rock cycle
sediment
sedimentary rock
sill
stock
strata
unfoliated

CONTENT REVIEW: MULTIPLE CHOICE

Choose the letter of the answer that best completes each sentence.

1. The classification of rocks into three main types is based on the rocks'
a. formation b. color c. surface area d. size

2. Rocks formed by cooling magma are called
a. sedimentary b. metamorphic c. igneous d. foliated

3. Rocks formed from sediments pressed and cemented together are called
a. igneous b. sedimentary c. porphyry d. metamorphic

4. Rocks formed as a result of changes in existing rocks are called
a. sedimentary b. metamorphic c. igneous d. foliated

5. The continuous changing of rocks from one type to another is called the
a. erosion cycle b. intrusion cycle
c. metamorphic cycle d. rock cycle

6. The most common fine-grained igneous rock is
a. basalt b. granite c. diorite d. peridotite

7. An igneous rock that has two or more different-sized crystals because of changes in cooling rate is called a (an)
a. geode b. intrusion c. porphyry d. sill

8. A huge, irregularly shaped intrusion that extends deep into the earth's crust is called a
a. stock b. laccolith c. dike d. batholith

9. An example of an organic rock is
a. shale b. limestone c. gypsum d. schist

10. Metamorphic rocks with mineral crystals arranged in parallel layers, or bands, are called
a. intrusive b. organic c. foliated d. unfoliated

CONTENT REVIEW: COMPLETION

Fill in the word or words that best complete each sentence.

1. Scientists who specialize in the study of rocks are called ________________.

2. Igneous rocks formed from lava at the earth's surface are called ________________ rocks.

3. An igneous rock that has two or more different-sized crystals because its cooling rate has changed is called a (an) ________________.

4. The process by which sediments are changed into rock by pressure on the lower layers is called ________________.

5. Sedimentary rocks formed either directly or indirectly from material that was once living are called ________________.

6. Sedimentary rocks formed by chemical means that do not involve any living organisms are called ________________.

7. Visible layers, fossils, ripple marks, and ________________ are features often found in sedimentary rocks.

8. The changing of one type of rock into another as a result of tremendous heat, great pressure, and chemical change is called ________________.

9. A metamorphic rock that does not have bands of crystals and does not break in layers has a (an) ________________ texture.

10. The metamorphic rock formed from limestone is ________________.

CONTENT REVIEW: TRUE OR FALSE

Determine whether each statement is true or false. If it is true, write "true." If it is false, change the underlined word or words to make the statement true.

1. Igneous rocks formed deep within the earth are called intrusive rocks.
2. Igneous rocks that cool quickly at the earth's surface have large crystals.
3. Seventy-five percent of the rocks on the earth's surface are metamorphic rocks.
4. The process by which sediments are joined together by minerals dissolved in water is called compaction.
5. Sedimentary rocks formed from broken pieces, or fragments, of rocks are called organic rocks.
6. Limestone is an example of an organic sedimentary rock.
7. Chemical sedimentary rocks formed when water evaporates and leaves behind mineral deposits are called evaporites.
8. The changing of one type of rock into another as a result of heat, pressure, and chemical change is called foliation.
9. Slate is an example of a foliated metamorphic rock.
10. The metamorphic rock marble is formed from the igneous rock granite.

CONCEPT REVIEW: SKILL BUILDING

Use the skills you have developed in the chapter to complete each activity.

1. **Making diagrams** Obtain samples of sedimentary, metamorphic, and igneous rocks. Using Figure 7–2 on page 170, illustrate the rock cycle with actual rocks.
2. **Making comparisons** On a piece of graph paper, compare the sizes of a batholith, whose exposed surface area is 10 kilometers wide and 10 kilometers long, and a stock, whose surface area is 10 kilometers wide and 4 kilometers long. Have each square on the graph paper represent 1 square kilometer.
3. **Identifying patterns** Explain why texture and chemical composition are the two most important properties in classifying igneous rocks.
4. **Relating cause and effect** Explain why fossils are present in sedimentary rocks but not usually in metamorphic or igneous rocks.
5. **Classifying rocks** What information would you use to determine whether a rock sample is limestone or marble?
6. **Making inferences** Suppose you have found a large mass of igneous rock between layers of sedimentary rock. Between the bottom of the igneous rock and the sedimentary rock you observe a thin layer of quartzite. The igneous rock itself is fine grained and very dark. What can you infer about the igneous formation's history?

CONCEPT REVIEW: ESSAY

Discuss each of the following in a brief paragraph.

1. How does an igneous rock become part of a sedimentary rock?
2. How can the shell of a snail become part of a sedimentary rock?
3. Explain why 75 percent of the rocks on the earth's surface are sedimentary rocks.
4. Relate the cooling rate of magma to crystal size in igneous rocks.

Adventures in Science

Colleen Cavanaugh Explores the Underwater World of TUBE WORMS

The seabed lies 2500 meters below the ocean's surface. Here, the pressure is nearly 260 times that at the earth's surface, and the temperature is close to the freezing point. The region is dark year round, as sunlight cannot penetrate these ocean depths.

Almost all organisms depend on light as their source of energy in manufacturing food. So scientists had expected to find only the simplest creatures inhabiting this dark area of the Pacific Ocean floor near the Galápagos Islands. To the surprise of a group of scientists from the Woods Hole Oceanographic Institution, however, communities of strange sea animals were found in this forbidding environment.

Among the animals observed by the Woods Hole team are giant clams that measure ⅓ meter in diameter, oversized mussels, and crabs. But perhaps the most striking organisms are giant tube worms. These worms are so different from anything seen before that scientists have placed them in a new family of the animal kingdom.

Although most of the worms are only 2½ to 5 centimeters in diameter, they can be as long as 2 meters! Like a sausage in a tube, each worm lives inside a tough rigid casing. One end of the tube worm is anchored to the seabed. At the other end, a red plumelike structure made of blood-filled filaments waves in the ocean water.

Internally, the body of the worm is very unusual. Approximately half of its body is made of a colony of densely packed bacteria. Dangerous though this may sound, these bacteria are the key to a worm's ability to survive in such a harsh environment. But exactly what is the relationship between the bacteria and the tube worms?

Enter Dr. Colleen Cavanaugh, a marine biologist and microbiologist at Harvard University, who studies these bacteria and their relationship to the larger life forms they support. She has found that the bacteria break down hydrogen sulfide, a common sulfur compound, to produce energy. This energy is then used by the tube worms. In this way, the seemingly worthless hydrogen sulfide—which smells like rotten eggs and is poisonous to most organisms—provides the energy for a fascinating aquatic ecosystem.

Hydrogen sulfide is not ordinarily found in sea water. But plenty of hydrogen sulfide is found near hydrothermal vents such as those in the Pacific Ocean areas where the tube worms were first discovered. Hydrothermal vents are openings in the ocean floor that allow ocean water to come into contact with the earth's hot, molten interior. In the vents, ocean water is heated to temperatures as high as 350 degrees Celsius. The hot water is ejected back into the ocean laced with many different chemical compounds, including hydrogen sulfide. Tube worms and other animals that are able to use sulfur abound in these regions.

Research on tube worms requires interest, dedication, and a broad knowledge of science. So it is not surprising that Colleen Cavanaugh is part of the team at Woods Hole exploring this fascinating underwater world. As a high-school student growing up in Michigan, Colleen Cavanaugh explored many fields of science. She then went on to study general ecology and biology at the University of Michigan. As a graduate student at Harvard, she developed an interest in microbial ecology. Now she combines these three fields, as well as others such as oceanography, in her work. The work Dr. Cavanaugh has already done on tube worms will be of help in her more general study of the nature of symbiosis, or cooperation, between animals and bacteria. As she points out, the sulfides and sulfide-based ecosystems such as that of the tube worms are not limited to just the ocean depths. They are also found in salt marshes, mud flats, and many other marine environments closer to home. Thus, scientific work in the dark reaches of the sea may shed new light on the nature of life on the surface as well.

Living on the ocean bottom near hydrothermal vents (left), tube worms (center) thrive as a result of a symbiotic relationship with bacteria (right).

Issues in Science

Seafloor Minerals

WHO OWNS THEM?

Six hundred meters below the ocean's surface, the strange and beautiful world of underwater plants and animals is suddenly pierced by a powerful beam of light. The light illuminates a vast array of fish, other sea animals, and sea plants. These life forms represent just a few of the many treasures of the ocean depths.

The light, which is carried aboard a strange-looking diving suit called the Wasp, suddenly focuses on another buried treasure. Potato-sized lumps of rocks cover the ocean bottom in many places. These rock lumps, or nodules, represent trillions of tons of minerals sitting on the ocean floor just waiting to be scooped up.

Geologists believe that more than 1.5 trillion tons of these nodules occur in the Pacific Ocean, with lesser amounts in the

other oceans of the world. Scientists estimate that there may be more than $3 trillion worth of minerals in the nodules!

The nodules are rich in a variety of minerals, including manganese, copper, nickel, cobalt, tungsten, vanadium, tin, titanium, silver, platinum, and gold. Land reserves of these minerals are steadily being depleted. So harvesting the nodules from the ocean floor seems to be a sensible and perhaps even essential idea. Why then do the nodules remain unmined along the ocean floor as the need for the minerals continues to grow?

This vast and valuable natural resource remains untapped because two important questions remain unanswered: How can the minerals be mined? and Who owns the right to mine the minerals? Scientists and world leaders are now trying to answer these questions.

Developing the technologies to recover the nodules needs careful research and testing. Several techniques to retrieve the nodules have already been tried, but the attempts have met with only partial success. One approach uses a series of huge metal buckets strung along a belt that moves between a ship and the ocean floor. The buckets scrape along the ocean floor, pick up the nodules, and carry them to the ship. Another method employs a giant vacuum that sucks up the ooze along the ocean bottom and the nodules as well. A third scheme involves the use of robots to find and retrieve the mineral treasures.

With technological advances, the problem of mining the minerals may soon be answered. But the international political questions still remain. Who has the right to mine the ocean depths? Where should this mining be allowed? Who should set the rules? And who should benefit from ocean mining?

These questions are difficult to answer. Since 1959, representatives from many nations have been meeting to try to create a Law of the Sea. This law would regulate ocean mining, oil drilling, fishing, energy usage, dumping of wastes, exploration, and research. Finally, in 1982, 119 nations signed a Law of the Sea treaty. But the United States was not one of them.

Under provisions of the treaty, each coastal nation is given an exclusive economic zone of 200 nautical miles from its shore. Within that zone, a nation controls all natural resources, dumping, economic use, and scientific research. Where economic zones of different nations overlap, the nations must work out agreements.

Outside of the economic zones, no single nation controls the ocean floor. The International Seabed Authority administers this vast ocean floor region, called the International Seabed Area. The Authority sets the rules for mining in the International Seabed Area. And further, all mining technology must be shared with the Authority.

The United States could not accept these provisions and did not sign the Law of the Sea treaty. On March 10, 1983, the United States declared its own economic zone extending 200 nautical miles off the coasts of the United States and all its territories.

Conflict over the zone has already arisen. And it is likely that many disputes will come up when people start mining the ocean floor for its mineral wealth. Who do you think should own these valuable and vital minerals?

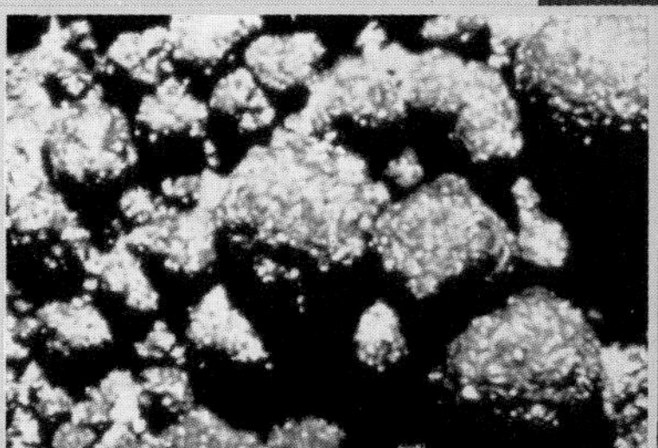

Manganese nodules are part of the wealth of the ocean floor. Manganese is important in the manufacture of steel and other alloys.

UNIT THREE

Structure of the Earth

Driven by forces unleashed in the atmosphere, thundering waves break against a rocky shore. In time, the waves will carve new shorelines along the earth's continents. Although they seem destructive, the pounding waves hide a gentle world. For beneath the waves, giant "rivers" flow slowly and silently for thousands of kilometers. Some of these rivers are icy cold. Others are comfortably warm. All of them help support the great variety of living things that inhabit the earth's oceans.

Deep beneath the ocean, another scene unfolds. Mountains rise from the ocean floor. Volcanoes hiss. The floor itself is on the move. The ocean depths are a place of constant change brought about by fiery forces set loose within the earth. In this unit, you will be taken on a journey that will crisscross the earth's interior and the ocean, land, and air above it. At the end of your journey, you will have discovered how these parts of the earth interact to form the world in which you live.

CHAPTERS

Waves crashing along the rocky California coast are one of many interactions that occur among the earth's interior, oceans, land, and air.

The Earth's Interior 8

CHAPTER SECTIONS

8–1 The Earth's Core
8–2 The Earth's Mantle
8–3 The Earth's Crust

CHAPTER OBJECTIVES

After completing this chapter, you will be able to

8–1 Relate seismic wave movements to the composition of the earth's core.
8–1 Describe the characteristics of the inner core and the outer core.
8–2 Describe the properties and composition of the mantle.
8–2 Define the term Moho.
8–3 Compare continental crust and oceanic crust.

In 1864, the well-known author Jules Verne wrote a book called *Journey to the Center of the Earth.* In this exciting and imaginative story, Verne described his idea of what lies below the earth's surface.

Verne was not the only one to be fascinated by this unknown world. For many years, scientists have been exploring the interior of the earth. But they have not been able to use mechanical probes such as those that explore outer space. The tremendous heat and pressure in the earth's interior make this region harder to explore than planets millions of kilometers away.

The information scientists have gathered about the earth's interior has come from earthquakes! Earthquakes produce shock waves that travel through the earth. These shock waves penetrate the depths of the earth and return to the surface. During this passage, the speed and the direction of the waves change. The changes in the movements of the waves are caused by differences in the structure and composition of the earth's interior. By recording and studying the waves, scientists have been able to "see" into the interior of the earth. As a result of their observations, scientists believe that the earth is made of four different layers.

In this chapter, you will learn about the structure and composition of each layer of the earth. Perhaps you will then consider reading *Journey to the Center of the Earth* and comparing Jules Verne's description with the scientific model of the earth's interior.

Descending into the earth to find out what the earth's interior is made of

Section Objective

To relate seismic wave evidence to the structure of the earth's core

8–1 The Earth's Core

The shock waves produced by an earthquake are called **seismic** (SIGHZ-mihk) **waves.** All earthquakes produce at least two types of seismic waves at the same time: P waves and S waves. These waves are detected and recorded by a special instrument called a **seismograph** (SIGHZ-muh-grahf).

After observing the speeds of P waves and S waves, scientists have concluded that the earth's core, or center, is actually made of two very different layers. Both layers of the core are made of iron and nickel.

The solid, innermost layer of the earth is called the **inner core.** The inner core is very dense. Here the iron and nickel are under a great deal of pressure. The temperature of the inner core reaches about 5000°C. Iron and nickel will usually melt at this temperature. But the enormous pressure at this depth pushes the particles of iron and nickel so tightly together that they remain solid.

The radius, or distance from the center to the edge, of the inner core is about 1300 kilometers. The inner core begins at a depth of about 5150 kilometers below the earth's surface. The presence of dense iron in the inner core may help explain the existence of the magnetic field around the earth. Scientists think that the iron produces an effect similar to the magnetic field around a magnet.

Sharpen Your Skills

Speed of Seismic Waves

Seismic waves travel at a speed 24 times the speed of sound. The speed of sound is 1250 km/hr. How fast do seismic waves travel?

Figure 8–1 *A very powerful earthquake in Caracas, Venezuela, ripped a hole in the ground into which this house fell.*

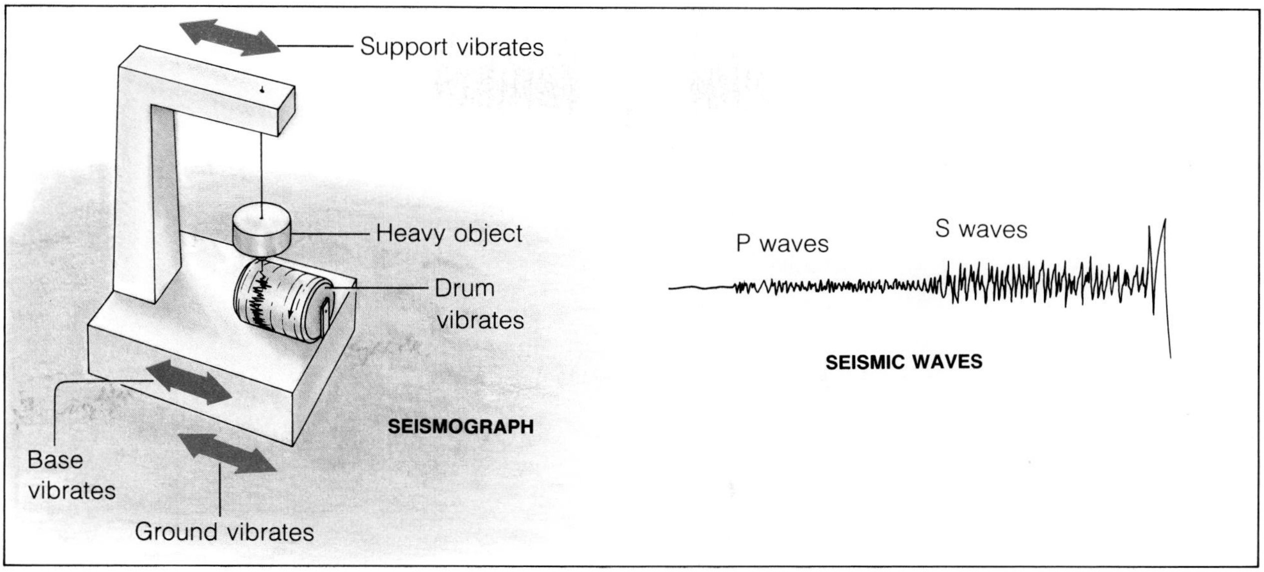

Figure 8–2 *A seismograph (left) detects and records earthquake waves, or seismic waves. A typical pattern of seismic waves is shown (right). What are the two types of seismic waves?*

Surrounding the inner core is the second layer of the earth, called the **outer core.** The outer core begins at a depth of about 2900 kilometers below the earth's surface. It is about 2250 kilometers thick. The outer core is made of liquid iron and nickel. In this layer, the temperature ranges from about 2200°C in the upper part to almost 5000°C near the inner core. This tremendous heat makes the iron and nickel in the outer core molten, or a hot liquid.

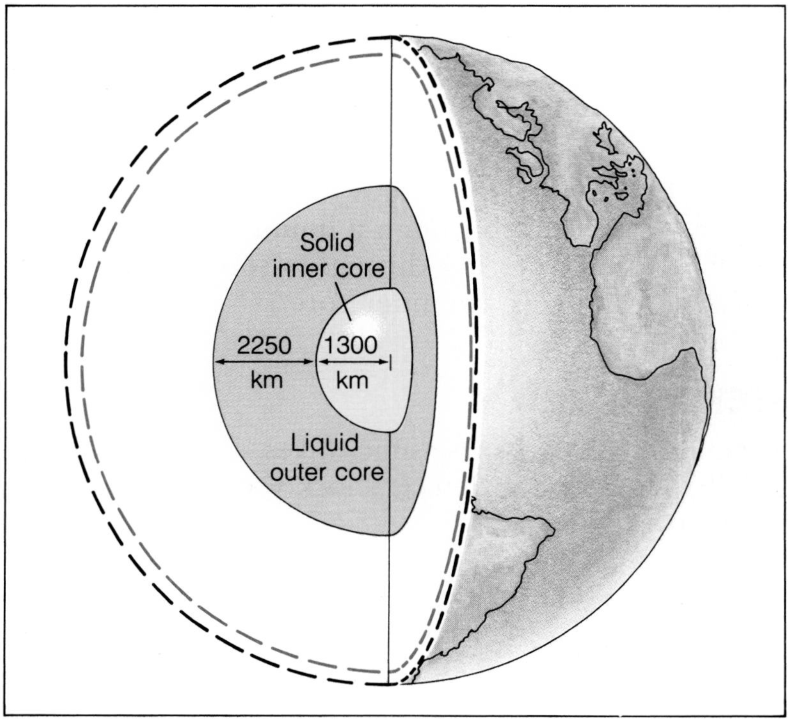

Figure 8–3 *This cross section of the earth shows the location and radius of the inner core and the outer core. What is each core made of?*

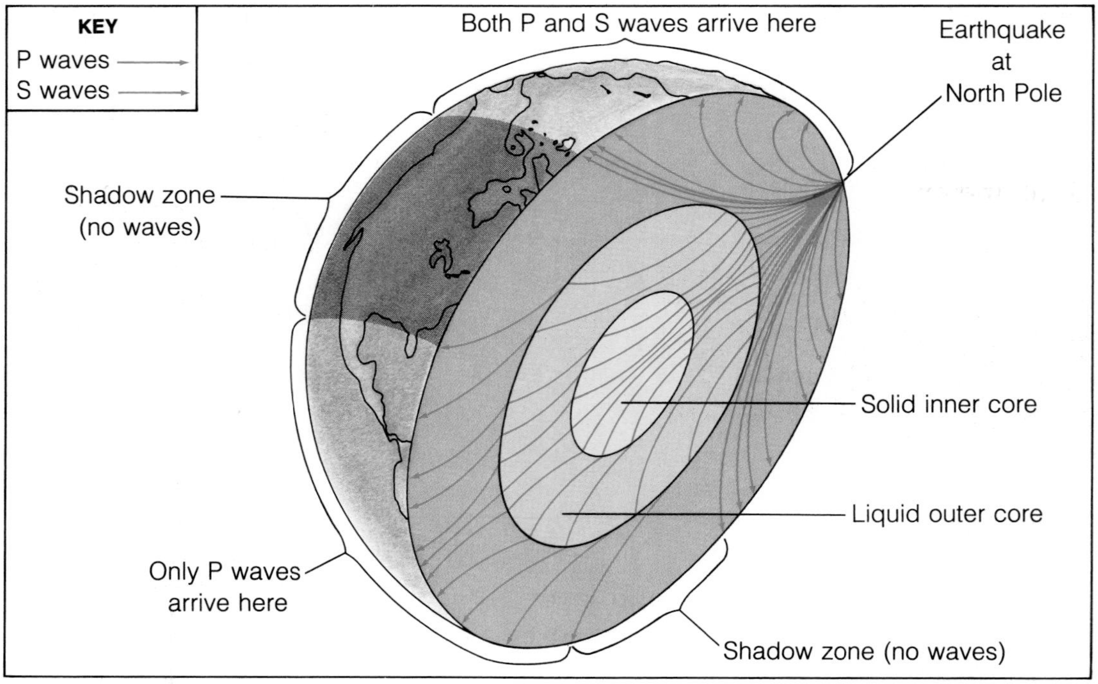

Figure 8–4 *The paths of seismic waves change as they travel through the earth. P waves slow down as they pass through the liquid outer core. As they leave the outer core and pass through the inner core, P waves speed up. This change in speed bends the waves. S waves disappear as they enter the outer core. Why? A wave-free shadow zone that extends all the way around the earth is produced by the bending of seismic waves.*

How have P waves and S waves helped scientists determine the structure of the earth's core? At a depth of 2900 kilometers below the earth's surface, P waves passing through the earth slow down rapidly. S waves disappear. Scientists know that P waves do not move very well through liquids and that S waves are stopped completely. So these changes in the movement of the two seismic waves at a depth of 2900 kilometers indicate the beginning of a liquid layer of the earth. This layer is the outer core. At a depth of 5150 kilometers, P waves increase their speed. This increase indicates that the P waves are no longer traveling through a liquid layer. Instead the P waves are passing through a solid layer of the earth. This layer is the inner core.

SECTION REVIEW

1. Name two types of seismic waves.
2. What instrument detects shock waves produced by an earthquake?
3. What is the inner core made of? What is the outer core made of?
4. How do scientists know that the outer core is a liquid layer?

8–2 The Earth's Mantle

Section Objective

To describe the features of the mantle

The layer of the earth that lies above the outer core is the **mantle.** The mantle extends to a depth of about 2900 kilometers below the earth's surface. It makes up 80 percent of the earth's volume. It also makes up 68 percent of the earth's mass.

In 1909, a Yugoslav scientist named Andrija Mohorovičić (moh-hoh-ROH-vuh-chihch) observed a change in the speed of seismic waves as they moved through the earth. When they reached a depth of 32 to 64 kilometers below the earth's surface, the waves increased in speed. The change in the speed of the waves indicated a difference in either the density or the composition of the rock at that depth. Mohorovičić discovered a boundary between the earth's outermost layer and the mantle. This boundary is now called the **Moho.**

Scientists have made many attempts to determine the composition of the mantle. They have studied rocks from volcanoes because these rocks were

Sharpen Your Skills

Mohorovičić's Discovery

Write a 250-word essay explaining how the boundary between the earth's mantle and the earth's crust was discovered. In your essay, use the following words:

crust	P waves
earthquake	S waves
mantle	seismograph
Moho	

Figure 8–5 *The mantle is the layer that lies above the outer core. What is the name of the boundary between the mantle and the outermost layer?*

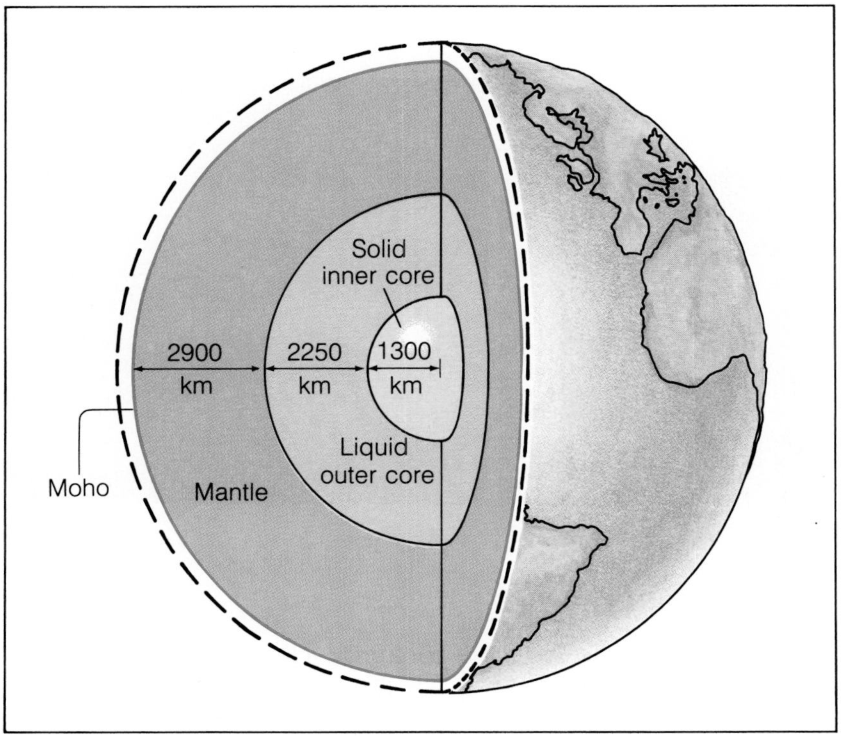

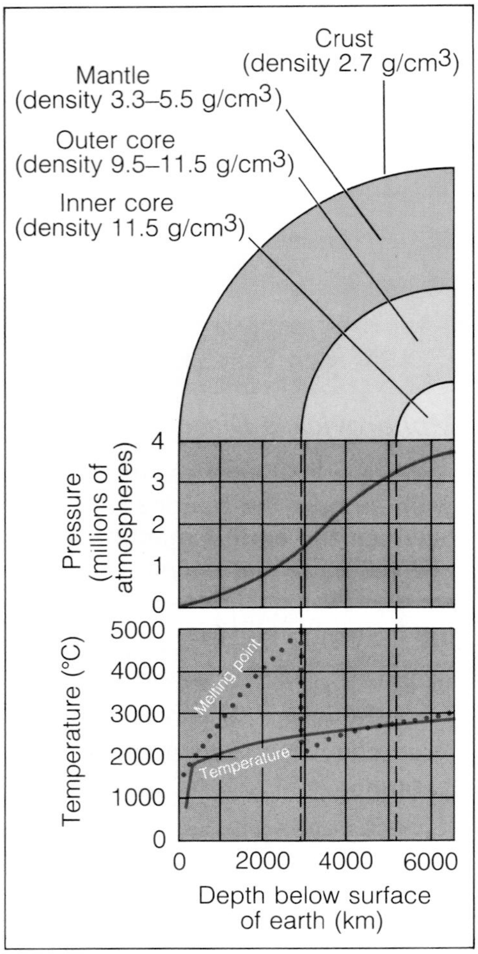

Figure 8–6 *These graphs show how pressure and temperature increase below the earth's surface. In which layer is the pressure the greatest?*

formed deep in the earth. They have also studied rocks from the ocean floor. **After studying rock samples, scientists have determined that the mantle is made mostly of the elements silicon, oxygen, iron, and magnesium.** The lower mantle has a greater percentage of iron than the upper mantle.

The mantle is more dense than the outermost layer of the earth. The density of the mantle increases with depth. This increase in density is perhaps due to the greater percentage of iron in the lower mantle. The temperature and the pressure within the mantle also increase with depth. The temperature ranges from 870°C in the upper mantle to about 2200°C in the lower mantle.

Studies of seismic waves suggest that the rock in the mantle can flow like a thick liquid. The high pressure and temperature in the mantle allow the solid rock to flow slowly, or change shape. When a solid has the ability to flow, it has the property known as **plasticity** (plas-TIHS-uh-tee).

Figure 8–7 *Scientists study rocks from volcanoes and from the ocean floor to determine the composition of the mantle. The partially molten rock (right) has been "frozen" while flowing from a deep valley in the ocean floor.*

SECTION REVIEW

1. Where is the mantle located? How far does it extend below the earth's surface?
2. What is the Moho?
3. What is plasticity?

8–3 The Earth's Crust

Section Objective

To compare oceanic crust with continental crust

The earth's crust is the thin outermost layer of the earth. The **crust** is like the peel on an apple. It is much thinner than the thick inner layers of the earth. All life on the earth exists on or within a few hundred meters above the crust.

The crust is made of three types of solid rocks: igneous, sedimentary, and metamorphic. These rocks contain mostly the elements oxygen and silicon. Other abundant elements in the earth's crust are aluminum, iron, calcium, sodium, potassium, and magnesium.

The thickness of the earth's crust varies. Crust beneath the oceans, called oceanic crust, is less than 10 kilometers thick. Its average thickness is only about 8 kilometers. Oceanic crust is made mostly of silicon, oxygen, iron, and magnesium.

Crust beneath the continents, called continental crust, has an average thickness of about 32 kilometers. Beneath mountains, continental crust is much

Figure 8–8 *The crust is only a very thin layer of the earth. Most of the crust cannot be seen. It is covered with soil, rock, and water. However, the crust of the earth is visible on some mountains. What are the three types of rocks in the crust?*

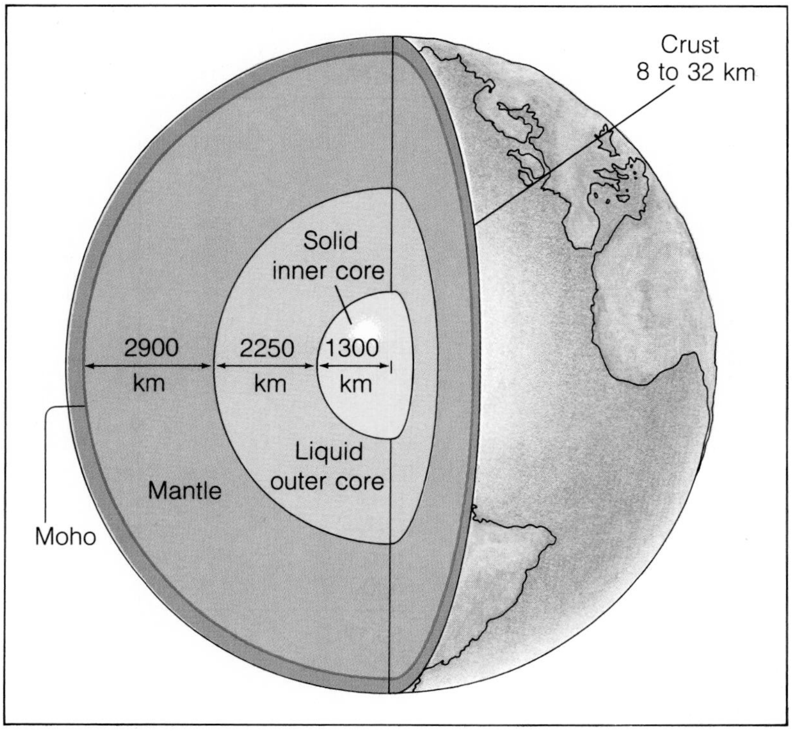

Figure 8–9 *The elements that make up the earth's crust are listed in this chart. What two elements are the most abundant?*

ELEMENTS IN THE EARTH'S CRUST

Element	Percentage in Crust
Oxygen	46.60
Silicon	27.72
Aluminum	8.13
Iron	5.00
Calcium	3.63
Sodium	2.83
Potassium	2.59
Magnesium	2.09
Titanium	0.40
Hydrogen	0.14
Total	99.13

thicker. Under some mountains, its thickness is more than 70 kilometers. Continental crust is made mostly of silicon, oxygen, aluminum, calcium, sodium, and potassium.

Continental crust has two layers of rocks. The top layer is made of granite, a light-colored igneous rock. The bottom layer is made of basalt, a dark-colored igneous rock denser than granite. The granite layer does not extend beyond the continents. The basalt layer extends beneath the earth's oceans to form oceanic crust.

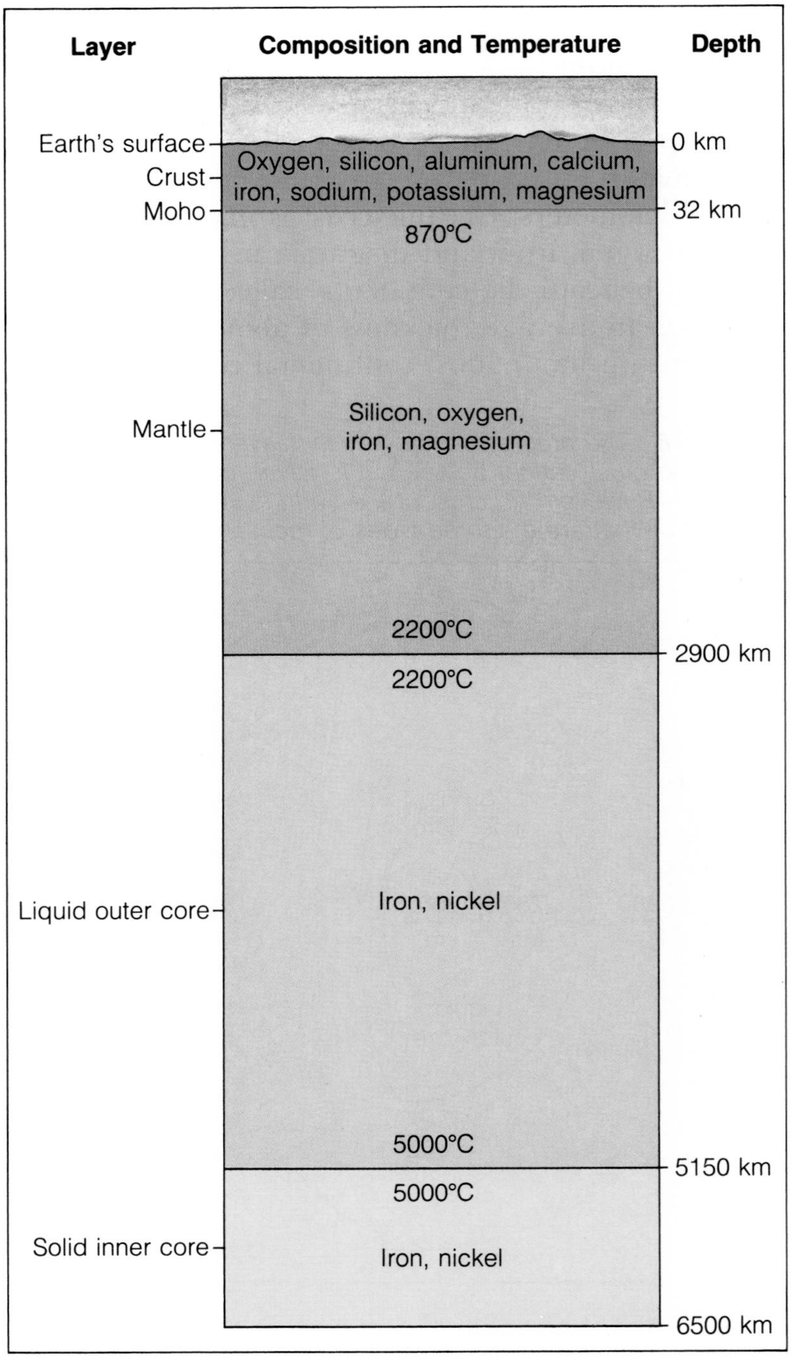

Figure 8–10 *This diagram summarizes the major characteristics of the four layers of the earth.*

Sharpen Your Skills

Model of the Earth's Interior

1. Obtain a Styrofoam ball 15 cm or more in diameter.

2. Carefully cut out a wedge from the ball so that the ball looks similar to Figure 8–8.

3. Draw lines on the inside of the ball and of the wedge to represent the four layers of the earth.

4. Label and color each layer on the ball and wedge.

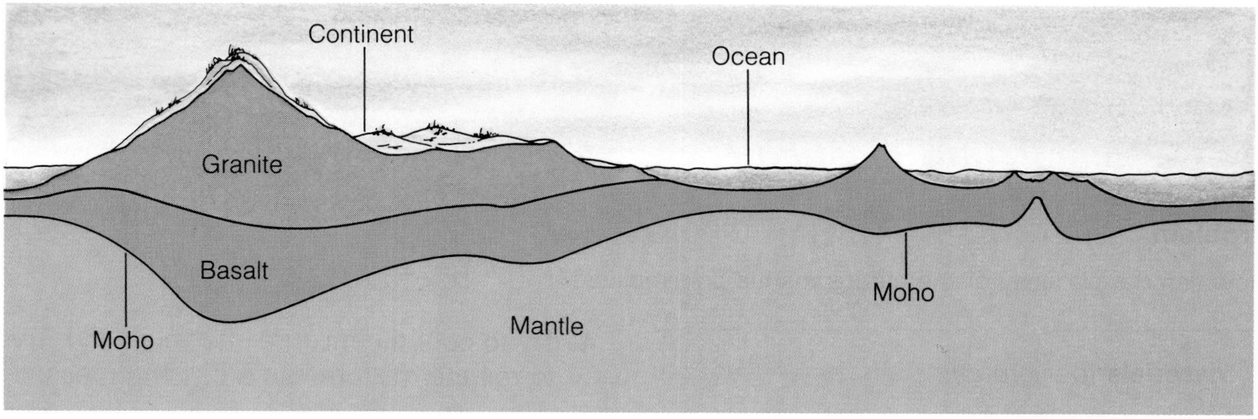

Figure 8–11 *The earth's crust has two layers. The top layer is made of granite and is found only under the continents. The bottom layer is made of basalt and is found under both the continents and the oceans.*

The earth's crust forms the upper part of the **lithosphere** (LIHTH-uh-sfir). The lithosphere is the topmost solid part of the earth. The lithosphere is broken up into large sections called lithospheric plates. There are at least seven major plates. These plates drift on hot, molten material. You will learn more about these plates in Chapter 19.

SECTION REVIEW

1. What are the eight most abundant elements in the earth's crust?
2. What is the average thickness of oceanic crust? Of continental crust?
3. What rock makes up continental crust? Oceanic crust?

CAREER — *Geologist*

HELP WANTED: GEOLOGIST Position available for geologist with background in microscopic examination of rock samples. Candidate must have a B.S. degree in geology. Some training in chemical study of rocks helpful.

Were all of the continents once a large landmass? Why is so much of the earth covered with water? What causes mountains to form?

People who try to answer such questions are called **geologists.** Geologists study the structure, composition, and history of the earth. Some of their time is spent examining rocks and minerals. They use instruments such as gravity meters and seismographs.

Geologists usually specialize in a specific area of geology. For example, mineralogists study and classify minerals. Paleontologists study the fossils in rocks to understand the history of the earth.

To learn more about this field, write to the American Geological Institute, 5202 Leesburg Pike, Falls Church, VA 22041.

8 LABORATORY INVESTIGATION

Simulating Plasticity

Problem

How can the plasticity of the earth's mantle be simulated?

Materials *(per group)*

15 g cornstarch
10 mL water
2 small beakers
Metal stirring rod or spoon
Medicine dropper

Procedure

1. Put 15 g of cornstarch in one of the beakers. Into the other beaker, pour 10 mL of water.
2. Using the medicine dropper, gradually add one dropperful of water to the cornstarch. Stir the mixture.
3. Continue adding water, one dropperful at a time. Stir the mixture after each addition. When the mixture becomes difficult to stir, stop adding water.
4. Try to pour the mixture into your hand. Try to roll the mixture into a ball and press it.

Observations

1. Before the addition of water, is the cornstarch a solid, liquid, or gas? What is the phase of the water?
2. When you try to pour the mixture into your hand, does the mixture have the properties of a solid, liquid, or gas?
3. When you try to roll the mixture into a ball and apply pressure, does the mixture act like a solid, liquid, or gas?

Conclusions

1. How is the mixture of cornstarch and water similar to the earth's mantle? Different from the earth's mantle?
2. How might the plasticity of the mantle influence the movement of the earth's lithospheric plates?

CHAPTER REVIEW

SUMMARY

8–1 The Earth's Core

- Shock waves produced by an earthquake are called seismic waves.
- Seismic waves are detected and recorded by an instrument called a seismograph.
- Seismic waves called P waves and S waves are used to study the structure and composition of the core.
- The core is made of a liquid outer core and a solid inner core. Both layers are made of iron and nickel.
- The temperature of the very dense inner core reaches about 5000°C.
- Although the temperature is enough to melt iron and nickel, the inner core is solid because of the enormous pressure. Particles of iron and nickel are pushed so tightly together that they remain solid.
- The inner core begins at a depth of about 5150 kilometers below the earth's surface. Its radius is about 1300 kilometers.
- The dense iron and nickel in the inner core may be the cause of the earth's magnetic field.
- The outer core begins at a depth of about 2900 kilometers below the earth's surface and is about 2250 kilometers thick.
- The temperature in the outer core ranges from about 2200°C to almost 5000°C.
- P waves do not move very well through liquids. S waves do not move at all through liquids. This information has helped scientists determine that the outer core is liquid and the inner core is solid.

8–2 The Earth's Mantle

- The layer of the earth that lies above the outer core is the mantle.
- The mantle makes up 80 percent of the earth's volume and 68 percent of the earth's mass.
- The boundary between the earth's outermost layer and the mantle is called the Moho.
- The mantle is made mostly of silicon, oxygen, iron, and magnesium.
- Pressure and temperature increase with depth in the mantle.
- Because of the high heat and pressure in the mantle, rocks in the mantle exhibit the property of plasticity.

8–3 The Earth's Crust

- The earth's crust is the thin outermost layer of the earth.
- The crust is made of igneous, sedimentary, and metamorphic rocks.
- The most abundant elements in the crust are oxygen, silicon, aluminum, iron, calcium, sodium, potassium, and magnesium.
- Oceanic crust is about 8 kilometers thick. Continental crust is about 32 kilometers thick.
- Oceanic crust is made mostly of silicon, oxygen, iron, and magnesium. Continental crust is made mostly of silicon, oxygen, aluminum, calcium, sodium, and potassium.
- The crust forms the upper part of the lithosphere. The lithosphere is broken up into large sections called lithospheric plates.

VOCABULARY

Define each term in a complete sentence.

crust
inner core
lithosphere
mantle
Moho
outer core
plasticity
seismic wave
seismograph

CONTENT REVIEW: MULTIPLE CHOICE

Choose the letter of the answer that best completes each sentence.

1. Shock waves produced by an earthquake are measured with a
a. radiograph b. seismograph c. laser d. sonograph

2. The core of the earth is made of
a. oxygen and silicon b. iron and silicon
c. iron and nickel d. copper and nickel

3. When P waves and S waves reach the outer core,
a. both keep moving at the same speed b. both stop completely
c. P waves stop and S waves slow down d. S waves stop and P waves slow down

4. The layer that makes up most of the earth's mass and volume is the
a. mantle b. magma c. crust d. core

5. The boundary between the mantle and the outermost layer of the earth is called the
a. Moho b. outer core c. lithosphere d. bedrock

6. The ability of a solid to flow is called
a. ductility b. plasticity c. seismology d. porosity

7. The thin outermost layer of the earth is called the
a. mantle b. magma c. crust d. core

8. The crust of the earth is made mostly of
a. oxygen and silicon b. iron and silicon
c. iron and nickel d. copper and nickel

9. Oceanic crust is
a. thicker than continental crust b. as thick as continental crust
c. made of granite d. thinner than continental crust

10. The topmost solid part of the earth is called the
a. lithosphere b. atmosphere c. hydrosphere d. Moho

CONTENT REVIEW: COMPLETION

Fill in the word or words that best complete each sentence.

1. Shock waves produced by an earthquake are called ______________ waves.

2. The earth's core is actually made of two layers: the ______________ and the ______________.

3. The presence of ______________ in the inner core may explain the magnetic field around the earth.

4. ______________ waves do not pass through liquids.

5. The layer that makes up most of the earth's mass and volume is called the ______________.

6. The boundary between the mantle and the outermost layer of the earth is called the ______________.

7. The ability of solid rock to flow is called ______________.

8. The two most abundant elements found in the earth's crust are ______________ and ______________.

9. Continental crust is made of granite and ______________.

10. The topmost solid part of the earth is called the ______________.

CONTENT REVIEW: TRUE OR FALSE

Determine whether each statement is true or false. If it is true, write "true." If it is false, change the underlined word or words to make the statement true.

1. Shock waves produced by an earthquake are called laser waves.
2. The innermost layer of the earth is called the outer core.
3. The outer core is molten, or a hot liquid.
4. S waves slow down as they pass through liquids.
5. The mantle makes up more of the earth's mass than any other layer.
6. The boundary between the earth's outermost layer and the mantle is called the Moho.
7. Rock in the mantle has the property of porosity, or the ability to flow.
8. The outermost layer of the earth is called the crust.
9. Oceanic crust has a layer of granite and a layer of basalt.
10. The topmost solid part of the earth is broken up into lithospheric plates.

CONCEPT REVIEW: SKILL BUILDING

Use the skills you have developed in the chapter to complete each activity.

1. **Making models** Using the information in this chapter, construct a stratographic model of the four layers of the earth's interior. You may want to use a marble, clay of different colors, papier-mâché, or other materials to make your model. Keep the depth and thickness of each layer of your model relative to its actual depth and thickness. Include a key of relative measurements in your model. For example, 1 model centimeter might equal 1000 actual kilometers.
2. **Applying data** Suppose an earthquake occurs early one morning in Tokyo, Japan. A seismograph there records the shock waves. On the other side of the world, a seismograph in Potsdam, Germany, records a series of shock waves about an hour later. Describe or draw what each seismographic recording will look like. Explain each drawing.
3. **Analyzing data** The temperature of the inner core reaches about 5000°C. The temperature of the outer core begins at about 2200°C. Yet the outer core is liquid while the inner core is solid. Explain how this can be so.
4. **Making graphs** Construct a graph using the data in Figure 8–9. Plot each element in the earth's crust on the horizontal axis. Plot the percentage of each element in the earth's crust on the vertical axis. What general conclusions can you draw from your graph?

CONCEPT REVIEW: ESSAY

Discuss each of the following in a brief paragraph.

1. How have scientists learned about the composition of the earth's interior?
2. What is the difference between oceanic crust and continental crust?
3. What is the importance of P waves and S waves in learning about the structure of the earth's interior?

STALAME
HOIA
AOVSTA MAION
Toupa
Port Royal
C. de S. Helene
R. Jordan
MACEOV
R. Grande
R. Belle
R. de Gironde
R. de Garonne
R. de Charente
R. de Loyre
R. de Somme
R. de Seine
R. de May
VTINA
SATVRIONA
C. des Françoys
C. de Mont
OATCHAQVA
Bahama
CIGATEO
Les Jardinetz
CATOS
DE FLORIDE
IANI
GVANIMA

The Earth's Landmasses

9

CHAPTER SECTIONS

9–1 Continents
9–2 Topography
9–3 Mapping the Earth's Surface
9–4 Topographic Maps

CHAPTER OBJECTIVES

After completing this chapter, you will be able to

- **9–1** Name the earth's continents.
- **9–2** Identify some of the major characteristics of mountains, plains, and plateaus.
- **9–3** Explain the need for time zones and the international date line.
- **9–3** Compare a Mercator projection and an equal-area projection.
- **9–4** Interpret a topographic map.
- **9–4** Read a map's legend.

For thousands of years, most people thought that the earth was flat. But as early as 300 B.C., the ancient Greeks theorized that the earth was round. Yet they still drew maps of a flat earth.

As people explored more of the world, they were able to map larger areas of it. In 150 A.D., the famous Greek astronomer Ptolemy made maps that included Europe, Africa, and most of Asia. Even more important, these maps showed the earth as round!

For hundreds of years after Ptolemy's work, mapping was neglected. Much knowledge of the world, as well as the idea of a round earth, was forgotten. In the fourteenth century, interest in Ptolemy's work was renewed. Once again, people believed that the earth might be round. Columbus's voyage to the New World was final proof that it was indeed round.

After Columbus's voyage, maps were redrawn to include the newly discovered land. With each exploration of the New World, maps became more and more accurate. By the middle of the eighteenth century, maps showed the earth's land areas in the same shapes and sizes you see on maps today.

In this chapter, you will learn about different land features. You will also learn how they are represented on maps. And you will gain a better understanding of maps in general.

This 400-year-old map shows the eastern coast of the United States from Florida to Virginia. Both the size and shape of the land are drawn inaccurately.

9–1 Continents

Section Objective

To identify the earth's landmasses

All of the land on the earth is surrounded by oceans. There are many **islands,** or small landmasses completely surrounded by water, scattered throughout the oceans. But there are only four major landmasses on the earth. Each major landmass is made up of one or more **continents.** A continent is a large land area that measures millions of square kilometers and rises a considerable distance above sea level.

There are seven continents on the earth: Asia, Africa, Europe, Australia, North America, South America, and Antarctica. Some of these continents are joined. Together they form a landmass. See Figure 9–1. Asia and Europe are joined and thus are often considered one continent, called Eurasia. And Africa is connected to Asia by a small piece of land. These three continents together—Asia, Europe, and Africa—make up one giant landmass. It is the largest landmass on the earth.

The second largest landmass is made up of the continents of North America and South America. Just south of the United States is an area called Central America. Central America is part of the North American continent. At the point where Central America is connected to South America, the continents of North and South America are joined.

Figure 9–1 *This map shows the major islands and the seven continents of the world. Which continents together make up the largest landmass on the earth?*

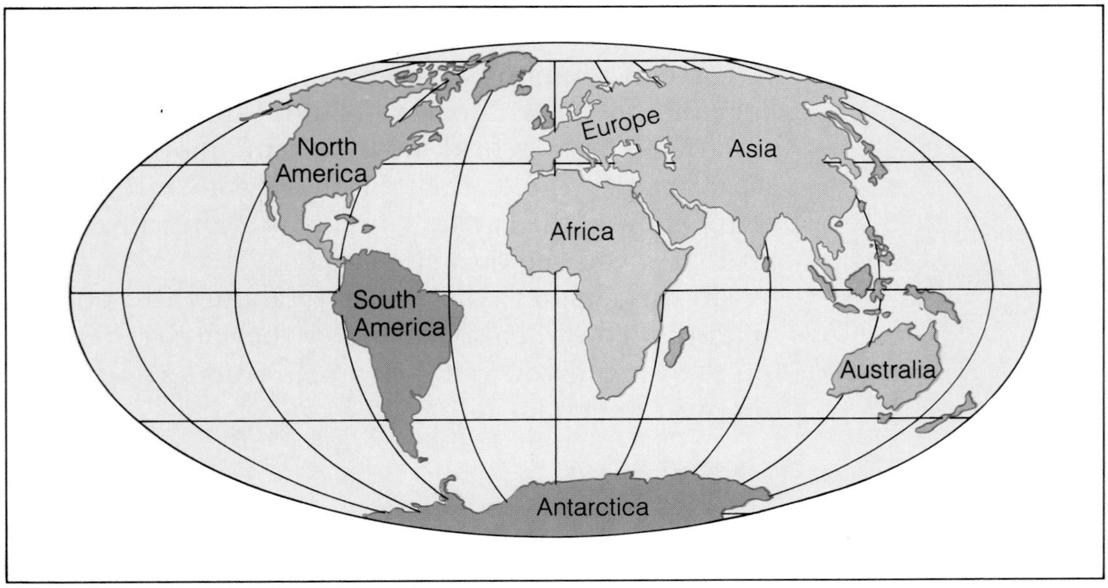

Figure 9–2 *This is a photograph of an Antarctic glacier that reaches out into the frozen Ross Sea. The glacier is part of the huge icecap that covers Antarctica. What percentage of all the earth's ice is contained in the icecap?*

Sharpen Your Skills

Continental Sizes

1. From a globe, trace the outline of each of the seven continents. Cut out the outlines. Trace each cutout on a piece of graph paper. Shade in the outlined continents.

2. Consider each square on the graph paper as an area unit of 1. Calculate the area units for each of the seven continents to the nearest whole unit. For example, suppose a continent covers all of 45 units, about one-half of 20 units, and about one-fourth of 16 units. The total area units the continent covers will be 45 + 10 + 4, or 59.

List the continents from largest to smallest.

The third largest landmass is the continent of Antarctica. Antarctica is about twice the size of the United States. It is the most recently discovered continent. The first known exploration of Antarctica began in 1901.

Antarctica is very different from the other continents. It is almost completely covered by a thick icecap. The Antarctic icecap is the largest in the world. It has an area of 34 million square kilometers! It is so large that it extends out into the surrounding ocean. The icecap contains 85 percent of the ice on the earth's surface.

Antarctica is the coldest area on the earth. In July 1983, the temperature in Vostok, Antarctica, dropped to nearly −89.2°C, the lowest temperature ever recorded on the earth. Many scientific stations have been built on Antarctica to study the earth and the environment. Because of the extreme cold, only temporary visitors live on the continent.

The smallest landmass still considered a continent is Australia. Australia is the only continent that is a country. Sometimes Australia is referred to as an island-continent. Why do you think this term is used to describe Australia?

Each continent has at least one large area of very old rock exposed at its surface. This area is called a

Figure 9–3 *Australia is a continent completely surrounded by water. These steep cliffs in southwestern Australia border on the Indian Ocean.*

shield. Shields form the cores of the continents. The shield of North America is found in Canada.

SECTION REVIEW

1. What is an island?
2. What are the names of the seven continents?
3. Predict what would occur if the average temperature in Antarctica were 5°C.

Section Objective

To compare the three main types of landscape regions

9–2 Topography

Over billions of years, the earth's surface has changed in appearance many times. These changes are the result of several factors. Weather conditions such as wind and heat change the surface. Running water reshapes the land. Earthquakes and volcanoes cause major changes in the earth's surface. Even people alter the earth's appearance. What human activities can you think of that might change the shape of the land?

Scientists refer to the shape of the earth's surface as its **topography** (tuh-PAHG-ruh-fee). The earth's

Figure 9–4 *This map shows the major landscape regions of the United States mainland. What type of landscape region covers most of the United States?*

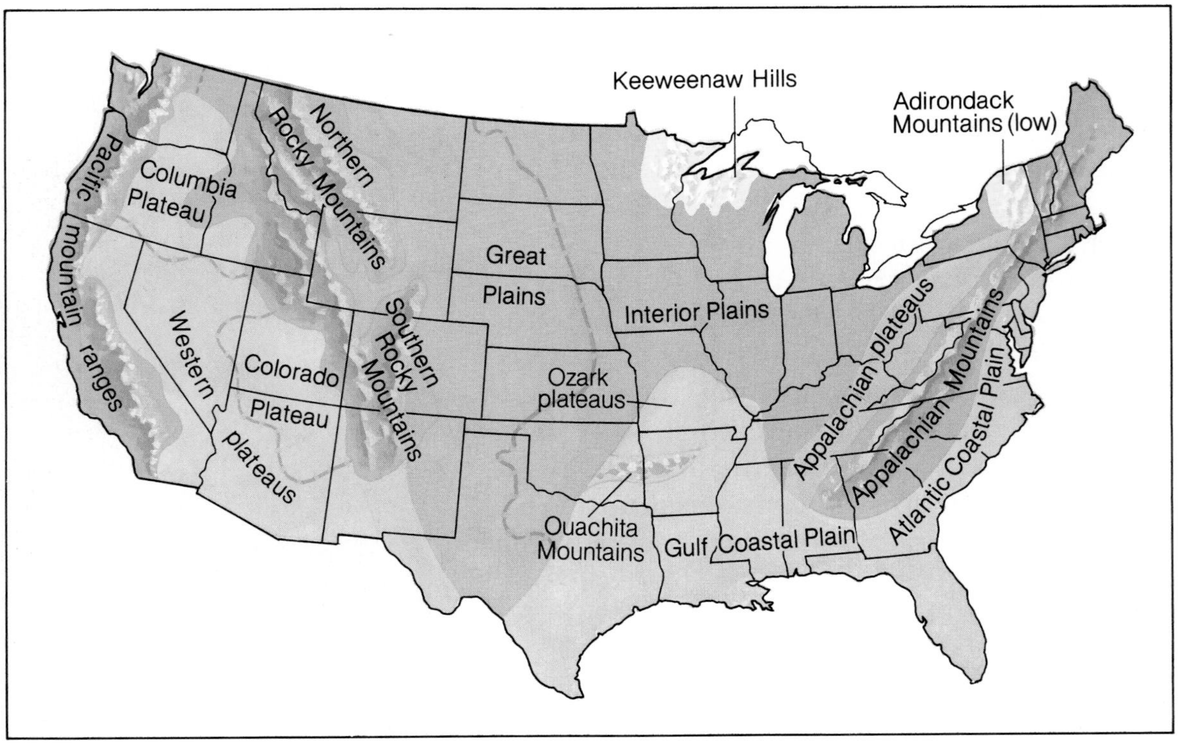

topography is made up of different kinds of **landscapes.** A landscape is the physical features of the earth's surface found in an area. Figure 9–4 shows landscape regions in the United States. In which landscape region do you live?

There are three main types of landscape regions: mountains, plains, and plateaus. Each type has different characteristics. One characteristic is **elevation,** or height above sea level. Some landscape regions have high elevations. Others have low elevations. Within a landscape region, the elevation can vary from place to place. This difference in a region's elevations is called its **relief.** If a landscape region has high relief, there is a large difference in the elevations of different areas within the landscape region.

Sharpen Your Skills

Mountain Landscapes

Mountain landscapes cover about one-fifth of the earth's surface. The total land area of the earth's surface is about 148,300,000 sq km. How much of the surface has a mountain landscape?

Mountains

Mountains make up one type of landscape region. Mountains are natural landforms that reach high elevations. Mountains have narrow summits, or tops, and steep slopes, or sides. Mountain landscapes have very high relief. Their summits are at least 600 meters above the surrounding area.

The highest mountain in the world is Mount Everest. Mount Everest is part of the Himalayas, a great chain of mountains extending from Tibet to Pakistan. The peak of Mount Everest soars to over 8 kilometers! The highest mountain in the United States is Mount McKinley in the state of Alaska. It is more than 6 kilometers high. What mountains are closest to your home?

Mountains can be formed in several ways. Some mountains result from the folding and breaking of the earth's surface. Other mountains are created when hot magma rises through the earth's surface.

Streams and rivers in mountain areas move very quickly. The higher and steeper the mountain slopes, the faster the water flows. Mountain streams and rivers carry rocks of all sizes. When there is heavy rainfall or when snow melts, the streams and rivers become so swollen that they can even carry small boulders.

Streams and rivers often carve valleys in mountains. Valleys in older mountains are usually wide.

Figure 9–5 *This mountain stream, swollen by water from melting snow, is flowing very quickly. What might this stream eventually do to the mountain?*

Figure 9–6 *Mount Kilimanjaro, the highest mountain in Africa, is a single mountain. How do you think this mountain formed?*

Valleys in younger mountains are usually narrow. Why do you think this is so?

Individual mountains can be found in all parts of the world. These mountains are usually volcanic mountains, which are created by magma flowing onto the earth's surface. Examples of volcanic mountains are Fujiyama in Japan, Vesuvius in Italy, and Kilimanjaro in Africa.

Most mountains, however, are part of a group of mountains called a **mountain range.** Mountain ranges are roughly parallel series of mountains that have the same general shape and structure. A group of mountain ranges in one area is called a **mountain system.** The Great Smoky, Blue Ridge, Cumberland, and Green mountains are all mountain ranges in the Appalachian mountain system in the eastern United States.

Most mountain ranges and mountain systems are part of an even larger group of mountains called a **mountain belt.** The pattern of mountain belts on the earth is shown in Figure 9–7.

There are two major mountain belts in the world. The circum-Pacific belt rings the Pacific Ocean. The Eurasian–Melanesian belt runs across northern Africa, southern Europe, and Asia. The Eurasian–Melanesian belt and the circum-Pacific belt meet in Indonesia, just north of Australia. These mountain belts may have been formed by movements of the earth's crust.

Figure 9–7 *Most of the earth's mountains are located within the two major mountain belts shown on this map: the Circum-Pacific belt and the Eurasian-Melanesian belt. Which major mountain belt runs through the United States?*

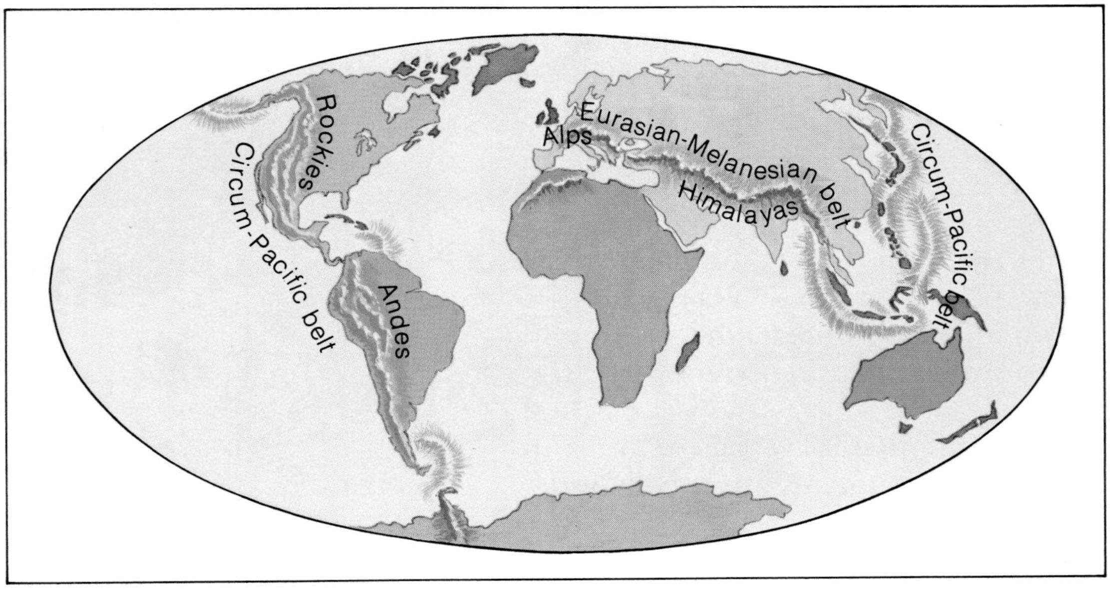

Plains

Another type of landscape region is made up of **plains.** Plains are flat land areas that are not far above sea level. So plains have very small differences in elevation. They are areas of low relief. The difference between the highest and lowest elevations in a plain may be less than 100 meters. Some plains are found at the edges of continents. Other plains are located in the continent's interiors.

COASTAL PLAINS A coast is a place where the land meets the ocean. Low, flat areas along the coast are called **coastal plains.** The Atlantic and Gulf coastal plains of the United States are typical coastal plains. The change in the elevation of the land from the Gulf of Mexico to southern Illinois is very small. Over a distance of more than 1000 kilometers, the land rises only about 150 meters above sea level.

The coastal plains of the United States were formed as soil and silt were deposited on the edge of the continent. In the past, shallow oceans covered this area. As these shallow oceans disappeared, large deposits of sand and silt were left behind. More sediments have been deposited onto the coastal plains by rivers and streams.

The soils of coastal plains are usually very rich. These areas are easy to farm. Agriculture is often the major activity on coastal plains. In the United States, cotton, tobacco, vegetables, and citrus crops are grown in these areas.

Sharpen Your Skills

Landscape Features of the United States

Imagine that you are taking a trip around the United States. You will see many different landscape features. Write a 200-word essay about what you see on your trip. Include the following vocabulary words in your essay: coastal plain, interior plain, mountain, mountain range, plateau, and elevation. Be sure to mention specific locations such as the Gulf Coastal Plain and the Colorado Plateau.

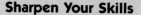

Figure 9–8 *This area in Jacksonville Beach, Florida, is located within the Atlantic coastal plain. What characteristic of plains regions is visible in this photo?*

Figure 9–9 *In interior plains regions, the flat land has fertile soil that is good for growing wheat. How was the soil deposited here?*

INTERIOR PLAINS Some low, flat areas are also found inland on a continent. These areas are called **interior plains.** Interior plains are somewhat higher above sea level than coastal plains. For example, the interior plains of the United States have an elevation of about 450 meters above sea level. This is considerably greater than the elevation of the Atlantic and Gulf coastal plains. But within the interior plain itself, the differences in elevation are small. So interior plains have low relief.

The Great Plains of the United States are large interior plains. They were formed as mountains and hills were worn down by wind, streams, and glaciers. Large interior plains are also found in the Soviet Union, central and eastern Europe, and parts of Africa and Australia.

Interior plains have good soil. The sediments deposited by streams make the soil suitable for farming. In the United States, grasses and grains such as wheat, barley, and oats are grown in the interior plains. Cattle and sheep are raised in these areas, too.

Plateaus

A third type of landscape region consists of **plateaus.** Plateaus are broad, flat areas of land that rise more than 600 meters above sea level. Some plateaus reach elevations of over 1500 meters. Plateaus are not considered mountains because their surfaces are fairly flat. Like plains, plateaus have low relief, or small differences in elevation. But unlike plains, plateaus rise much higher above sea level.

Most plateaus are located inland. But a few plateaus are near oceans. The plateaus near oceans often end in a cliff at the edge of a coastal plain. If a plateau is directly next to an ocean, it ends in a cliff at the coast.

Plateaus often have the same landscape for thousands of kilometers. Some plateaus have been deeply cut by streams and rivers that form canyons. The Colorado River cuts through the Colorado Plateau to form the Grand Canyon in Arizona. The river flows 1.5 kilometers lower than the surface of the surrounding plateau.

Many plateaus of the world are dry, nearly desert areas. They are often used for grazing cattle,

Figure 9–10 *In this photograph of the Grand Canyon, the broad, flat surface of the Colorado Plateau is visible. What makes this and other plateaus different from plains?*

sheep, and goats. Plateaus in the western United States are rich in coal and mineral deposits such as copper and lead.

SECTION REVIEW

1. What is topography?
2. What are the three main types of landscape regions?
3. What is a coastal plain?

9–3 Mapping the Earth's Surface

Section Objective

To describe the features of maps and globes

A **map** is a drawing of the earth, or part of the earth, on a flat surface. **There are many ways to show the earth's surface on maps and globes.** Some maps show only a small area of the earth. Others show the entire surface. A book of maps is called an atlas.

The most accurate representation of the entire surface of the earth is a **globe.** A globe is a spherical, or round, model of the earth. It shows the shapes, sizes, and locations of all the earth's landmasses and bodies of water.

Figure 9–11 *The scale on this map is useful in finding the distance between two cities. If you took a plane ride from Unalakleet to Old Crow, how many kilometers would you fly?*

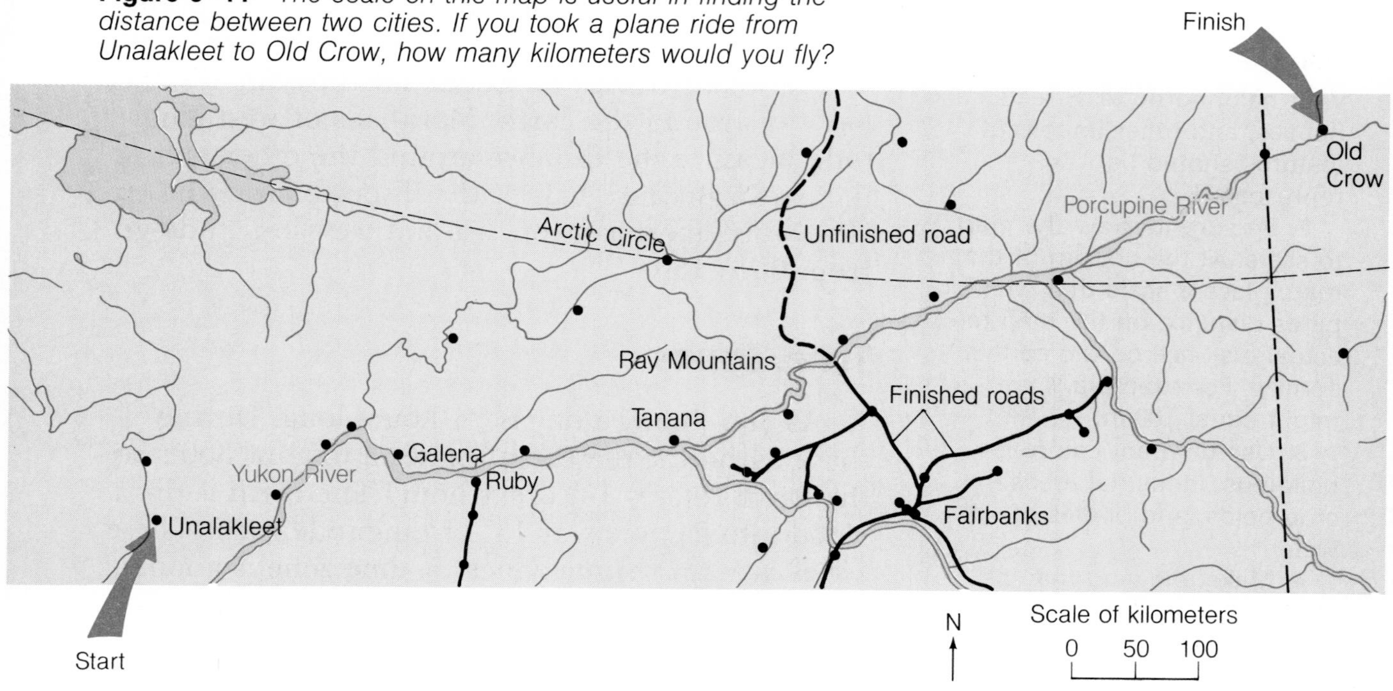

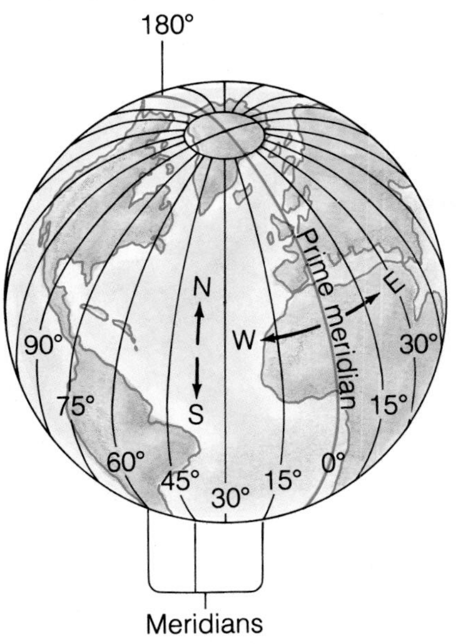

Figure 9–12 *Meridians are lines running north to south on a map or globe. What are meridians used to measure?*

Both maps and globes are drawn to **scale.** A scale compares distance on a map or globe to actual distance on the earth's surface. For example, 1 centimeter on a map might equal 10 kilometers on the earth's surface. Different maps may have different scales. See Figure 9–11 on page 221.

Meridians

When you look at a globe or a map, you see many straight lines on it. Some of the lines run between the points that represent the geographic North and South poles of the earth. These lines are called **meridians** (muh-RIHD-ee-uhnz).

Each meridian is half of an imaginary circle around the earth. Geographers have named the meridian that runs through Greenwich, England, the **prime meridian.** The measure of distance east or west of the prime meridian is called **longitude.** Meridians are used to measure longitude.

The distance around any circle, including the earth, is measured in degrees. The symbol for degree is a small circle written at the upper right of a number. All circles contain 360°. Each meridian marks 1° of longitude around the earth. But not all meridians are drawn on most globes or maps.

The prime meridian is labeled 0° longitude. Meridians to the east of the prime meridian are called east longitudes. Meridians to the west of the prime meridian are called west longitudes.

Meridians of east longitude measure the distance halfway around the earth. Meridians of west longitude measure the distance around the other half of the earth. Because half of the distance around a circle is 180°, meridians of east and west longitude go from 0° to 180°.

Time Zones

As you know, a day is 24 hours long. During these 24 hours, the earth rotates a total of 360°. So the earth rotates 15° every hour. The earth is divided into 24 zones of 15° of longitude each. These zones are called **time zones.** A time zone is a longitudinal belt of the earth in which all areas have the same local time.

Sharpen Your Skills

Mapping Your Neighborhood

1. Draw a detailed map of your neighborhood. Streets, houses, and other important features should be represented.

2. Be sure to draw the map to scale. At the bottom of the map, place a scale that compares distance on the map to actual distance on the earth's surface. For example, 1 cm might equal 100 m.

3. Use different colors for buildings, industrial areas, crop fields, and bodies of water.

4. Make a legend that includes the symbols in the map and their meanings.

Suppose it is 6:00 A.M. in Miami, Florida. It is also 6:00 A.M. in Washington, D.C., because Miami and Washington are in the same time zone. But in Dallas, Texas, it is *not* 6:00 A.M. Dallas is one time zone away from Miami and Washington. How can you tell whether it is earlier or later in Texas?

The earth rotates on its axis from west to east. This direction of rotation makes the sun appear to rise in the east and travel west. So the sun comes into view first in the east. Suppose the sun rises in New York City at 6:00 A.M. After the earth rotates 15°, the sun rises in Dallas. It is 6:00 A.M. in Dallas. But it is one hour later, or 7:00 A.M., in New York City. Dallas is one time zone west of New York City.

After the earth rotates another 15°, the sun rises in Denver. It is 6:00 A.M. in Denver. But by now it is 7:00 A.M. in Dallas and 8:00 A.M. in New York City. Denver is one time zone west of Dallas and two time zones west of New York City.

If it were not for time zones, the sun would rise in New York City at 6:00 A.M., in Dallas at 7:00

Figure 9–13 *The earth is divided into 24 time zones. Here you see the time zones of North America. All areas within a time zone have the same local time. If it is 10 P.M. in Miami, what time is it in Hawaii?*

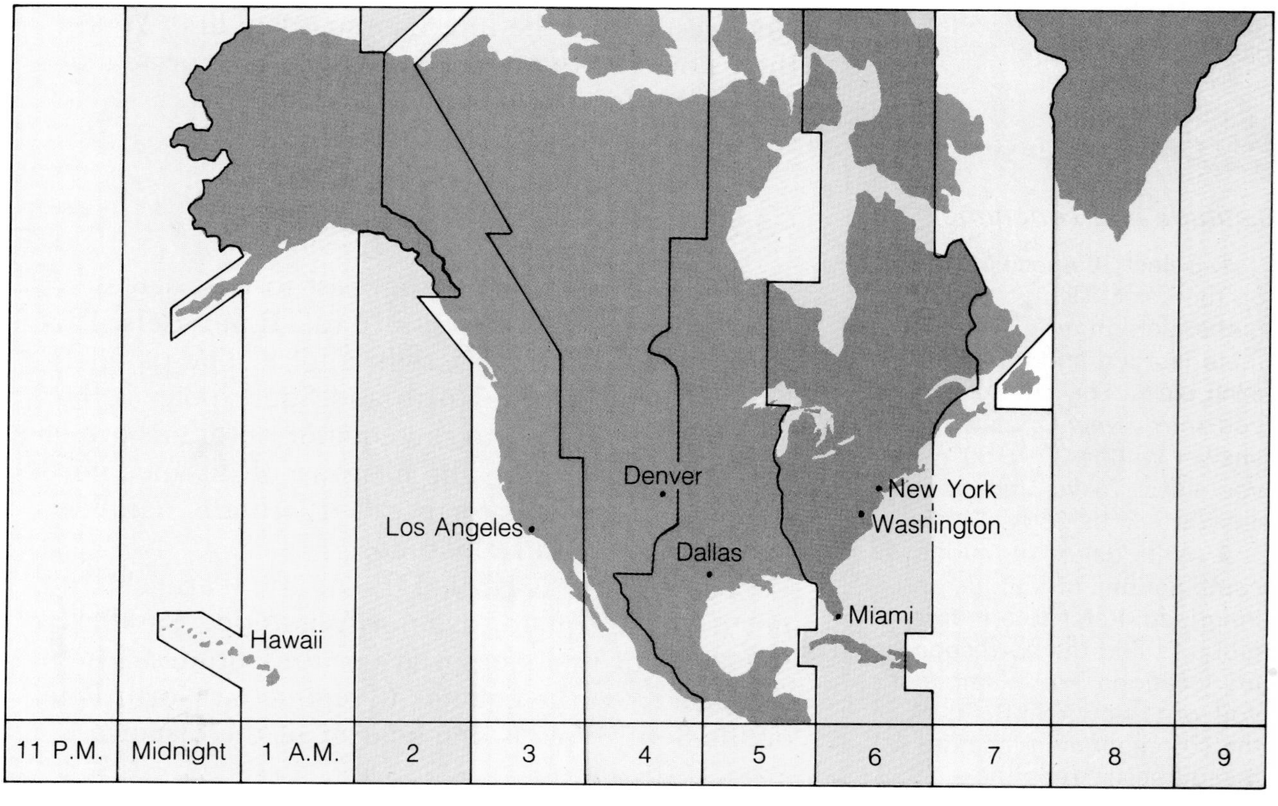

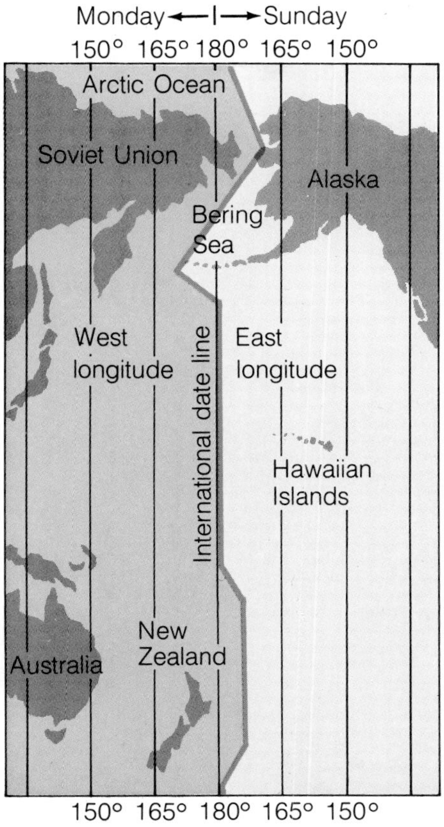

Figure 9–14 *Travelers going west across the international date line gain a day. Those going east across it lose a day. Why does the international date line zigzag?*

Sharpen Your Skills

Latitude and Longitude

1. Select 10 specific places on the earth. Using a map or globe, determine the approximate latitude and longitude of each place. For example, if you select New Orleans, your answer will be 30°N, 90°W. If you select Tokyo, Japan, your answer will be 35°N, 140°E.

2. Write down 10 random combinations of latitude and longitude. Refer to a map or globe to find the corresponding locations. For example, if you write down 50°S, 70°W, the corresponding location will be southern Argentina.

A.M., in Denver at 8:00 A.M., and in Los Angeles at 9:00 A.M. And the sun would not rise in Hawaii until 11:00 A.M.! Because of time zones, the sun rises in each city at 6:00 A.M.

When you cross from one time zone to another, the local time changes by one hour. If you are traveling east, you add one hour for each time zone you cross. If you are traveling west, you subtract one hour.

Now suppose you are taking a 24-hour trip around the world. You travel west, leaving Miami, Florida, at 1:00 P.M. Sunday. Because you are going west, you subtract one hour for each time zone you cross. One day later, you arrive back in Miami. It is now 1:00 P.M. Monday. But because you have subtracted a total of 24 hours as you traveled, you think that it is still 1:00 P.M. Sunday!

This situation is quite confusing. But geographers have established the **international date line** to simplify matters. The international date line is located along the 180th meridian. If you cross this line going east, you subtract one day. If you cross this line going west, you add one day. So in your trip around the world, you should have added one day, or gone from Sunday to Monday, as you traveled west across the international date line. You then would have arrived in Miami, as expected, at 1:00 P.M. Monday afternoon.

Parallels

There are also lines from east to west across a map or globe. These lines are called **parallels.** Parallels cross meridians at right angles. The parallel halfway between the North and South poles is the **equator.** In relation to the equator, locations are either north or south. The measure of distance north or south of the equator is called **latitude.** Parallels are used to measure latitude.

The equator is labeled 0° latitude. Parallels to the north of the equator are north latitudes. Parallels to the south of the equator are south latitudes. The distance from the equator to either the North Pole or the South Pole is one-quarter of the distance around the earth.

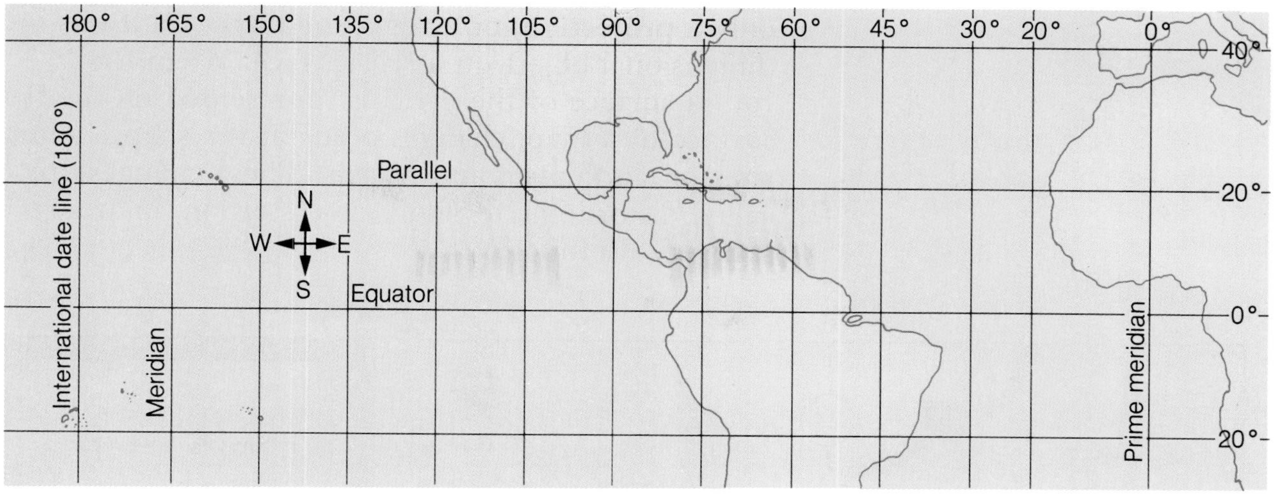

Figure 9–15 *Parallels are lines that run from east to west on a map or globe. Parallels and meridians form a grid used to determine exact locations. On what continent is 40° north latitude and 90° west longitude located?*

Because one-quarter of the distance around a circle is 90°, north and south parallels are labeled from 0° to 90°. The North Pole is at 90° north latitude, or 90°N. Just as there is a meridian for every degree of longitude, there is a parallel for every degree of latitude. But not all parallels are drawn on most globes or maps.

Meridians and parallels form a grid, or network of crossing lines, on a globe or map. They can be used to determine exact locations east and west of the prime meridian and north and south of the equator. For example, if a ship reported its position as 30° south latitude and 165° east longitude, it would be off the coast of Australia. Why is this system of locating points helpful in shipping?

Figure 9–16 *This photograph of San Francisco, California, was taken from space. Scientists use photographs such as this one to make detailed maps of cities.*

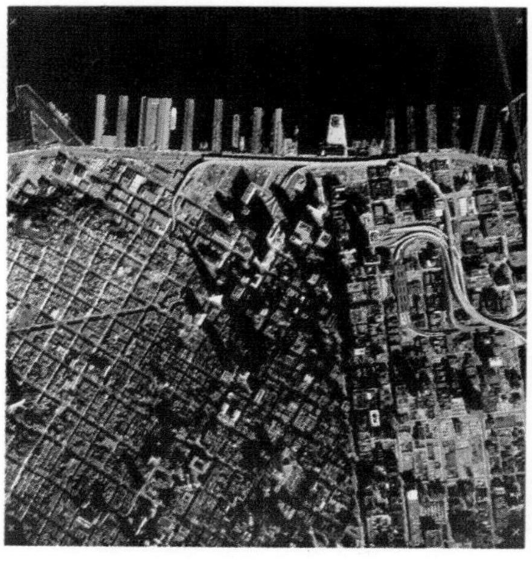

Types of Maps

Maps of the earth are very useful. They show locations and distances on the earth's surface. They also show many different local features. Some maps show the soil types in an area. Some show currents in the ocean. Some maps show small, detailed areas of the earth. Maps of cities may show every street in those cities.

Maps have one serious drawback. Because they are flat, maps cannot accurately represent a round surface. Like a photograph of a person, a map is only a **projection,** or a representation of a three-dimensional object on a flat surface. When the round surface of the earth is represented on the flat surface of a map, changes occur in the shapes and sizes of landmasses and oceans. These changes are called distortion. Despite such distortion, maps are still very useful.

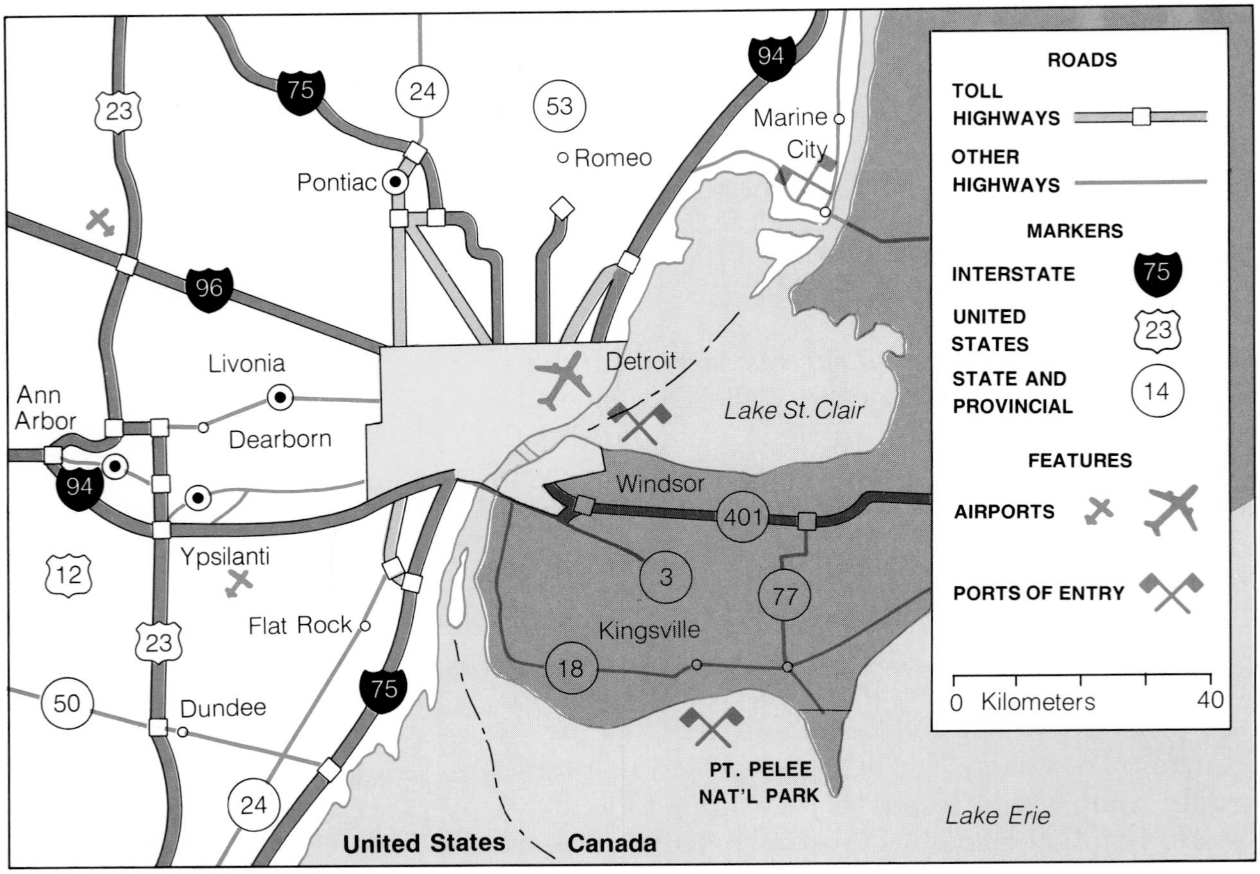

Figure 9–17 *One of the most familiar types of maps is a road map. Notice the legend, which supplies valuable information about the scale and symbols used on the map.*

MERCATOR PROJECTIONS There are many different ways to project the earth's image onto a map. One type of map projection is a **Mercator projection.** Mercator projections are used for navigation. They show the correct shapes of the coastlines. But the sizes of land and water areas become distorted in latitudes far from the equator. For example, on the Mercator projection in Figure 9–18, Greenland appears much larger than it really is.

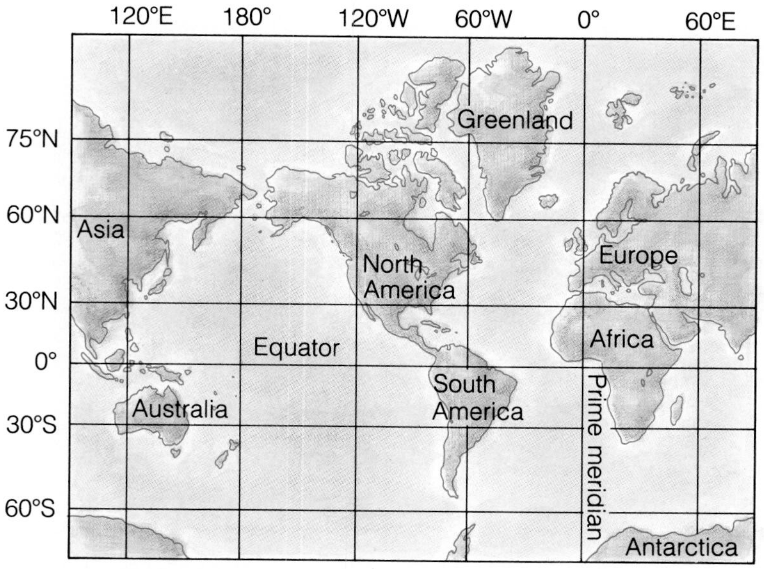

Figure 9–18 *This type of map is called a Mercator projection. What feature of this map is distorted?*

Sharpen Your Skills

The History of Map Making

Using reference materials in the library, write a short essay on the history of map making from the time of the Babylonians to the present. Include information on the following:

Gerhardus Mercator
Christopher Columbus
Claudius Ptolemy
Amerigo Vespucci
Satellite mapping

Include drawings and illustrations with your essay.

EQUAL-AREA PROJECTIONS Another type of map projection is called an **equal-area projection.** Equal-area projections show area correctly. The meridians and parallels are placed on the map in such a way that every part of the earth is the same size on the map as it is on a globe. But the shapes of the areas are distorted on an equal-area projection. What areas in Figure 9–19 look distorted to you?

Figure 9–19 *The correct areas of the earth's landmasses are shown on this map. But the correct shapes are not. What type of map is this?*

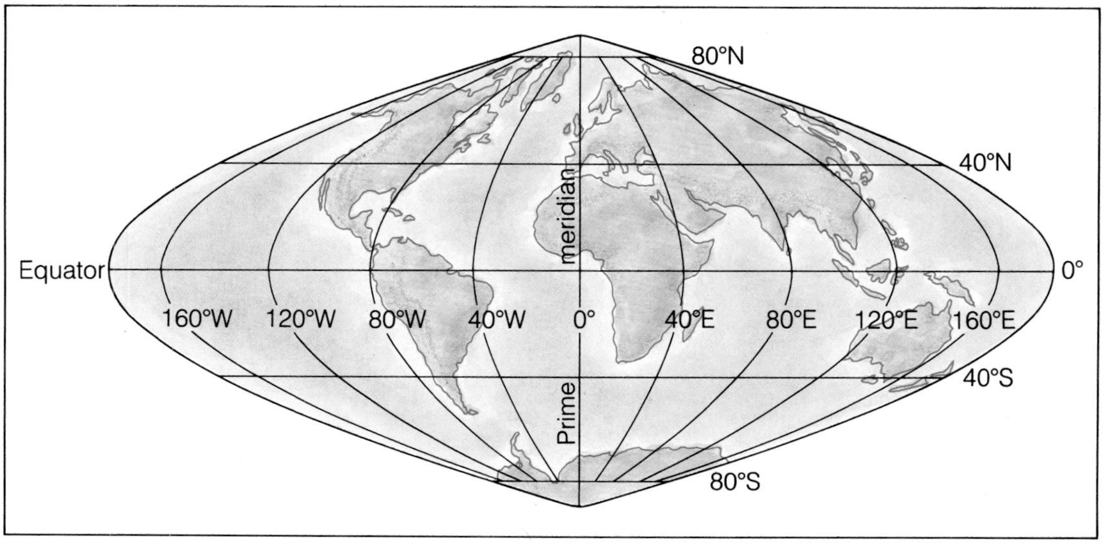

CAREER — *Surveyor*

HELP WANTED: SURVEYOR For private mapping company. Bachelor's degree in surveying required. Good writing skills helpful. Mostly outdoor work.

Before a highway can be planned, engineers must know the height and shape of the land on which the highway is to be built. The measuring of the elevation, size, and shape of any part of the earth's surface is done by **surveyors** and their assistants. A surveying team usually consists of from three to six workers. Based on the information the surveyors obtain, sketches, maps, and reports describing the land are prepared.

Surveyors spend a great deal of their time outdoors. They work in all kinds of environments. Many surveyors are employed by construction companies. Some surveyors work for government agencies such as the highway department. Others work for companies that conduct land surveys for a fee.

To learn more about this field, write to American Congress on Surveying and Mapping, 210 Little Falls Street, Falls Church, VA 22046.

SECTION REVIEW

1. What are time zones?
2. Compare a Mercator projection with an equal-area projection.
3. Under what circumstances would a globe be more useful than a map?

Section Objective

To apply topographic maps to the structure of the earth's landmasses

9–4 Topographic Maps

You have learned that the earth has a varied topography. There are mountains, plains, valleys, and other features. A map that shows the different shapes and sizes of a land surface is called a **topographic map.** This type of map may also show cities, roads, parks, and railroads.

Topographic maps show the relief of the land. Some topographic maps show relief by using different colors for different elevations. But most topographic maps use **contour lines** to show relief. A contour line is a line that passes through all points on a map that have the same elevation.

The difference in elevation from one contour line to the next is called the **contour interval.** For example, in a map with a contour interval of 5 meters, contour lines are drawn only at the elevations of 0 meters, 5 meters, 10 meters, 15 meters, and so on. Look at the contour lines in Figure 9–20. What contour interval is used? What is the highest elevation on the hill?

Like other maps, topographic maps use symbols to represent the features shown. Symbols for buildings and roads are usually black. Symbols for bodies of water such as rivers, lakes, and streams are blue. Green represents woods and swamps. And contour lines are brown or red. All symbols on a map are placed in a **legend.** The legend explains what each symbol represents. See the legend in Figure 9–21 for some common map symbols and their meanings.

The information on a topographic map is very useful in understanding the landscape features of an area. But the many lines on a topographic map can be quite confusing. The following rules will make it easier for you to read this type of map.

1. A contour line of one elevation never crosses or divides a contour line of another elevation. Each contour line represents only one elevation. The contour lines cannot intersect since one point cannot have two different elevations.

2. Closely spaced contour lines represent a steep slope. The lines are closely spaced because the elevation of a steep slope changes greatly over a very short distance. Contour lines spaced far apart represent a gentle slope. The lines are far apart because the elevation of a gentle slope changes only slightly from one point to another.

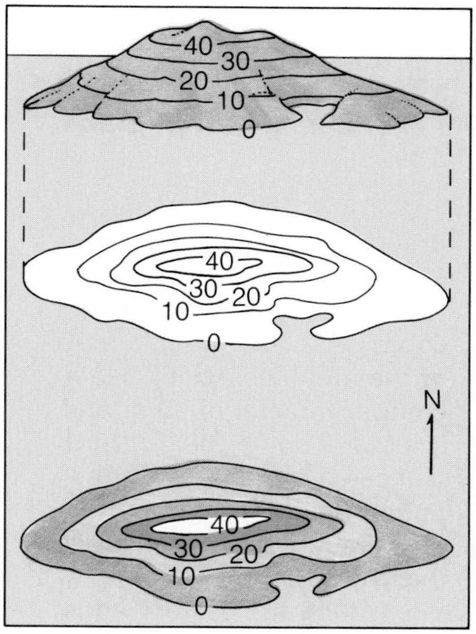

Figure 9–20 *Some topographic maps use colors to indicate different elevations. Others use contour lines to show different elevations.*

Figure 9–21 *The symbols in this legend are commonly found on topographic maps. Different colors are used for different types of symbols. What color would the symbol for an office building be?*

TOPOGRAPHIC MAP SYMBOLS

Symbol	Meaning	Symbol	Meaning	Symbol	Meaning
	House	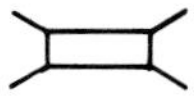	Bridge		Pond or lake
	School		Railroad		Contour line
	Road		Stream		Depression
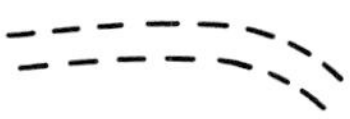	Unpaved road		Seasonal stream		Swamp

Sharpen Your Skills

Constructing a Topographic Map

1. On a sheet of paper, draw a rectangle 11 cm by 8 cm. This is your map area.

2. Use the following data to construct a topographic map of the area described. Use a contour interval of 10 m and a scale of 1 cm = 100 m. North is located at the top of the paper. Read through all the information before constructing your map.

a. Along the eastern edge of the map area, the elevation of the relatively flat landscape is 10 m. Elevation increases 10 m every 100 m to the west.

b. A mountain is located 650 m from the eastern edge of the map area. The circumference of the mountain's base is 2000 m. The mountain's peak is at an elevation of 950 m. The northern slope is the steepest.

c. A river flows from west to east along the southern edge of the mountain.

3. Contour lines that cross a valley are V shaped. If a stream flows through the valley, the V will point upstream, or in the direction opposite to the flow of the stream.

4. Contour lines form closed loops around hilltops and depressions. Elevation numbers on the contour lines indicate whether a feature is a hilltop or depression. If the numbers increase toward the center of the closed loop, the feature is a hilltop. If the numbers decrease, the feature is a depression. Sometimes elevation numbers are not given. Instead short dashes called hachures (HASH-oorz) are used to indicate a depression. Hachures are drawn perpendicular to the contour line that loops around a depression. The hachures point to the inside of the loop.

See Figure 9–22. You should be able to understand all of the information on the map. What is the location of the depression? Which mountain has the steeper slope? In what direction does the Campbell River flow? Now see Figures 9–24 on page 232 and 9–25 on page 233. Use the legend in Figure 9–21 and the rules you have just learned to identify other topographic features.

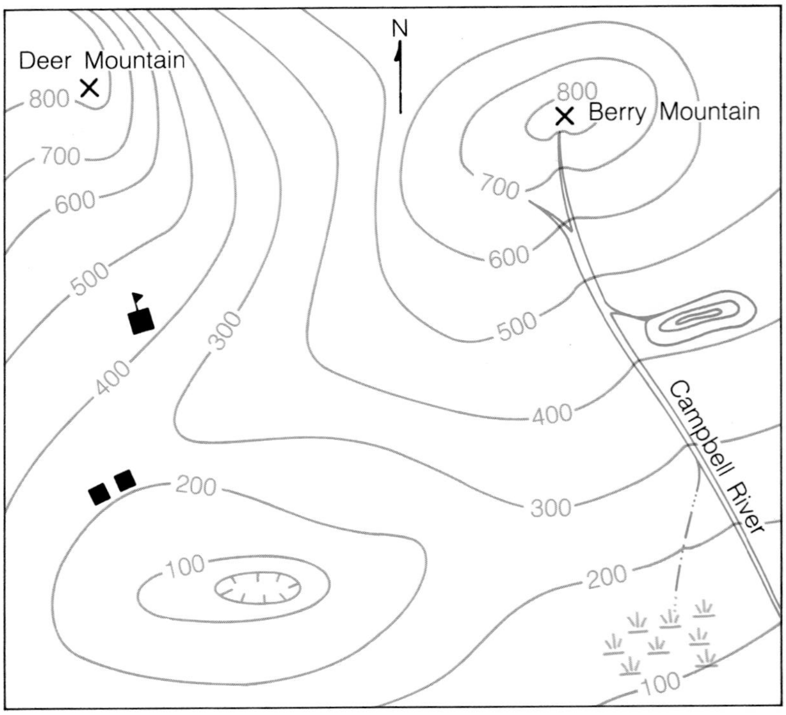

Figure 9–22 *Once you learn the meanings of map symbols, topographic maps such as this one are easy to understand. What is the symbol in green in the bottom right corner of the map?*

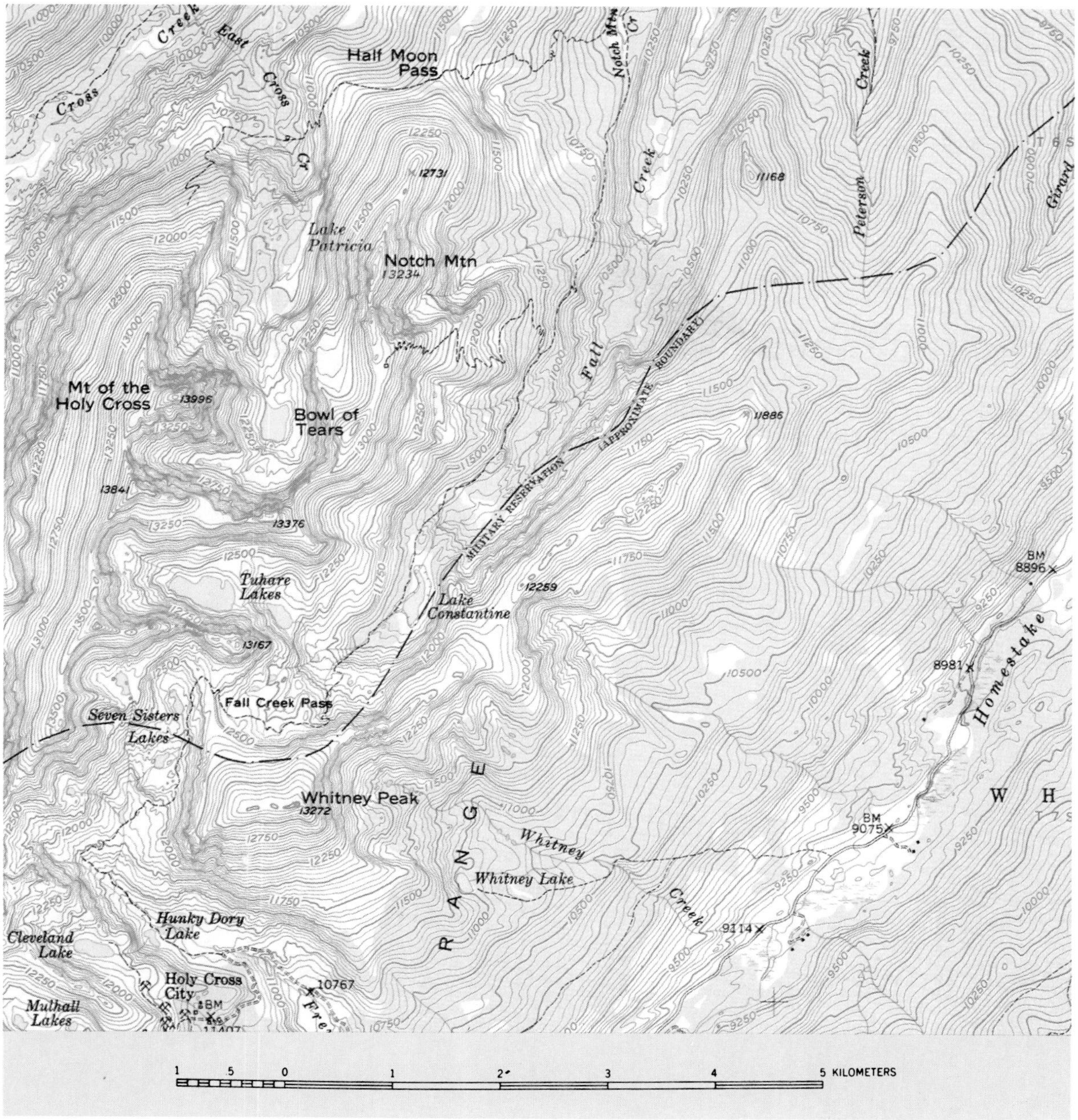

Figure 9–23 *This is a topographic map of Holy Cross Quadrangle, Colorado. What type of landscape region do you think this area is part of? How are changes in elevation shown? What is the highest point shown on this map?*

SECTION REVIEW

1. What is a contour line?
2. Why would it be difficult to show a vertical cliff on a topographic map?
3. Why is a larger contour interval used for mapping mountains than is used for mapping flat areas?

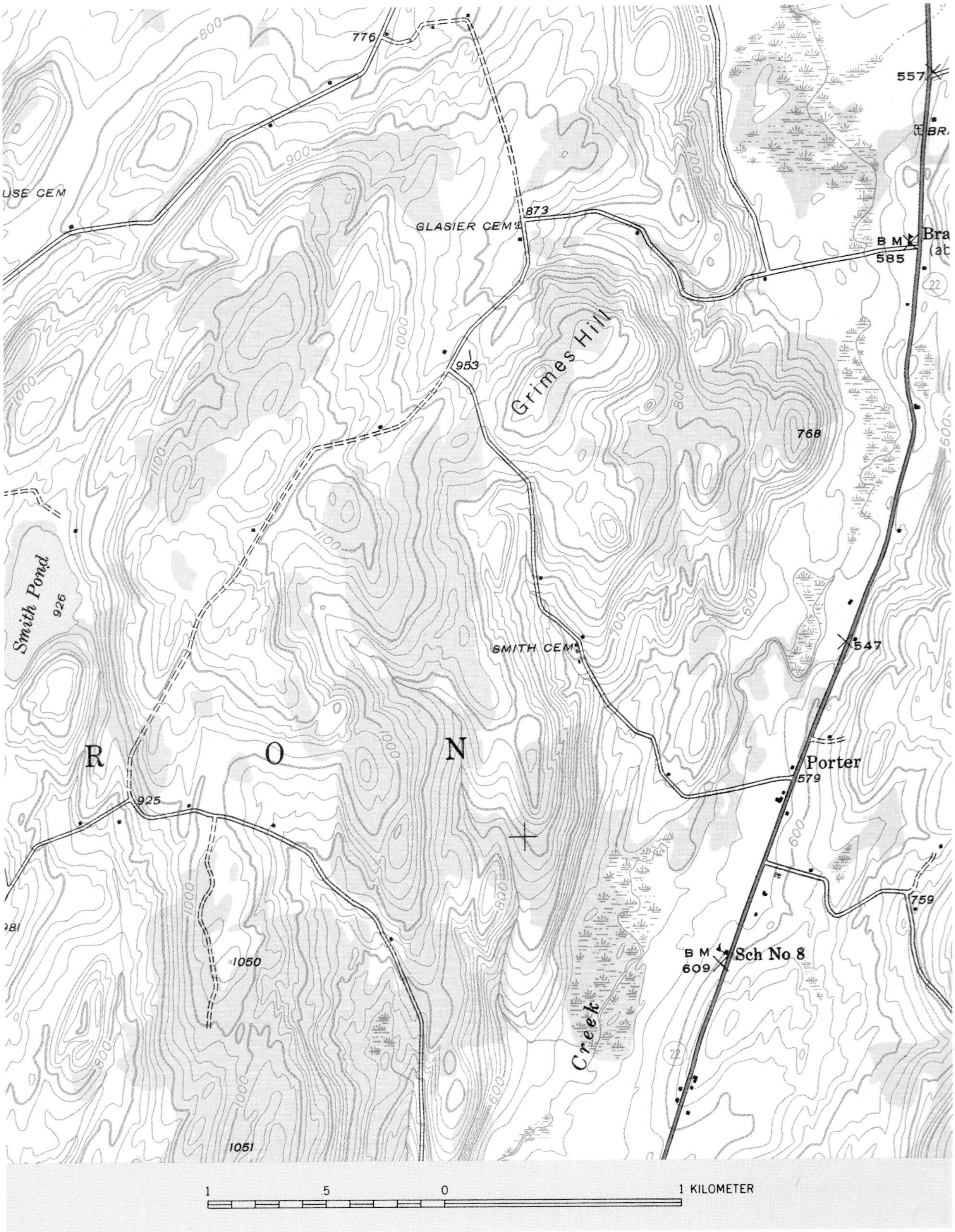

Figure 9–24 *This is a topographic map of Hebron County, New York. What landscape features can you identify?*

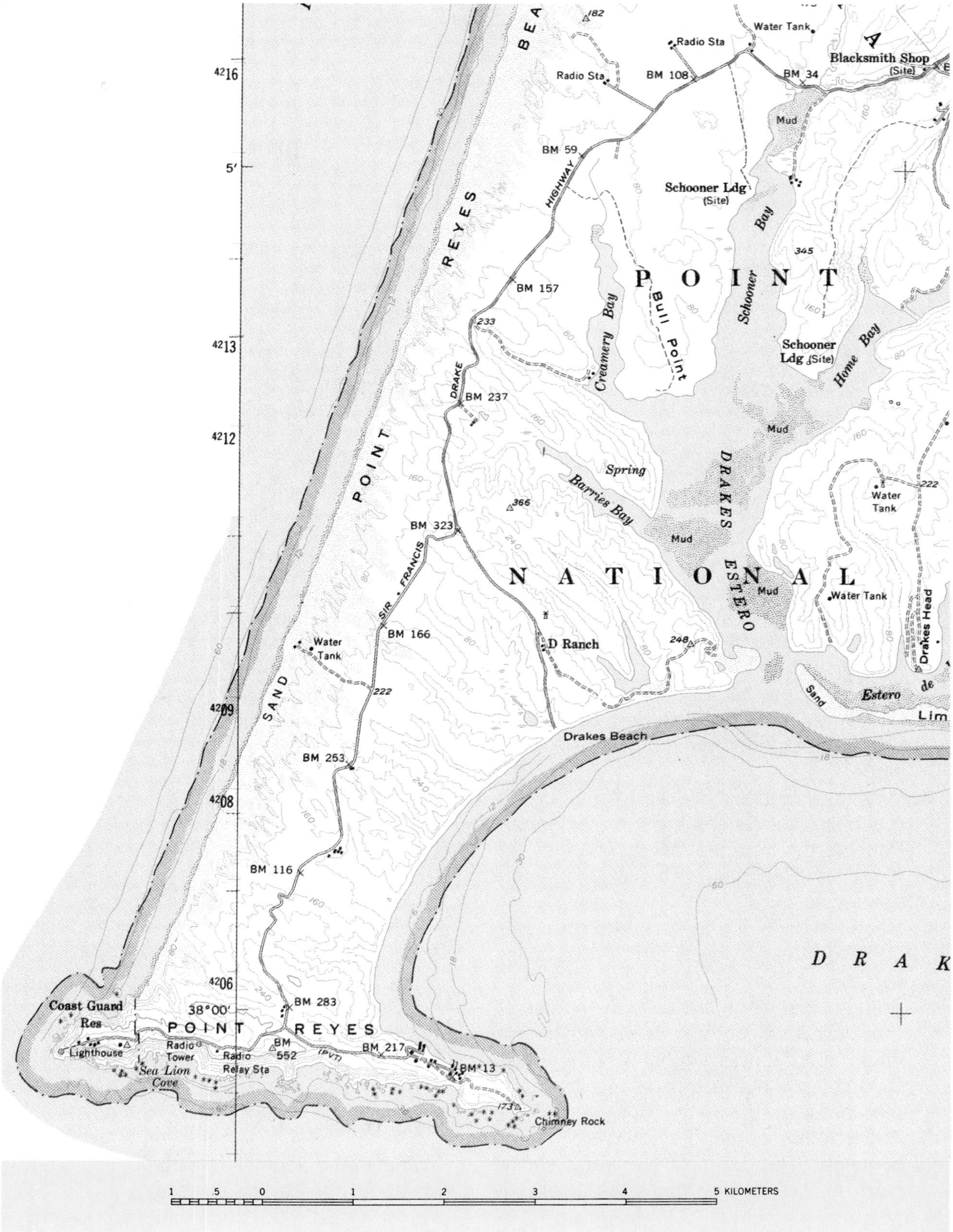

Figure 9–25 *This topographic map of Point Reyes, California, shows a shoreline. What type of landscape region do you think this is part of?*

9 LABORATORY INVESTIGATION

Making a Topographic Map

Problem

What information can topographic maps provide about the earth's surface?

Materials *(per group)*

Aquarium tank or deep-sided pan
Modeling clay
Metric ruler
Rigid cardboard
Pane of clear glass
Grease pencil
Sheet of unlined, white paper
1 L water
Pencil

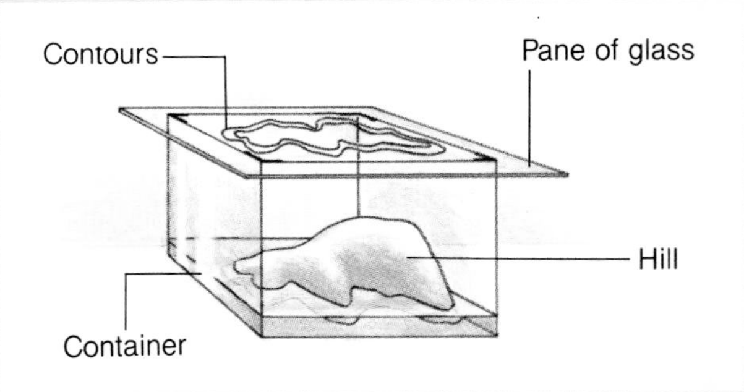

Procedure

1. Cut the cardboard to fit the bottom of the tank or pan.
2. On top of the cardboard, shape the clay into a model of a hill. Include on the model some gullies, a steep slope, and a gentle slope.
3. When the model is dry and hard, place the model and cardboard into the tank or pan. Pour water into the container until the water is 1 cm deep. This will represent sea level.
4. Place the pane of glass over the container. Looking straight down into the container, use the grease pencil to trace the outline of the container on the glass. Also trace on the glass the contour, or outline, of the water around the edges of the model. Carefully remove the pane of glass from the container.
5. Add another centimeter of water to the container. The depth of the water should now be 2 cm. Place the glass in exactly the same position as before. Trace the new contour of the water on the pane of glass.
6. Repeat step 5, adding 1 cm to the depth of the water each time. Stop when the next addition of water would completely cover the model.
7. Remove the glass. With a pencil, trace the contours on the glass onto the sheet of paper. This will be your topographic map.
8. Assume that every centimeter of water above sea level equals 100 m of elevation on the map. Label the elevation of each contour line.

Observations

1. What is the approximate elevation of the top of the hill?
2. How can you determine if the hill has a steep slope by looking at the contour lines?
3. How can you determine if the hill has a gentle slope by looking at the contour lines?
4. How do the contour lines look where they show the gullies on the model?

Conclusions

What information can topographic maps provide about the earth's surface?

CHAPTER REVIEW

SUMMARY

9–1 Continents

❑ There are four major landmasses and many islands scattered throughout the oceans.

❑ There are seven continents on the earth: Africa, Antarctica, Asia, Australia, Europe, North America, and South America.

❑ Antarctica is almost completely covered by an icecap and is the coldest area on the earth.

❑ Australia is the smallest continent.

9–2 Topography

❑ The shape of the earth's surface is called its topography.

❑ The different physical features of an area are called its landscape.

❑ The three main types of landscape regions are mountains, plains, and plateaus.

❑ Mountains have high elevations. They are areas of very high relief.

❑ Mountains are usually part of larger groups called mountain ranges, mountain systems, and mountain belts.

❑ Plains are flat land areas that are not far above sea level. They are areas of low relief.

❑ Low, flat areas along the coast are called coastal plains. Low, flat areas found inland are called interior plains.

❑ Plateaus are broad, flat areas that rise more than 600 meters above sea level.

9–3 Mapping the Earth's Surface

❑ A map is a drawing of the earth, or part of the earth, on a flat surface. The most accurate representation of the earth is a globe.

❑ The earth is divided by lines that run from north to south, called meridians, and by lines that run from east to west, called parallels.

❑ Meridians are used to measure longitude. Parallels are used to measure latitude.

❑ The earth is divided into 24 time zones in which all areas have the same local time.

9–4 Topographic Maps

❑ Topographic maps show the different shapes and sizes of land surfaces.

❑ Topographic maps use contour lines to show relief.

❑ A legend explains the symbols used on a map.

VOCABULARY

Define each term in a complete sentence.

coastal plain
continent
contour interval
contour line
elevation
equal-area projection
equator
globe
interior plain
international date line
island
landscape
latitude
legend
longitude
map
Mercator projection
meridian
mountain
mountain belt
mountain range
mountain system
parallel
plain
plateau
prime meridian
projection
relief
scale
shield
time zone
topographic map
topography

CONTENT REVIEW: MULTIPLE CHOICE

Choose the letter of the answer that best completes each sentence.

1. Land areas that measure millions of square kilometers and rise a considerable distance above sea level are called
a. continents b. mountains c. parallels d. contours

2. The smallest landmass still considered a continent is
a. North America b. Australia c. Greenland d. Antarctica

3. Large areas of very old, exposed rock that form the core of each continent are called
a. icecaps b. mountains c. shields d. meridians

4. Tops of mountains are called
a. gorges b. elevations c. summits d. projections

5. Individual mountains are usually
a. volcanic mountains b. mountain systems
c. plateaus d. none of these

6. The landscape region with the lowest overall elevation is a (an)
a. mountain belt b. coastal plain c. plateau d. interior plain

7. Broad, flat areas of land over 600 meters above sea level are called
a. plains b. plateaus c. farmland d. mountains

8. The measure of distance east or west of the prime meridian is called
a. latitude b. parallel c. projection d. longitude

9. A map projection that shows the correct shapes of coastlines but distorts the sizes of regions far from the equator is called a (an)
a. Mercator projection b. equal-area projection
c. topographic map d. contour projection

10. Lines on a map that pass through points with the same elevation are called
a. meridians b. contour lines c. parallels d. lines of relief

CONTENT REVIEW: COMPLETION

Fill in the word or words that best complete each sentence.

1. The seven large landmasses on the earth are called ________.

2. The coldest continent is ________.

3. The shape of the earth's surface is called its ________.

4. The difference in elevations within a landscape region is called ________.

5. Most mountain ranges and mountain systems are part of a larger group of mountains called a (an) ________.

6. A (An) ________ compares distance on a map to actual distance on the earth's surface.

7. The ________ runs through Greenwich, England.

8. The network of crossing lines formed by meridians and parallels on a globe or map is called a (an) ________.

9. Contour lines on a globe or map indicate points of equal ________.

10. ________ are short dashes drawn perpendicular to the contour line that loops around a depression.

CONTENT REVIEW: TRUE OR FALSE

Determine whether each statement is true or false. If it is true, write "true." If it is false, change the underlined word or words to make the statement true.

1. Europe, Africa, and Asia together form the earth's largest landmass.
2. Central America is part of the continent of South America.
3. The three main types of landscape regions are mountains, plains, and continents.
4. There are two major mountain ranges on the earth's surface.
5. Coastal plains are higher in elevation than interior plains.
6. Plains are broad, flat areas of land that rise more than 600 meters above sea level.
7. Many plateaus of the world are dry areas.
8. The distance around the earth is measured in degrees.
9. The prime meridian divides the parallels of north latitude from those of south latitude.
10. The time in a city one time zone west of another city will be one hour earlier.

CONCEPT REVIEW: SKILL BUILDING

Use the skills you have developed in this chapter to complete each activity.

1. **Making predictions** Most of the earth's ice is found on or around Antarctica. Suppose the temperature of the South Pole rises high enough to melt all of Antarctica's ice. Which landscape region will be most affected? Why?
2. **Interpreting maps** In Figure 9–24, what contour interval is used? At what elevation is School Number 8? If you wanted to take an easy hike up Grimes Hill, which slope would you choose to climb? Why? Why would you not want to hike in the area just west of the major highway? Locate the unpaved road west of Grimes Hill. If you walked from one end of the road to the other, how many kilometers would you have walked? Does the stream flow in or out of Lake Smith? How can you tell?
3. **Applying concepts** Look at the contour lines in Figure 9–25. What contour interval is used? Which area has the steepest cliffs? Explain your answer. Which area has the lowest relief? Explain your answer. What do you think will happen to the Bull Point area if sea level rises 100 feet?
4. **Making maps** Draw topographic maps of three imaginary areas. The first area has a mountain landscape, the second has a landscape of a plain, and the third has a landscape of several plateaus separated by rivers.

CONCEPT REVIEW: ESSAY

Discuss each of the following in a brief paragraph.

1. Describe a shield and its relationship to a continent.
2. What are the similarities and differences between interior plains and coastal plains?
3. Explain the need for the international date line.
4. What are some ways that maps and globes are useful?
5. Why is it that the distance measured by degrees of latitude always stays the same while the distance measured by degrees of longitude varies?

The Earth's Fresh Water

10

CHAPTER SECTIONS

10–1 Fresh Water on the Earth's Surface

10–2 Fresh Water Beneath the Earth's Surface

10–3 Water as a Solvent

CHAPTER OBJECTIVES

After completing this chapter, you will be able to

10–1 Identify the processes of the water cycle.

10–1 List the major sources of fresh water on the earth's surface.

10–2 Explain the relationship between groundwater, the water table, and the structure of the ground.

10–3 Describe how water can dissolve substances.

10–3 Determine how the earth's water resources can be kept clean.

The newspaper headlines said it all. Water, a substance most people take for granted, seemed to be creating problems all over the country. In some places there was too much of it, and in other places too little!

A severe drought in the West had left hundreds of square kilometers of forest dry and parched. Forest fires raged in these areas and caused heavy damage to property. Firefighters battled in vain to stem the fire's path of destruction.

Several northeastern states faced one of the worst water shortages ever. Reservoirs, which supplied water for millions of people, were far below their normal level. Plans were quickly being made to use nearby rivers as sources of water.

Meanwhile heavy rains in some southern states had flooded rivers, lakes, and streams. Dams could no longer contain the huge quantities of water. In several areas, the force of this water had caused the collapse of dams. Water and thick streams of mud rushed forward. They buried land and homes under a sheet of wet, brown dirt. The safety of the people was threatened. Millions of dollars in property was lost forever.

Perhaps you do not often think of water as the cause of such problems. To you, water is a "friend"—a natural resource you use every day to stay alive. In fact, more than 500 billion liters of water are used every day by people, industry, and agriculture in the United States alone. This amount will probably double in the next 20 years. Where does the earth's fresh water come from? Will there be enough for everyone? In this chapter, you will learn about the earth's supply of fresh water and the answers to these questions.

Fresh water is one of the earth's most important natural resources and a substance most living things need to stay alive.

10–1 Fresh Water on the Earth's Surface

Section Objective

To identify sources of fresh water on the earth's surface

Sharpen Your Skills

I'm Thirsty

An average person needs about 2.5 L of water a day to live. How much water will each person need in a year? How much water will your class need in a day to live? In a year?

Water is one of the most abundant substances on the earth's surface. You see that this is true from photographs of the earth taken from space. See Figure 10–1. In fact, astronauts have described the earth as the blue planet!

A casual glance at a world map might make you think that the earth has enough water to meet the needs of living things forever. After all, oceans cover more than 70 percent of the earth's surface. In fact, about 97 percent of the earth's water is found in the oceans. But most of the ocean water cannot be used by living things because it contains salt. The salt would have to be removed before the water could be used.

Fresh water makes up about 3 percent of the earth's water. But most of this fresh water cannot be used because it is locked up in ice, mainly in icecaps near the North and South poles and in glaciers. In fact, only 15 percent of the earth's fresh water is available for use by living things. This very small percent represents the earth's total available supply

Figure 10–1 *You can see from this fantastic photo taken from an Apollo spacecraft why astronauts describe the earth as the blue planet (right). Although the Mississippi River (left) may seem to contain a tremendous amount of water, it holds only a small fraction of all the water on Earth.*

of fresh water. With such a limited supply, you might wonder why the earth does not run out of fresh water. It does not because the supply of fresh water is continuously being renewed.

The Water Cycle

Most of the fresh water on the earth's surface is found in moving water and in standing water. Rivers, streams, and springs are moving water. Ponds, lakes, and swampy wetlands are standing water.

Water moves among these sources of fresh water, the salty oceans, the air, and the land in an endless cycle. A cycle is a continuous chain of events. The **water cycle** is the continuous movement of water from the oceans and freshwater sources to the air and land and then back to the oceans. The water cycle, also called the hydrologic cycle, constantly renews the earth's supply of fresh water. Three main steps make up the water cycle.

The first step of the water cycle involves the heat energy of the sun. This energy causes the water on the surface of the earth to change to a vapor, or gas. This process is called **evaporation** (ih-vap-uh-RAY-shuhn). Enormous amounts of water evaporate from the oceans. Water also evaporates from freshwater sources, as well as from the soil, animals, and plants. The water vapor is then carried by winds over the land and oceans.

The second step of the water cycle involves a process called **condensation** (kahn-duhn-SAY-shuhn). Condensation is the process by which vapor changes back into a liquid. For condensation to occur, the air containing the water vapor must be cooled. And this is exactly what happens as the warm air close to the earth's surface rises. The warm air cools and can no longer hold as much water vapor. Most of the water vapor condenses into droplets of water that form clouds. But these clouds are not "salty" clouds. When the water evaporates from the oceans, the salt is left behind. Why do you think this is important?

During the third step of the water cycle, the water returns to the earth in the form of rain, snow, sleet, or hail. This process is called **precipitation** (prih-sihp-uh-TAY-shuhn). Precipitation occurs when

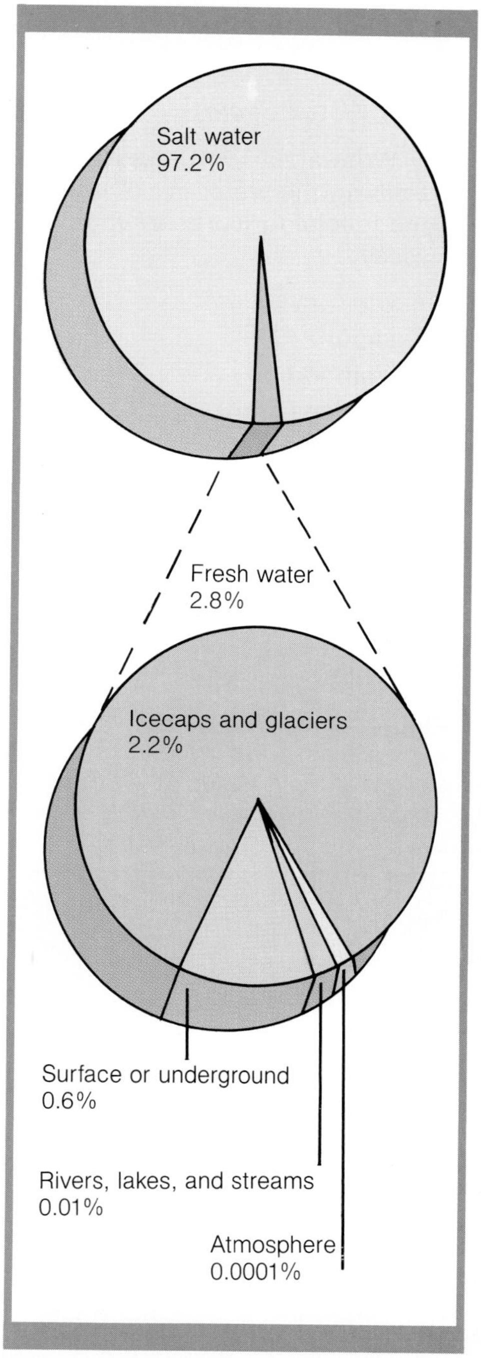

Figure 10–2 *This graph shows the distribution of the earth's water. What percent of the earth is fresh water? Is all this water available for use? Why?*

Sharpen Your Skills

The Water Cycle

Write a 250-word essay describing the water cycle. Use the following words in your essay:

water cycle
vapor
evaporation
condensation
precipitation
groundwater

the water droplets that form clouds become too numerous and too heavy to remain floating in the air. Water that falls to the earth as rain, snow, sleet, or hail is fresh water.

After the water falls to the earth, some of the water returns to the atmosphere through evaporation. Then the cycle begins again. As a result of the water cycle, the earth's supply of fresh water is continuously renewed.

Some of the remaining water that is returned to the earth may run off into ponds, lakes, streams, rivers, or oceans. Some may soak into the ground and become **groundwater.** Groundwater is the water that remains in the ground. At some point, the groundwater flows underground to the oceans. This water then reenters the water cycle. You will learn more about groundwater in Section 10–2.

Frozen Water

If you make a snowball out of freshly fallen snow and hold it tightly for a while, the warmth from your hands will cause the snow to melt. The

Figure 10–3 *The water cycle constantly renews the earth's supply of fresh water. What three processes make up the water cycle?*

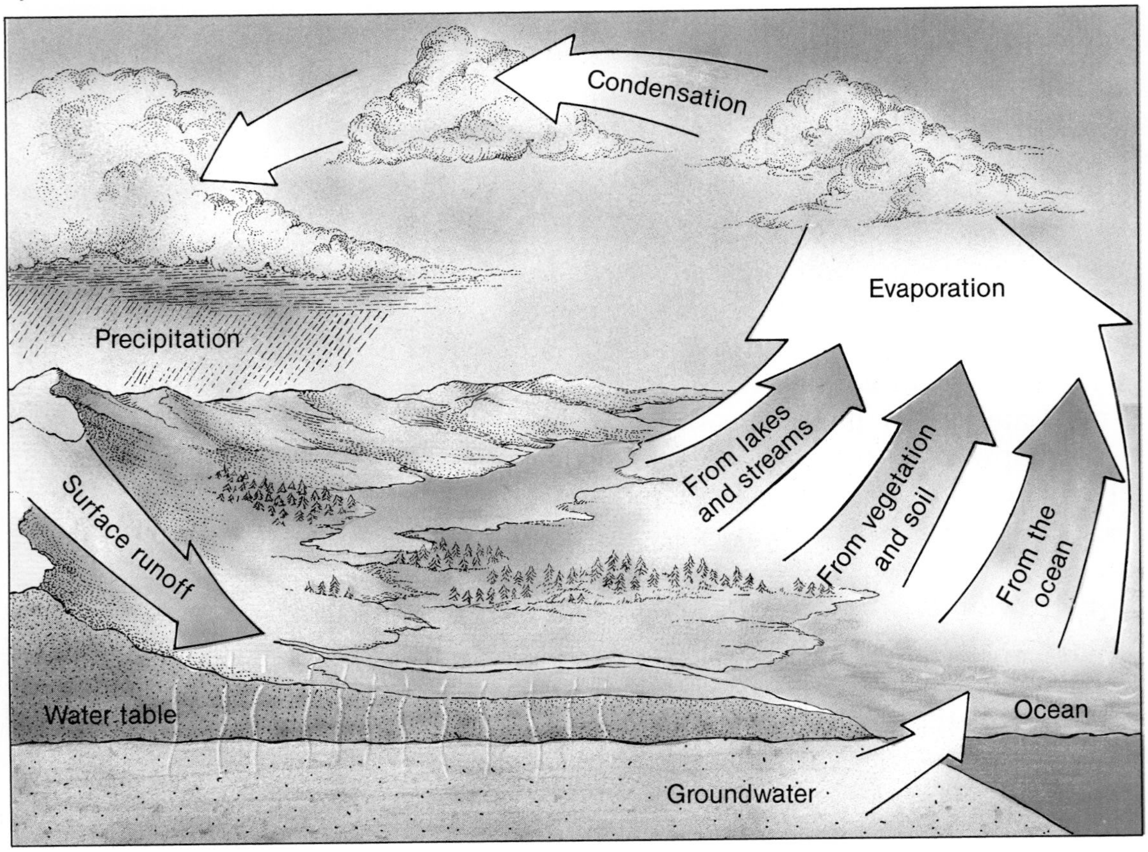

CAREER

Wastewater-Treatment-Plant Operator

HELP WANTED: OPERATOR FOR WASTEWATER-TREATMENT-PLANT
Trainee needed. Duties will include testing water samples and maintaining equipment. High school diploma necessary.

Every day, large quantities of sewage and other wastewaters pour out of homes, schools, and factories. This water must be cleaned. Harmful bacteria, discarded objects, and other impurities must be removed.

The wastewater that enters sewer systems is carried through a network of pipes to treatment plants. The people who operate treatment plants are **wastewater-treatment-plant operators.** They control and maintain the equipment that removes pollutants from the water. During various steps of the treatment process, they take water samples for testing. Testing the water samples assures that the treatment process is proceeding correctly. Wastewater-treatment-plant operators also regulate the amount of chemicals used to purify the water.

Many people who work in wastewater treatment plants begin as helpers. They get on-the-job training and gradually receive more responsibility. Some operators take special two-year programs in wastewater technology. To learn more about this career, write to the Water Pollution Control Federation, 2626 Pennsylvania Avenue NW, Washington, DC 20037.

snow is a solid form of water. You may also notice that some of the snow in your hands will get pressed together and form ice. The same thing happens when new snow is piled on top of old snow. The pressure of the piled-up snow causes some of the snow to change into ice. A **glacier** is formed. A glacier is a large mass of moving ice and snow.

Glaciers form in very cold areas, such as high in mountains and near the North and South poles. The snow that falls in these areas does not completely melt because of the very cold temperatures. As more snow falls, it buries the older snow. As the snow builds up, the pressure on the older snow squeezes the snow crystals together. Eventually ice forms. When the layers of ice become very thick and heavy, the ice begins to move.

Glaciers contain about 2 percent of the available fresh water of the earth. As sources of fresh water become more and more scarce, scientists are trying to develop ways of using this frozen water to provide fresh water.

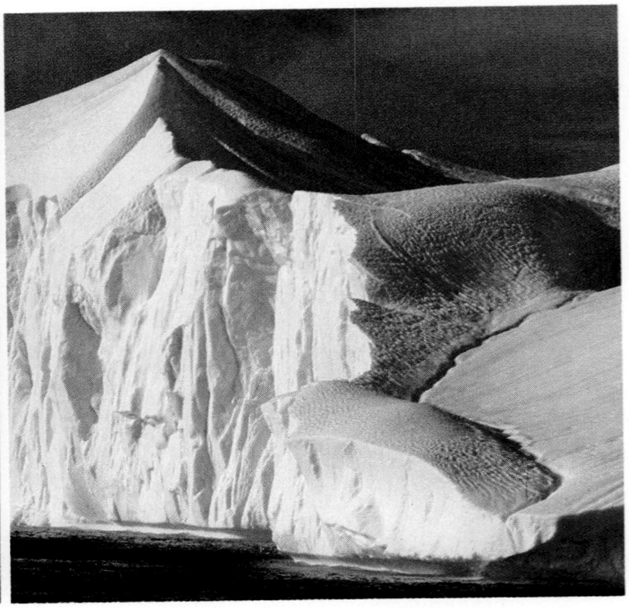

Figure 10–4 *Most of the earth's fresh water is frozen in valley glaciers, such as Davidson Glacier in Alaska (left), and in continental glaciers, such as this Greenland glacier (right).*

Sharpen Your Skills

Simulating the Water Cycle

1. Stir salt into a small jar filled with water until no more salt will dissolve. Pour a 1-cm deep layer of the salt water into a large, wide-mouthed jar.

2. Place a paper cup half filled with sand in the center of the jar.

3. Loosely cover the jar's mouth with plastic wrap. Seal the wrap around the jar's sides using a rubber band.

4. Place a small rock or weight on the plastic wrap directly over the paper cup.

5. Place the jar in direct sunlight. After several hours, observe the setup.

What is the purpose of sealing the jar? What do you notice about the taste of the water on the plastic wrap? What processes of the water cycle can you identify?

VALLEY GLACIERS Long, narrow glaciers that move downhill between the steep sides of mountain valleys are called **valley glaciers.** Usually they follow channels worn by running water in the past. As valley glaciers move downhill, they bend and twist to fit the shape of the surrounding land. The valley walls and the weight of the ice itself keep the glaciers from breaking apart. But on the surface, the ice cracks. Cracks on the surface of glaciers are called **crevasses** (krih-VAS-sehz).

As a valley glacier slides downward, it tears rock fragments from the mountainside. The fragments become frozen in the glacier. They cut deep grooves in the valley walls. Finer bits of rock act like sandpaper, smoothing the surface of the walls.

Mountains located anywhere from the equator to the poles can contain glaciers. There are many glaciers in the United States. Mount Rainier in Washington and Mount Washington in New Hampshire contain small glaciers. There are also glaciers in many of the mountains of Alaska.

As a valley glacier moves, some of the ice begins to melt. A stream of water is formed. This water is called **meltwater.** Meltwater is usually nearly pure. Some cities use meltwater as a source of fresh water. Many cities also use streams of meltwater to generate electricity in hydroelectric plants. But there are some problems in using meltwater in these ways. Building channels or pipelines from glaciers to cities to transport meltwater can be very costly. The construction of hydroelectric plants in the undeveloped areas where glaciers are found could change the environment. What do you think are some environmental problems that might be caused by building hydroelectric plants in these areas?

CONTINENTAL GLACIERS In the polar regions, snow and ice have built up into very thick sheets. These thick sheets of ice are called **continental glaciers,** or polar ice sheets. Continental glaciers cover millions of square kilometers of the earth's surface and may be several thousand meters thick. They move out slowly in all directions.

Large continental glaciers are found in Greenland and Antarctica. Nearly 80 percent of Greenland is covered by ice. More than 90 percent of Antarctica is covered by ice. These huge piles of ice have a thickness of more than 3200 meters at the center. Continental glaciers could be another source of fresh water.

ICEBERGS At the edge of the sea, continental glaciers form overhanging cliffs. Large chunks of ice often break off from the glaciers and drift into the sea. These large chunks of ice are called **icebergs.** Some icebergs are as large as the state of Rhode Island! The continental glaciers of Greenland and Antarctica are the major sources of icebergs in the ocean waters.

Figure 10–5 *Icebergs are large chunks of ice that break off glaciers and drift into the sea. Icebergs often have spectacular shapes, as does this one in the waters off the coast of Labrador, Canada. Only a small part of an iceberg rises above the water's surface. The rest is beneath the surface.*

Icebergs can be a major hazard to ships. In 1912, the ocean liner *Titanic* sank after smashing into an iceberg in the North Atlantic Ocean. Today sea lanes are patrolled constantly by ships and planes on the lookout for icebergs.

There is much fresh water in icebergs. Attempts have been made to develop ways of towing icebergs to areas in need of fresh water, such as deserts. But transporting icebergs from Greenland and Antarctica poses several problems. First, the effect of an iceberg on local weather conditions must be evaluated. Second, the cost and time involved in moving an iceberg to a desert area must be considered. Third, scientists would have to find ways of keeping the iceberg from melting during the journey. What ideas do you have for using and moving icebergs?

Running Water

Rivers and streams are very important sources of fresh water. Many cities and towns were built near rivers and streams. The water was used for irrigating, generating electric power, and drinking. Industry and commerce depend on rivers for transporting supplies and equipment. Rivers and streams are also used for fishing, boating, and swimming.

Figure 10–6 *Rain and melted snow that do not evaporate or soak into the soil form surface runoff. What are the probable destinations of this surface runoff?*

Rain and melted snow that do not evaporate or soak into the soil flow into rivers and streams. The water entering a river or stream after a heavy rain or during a spring thaw of snow or ice is called **surface runoff.**

The amount of surface runoff is affected by several factors. One factor is the type of soil the rain or snow falls on. Some soils soak up more water than others. Such soils have more space between their particles. The space between particles of soil is called the **pore space.** The more pore space a soil has, the more water it will hold. The condition of the soil also affects the amount of runoff. If the soil is dry, it will soak up a great deal of water and thus reduce the surface runoff.

The number of plants growing in the soil also affects the amount of runoff. Plant roots absorb water from the soil. In areas where there are many plants, large amounts of water are absorbed. So the runoff there is less. The seasons are another factor in the amount of runoff. There will be more runoff in rainy seasons and in the spring when large amounts of snow are melting.

A land area in which surface runoff drains into a river or a system of rivers and streams is called a **watershed.** Watersheds can be very small or very large. Some watersheds cover millions of acres and drain their water into the oceans. Watersheds prevent floods and water shortages by controlling the amount of water that feeds into streams and rivers. They also help to provide a steady flow of fresh water to the oceans. How do you think the construction of roads in a watershed area might affect the nearby rivers and streams?

Many rivers are sources of fresh water. The amount of water in a river and the speed at which the water flows affect the usefulness of a river as a source of fresh water. Rivers that move quickly carry a lot of water. But because the water is moving rapidly, they also carry a large amount of soil, pebbles, and other sediments. The water in these rivers often looks cloudy. Slow-moving rivers do not churn up as much sediment. Their water is clearer. These rivers are better sources of fresh water.

In recent years, pollution has had an effect on the usefulness of rivers as sources of fresh water. If a river has many factories along its banks that are

Sharpen Your Skills

Comparing Pore Space

1. Fill a plastic cup half full with sand and another cup half full with gravel.

2. Shake the cups to settle the contents of each.

3. Fill a measuring cup with 100 mL of water. Slowly pour just enough water into the cup of sand to cover the top of the particles. Record the amount of water used.

4. Repeat step 3 using the cup of gravel.

Compare the amount of water each cup of particles held. Compare the pore space in each. What might be the effect of planting crops in soil containing a large amount of gravel? A large amount of sand?

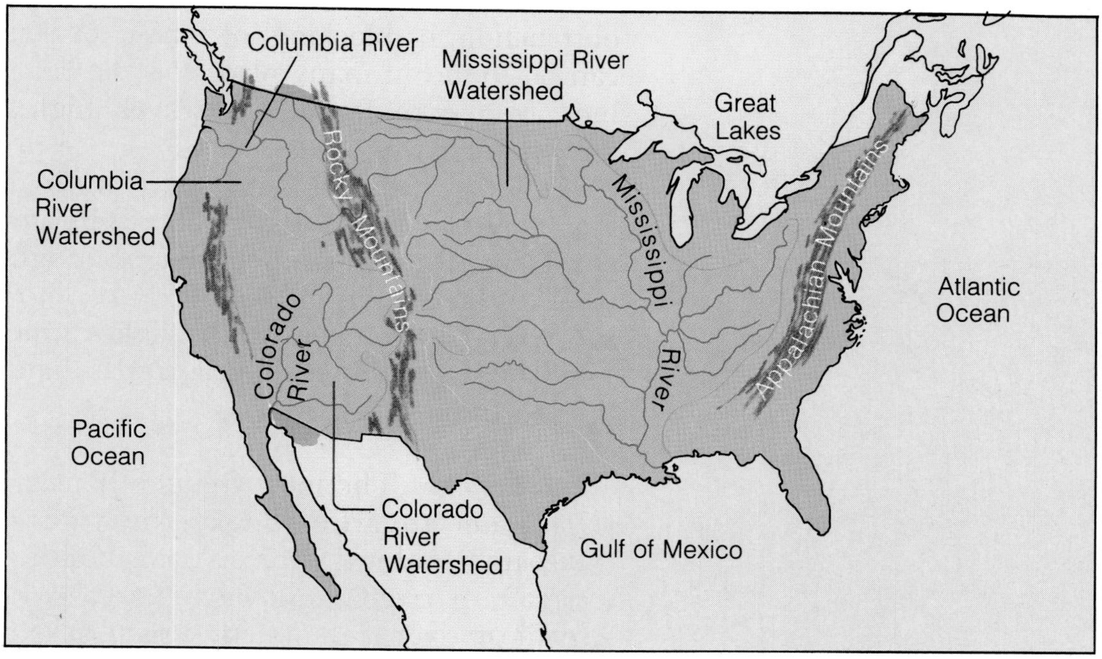

Figure 10–7 *The major watersheds of the United States are shown here. Which watershed is the largest?*

Figure 10–8 *Pollution of fresh water is a major problem today. Water can be polluted by poisonous chemicals, untreated wastes, oil spills, and litter from people and industry. Would you want to get your fresh water from the source pictured here?*

discharging wastes into the river, the water will become polluted. The water must be cleaned before it can be used. Some rivers are so heavily polluted that they cannot be used as sources of fresh water.

Standing Water

Within a watershed, some of the surface runoff gets caught in low places. Standing bodies of fresh water are formed there. These standing bodies of water are called lakes and ponds, depending on their size.

Like streams and rivers, lakes and ponds continually receive runoff from the land. The runoff keeps them from drying up. These standing bodies of water are important sources of fresh water. Moosehead Lake, in Maine, is a natural source of fresh water. It is 56 kilometers long and 3 to 16 kilometers wide. The pine-forested shores of the lake can hold huge amounts of water from rains and melting snow. The water is released slowly to the lake. So flooding is not likely. During times of drought, the lake holds a huge supply of water in reserve.

LAKES AND PONDS Lakes are usually deep depressions in the earth's crust that have filled with fresh water. Rain, melting snow, water from springs and rivers, and surface runoff fill these depressions. A lake is sometimes formed when there is a natural obstruction, or blocking, of a river or stream. Lakes can be found in many places on the earth. They are most frequently found at relatively high altitudes and in areas where glaciers were once present.

Ponds are shallow depressions in the earth's crust that have filled with fresh water. They are usually smaller and not as deep as lakes. Sunlight can penetrate to the bottom of a pond. Lakes, however, have some very deep areas that sunlight cannot reach. Ponds also have more plant growth than lakes. Why do you think this is so?

RESERVOIRS The most frequently used sources of fresh water are artificial lakes known as **reservoirs** (REHZ-uhr-vwahrz). A reservoir is built by damming a stream or river in a low-lying area. When the stream or river is dammed, water backs up behind the dam. Reservoirs have been built near cities

Figure 10–9 *Many large lakes are used by cities as sources of fresh water (left). Ponds can also be used as sources of fresh water but only for a small, local area (right). Why would a pond not be a good source of fresh water for a city?*

and towns and in mountainous regions throughout the country.

Reservoirs serve several purposes. They help control water flow during periods of heavy rain and runoff. This prevents flooding. During periods of little rain or runoff, reservoirs store water. They serve as sources of drinking water for nearby towns and cities and provide irrigation water for farms. Reservoirs can also be used in the generation of electrical power. The water stored behind the dams can be moved through hydroelectric plants. These plants convert the energy of the running water into electrical power.

A reservoir, however, cannot be used for all purposes at the same time. Why is this so? Suppose a reservoir is being used to store water. To use it also in the generation of electricity, the water would have to be drawn from the reservoir and moved through the hydroelectric plant. The reservoir would no longer be storing water.

SECTION REVIEW

1. What are the major sources of fresh water on the earth's surface?
2. What is the water cycle?
3. Why are watersheds important?
4. Explain why a reservoir cannot be used to control flooding and store water at the same time.

Sharpen Your Skills

Hydroelectric Power

The total potential hydroelectric power of the world is 2.25 billion kilowatts. But only 363 million kilowatts of this is being utilized. The United States uses one-sixth of the world's hydroelectric power. Calculate the percent of the world's hydroelectric power that is used compared to the worldwide potential. Then calculate the percent of the world's water power now used in the United States.

10–2 Fresh Water Beneath the Earth's Surface

Section Objective

To identify the relationship between groundwater and the rock and soil through which it moves

Not all of the water that falls to the earth as rain, snow, sleet, or hail runs off into lakes, ponds, and rivers. Some of the water soaks into the ground. Water contained in the ground is one of the earth's most important natural resources. **There is more fresh water below the surface of the land than in all of the lakes and reservoirs on the earth's surface.**

Figure 10–10 *Some of the water that falls to the earth as rain, snow, sleet, or hail soaks into the ground. In some places, this water is very close to the earth's surface. So a well such as this can be used to obtain water.*

Groundwater

If you live in a rural, or country, area, you probably do not get your drinking water from a reservoir or a river. More likely, your water is pumped from a well below the ground. The water stored in the ground is known as groundwater. In many areas, groundwater provides a continuous supply of fresh water.

Groundwater is present because the various forms of precipitation—rain, snow, sleet, and hail—do not stop traveling when they hit the ground. Instead the precipitation continues to move slowly downward through pores in the rocks and soil. If the rocks and soil have many pores between their particles, they can hold large quantities of groundwater. Sand and gravel are two such types of soil.

As the water seeps down, it passes through layers of rocks and soil that allow it to move quickly. Material through which water can move quickly is described as **permeable** (PER-mee-uh-buhl). Sandstone is a rock that is very permeable. But clay, which has small pores between each particle, is not as permeable. Clay is sometimes described as **impermeable.**

UNDERGROUND ZONES Groundwater continues to move downward through permeable rock and soil until it reaches an impermeable layer of rock. It can go no further. So the groundwater fills up all the pores above the impermeable layer. This underground region in which all the pores are filled with water is called the **zone of saturation** (sach-uh-RAY-shuhn).

Above this water-filled zone, the ground is not as wet. Pores in the soil and rocks are filled mostly with air. This drier region in which the pores are filled mostly with air is called the **zone of aeration** (ehr-AY-shuhn).

The surface between the zone of saturation and the zone of aeration is an important boundary. It marks the level below which the ground is saturated, or soaked, with water. This level is called the **water table.** See Figure 10–11.

The water table at the seashore is easy to find. After you dig down a few centimeters, you may notice that the hole you are digging fills with water. At this point, you have found the water table. In general, the water table is not very deep near a large body of water.

In areas near hills or mountains, the water table may be deep in the ground. In low-lying areas such as valleys with swamps and marshes, the water table may be close to or at the surface. The depth of the water table also varies with the climate of the area. It may be very deep in very dry areas such as deserts. It may be close to the surface in wet, low-lying forest areas. In very moist climate regions, the water table may come right to the surface and form a swamp, lake, or spring. Why do you think low-lying areas have a water table close to the surface?

Sharpen Your Skills

Drought and the Water Table

1. Fill a deep clear-glass baking dish about halfway with sand. Make sure the sand covers the bottom of the dish.

2. Slowly add enough water so that the sand becomes saturated and about 1 cm of water is visible above the surface of the sand.

3. Add more sand on top of the water in *only one-half* of the baking dish. You can now see how the water table looks above and below the "earth's" surface after a period of rain.

4. Observe the water level above and below the sand's surface. Continue to observe the water level during the next few days.

What changes do you notice in the water level? How do you think the lowering of the water table during drought might affect people in the area?

Figure 10–11 *A cross section of the zones of underground water is shown here. What separates the zone of aeration from the zone of saturation?*

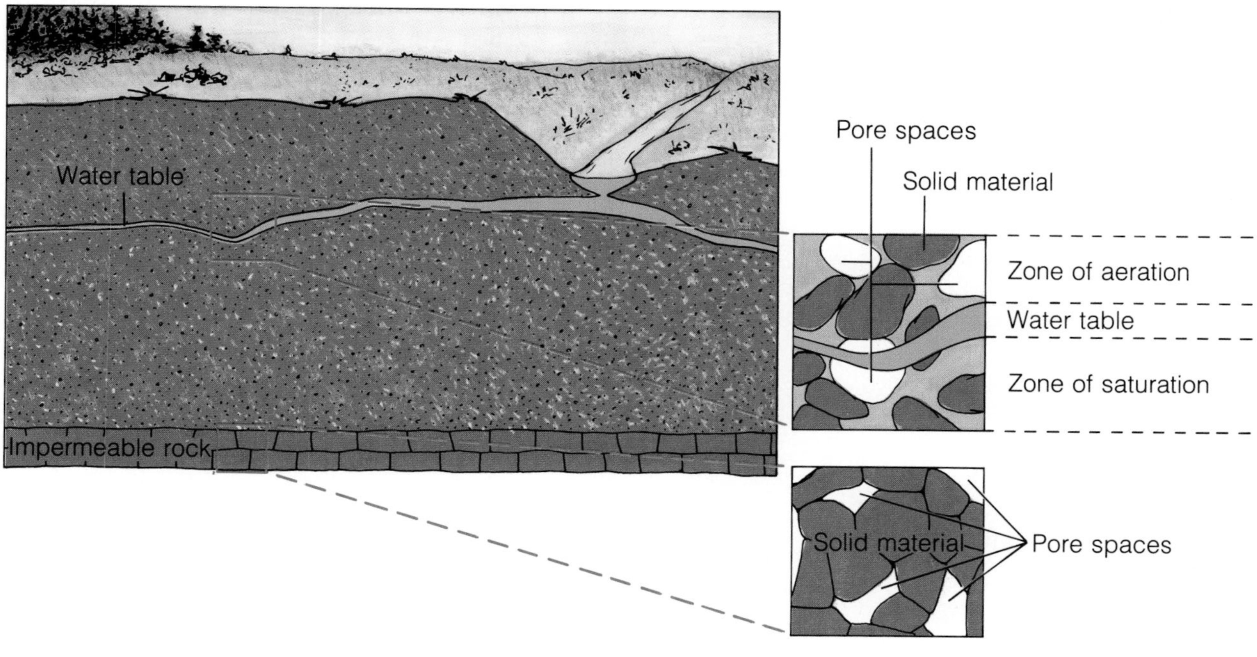

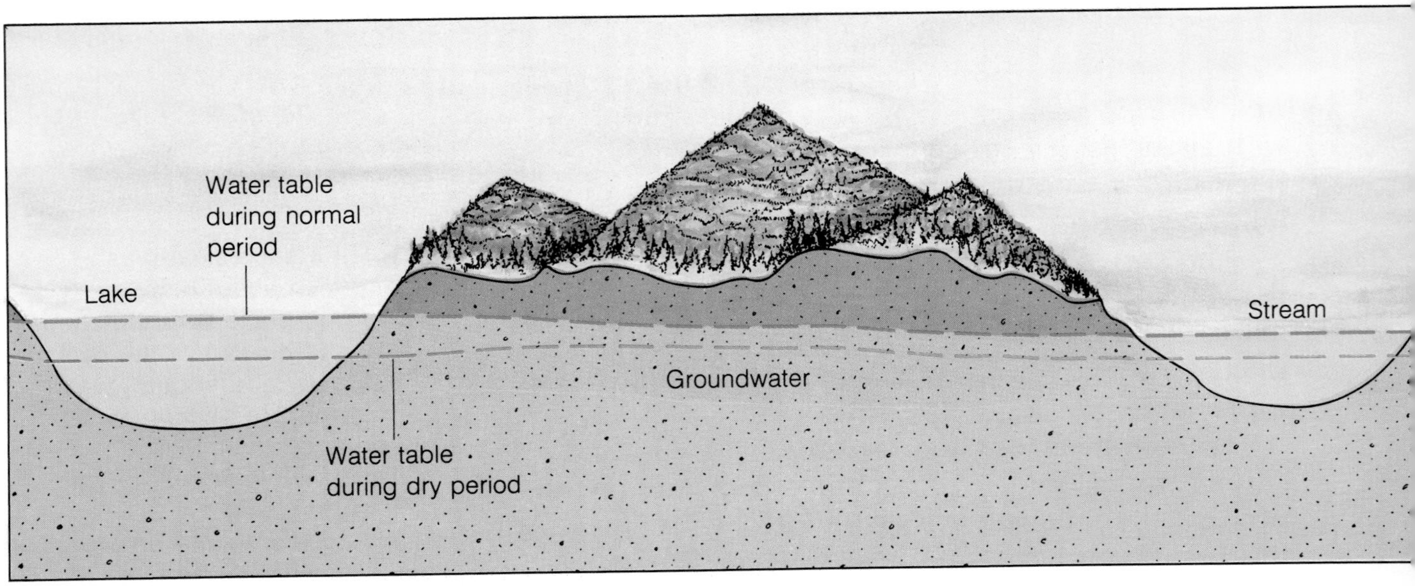

Figure 10–12 *The water table follows the shape of the land. Springs, swamps, and ponds sometimes form where the water table meets the land's surface. What happens to the water table during a dry period?*

Even in the same area, the depth of the water table may change. Heavy rains and melting snows will make the water table rise. If there is a long, dry period, the water table will fall. The depth of the water table may also change if wells are overused or if many wells are located in a small area. Wells are holes dug or drilled to the water table to get water. The use of several wells in one area may lower the water table so much that only very deep wells will be able to pump water. Figure 10–12 shows some characteristics of the water table.

AQUIFERS As groundwater moves through a permeable rock layer, it often reaches an impermeable rock layer or the water table. At this point, the groundwater may move sideways through a layer of rock or sediment that allows it to pass freely. Such a layer is called an **aquifer** (AK-wuh-fuhr). Aquifers are usually layers of sandstone, gravel, sand, or cracked limestone.

Because rocks form in layers, a layer of permeable rock may become trapped between two layers of impermeable rock. Sandstone trapped between layers of shale is an example. If the layer of sandstone contains water, an aquifer forms. An aquifer may also form when soil saturated with groundwater is located above an impermeable rock layer.

An aquifer is a source of groundwater. To reach this water, a well is often dug or drilled into the aquifer. Groundwater moves into the well hole and forms a pool. Each time water is pumped from the

Sharpen Your Skills

Water Bill

An average household uses 38,000 L of water a month, and the cost of water is $0.50 per 1000 L. How much is the water bill at the end of the month?

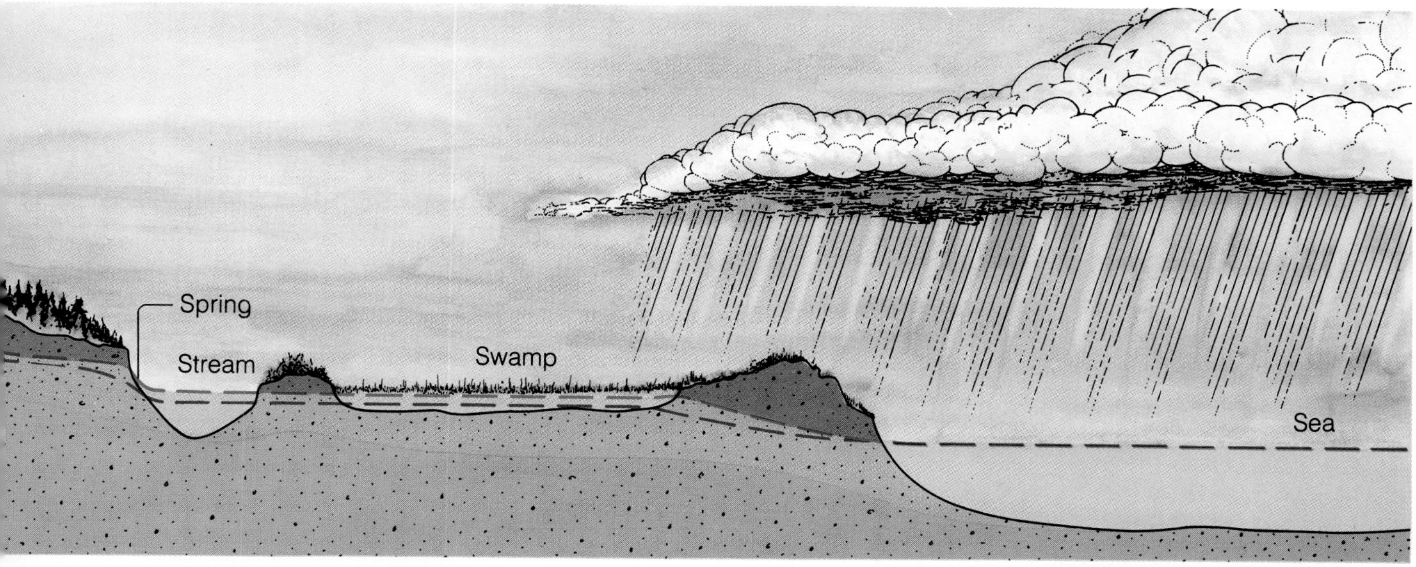

well, more water moves through the aquifer into the well hole.

In some places where the underground rock layers slope, an aquifer carries water from a higher altitude to a lower altitude. If the aquifer is trapped between two layers of impermeable rock, pressure may build up at the lower altitude. A well drilled into the aquifer at this point will provide water without pumping. A well from which water flows on its own without pumping is called an **artesian** (ahr-TEE-zhuhn) **well.** See Figure 10–13.

Figure 10–13 *An aquifer is a source of groundwater. Water can be obtained from an aquifer by means of an ordinary well or an artesian well. The amount of water pressure in an artesian well depends on how close the well is to the water table. Would there be more pressure in a regular artesian well or a gushing artesian well? Why?*

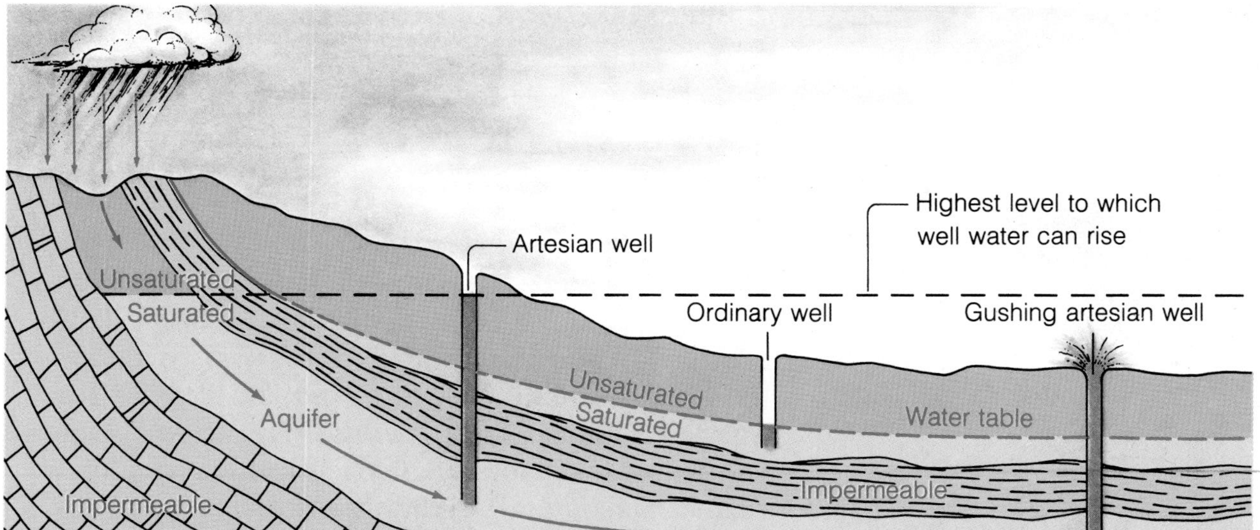

Figure 10–14 *In many caverns, underground lakes are formed as groundwater moves through limestone. This is Dream Lake in Luray Caverns, Virginia. What are the formations hanging from the cavern ceiling called?*

Groundwater Formations

In areas where the underlying rock is limestone, underground **caverns** (KAV-uhrnz) may be found. Limestone is affected by groundwater in a particular way. As water moves down through the soil, it combines with carbon dioxide to form a weak acid that can dissolve limestone. When groundwater enters cracks in the limestone, the cracks gradually get wider. If this process goes on long enough, underground passages big enough to walk through may be formed!

Sometimes large underground caverns with many passageways are formed. If you go into these caverns, you will see what look like long stone icicles hanging from the ceilings. These formations are called **stalactites** (stuh-LAK-tights). **Stalagmites** (stuh-LAG-mights) look like stone icicles built up on the floors of the caverns. Stalactites and stalagmites are formed from dissolved substances in groundwater. You will learn more about how water can dissolve substances in the following section.

SECTION REVIEW

1. What are the three underground zones through which groundwater moves?
2. What causes differences in the depth of the water table?
3. How is an aquifer related to an artesian well?
4. What would you predict might happen to the water table if a large industry using a well were built in an area?

Section Objective

To relate a water molecule's structure to its ability to dissolve substances

10–3 Water as a Solvent

Water is the most common substance on the earth. It can exist on the earth as a solid, a liquid, or a gas. Water moves in a continuous cycle among the oceans, the air, and the land. Water changes form as it moves through this cycle. In this section, you will take a look at the chemical makeup of water and some of its important properties.

Composition of Water

A water molecule (MAHL-uh-kyool) is the smallest particle of water that has all the properties of water. It is formed when two hydrogen atoms and one oxygen atom combine. In the molecule, the atom of oxygen has a slight negative charge (−). Each hydrogen atom has a slight positive charge (+). So the water molecule has oppositely charged ends. See Figure 10–15. These charged ends give water the property known as **polarity** (poh-LAR-uh-tee).

The polarity of water molecules makes water a **solvent** (SAHL-vuhnt). A solvent is a substance in which another substance dissolves. The dissolving process produces a **solution.** A solution contains two or more substances mixed on the molecular level.

If you pour a small quantity of salt into a container of water, the salt will dissolve in the water. Although you will not see the salt, you will know that it is there if you taste the water. The water molecules, having oppositely charged ends, attract the ions, or charged particles, that make up the salt. It is as if the water molecules "pull" the ions out of the solid salt, dissolving the salt.

Water can dissolve many different substances. You probably use water as a solvent every day without realizing it. For example, flavoring and carbon dioxide gas are dissolved in water to form soft

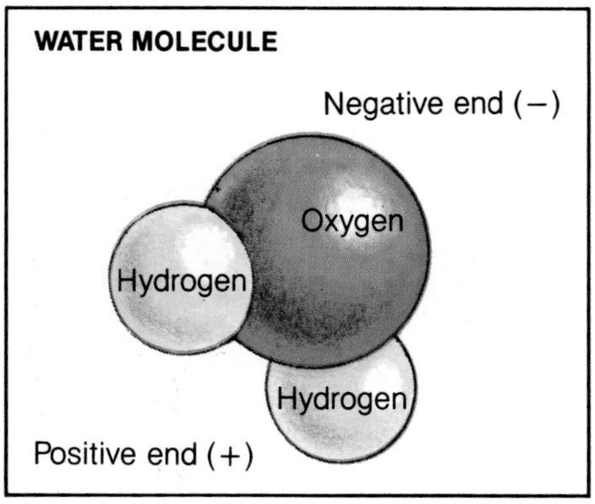

Figure 10–15 *A molecule of water exhibits the property of polarity. Why is this property important?*

Figure 10–16 *This giant sinkhole in Venezuela was caused by the collapse of an underground cavern. How did the cavern first form?*

drinks. In fact, all of the beverages you drink contain substances dissolved in water. What other products can you name that are made with water?

Farmers use water to mix fertilizers for crops. Many of the medicines you buy use water to dissolve the medication. Certain minerals and chemicals are dissolved in water in water-treatment plants to remove harmful minerals, chemicals, and wastes. For example, chlorine, a chemical that kills bacteria, is added to drinking water. In some cities and towns, water-treatment plants also add fluorides to water. The dissolved fluorides help prevent tooth decay.

Sharpen Your Skills

Sudsing Power

1. Separately add 0 mL, 10 mL, 20 mL, and 40 mL of salt to four 1-L jars containing 500 mL of water each. Stir the water until the salt dissolves.

2. Add 10 mL of laundry soap to each jar.

3. Cap the jars and vigorously shake each jar for 20 seconds.

How did the different concentrations of salt affect the sudsing action of the laundry soap? What effect do you think hard water has on washing clothes and bathing?

Hardness of Water

The taste, odor, and appearance of water vary from area to area. The differences depend on the amount and type of material dissolved in the water.

The water you drink may come from either a groundwater or a surface source. This water may be "hard" or "soft." The hardness or softness of water depends on the source of the water and the types of rocks and soil the water comes in contact with. **Hard water** contains large amounts of dissolved minerals, especially calcium and magnesium. Soap does not lather easily in hard water. Also, hard water causes mineral deposits to build up in hot-water heaters and plumbing systems. **Soft water** does not contain these minerals. It does not present problems with lathering of soap or mineral deposits.

Some water is softened naturally as it passes through and reacts with rock formations containing certain minerals. These minerals remove the calcium and magnesium and make the water soft. Many homes with hard water have water softeners to remove the minerals that make it hard. What type of water do you have in your home? How can you tell?

Quality of Water

Water is necessary to all life on the earth. So it is important to maintain the quality of water. Yet many of the earth's sources of fresh water are becoming polluted. Normally water is naturally filtered through soil and sand, which help to remove impurities. But carelessness in dumping sewage, silt, industrial wastes, and pesticides into water has caused serious problems. Since these substances are easily

Figure 10–17 *On March 29, 1989, the Exxon Valdez struck a reef in Prince William Sound off the coast of Alaska and released millions of liters of oil into the water. The result was one of the worst environmental disasters in U.S. history and the destruction of important natural resources.*

dissolved in water, water is becoming more and more polluted.

Water pollution limits the amount of wildlife that can live in the water, affects supplies of drinking water, and destroys recreational areas. Among the chemicals that cause water pollution are phosphates and nitrates. These chemicals are used on farmlands to improve the growth of plants or to kill harmful insects. Phosphates and nitrates have entered the groundwater in many areas and must be removed so water can be used for drinking or swimming.

Federal laws have been passed to prevent industry from dumping certain chemical wastes into the earth's waters. Wastewater treatment systems are being constructed to remove pollution from rivers and lakes. What other steps might be taken to stop water pollution and save one of the earth's most important natural resources?

Sharpen Your Skills

Water as a Solvent of Earth Materials

1. Chalk is composed of calcium carbonate, a substance which makes up many rocks. Add a piece of chalk to a glass of water. To another glass of water, add some quartz sand.

2. Allow both to soak for thirty minutes then feel both samples.

What happened to the chalk? What happened to the sand? Why do you think some rocks dissolve in water more quickly than others? Why is most beach sand made of quartz?

SECTION REVIEW

1. What is the structure and composition of a water molecule?
2. What is the difference between hard water and soft water?
3. How does the amount of dissolved minerals in water affect the sudsing action of soap?
4. What are some effects of water pollution?

10 LABORATORY INVESTIGATION

Porosity of Various Soils

Problem

How can the water-holding capability, or porosity, of various soils be determined?

Materials *(per group)*

2 L water
500-mL graduated cylinder
250 mL sand
250 mL clay
250 mL gravel
4 small paper cups

Procedure

1. Fill the first paper cup about three-fourths full of sand. Fill the second paper cup about three-fourths full of clay. Fill the third paper cup about three-fourths full of gravel. Fill the fourth paper cup about three-fourths full of a mixture of sand, clay, and gravel.
2. Fill the graduated cylinder with water to the 500-mL mark. Slowly pour water into the first cup. Let the water seep through the sand. Slowly add more water until a small pool of water is visible at the surface of the sand. At this point, the sand can hold no more water.
3. Record the amount of water you added to the sand by subtracting the amount of water left in the graduated cylinder from 500 mL. Write your answer in a chart like the one on this page.
4. Repeat steps 2 and 3 for the cups of clay, gravel, and mixture of sand, clay, and gravel.

Observations

Which soil sample is able to hold the most water? The least water?

Conclusions

1. What can you conclude about the porosity of the soils?
2. Why can some soils hold more water than others?
3. If you wished to test the porosity of the soil found on your school grounds, what procedure would you follow? Which tested soil sample do you think your school-grounds soil would be most like?

Soil	Amount of Water Added to Soil
Sand	
Clay	
Gravel	
Sand, clay, gravel	

CHAPTER REVIEW

SUMMARY

10–1 Fresh Water on the Earth's Surface

❑ Fresh water, one of the earth's most important natural resources, is found in lakes, ponds, rivers, streams, springs, and glaciers.

❑ The water cycle is the continuous movement of water from the oceans and the sources of fresh water to the air and land and then back to the oceans. The three steps in the water cycle are called evaporation, condensation, and precipitation.

❑ A land area in which surface runoff drains into a river or system of rivers and streams is called a watershed.

10–2 Fresh Water Beneath the Earth's Surface

❑ Fresh water beneath the earth's surface is called groundwater.

❑ The water table is the underground level below which all of the pore spaces are filled with water. The water table separates the zone of aeration from the zone of saturation.

❑ The depth of the water table depends on the location of the groundwater, the climate of the area, the amount of rainfall, the type of soil, and the number of wells drawing water.

❑ Groundwater formations include caverns, stalactites, and stalagmites.

10–3 Water as a Solvent

❑ Because of the polarity of water molecules, water is a good solvent. It can dissolve most substances.

❑ Water may be hard or soft and can easily become polluted.

❑ People must conserve and protect their sources of fresh water.

VOCABULARY

Define each term in a complete sentence.

aquifer
artesian well
cavern
condensation
continental glacier
crevasse
evaporation
glacier
groundwater
hard water
iceberg
impermeable
meltwater
permeable
polarity
pore space
precipitation
reservoir
soft water
solution
solvent
stalactite
stalagmite
surface runoff
valley glacier
water cycle
watershed
water table
zone of aeration
zone of saturation

CONTENT REVIEW: MULTIPLE CHOICE

Choose the letter of the answer that best completes each sentence.

1. The continuous movement of water from the oceans and freshwater sources to the air and land and back to the oceans is called the
a. nitrogen cycle b. water cycle
c. runoff cycle d. oxygen cycle

2. The process in which water vapor changes to a liquid is called
a. precipitation b. evaporation
c. condensation d. sublimation

3. Very thick sheets of ice found mainly in the polar regions are called
a. valley glaciers b. crevasses
c. continental glaciers d. aquifers

4. The space between particles of soil is called
a. pore space b. zone of aeration
c. surface runoff d. watershed

5. The land area in which runoff drains into a river or river system is called the
a. water table b. groundwater c. meltwater d. watershed

6. The underground region in which all the pores are filled with water is called the
a. zone of saturation b. aquifer
c. watershed d. zone of aeration

7. The level below which all of the pore spaces in the soil are filled with water is called the
a. water table b. groundwater c. meltwater d. watershed

8. The property of water that enables it to dissolve many substances easily is called
a. hardness b. polarity c. softness d. permeability

9. A substance in which another substance dissolves is called a
a. solution b. saturated substance c. solvent d. molecule

10. Water pollution affects
a. wildlife b. drinking water
c. recreational areas d. all of these

CONTENT REVIEW: COMPLETION

Fill in the word or words that best complete each sentence.

1. Oceans cover about ______ percent of the earth's surface.

2. Another name for the water cycle is the ______ cycle.

3. The return of water to the earth in the form of rain, snow, sleet, or hail is called the process of ______.

4. Cracks on the surface of glaciers are called ______.

5. The stream of liquid formed by a moving valley glacier is called ______.

6. The space between particles of soil is called ______.

7. Water stored in the ground is called ______.

8. Material through which water can move quickly is called ______ material.

9. A well from which water flows on its own without pumping is called a (an) ______ well.

10. Water containing large amounts of dissolved minerals, especially calcium and magnesium, is called ______ water.

CONTENT REVIEW: TRUE OR FALSE

Determine whether each statement is true or false. If it is true, write "true." If it is false, change the underlined word or words to make the statement true.

1. About 97 percent of the earth's water is found in the oceans.
2. The process by which water changes to a gas is called condensation.
3. Rain, snow, sleet, and hail are forms of precipitation.
4. Cracks on the surface of glaciers are called pores.
5. Water entering a river or stream after a heavy rain or during thawing of snow or ice is called groundwater.
6. Lakes and ponds are examples of running water.
7. Artificial lakes built by damming a stream or river in a low-lying area are known as reservoirs.
8. Material through which water can move quickly is described as saturated.
9. In very dry areas such as deserts, the water table is usually very shallow.
10. Because water can dissolve almost all other substances, it is sometimes called the universal solvent.

CONCEPT REVIEW: SKILL BUILDING

Use the skills you have developed in the chapter to complete each activity.

1. **Making diagrams** Two different areas in the United States receive the same amount of rainfall during a day. Area A has soil that contains many large pores and rocks made of sandstone. The soil in Area B is mainly clay. Area A is a desert. Area B is a swamp. Drawing two diagrams of each area, show the depth of the water table both *before* and *after* a day of rain.
2. **Applying concepts** Water molecules are polar. Explain how they can be attracted to each other and line up in groups of molecules. Illustrate your explanation.
3. **Making generalizations** Three factors affect the rate at which a substance dissolves in water. Use the following observation to determine what these three factors are: In preparing your tea, you stir the sugar powder into the cup of hot liquid to make a sweet drink.
4. **Designing an experiment** Clouds are not salty. The salt from the oceans is left behind when the water evaporates. Devise an experiment to illustrate this fact. Describe the problem, materials, procedure, expected observations and conclusion.

CONCEPT REVIEW: ESSAY

Discuss each of the following in a brief paragraph.

1. Explain how the water cycle constantly renews the earth's supply of fresh water.
2. Why is it important to find new sources of fresh water and to conserve the sources now available?
3. How does the structure of water affect its ability to dissolve substances?
4. Why is it important for industry to reduce the amount of chemical wastes it dumps into the earth's waters?

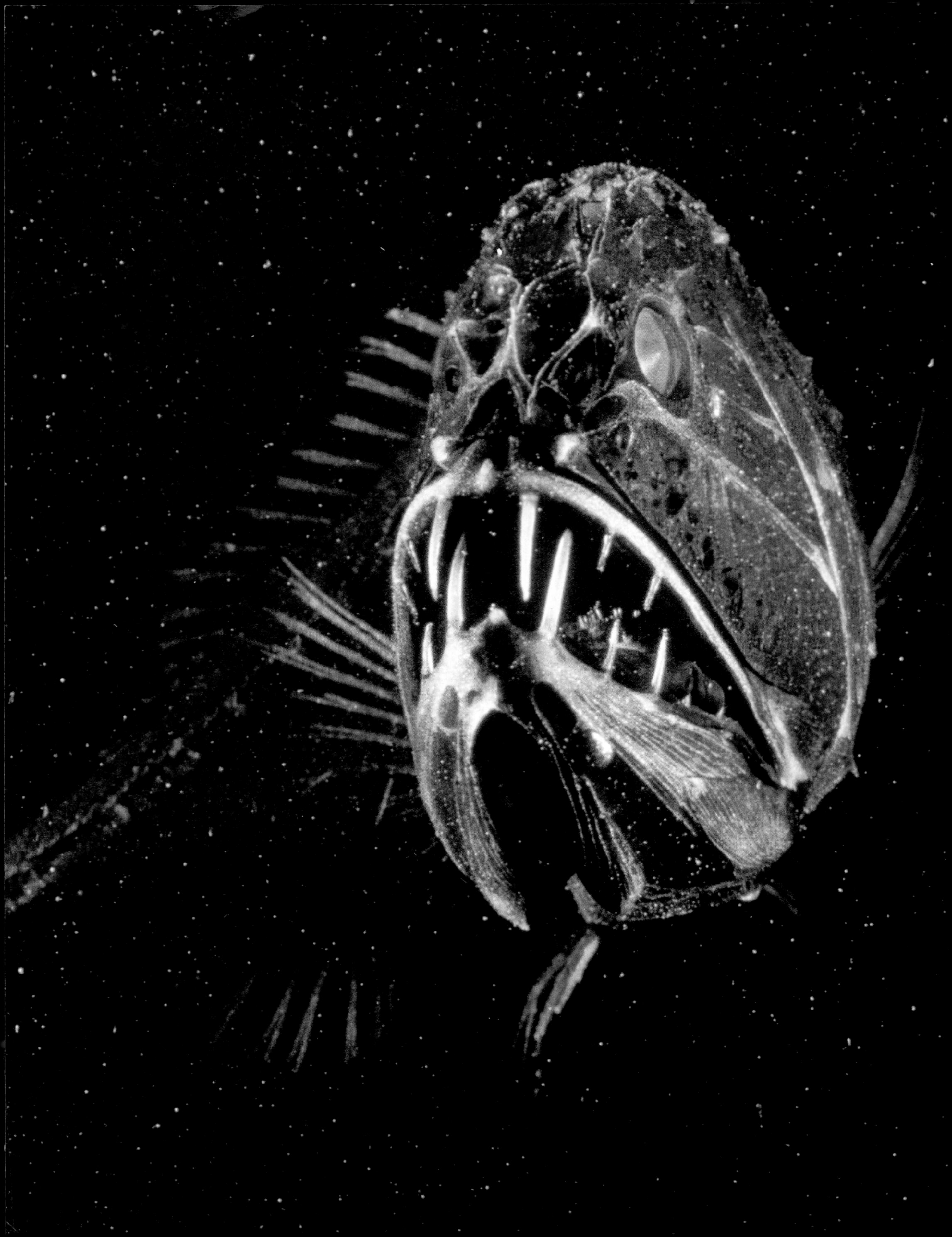

The Earth's Oceans 11

CHAPTER SECTIONS

CHAPTER OBJECTIVES

After completing this chapter, you will be able to

11–1 List the earth's major oceans and seas.
11–2 Describe the makeup and temperature of ocean water.
11–3 Describe the major features of the ocean floor.
11–4 Compare the ocean-life zones.
11–5 Explain how the ocean floor is mapped.
11–6 Identify the motions of the ocean and their effects.

Deep beneath the ocean waves, life seems to imitate science fiction. The anoplogaster on the opposite page is but one of many examples. With its needlelike teeth bared, the 15-centimeter fish stalks its prey. Food is hard to find in the ocean depths the anoplogaster calls home. Swimming in waters nearly 6000 meters deep, this strange-looking creature must contend with near-freezing temperatures, tremendous pressure, and a limited food supply. But in the blue-black ocean water where no sunlight penetrates, the anoplogaster is a fearsome predator.

The ocean is rich in many forms of life. From microscopic plants to mammoth animals, a huge variety of organisms obtain from ocean water the gases and foods necessary for survival. The ocean plays an important role in your survival, too. It is a direct source of food and an indirect source of fresh water for all living things.

In this chapter, you will learn about the ocean—its properties, topography, and motions. And you will become familiar with the variety of living things that make the ocean their home.

Tiny but terrifying, an anoplogaster patrols the ocean depths in search of food.

Section Objective

To identify the major oceans of the world

11–1 Oceans of the World

If you were asked to rename the earth, what would you call it? If you looked at its surface features, you might call it Oceanus. About 71 percent of the earth's surface is covered by ocean water. In fact, the ocean contains most of the earth's water—about 97 percent. Although people refer to separate oceans and seas, all of the oceans and seas are part of one continuous body of water.

The Atlantic, Indian, and Pacific oceans are the three major oceans. Smaller bodies of ocean water, such as the Mediterranean Sea, the Black Sea, and the Arctic Ocean, are considered part of the Atlantic Ocean. A sea is a part of an ocean that is nearly surrounded by land. What seas can you name?

The Pacific Ocean is the largest ocean. Its area and volume are greater than those of the Atlantic and Indian oceans combined. The Pacific Ocean is also the deepest ocean. Its average depth is 3940 meters. The Atlantic Ocean is the second largest ocean. It has an average depth of 3350 meters. The Indian Ocean is much smaller than the Atlantic Ocean, but its average depth is greater.

The ocean, which is made of salt water, plays an important role in the water cycle. During this cycle, the sun's rays heat the surface of the ocean. The

Figure 11–1 *The major oceans and seas of the world are actually part of one continuous body of water. What are the three major oceans?*

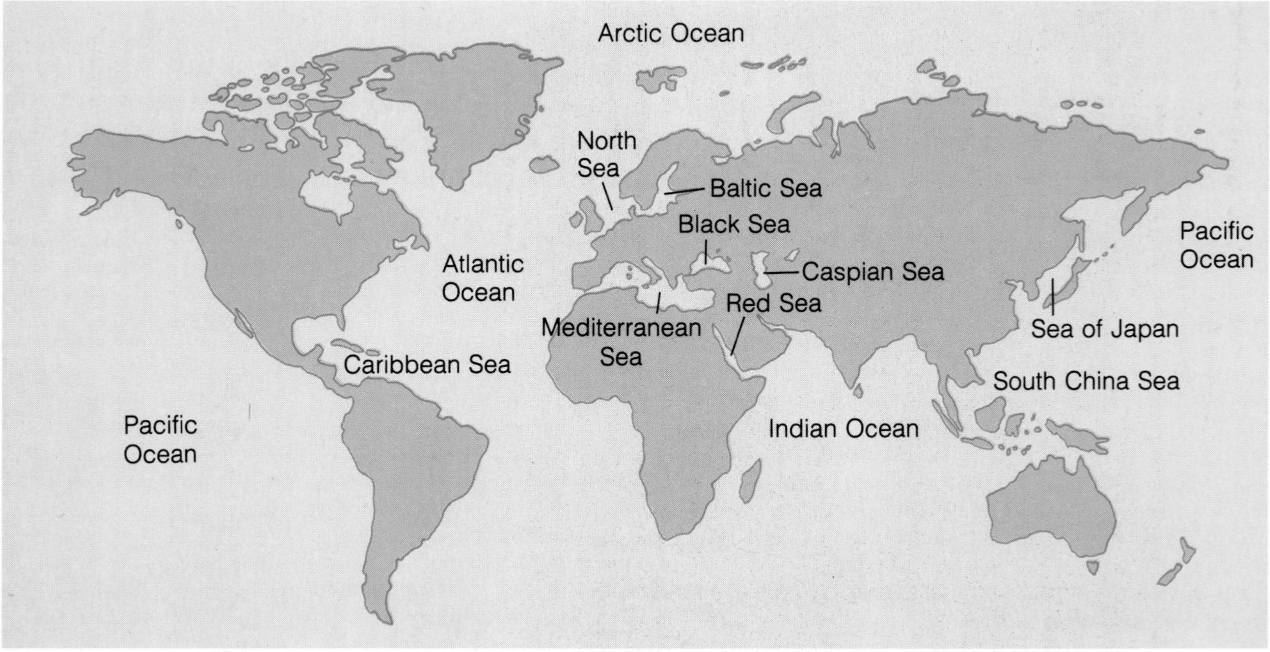

heat causes the water to evaporate. When the water evaporates, it enters the atmosphere as water vapor. The salts the water contained remain in the ocean.

Winds carry much of the water vapor over land areas. Some of the water vapor in the atmosphere condenses to form clouds. Under the right conditions, the water in clouds falls as precipitation. This water is fresh water. Some of it runs into streams and rivers that flow directly back to the ocean. Some of it seeps deep into the soil and rocks to become part of the groundwater beneath the earth's surface. So indirectly, the ocean is a source of fresh water for all living things.

SECTION REVIEW

1. Name the three major oceans of the world.
2. What is the difference between an ocean and a sea?
3. Why is the ocean an indirect source of fresh water?

11–2 Properties of Ocean Water

Section Objective

To describe the composition and characteristics of ocean water

Ocean water is a mixture of gases and solids dissolved in pure water. Scientists who study the ocean, or **oceanographers** (oh-shuh-NAHG-ruh-fuhrz), believe that ocean water contains all of the natural elements on the earth. There are 90 elements known to exist in nature. About 85 of these elements have already been found in ocean water. With advances in technology, oceanographers hope to find the remaining elements.

Ocean water is about 96 percent pure water, or H_2O. So the most abundant elements in ocean water are hydrogen and oxygen. The remaining 4 percent is dissolved elements. Figure 11–2 on page 266 shows the major elements in ocean water.

Salts in Ocean Water

Sodium chloride is the most abundant salt in ocean water. If you have ever accidentally swallowed

MAJOR ELEMENTS IN OCEAN WATER

Element	Percent of Total (%)
Oxygen Hydrogen	96.5
Chlorine	1.9
Sodium	1.1
Magnesium Sulfur Calcium Potassium Bromine Carbon Strontium Silicon Fluorine Aluminum Phosphorus Iodine	0.5
	100

Figure 11–2 *Ocean water is composed of hydrogen, oxygen, and about 85 other elements. Of these other elements, which two are the most abundant?*

a mouthful of ocean water, you have probably recognized the taste of the sodium chloride. Sodium chloride is, in fact, common table salt. Sodium chloride is made of the elements sodium and chlorine.

Sodium chloride is one of many salts dissolved in ocean water. Figure 11–3 shows the other salts in ocean water. Oceanographers use the term **salinity** (suh-LIHN-uh-tee) to describe the amount of dissolved salts in ocean water. Salinity is the number of grams of dissolved salts in 1 kilogram of ocean water. When 1 kilogram of ocean water evaporates, 35 grams of salts are left. Of these 35 grams, 27.2 grams are sodium chloride. How many grams are magnesium chloride?

The salinity of ocean water is expressed in parts per thousand. It ranges between 33 and 37 parts per thousand. The average salinity is 35 parts per thousand. How many grams of table salt and fresh water do you need to make a solution with the same salinity as ocean water?

The salts and other materials dissolved in ocean water come from several different sources. One

Figure 11–3 *This figure shows the amounts, in parts per thousand, of the seven most abundant salts in ocean water. What three salts are the most abundant?*

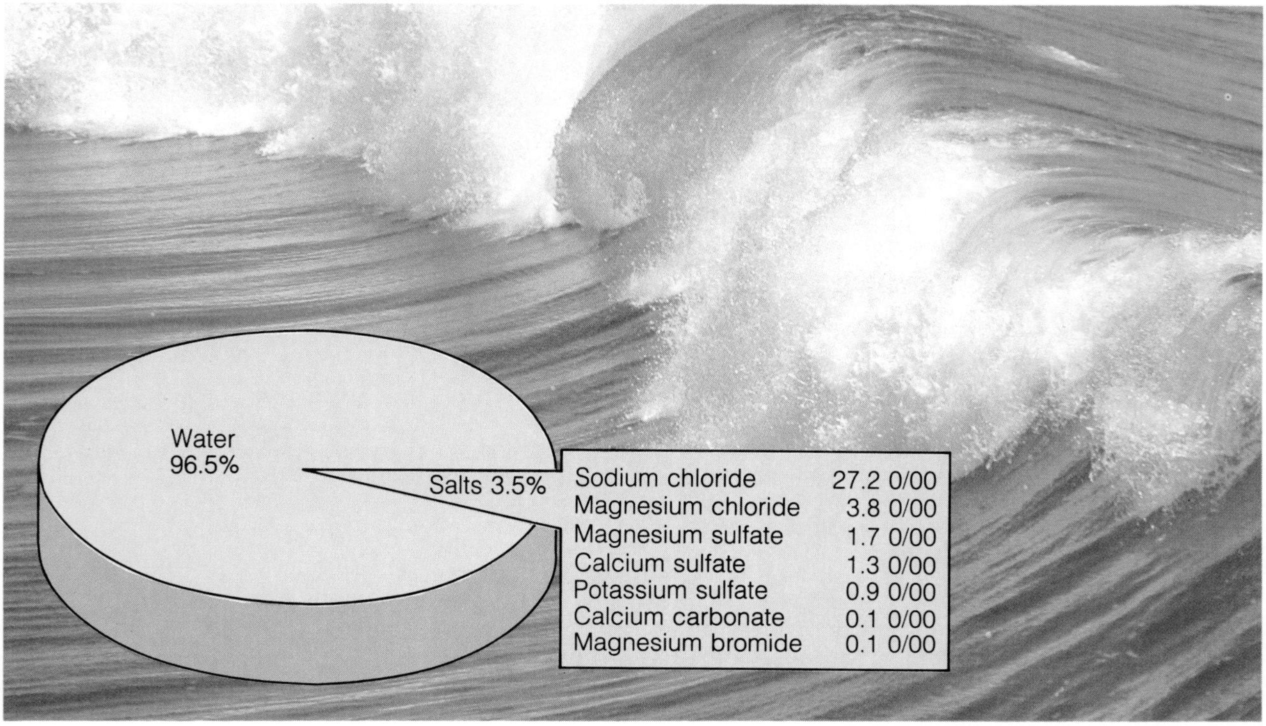

source is volcanic activity in the ocean. When volcanoes erupt, rock material and gases spew forth. These substances are dissolved in ocean water. Chlorine gas is one substance that is added to ocean water by volcanic action.

Another source is erosion of land areas by rivers and glaciers. As rivers and glaciers pass over rocks and soil, they dissolve the salts in them. Sodium, magnesium, and potassium are probably carried to the ocean this way.

Wave action along shorelines is also a source of salts and other materials. As waves pound the shorelines, they dissolve the salts contained in rocks along the coasts.

In many areas of the ocean, the salinity is about the same. But in other areas, greater or lesser amounts of dissolved salts cause differences in the salinity. There are several reasons for these differences. The salinity is much lower in areas where freshwater rivers flow into the ocean. This is especially true where major rivers such as the Mississippi, Amazon, and Congo flow into the ocean. Why do the areas where major rivers reach the ocean have lower salinity?

In warm ocean areas where there is little rainfall and much evaporation, the amount of dissolved salts in the ocean water is greater than average. The salinity is higher. The salinity is also higher in the polar regions. Here ocean water freezes, removing pure water and leaving the salts behind.

Scientists believe that the salinity of ocean water is also affected by animal life. Animals such as clams and oysters use calcium salts to build their shells. How does this affect the salinity of ocean water?

Gases in Ocean Water

The most abundant gases dissolved in ocean water are nitrogen, carbon dioxide, and oxygen. Two of these gases, carbon dioxide and oxygen, are vital to ocean life. Plants use carbon dioxide to make food. In the presence of sunlight, plants combine carbon dioxide with water to make simple sugars. During this process, oxygen is released into the water. Plants and animals use oxygen to break down food and provide energy for all life functions.

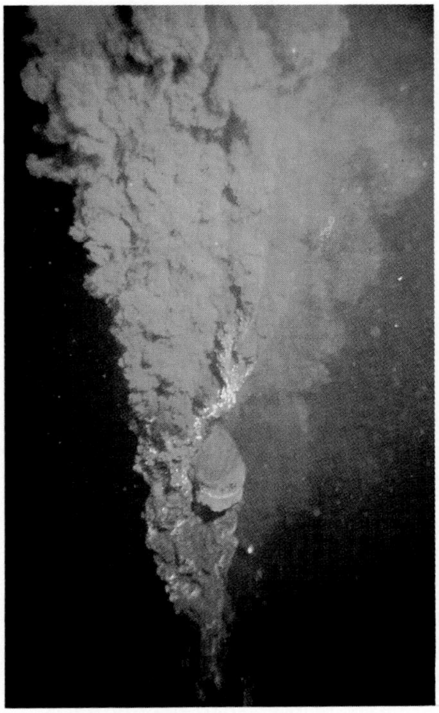

Figure 11–4 *Superheated water, gases, and minerals pour out of a natural chimney or volcanic deep-sea vent in the ocean floor. What happens to these materials?*

Sharpen Your Skills

Relating Temperature and Salinity

1. Pour 100 mL of hot tap water into a glass.

2. Add salt, one teaspoonful at a time, to the water. Stir the water after each addition. Stop adding salt when no more can be dissolved. Record the number of teaspoons of salt added.

3. Using 100 mL of cold tap water, repeat steps 1 and 2.

In which glass did more salt dissolve? What is the relationship between temperature and salinity?

Figure 11–5 *A wide variety of plants live in the ocean. During the food-making process, these plants take in carbon dioxide dissolved in ocean water and release oxygen. Oxygen is used by both plants and animals to provide energy for all life activities. Here you see a plant called kelp.*

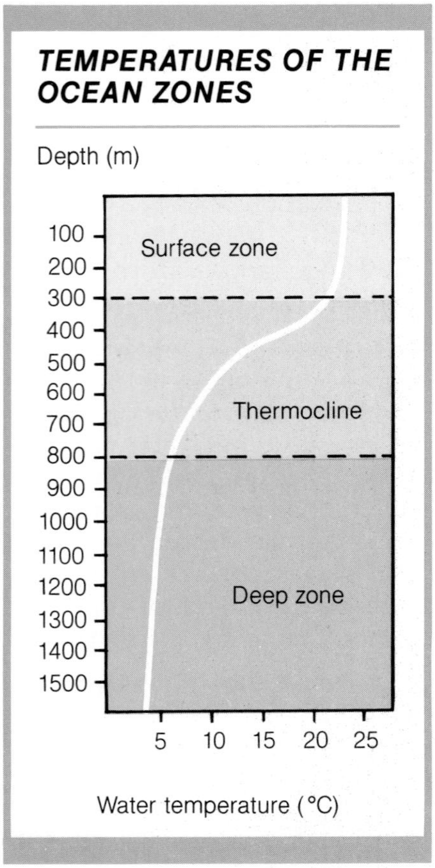

The amount of nitrogen, carbon dioxide, oxygen, and other gases in ocean water varies with depth. Nitrogen, carbon dioxide, and oxygen are more abundant at the surface of ocean water. At the surface, sunlight easily penetrates and plant growth abounds. So there is a large amount of oxygen here. Why is there more oxygen at the surface of ocean water than in the ocean depths?

The amount of dissolved gases is also affected by the temperature of the ocean water. Warm water holds less dissolved gas than cold water. When ocean water cools, as in the polar regions, it sinks. It carries oxygen-rich water to the ocean depths. As a result, fish and other animals can live in the deepest parts of the ocean.

Temperature of Ocean Water

The sun is the major source of heat for the ocean. Since solar energy is received at the surface of ocean water, water temperatures are highest there. Motions of the ocean, such as waves and currents, mix the surface water and transfer the heat downward. The zone where the water is mixed by waves and currents is called the **surface zone.** The surface zone extends to a depth of at least 100 meters. Sometimes it extends as deep as 400 meters.

Within a surface zone, the temperature remains fairly constant. It does not change with depth. But the temperature of a surface zone does change with location and with season. Water near the equator is warmer than water in regions farther north and south. And summer water temperatures are warmer than winter water temperatures. For example, the summer water temperature near the surface of the Caribbean Sea may be 26°C. Off the coast of England, it may be 15°C. What do you think happens to these temperatures in the winter?

Below the surface zone, the temperature of the water falls very rapidly. This zone of rapid temperature change is called the **thermocline** (THER-muh-klighn). The thermocline does not have

Figure 11–6 *There are three different temperature zones in the ocean, except in the polar regions. In which zone is the temperature constant? In which zone is there a rapid temperature change?*

Figure 11–7 *Although ocean water temperatures in the polar regions are very low, plants such as algae can survive. Here you see blue-green algae that grow below the frozen surface of Lake Hoare in Antarctica.*

a specific depth. The season of the year and the flow of ocean currents affect its depth.

The thermocline exists because warm surface water does not mix easily with cold deep water. The difference in the densities of the warm water and the cold water keeps them from mixing. The less dense warm water floats on the denser cold water.

The thermocline is the transition zone between the surface zone and the **deep zone.** The deep zone is an area of very cold water that extends from the bottom of the thermocline to depths of 4000 meters or more. Within the deep zone, the temperature decreases slightly. At depths of more than 1500 meters, the temperature is about 4°C. So the temperature of most ocean water is just above freezing!

The three ocean zones are not found in the polar regions. In the Arctic and Antarctic oceans, the surface waters are very cold. The temperature changes only slightly as the depth increases.

SECTION REVIEW

1. What is the most abundant salt in ocean water?
2. What is salinity?
3. What are the most abundant gases in ocean water?
4. What are the three zones of the ocean? On what property of ocean water are these zones based?

Sharpen Your Skills

Fresh Water From the Ocean

1. Using your knowledge of the properties of ocean water, including density, devise a procedure for obtaining fresh water from ocean water by freezing. Describe the steps.
2. Try out the procedure using a solution of 100 mL of tap water and 3 g of salt. Report your results.

11–3 Topography of the Ocean Floor

Section Objective

To describe the major ocean-floor features

The topography of the ocean floor is different from the topography of the continents. **The ocean floor has higher mountains, deeper canyons, and larger, flatter plains than the continents.** The ocean floor has more volcanoes than the continents. Earthquakes occur more often under the ocean than on the land. The rocks that form the ocean floor are very different from the rocks that form continental crust. The crust of the earth is much thinner under the ocean than under the continents.

Edges of the Continents

The edge of a continent extends into the ocean. The area where the underwater edge of a continent meets the ocean floor is called a **continental margin.** Although a continental margin forms part of the ocean floor, it is more a part of the land than it is of the ocean.

On a continent, there is a boundary where the land and the ocean meet. This boundary is called a shoreline. A shoreline marks the average position of sea level. It does *not* mark where the continent ends. As you just read, a continent extends *into* the ocean.

Figure 11–8 *In this illustration, you can see the major features of the ocean floor. What are some of these features?*

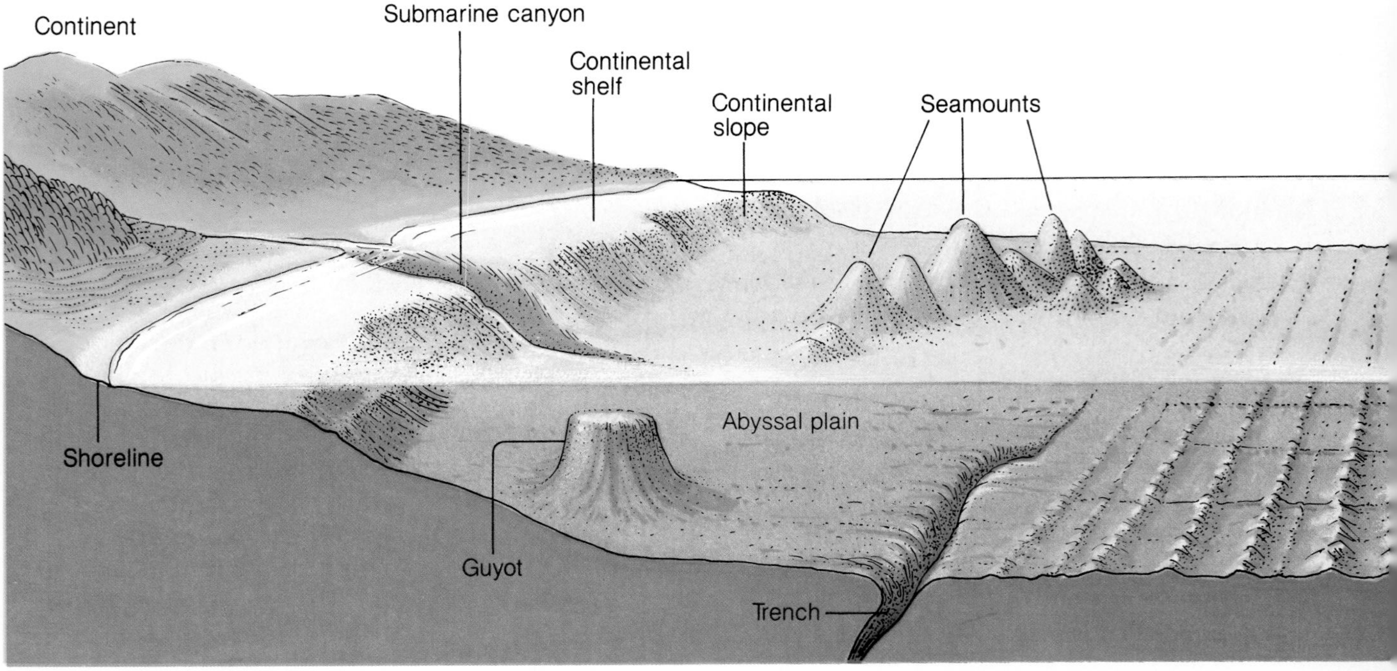

A continental margin generally consists of a continental shelf, a continental slope, and a continental rise. Sediments eroded from the land are deposited in these parts of a continental margin.

The relatively flat part of a continental margin that is covered by shallow ocean water is called a **continental shelf.** A continental shelf usually slopes very gently downward from the shoreline around the continent. In fact, it usually slopes less than 1.2 meters for every 100 meters from the shoreline.

The width of a continental shelf varies. Off the Atlantic Coast, the continental shelf extends more than 200 kilometers into the ocean. Off the Arctic shore of Siberia, the continental shelf extends over 1200 kilometers into the ocean. On the other hand, there is almost no continental shelf off the coast of southeastern Florida.

The waters over a continental shelf are the best fishing areas in the ocean. Large mineral deposits and deposits of oil and natural gas are also found on a continental shelf. Because of the resources a continental shelf contains, many countries of the world have extended their natural boundaries to include the continental shelf off their shores.

At the edge of a continental shelf, the ocean floor plunges steeply 4 to 5 kilometers. This part of a continental margin is called a **continental slope.** A continental slope marks the boundary between

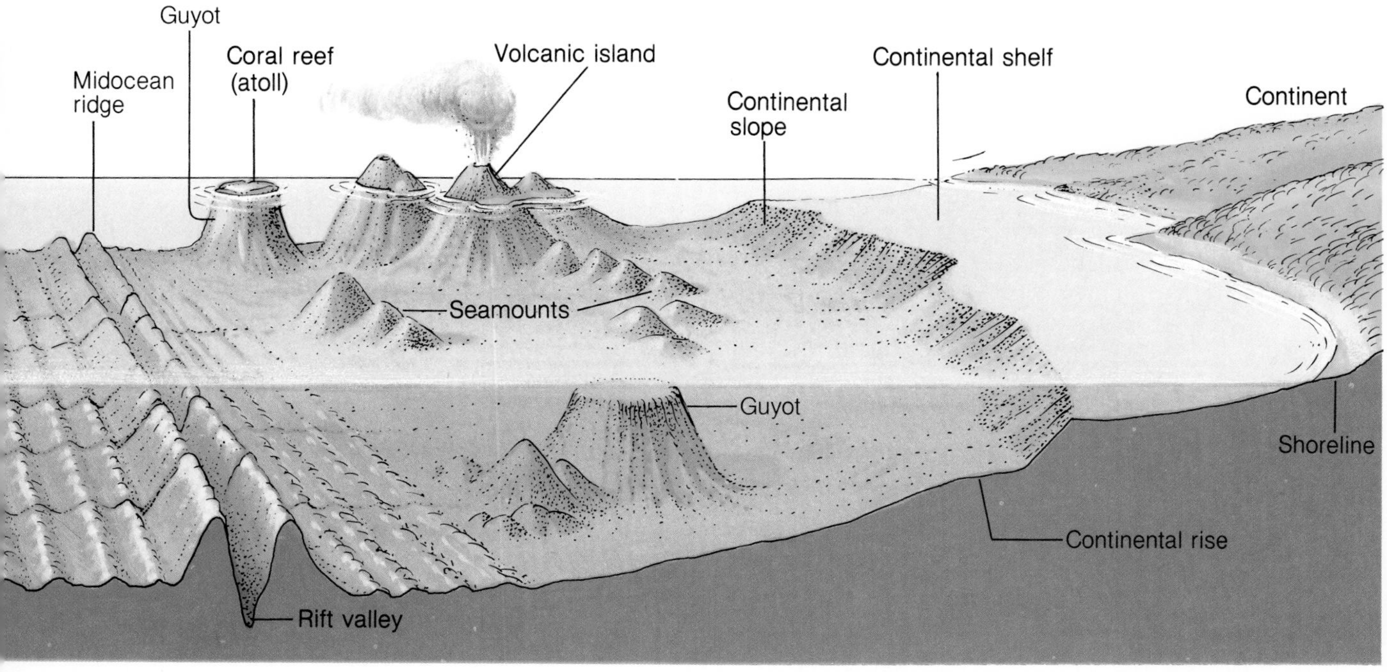

Figure 11–9 *These divers are swimming toward a submarine canyon cut into the continental shelf. What do scientists believe form submarine canyons?*

continental crust and oceanic crust. Separating a continental slope from the ocean floor is a **continental rise.** You can see the parts of a continental margin and other ocean-floor features in Figure 11–8.

A continental rise is made of a large amount of sediments. These sediments, composed of small pieces of rocks and plant and animal remains, have been washed down from the continent and the continental slope. Sometimes the sediments are carried down the slope in masses of flowing water called **turbidity** (ter-BIHD-uh-tee) **currents.** A turbidity current is a flow of water that is very dense because of the sediments it carries. A turbidity current is like an underwater avalanche.

In many areas, a continental shelf and slope are cut through by **submarine canyons.** Submarine canyons are deep, V-shaped valleys that have been cut in hard rock. Some of these canyons are very deep. For example, the Monterey Submarine Canyon off central California reaches depths of over 2000 meters. It is deeper than the Grand Canyon!

Many scientists believe that submarine canyons are formed by powerful turbidity currents. Submarine canyons may also be caused by earthquakes or other movements on a continental slope. Scientists still have much to learn about the origin and nature of submarine canyons.

Sharpen Your Skills

Ocean Floor Models

1. Use papier-mâché, plaster, or modeling clay to construct a model of the ocean floor. Include at least one example of each of the features shown in Figure 11–8.
2. Label each feature on your model.

Features of the Ocean Floor

Scientists have identified several major features of the ocean floor. As you read about these features, refer back to Figure 11–8.

ABYSSAL PLAINS Large flat areas on the ocean floor are called **abyssal** (uh-BIHS-uhl) **plains.** The abyssal plains are larger in the Atlantic and Indian oceans than in the Pacific Ocean. Scientists believe that there are two reasons for the difference in size.

First, the world's greatest rivers all flow directly or indirectly into the Atlantic and Indian oceans. These rivers include the Mississippi, Congo, Nile, and Amazon, which flow into the Atlantic Ocean. The Ganges and Indus rivers flow directly into the Indian Ocean. These major rivers and many smaller rivers deposit large amounts of sediments on the abyssal plains.

Second, the floor of the Pacific Ocean contains a number of deep cracks along the edges of the continents. These long, narrow cracks trap the sediments carried down a continental slope.

Deep-sea drilling operations and sound-wave detection equipment have shown that the sediments of the abyssal plains close to continents consist of thick layers of mud, sand, and silt. Farther out on the abyssal plains, some of the sediments are made of the remains of tiny organisms. These organisms can only be seen with a microscope. They form a sediment called ooze. Where ocean life is not abundant, the ocean floor is covered with a different sediment called red clay. Red clay is composed of sediments carried to the oceans by rivers.

SEAMOUNTS AND GUYOTS Scattered along the ocean floor are thousands of underwater mountains called **seamounts.** Seamounts are volcanic mountains that rise more than 1000 meters above the surrounding ocean floor. They have steep sides leading to a narrow summit. Oceanographers have located over 1000 seamounts. They expect to find thousands of others in the future. There are more seamounts in the Pacific Ocean than in either the Atlantic or Indian ocean.

Some seamounts reach above the surface of the ocean to form islands. The Azores and the Ascension Islands in the Atlantic Ocean are examples of such volcanic islands. Perhaps the most dramatic volcanic islands are the Hawaiian Islands in the

Figure 11–10 *The Hawaiian island of Molokai is the top of a seamount that extends above the surface of the ocean. What kind of mountains are seamounts?*

MAJOR OCEAN TRENCHES

Trench	Depth (*m*)
Pacific Ocean	
Aleutian	8100
Kurile	10,542
Japan	9810
Mariana (Challenger Deep)	11,034
Philippine	10,497
Tonga	10,882
Kermadec	10,047
Peru-Chile	8055
New Hebrides	9165
Atlantic Ocean	
Puerto Rico	8648
South Sandwich	8400

Figure 11–11 *Ocean trenches are the deepest parts of the ocean floor. Which ocean, the Atlantic or Pacific, has the most trenches?*

Pacific Ocean. The island of Hawaii is the top of a great volcano that rises more than 9600 meters from the ocean floor. It is the highest mountain on Earth when measured from base to peak.

During the mid-1940s, scientists discovered that many seamounts do not rise to a peak. Instead, they have a flat top. These flat-topped seamounts are called **guyots** (gee-OHZ). Scientists believe that the flat tops are the result of wave erosion. The waves broke apart the tops of the seamounts that once were at sea level. The flattened volcanic seamounts were later submerged.

TRENCHES The deepest parts of the ocean are not in the middle of the ocean floor. The greatest depths are found in **trenches** along the edges of the ocean floor. Trenches are long, narrow crevices, or cracks, that can be more than 11,000 meters deep.

The Pacific Ocean has more trenches than the other oceans. The Mariana Trench in the Pacific Ocean contains the deepest spot known on the earth. This spot is called Challenger Deep. Challenger Deep is over 11,000 meters deep.

MIDOCEAN RIDGES Some of the largest mountain ranges on the earth are not located on the land but

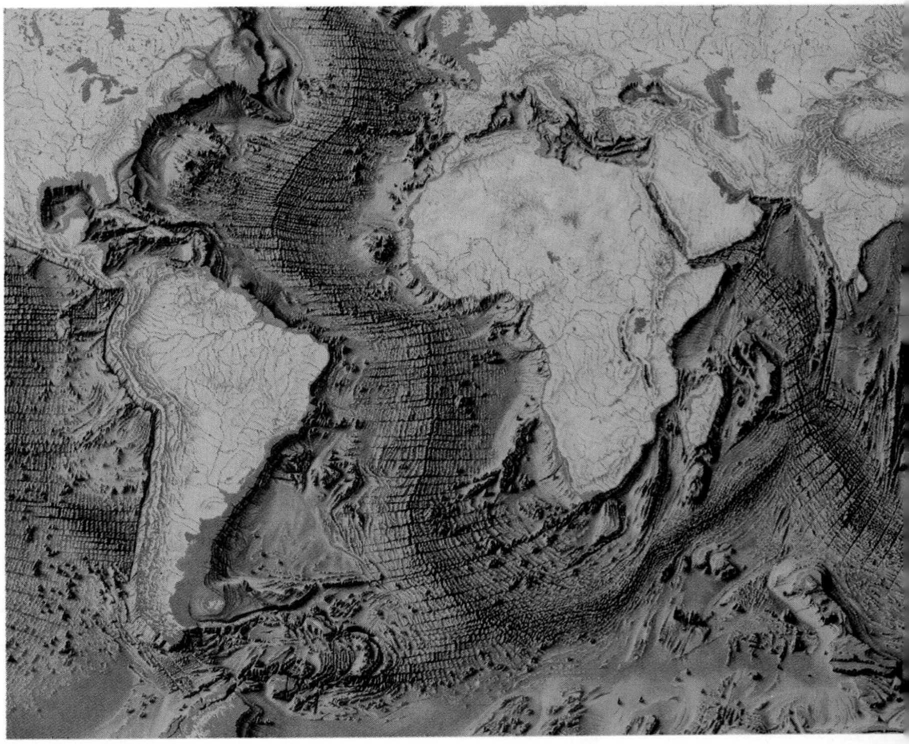

Figure 11–12 *The land beneath the ocean has varied features. This map shows the topography of the ocean floor. What ocean-floor feature extends lengthwise between South America and Africa?*

under the ocean. These mountain ranges are called **midocean ridges.** They form an almost continuous mountain belt that extends from the Arctic Ocean, down through the middle of the Atlantic Ocean, around Africa into the Indian Ocean, and then across the Pacific Ocean north to North America. In the Atlantic Ocean, the mountain belt is called the Mid-Atlantic Ridge. In the Pacific Ocean, the mountain belt is called the Pacific–Antarctic Ridge or East Pacific Rise or Ridge.

The midocean ridges are unlike any mountain ranges on the land. Mountain ranges on the land are formed by the folding and compressing of the earth's crust. Midocean ridges are areas where molten material from the mantle flows up to the surface. At the surface, the molten material cools and piles up to form new crust.

Running along the middle of the midocean ridges are deep crevices, or rift valleys. Rift valleys are about 25 to 50 kilometers wide and 1 to 2 kilometers below the surrounding midocean ridges. Rift valleys may mark the center of the areas where new crust is formed. There are many earthquakes and volcanic eruptions in these areas. Scientists have learned about changes in the earth's crust by studying the rocks in and around the midocean ridges.

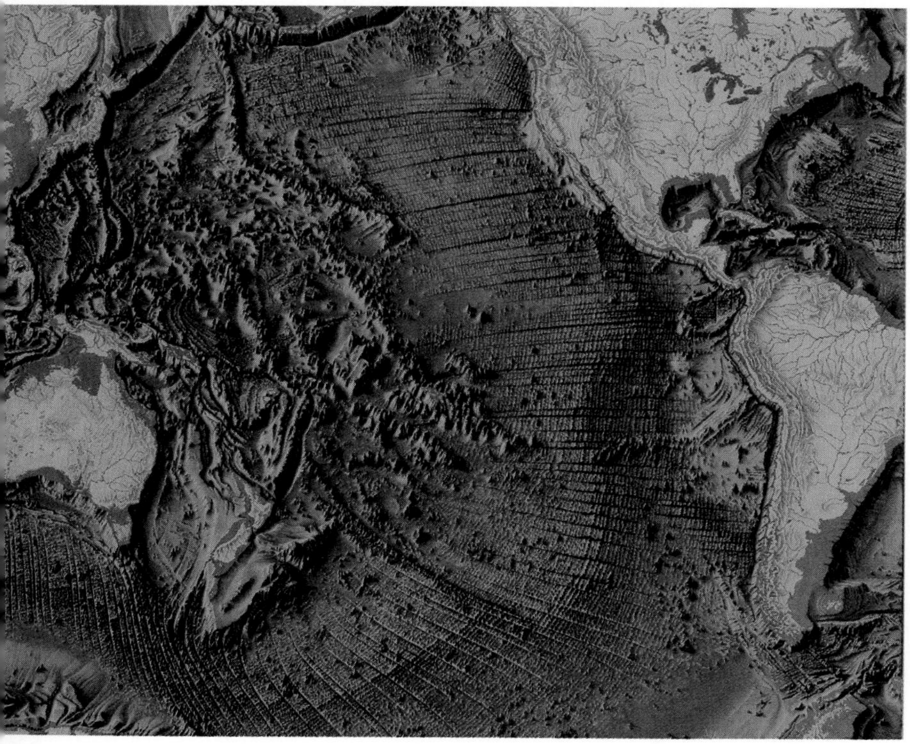

Sharpen Your Skills

Journey Across the Ocean Floor

Imagine that all the water has been drained from the ocean. You and a companion decide to take a hike across the newly revealed ocean floor. Choose a starting point and destination. Then describe in a report all the ocean floor features you saw on your way.

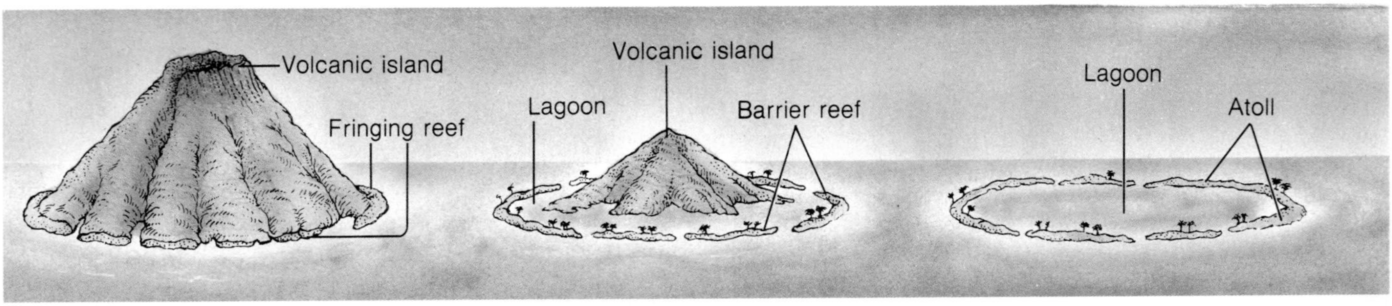

Figure 11–13 *The development of the three types of coral reefs is shown in this illustration. What happens to the volcanic island by the time an atoll forms? What is the area of water within an atoll called?*

Figure 11–14 *The island of Morea in Polynesia is separated from a barrier reef by a lagoon (top). An atoll surrounds only a lagoon because the island has been worn away and is no longer above the ocean surface (bottom).*

REEFS In tropical waters near a continental shelf, unusual-looking volcanic islands can be seen. Surrounding these islands offshore are large masses and ridges of limestone rocks. The limestone structures contain the shells of animals. These structures are called **coral reefs.** Reef-building organisms cannot live in waters colder than 18°C. So reefs are found only in tropical waters, such as those of the South Pacific Ocean and Caribbean Sea. Reef-building organisms also cannot live at depths greater than about 55 meters. They need sunlight to make their hard limestone skeletons. And there is not enough sunlight below this depth.

There are three types of coral reefs. One type is called **fringing reefs.** Fringing reefs are coral reefs that touch the shoreline of a volcanic island. The width of fringing reefs may be several hundred meters but generally is less than 30 meters.

Another type of coral reef is called **barrier reefs.** Barrier reefs are separated from the shore by an area of shallow water called a lagoon. Barrier reefs are generally larger than fringing reefs. And the islands barrier reefs surround usually have sunk farther into the ocean than the islands fringing reefs surround. The Great Barrier Reef of Australia is from 40 to 320 kilometers wide and about 2300 kilometers long. It is rich in many kinds of plant and animal life.

The third type of coral reef can be found farther out in the ocean. It is a ring of coral reefs called an **atoll.** An atoll surrounds an island that has been worn away and has sunk beneath the waves. Figure 11–13 shows the three types of coral reefs.

SECTION REVIEW

1. What is a continental margin? Describe the parts of a continental margin.
2. List six features of the ocean floor.
3. How are seamounts and guyots related?
4. What are the three types of coral reefs?

11–4 Ocean-Life Zones

Section Objective

To classify ocean life and ocean-life zones

A wide variety of plant and animal life exists in the ocean. Ocean life is affected by several factors. One factor is the amount of sunlight that penetrates the environment. Another factor is temperature. There is less sunlight deep in the ocean. And the temperature is lower. So more plants and animals are found in the upper parts of the ocean and near the shore than in the deeper parts. Another factor that affects ocean life is water pressure. Water pressure increases as depth increases. Organisms that live deep in the ocean must be able to withstand great pressure.

The animals and plants in the ocean can be classified into three major groups by their habits and the depth of ocean water in which they live. The largest group of animals and plants is called **plankton** (PLANGK-tuhn). Plankton float at or near the surface of the ocean where sunlight penetrates. Near the shore, they live at depths of about 1 meter. In the open ocean, they live at depths of nearly 200 meters.

Plankton are usually very small organisms. Many forms of plankton are microscopic. These organisms move by drifting with the currents and tides of the ocean. Tiny shrimplike animals and various forms of algae, such as diatoms, are all plankton. Plankton are the main food for many larger organisms, including whales.

Figure 11–15 *This microscopic animal is an example of plankton. Where in the ocean are plankton found?*

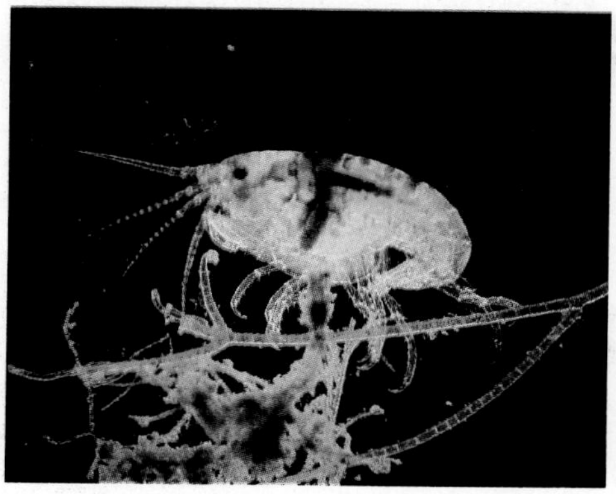

Forms of ocean life that swim are called **nekton** (NEHK-tahn). Whales, dolphins, squid, and fish are nekton. Nekton are able to search for food and avoid predators. Predators are organisms that eat other organisms.

Nekton can be found near the ocean surface and near the ocean floor. Because they can swim, they

Figure 11–16 *The grouper (left) and shark (right) are forms of ocean life called nekton. Nekton can be found near the ocean surface and near the ocean floor. Why is this so?*

Figure 11–17 *These brown tube sponges (top) and this sea anemone (bottom) are organisms that live on the ocean floor. What is this group of organisms called?*

move from one area of the ocean to another. But they remain in areas where environmental conditions are favorable to them. What conditions might affect where these organisms live?

Organisms that live on the ocean floor are called **benthos** (BEHN-thahs). Some benthos are plants that grow on the ocean floor in shallow waters. Some are animals such as barnacles, oysters, starfish, and crabs. Many benthos, such as sea anemones, actually attach themselves to the ocean floor. Others live in shore areas. A few live on the ocean floor in the deepest parts of the ocean.

Intertidal Zone

The **intertidal zone** lies between the low- and high-tide lines. This is the most changeable zone in the ocean. It is difficult for living things to exist in the intertidal zone. The tides and the breaking waves constantly move materials in this zone. Since the tide goes in and out, organisms must be able to live without water some of the time.

Some of the organisms in the intertidal zone are anemones, crabs, clams, mussels, and plants such as seaweed. To keep from being washed out to sea, many of these organisms attach themselves to the sand and rocks of the shore. Others, such as marine worms, burrow into the wet sand for protection.

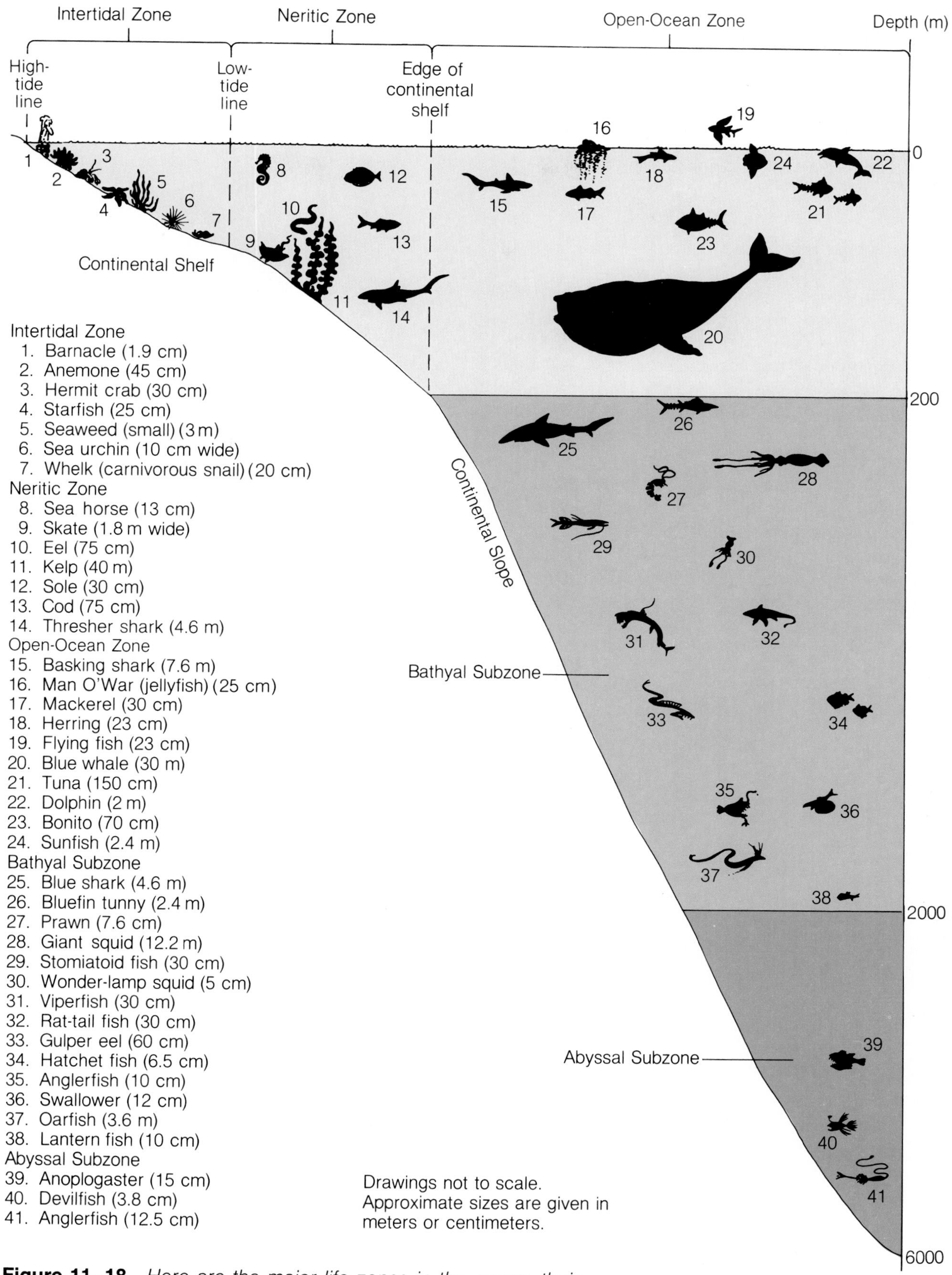

Figure 11–18 *Here are the major life zones in the ocean, their depths, and some of the living things usually found in these zones. Above what depth is most ocean life found?*

CAREER — *Oil-Rig Worker*

HELP WANTED: OIL-RIG WORKER Men and women needed to help build and maintain off-shore oil rigs in the Gulf of Mexico. Hard outdoor work and good pay.

When marine organisms die, they sink into the ocean depths and are gradually covered with layers of sediments. Those remains that were buried millions of years ago have since been exposed to great heat and pressure—turning them into fossil fuels. Today fossil fuels, crude oil and natural gas, provide three-fourths of the energy used in the United States.

To recover the oil and gas stored beneath a continental shelf, the petroleum industry hires many scientists and nonscientists to locate the fuels and bring them to the surface. A team of **oil-rig workers** is sent to the drill site many kilometers off the coast. They build a drilling rig to support the equipment. Other drill team workers periodically connect lengths of pipe and apply mud for lubrication during the drilling process.

Oil-rig work is a dangerous and exciting job done in isolated places. Anyone interested should enjoy working outdoors under a variety of weather conditions. Mechanical ability is also needed to work with tools and machinery. To learn more, write to the American Petroleum Institute, 1220 L Street, NW, Washington, DC 20005.

Neritic Zone

The **neritic** (nuh-RIHT-ihk) **zone** extends from the low-tide line to the end of a continental shelf. This zone extends to a depth of about 200 meters.

The neritic zone has plenty of sunlight. The water pressure is low. The temperature remains fairly constant. And the floor of the zone is covered with seaweed. Many different animals and plants live in this zone, including plankton, nekton, and benthos. Fish, clams, snails, some types of whales, and lobsters are just some of the organisms in the neritic zone. This zone is the source of much of the seafood people eat. The neritic zone ends where seaweed stops growing because there is too little sunlight. How would this affect other living things?

Open Ocean

There are two open-ocean zones. The first is the **bathyal** (BATH-ee-uhl) **zone.** It begins at a continental slope and extends down about 2000 meters. Sunlight does not penetrate to the bottom of this zone.

There are many forms of nekton in the bathyal zone, including squid, octopus, and large whales. Because there is little sunlight in the lower parts, plants do not grow near the bottom of this zone.

About 2000 meters down, the **abyssal zone** begins. This is the second open-ocean zone. It extends to an average depth of 6000 meters. The abyssal zone covers the large, flat plains of the ocean. There is no sunlight in this zone. Little food is available. The pressure of the water is very high. What do you think the temperatures are like here?

Despite these harsh conditions, life exists in the abyssal zone. Most of the animals are small. Many are very strange looking. Some of the animals make their own light.

Sharpen Your Skills

Food From the Ocean

Visit a supermarket or fish market. List the different seafoods available. Answer the following questions about the seafoods:

1. Which are plankton? Nekton? Benthos?
2. From which ocean-life zone did each come?
3. Where did the store obtain them?
4. Which are fresh? Frozen? Canned?
5. Which do you eat?

SECTION REVIEW

1. What are some factors that affect ocean life?
2. What are the three main groups of ocean life?
3. Which zone contains the greatest variety of ocean life? Why?

11–5 Mapping the Ocean Floor

Section Objective

To describe how the ocean floor is mapped

In 1872, the first expedition to explore the ocean began when the *Challenger* sailed from England. Equipped for ocean exploration, the *Challenger* remained at sea for 3½ years. Scientists aboard the *Challenger* had only piano wire to measure ocean depth. They used nets attached to heavy ropes to gather plants and animals from the ocean floor. Special thermometers enabled them to record deep-ocean temperatures. And samples of ocean water were collected in special bottles.

Today oceanographers use many modern instruments to explore the ocean. Underwater cameras provide pictures of the ocean floor. Devices called corers bring up samples of mud and sand from the ocean floor. And a variety of diving vehicles, including bathyspheres, bathyscaphs, and submersibles, are used to inspect the ocean depths. You can read more about these devices in Chapter 23.

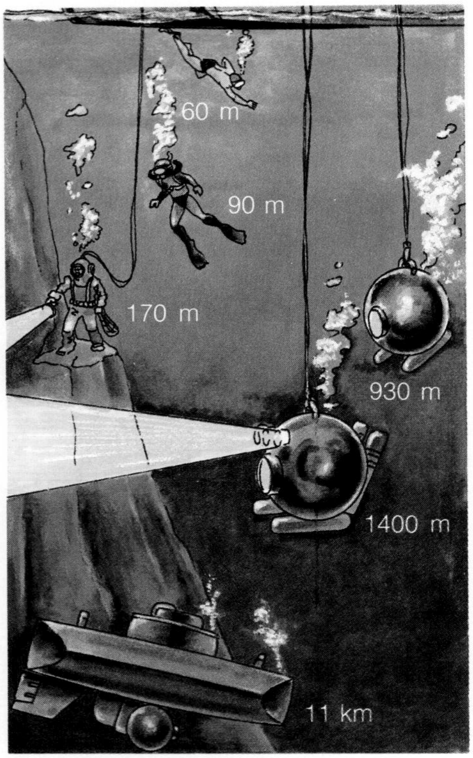

Figure 11–19 *Different instruments are used to explore the ocean. The type of instrument used is determined by the ocean depth. To what depth can a person descend without special breathing equipment?*

One of the most important goals of oceanographers is to map the ocean floor. **Mapping the ocean floor can only be done by indirect methods, such as echo sounding, radar, sonar, and seismographic surveys.** All of these methods are based on the same principle: Energy waves such as sound waves sent down from the ocean surface are reflected from the ocean floor and recorded at the surface. Knowing the speed of sound in water, which is about 1500 meters per second, and the time it takes sound waves to make a round trip, oceanographers can determine the ocean depth at any location along the ocean floor.

The most complete picture of the ocean floor has been obtained from information gathered by *Seasat,* a scientific satellite launched in 1978. From the 8 billion readings radioed back by *Seasat,* scientists have created the most accurate map yet of the ocean floor.

SECTION REVIEW

1. Name three instruments used by oceanographers today to explore the ocean.
2. What two pieces of information are needed to determine ocean depth?
3. How has the most complete picture of the ocean floor been obtained?

Section Objective

To describe the causes of waves, currents, and tides

11–6 Motions of the Ocean

Ocean water never stops moving. **There are three basic motions of ocean water: the up and down movement of waves, the steady movement of ocean currents, and the rise and fall of ocean water in tides.** In this section you will learn more about each of these ocean motions.

Waves

Waves are pulses of energy that move through the ocean. Waves are set in motion by winds, earthquakes, and the gravitational pull of the moon. But the most common source of energy for waves is wind blowing across the surface of the ocean.

Figure 11–20 *The "Pipeline" in Oahu, Hawaii, is one of the most spectacular examples of ocean motion.*

Ocean waves begin as wind-stirred ripples on the water's surface. As more energy is transferred from the wind to the water, the waves look like great surges of rapidly moving water. But the water is not moving forward at all! It is actually energy that moves forward through the water, producing one wave after another. The energy is passed from one particle of water to another. The particles themselves stay in their relative positions.

Wave energy is not only passed forward from one particle to another. It is also passed downward from particle to particle. With increasing depth, the motion of the particles decreases. At a certain depth, motion stops. In deep water, there are no waves except for those that are caused by tides and earthquakes.

The height of surface waves depends on three factors. These factors are the wind's speed, the length of time the wind blows, and the distance the wind blows over the water. In which ocean, the Atlantic or Pacific, would you expect the larger waves to occur?

Figure 11–21 *As energy is transferred from the wind to the water, waves are set in motion. The wave pulses of energy are passed forward from particle to particle, as well as downward from particle to particle. Notice that it is not the water that is moving forward, but the pulse of energy.*

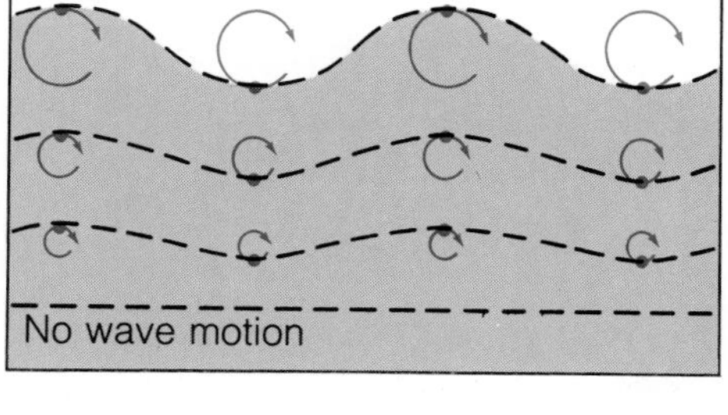

WAVE CHARACTERISTICS Ocean waves, like all other waves, have several characteristics. The highest point of a wave is called the **crest.** The lowest point of a wave is called the **trough** (trawf). The horizontal distance between two consecutive crests or two

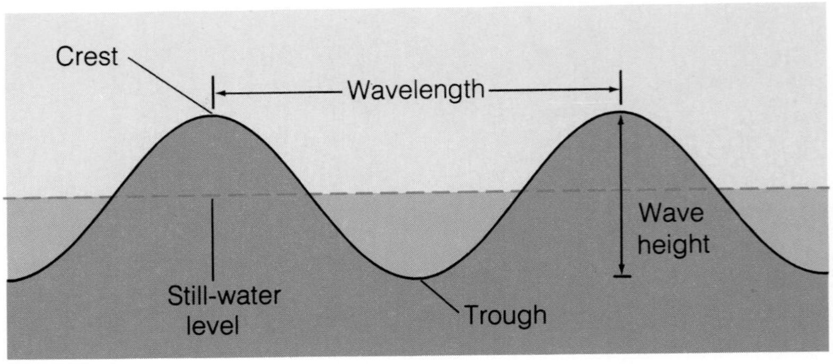

Figure 11–22 *Characteristics of ocean waves are shown in this diagram. What is the distance between two consecutive crests called? What is the lowest point of a wave called?*

consecutive troughs is called the **wavelength.** The vertical distance between a crest and a trough is called the wave height. All of these characteristics are shown in Figure 11–22. Waves can have various wavelengths and wave heights.

The amount of time it takes consecutive crests or troughs to pass a given point is called the wave period. The number of crests or troughs passing a given point in a certain wave period is called the wave frequency. What is the relationship between wavelength and wave frequency?

Out in the ocean, waves stay about the same distance apart for thousands of kilometers. So wavelength is usually constant. These waves are called swells. Swells are long, wide waves that are not very high.

But waves change as they near the shore. The waves slow down. They also get closer and closer together. Their wavelength decreases and their wave height increases. They finally crash forward as breakers and surge onto the shore. The surging water is called the surf.

The water then flows back toward the ocean. Bits of seaweed, sand, and pebbles are pulled back by the retreating water. This retreating water is called an undertow. Undertows can be very strong and extend for several kilometers.

Figure 11–23 *The pattern of a swell as it reaches a sloping beach is shown in this diagram. What happens to the wavelength and the wave height as the wave nears the beach?*

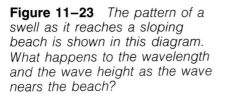

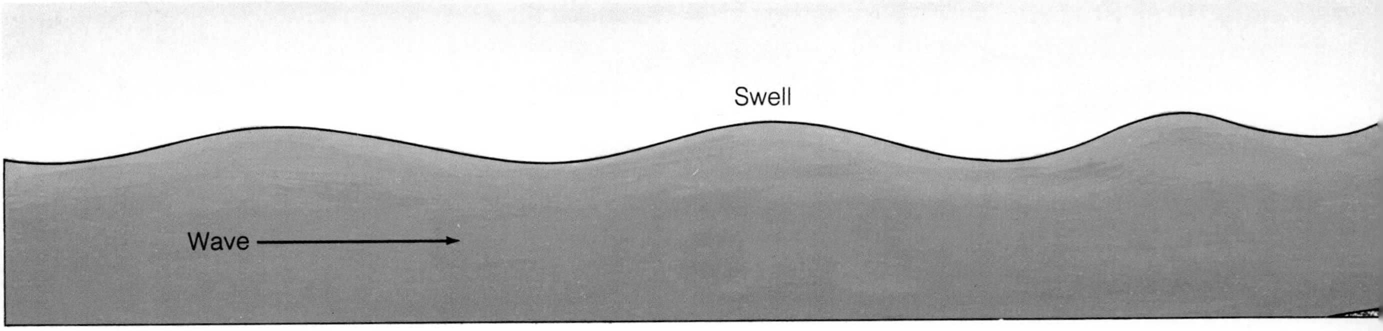

TSUNAMIS Some waves are caused by earthquakes. These waves are called **tsunamis** (tsoo-NAH-meez). Tsunamis are the largest ocean waves.

Tsunamis have very long wavelengths and are very deep. They carry a huge amount of energy. As tsunamis slow down in shallow water, they pile closer together and get very high. The energy that was once spread throughout a great depth of water is now concentrated in much less water. This energy produces the tsunamis, which can reach heights of 35 meters or more when they strike the shore.

Currents

You can see water moving on the surface of the ocean in the form of waves. But water below the surface also moves. This water moves in streams called currents. Some currents might better be described as "rivers" in the ocean because they are thousands of kilometers long. In fact, the mighty Mississippi River is a mere brook compared with the largest of the ocean currents. But long or short, all ocean currents are caused by the same major factors: wind patterns and differences in water density.

SURFACE CURRENTS Currents caused mainly by wind patterns are called **surface currents.** These currents usually have a depth of several hundred meters. Some of these currents are warm-water currents. Others are cold-water currents. The temperature of a current depends on where the current originates. A warm current comes from a warm area. A cold current comes from a cold area.

Some surface currents travel long distances. Surface currents that travel thousands of kilometers are called long-distance surface currents. The Gulf

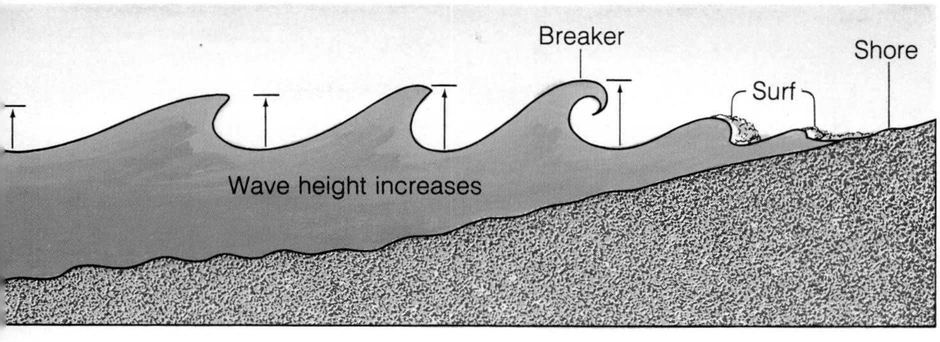

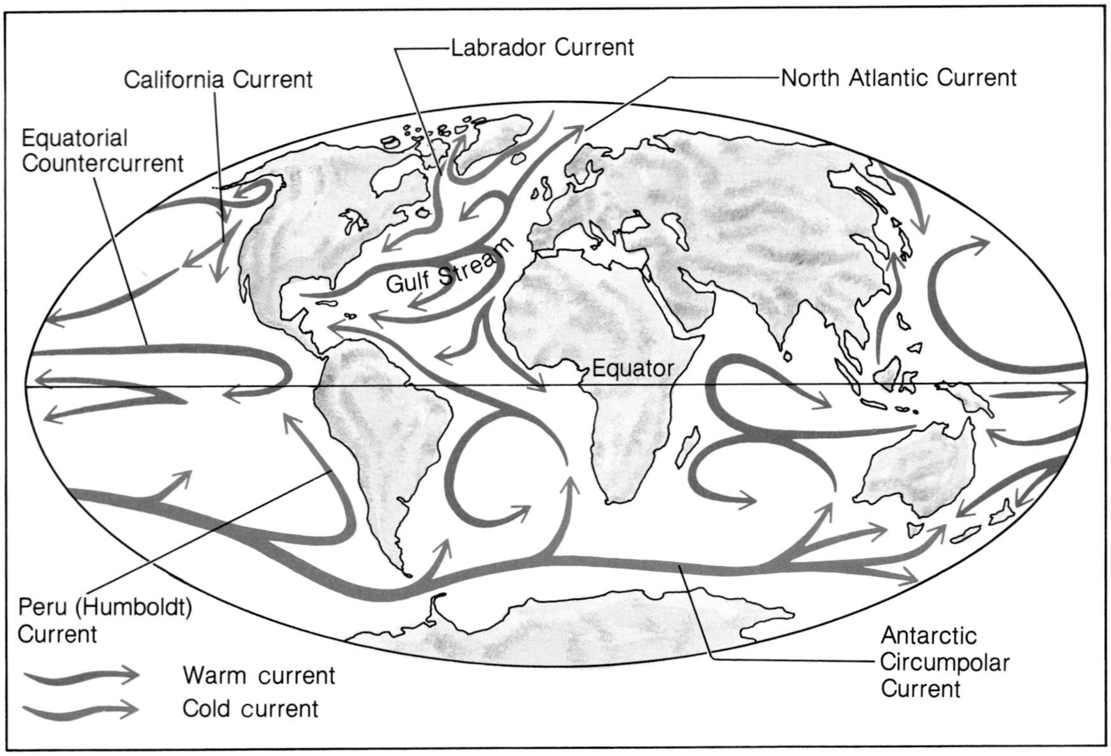

Figure 11–24 *The general directions of flow of the major warm and cold long-distance surface currents of the world are shown on this map. Which current would affect the climate in your area?*

Stream is a well-known surface current. It is about 150 kilometers wide and may reach a depth of about 1000 meters. It carries warm water from the southern tip of Florida north along the eastern coast of the United States. It moves at speeds greater than 1.5 meters per second. And more than 150 million cubic meters of water may pass a given point each second!

Figure 11–24 shows the major warm and cold surface currents of the world and the general directions in which they flow. Because all of the oceans are connected, these ocean currents form a continuous worldwide pattern of water circulation.

You will notice from Figure 11–24 that the water in each ocean moves in a large, almost circular pattern. In the Northern Hemisphere, the currents move clockwise. In the Southern Hemisphere, the currents move counterclockwise. These motions correspond to the direction of wind circulation in each hemisphere.

Surface currents that move over short distances are called short-distance surface currents. These currents usually are found near a shoreline where waves hit at an angle. When the waves hit the shoreline, the water turns and produces currents that flow parallel to the shoreline. These streams of water are called longshore currents.

As longshore currents move parallel to the shoreline, they pick up large quantities of material, such as sand from the beach. The sand is deposited in water close to the shoreline. A long, underwater pile of sand called a sand bar builds up.

Longshore currents can become trapped on the shoreline side of a sand bar. These currents may eventually cut an opening in the sand bar. The currents then return to the ocean in a powerful narrow flow called a rip current. A rip current is the type of strong undertow that you read about earlier in this chapter.

DEEP CURRENTS Some currents are caused mainly by differences in water density deep in the ocean. Such currents are called **deep currents.** The density, or mass per unit volume, is affected by temperature and salinity. Cold water is more dense than warm water. And the saltier the water is, the more dense it is. For example, cold dense water flowing out of the polar regions moves downward under less dense warm water.

Cameras lowered to the ocean floor in places have photographed evidence of these powerful deep

Sharpen Your Skills

Observing a Current

1. Fill a glass half full with ice-cold water. Add several drops of food coloring.

2. Fill a clear glass bowl one-half to three-quarters full with warm water.

3. Carefully pour the cold water down the side of the bowl. Observe the current.

Explain why the current forms. Which type of ocean current is it most like?

Figure 11–25 *When longshore currents cut through a sand bar, a rip current is formed. Why are rip currents dangerous?*

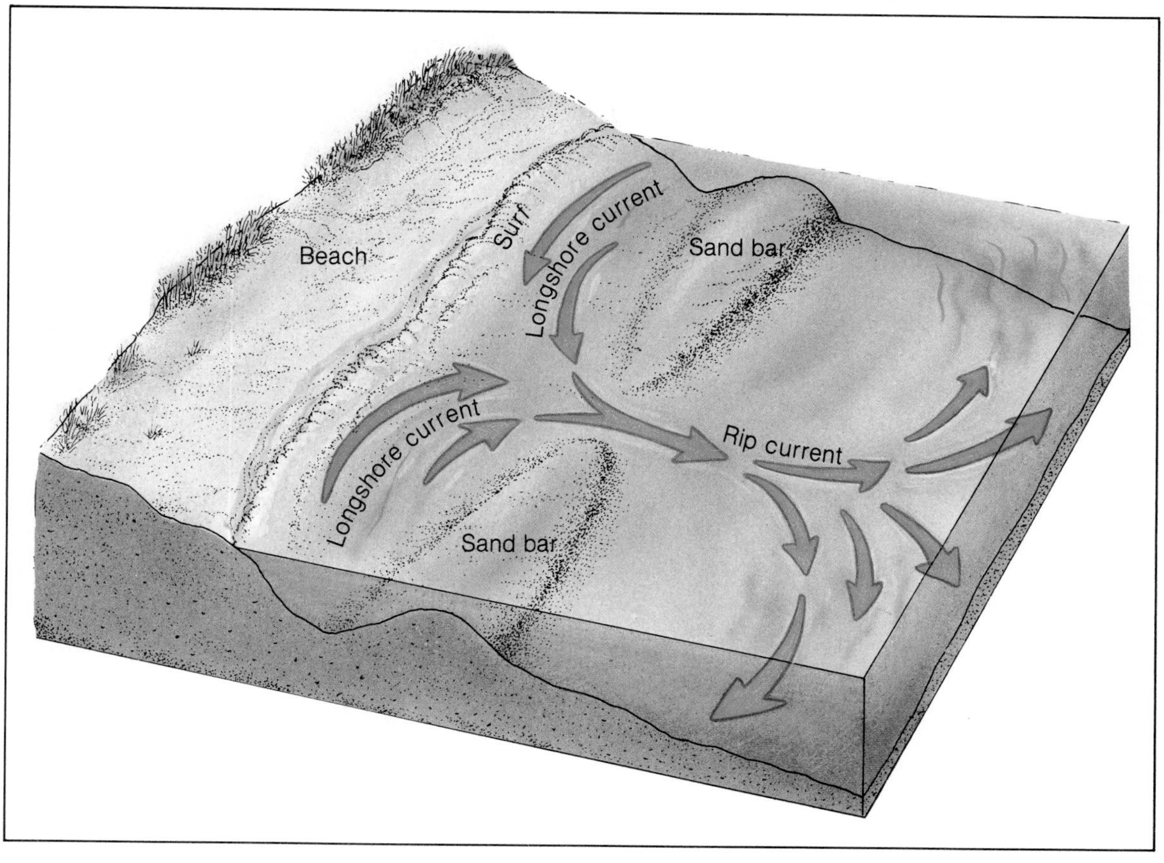

Figure 11–26 *Areas of upwelling are important fishing areas because ocean life is plentiful.*

currents. The photographs show ripples carved into the sand of the ocean floor. In places on the floor, heavy clay has been piled into small dunes, as if shaped by winds. These "winds," scientists conclude, must be very strong ocean currents.

Most deep currents flow in the opposite direction from surface currents. For example, in the summer the Mediterranean Sea loses more water by evaporation than it gets back as rain. The salinity of the Mediterranean increases and so does its density. As a result, deep currents of dense Mediterranean water flow out along the ocean floor into the Atlantic Ocean. At the same time, Atlantic Ocean water that is less salty, and thus less dense, flows into the Mediterranean at the ocean surface.

The densest ocean water in the world lies off the Antarctic coast. This dense, cold Antarctic water sinks to the ocean floor and tends to flow north through the world's oceans. These deep Antarctic currents travel for thousands of kilometers. At the same time, warm surface currents near the equator tend to flow south toward Antarctica.

As the deep Antarctic currents near the land, the ocean floor rises, forcing these cold currents upward. The rising of deep cold currents to the ocean surface is called **upwelling.** Upwelling is very important because the rising currents carry with them rich foodstuffs that have drifted down to the ocean floor—the remains of dead animals and plants. Wherever these deep currents rise, they turn the ocean into an area of plentiful ocean life. For example, deep currents move upward off the coasts of Peru and Chile. There are important fishing industries in both of these areas.

Tides

Tides are the regular rise and fall of ocean water caused by the gravitational attraction among the earth, moon, and sun. The earth's gravity pulls on the moon. But the moon's gravity also pulls on the earth, producing a bulging of the ocean. The ocean bulges in two places: on the side of the earth facing the moon and on the side of the earth facing away from the moon. Both bulges cause a high tide, or rising of ocean water, on nearby shorelines.

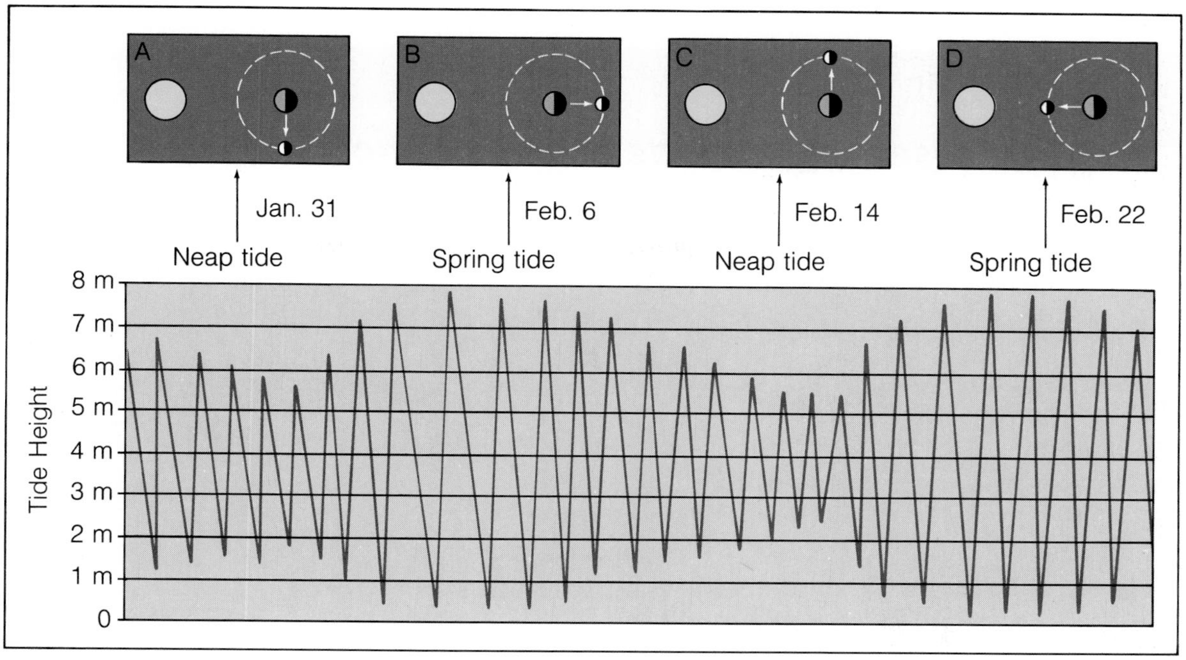

Figure 11–27 *Spring tides occur when the sun and moon are in line with the earth. During what phases of the moon does this occur? Neap tides occur when the sun and moon are at right angles to the earth. During what phases does this occur?*

At the same time that the high tides occur, low tides occur between the two bulges. Observations show that at a given place on the earth there are two high tides and two low tides every 24 hours.

Some high tides are higher than other high tides. For example, when the moon is at its full- and new-moon phases, the earth has higher tides than at other times. These higher tides are called spring tides. Spring tides occur when the sun and the moon are in line with the earth. The increased gravitational effect due to the sun's gravity causes the ocean bulges to become larger than usual.

When the moon is at its first- and last-quarter phases, its gravitational pull on the oceans is partially canceled by the sun's gravitational pull. Lower high tides than usual result. These minimum tides are called neap tides. What is the position of the sun and moon with respect to each other during neap tides?

SECTION REVIEW

1. What are the three motions of the ocean?
2. What are waves? Describe four characteristics of a wave.
3. What is the difference between surface currents and deep currents?
4. What causes ocean tides?

Sharpen Your Skills

Tides and the Moon

Tide forecasts for each month are usually given in the newspaper on the first day of the month or in the *Farmer's Almanac.*

1. Using the information for a particular coastal area, plot a graph of the daily high- and low-tide heights for the month. Because there are two high- and two low-tide heights each day, plot only the earlier heights.

2. Determine how the phases of the moon are reflected in the graph.

11 LABORATORY INVESTIGATION

Observing a Model Thermocline

Problem

How can a model of a thermocline be constructed and interpreted?

Materials (*per group*)

2-L plastic soda bottle with top cut off
6 thermometers (100°C)
Light source
Sheet of plastic (transparency or plastic folder)
Clear tape
Safety goggles
Clock or watch with sweep second hand
Graph paper
Colored pencils or crayons
Water

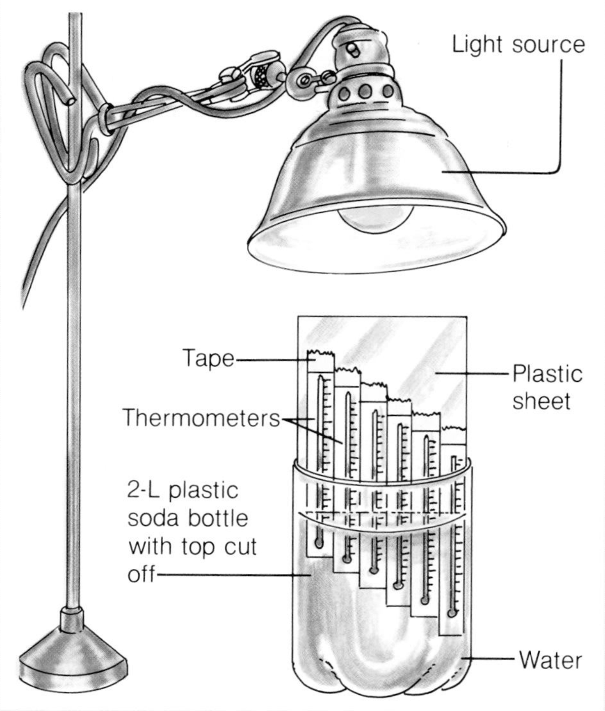

Procedure

1. Put your safety goggles on.
2. Fill a plastic container with water to a height of 16 cm.
3. Tape six thermometers to a plastic sheet so that the top one is just below the surface of the water in the container. The remaining thermometers should be placed so that they record temperatures at depths of 2, 4, 6, 8, and 10 cm below the water's surface. Allow a minute or two for all of the thermometers to reach water temperature. Then record the temperature at each level.
4. Adjust the light source so that it is about 15 cm above the surface of the water and turn it on. **CAUTION:** *Do not allow any part of the cord to come in contact with the water.* Observe and record the temperatures at each level every 2 minutes for a total of 20 minutes.
5. At the end of the 20-minute heating period, turn off the light source.

Observations

1. From your recorded data, make a graph of the temperature at each level versus time. Use a different-colored pencil or crayon for each different thermometer. Label the temperature curves drawn for each level.
2. On another piece of graph paper, make a second graph. Plot the data for temperature versus depth at the end of the 20-minute heating period only. This graph should show a single curve.

Conclusions

1. At which depth did you observe the greatest range in temperature? In °C, what was the extent of this temperature range?
2. At which depth did you observe the smallest range in temperature? In °C, what was the extent of this temperature range?
3. What is the approximate depth and thickness of the zone in which temperatures changed most rapidly? What is this zone called?

CHAPTER REVIEW

SUMMARY

11–1 Oceans of the World

❑ About 71 percent of the earth's surface is covered by ocean water.

❑ The Atlantic, Pacific, and Indian oceans are the three major oceans.

11–2 Properties of Ocean Water

❑ Salinity describes the amount of dissolved salts in ocean water.

❑ Ocean water is classified into three zones according to its temperature: surface zone, thermocline, and deep zone.

11–3 Topography of the Ocean Floor

❑ A continental margin consists of a continental shelf, a continental slope, and a continental rise.

❑ Major features of the ocean floor include abyssal plains, seamounts, guyots, trenches, midocean ridges, rift valleys, and reefs.

11–4 Ocean-Life Zones

❑ Ocean-life forms are classified as plankton, nekton, and benthos.

❑ The three ocean zones are the intertidal zone, neritic zone, and open ocean.

11–5 Mapping the Ocean Floor

❑ Methods of mapping the ocean floor are based on the speed of sound in water and the time it takes sound waves to make a round trip.

11–6 Motions of the Ocean

❑ Motions of the ocean include waves, currents, and tides.

❑ All waves have the following characteristics: crests, troughs, wavelength, wave height, wave period, and wave frequency.

❑ Currents caused mainly by wind patterns are called surface currents. Currents caused mainly by differences in water density are called deep currents.

❑ Tides are the regular rise and fall of ocean water caused by the gravitational attraction among the earth, moon, and sun.

VOCABULARY

Define each term in a complete sentence.

abyssal plain
abyssal zone
atoll
barrier reef
bathyal zone
benthos
continental margin
continental rise
continental shelf
continental slope
coral reef
crest
deep current
deep zone
fringing reef
guyot
intertidal zone
midocean ridge
nekton
neritic zone
oceanographer
plankton
salinity
seamount
submarine canyon
surface current
surface zone
thermocline
trench
trough
tsunami
turbidity current
upwelling
wavelength

CONTENT REVIEW: MULTIPLE CHOICE

Choose the letter of the answer that best completes each sentence.

1. The three major oceans of the world are the
a. Atlantic, Pacific, and Arctic b. Indian, Arctic, and Mediterranean
c. Atlantic, Pacific, and Indian d. Atlantic, Pacific, and Caribbean

2. The amount of dissolved salts in ocean water is called
a. salinity b. turbidity c. density d. upwelling

3. The zone of rapid temperature change in ocean water is called the
a. surface zone b. intertidal zone c. deep zone d. thermocline

4. The deepest parts of the ocean are found in long, narrow crevices called
a. guyots b. trenches c. seamounts d. reefs

5. Organisms that live on the ocean floor are called
a. nekton b. plankton c. diatoms d. benthos

6. The most common source of energy for waves is
a. wind b. earthquakes c. tides d. volcanoes

7. The amount of time it takes consecutive crests or troughs to pass a given point is called the
a. wavelength b. wave period c. wave height d. frequency

8. All ocean currents are caused by
a. winds and earthquakes b. volcanoes and tides
c. winds and differences in water density
d. tides and differences in water density

9. The rising of deep cold currents to the ocean surface is called
a. surfing b. upwelling c. mapping d. reefing

10. High tides that are higher than other high tides are called
a. neap tides b. moon tides c. ebb tides d. spring tides

CONTENT REVIEW: COMPLETION

Fill in the word or words that best complete each sentence.

1. Scientists who study the ocean are called ________.

2. The most abundant gases dissolved in ocean water are nitrogen, oxygen, and ________.

3. Large flat areas on the ocean floor are called ________.

4. Underwater volcanic mountains are called ________.

5. The highest point of a wave is called the ________.

6. The horizontal distance between two consecutive troughs on a wave is called the ________.

7. Giant waves caused by earthquakes are called ________.

8. Currents caused mainly by windpatterns are called ________ currents.

9. The two factors that affect the density of water are ________ and ________.

10. The regular rise and fall of ocean water is called the ________.

CONTENT REVIEW: TRUE OR FALSE

Determine whether each statement is true or false. If it is true, write "true." If it is false, change the underlined word or words to make the statement true.

1. The most abundant salt in ocean water is magnesium bromide.
2. The zone of ocean water where the water is mixed by waves and currents is called the thermocline.
3. The relatively flat part of a continental margin covered by shallow ocean water is called a continental slope.
4. Very small plants and animals found at or near the surface of the ocean are called plankton.
5. The lowest point of a wave is called the crest.
6. Long, wide waves far out in the ocean are called breakers.
7. The Gulf Stream is a long-distance surface current.
8. Ocean waters off the coasts of Peru and Chile are important fishing areas because of upwelling.
9. Tides are caused mainly by the gravitational attraction of the moon.
10. Spring tides occur during the first- and last-quarter phases of the moon.

CONCEPT REVIEW: SKILL BUILDING

Use the skills you have developed in the chapter to complete each activity.

1. **Making generalizations** Describe what the ocean would be like at a depth of 3000 meters. Include all of the physical and chemical features you have learned.
2. **Making inferences** For many years, Peru's fishing industry was first in the world. The waters along Peru's coast were rich in fish. El Niño changed things. El Niño is a warm-water current that flows south along the coast of Ecuador. About every seven years, wind patterns change, and El Niño extends down the coast of Peru. The warm water lies along the coast. Why has El Niño harmed Peru's fish industry.
3. **Drawing conclusions** What special features should a diving suit have to help a diver survive in the abyssal zone?
4. **Relating concepts** The interval of time required for consecutive crests or troughs to pass a given point is the wave period. Using this definition, develop a formula that shows the relationship between the wave period in seconds, wavelength in meters, and speed in meters per second of a wave.

CONCEPT REVIEW: ESSAY

Discuss each of the following in a brief paragraph.

1. Many legends tell of the appearance and disappearance of islands. Explain why such legends could be true.
2. Draw and label a typical wave.
3. Why do you think oceanography is an important science?

The Earth's Atmosphere

12

CHAPTER SECTIONS

CHAPTER OBJECTIVES

After completing this chapter, you will be able to

- **12–1** Identify the gases that make up the earth's atmosphere.
- **12–1** Describe the processes that changed the earth's early atmosphere.
- **12–1** Explain the nitrogen, carbon dioxide, and oxygen cycles.
- **12–2** Compare the various layers of the atmosphere.
- **12–3** Describe the features of the magnetosphere.

The airborne wicker basket could not compare with the complex satellites that orbit the earth today. But the huge basket hanging from a hydrogen-filled balloon was the ship of exploration for scientists of the 1800s. Aboard such a vehicle, weather scientists began exploring the earth's envelope of air.

James Glaisher and Henry Coxwell, two early explorers, boarded their ship one warm September day in 1862 and began their balloon trip. Shortly after liftoff, the men found themselves in serious trouble.

Twenty-five minutes into their flight, and at a height of 4.8 kilometers, the temperature was a very cold −11°C. Ice coated the basket and the rigging of the balloon. But the two scientists chose to continue. At their final altitude of 11 kilometers, the temperature had plunged to −52°C.

The scientists were numbed with cold and had difficulty breathing. They knew that they would soon die if they did not bring the balloon down. The task fell to Coxwell. He managed to open the gas valves and bring the balloon back down to safety. Since his hands were frostbitten, he accomplished this feat by grabbing the valve cord with his teeth!

Glaisher and Coxwell learned two important facts about the air: As the altitude increases, the air becomes colder and less dense. Luckily they lived to tell their story and make other balloon flights of exploration. As you read this chapter, you will learn what scientists have discovered about the earth's envelope of air.

Towering clouds are a familiar sight in the earth's atmosphere. The atmosphere extends for thousands of kilometers and envelops the earth in layers of gases that support all forms of life.

12–1 Composition of the Atmosphere

Section Objective

To identify the gases in the atmosphere

When astronauts walk in space, they wear space suits. The space suits provide a protective covering. They enclose the astronauts in an artificial environment, providing them with comfortable temperatures as well as moisture and oxygen. They also protect the astronauts from harmful ultraviolet rays given off by the sun. In much the same way, the **atmosphere** (AT-muhs-fir) of the earth provides protection for you. The atmosphere is the envelope of gases surrounding the earth. The atmosphere provides materials necessary to support all forms of life on the earth.

Cameras and other instruments aboard space satellites have provided much data about the structure and composition of the present atmosphere. From this information and other studies, earth scientists have developed a picture of what the earth's atmosphere may have been like billions of years ago. They are certain that the earth's atmosphere has changed greatly. And they believe that the present atmosphere is changing! What conditions might be responsible for changes in the atmosphere?

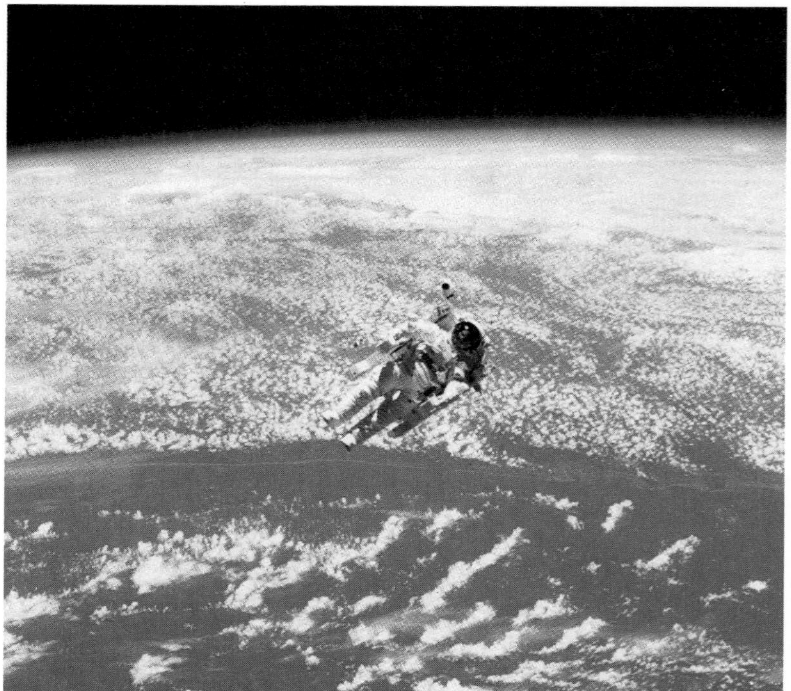

Figure 12–1 *When astronaut Robert L. Stewart walked in space, his space suit provided comfortable temperature, moisture, oxygen, and protection from harmful ultraviolet rays. In much the same way, the earth's atmosphere encloses you in a comfortable and safe environment.*

Figure 12–2 *Scientists obtain information about the earth's atmosphere from a variety of instruments. Weather satellites (left) carry cameras to take photographs of cloud patterns and special equipment to study the atmosphere. High-altitude balloons (top right) record temperatures at different heights in the earth's atmosphere. And dust trapped in ice samples (bottom right) helps scientists study changes in the earth's early atmosphere.*

The Past Atmosphere

It is theorized that the earth's atmosphere 4 billion years ago contained two deadly gases: **methane** and **ammonia.** Methane is a poisonous compound made up of hydrogen and carbon. Ammonia, also a poisonous gas, is composed of nitrogen and hydrogen. There was also some water in the air.

As you well know, the air is no longer deadly. In fact, you could not live without it. How did this important change in the atmosphere occur?

To explain this change, it is necessary to picture the earth's atmosphere 3.8 billion years ago. Sunlight triggered chemical reactions among the substances in the air—methane, ammonia, and water. As a result of many chemical reactions, new materials formed in the air. Among them were nitrogen, hydrogen, and carbon dioxide. The methane and ammonia vanished. But the water still remained.

Hydrogen, a very lightweight gas, escaped the earth's gravity and disappeared into space. That left nitrogen in greatest abundance, as well as carbon dioxide and water vapor. Sunlight began breaking down water vapor in the upper parts of the earth's atmosphere. The water vapor broke down into hydrogen and oxygen gases. As before, the hydrogen gas escaped into space. But the atoms of oxygen gas began to combine with each other to form **ozone.** The end result was a layer of ozone gas about 30 kilometers above the earth's surface.

The ozone layer is sometimes referred to as an "umbrella" for life on earth. This is because the

Figure 12–3 *An artist's conception of what the earth's atmosphere may have looked like billions of years ago. What two gases were most abundant then?*

Figure 12–4 *The ozone layer absorbs most of the harmful ultraviolet radiation before it reaches the earth's surface. Visible light is not absorbed. What is the nickname for the ozone layer?*

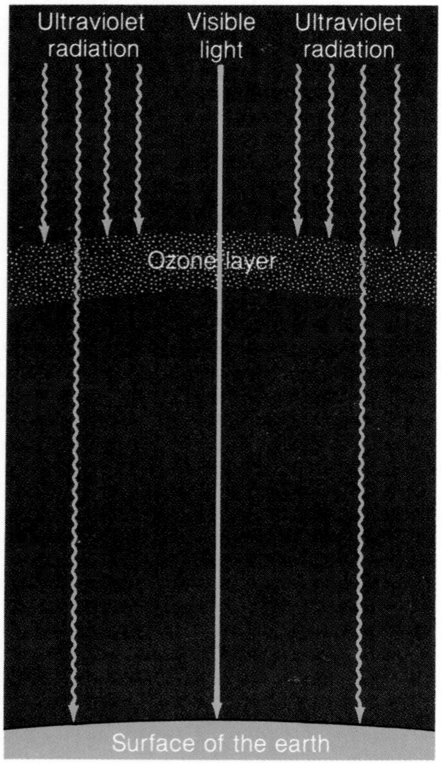

ozone layer absorbs most of the harmful ultraviolet radiation from the sun. Without the protection of the ozone shield, few living things could survive.

Before the ozone layer formed, the only living things on the earth were microscopic organisms that lived far below the surface of the oceans. Here they were protected from most of the ultraviolet radiation. After the formation of the ozone layer, certain types of organisms called blue-green algae started to appear on or near the water's surface. These algae used the energy in sunlight to combine carbon dioxide from the air with water to produce food.

A waste product of this food-making process would soon change the planet forever. This waste product was oxygen. Unlike ozone, oxygen stayed near the bottom of the atmosphere. It would be this oxygen that animals would later breathe.

In time, green plants began to grow on the land. And they, too, took in carbon dioxide and released oxygen during the food-making process. The oxygen content in the atmosphere greatly increased. Then, around 600 million years ago, the amount of oxygen and carbon dioxide in the air leveled off. Since that time, the composition of the atmosphere has remained about the same.

The Present Atmosphere

The atmosphere that surrounds the earth today contains gases necessary for the survival of all living things. The air you breathe is the earth's most important natural resource. What is the air made of?

The atmosphere is a mixture of gases. **The atmospheric gases include nitrogen, oxygen, carbon dioxide, water vapor, and argon.** Nitrogen gas makes up about 78 percent of the atmosphere. Another 21 percent of the atmosphere is oxygen. The remaining 1 percent is a combination of carbon dioxide, water vapor, argon, and trace gases.

Trace gases are gases present in only very small amounts. The trace gases include neon, helium, krypton, and xenon. As you can see from Figure 12–6, there is still some methane in the atmosphere. But the earth's atmosphere has changed greatly in the past 4 billion years!

Figure 12–5 *Without the atmosphere, scenes such as this would be impossible on the earth. Why?*

NITROGEN The most abundant gas in the atmosphere is nitrogen. Living things need nitrogen to make proteins. Proteins are complex nitrogen

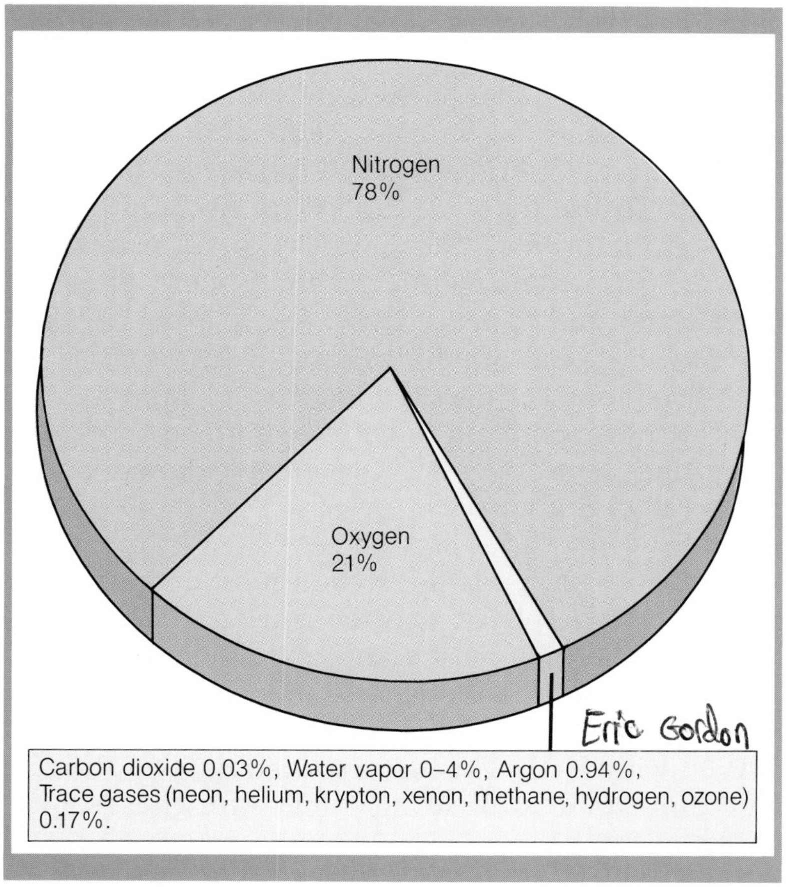

Figure 12–6 *The atmosphere is a mixture of many gases. Which two gases make up most of the earth's atmosphere?*

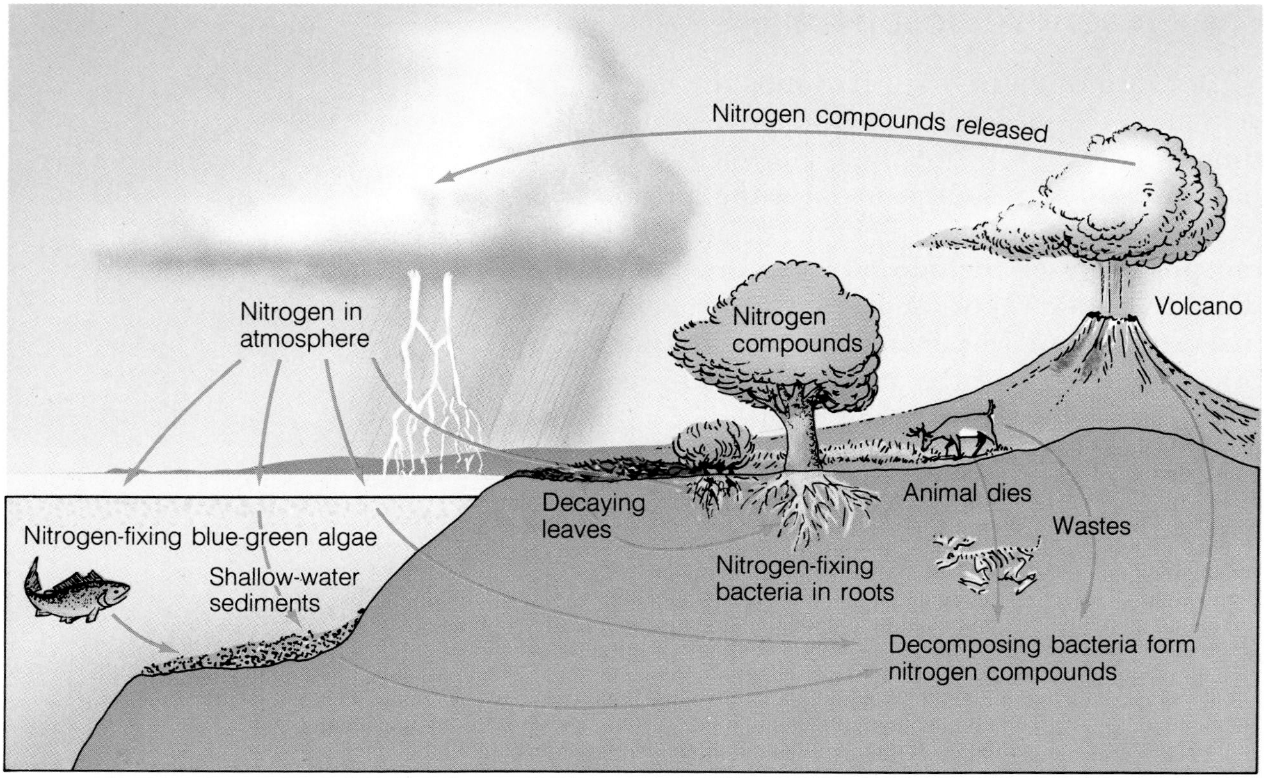

Figure 12–7 *This diagram shows the nitrogen cycle. How is nitrogen returned to the soil?*

compounds needed for growth and repair of body parts. But plants and animals cannot use the nitrogen in the atmosphere directly. Bacteria in the soil combine the nitrogen in the atmosphere with other chemicals in the soil to make compounds called nitrates. These bacteria are called nitrogen-fixing bacteria. Plants use the nitrates to form proteins. Animals get the proteins they need by eating plants.

Nitrogen is returned to the atmosphere when dead plants and animals decay. Decay is the breaking down of dead organisms, usually by bacteria, into the substances they are made of. The movement of nitrogen from the atmosphere and soil to living things and then back to the atmosphere and soil is called the nitrogen cycle.

OXYGEN Oxygen is the second most abundant gas in the atmosphere. Oxygen is used directly from the atmosphere by most plants and animals. It is essential for respiration (rehs-puh-RAY-shuhn). During respiration, living things chemically combine oxygen with food. This process breaks down the food and supplies the living things with energy.

Sharpen Your Skills

Atmospheric Gases

You have read about the various gases that make up the earth's atmosphere. Using reference books and other materials in the library, describe some of the uses of each gas. Name some household materials that use these gases in their production.

Oxygen is also necessary for the combustion, or burning, of fuels such as oil, coal, and wood. Combustion will not take place without oxygen. Why do you think combustion is important to people?

CARBON DIOXIDE The amount of carbon dioxide in the atmosphere is very small. But carbon dioxide is one of the raw materials needed by plants to make food.

Carbon dioxide is removed from the atmosphere by plants during the food-making process. It is returned to the atmosphere by the respiration of plants and animals. The decay of dead plants and animals also returns carbon dioxide to the air.

Scientists believe that the amount of carbon dioxide used by plants is equal to the amount returned to the atmosphere by respiration, decay, and other natural processes. But the burning of fossil fuels, such as oil and coal is adding even more carbon dioxide to the atmosphere. Scientists are concerned that the burning of these fuels is increasing the amount of carbon dioxide in the atmosphere to a

Sharpen Your Skills

Oxygen Calculation

1. With some melted candle wax, attach a small candle to the center of a small pie pan.
2. Fill the pan with 2 cm of water.
3. Light the candle and cover it with a 100-mL graduated cylinder.
4. After the candle has burned out, measure the height to which the water rose in the graduated cylinder.
5. Calculate the percentage of oxygen in the air by dividing the height of the water in the graduated cylinder by the height of the graduated cylinder and multiplying by 100.

How does your answer compare with the percentage of oxygen in the air given in this chapter?

Figure 12–8 *Carbon dioxide and oxygen are continuously exchanged among plants and animals. How is oxygen returned to the atmosphere?*

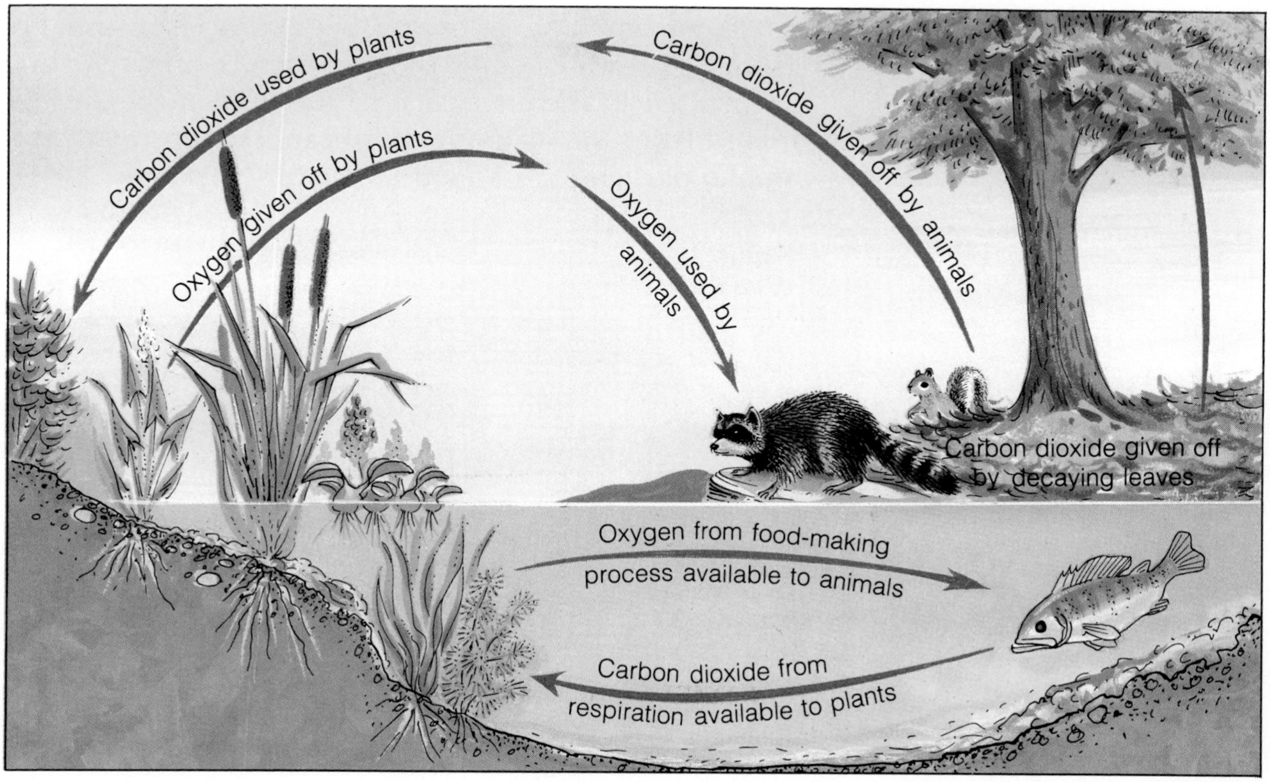

Figure 12–9 *The amount of water vapor in the atmosphere varies from place to place. The amount of water vapor is very small in desert regions such as Death Valley, California (top). In the tropical rain forest of Tanzania, there is much more water vapor in the atmosphere (bottom). How does the amount of water vapor in the air affect plant life in each area?*

dangerously high level. Why do you think scientists are concerned about an increase in the level of carbon dioxide in the atmosphere?

WATER VAPOR Water vapor plays a very important role in the weather on the earth and in the heating of the atmosphere. Water vapor absorbs heat energy from the sun. The amount of water vapor in the atmosphere varies from place to place. In desert regions, the amount of water vapor may be very small. In tropical regions, the amount of water vapor may be as high as 4 percent. Where else on earth would you expect to find a great deal of water vapor in the atmosphere?

SOLID PARTICLES Many tiny particles of solid material are mixed with the air's gases. These particles are dust, smoke, dirt, and tiny pieces of salt. Where do these particles come from?

Every time a wave breaks, tiny particles of salt from ocean water enter the atmosphere and remain suspended in the air. Much of the dust in the air comes from the eruption of volcanoes. Dirt and smoke particles are added to the air by people.

Figure 12–10 *Some air pollutants are emissions from a power plant (left), asbestos particles (center), and acid rain (right).*

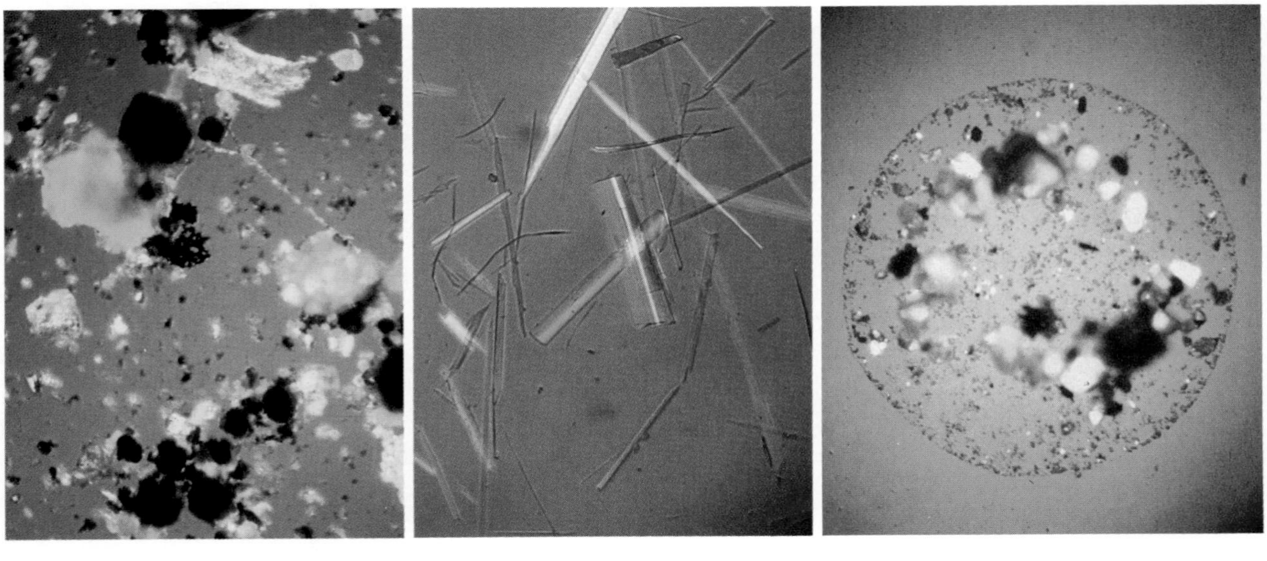

These harmful pollutants are products of the burning of fuels such as coal and oil.

SECTION REVIEW

1. What two deadly gases made up the earth's early atmosphere?
2. Name the four most abundant gases found in the atmosphere today.
3. Recently, scientists have discovered a "hole" in the ozone layer above Antarctica. Predict what might happen if this "hole" becomes larger.

Sharpen Your Skills

Earth's Atmosphere—Past, Present, and Future

Write a 250-word essay comparing the earth's atmosphere in the past with the atmosphere today. In your essay, predict what the earth's future atmosphere might be like and what life on the earth would then be like.

12–2 Layers of the Atmosphere

Section Objective

To relate changes in atmospheric temperature to the layers of the atmosphere

The mixture of gases, the temperature, and the electrical and magnetic forces of the atmosphere change as the distance above the earth's surface increases. For example, there is less oxygen in the upper atmosphere than in the lower atmosphere. You may have seen pictures of mountain climbers wearing oxygen masks when they were climbing very high mountains. They do so because there is only half as much oxygen available 5.5 kilometers above the earth's surface as there is available at the earth's surface.

If you ever climb a very high mountain yourself, you will notice that as you climb the air gets colder. At an altitude of 3 kilometers, you will probably need a heavy jacket to keep you warm! The temperature of the air decreases as the altitude increases because the air becomes less dense. That is, there are fewer and fewer particles of air in a given amount of space. The thin, less dense air cannot hold as much heat.

The atmosphere is divided into layers according to major changes in its temperature. The layers of air that surround the earth are held close to it by gravity. Gravity is a force by which objects are pulled toward one another. Gravity is a force of attraction. Because of gravity, the layers of air surrounding the earth push down on the earth's surface. This push is called air pressure.

Figure 12–11 *Climbers need heavy clothing on a high mountain because the air is colder. As they climb higher, the air thins and they must use oxygen masks.*

The upper layers of air push down on the lower layers. So the air pressure near the surface of the earth is greater than the air pressure farther away from the surface. If you have ever taken an airplane trip, you may have felt your ears "pop." This was caused by a change in air pressure. Where else might you experience a change in air pressure?

It is interesting to note that 99 percent of the total mass of the atmosphere of the earth is below an altitude of 32 kilometers. Only 1 percent of the total mass of the air is in the remaining hundreds of kilometers above an altitude of 32 kilometers.

Figure 12–12 *The troposphere is the weather layer of the atmosphere. Which two weather characteristics can be seen in these photographs?*

The Troposphere

The lowest layer of the atmosphere is called the **troposphere** (TRAHP-uh-sfir). The troposphere is the region that touches the earth's surface. It is the layer in which you live. Almost all of the earth's weather occurs in the troposphere.

The height of the troposphere varies from the equator to the poles. Around the equator, the height of the troposphere is about 17 kilometers. In the areas north and south of the equator, the height of the troposphere is about 12 kilometers. At the poles, the height of the troposphere is between 6 kilometers and 8 kilometers.

As the heat energy from sunlight travels through the atmosphere, only a small part of it is trapped by the atmosphere. Most of the heat energy is absorbed by the ground. The ground then warms the air above it. The warm, less dense air rises and is replaced by cooler, denser air. Currents of air that carry heat up into the atmosphere are produced. These air movements are called **convection** (kuhn-VEHK-shuhn) **currents.** Why do you think the air moves upward?

Temperature decreases with increasing altitude in the troposphere. The temperature of the troposphere drops about 6.5°C for every kilometer above the earth's surface. But at an altitude of about 12 kilometers, the temperature seems to stop dropping. The zone of the troposphere where the temperature remains fairly constant is called the **tropopause** (TRAHP-uh-pawz). The tropopause divides the troposphere from the next layer of the atmosphere.

Figure 12–13 *This colorful sunset results from the scattering of sunlight by dust and water droplets in the atmosphere (left). Rainbows are also produced by the scattering of sunlight (right). When might you see a rainbow?*

The Stratosphere

The **stratosphere** (STRAT-uh-sfir) extends from the tropopause to an altitude of about 50 kilometers. In the lower stratosphere, the air temperature remains constant and very cold—around −60°C. The lower stratosphere interacts with the tropopause. Here very strong eastward winds blow horizontally around the earth. These winds, called the **jet stream,** reach speeds of more than 320 kilometers per hour. What effect does the jet stream have on weather patterns in the United States?

A special form of oxygen called ozone is present in the stratosphere. Ozone is formed when three atoms of oxygen combine to form one molecule (O_3). The oxygen that you breathe has two atoms of oxygen (O_2). Ozone has a clean, sharp smell. You have probably smelled ozone after a thunderstorm. The air seems to have a clean odor. The clean odor is caused by the ozone formed when lightning passed through the atmosphere.

Most of the ozone in the atmosphere is found in the ozone layer between 16 kilometers and 60 kilometers above the earth's surface. Below and above these altitudes, there is little or no ozone. Even though the total amount of ozone in the stratosphere is very small, ozone is very important to life on the earth. Ozone acts as a shield for the earth's surface. As you read, ozone absorbs most of the ultraviolet radiation from the sun. Ultraviolet radiation is harmful to living things.

Sharpen Your Skills

Temperature Changes in the Troposphere

1. At three times during both the day and evening, use an outdoor thermometer to measure air temperature 1 cm above the ground and 1.25 m above the ground. You may have to leave the thermometer in place for a few minutes.

2. On a chart, record the time of day and the temperature for both locations.

3. On graph paper, plot time versus temperature for each thermometer location. Label both graphs.

In which area did temperature change more rapidly? By a greater amount over the entire time period? Why?

HELP WANTED: AIR ANALYST For coal mining company. Good math skills and chemistry background necessary.

Air is considered "pure" when it contains only nitrogen, oxygen, and other harmless gases. But in today's industrialized world, many pollutants enter the atmosphere every day. Pollutants can be harmful to your health. They can also kill crops and other plants.

It is important for people to know what pollutants are in the air and how high the pollution level is. This information is gathered by **air analysts.** Air analysts collect air samples, often from a city, mine, or factory area. They determine which pollutants are in the air and how much of each pollutant is present. They summarize their findings and issue a report. The report may suggest ways to improve pollution control methods.

Air analysts should have some mechanical ability and know basic mathematics and chemistry. You can learn more about air analysts and about other careers in air pollution control by writing to the Air Pollution Control Association, P.O. Box 2861, Pittsburgh, PA 15230.

Ozone is responsible for the temperature increase in the upper stratosphere. As the ozone reacts with ultraviolet radiation, heat is given off. This heat warms the upper stratosphere to temperatures around 18°C. The zone in which the temperature is at its highest is called the **stratopause** (STRAT-uh-pawz). The stratopause separates the stratosphere from the next layer of the atmosphere.

The Mesosphere

Above the stratopause, the temperature begins to decrease. This drop in temperature marks the beginning of the **mesosphere** (MEHS-uh-sfir). The mesosphere extends from about 50 kilometers to about 80 kilometers above the earth's surface. In the mesosphere, the temperature drops to nearly −100°C. The upper mesosphere is the coldest region of the atmosphere. If water vapor is present, thin clouds of ice form. You can see these feathery clouds if sunlight strikes them after sunset.

The mesosphere helps protect the earth from large rocklike objects in space known as meteoroids (MEET-ee-uh-roidz). When meteoroids enter the atmosphere, they burn up in the mesosphere. The

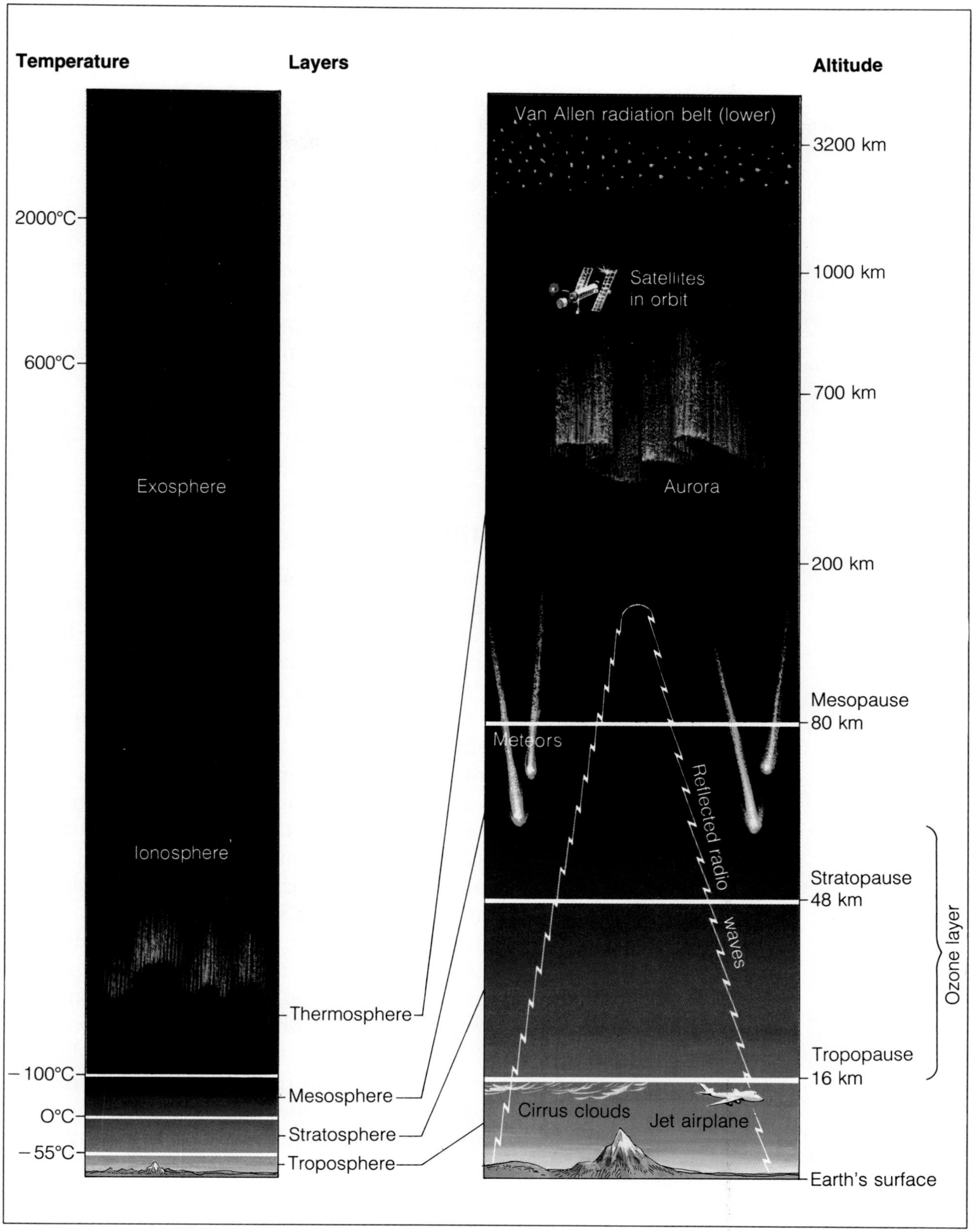

Figure 12–14 *The four main layers of the atmosphere and their characteristics are shown here. In which layer do you live? In which layer is the temperature the highest?*

Sharpen Your Skills

Meteor Hunt

1. On a clear night, go outside and observe the sky. If you live in an area that has considerable light pollution, find a location away from most lights.

2. Observe the stars and record the number of meteors you see. Do this for several nights.

3. Determine whether there is any increase in meteor activity.

heat caused by the friction, or rubbing, between the meteoroid and the atmosphere causes this burning. At night, you may see a streak of light, or "shooting star," in the sky. What you are actually seeing is a bright trail of hot, glowing gases known as a meteor (MEET-ee-uhr).

Most meteoroids burn up completely as they pass through the earth's atmosphere. But some are large enough to survive the passage and actually hit the earth. These pieces are called meteorites (MEET-ee-uh-rights). When artificial satellites fall from orbit, they also burn up as they pass through the atmosphere. But pieces of the United States' *Skylab* and a Russian *Cosmos* satellite have fallen out of orbit and reached the earth's surface. Why do you think some meteoroids and satellites do not burn up completely as they pass through the atmosphere?

The Thermosphere

The **thermosphere** (THER-muh-sfir) begins above the mesosphere at a height of about 80 kilometers. The thermosphere has no well-defined upper limit. The air in the thermosphere is very thin. The density of the atmosphere and the air pressure are only about one ten-millionth of what they are at the earth's surface.

The word *thermosphere* means "heat sphere," or "warm layer." The temperature is very high in this layer of the atmosphere. In fact, the temperature of the thermosphere may reach 2000°C or more! Why? Nitrogen and oxygen absorb a great deal of ultraviolet radiation and turn it into heat.

The temperature in the thermosphere is measured with special instruments, not with a thermometer. If a thermometer were placed in the thermosphere, it would register far below 0°C! How can this be so? Temperature is a measure of how fast particles in air move. The faster the air particles travel, the higher the temperature is. And the particles in this layer of the atmosphere are moving very fast. So the particles themselves are very hot.

But these particles are very few and very far apart. There are not enough of them to bombard the thermometer and warm it. So the thermometer would record a temperature far below 0°C.

Sharpen Your Skills

Atmospheric Layers

Figure 12–14 shows the layers of the earth's atmosphere and the altitudes at which they begin and end. Using the information in the diagram, calculate the average thickness of each layer.

THE IONOSPHERE The lower thermosphere is called the **ionosphere** (igh-AHN-uh-sfir). The ionosphere extends from 80 kilometers to 550 kilometers above the earth's surface. The size of the ionosphere varies with the amount of ultraviolet and X-ray radiation. These two types of radiation are forms of invisible energy given off by the sun.

Nitrogen oxide, oxygen, and other gas particles in the ionosphere absorb the ultraviolet and X-ray radiation from the sun. The particles of gas become electrically charged. These electrically charged particles are called **ions.** Ions are atoms that have either lost or gained electrons.

The ions in the ionosphere are important to radio communication. AM radio waves are bounced off the ions in the ionosphere and back to the earth's surface. As a result, radio messages can be sent over very great distances. See Figure 12–15.

Sometimes large disturbances on the sun's surface known as solar flares cause the number of ions in the ionosphere to increase. This increase in ions can interfere with the transmission of some radio waves. What other communication system on the earth do you think might be disrupted?

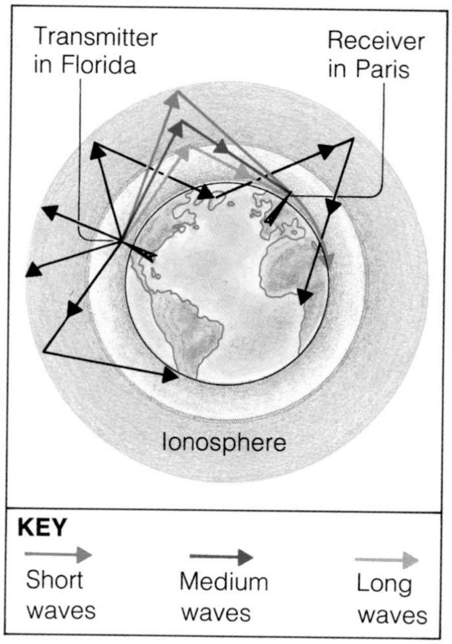

Figure 12–15 *Radio waves are bounced off the ionosphere to transmit radio messages overseas or across continents. Which type of wave travels the highest in the ionosphere?*

THE EXOSPHERE The upper thermosphere is called the **exosphere** (EK-suh-sfir). The exosphere extends from about 550 kilometers above the earth's surface for thousands of kilometers. The air is so thin in the exosphere that particles can travel great distances without hitting each other.

It is in the exosphere that artificial satellites orbit the earth. Satellites play an important role in television transmission and telephone communication. Satellites are also used to keep a 24-hour watch on the world's weather. And because the very thin air of the exosphere makes viewing sky objects easier, telescopes are often carried aboard satellites.

Figure 12–16 *Weather satellites orbit the earth in the exosphere. They keep a 24-hour watch on the world's weather and transmit information used by scientists to track weather patterns. What type of weather do you think the southeastern United States is having?*

SECTION REVIEW

1. Describe the temperature changes in the four main layers of the atmosphere.
2. Why is ozone important to life on the earth?
3. What characteristic of the ionosphere enables radio waves to travel thousands of kilometers?

12–3 The Magnetosphere

Section Objective

To describe the magnetic field of the earth

The area around the earth that extends beyond the atmosphere is called the **magnetosphere** (mag-NEET-uh-sfir). The earth's magnetic force operates in the magnetosphere. The magnetosphere begins at an altitude of about 1000 kilometers. On the side of the earth that faces the sun, it extends out into space about 4000 kilometers. It extends even farther out into space on the other side, as shown in Figure 12–17. The difference is caused by the solar wind, a stream of fast-moving ions given off by the outermost layer of the sun's atmosphere. The solar wind pushes the magnetosphere farther into space on the side of the earth away from the sun.

The magnetosphere is made up of positively charged protons and negatively charged electrons. These particles are given off by the sun and captured by the earth's magnetic field. The charged particles are concentrated into belts or layers of high radiation. These belts are called the **Van Allen radiation belts.** They were discovered by satellites in 1958. These belts are named after James Van Allen, the scientist whose work led to their discovery.

The Van Allen belts are a problem for space travelers. Either space flights have to be programmed to avoid the radiation or suitable protection must be given to the astronauts. But the Van Allen radiation belts are important to life on the

Figure 12–17 *The earth's magnetosphere is pushed far into space by the solar wind. On which side of the earth does it extend farther?*

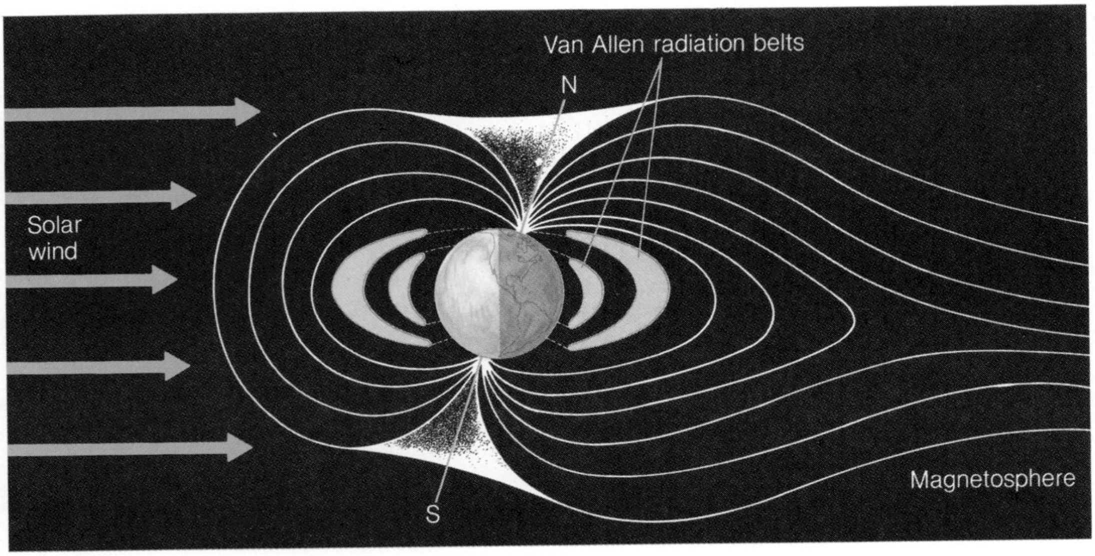

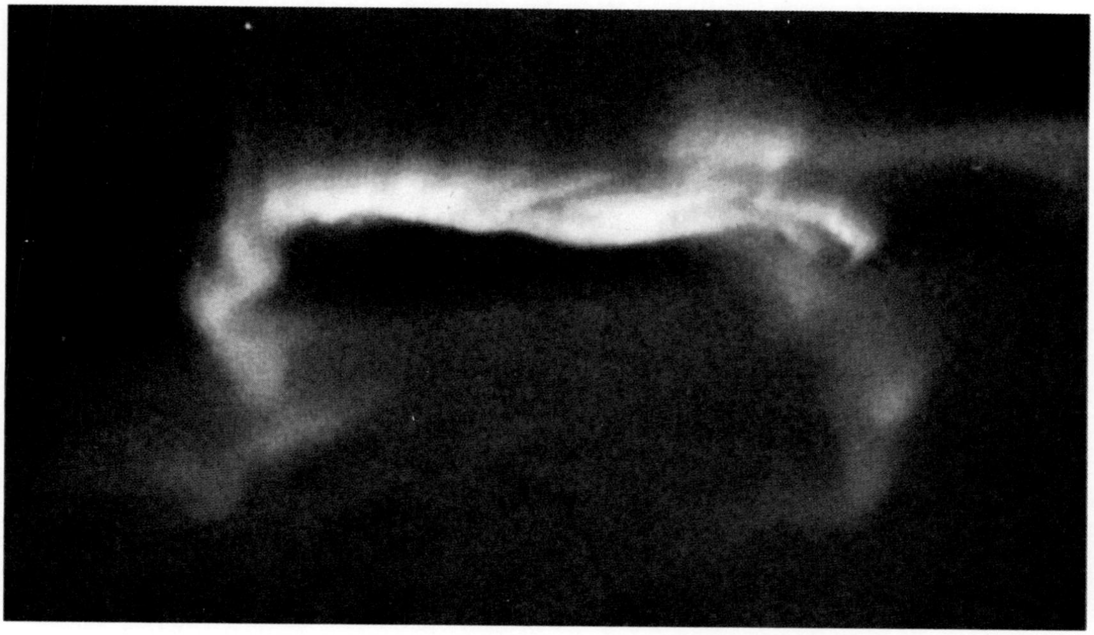

Figure 12–18 *This photo of the aurora australis, or southern lights, was taken from the Skylab space station in orbit around the earth. The space station was moving into the sunlight when the picture was taken. The surface of the earth is in the foreground.*

earth. They provide protection by trapping other deadly radiation. What might happen to life on the earth if the radiation reached the surface?

When there is a solar flare, the magnetosphere is bombarded by large quantities of electrically charged particles from the sun. These charged particles get trapped in the magnetosphere. Here they collide with other particles in the upper atmosphere. The collisions cause the atmospheric particles to give off light. The multicolored lights are called the aurora borealis, or northern lights, and the aurora australis, or southern lights.

After a heavy bombardment of solar particles, sometimes called a magnetic storm, the magnetic field of the earth may change temporarily. A compass needle may not point north. Radio signals may be interrupted. Telephone and telegraph communications may also be affected.

SECTION REVIEW

1. What is the magnetosphere made up of?
2. Why are the Van Allen radiation belts important to life on the earth?
3. How can scientists predict when an aurora will be visible?
4. Why do auroras appear near the magnetic poles?

Sharpen Your Skills

Science Concentration

Using the vocabulary words in the chapter, develop a game of concentration. On a note card, write one vocabulary word. On another note card, write its definition. When you have written all of the vocabulary words and their definitions, randomly place the cards face down on a table in front of two classmates. Have each player take a turn trying to match a vocabulary word with its definition. Each time a player makes a correct match, remove the two cards from the table and give the player a point. The player with the most points wins the game.

12 LABORATORY INVESTIGATION

Radiant Energy and Surface Temperature

Problem

Does the type of surface affect the amount of heat absorbed both in and out of direct sunlight?

Materials *(per group)*

10 thermometers
Stopwatch
2 shallow containers of water

Procedure

1. Place a thermometer on the grass in the sun. Place a second thermometer on the grass in the shade.
2. Place two of the remaining thermometers—one in the sun and one in the shade—on bare soil, on concrete, on a blacktop surface, and in water.
3. After 2 minutes, record the temperature of each surface.
4. Continue recording the temperature of each surface every 2 minutes for a period of 10 minutes.
5. Record your results in a chart similar to the one on this page.

Observations

1. Which surface was the warmest? Which surface was the coolest?
2. By how many degrees did the temperature of each surface in the sun change during the 10-minute time period?
3. By how many degrees did the temperature of each surface in the shade change during the 10-minute time period?

Conclusions

1. Why do you think the blacktop surface was the warmest?
2. Why do you think the water had the smallest temperature gain?
3. What conclusions can you reach about the amount of heat energy different surfaces absorb from the sun?
4. In what ways do the results of this experiment affect people's lives?

Surface	Temperature in the Sun					Temperature in the Shade				
	2 min	*4 min*	*6 min*	*8 min*	*10 min*	*2 min*	*4 min*	*6 min*	*8 min*	*10 min*
Grass										
Soil										
Concrete										
Blacktop										
Water										

CHAPTER REVIEW

SUMMARY

12–1 Composition of the Atmosphere

❑ The earth's atmosphere is the envelope of gases surrounding the earth.

❑ Scientists have learned about the structure and composition of the present atmosphere from data gathered by cameras and other instruments aboard space satellites.

❑ The earth's past atmosphere contained mostly methane and ammonia, two poisonous gases.

❑ The ozone layer, sometimes referred to as an "umbrella" for life on the earth, absorbs most of the harmful ultraviolet radiation from the sun.

❑ The present atmosphere consists mainly of nitrogen, oxygen, carbon dioxide, water vapor, and other trace gases.

❑ Nitrogen gas makes up about 78 percent of the atmosphere, and oxygen makes up about 21 percent. The remaining 1 percent is a combination of carbon dioxide, water vapor, argon, and trace gases.

12–2 Layers of the Atmosphere

❑ The four main layers of the atmosphere are the troposphere, the stratosphere, the mesosphere, and the thermosphere. These layers are determined mainly by differences in temperature.

❑ The troposphere is the lowest layer of the atmosphere. Almost all of the earth's weather occurs in the troposphere.

❑ Currents of air that carry heat up into the troposphere are called convection currents.

❑ Temperature decreases with increasing altitude in the troposphere. The zone of the troposphere where the temperature remains fairly constant is called the tropopause.

❑ Most of the ozone in the atmosphere is found in a layer of the stratosphere.

❑ The upper mesosphere is the coldest region of the atmosphere.

❑ The mesosphere helps protect the earth from meteoroids.

❑ The thermosphere is made up of the ionosphere and the exosphere.

❑ The ionosphere contains electrically charged particles called ions, which are important to radio communication.

❑ Artificial satellites orbit the earth in the exosphere.

12–3 The Magnetosphere

❑ The magnetosphere extends from an altitude of about 1000 kilometers far into space.

❑ The magnetosphere is made up of protons and electrons.

❑ The Van Allen belts are layers of high radiation because of the concentration of charged particles.

VOCABULARY

Define each term in a complete sentence.

ammonia
atmosphere
convection current
exosphere
ion
ionosphere
jet stream
magnetosphere
mesosphere
methane
ozone
stratopause
stratosphere
thermosphere
tropopause
troposphere
Van Allen radiation belt

CONTENT REVIEW: MULTIPLE CHOICE

Choose the letter of the answer that best completes each sentence.

1. Four billion years ago the earth's atmosphere contained the deadly gases
a. nitrogen and oxygen b. methane and ammonia
c. methane and oxygen d. nitrogen and ozone

2. The gas in the earth's atmosphere referred to as an "umbrella" for life is
a. oxygen b. nitrogen c. carbon dioxide d. ozone

3. The most abundant gas in the atmosphere is
a. oxygen b. nitrogen c. carbon dioxide d. methane

4. The lowest layer of the atmosphere is called the
a. stratosphere b. mesosphere c. thermosphere d. troposphere

5. Air movements in which warm, less dense air rises and cooler, denser air replaces it are called
a. convection currents b. conduction currents
c. jet streams d. meteoroids

6. Ultraviolet radiation from the sun is absorbed by ozone in the
a. troposphere b. stratosphere c. thermosphere d. ionosphere

7. The layer of the atmosphere in which temperatures may reach 2000°C is called the
a. stratosphere b. mesosphere c. thermosphere d. troposphere

8. The lower thermosphere is called the
a. stratosphere b. exosphere c. ionosphere d. troposphere

9. Artificial satellites orbit the earth in the part of the thermosphere called the
a. ionosphere b. mesosphere c. exosphere d. magnetosphere

10. The area containing protons and electrons given off by the sun is called the
a. magnetosphere b. exosphere c. ionosphere d. thermosphere

CONTENT REVIEW: COMPLETION

Fill in the word or words that best complete each sentence.

1. The envelope of gases surrounding the earth is called the ________________.

2. The two gases that composed the earth's atmosphere billions of years ago are ________________ and ________________.

3. A gas essential for respiration is ________________.

4. The atmosphere is divided into layers according to major changes in its ________________.

5. The weather layer of the atmosphere is called the ________________.

6. The zone of the troposphere in which the temperature remains fairly constant is called the ________________.

7. Very strong winds blowing from the west horizontally around the earth at the boundary between the troposphere and stratosphere are called ________________.

8. The form of oxygen that has the formula O_3 is called ________________.

9. Large rocklike structures from space that pass through the atmosphere and strike the earth are called ________________.

10. Belts of charged particles and high radiation are called the ________________.

CONTENT REVIEW: TRUE OR FALSE

Determine whether each statement is true or false. If it is true, write "true." If it is false, change the underlined word or words to make the statement true.

1. The envelope of gases surrounding the earth is called the hydrosphere.
2. Few things could survive without the presence of methane, the gas that absorbs ultraviolet radiation.
3. The two most abundant gases in the atmosphere are nitrogen and oxygen.
4. As the altitude increases, the temperature of the air increases.
5. The layer of the atmosphere in which you live is the troposphere.
6. The stratopause is the boundary between the stratosphere and the mesosphere.
7. Temperatures may reach 2000°C or more in the mesosphere.
8. Atoms that have either lost or gained electrons are called molecules.
9. The area that extends beyond the atmosphere is called the magnetosphere.
10. Multicolored lights formed when the magnetosphere is bombarded by large quantities of electrically charged particles from the sun are called auroras.

CONCEPT REVIEW: SKILL BUILDING

Use the skills you have developed in the chapter to complete each activity.

1. **Making diagrams** The diagrams on pages 300 and 301 show the nitrogen cycle and the oxygen-carbon dioxide cycle. Using these figures as a guide, draw a picture of each cycle as it would occur in your surroundings. Include plants and animals common to your area.
2. **Sequencing events** Using a series of drawings, illustrate the various steps by which the past atmosphere of the earth changed into its current composition.
3. **Interpreting graphs** Compare the temperatures found in the four main layers of the atmosphere by drawing a line graph of the data. Plot the altitude of the layers as the X-axis and the temperatures as the Y-axis. Use the average winter or summer temperature in your area as the beginning of the troposphere. Then explain why your graph is *not* a straight line.
4. **Applying concepts** Travel time by airplane from New York to San Francisco, California, is about 5 hours 30 minutes. The reverse flight from San Francisco to New York is about 5 hours. Applying what you know about the jet stream, explain this difference in travel time.

CONCEPT REVIEW: ESSAY

Discuss each of the following in a brief paragraph.

1. What might happen if pollution of the earth's atmosphere continues? What can be done to prevent air pollution?
2. Explain why air pressure decreases as altitude increases.
3. How might life on the earth be affected if the ozone layer were destroyed by the use of certain chemicals?
4. Why is it important that most meteoroids burn up in the atmosphere?

Adventures in Science

William Haxby Maps a Strange World

BENEATH

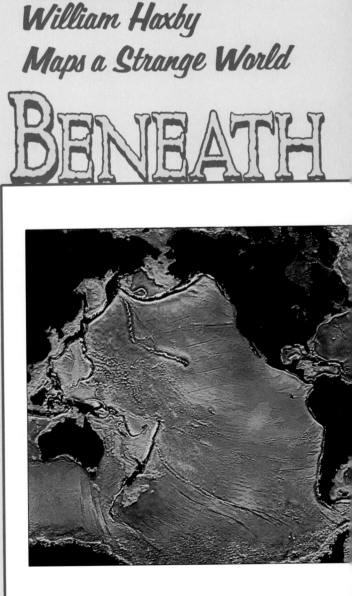

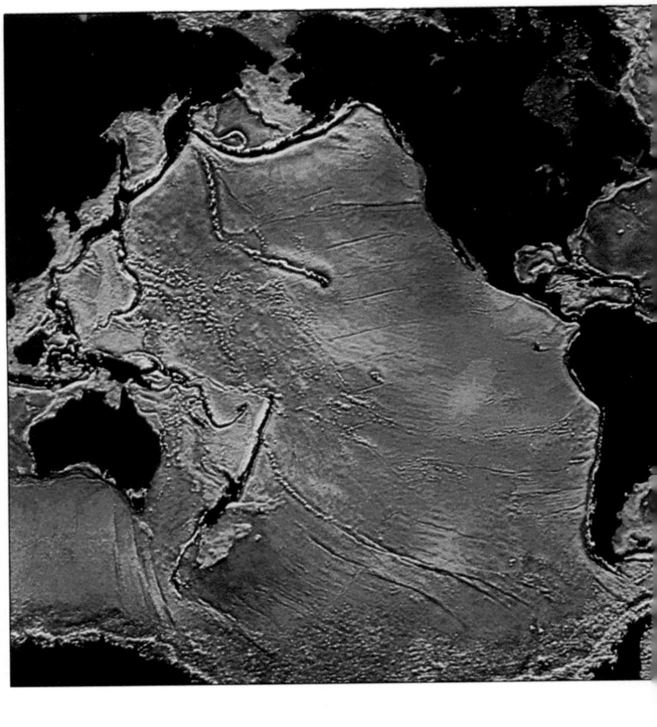

Vast canyons and craggy mountains make the ocean floor as mysterious as the surface of a far-off planet. It may be centuries before the bottom of the world's seas are fully explored. Yet using information from space satellites, geologist William Haxby has created startling maps of the undersea landscape. The remarkable maps are almost as detailed as if the water had been drained from the seas to reveal the features of the ocean floor.

William Haxby works at the Lamont Doherty Geological Observatory in Palisades, New York. Using data from space satellites and a computer, Haxby produces three-dimensional maps in vivid colors. These maps provide a view of the ocean floor never before seen. Cracks in the sea bottom, underwater volcanoes, and other features of the ocean floor are easily observed on Haxby's maps. The existence of such features provides new evidence about some of the most important earth science theories.

One theory, called plate tectonics, states that the earth's crust is made up of a number of very large plates. Heat and motion deep within the earth cause the plates to move slowly but constantly. The movement of plates triggers earthquakes, thrusts up mountain ranges, and cuts deep ridges.

Haxby's maps show many signs of plate movement along the ocean floor. One deep crack under the Indian Ocean may have been made when India drifted away from Antarctica and moved toward Asia millions of years ago. Geologists believe a twisting ridge on the ocean floor off the southern tip of Africa was also formed millions of years ago, when Africa, South America, and Antarctica separated. The ridge, concealed under layers of sediment, was detected by Haxby's computer imaging.

Haxby started his mapping project, which took 18 months, in 1981. His work was based on data from the space satellite *Seasat*. *Seasat*'s measurements showed that there were height differences on the ocean's surface. Haxby discovered that the height of the ocean's surface varies by dozens of meters from one place to another. And as he points out, these differences are not due to waves or wind. The surface of the ocean is simply not flat.

The reason for the variations in the ocean's surface is the gravitational pull of structures on the ocean bottom. Structures with large mass, such as underwater mountains, pull on the water with more force than structures with less mass, such as canyons. The stronger the pull of the underwater structure, the greater the amount of water that is attracted to a place above it. "As a result," says Haxby, "water piles up and there is a bump in the ocean over a big object." So the ocean surface imitates the ocean bottom.

Launched in 1978 for a five-year orbit, *Seasat* became silent after three months due to a short circuit in its electrical system. But the eight billion readings it had radioed back to tracking stations on the earth were enough for Haxby to begin working on his maps. And today, data collected by another space satellite, *Geosat,* allows Haxby to continue.

Haxby has been interested in geology since his boyhood, when he was a "rockhound." At the University of Minnesota, he became interested in continental drift and plate tectonics. He eventually did graduate work in geophysics, leading to a doctoral degree from Cornell University. When he first began computer analysis of the satellite information, he did not intend to map the entire ocean bottom. All he wanted to do was chart some small areas by matching ocean surface heights with the gravitational forces that created them. His first maps were so detailed, however, that he decided to go further.

The detail—Haxby can pinpoint objects as small as 30 kilometers across—and colors reveal structures that are not on other large maps of the ocean bottom. In fact, the images produced by Haxby's computer look so real that people looking at them feel as if they are standing on the bottom of the ocean. And around the world, scientists use Haxby's maps to help them learn more about the ever-changing earth.

The SEA

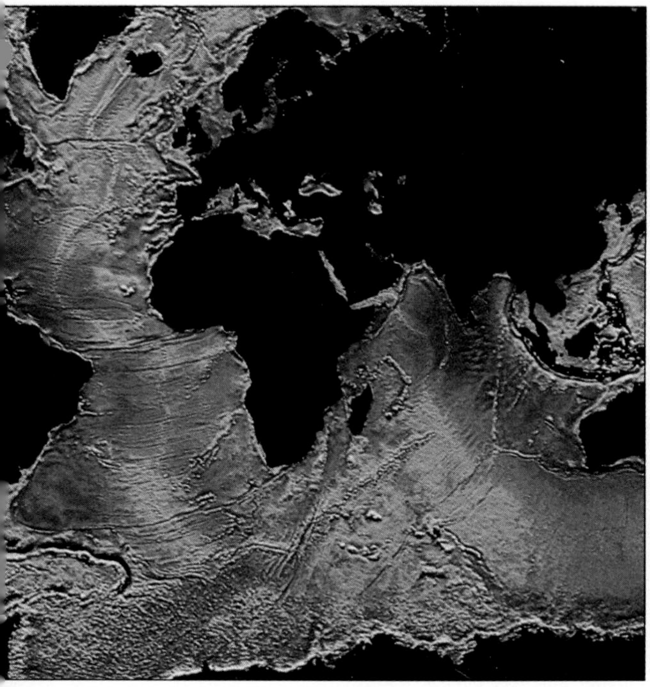

This is an example of the type of map that William Haxby draws with the help of a computer that analyzes measurements taken by an orbiting satellite.

Issues in Science

TOXIC WASTE D·I·S·P·O·S·A·L

How Should We Deal with Deadly Garbage?

In December 1982, Times Beach, Missouri, was changed from a busy riverside community into the ghost town that it is today. The signs on Interstate-44 that once indicated the Times Beach exit now read HAZARDOUS WASTE. And the inhabitants, who long ago fled their town, continue to suffer from cancers, seizures, and stomach problems.

In 1982, government officials found high levels of dioxin, an extremely toxic chemical waste, in Times Beach. They investigated the contamination and discovered that the problem started in the 1970s. At that time, oil was sprayed on unpaved streets of Times Beach to prevent dust from being blown around by the wind. This oil had been illegally mixed with dioxin, and the roads had actually been sprayed with a toxic chemical goo! Because of an unfortunate mistake, the town of Times Beach had become the victim of toxic waste pollution.

Today, toxic waste pollution is becoming one of the greatest threats to our nation's environment. Our towns, rivers, underground water supplies—even the air we breathe—are being polluted with a variety of different chemicals. Industrial wastes, farm chemicals, and human sewage are but a few. What should be done about this alarming and growing problem?

For more than five years now, the government-funded Environmental Protection Agency (EPA) has been administering a program called Superfund. Superfund is aimed at cleaning up the most critical sites of toxic waste. The program, which is still in effect today, has spent nearly $1.6 billion in this effort.

Under the supervision of the EPA, most of the toxic waste is hauled away in barrels and buried in specially designed dumps called landfills. But this waste-disposal method is almost as dangerous as the chemicals themselves. For landfills develop leaks. Experts say that when landfills leak, poisonous chemicals seep into the ground. The toxins then pass through layers of soil into underground water reservoirs called aquifers. Aquifers, which are major sources of America's drinking water, are becoming more and more polluted.

What happens when a landfill begins to leak? The EPA deals with this problem by simply moving the wastes to another dump. Here they remain until that landfill starts to leak. Thus, the EPA seems to be playing a sort of "toxic leapfrog," moving wastes from landfill to landfill without really solving the problem.

Critics of the EPA's actions say that the agency is not using Superfund effectively. They also claim that the EPA has failed to find new ways of removing toxic waste. Government officials claim that the problem of toxic waste is bigger than they originally believed. They also say that they lack the money and staff to deal with the problem the nation is facing. So in the meantime, the EPA continues to bury toxic wastes.

New methods of dealing with toxic waste are currently being tried—and with some success. Scientists are attempting to use certain bacteria to feed on chemical waste. Under the right conditions, the waste-munching bacteria break down toxic chemicals into nontoxic ones.

While scientists are developing new technologies, some people are arguing that the way to control toxic-waste disposal is through laws. They support enacting stricter laws against waste disposal and enforcing harsher punishments on companies that violate the laws. Such actions would encourage companies to develop new ways of recycling their wastes. It might also encourage companies to seek other manufacturing methods and products that do not produce toxins.

Meanwhile, steps must be taken to clean up polluted areas—especially the nation's water supplies. Experts estimate that it will cost $100 billion to clean up the country's 10,000 waste sites. So no matter how one looks at it, toxic waste is an expensive problem. Either taxes will have to be increased to finance a more effective Superfund program or product prices will have to be raised so that companies can afford safer waste disposal. If such choices are not made, Americans will end up paying with their personal health and the health of their environment. Who do you think should bear the cost of disposing of this deadly waste?

Many of the chemicals stored in landfills are so dangerous that people who work with them must be completely covered with protective clothing.

◀ In many places in the United States, toxic wastes are stored in large drums dumped in landfills. Over time these drums decompose, releasing the toxic chemicals.

UNIT FOUR

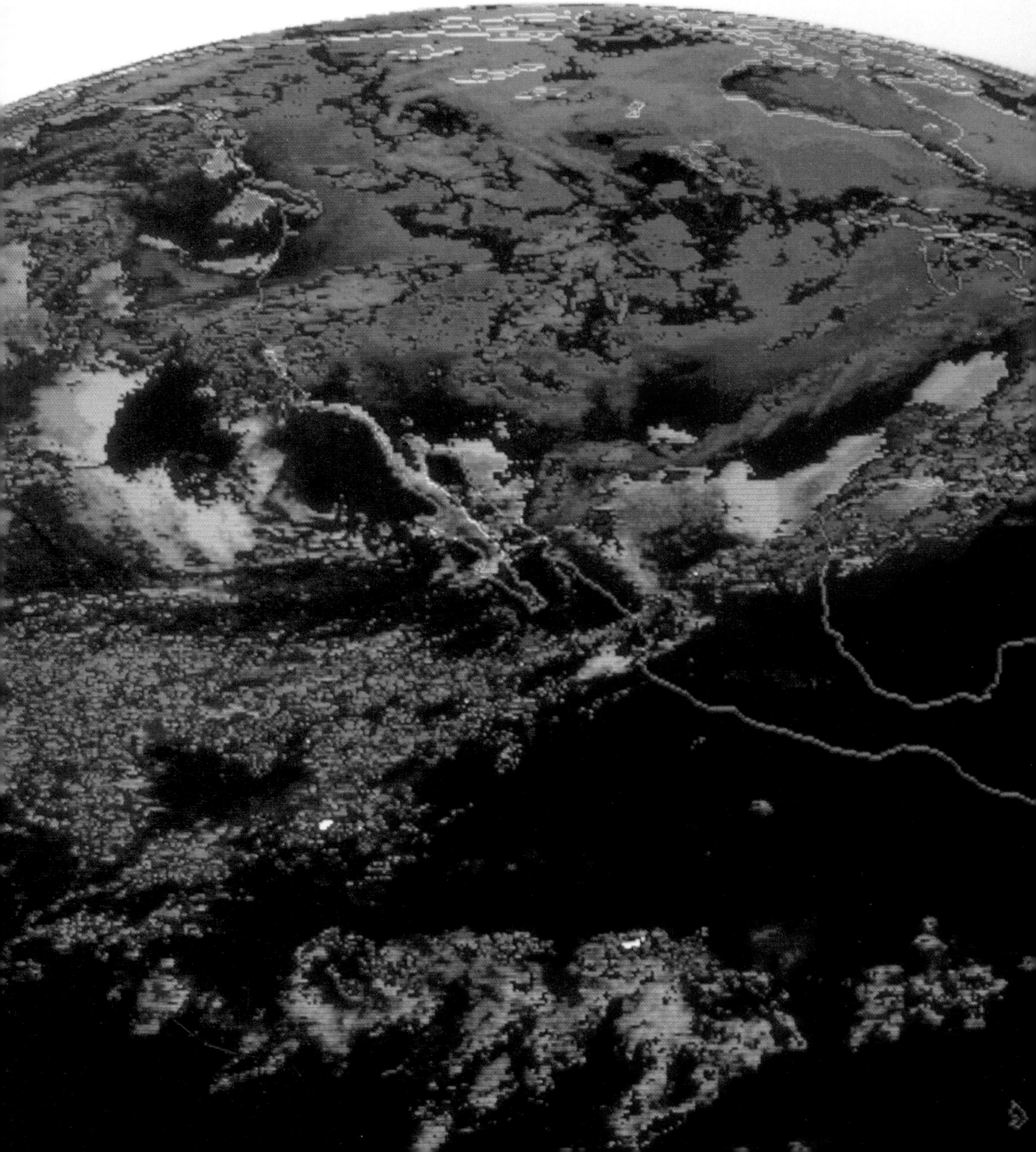

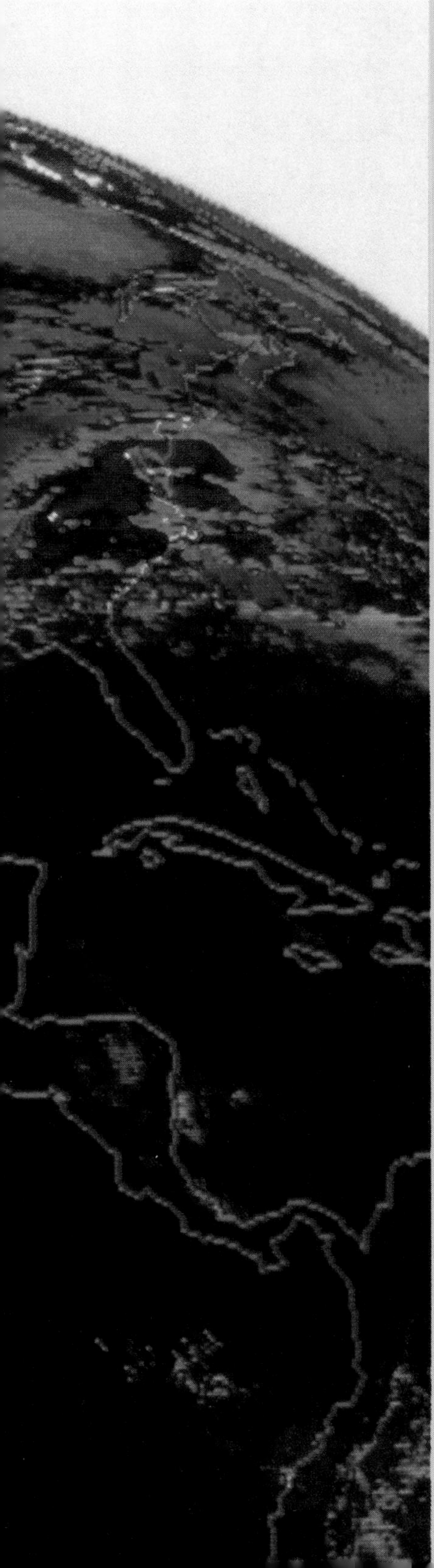

The Changing Earth: Surface Activity

Somewhere in the Gulf of Mexico a hurricane is forming. A few thousand kilometers to the north, dark clouds roll across the Kansas sky. To the northeast, thunderheads billow over New England. Bad weather is on its way! But will the hurricane slam into Texas or make a sharp turn toward Florida? Will tornadoes cut a path through Wichita or Topeka? Will torrents of rain flood lowlands in western Massachusetts or southern Vermont? Severe weather conditions such as these cannot be prevented. But an early warning may save countless lives and millions of dollars in property. The warning comes from weather forecasters who use a variety of instruments to help predict the weather. One of their most valuable tools is satellites. Traveling in orbits around the earth, weather satellites continuously take pictures of the land, the waters, and the clouds below.

CHAPTERS

To a weather forecaster, this satellite view of the earth's cloud cover provides many clues to the weather conditions down below. With such clues, forecasters can better predict violent storms and save many lives.

Weather

13

CHAPTER SECTIONS

CHAPTER OBJECTIVES

After completing this chapter, you will be able to

13–1 Describe the factors that interact to cause weather.

13–2 Discuss the three basic methods of heat transfer.

13–3 Describe the three factors that affect air pressure.

13–4 Compare local and global wind patterns.

13–5 Identify the three basic types of clouds.

13–6 Compare the four major types of air masses.

13–6 Explain how fronts affect weather patterns.

13–7 Interpret a weather map.

13–8 Describe cloud seeding.

Perhaps you think it strange to see a photo of a groundhog in a chapter on weather. But it really is not strange. Many people believe that a groundhog can forecast the weather. In fact, on February 2 in most countries in the Northern Hemisphere, people anxiously wait to find out just what the groundhog will see! If he sees his shadow, six more weeks of winter are on the way.

The groundhog's foretelling extra weeks of cold is one of many examples of weather folklore. You have probably heard the weather proverb "Red sky at night, sailors delight. Red sky at morning, sailors take warning." Or perhaps you have heard "Goose honks high, weather fair. Goose honks low, weather foul."

Weather influences almost every aspect of people's daily lives. So people have been trying to make accurate weather predictions for centuries. In doing so, they have relied on many devices. Some are scientific and others are not. There is truth to the saying that bees stick close to the hive before a storm. But there is no truth to the proverb that the width of a woolly bear caterpillar's brown band predicts how severe a winter will be.

Today scientists know a great deal about the conditions that determine weather. Advanced instruments help them predict the weather more accurately than ever before. These scientists use weather satellites and computers, not colored skies and geese, to make their forecasts. And you, too, are a weather forecaster whether you rely on folklore, glance at a thermometer, or just step outside!

If this groundhog sees its shadow when it emerges from its burrow, weather folklore says there will be six more weeks of winter.

13–1 Weather Factors

Section Objective

To identify the atmospheric factors that influence weather

When you woke up this morning, did you stop to think about the weather? Was it warm or cold? Windy or calm? Did you take an umbrella with you? Were you able to have your picnic?

Weather affects you daily and influences you and the world around you. The type of homes people build, the clothes they wear, the crops they grow, the jobs they work at, and the ways they spend their leisure time are all determined by the weather.

Today people have a good understanding of the weather. Weather satellites, computers, and other kinds of weather instruments provide accurate information about weather conditions. **Meteorologists** (meet-ee-uh-RAHL-uh-jihsts), people who study the weather, use this information to predict the weather. Their forecasts help you plan your daily activities.

Weather is caused by the interaction of several factors in the earth's **atmosphere** (AT-muhs-fir). The atmosphere is a mixture of gases that surrounds the earth. **The atmospheric factors that interact to cause weather are heat energy, air pressure and winds, and moisture.**

SECTION REVIEW

1. What are people who study the weather called?
2. What atmospheric factors cause weather?

Figure 13–1 *Weather plays an important role in daily life. The interaction of several factors in the earth's atmosphere causes weather. What extreme weather conditions are shown in these photographs?*

13–2 Heat Energy and the Atmosphere

Section Objective

To describe how the earth's atmosphere is heated

Almost all of the earth's energy comes from the sun. This energy is called **radiant** (RAY-dee-uhnt) **energy.** The sun's radiant energy is in the form of visible and invisible light.

The sun's radiant energy helps warm the earth. The atmosphere also helps warm the earth by absorbing, storing up, and recycling the sun's radiant energy. Let's see how this happens.

As the sun's energy reaches the atmosphere, part of it is reflected back into space. This happens because incoming rays strike water droplets and dust particles suspended in the atmosphere. Some of the sun's rays reflect off particles in the atmosphere but do not go into space. Instead these rays are scattered throughout the atmosphere.

Much of the sun's energy is absorbed by the atmosphere. A layer of ozone (O_3) gas in the upper atmosphere absorbs ultraviolet rays. Ultraviolet radiation is one form of invisible radiant energy. Ultraviolet radiation, which causes sunburns, can be dangerous to people if absorbed in large quantities. Fortunately, a lot of the ultraviolet energy that is

Figure 13–2 *The sun's radiant energy helps warm the atmosphere. The atmosphere then warms the earth. What six things happen to the sun's radiant energy according to this diagram?*

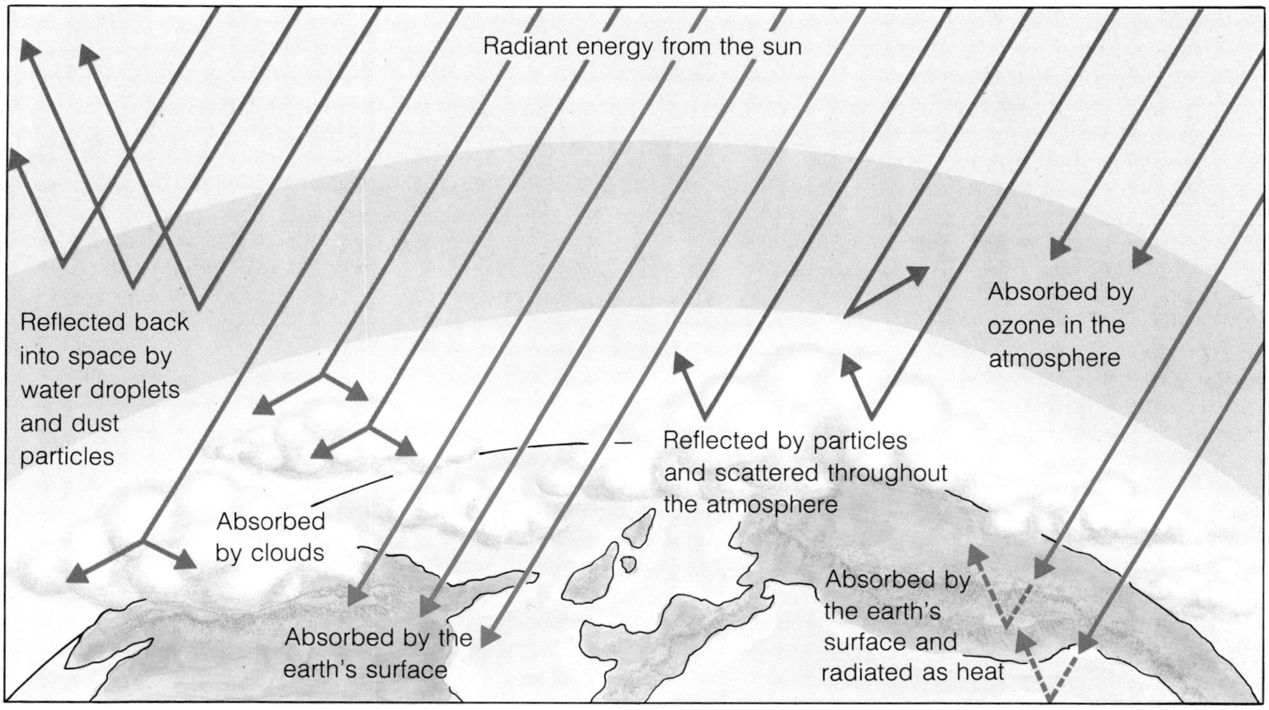

not absorbed by ozone is absorbed by water vapor and carbon dioxide in the lower atmosphere.

The remaining ultraviolet radiation that is neither reflected nor absorbed by the atmosphere reaches the earth's surface. Here it is absorbed by the earth and changed into heat.

Sharpen Your Skills

Convection Currents

1. Pour water into a small beaker until it is almost full.

2. Add two or three drops of food coloring to the surface of the water.

3. Put on safety goggles and light a candle. Put on heat-resistant gloves. Using laboratory tongs, hold the beaker about 10 centimeters above the flame.

What happens to the food coloring? Relate your observations to the way convection currents work in air. At what location on the earth would air constantly be rising because of convection currents?

Conduction, Convection, and Radiation

The sun's energy that is absorbed by the earth is spread throughout the atmosphere in three basic ways: conduction, convection, and radiation.

Conduction is the direct transfer of heat energy from one substance to another. As air above the earth's surface comes in contact with the warm ground, the air is warmed. So temperatures close to the ground are usually higher than temperatures a few meters above the surface. Soil, water, and air are poor heat conductors. So conduction plays only a minor role in spreading heat energy through land, sea, and atmosphere.

Convection is the transfer of heat in a fluid. Air is a fluid. When air near the earth's surface is heated, it becomes less dense and rises. Cooler, more dense air from above sinks. As it sinks, it is heated by the ground and begins to rise. The process of warm air rising and cool air sinking continues. **Convection currents** are formed. Convection currents are caused by the unequal heating of the atmosphere. Most of the heat energy in the atmosphere is transferred by convection currents.

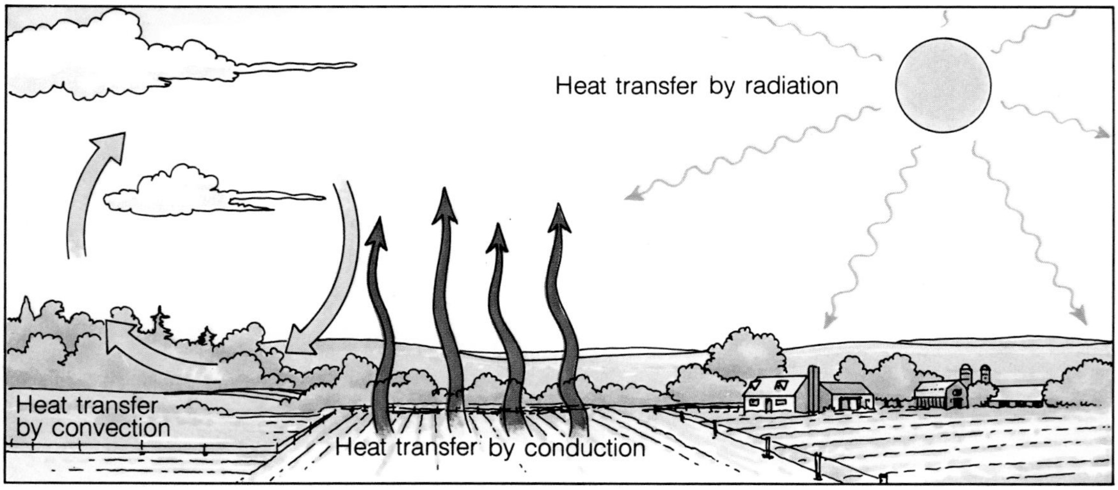

Figure 13–3 *Conduction is the direct transfer of heat energy from one substance to another. Convection is the transfer of heat in a fluid. And radiation is the transfer of heat energy in the form of waves. How is most of the heat energy in the atmosphere transferred?*

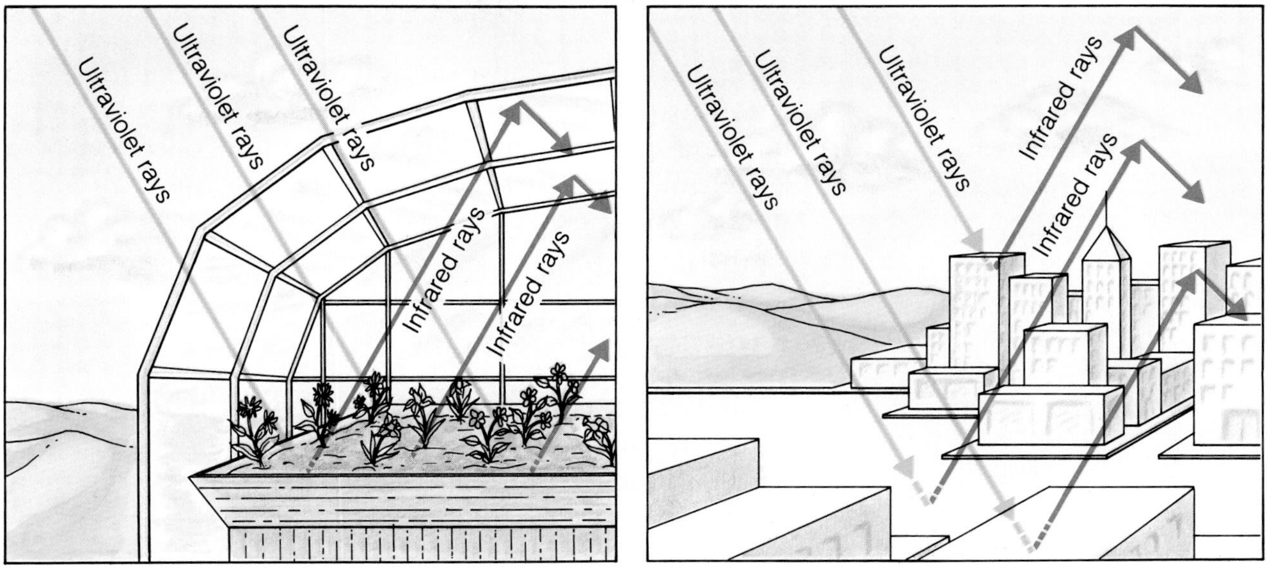

Figure 13–4 *The greenhouse effect occurs in a greenhouse because the glass windows prevent heat from escaping (left). Carbon dioxide and other gases in the atmosphere act like the glass windows in a greenhouse (right). These gases form a "heat blanket" around the earth. In what form is the energy of ultraviolet rays radiated from the earth to the atmosphere?*

Radiation is the transfer of heat energy in the form of waves. When the sun's energy moves by radiation, it does not need the presence of a solid, liquid, or gas. It can travel right through space.

As you read before, some of the sun's energy, in the form of ultraviolet rays, is absorbed by the earth and changed into heat. Ultraviolet rays pass easily through the atmosphere and penetrate the earth. Later this energy is radiated back from the earth to the atmosphere in the form of infrared rays. You cannot see infrared rays. But you can feel them as heat.

Infrared energy cannot pass through the atmosphere into space. Carbon dioxide and other gases in the atmosphere absorb the infrared rays, forming a kind of "heat blanket" around the earth. This process is called the **greenhouse effect** because the carbon dioxide acts like the glass in a greenhouse. The greenhouse effect makes the earth a comfortable place to live. What do you think would happen to the temperature at the earth's surface if there were no greenhouse effect?

Because most of the infrared rays are absorbed by carbon dioxide, the amount of this gas in the atmosphere is very important. If there is too much carbon dioxide in the atmosphere, more infrared rays than normal will be absorbed. The greenhouse effect will increase, and temperatures around the world will become higher. Summers might become hotter, rainfall might be altered, and the polar icecaps might melt!

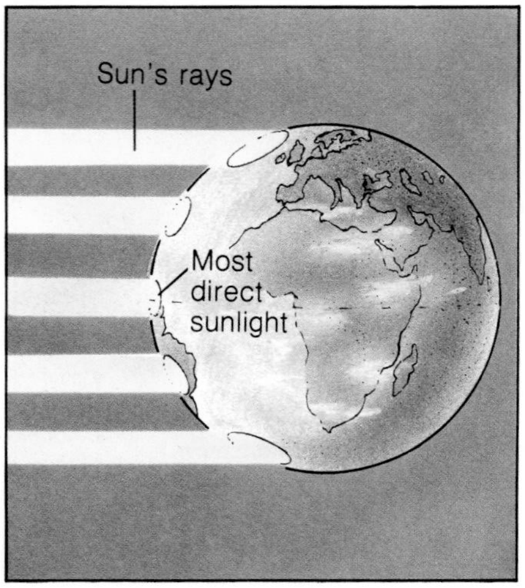

Figure 13–5 *Radiant energy from the sun strikes the earth at different angles, causing uneven heating of the earth's surface. Which area receives the most direct sunlight? In which areas is the same amount of radiant energy spread over a wider area?*

Figure 13–6 *The temperature of the air is measured with a thermometer in units called degrees. What is the freezing point of water on the Celsius scale? The boiling point?*

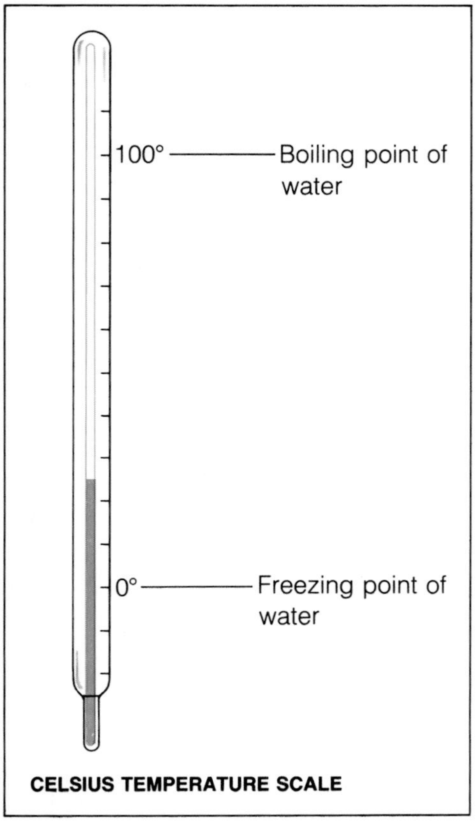

Scientists are concerned about the increasing amount of carbon dioxide in the atmosphere. The burning of fossil fuels such as coal and oil releases large quantities of carbon dioxide into the atmosphere. What are some possible ways of dealing with this situation?

Variations in Temperature

If the whole atmosphere is warmed by heat rising from the earth, how can the air temperature vary so much from place to place? To help you answer this question, look at Figure 13–5.

The angle at which the sun's rays strike the earth's surface is not the same everywhere on the globe. At the equator, the sun is nearly overhead. The sun's rays strike the earth at an angle of 90° all year long. The greatest heating occurs when the sun's rays strike the earth at or near an angle of 90°. So areas at or near the equator receive the most direct rays and have the highest temperatures.

The farther an area is from the equator, the less radiant energy it receives. Why is this so? The angle at which the sun's rays strike the earth is smaller than 90°. The same amount of radiant energy is spread over a wider area. The result is less heat and lower temperatures. As the angle of the sun's rays decreases from 90°, the rays become less direct. The amount of energy received at a location decreases.

Measuring Temperature

The temperature of the air can be measured with a thermometer. Most thermometers consist of a thin, sealed tube with a glass bulb at one end. The bulb is filled with either mercury or alcohol colored with dye. Thermometers make use of the ability of such liquids to expand and contract. When a liquid is heated, it expands, or takes up more space. When a liquid is cooled, it contracts, or takes up less space. What will happen to the liquid in the thermometer if the air temperature rises? What will happen if the air temperature drops?

Temperature is measured in units called degrees. The temperature scale used by scientists is called the Celsius (SEHL-see-uhs) scale. On the Celsius scale, the freezing point of water is 0°. The boiling point of water is 100°.

SECTION REVIEW

1. What three things happen to the sun's rays when they reach the atmosphere?
2. What are the three ways by which heat energy is spread throughout the atmosphere?
3. What is the greenhouse effect?
4. What factor causes unequal heating of the earth?

13–3 Air Pressure and the Atmosphere

Section Objective

To relate the density of air to air pressure

The gases and suspended particles in the air have mass. So the earth's gravity pulls the air toward the earth's surface. The air exerts pressure on the earth. This pressure is called **air pressure.**

Air pressure often varies from one point to another across the earth's surface. It varies according to the density of the air. Denser air has more mass per unit volume than less dense air. So denser air exerts greater pressure against the earth's surface than less dense air.

Factors That Influence Air Pressure

The density of the earth's atmosphere, and thus the air pressure, is affected by three factors: temperature, water vapor, and elevation.

You read before that when a fluid is heated, its density decreases. Less dense air exerts less air pressure. So you can expect lower air pressure in places with higher temperatures.

Water molecules have less mass than molecules of the other gases found in the air. So as the amount of water vapor in the air increases, the mass of the air decreases. The air becomes less dense. Air with a large amount of water vapor in it exerts less air pressure.

Elevation, or height above sea level, also affects air pressure. As the elevation increases, the air gets

Figure 13–7 *When air pressure increases, the column of mercury rises in the barometer tube (right). What happens to the column of mercury when the air pressure decreases (left)?*

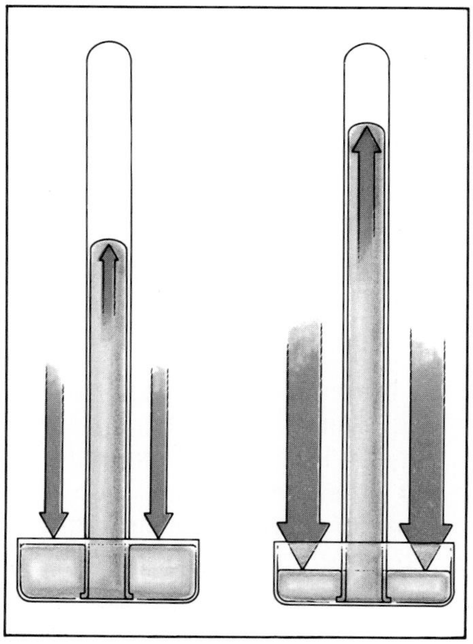

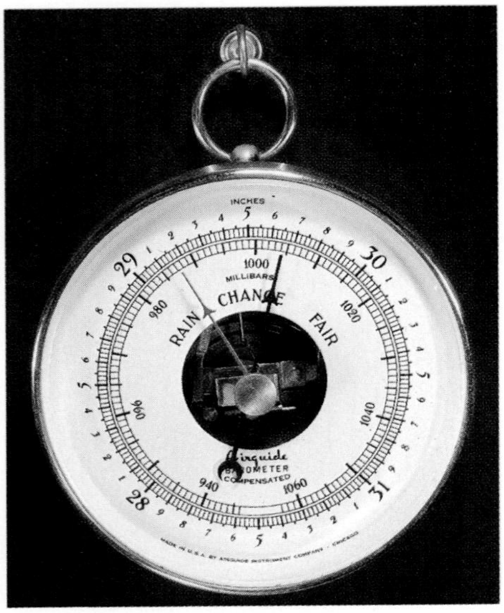

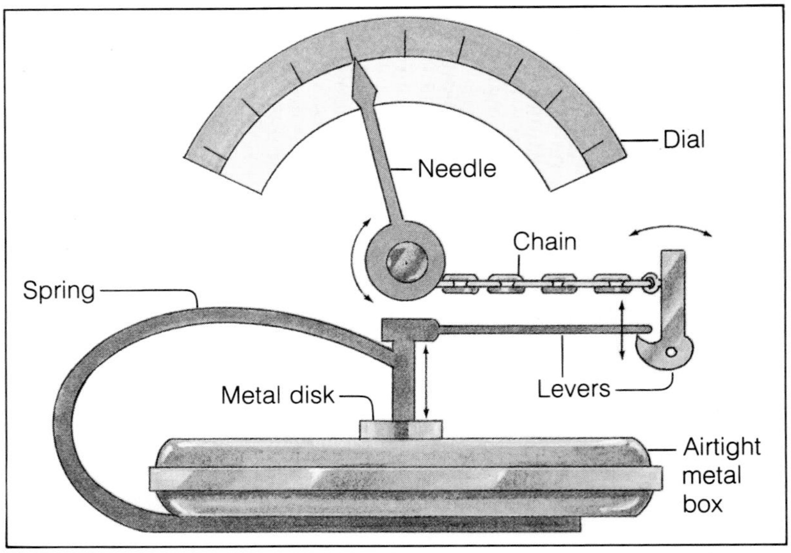

Figure 13–8 *An aneroid barometer is often used in homes, offices, and classrooms. What effect do changes in air pressure have on the barometer?*

thinner. It is less dense. So the air pressure decreases. Because air pressure changes with temperature, water vapor, and elevation, standard air pressure is measured at 0°C and at sea level.

Measuring Air Pressure

Air pressure is measured with an instrument called a **barometer** (buh-RAHM-uh-tuhr). There are two types of barometers. One type is a mercury barometer. A mercury barometer consists of a glass tube closed at one end and filled with mercury. The open end of the glass tube is placed in a container of mercury. At sea level, air pushing down on the mercury in the container supports the column of mercury at a certain height in the tube. As the air pressure decreases, the column of mercury drops. What will happen to the column of mercury if the air pressure increases?

At sea level and 0°C, air pressure is able to support a column of mercury 760 millimeters high. This value is called standard air pressure and is often expressed as one atmosphere. Air pressure is also measured in millibars. Millibars are most commonly used on weather maps. Standard air pressure, or 760 millimeters of mercury, is equal to 1013.20 millibars.

A more common type of barometer is called an aneroid (AN-uhr-oid) barometer. See Figure 13–8. An aneroid barometer consists of an airtight metal

Sharpen Your Skills

A Water Barometer

Mercury has a density of 13.5 g/cm^3. Water has a density of 1.0 g/cm^3. If standard air pressure supports a column of mercury 76 cm high, how high a column of water would be supported at this pressure?

box from which most of the air has been removed. A change in air pressure causes the needle to move and indicate the new air pressure.

SECTION REVIEW

1. Why does air exert pressure on the surface of the earth?
2. What three factors affect the density of the earth's atmosphere?
3. What instrument is used to measure air pressure?

13–4 Air Currents: Wind

Section Objective

To compare the movements of local and global winds

When air is heated, its density decreases. The warm air rises and produces an area of low pressure. Cooler, denser air, which produces an area of high pressure, moves in underneath the rising warm air. So air moves from an area of high pressure to an area of low pressure. **Winds** are formed by this movement of air.

There are two general types of winds: local winds and global winds. Local winds are the type you are most familiar with. They blow from any direction and usually cover short distances. Global winds blow from a specific direction and almost always travel longer distances. **Both local winds and global winds are caused by differences in air pressure due to unequal heating of the air.**

Figure 13–9 *Wind is air in motion. The force of the wind enables these boaters to enjoy an exciting ride.*

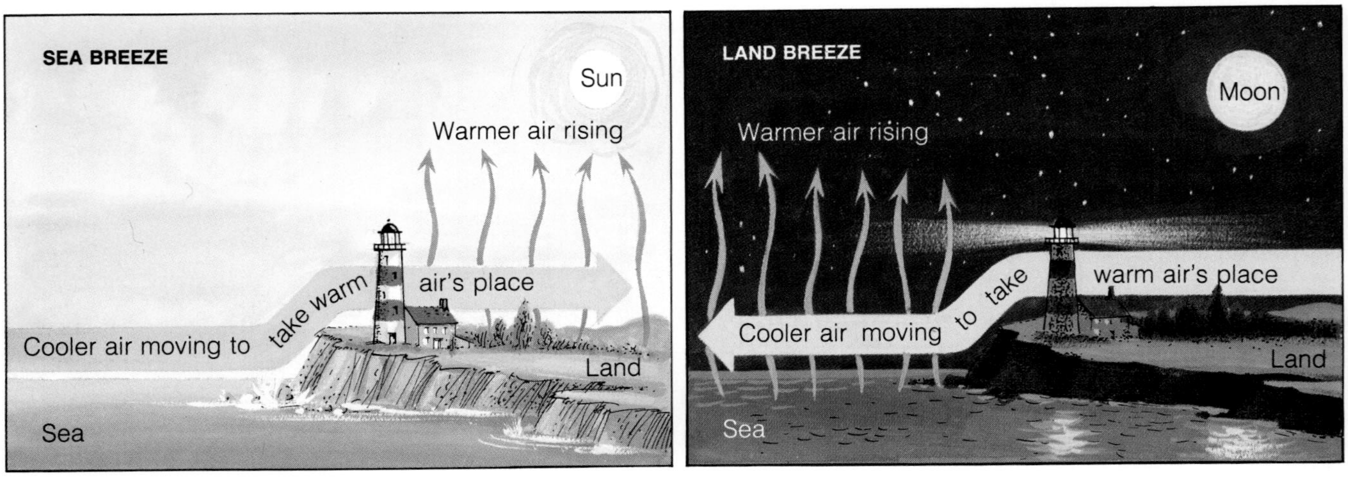

Figure 13–10 *Land and water absorb and lose heat at different rates, causing a sea breeze during the day and a land breeze during the night. Which heats up faster, land or water?*

Local Winds

During the daytime, the air over a land area is often warmer than the air over a nearby lake or sea. The air is warmer because the land heats up faster than the water. As the air over the land rises, the cooler air over the sea moves inland to take its place. This flow of air from the sea to the land is called a **sea breeze.**

During the night, the land cools off faster than the water. The air over the sea is now warmer than the air over the land. This warm air over the sea rises. The cooler air over the land moves to replace the rising warm air over the sea. A flow of air from the land to the sea, called a **land breeze,** is formed.

The name of a wind tells you where the wind is coming *from.* A land breeze flows from the land to the sea. A sea breeze flows from the sea to the land. You are probably familiar with winds that have a direction in their name. For example, a northwest wind flows from northwest to southeast. From what direction does a southwest wind come? In what direction is it blowing?

A major land and sea breeze is called a **monsoon** (mahn-SOON). A monsoon is a seasonal wind. During part of the year, the wind blows from the continent to the ocean. During the rest of the year, it blows from the ocean to the continent. When the wind blows from the ocean, it brings in warm, moist air. Huge amounts of rain and warm temperatures over land areas result. This rainy season is important to many countries. It supplies fresh water for farming. Many monsoon winds occur on the Asian continent.

Sharpen Your Skills

Heating the Land and Sea

1. Place equal amounts of water and sand in separate beakers.

2. Expose the beakers to sunlight or to a very bright light bulb. Make sure each beaker is the same distance from the light source.

3. Note the temperature of the beakers at regular intervals.

4. Remove the beakers from the source of heat and again note the temperature as each cools.

Which heats up faster? Which cools faster? Which holds its heat longer? Based on your answers, explain why land and sea breezes occur.

Global Winds

Unequal heating of the earth's surface also forms large global wind systems. In areas near the equator, the sun is almost directly overhead for most of the year. The direct rays of the sun heat the earth's surface rapidly. The polar regions receive slanting rays from the sun. The slanting rays do not heat the earth's surface as rapidly as the direct rays do. So temperatures in the polar regions are lower than those in areas near the equator. At the equator, the warm air rises and moves toward the poles. At the poles, cooler air sinks and moves toward the equator. This movement produces a global pattern of air circulation.

Global winds do not move directly from north to south or from south to north, as you might expect. Because the earth rotates, the paths of the winds shift in relation to the earth's surface. All winds in the Northern Hemisphere curve to the right as they move. In the Southern Hemisphere, winds curve to the left. This effect is called the **Coriolis effect.**

The Coriolis effect is the apparent shift in the path of any fluid or object moving above the surface of the earth due to the rotation of the earth. For example, suppose an airplane is traveling south from Pittsburgh, Pennsylvania, to Miami, Florida. If the pilot does not make adjustments for the Coriolis effect, the airplane will land west of the point from which it started. It would appear as if an invisible force were pushing it west.

DOLDRUMS At the equator, surface winds are very calm. These winds are called the doldrums (DOHL-druhmz). A belt of air around the equator gets much of the sun's radiant energy. The warm, rising air produces a low-pressure area that extends many kilometers north and south of the equator. Normally, cooler, high-pressure air flows into such an area, creating winds. But the cooler air is warmed so rapidly near the equator that the winds that form cannot go into the low-pressure area. If there are any winds, they will be weak.

The doldrums can be a problem for sailing ships. Because there may be no winds, or very weak winds at best, sailing ships can be stuck in the doldrums for many days.

Figure 13–11 *Because of the earth's rotation, winds appear to curve to the right in the Northern Hemisphere and to the left in the Southern Hemisphere. What is the name of this shift in winds?*

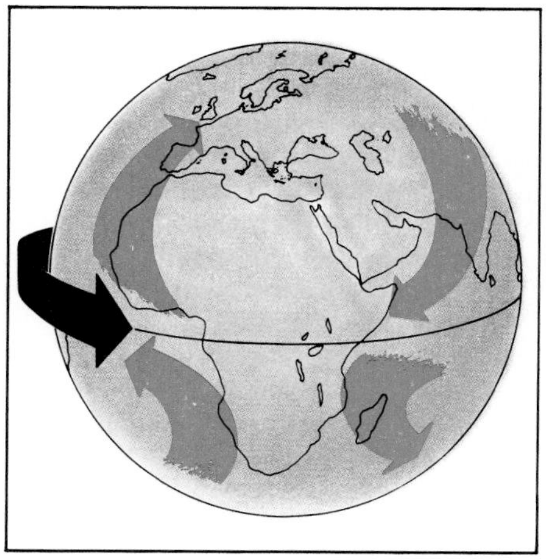

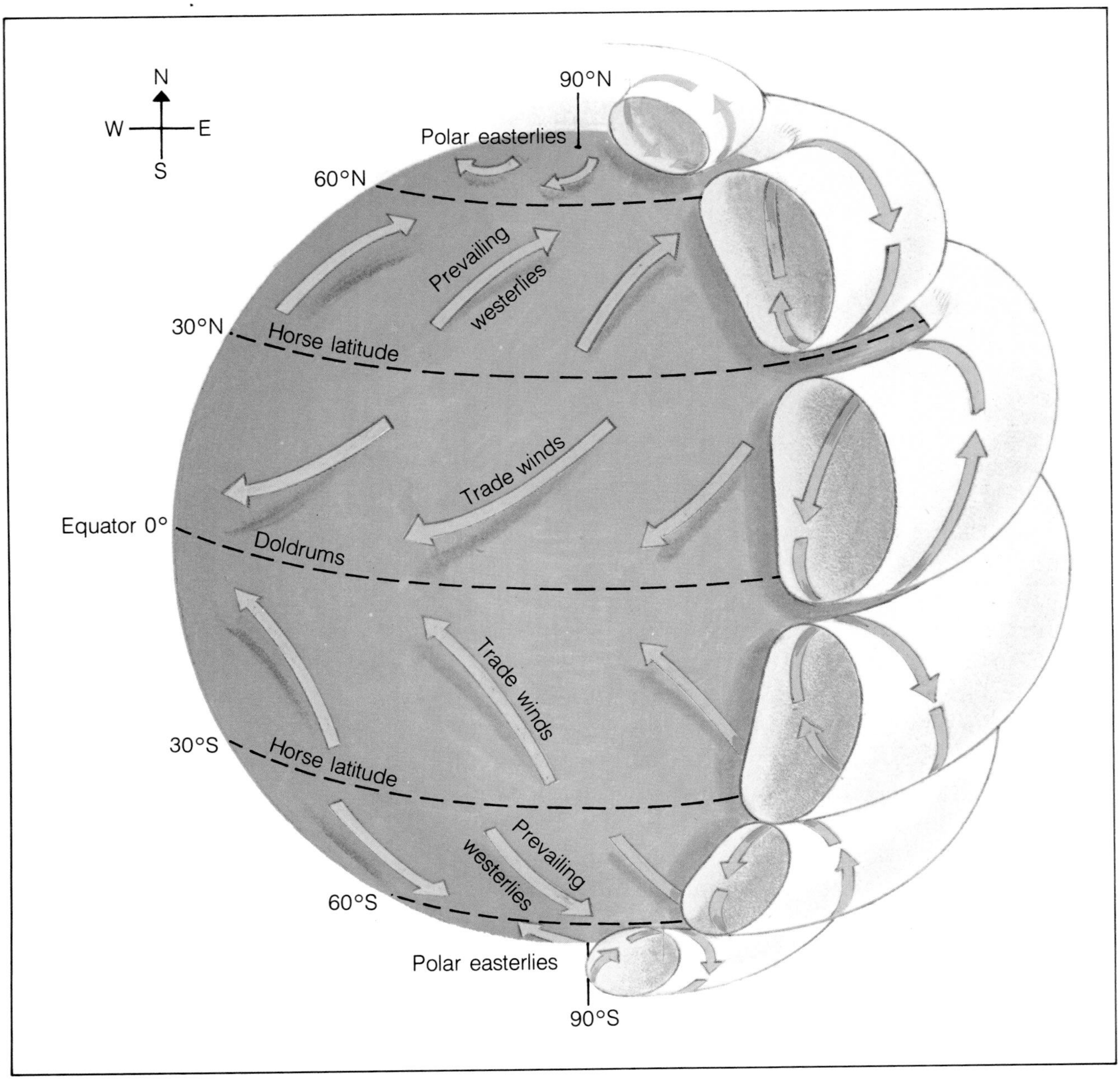

Figure 13–12 *Global wind patterns are caused by unequal heating of the earth's surface and by the rotation of the earth. Warm air rises. Cold air sinks. And the Coriolis effect bends the winds. What are the three major global winds?*

HORSE LATITUDES AND TRADE WINDS At about 30° north and south latitude, the air moving from the equator cools and begins to sink. The sky is clear most of the time. There are few clouds and very little rainfall. The winds are very calm here, too. Centuries ago, sailors on voyages to the New World were sometimes unable to move for days or weeks because of the lack of winds. They sometimes had to throw horses overboard because they ran out of food for them. So the 30° north and south latitudes are called the horse latitudes.

At the horse latitudes, some of the sinking air travels back toward the equator. The rest of the sinking air continues to move toward the poles. The air moving back toward the equator forms a belt of warm, steady winds. These winds are called trade winds. See Figure 13–12.

In the Northern Hemisphere, the Coriolis effect deflects the trade winds to the right. Known as the northeast trades, they blow from northeast to southwest. In the Southern Hemisphere, the trade winds are deflected to the left. They become the southeast trades. How are the southeast trades blowing?

Sailors used the trade winds when they traveled to the New World. The trade winds provided a busy sailing route between Europe and America. Today airplane pilots use the trade winds to increase their speed and save fuel when they fly from east to west in the tropics.

PREVAILING WESTERLIES The sinking air that continues to move toward the North and South poles is also affected by the Coriolis effect. In the Northern Hemisphere, the air is deflected to the right. In the

CAREER — *Weather Observer*

HELP WANTED: WEATHER OBSERVER Strong interest and some coursework in meteorology required. Experience in using weather instruments a plus. Position involves outdoor work in all kinds of weather.

Another school day! The sun shines brightly through your bedroom window. As you enter the kitchen, however, you notice boots and rain gear set by the door for you to wear to school. Someone obviously heard a forecast of rain over the radio. You wonder how anybody can tell that it will rain on a day that starts with the sun out.

Amazingly there are hundreds of **weather observers** located at points all around the world. At the same times each day, four times a day, they cart their data charts out toward an instrument shelter station. The weather data collected at these stations, such as wind speed, wind direction, air pressure, and relative humidity, are radioed or phoned to the National Meteorological Center in Maryland. There the information is fed into large computers that print out maps based on the weather observations. Meteorologists study the maps before making a forecast. If you wish to learn more about weather observing, write to the United States Department of Commerce, NOAA, National Weather Service, Silver Spring, MD 20910.

Figure 13–13 *Strong winds are often associated with rain storms, such as this one along the coast of Florida (left). But winds can also be strong enough to create a dust storm, such as this one on the Alaskan Range (right).*

Southern Hemisphere, it is deflected to the left. So the winds appear to travel from west to east. These winds are called the prevailing westerlies. See Figure 13–12. Remember, winds are named according to the direction from which they come.

The prevailing westerlies in both hemispheres are located in a belt between 40° and 60° latitude. Unlike the trade winds, the prevailing westerlies are often very strong winds.

POLAR EASTERLIES In both hemispheres, the westerlies start rising and cooling between 50° and 60° latitude. Here they meet very cold air flowing toward the equator from the poles. This band of cold air is deflected west by the Coriolis effect. The winds appear to travel from east to west and are called the polar easterlies. See Figure 13–12.

The polar easterlies are cold but weak winds. In the United States, many changes in the weather are caused by these winds.

Figure 13–12 shows the complete picture of global wind systems. Remember, wind systems describe an overall pattern of air movement. At any particular time or place, local conditions can influence and change the pattern.

JET STREAMS For centuries, people have been aware of the global winds you just read about. But it was not until the 1940s that another global wind

Figure 13–14 *A high-altitude jet stream moves over the Nile Valley and the Red Sea.*

was discovered. This wind is a narrow belt of strong, high-speed air called a jet stream.

Jet streams are high-pressure belts of air that flow from west to east. Generally found at altitudes above 12 kilometers, they are near the tropopause. Wind speeds in the jet streams can reach 180 kilometers per hour in the summer and 220 to 350 kilometers per hour in the winter.

Jet streams do not flow around the globe in regular bands. They wander up and down as they circle. At times, they take great detours north and south. Changes in the latitude, altitude, and depth of the jet streams can occur daily or seasonally.

The wandering jet streams affect the atmosphere below them. The rush of a jet stream creates waves and eddy currents, or swirling motions opposite to the flow of the main stream, in the lower atmosphere. These disturbances cause air masses in the lower atmosphere to spread out. This produces areas of low pressure. And the low-pressure areas serve as the centers of local storms. Unusually severe storms can also occur when a jet stream interferes with the surface wind systems.

Measuring Wind

Two measurements are needed to describe wind: wind direction and wind speed. Meteorologists and weather observers use a wind vane to determine the

Sharpen Your Skills

The Beaufort Scale

Wind speed can be estimated and given a descriptive name by using the Beaufort scale. This scale was established by Admiral Francis Beaufort in the 19th century. According to this scale, wind speeds are placed in specific categories. These categories are determined by observing the movements of objects on land.

1. Locate copies of the Beaufort scale in two or three reference books.

2. Use the information from the references to prepare a complete chart of this scale.

3. Your chart should have columns for Beaufort numbers, wind speeds in kilometers per hour, and effects of wind speed on land objects.

4. Using the Beaufort scale, make a record of wind speeds in your area each day for ten days. Make two observations a day.

Figure 13–15 *Wind speed can be determined by counting the number of times the cups of the anemometer revolve. What other weather instrument can you see?*

direction of wind on the earth's surface. A wind vane points into the wind.

An anemometer (an-uh-MAHM-uh-tuhr) is used to measure wind speed. Wind speed is usually expressed in meters per second, miles per hour, or knots. A knot is equal to 1850 meters per hour.

SECTION REVIEW

1. What are the differences between local winds and global winds?
2. What causes winds in the Northern Hemisphere to curve to the right as they move?
3. What are the four major wind belts in the world?
4. Explain the specific movements of the three major global winds in terms of unequal heating and the Coriolis effect.

13–5 Moisture and the Atmosphere

Section Objective

To describe the forms of water vapor in the air

Water vapor, or moisture, in the air is called humidity (hyoo-mihd-uh-tee). The atmosphere gains moisture through evaporation of water from oceans, lakes, rivers, soil, plants, and animals. Winds trans-

Figure 13–16 *Fog, such as this enveloping the Golden Gate Bridge in San Francisco, California, is formed when water vapor in the air condenses at a temperature called the dew point (right). If the dew point is below freezing, frost forms (left).*

port the moisture all over the earth. At any given time, there is about 14 million tons of moisture in the atmosphere.

The amount of moisture in the air can vary greatly from place to place and from time to time. The amount of moisture in the air is often stated in terms of **relative humidity,** or the percentage of moisture the air holds relative to the amount it can hold at a particular temperature.

Warm air can hold more moisture than cold air. If a space holding 1 kilogram of air could hold 12 grams of water vapor, but actually holds 9 grams, the relative humidity is 9/12, or 75 percent. If the same kilogram of air held 12 grams, it would be holding all the moisture it could. The relative humidity would be 100 percent. When the relative humidity is 100 percent, the air is saturated. It is holding all the water vapor it can hold at that particular temperature.

If warm, moist air rises to cooler regions, its temperature begins to drop. Because cool air cannot hold as much water vapor as warm air, the air soon reaches its saturation point. The water vapor in the air begins to condense, or change to a liquid. The temperature at which water vapor condenses is called the **dew point.** Dew, clouds, or fog form. If the dew point is below freezing, frost will form.

Measuring Relative Humidity

Meteorologists measure relative humidity with a psychrometer (sigh-KRAHM-uh-tuhr). The psychrometer consists of two thermometers. The bulb of one thermometer is covered with a moist cloth. This thermometer is the wet-bulb thermometer. The other thermometer is the dry-bulb thermometer.

When air passes over the wet bulb, the water in the cloth evaporates. Evaporation requires heat energy. So the evaporation of the water from the cloth cools the thermometer bulb. If the humidity is low, the evaporation will be fast and the temperature of the wet-bulb thermometer will drop rapidly. If the humidity is high, the evaporation will be slow and the temperature of the wet-bulb thermometer will remain high.

To determine the relative humidity, first find the difference between the dry-bulb temperature and

RELATIVE HUMIDITY

Dry-Bulb Thermometer Readings (°C)	Difference Between Wet- and Dry-Bulb Thermometer Readings (°C)				
	1	2	3	4	5
10	88	77	66	55	44
11	89	78	67	56	46
12	89	78	68	58	48
13	89	79	69	59	50
14	90	79	70	60	51
15	90	80	71	61	53
16	90	81	71	63	54
17	90	81	72	64	55
18	91	82	73	65	57
19	91	82	74	65	58
20	91	83	74	66	59
21	91	83	75	67	60
22	92	83	76	68	61
23	92	84	76	69	62
24	92	84	77	69	62
25	92	84	77	70	63
26	92	85	78	71	64
27	92	85	78	71	65
28	93	85	78	72	65
29	93	86	79	72	66
30	93	86	79	73	67

Figure 13–17 *If the difference between the readings on the wet-bulb and dry-bulb thermometers is 3° and the air temperature is 17°C, what is the relative humidity?*

Sharpen Your Skills

Relative Humidity

Use the table in Figure 13–17 to find the relative humidity for each set of dry-bulb and wet-bulb temperatures given below. To use the table, you must calculate the difference between the dry-bulb and the wet-bulb temperature.

Dry-bulb	Wet-bulb
17°C	13°C
12°C	10°C
15°C	14°C
23°C	20°C
20°C	15°C

the wet-bulb temperature. Then using a chart similar to the one in Figure 13–17 on page 339, find the relative humidity expressed as a percentage. Suppose the dry-bulb thermometer reads 25°C. The difference between the two thermometer readings is 5°C. What will be the relative humidity?

Clouds

Clouds form when moisture in the air condenses on small particles of dust or other solid particles in the air. The tiny droplets of water that form make up the clouds.

Clouds have different shapes and sizes. Clouds are classified according to shape and altitude. There are three main types of clouds: **cumulus clouds, stratus clouds,** and **cirrus clouds.**

Figure 13–18 *Clouds are classified according to their shape and altitude. Cumulus and stratus clouds that develop at altitudes between 2 km and 7 km have the prefix* alto- *in their names. What prefix is used for these clouds if they are at an altitude above 7 km? What prefix means storm cloud?*

Figure 13–19 *The three basic cloud types are fluffy cumulus (left), layered stratus (center), and wispy cirrus (right). What type of weather is usually associated with each cloud type?*

Cumulus (KYOOM-yuh-luhs) clouds look like piles of cotton balls in the sky. These clouds are very puffy and have flat bottoms. They form at altitudes of 2.4 to 13.5 kilometers.

Cumulus clouds usually indicate fair weather. But sometimes they develop into the larger clouds that produce thunderstorms. These large clouds are called **cumulonimbus clouds.**

Gray, smooth clouds that cover the whole sky and block out the sun are called stratus (STRAT-uhs) clouds. They form at an altitude of about 2.5 kilometers. Light rain and drizzle are usually associated with stratus clouds. Nimbostratus clouds bring rain or snow.

Stratus clouds that form close to the ground are called fog. Ground fog is formed when air above the ground cools rapidly at night. Warmer temperatures during the day cause the fog to disappear.

Very feathery or fibrous clouds are called cirrus (SIR-uhs) clouds. Cirrus clouds form at very high altitudes. They are usually found at altitudes between 6 and 12 kilometers. Cirrus clouds are made of ice crystals. Sometimes these clouds are called mare's tails. You can see cirrus clouds when the weather is fair, but they often indicate rain or snow within several hours.

Precipitation

Water vapor that condenses and forms clouds often falls to the earth as rain, sleet, snow, or hail. Water that falls from the atmosphere to the earth is called **precipitation** (prih-sihp-uh-TAY-shuhn).

Sharpen Your Skills

Fog in a Bottle

1. Fill a narrow-necked bottle with hot water. **CAUTION:** *Do not use water hot enough to cause burns.*

2. Pour out almost all the water, leaving about three centimeters at the bottom.

3. Place an ice cube on the mouth of the bottle.

4. Set up another experiment using cold water in the same type of bottle instead of hot water.

Why does fog form in the bottle with hot water but not in the bottle with cold water? Why is it helpful to set up an experiment with cold water?

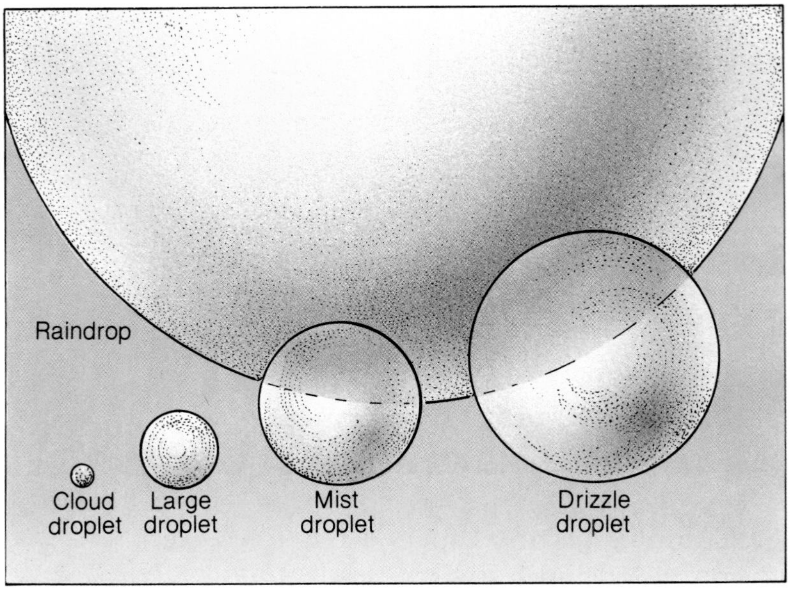

Figure 13–20 *Notice the relative sizes of water droplets in a cloud. Which droplet is the smallest? The largest? When water droplets get large enough, they fall to the earth.*

Before water falls to the earth as precipitation, cloud droplets must increase in size. Cloud droplets increase in size by colliding and combining with other droplets. At some point, the droplets become too large to remain suspended in the cloud. The average raindrop contains about 1 million times the amount of water contained in a cloud droplet!

Gravity pulls the larger drops of water to the earth as rain. Sometimes when falling raindrops pass through a very cold layer of air, they freeze into small ice pellets. These small ice pellets are called sleet. Sleet reaches the earth only in the winter. In the summer, sleet melts and turns to rain before it hits the ground.

Snow is ice in the form of flat, six-sided crystals, which have beautiful shapes. Snow forms when water vapor changes directly to a solid. Because snowflakes sometimes clump together, it is often hard to see the separate crystals.

Hail is one of the most damaging forms of precipitation. It is usually formed in cumulonimbus clouds. Hailstones are small balls or chunks of ice ranging in diameter from 5 to 75 millimeters. Hailstones are formed when water droplets hit ice pellets in a cloud and freeze. If the updraft, or upward movement of the wind, is strong enough, the hailstones remain above the freezing level for a long time. As more water droplets strike them, new layers of ice are added on. The hailstones get so big and heavy that they fall to the ground.

Figure 13–21 *These hailstones became large and heavy enough to fall to the ground.*

Measuring Precipitation

Precipitation in the form of rain is measured with a rain gauge. A rain gauge is a straight-sided container with a flat bottom that collects rain as it falls. The amount of rain collected in the rain gauge over a given period of time is expressed in millimeters or centimeters. Weather observers in the United States usually express the amount of rain in inches.

Figure 13–22 *A rain gauge is used to collect and measure the amount of rain or snow that falls in an area.*

SECTION REVIEW

1. What are the three main types of clouds? What are the four main kinds of precipitation?
2. What type of clouds form at low altitudes and indicate fair weather?
3. Suppose 1 kilogram of air can hold 16 grams of water vapor, but actually holds 8 grams. What will be the relative humidity?

13–6 Weather Patterns

Section Objective

To classify air masses

Changes in the weather are caused by movements of air called **air masses.** Air masses have the same temperature and humidity throughout. They usually cover thousands of square kilometers. They are classified according to where they form. Some form over continents. Others form over oceans. The amount of moisture in an air mass depends on where the air mass develops. **There are four major types of air masses that affect the weather in the United States: maritime tropical, maritime polar, continental tropical, and continental polar.**

The **maritime tropical** air mass forms over the ocean near the equator. It holds warm, moist air. In the summer, the maritime tropical air mass brings very hot, humid weather. But if the warm, moist air comes in contact with a cold air mass in the winter, rain or snow will fall.

The **maritime polar** air mass forms over the Pacific Ocean in both the winter and the summer. It forms over the cold North Atlantic waters in the summer. During the summer, the maritime polar air mass brings cooler temperatures to the eastern states and fog to California and other western states.

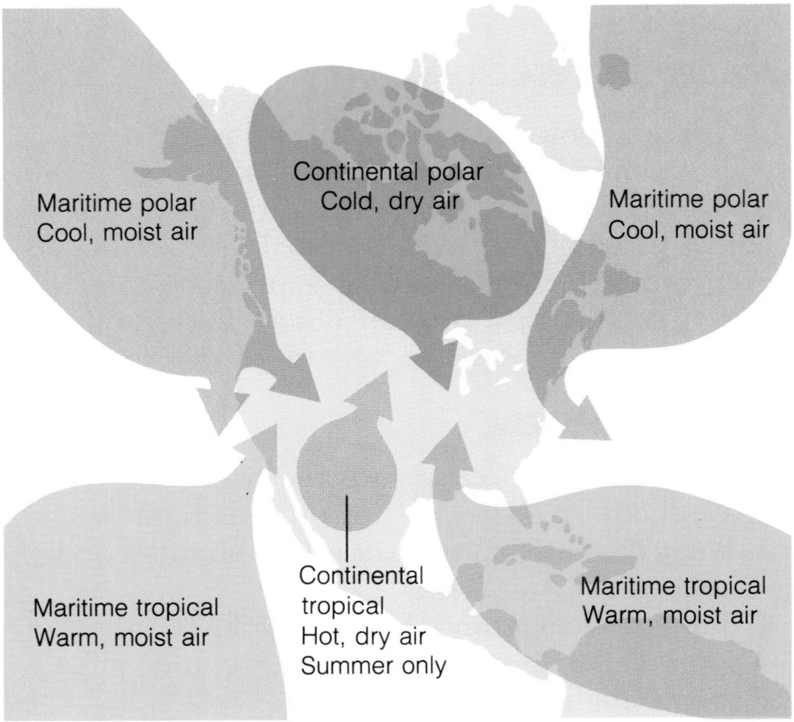

Figure 13–23 *Four major air masses affect the weather of the United States. Each type brings different weather conditions. Which air masses affect the weather where you live?*

Heavy snow and very cold temperatures are produced by the maritime polar air mass in the winter.

During the summer, a **continental tropical** air mass forms over land in Mexico. It brings dry, hot air to the southwestern states. The **continental polar** air mass forms over land in northern Canada. In the winter, this cold, dry air mass causes very cold temperatures in the United States.

Fronts

When two air masses meet, a **front** forms. A front is the boundary between air masses that have

Figure 13–24 *A cold front forms when a mass of cold air meets and replaces a mass of warm air, as shown in the illustration (right). Notice the weather symbols showing the edge of the cold front on the satellite weather photograph (left).*

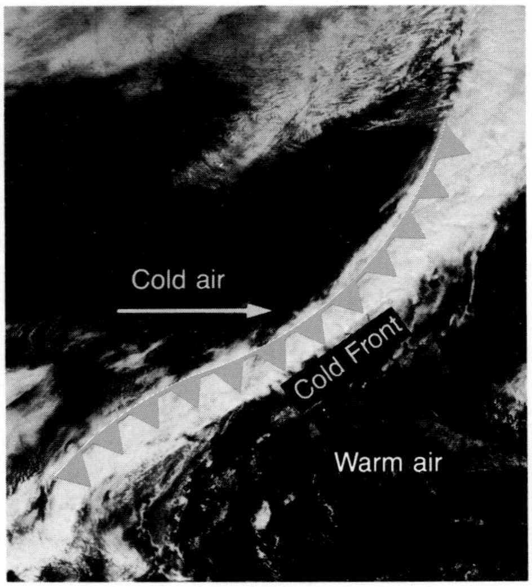

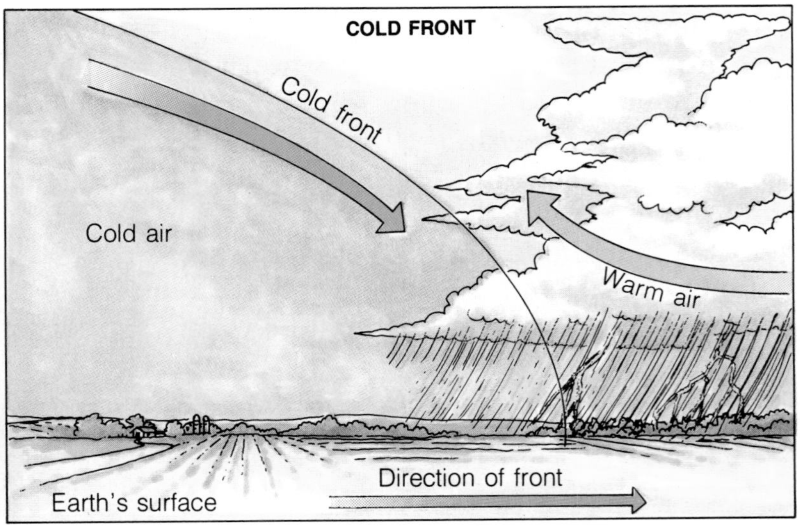

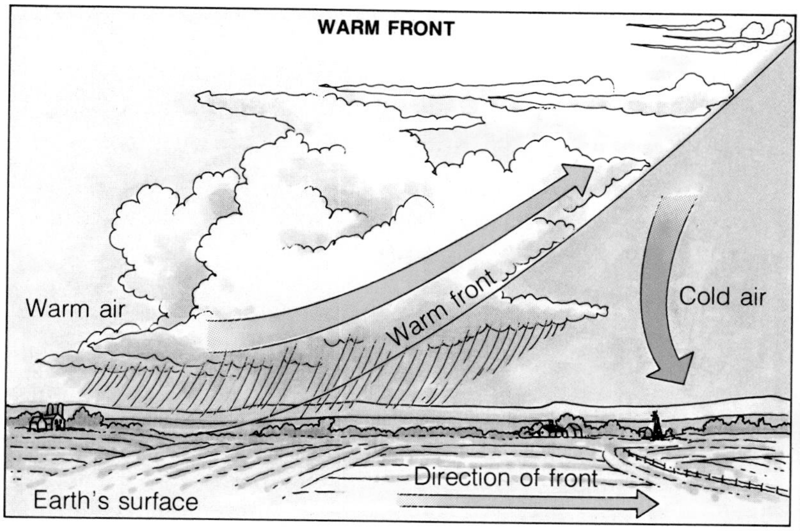

Figure 13–25 *A warm front forms when a mass of warm air overtakes a cold air mass and moves over it, as shown in the illustration (left). Notice the weather symbols showing the edge of the warm front on the satellite weather photograph (right).*

different temperatures and humidity. The weather at a front is usually unsettled and stormy. Four different types of fronts are possible.

A **cold front** forms when a mass of cold air meets and replaces a mass of warm air. See Figure 13–24. The cold air mass forces its way underneath the warm air mass and pushes it upward. Violent storms are associated with a cold front. Fair, cool weather usually follows.

A **warm front** forms when a mass of warm air overtakes a cold air mass and moves over it. See Figure 13–25. Rain and showers usually accompany a warm front. Hot, humid weather usually follows.

A cold front travels faster than a warm front. When a cold front overtakes a warm front, an **occluded front** occurs. See Figure 13–26. The warm air is pushed upward, and the cold air meets cool air. As a result, the occluded front produces less extreme weather than a cold or a warm front. An

Figure 13–26 *An occluded front occurs when a cold front overtakes a warm front, as shown in the illustration (left). Notice the weather symbols showing the occluded front on the satellite weather photograph (right).*

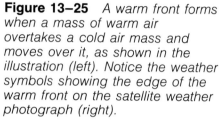

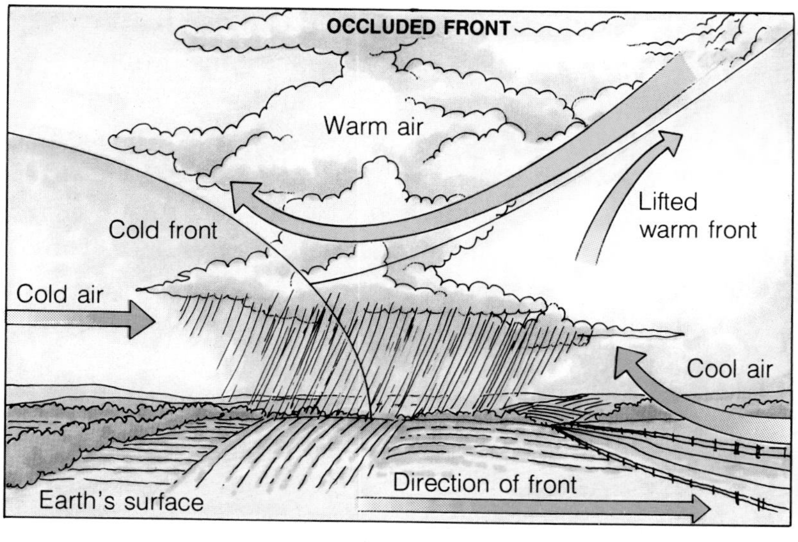

occluded front may also occur when cool air overtakes a cold front and warm air is pushed upward.

When a warm air mass meets a cold air mass and no movement occurs, a **stationary front** forms. Rain may fall in an area for many days when a stationary front is in place.

Figure 13–27 *If the temperature is below −7°C and the wind speed is more than 56 km/hr when two fronts collide, a blizzard will form.*

Rainstorms and Snowstorms

When two different fronts collide, rainstorms and snowstorms form. When a warm front moves in and meets a cold front, heavy nimbostratus clouds develop. In the summer, the result is a steady rainfall that lasts for several hours. In the winter, a heavy snowfall occurs. If the wind speed is more than 56 kilometers per hour and the temperature is below −7°C, a blizzard will form.

When a cold front moves in and meets a warm front, cumulonimbus clouds produce thunderstorms. Thunderstorms are heavy rainstorms with thunder and lightning. These storms can be violent. During a thunderstorm, areas of positive and negative electrical charges build up in the storm clouds. Lightning results. Lightning is a sudden discharge, or spark, of electricity between these cloud areas or between a cloud and the ground. The lightning causes the air to heat and expand explosively. The result is thunder. Sometimes hail is produced during a thunderstorm.

Sharpen Your Skills

How Many Storms? How Much Lightning?

Storms and lightning are very common weather effects. See if you can determine just how common they are.

1. Every day, an average of 45,000 storms occur across the earth's surface. During these storms, water falls to the earth in various forms of precipitation. How many storms occur in a year across the earth's surface?

2. Lightning can occur with or without storms. The United States is struck by lightning about 50 million times a year. On the average, how many times each day does lightning strike the United States?

Cyclones and Anticyclones

Air pressure has a great effect on the weather. An area of low pressure containing rising warm air is called a **cyclone.** In a cyclone, cooler air moves in to take the place of the rising warm air. The air currents begin to spin. Winds spiral around and into the center of the cyclone. They move in a counterclockwise direction in the Northern Hemisphere. Cyclones usually cause rainy, stormy weather. What do you think causes the air currents of a cyclone to spin?

A high-pressure area containing cold, dry air is called an **anticyclone.** Winds spiral around and out from the centers of anticyclones. They move in a clockwise direction in the Northern Hemisphere.

The weather anticyclones bring is usually clear, dry, and fair.

Cyclones and anticyclones can be very small or very large. They travel across the United States, forming areas of high or low air pressure called highs and lows. Many changes in the weather are related to the movement of these highs and lows.

Hurricanes and Tornadoes

A hurricane is a powerful cyclone. It forms over tropical oceans. During the late summer and the early fall, low-pressure areas form over the ocean. Warm, moist air begins to rise rapidly. Cooler air moves in, and the air begins to spin. As the air pressure in the center drops, more air is drawn into the spinning system. It begins to spin faster. The rapidly spinning, rising air forms a cylindrical wall of strong winds, clouds, and rainfall. Inside the wall, the air is calm. This calm center is called the eye of the hurricane. Outside the eye, winds may reach speeds between 120 and 320 kilometers per hour. In terms of the total energy involved, hurricanes are the most powerful storms on the earth.

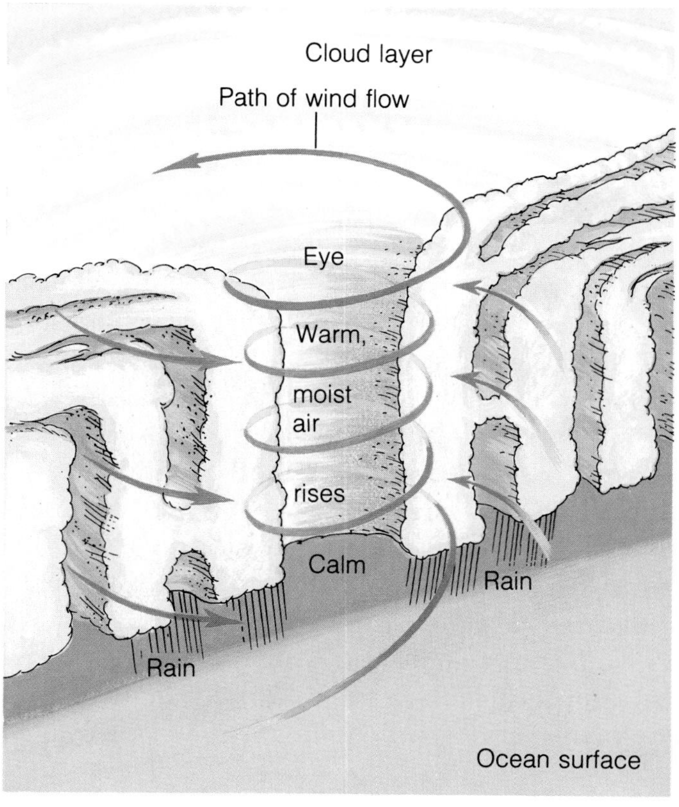

Figure 13–28 *This photo taken from space shows a hurricane over the Atlantic Ocean (right). The storm has a large, circular, counterclockwise movement of air surrounding a low pressure center (left). What is the name of the calm center of a hurricane?*

Figure 13–29 *A tornado lasts no more than a few minutes, but is the most violent storm on the earth (right). A tornado over a lake or an ocean is called a waterspout (left).*

As hurricanes move inland, they lose their force and power. But the heavy rains cause flooding and very high waves. The waves and high winds cause great damage.

Tornadoes are also very destructive. A tornado is a whirling, funnel-shaped cloud. It develops in low, heavy cumulonimbus clouds. The area at the bottom of this funnel of swirling air is extremely low in air pressure. When this low-pressure point touches the ground, it acts like a giant vacuum cleaner.

Scientists are not sure how tornadoes form. Tornadoes occur most often in the spring during the late afternoon and early evening. In the United States, they are most common on the Great Plains. Cool, dry air from the West collides there with moist, warm air from the Gulf of Mexico. Some tornadoes occur over water. A tornado over a lake or ocean is called a waterspout.

The diameter of an average tornado is only about 0.4 kilometer. The length of a tornado's path varies, but it averages 6 kilometers. Tornadoes generally last only a few minutes. But they are the most violent storms on the earth. Tornadoes have very strong winds that can reach speeds of more than 350 kilometers per hour. Roofs and walls of buildings may be blown out by the winds. Houses, railroad cars, automobiles, and people may be thrown hundreds of meters.

Sharpen Your Skills

Hurricane Tracking Chart

1. Get a hurricane tracking chart from a local store, radio station, or TV station.

2. When you hear a tropical cyclone advisory, note the advisory number, eye position, intensity, and predicted direction of movement.

3. Record the eye position of the hurricane on your tracking chart. Hurricane eye positions are given by latitude and longitude to the nearest tenth of a degree.

4. Tropical cyclone advisories are usually issued at six-hour intervals. Record each new eye position on your chart.

Note whether or not the hurricane followed its predicted direction of movement. If not, find out why the direction changed.

SECTION REVIEW

1. What are the four major types of air masses that affect weather in the United States?
2. What is the term for the boundary between two air masses that have different temperatures and humidity?
3. Explain in terms of major air masses why Saskatchewan, Canada, has hot summers, cold winters, and stormy weather in spring and fall.

13–7 Predicting the Weather

Section Objective

To interpret weather data

Information about future weather conditions is important to most people. Farmers need to know the best times to plant and harvest their crops. Airplane takeoffs, landings, and flight paths are scheduled according to weather conditions. Accurate weather forecasts alert people to severe weather conditions that could endanger life or property.

Meteorologists interpret weather information from local weather observers, balloons, satellites, and weather stations around the world. Weather stations are located on land and on ships at sea. Meteorologists also use computers to help interpret weather conditions.

Figure 13–30 *Meteorologists work in all kinds of weather! Here you see the observatory in Mt. Washington, New Hampshire, in winter.*

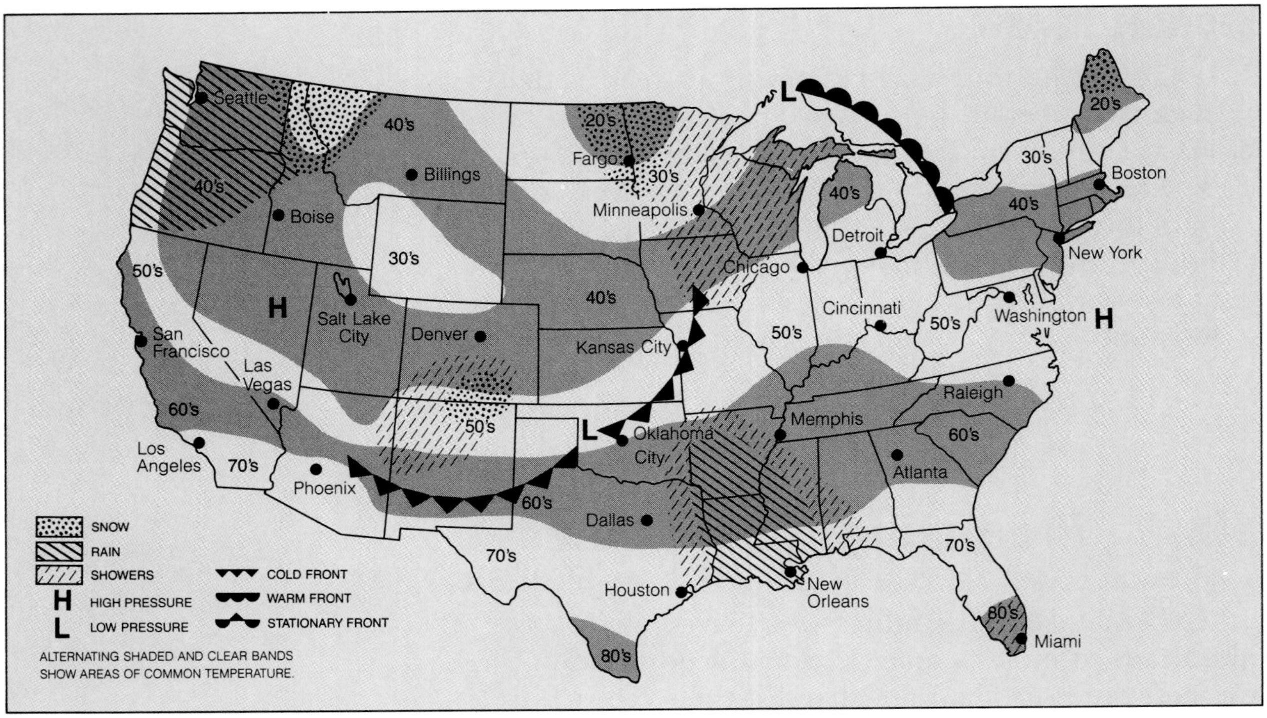

Figure 13–31 *This weather map is similar to ones often shown in newspapers. The legend at the bottom tells you how to read the different symbols on this map. These symbols are not all exactly the same as those on an official weather map produced by the National Weather Service. What was the temperature in Oklahoma City on this particular day?*

Accurate weather forecasting is made possible by studying information about atmospheric conditions at several places. In the United States, weather data are gathered from more than 300 local weather stations. These data include temperature, air pressure, precipitation, and winds. They are used to prepare a daily weather map. Very often, information about sky conditions, air masses, and fronts is also included. So a weather map is a "picture" of weather information.

The information on weather maps is often recorded in the form of numbers, symbols, or lines. Symbols are used to show wind speed and direction, cloud cover, precipitation, position and direction of fronts, and areas of high pressure and low pressure. The symbols found on official weather bureau weather maps are used by all nations. However, these symbols may differ from those used on the simplified weather maps often shown in newspapers. See Figure 13–31.

Look closely at Figure 13–32, which shows how data from a particular location are presented. The circle represents an observation station. Weather

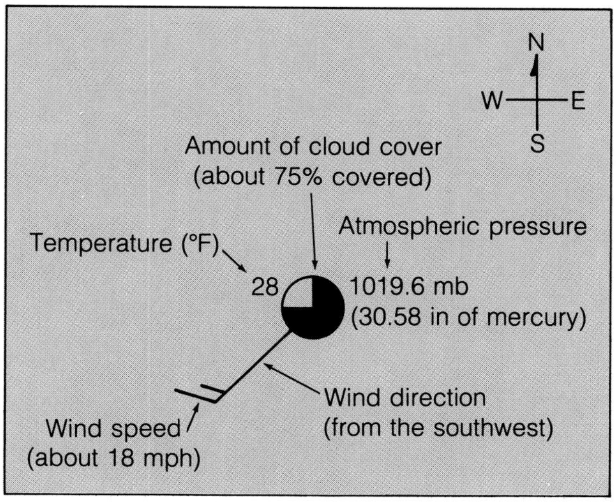

Figure 13–32 *These data indicate the weather readings taken at a weather observation station. Data from thousands of such stations are used by meteorologists to produce detailed weather maps. What do you think the amount of cloud cover would have been if the entire inner circle was filled in?*

data are placed in specific positions inside and outside the station circle. Think of the station circle as the point of an arrow. Attached to the station circle is a line, the shaft of an arrow. The wind direction is represented as moving along the arrow's shaft toward the center of the station circle. The wind direction is the direction from which the wind is blowing. In this station circle, the wind is blowing from southwest to northeast.

Often there are small lines at the end of the shaft. These lines are symbols for the wind speed. Each full line represents an increase in speed of about six miles per hour. In this station circle, the wind speed is about 18 miles per hour. Other data presented include percentage of cloud cover, temperature in degrees Fahrenheit, and atmospheric pressure in millibars and inches of mercury. What were the temperature and percentage of cloud cover when the data at this station were recorded?

On some weather maps, you may see curved lines called **isotherms** (IGH-suh-thermz). Isotherms are lines connecting locations that have the same temperature. The number on the end of an isotherm indicates the temperature at all points along the isotherm line.

The data from weather stations all around the country are assembled into weather maps by meteorologists at the weather bureau. Figure 13–33 on page 352 shows such a weather map. You will notice that this map includes most of the weather station

Sharpen Your Skills

Predicting and Observing the Weather

1. Each day cut out the weather map from your local newspaper. What type of weather is predicted for your area?

2. Each day write down a brief description of your actual weather conditions.

3. Obtain a copy of the *Farmer's Almanac* and read the weather predictions for those days.

4. How do the long-range *Almanac* predictions compare with the daily weather map predictions and your description of the actual weather?

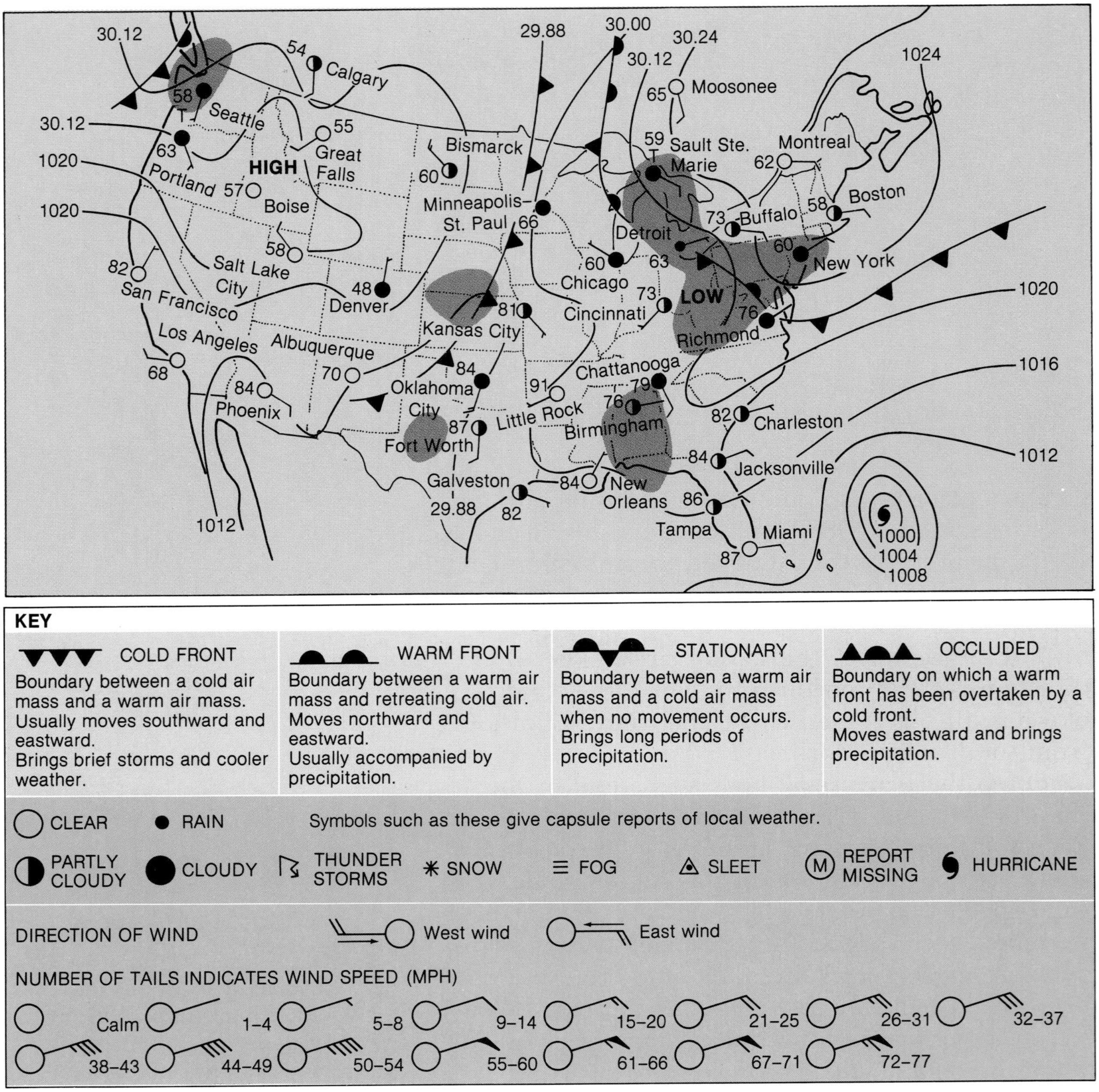

Figure 13–33 *This illustration shows a typical weather map with data from observation stations all over the country. Use the symbol key below the map to determine the weather conditions in your home state on this particular day.*

data you see in Figure 13–32 on page 351. How does this weather map compare to the kinds of weather maps you see in your local newspapers?

Notice the curved lines running through the weather map. These lines are called **isobars** (IGH-suh-barz). Isobars are lines joining places on a weather map that have the same atmospheric pressure. The numbers at the ends of these lines are the atmospheric pressure recorded at each observation station along the lines. Atmospheric pressure can be given in inches or millibars of mercury. A millibar equals about 0.03 inch of mercury. In this map, isobars are marked at one end with barometric pressure in inches and at the other end with barometric pressure in millibars. Inches of mercury are usually given to the hundredths place and range from 28.00 to 31.00.

Average daily temperature is given in degrees Fahrenheit next to the station circle. Shaded areas mark precipitation such as rain. Other symbols for sky conditions are explained in the key. A warm front is shown as a line with half circles pointing in the direction of its movement. A cold front is shown as a line with triangles pointing in the direction of its movement. For a stationary front, the symbols for a warm front and a cold front are combined. They are shown as pushing against each other to illustrate that a stationary front does not move in either direction. To indicate an occluded front, the symbols for a warm front and a cold front are also combined. But the symbols are on the same side to illustrate that both fronts are moving in the same direction.

SECTION REVIEW

1. What are some sources of weather information used by meteorologists?

2. What lines on a weather map connect areas of equal pressure? Areas of equal temperature?

3. Using the weather map in Figure 13–33:

- **a.** Describe the weather conditions in Fort Worth.
- **b.** What is the wind speed in Denver? In Bismarck? In Boise?
- **c.** Find the isobar passing through New York. What is the air pressure in New York? What other locations have the same air pressure?
- **d.** A stationary front is located over Detroit. What type of weather is Detroit having?
- **e.** Is atmospheric pressure increasing or decreasing toward the center of a hurricane? How does your answer relate to what you know about a hurricane?
- **f.** Predict the probable weather conditions in Kansas City the day after this map was issued.

13–8 Controlling the Weather

Section Objective

To relate weather technology to weather control

The American writer and humorist Mark Twain once said, "Everybody talks about the weather, but nobody does anything about it." But if something could be done about it, the results might be very important to many people. If the weather could be controlled, damage by hailstorms, tornadoes, lightning, and hurricanes could be prevented. If people could control the weather, they could cause rain to fall in dry areas. Farming in these areas would then be possible.

At the present time, weather control has been limited to the seeding of clouds. Cloud seeding is the sprinkling of dry ice or silver iodide crystals into supercooled layers of stratus clouds. Supercooling occurs when water remains in the liquid phase below its freezing point. Seeding causes droplets of water to evaporate, or turn into a gas. As they evaporate, these droplets absorb heat from nearby supercooled droplets. The supercooled droplets then freeze and form ice crystals. The crystals grow rapidly. At some point, the crystals grow large enough to fall out of the cloud as rain or snow.

Figure 13–34 *Controlling the weather by cloud seeding can sometimes damage the environment by producing too much rain and subsequent flooding.*

Figure 13–35 *Notice how this airplane is releasing silver iodide crystals from the back of the wing as it flies through the clouds. Cloud seeding is a common method of producing rain in areas that need precipitation during dry periods.*

The most successful use of cloud seeding has been the partial removal of cool fog at airports. Dry ice is sprinkled on the fog. This causes the fog to give up some of its moisture as ice crystals. In this way, some of the fog particles are removed, providing a clear area or "hole" in the fog so airplanes can take off and land. Unfortunately, most fogs are warm and seeding does not work with warm fog. But warm fog has been removed by mechanical mixing of the fog with drier, warmer air from above, or by heating the air from the ground. Fog evaporates when it is heated.

Experiments have shown that seeding hailstorms and hurricanes decreases their force. Controlling weather environments in the future may improve living conditions on the earth. In what way could weather control damage the environment?

SECTION REVIEW

1. Why is controlling the weather important?
2. What are several ways of removing fog?
3. Explain how clouds are seeded.
4. Predict how your life might change if weather could be carefully controlled.

13 LABORATORY INVESTIGATION

Using a Sling Psychrometer to Determine Relative Humidity

Problem

How can relative humidity be determined using a hand-made sling psychrometer?

Materials *(per group)*

2 metal or plastic-backed thermometers
Wooden dowel (for handle)
Hammer
2 washers
Thread
Two-sided foam tape
Large-headed nail
Small piece of gauze

Procedure

1. Attach two thermometers back-to-back with two-sided foam tape.
2. Wrap gauze around the bulb of one thermometer. Using thread, tie the gauze to the bulb. This thermometer will now be referred to as the wet-bulb thermometer.
3. Slide the thermometers and washers onto the nail. As shown in the diagram, place a washer in front of each thermometer.
4. Gently hammer the nail into the dowel. See the diagram. **CAUTION:** *Be extremely careful when hammering the nail into the dowel. Do not hit the thermometers with the hammer.*
5. Using a medicine dropper, add a few drops of water to the gauze of the wet-bulb thermometer.
6. Holding the dowel in your hand, slowly whirl the psychrometer. This whirling motion will speed the evaporating process.
7. Periodically check the temperature recording of the wet-bulb thermometer until the temperature has stopped decreasing.
8. When the wet-bulb temperature has stopped decreasing, read the wet-bulb and dry-bulb temperatures. Determine the difference between the two readings.

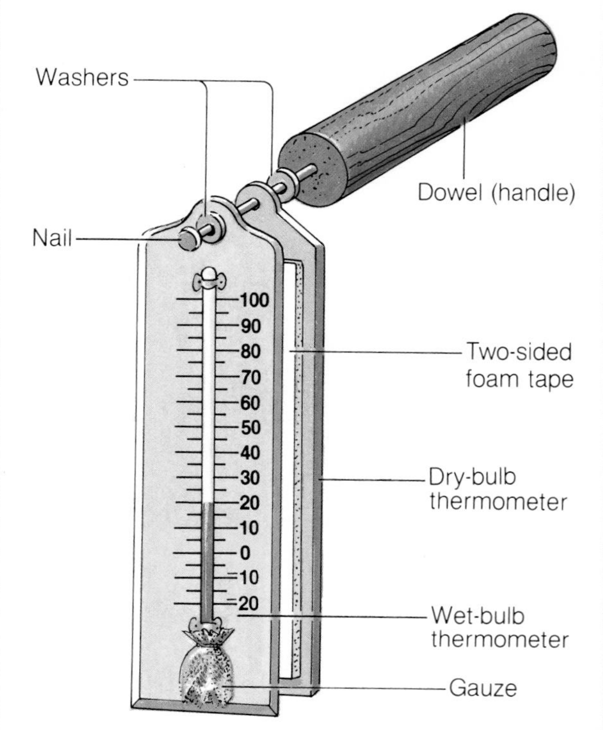

9. Using the dry-bulb temperature, and the difference between the dry-bulb and wet-bulb temperatures, refer to Figure 13–17 to determine the relative humidity. Note: Add a percent sign to your answer.

Observations

Which thermometer measures the temperature of the air?

Conclusions

1. What is the relative humidity in your classroom?
2. What is the relationship between evaporation and the wet-bulb temperature?
3. What is the relationship between evaporation and relative humidity?
4. What would the relative humidity be if the two thermometers measured the wet-bulb and the dry-bulb temperatures to be the same? Explain your answer.

CHAPTER REVIEW

SUMMARY

13–1 Weather Factors

❑ Weather is caused by the interaction of heat energy, air pressure and winds, and moisture.

13–2 Heat Energy and the Atmosphere

❑ Heat is spread throughout the atmosphere by conduction, convection, and radiation.

❑ The greenhouse effect heats the earth.

13–3 Air Pressure and the Atmosphere

❑ Air pressure is affected by temperature, water vapor, and elevation.

❑ A barometer is an instrument that measures air pressure.

13–4 Air Currents: Wind

❑ Winds are caused by differences in air pressure due to unequal heating of the air.

❑ The Coriolis effect is the curving of all global winds in the Northern Hemisphere to the right and in the Southern Hemisphere to the left.

13–5 Moisture and the Atmosphere

❑ Relative humidity is the percentage of moisture the air holds relative to the amount it can hold at a particular temperature.

❑ Clouds are classified according to shape and altitude as cumulus, stratus, or cirrus clouds.

13–6 Weather Patterns

❑ Large bodies of air with the same temperature and humidity throughout are air masses.

❑ The boundary between two different air masses is called a front.

❑ A cyclone is an area of low pressure containing rising warm air with winds spiraling into the center. An anticyclone is an area of high pressure containing cold, dry air with winds spiraling out from the center.

13–7 Predicting the Weather

❑ Weather maps summarize and organize weather information.

❑ Weather maps contain data such as temperature, precipitation, and atmospheric pressure.

13–8 Controlling the Weather

❑ Seeding clouds sometimes produces snow or rain.

VOCABULARY

Define each term in a complete sentence.

air mass
air pressure
anticyclone
atmosphere
barometer
cirrus cloud
cold front
conduction
continental polar
continental tropical
convection
convection current
Coriolis effect
cumulonimbus cloud
cumulus cloud
cyclone
dew point
front
greenhouse effect
isobar
isotherm
land breeze
maritime polar
maritime tropical
meteorologist
monsoon
occluded front
precipitation
radiant energy
radiation
relative humidity
sea breeze
stationary front
stratus cloud
warm front
wind

CONTENT REVIEW: MULTIPLE CHOICE

Choose the letter of the answer that best completes each sentence.

1. Unequal heating of the air causes
a. radiation currents b. convection currents
c. precipitation d. conduction coils

2. The process by which the earth's atmosphere is heated is called the
a. Coriolis effect b. convection effect
c. relative humidity d. greenhouse effect

3. The greatest heating occurs when the sun's rays strike the earth at or near an angle of
a. 90° b. 60° c. 30° d. 120°

4. Air pressure is measured with an instrument called a (an)
a. thermometer b. barometer c. psychrometer d. altimeter

5. High-pressure belts of air flowing west to east at altitudes above 12 kilometers are called
a. polar easterlies b. hurricanes
c. prevailing westerlies d. jet streams

6. The amount of water vapor in the air is called
a. humidity b. dew point c. precipitation d. fog

7. Feathery, high-altitude clouds that often indicate rain or snow are called
a. cirrus clouds b. cumulus clouds
c. stratus clouds d. nimbostratus clouds

8. Water that falls from the atmosphere to the earth is called
a. evaporation b. condensation c. precipitation d. dew

9. Large bodies of air with the same temperature and humidity throughout are called
a. air masses b. isobars c. isotherms d. air fronts

10. Curved lines connecting locations on a weather map that have the same barometric pressure are called
a. isotherms b. anticyclones
c. isobars d. cyclones

CONTENT REVIEW: COMPLETION

Fill in the word or words that best complete each sentence.

1. The three factors in the atmosphere that interact to cause weather are __________, __________, and __________.

2. __________ rays cannot pass through the atmosphere into space and instead get absorbed by gases in the air.

3. The increasing amount of __________ gas in the atmosphere is a concern to scientists because it might make temperatures around the earth higher.

4. Three factors that affect air pressure are __________, __________, and __________.

5. The apparent shift in the paths of winds due to the rotation of the earth is called the __________.

6. The very calm surface winds at the equator are called the __________.

7. The temperature at which water vapor condenses is called the __________.

8. The boundary between air masses with different temperatures and humidity is called a (an) ______________.

9. An area of low pressure containing rising warm air is called a (an) ______________.

10. Curved lines connecting locations on a weather map that have the same temperature are called ______________.

CONTENT REVIEW: TRUE OR FALSE

Determine whether each statement is true or false. If it is true, write "true." If it is false, change the underlined word or words to make the statement true.

1. People who study the weather are called meteorologists.

2. A layer of oxygen gas in the upper atmosphere absorbs ultraviolet rays.

3. Convection is the direct transfer of heat energy from one substance to another.

4. Warm air is more dense than cold air.

5. The instrument used to measure temperature is a thermometer.

6. Standard air pressure is 300 millimeters of mercury.

7. A major land and sea breeze is called a (an) monsoon.

8. The percentage of moisture the air holds relative to the amount it can hold at a particular temperature is called relative humidity.

9. Fair-weather clouds are cirrus clouds.

10. In terms of total energy, hurricanes are the most powerful storms on the earth.

CONCEPT REVIEW: SKILL BUILDING

Use the skills you have developed in the chapter to complete each activity.

1. Applying concepts The "comfort index" is often included in a weather forecast. The comfort index includes the effects of temperature and humidity on people. Explain how temperature and humidity affect human comfort.

2. Making predictions What influence might the jet stream have on temperature? On air pressure? On air travel from coast to coast?

3. Making inferences Explain how both the temperature and the amount of water vapor in the air could change and yet the relative humidity could stay the same.

4. Making calculations The air pressure reported by a forecaster for location X is 757.7 mm of mercury. Describe the temperature and humidity that would correspond to this pressure. If this were normal air pressure, what might the elevation of X be?

5. Developing a model Devise a way to illustrate convection currents using a classroom window and several strips of colored paper of the same size.

CONCEPT REVIEW: ESSAY

Discuss each of the following in a brief paragraph.

1. Describe the greenhouse effect.

2. Suppose you are setting up a weather station. What instruments will you need to measure atmospheric conditions?

3. Describe how a tropical cyclone forms.

4. Explain why hail, made of ice, commonly forms during the summer.

5. What are some conditions that make accurate weather prediction difficult?

Climate

14

CHAPTER SECTIONS

CHAPTER OBJECTIVES

After completing this chapter, you will be able to

- **14–1** Identify the factors that determine climate.
- **14–1** Describe the factors that affect temperature and precipitation.
- **14–2** Classify the earth's climate zones.
- **14–3** Compare the major climate regions of the United States.
- **14–4** Identify the factors that cause climate to change.

With the help of an imaginary time machine, you are about to embark on an incredible journey. Your journey begins in the Midwest of the United States at the present time. Now, step inside the time machine and turn a few dials. Suddenly the lights flash and flutter. After a few seconds, however, everything returns to normal. Or does it? You open the hatch of the time machine and step outside—into the world of 6000 years ago!

The air is warm. But it is also much more humid than you are used to. Tall grasses are everywhere. Many different types of flowers add splashes of brilliant color to the grasslands.

The world you have reached looks and feels more like a tropical grassland than the midwestern area from which your journey began. Obviously the climate of 6000 years ago was very different from the climate of today. What might it have been like at a much earlier time?

Back in the time machine, you set the dials to 16,000 years ago. When you step out of the machine again, a blast of cold air sets you shivering. Stretching away to the north is an endless sheet of ice. To the south is a bleak landscape of mossy grassland. In the distance, a herd of elephantlike woolly mammoths graze on low bushes.

As you head back to the warmth of the time machine you think about how drastically the climate has changed over the last 20,000 years. What can the future hold in store? Back in the time machine, you set the dials to 30,000 years in the future and wonder what type of climate awaits you. . . .

Woolly mammoths grazed the snow-covered grassland of the Midwest United States about 16,000 years ago.

Section Objective

To describe the factors that determine climate

14–1 What Causes Climate?

On your way to school today, you probably made some observations about the weather. You were probably aware of two important weather factors—temperature and precipitation. You noticed that the morning was either cold, cool, warm, or hot. You also noticed whether or not it was raining or snowing.

If you kept a record of the weather for an extended period of time, you would discover some general conditions of temperature and precipitation for your area. Such general conditions are described as the average weather for a region. Scientists call the general conditions of temperature and precipitation for an area **climate.** Every place in the world has its own special climate. For example, the climate of the southwestern United States tends to be warm and dry all year round. The climate of Florida is warm but much wetter.

The climate in any region of the world is determined by two basic factors: temperature and precipitation. Different combinations of temperature and precipitation are used to classify the earth's major climates. Temperature and precipitation are in turn influenced by several factors.

Figure 14–1 *Climate is the characteristics of the weather in an area over a long period of time. In certain climates, winter brings cold temperatures and lots of precipitation (left). Summer brings warm, dry conditions that evoke thoughts of the beach (right). What is the climate like where you live?*

Factors That Affect Temperature

Latitude, altitude, and the nearness of ocean currents are three natural factors that affect temperatures at a particular location. The extent to which these factors affect climate varies from place to place.

LATITUDE Latitude is a measure of distance north and south of the equator. Areas close to the equator, or 0° latitude, receive direct rays of the sun. Direct rays provide more radiant energy. So these areas near the equator have a warm climate. Farther from the equator, the sun's rays are not as direct. Less radiant energy is received by areas farther from the equator. So climates are cooler. In general, the lowest average temperatures occur near the polar regions, where the sun's rays are least direct.

ALTITUDE Altitude is distance above sea level. As altitude increases, the air becomes less dense. This means that there are fewer particles of air and they are spread farther apart. Less dense air cannot hold as much heat. So as altitude increases, the temperature decreases.

OCEAN CURRENTS An ocean current is a stream of water in the ocean that flows in a definite path. Some ocean currents are warm water currents. Other ocean currents are cold water currents. See Figure 14–3 on page 364. The surface temperature of water affects the temperature of the air above it. Warm water warms the air. Cold water cools the air. So land areas near warm water currents have warmer temperatures. And land areas near cold water currents have cooler temperatures.

Ocean currents traveling away from the equator are warm water currents. Land areas located near these currents have warmer temperatures. The Gulf Stream is a current that carries warm water from the southern tip of Florida along the eastern coast of the United States. How do you think the warm waters of the Gulf Stream affect the climate of the eastern United States?

Ocean currents traveling toward the equator are cold water currents. Areas located near these

Figure 14–2 *Although these two locations have the same latitude, their difference in altitude produces a dramatic difference in climate. In the cool, dry Andes Mountains (top), snow is visible and vegetation is sparse. Thick vegetation is plentiful in the hot, humid Amazon jungle (bottom). What factor other than latitude and altitude affects climate?*

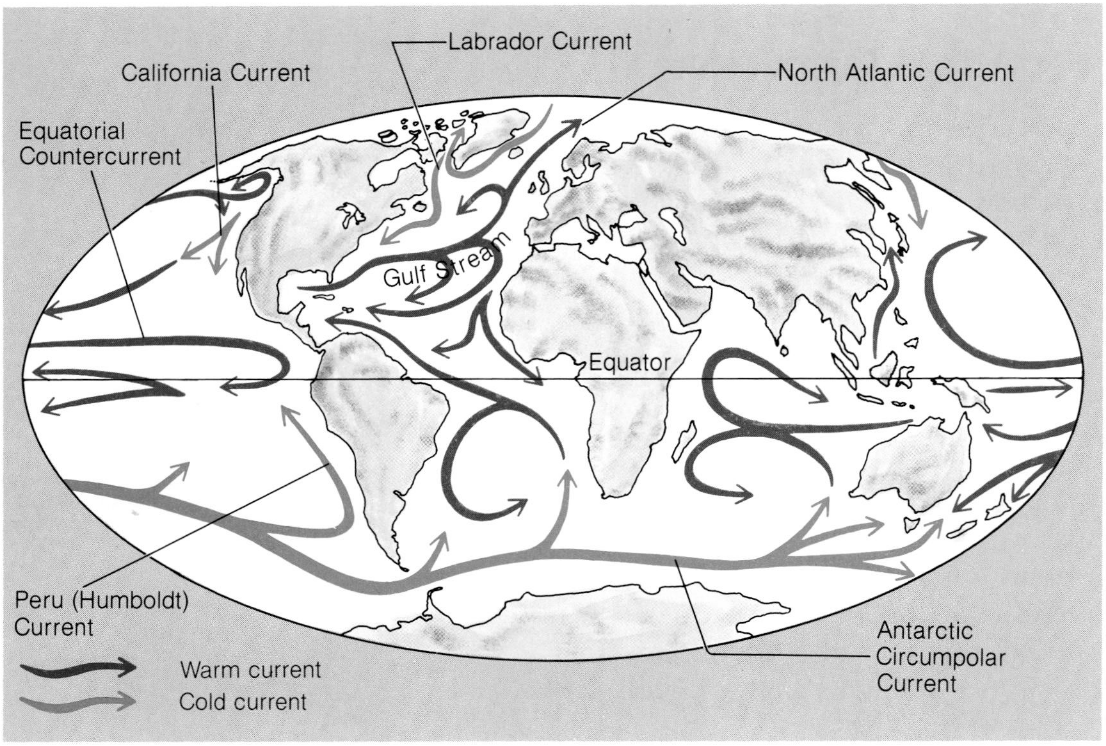

Figure 14–3 *This map shows the general direction of flow of the major warm and cold ocean currents of the world. Which ocean current affects the area where you live?*

currents have cooler temperatures. Off the western coast of the United States, the California Current flows toward the equator. Coastal locations in this area have cooler temperatures.

Factors That Affect Precipitation

The two natural factors that affect the amount of precipitation at a particular location are prevailing winds and mountain ranges. As with temperature factors, the effects of precipitation factors vary from place to place.

PREVAILING WINDS A **prevailing wind** is a wind that blows more often from one direction than from any other direction. Prevailing winds have a great influence on the climate of regions in their paths. Different prevailing winds carry different amounts of moisture. The amount of moisture carried by a prevailing wind affects the amount of precipitation a region receives.

Warm air is able to hold more moisture than cold air. As warm air rises, it cools and cannot hold as much moisture. The moisture it can no longer hold falls to the earth as some form of precipitation. Winds formed by rising warm air tend to bring

Sharpen Your Skills

Factors Affecting Climate

The climate of a region is determined by several different factors. Using reference materials in the library, write an essay describing the climate of one of the following cities.

Juneau, Alaska
Tokyo, Japan
Athens, Greece
Santiago, Chile

Be sure to explain which factors determining the climate of your chosen city are more important than others and why.

precipitation. Winds formed by sinking cold air become warmer and can then hold more moisture. So winds formed by sinking cold air tend to bring very little precipitation.

The direction from which a prevailing wind blows also affects the amount of moisture it carries. Some prevailing winds blow from land to water. Others blow from water to land. The prevailing winds that blow from water carry more moisture than those from land. So regions in the paths of winds originating over water receive more precipitation.

The combined effect of a prevailing wind's moisture content and direction makes it possible for a desert to exist next to a large body of water. The Sahara Desert in northern Africa is one of the driest places on the earth. Yet it is bordered on the west by the Atlantic Ocean. However, the prevailing winds flowing over this region are from a source of dry, sinking air. The prevailing winds are also dry because they originate far inland. So, little precipitation ever reaches the Sahara Desert, even though there is a large source of water nearby.

MOUNTAIN RANGES The amount of precipitation at a particular location is also affected by mountain ranges. Mountain ranges act as a barrier to prevailing winds. Mountains cause air to rise. See Figure 14–5 on page 366. As air rises, it cools, and most of the moisture it contains condenses, or becomes a liquid. As a result, there is much precipitation on the **windward side** of the mountain, which is the side facing toward the wind. The region on the windward side of a mountain has a wet climate.

Conditions are very different on the **leeward side** of the mountain, which is the side facing away from the wind. By the time the prevailing winds reach the top of the mountains, they have lost most of their moisture in the form of precipitation. So relatively dry air moves down the leeward side. As a result, there is very little precipitation on the leeward side of the mountain. The region has a dry climate.

The Cascade Mountains run through western Oregon and Washington. Land areas of these two states west of the Cascades receive a great amount

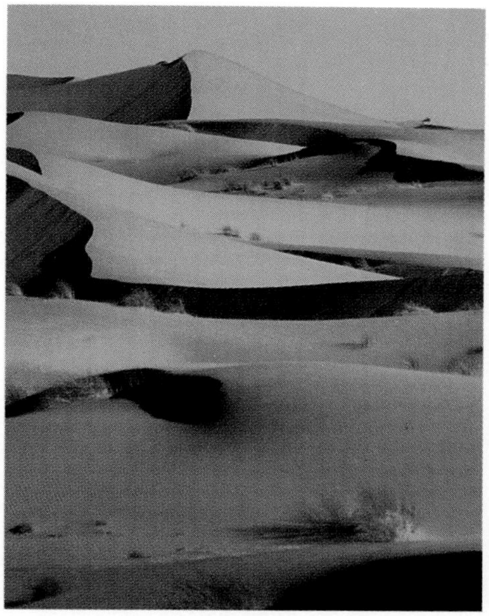

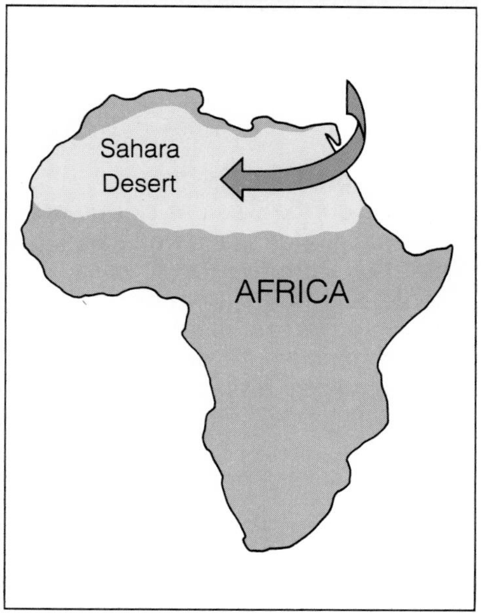

Figure 14–4 *Although the Sahara Desert in Africa is bordered on the west by the Atlantic Ocean, it is one of the driest places on the earth (top). The prevailing winds, which originate far inland, carry very little moisture as they sweep south and then west across the region (bottom).*

Figure 14–5 *There is a rainy climate on the western slopes of the Rocky Mountains because moist air from the Pacific rises, cools, and forms rain clouds. Dry air moving down the eastern slopes results in a desert climate. Which slopes represent the windward side? The leeward side?*

of precipitation from the prevailing winds, which blow in from the Pacific Ocean. Land areas east of the Cascades receive very little precipitation because the prevailing winds have lost most of their moisture by the time they have moved across the mountain range.

SECTION REVIEW

1. What two factors determine climate? What conditions influence these factors?
2. Explain how cold water currents and warm water currents affect the climate of a location.
3. Explain the following conditions.
   a. A mountain near the equator has snow on its peak throughout the year.
   b. Deserts exist on the eastern side of the Rocky Mountains.

Section Objective

To classify the earth into major climate zones

14–2 Climate Zones

The earth's climates can be divided into general zones according to average temperatures. These climate zones can be broken down into subzones. And even the subzones have further subdivisions. In fact, scientists often talk of very localized climates called **microclimates.** A microclimate can be as small as your own backyard!

The three major climate zones on the earth are the polar, tropical, and temperate zones. Temperatures in these three zones are determined by the location of the zone and the kind of air masses commonly found there. See Figure 14–6.

Polar Zones

In each hemisphere, the **polar zone** extends from the pole to about 60° latitude. Polar climates have the coldest average temperatures. Within this region, the average yearly temperature remains below freezing. Even during the warmest month, the average temperature does not rise above 10°C. There is little precipitation in the polar zones.

Polar zones are also known as high-latitude or arctic climates. The polar zones include the icecaps of Greenland in the Northern Hemisphere and Antarctica in the Southern Hemisphere. These icecaps remain frozen throughout the year. Places

Sharpen Your Skills

Examining a Microclimate

In this activity, you can investigate the factors that determine a microclimate.

1. Locate two separate areas in your neighborhood that appear to have different microclimates.

2. Carefully observe each area for several days.

3. Record the following information for each microclimate: temperature, type of organisms found, type of vegetation found, description of the soil, and any other features you notice.

Describe the similarities and differences in your two microclimates. What factors play a role in the differences? How does a microclimate relate to major climate zones of the earth?

Figure 14–6 *The three major types of climate zones on the earth are shown in this diagram. In which zone is most of the United States located?*

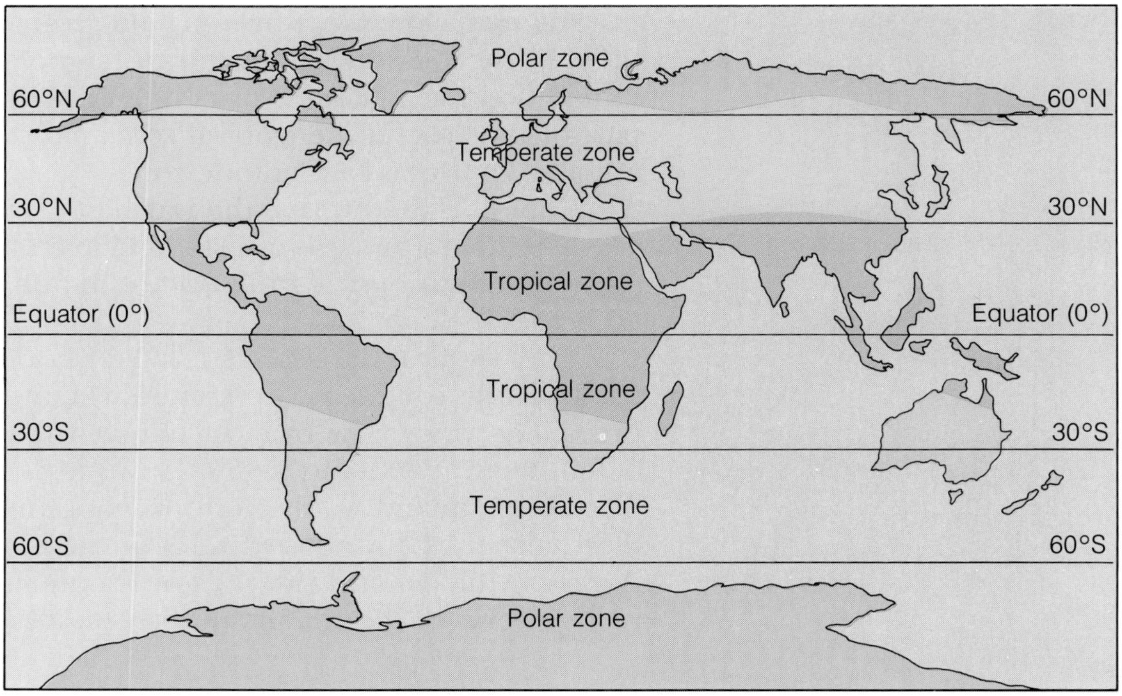

Figure 14–7 *As you can see from these photographs, the climate on a typical winter day is very different in the polar zone of Ross Island, Antarctica (left), and the tropical zone of the Namib Desert, Namibia (right). Which zone is the high-latitude zone? The low-latitude zone?*

where the snow does melt in the cool summer are also found in polar zones. The northern coasts of Canada and Alaska and the southern tip of South America are examples.

Tropical Zones

The **tropical zone,** which extends from 30° latitude to the equator, has very high temperatures and humidity. Precipitation is usually very heavy during part of the year in the tropical zone. Tropical zones are also known as low-latitude zones.

Tropical climates have the warmest average yearly temperatures. In a tropical climate, the average temperature during the coldest month does not go below 18°C.

Many tropical deserts are located on the western coasts of the continents. In tropical climates, the prevailing winds flow from inland west toward the ocean. High mountains along the western coasts block these inland winds from reaching the coasts. Rain falls on the windward sides of the mountains. Areas on the leeward sides of the mountains do not receive very much rainfall and become deserts.

Temperate Zones

In each hemisphere, the **temperate zone** is found between 30° and 60° latitude. In the areas of the temperate zone farther from the equator, snow is common in the winter. In the areas of the temperate zone closer to the equator, rain normally falls during all of the seasons. But the average amount of precipitation is about the same throughout the temperate zone.

Temperatures in the temperate zone are affected by both polar and tropical air masses. Average temperatures fall between the average temperatures of the polar and tropical zones. In the temperate zone, the average temperatures range from about 6°C in the coldest months to about 28°C in the warmest months.

Temperate zones, or middle-latitude climates, cover a huge portion of the globe. So a temperate zone can range from the cool rain forests of Washington State to the hot rain forests of southeastern China, with many different climates in between.

Deserts in temperate zones are generally located inland, far away from the oceans. The air that reaches these deserts contains little moisture. There are inland deserts in the United States and Central Asia.

A common misconception is that temperate deserts are always hot. This is true of deserts during the day. But at night, the temperature can drop to below freezing! The low humidity and cloudless skies allow a tremendous amount of solar radiation to reach the ground and heat it during the day. The same conditions allow the heat to escape rapidly at night, causing the temperature to drop dramatically. So there can be a range in temperature from 20°C at 2:00 P.M. to 0°C at 2:00 A.M.

Figure 14–8 *Temperate zones can contain many different climates. The rain forests of Washington State are cool (top), while those of India are hot and steamy (bottom). What are two general characteristics of the temperate zones?*

Marine and Continental Climates

Within each of these three major climate zones, there may be **marine climates** and **continental climates.** A marine climate is found in areas near an ocean. A continental climate is found in areas located within a large landmass.

Sharpen Your Skills

Radiant Energy and Climate

Radiant energy from the sun strikes the earth at different angles. To demonstrate this effect, do the following activity.

1. Tape a piece of paper to a wall at waist level.

2. Using one hand, hold a flashlight 25 cm away from the paper.

3. Shine the light at a 5° angle onto the paper. Using your free hand, trace the outline of the circle of light.

4. Repeat steps 2 and 3 using angles of 45° and 90°.

At what angle is the radiant energy most concentrated? Least concentrated? What is the effect of spreading the same amount of radiant energy over a small area of the earth's surface? Over a large area? What climate zone is represented by each of the three circles of light?

Areas with a marine climate receive more precipitation than areas with a continental climate. The temperature in areas with a marine climate does not vary greatly. Areas with a marine climate have cooler temperatures in the summer than do inland areas. They also have warmer winters than inland areas. Nearness to oceans has a moderating effect on air temperature.

A continental climate is drier than a marine climate. There is usually a great variation in temperature. Areas with a continental climate have hot summers and cold winters. Most of the world's desert areas that are located just north and south of the equator have continental climates.

SECTION REVIEW

1. What are the earth's three major climate zones?
2. Describe the location and temperature–precipitation conditions of each climate zone.
3. Compare a marine climate with a continental climate.
4. Explain in terms of radiant energy why polar zones have the coldest average temperature and tropical zones have the warmest average temperature.

14–3 Climate Regions of the United States

Section Objective

To identify the major climate regions of the United States

The three climate zones—polar, tropical, and temperate—are all represented in various sections of the United States. Alaska is located in the polar zone. Hawaii and southern Florida are located in the tropical zone. Most of the United States, however, is located in the temperate zone.

Within the temperate zone, there are many different climates. To describe each climate more precisely, scientists have divided the mainland United States into six major climate regions. **The division of the mainland United States into six major climate regions is based on the amount of precipitation and the temperature in each region.** See Fig-

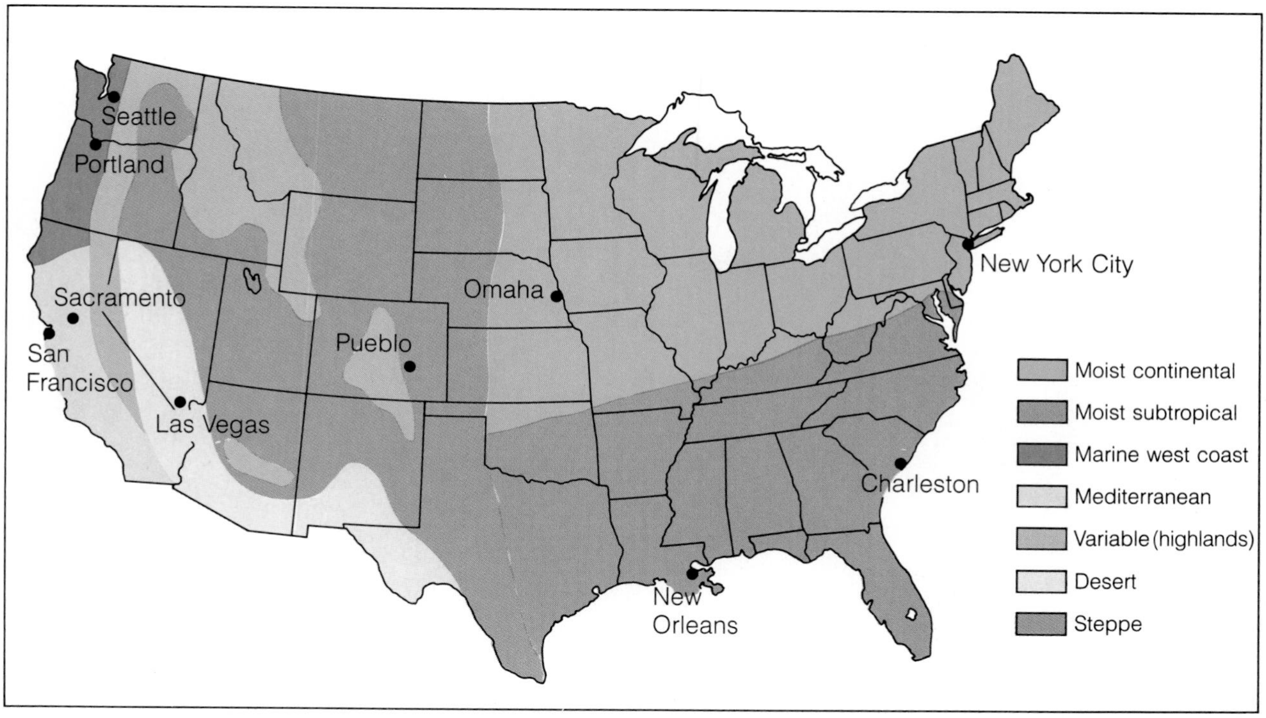

Figure 14–9 *The seven major climate regions of the United States are shown on this map along with representative cities in each region. Remember that these regions are generalized. The climate does not change suddenly if you cross one of the lines. The climates actually blend into one another. Notice the area called variable or highlands. This area is found in the mountain regions and is characterized by temperature and precipitation that vary with altitude and latitude. In which climate zone do you live?*

ure 14–9. But it is important to remember that even within a particular climate region, variations in precipitation and temperature exist.

Mediterranean Climate Region

The narrow coastal area of California has a **Mediterranean climate.** In winter, cyclones and moist maritime polar air masses bring heavy precipitation to this region. In summer, there is almost no rain. Winters throughout the Mediterranean climate region are cool. Summer temperatures are only slightly higher than winter temperatures. See Figure 14–10.

The Mediterranean climate of wet winters and dry summers results in two basic types of vegetation. One type of vegetation is a dense growth of shrubs and stunted trees. The other type consists of scattered oak and olive trees with a ground cover of grasses.

MEDITERRANEAN CLIMATE

	Summer	Winter
Average Temperature: (°C)		
San Francisco	17.3	10.0
Sacramento	24.0	9.0
Average Precipitation: (cm/month)		
San Francisco	0.2	9.8
Sacramento	0.2	8.0

Figure 14–10 *Within each particular climate region, variations in temperature and precipitation exist. San Francisco, California, and Sacramento, California, both have a Mediterranean climate.*

Figure 14–11 *Dense growth of shrubs and stunted trees are found in the Mediterranean climate (left). Dense forests of mixed red cedar, spruce, and firs are characteristic of the marine west coast climate (right).*

MARINE WEST COAST CLIMATE	Summer	Winter
Average Temperature: (°C)		
Seattle	17.0	5.3
Portland	18.5	5.0
Average Precipitation: (cm/month)		
Seattle	2.3	11.9
Portland	2.3	15.5

Figure 14–12 *Portland, Oregon, and Seattle, Washington, both have a marine west coast climate. What variations in temperature exist?*

Marine West Coast Climate Region

The northwest coast of the United States has a **marine west coast climate.** This is a rainy climate because moist air from the Pacific Ocean rises, cools, and releases precipitation on the western slopes of the Cascade Mountains. Cool winters and only slightly warmer summers are characteristic of the marine west coast climate. See Figure 14–12. The temperature range from one season to another is small due to the moderating effect of the nearby Pacific Ocean.

The type of vegetation most common to this climate region is forests of needleleafed trees. These heavy forests consist of mixed red cedar, spruce, and firs.

Moist Continental Climate Region

The portion of the United States extending from the northern Midwest to the North Atlantic coast has a **moist continental climate.** Continental polar air masses flowing south across the region produce very cold winters. In summer, tropical air masses flowing north across the region produce high temperatures throughout the region.

Figure 14–13 *This pine forest in Acadia National Park, Maine, is characteristic of the moist continental climate. What other type of vegetation is common to this climate?*

The region receives a moderate amount of precipitation throughout the year. During the summer, however, there is a marked increase in precipitation for all locations. During the winter, the decrease in precipitation varies from one place to another. See Figure 14–14.

In some sections of the moist continental climate region, forests of broadleafed and needleleafed trees are dominant. In other sections, much of the land is covered with tall grasses.

Moist Subtropical Climate Region

The southeastern United States has a **moist subtropical climate.** Summers are hot in this climate region. The average precipitation in summer is greater than it is in winter. See Figure 14–16 on page 374. The characteristic summer temperatures and precipitation of the moist subtropical region are very similar to those of the tropical zone. So in summer the climate of the moist subtropical region of the United States is very similar to the climate of the tropical regions of the world. Maritime tropical air masses moving inland from the tropics greatly influence the summer climate.

MOIST CONTINENTAL CLIMATE

	Summer	Winter
Average Temperature: (°C)		
New York City	22.0	−0.3
Omaha	23.7	−4.3
Average Precipitation: (cm/month)		
New York City	10.0	8.4
Omaha	8.7	2.2

Figure 14–14 *The moist continental climates of New York City, New York, and Omaha, Nebraska, show variations in temperature and precipitation.*

Figure 14–15 *Forests of oak, chestnut, and pine trees, such as those of South Carolina, are characteristic of the moist subtropical climate.*

MOIST SUBTROPICAL CLIMATE

	Summer	Winter
Average Temperature: (°C)		
New Orleans	26.3	12.7
Charleston	27.2	11.3
Average Precipitation: (cm/month)		
New Orleans	14.0	10.1
Charleston	15.0	7.6

Figure 14–16 *A moist subtropical climate is found in New Orleans, Louisiana, and in Charleston, South Carolina. Are the variations in temperature and precipitation extreme?*

The similarity between the moist subtropical climate and the tropical climate ends in winter. Although winters are generally cool and mild, the mixing of polar air masses with maritime tropical air masses causes the temperature to occasionally drop below freezing. Severe frosts in the northern areas of the region sometimes occur.

The vegetation of the moist subtropical climate region is forests of broadleafed and needleleafed trees. Oak, chestnut, and pine trees are commonly found in this region.

Desert and Steppe Climate Regions

Located within the western interior of the United States are two regions that have very similar climates. These climates are the **desert climate** and the **steppe climate.** The desert climate region and the steppe climate region begin just east of the west coast mountain ranges and end in the central midwest.

The desert and steppe climate regions receive the lowest amount of precipitation of any climate region of the United States. However, the steppe climate region receives slightly more precipitation than the desert climate region does. See Figure 14–18.

Figure 14–17 *Despite the harsh conditions of the desert climate of the Southwestern United States, short trees and flowering cacti are common sights.*

One reason precipitation is so low in these regions is that they are located far from the ocean sources of moist maritime air masses. In addition, high mountain ranges along the regions' western borders block most of the maritime air masses. Winter invasions of dry continental polar air masses further reduce the amount of precipitation.

Despite the harsh conditions of the desert climate, many plants—including cacti, yucca, and short trees—grow well here. The slightly higher precipitation of the steppe climate encourages the growth of short grasses and scattered forests of needleleaf evergreen trees.

DESERT AND STEPPE CLIMATES

	Summer	Winter
Average Temperature: (°C)		
Las Vegas	28.3	8.2
Pueblo	22.5	−0.3
Average Precipitation: (cm/month)		
Las Vegas	10.3	1.4
Pueblo	4.2	1.2

Figure 14–18 *The desert and steppe climates of Las Vegas, Nevada, and Pueblo, Colorado, receive the lowest amount of precipitation of any climate region of the United States. The steppe climate, however, receives slightly more precipitation than the desert climate.*

SECTION REVIEW

1. What are the major climate regions of the United States?
2. Why are summer temperatures cooler in San Francisco than in Sacramento?
3. What are three reasons for the low precipitation in desert and steppe climate regions?
4. Why do the middle and east coast portions of the United States receive more precipitation in the summer, while the west coast receives more precipitation in the winter?

Section Objective

To describe the causes of changes in climate

14–4 Changes in Climate

You know from experience that weather changes from day to day. Climates, however, seem to remain relatively unchanged. But climates do change slowly over time. In fact, the climate of a region can change from that of a temperate rain forest to that of a tropical desert within a relatively short time in the earth's history.

What causes climates to change? Scientists believe that major climate changes are caused by one or more of three natural factors. **The three factors responsible for climate changes are slow drifting of the continents, changes in the sun's energy output, and variations in the position of the earth in relation to the sun.** Some minor climate changes may be the result of changes in ocean and air currents.

As you might guess, major climate changes have a tremendous impact on the earth and the creatures that inhabit it. Major climate changes that have occurred in the past have had dramatic results on the earth: the flooding of huge land areas; the extinction of the dinosaurs; and severe personal and economic hardship for many people. Once scientists determine the cause of past climate changes, they will be better able to predict future climate changes and their effects on life on the earth.

Figure 14–19 *Most scientific evidence indicates that the white areas on this map were covered with ice during the last ice age. What is another name for an ice age?*

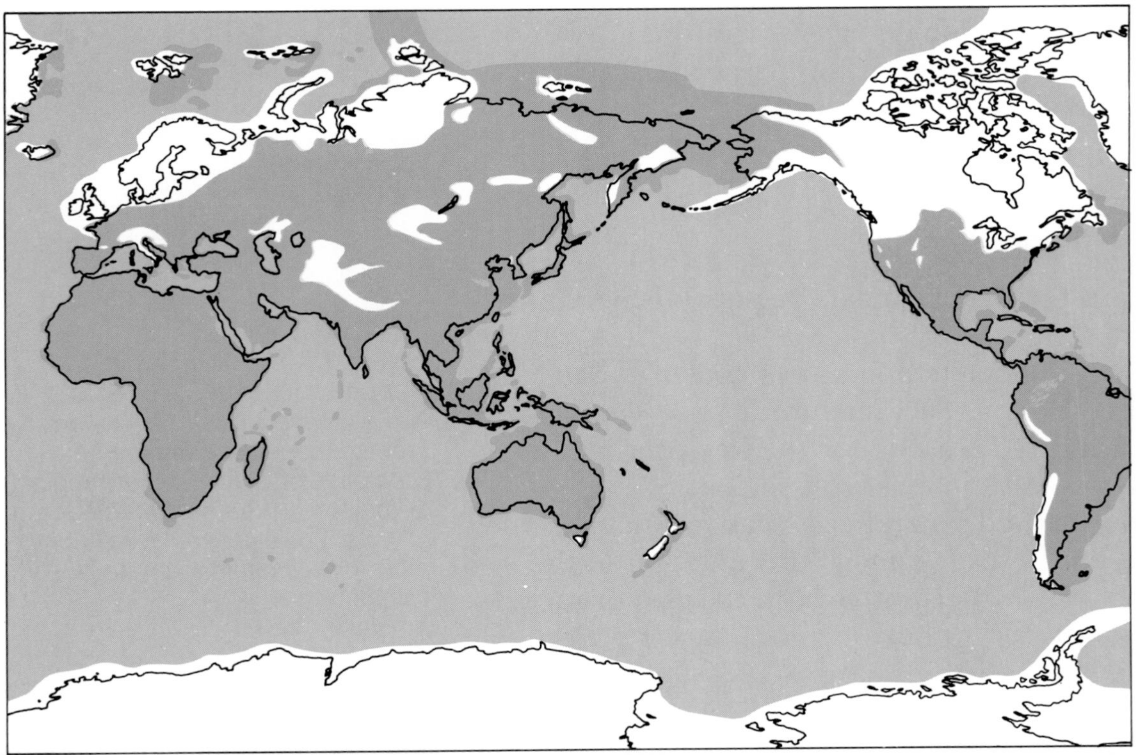

CAREER

Paleoclimatologist

HELP WANTED: PALEOCLIMATOLOGIST To study the climate from prehistoric times to the present. Graduate and undergraduate degrees must combine paleontology and meteorology. Experience in fossil study desirable.

Greenland is commonly known as a very cold place. Much of it is always frozen. Even its warmest region has summer temperatures rising no higher than 10°C. Yet fossils of palm trees and magnolia trees that were formed 80 million years ago have been discovered in Greenland. Only a warm, moist climate can support the growth of palms and magnolias. This means that 80 million years ago, the climate of Greenland was warm and moist.

Information about climates of the past comes from the study of fossils and other earth formations. Scientists who study the fossil record and other natural sources to learn about ancient climates are called **paleoclimatologists.** Their work has shown that the earth's history has included a series of major glaciations, or cold periods, falling between interglacials, or warm periods.

Paleoclimatologists study various types of records to gather information about the earth's past climates. One principle they use is that certain conditions needed by a plant or animal for survival today were also needed by that plant or animal for survival in the past. Such conditions include temperature and precipitation. So fossils from a specific time period can be evidence of what the climate was like at that time.

Anyone interested in a career in paleoclimatology should enjoy outdoor work, problem solving, and scientific study. For career information about paleoclimatology, write to the American Geological Institute, 5205 Leesburg Pike, Falls Church, VA 22041.

Ice Ages

From time to time throughout history, much of the earth's surface has been covered with enormous sheets of ice. Such periods are called **ice ages.** There is evidence that during the last two million years, there have been at least four major ice ages. Earth scientists call these ice ages **major glaciations.**

During an ice age, or major glaciation, the average temperature on the earth was about 6C° below the average temperature today. Glaciations lasted about 100,000 years or more. The most recent glaciation started about 1.75 million years ago and ended only about 10,000 years ago.

The time periods between major glaciations are called **interglacials.** Interglacials are warm periods. During an interglacial, the average temperature was about 3C° higher than the average temperature is today. During the last glaciation, a great sheet of ice moved as far south as Iowa and Nebraska. So much water was locked in the ice that average sea level rose about 85 meters when the glacier melted.

Although there are many theories about ice ages, the exact causes are not known. Many scientists believe that major glaciations are associated with gradual changes in the direction of the earth's axis and in variations in the distance between the earth and the sun.

Drifting Continents

About 230 million years ago, all the earth's landmasses were connected as one supercontinent. About 160 million years later, this supercontinent had broken apart and the different landmasses had drifted closer to their present positions.

The slow drifting apart of the continents caused worldwide climate changes. The drifting apart of the continents also caused a worldwide drop in sea level, a tremendous amount of volcanic activity, and the pushing up of much of the earth's surface. The combined effect of these occurrences was a decline in the temperature and precipitation of areas all over the world.

The climate changes caused by the drifting apart of the continents may have resulted in the extinction of the dinosaur. Dinosaurs could not adapt fast enough to these dramatic climate changes. Many of the plants the dinosaurs ate became extinct as a result of the climate changes. So the plant-eating dino-

Figure 14–20 *Climate changes caused by the drifting apart of continents may have caused the extinction of dinosaurs. As plants became extinct, plant-eating dinosaurs died out. Without these dinosaurs as a source of food, meat-eating dinosaurs also died out.*

saurs died out. Without the plant-eating dinosaurs as a food source, the meat-eating dinosaurs also died out. The theory of drifting continents and climatic change is only one explanation of dinosaur extinction. But it seems to be the most likely one.

El Niño

Ocean currents help transfer heat to the atmosphere, a process that generates global winds. The winds, in turn, help move the ocean currents. As you have already learned, ocean and wind currents have a strong influence on climate. Any major change in an ocean current can cause a change in climate.

El Niño is a warm water current that flows from west to east across the Pacific Ocean near the equator and down the west coast of South America. It strikes with little warning every two to seven years. The occurrence of El Niño brings with it dramatic changes in world climates. In 1982 and 1983, the strongest El Niño in history caused severe droughts in some regions. Other regions were subjected to unusually heavy rains and flooding. The extreme changes in climate resulted in more than 1000 deaths and much economic damage throughout the world.

Scientists have yet to discover just what causes El Niño to appear. However, important progress has been made in understanding the interaction of ocean and atmosphere. Many scientists believe that accurate predictions of future El Niños will be possible within a few years.

SECTION REVIEW

1. What factors do scientists believe may cause climate changes?
2. Describe three reasons for climate changes that have occurred in the past. What have been the effects of these climate changes?
3. How might the slow drifting of the continents have caused the extinction of the dinosaurs?
4. How might great amounts of volcanic dust in the atmosphere cause global temperature changes? Would the resulting temperatures be lower or higher than normal?

Figure 14–21 *The arrival of El Niño is unpredictable. But it usually results in surprising weather for much of the world. Such weather includes heavy rains and high waves along the California coast (above), dust storms in Australia, floods in South America, and a severe water shortage in Africa.*

Sharpen Your Skills

El Niño

Using reference materials from the library, find out about El Niño. Be sure to include information about the following topics.

1. What scientists believe may be the causes of El Niño.
2. Some of the worldwide weather changes that result from El Niño.
3. New methods of predicting El Niño.
4. The process of upwelling and its effect on ocean life in an area where it occurs.
5. The effect of El Niño on upwelling.

14 LABORATORY INVESTIGATION

Graphing Climate Characteristics

Problem

How are climate factors used to classify and compare different places in the world?

Materials *(per student)*

Graph paper, 2 sheets
Colored pencils, 3 colors

Procedure

1. Using the data in the table for average monthly rainfall in Winnipeg, Canada, construct a graph of the amount of rainfall for each month. Use the vertical axis for amount of rainfall and the horizontal axis for the months.
2. Connect the points on your graph.
3. Using the same colored pencil, construct a separate graph of average temperature for each month for Winnipeg. Use the vertical axis for average temperature and the horizontal axis for the months.
4. Connect the points on your graph.
5. Repeat steps 1 through 4 using the data for Izmir, Turkey, and Ulan Bator, Mongolia. Place the three graphs of precipitation on one sheet of graph paper and the three graphs of temperature on the other sheet. Be sure to use a different-colored pencil for each city.

Observations

1. Which city has the highest winter temperatures? The lowest?
2. Which city has the greatest range of temperature from winter to summer? Which has the smallest range?
3. Which city has the driest summer? The wettest?
4. Which city has the driest winter? The wettest?

Conclusions

1. What United States climate region is most similar to the climate of Winnipeg, Canada? Izmir, Turkey? Ulan Bator, Mongolia? Explain your answers.
2. Winnipeg is located in north-central North America. How does its climate differ from that of New York City? Why?
3. Izmir, Turkey, is located on the coast of the warm Mediterranean Sea. Compare its climate to that of San Francisco.

WINNIPEG, CANADA

Month	J	F	M	A	M	J	J	A	S	O	N	D	Year
Temperature (°C)	-18	-16	-8	3	11	17	20	19	13	6	-5	-13	3
Precipitation (cm)	2.6	2.1	2.7	3	5	8.1	6.9	7	5.5	3.7	2.9	2.2	51.7

IZMIR, TURKEY

Month	J	F	M	A	M	J	J	A	S	O	N	D	Year
Temperature (°C)	9	9	11	15	20	25	28	27	23	19	14	10	18
Precipitation (cm)	14.1	10	7.2	4.3	3.9	0.8	0.3	0.3	1.1	4.1	9.3	14.1	69.5

ULAN BATOR, MONGOLIA

Month	J	F	M	A	M	J	J	A	S	O	N	D	Year
Temperature (°C)	-26	-21	-13	-1	6	14	16	14	9	-1	-13	-22	-3
Precipitation (cm)	0.1	0.2	0.3	0.5	1	2.8	7.6	5.1	2.3	0.7	0.4	0.3	21.3

CHAPTER REVIEW

SUMMARY

14–1 What Causes Climate?

❑ Climate is determined by the two basic factors of temperature and precipitation.

❑ Temperature is influenced by latitude, altitude, and nearness to ocean currents.

❑ In general, highest temperatures occur near the equator and lowest temperatures occur near the polar regions.

❑ Temperature usually decreases as altitude increases.

❑ Areas located near cold water currents usually have cooler temperatures. Areas located near warm water currents usually have warmer temperatures.

❑ Precipitation is influenced by prevailing winds and mountain ranges.

❑ The direction and moisture content of prevailing winds is an important factor in the amount of precipitation an area receives.

❑ There are usually wet conditions on the windward side of mountains and dry conditions on the leeward side of mountains.

14–2 Climate Zones

❑ The three major climate zones on the earth are the polar, tropical, and temperate zones.

❑ Tropical deserts are usually located on the western coast of the continents. Temperate deserts are usually located farther inland.

❑ Each of the three major climate zones can have a marine climate and a continental climate.

❑ Areas with a marine climate have more moderate seasonal temperatures because nearness to oceans has a moderating effect on temperature.

❑ Areas with marine climates receive more precipitation than areas with continental climates.

14–3 Climate Regions of the United States

❑ The United States mainland can be divided into six different climate regions.

❑ Each climate region is characterized by differences in precipitation and temperature.

14–4 Changes in Climate

❑ Major climate changes may be caused by three natural factors: slow drifting of the continents, changes in the sun's energy output, and variations in the position of the earth in relation to the sun.

❑ Major glaciations have occurred alternately with interglacials throughout the earth's history.

❑ Dinosaur extinction may have been caused by worldwide climate changes resulting from the rearrangement of the continents.

❑ El Niño is a warm water current that causes climate changes.

VOCABULARY

Define each term in a complete sentence.

climate
continental climate
desert climate
El Niño
ice age
interglacial
leeward side
major glaciation
marine climate
marine west coast climate
Mediterranean climate
microclimate
moist continental climate
moist subtropical climate
polar zone
prevailing wind
steppe climate
temperate zone
tropical zone
windward side

CONTENT REVIEW: MULTIPLE CHOICE

Write the letter of the answer that best completes each statement.

1. Climate is determined by
a. temperature and pressure b. precipitation and pressure
c. temperature and cloud cover d. temperature and precipitation

2. The measure of distance north and south of the equator is called
a. altitude b. climate c. latitude d. steppes

3. In general, as altitude increases
a. temperature increases b. plant life increases
c. temperature decreases d. air pressure increases

4. A factor that affects precipitation at a particular location is
a. altitude b. ocean currents c. prevailing winds d. latitude

5. The climate zone with the coldest average temperatures is
a. tropical b. polar c. marine d. temperate

6. The climate zone with the greatest variations is the
a. polar zone b. temperate zone c. microclimate d. tropical zone

7. The southeastern part of the United States has a
a. moist subtropical climate b. moist continental climate
c. Mediterranean climate d. steppe climate

8. California has a climate of wet winters and dry summers that is called
a. marine west coast b. steppe c. Mediterranean d. moist subtropical

9. Ice ages are believed to be associated with changes in the
a. flow of rivers b. location of continents
c. earth's orbit and axis d. ocean and air currents

10. Dinosaur extinction may have resulted from changes in the
a. phases of the moon b. location of continents
c. earth's orbit and axis d. sun's energy output

CONTENT REVIEW: COMPLETION

Write the word or words that best complete each statement.

1. The average weather conditions in one place over a period of a year or longer is called __________.

2. Three factors that affect temperature are __________, __________, and __________.

3. Two factors that affect precipitation are __________ and __________.

4. Precipitation usually falls on the __________ side of a mountain.

5. There are __________ major climate zones on the earth.

6. Polar climate zones characteristically have the __________ (lowest or highest) average temperatures.

7. Tropical climate zones characteristically have the __________ (lowest or highest) average temperatures.

8. The United States mainland can be divided into __________ different climate regions.

9. Two very similar climate regions with low precipitation in the United States are __________ and __________.

10. Short warm periods between major glaciations are called __________.

CONTENT REVIEW: TRUE OR FALSE

Determine whether each statement is true or false. If it is true, write "true." If it is false, change the underlined word or words to make the statement true.

1. Climate is determined by temperature and pressure.
2. In general, areas located farther away from the equator receive a greater amount of solar energy.
3. The influence of prevailing winds helps explain why a desert can border an ocean.
4. Dry climates are usually found on the windward side of a mountain.
5. The localized climate of a backyard is called a microclimate.
6. The temperate zone extends from the pole to 60° latitude.
7. Many tropical deserts are located on the eastern coasts of continents.
8. The deserts of Arizona are found in a tropical zone.
9. The marine west coast climate of wet winters and dry summers is found along the California coast.
10. Two climate regions east of the Mississippi River are moist continental and steppe.

CONCEPT REVIEW: SKILL BUILDING

Use the skills you have developed in the chapter to complete each activity.

1. **Making predictions** If a warm ocean current flowing along a coastal area suddenly became a cold ocean current, describe what you think would happen to the climate along the coast.
2. **Analyzing data** A person is traveling up the west coast of the United States from Seattle, Washington, to Juneau, Alaska. The traveler notices that even though she has gone 1200 km to the north, the temperature has dropped only 5C°. On the same day, another person is traveling from Seattle due east over the Cascade Mountains to Spokane, Washington, a distance of only 375 km. This traveler also observes a temperature drop of 5C°. Explain why the temperature drop traveling 1200 km north was not greater than the temperature drop traveling 375 km due east.
3. **Making comparisons** What changes in climate would you expect to experience if you were to take a trip from New York to Louisiana during the summer? What if you were to take the trip during winter?
4. **Making inferences** Why does it make more sense for meteorologists to study both the minimum and maximum temperatures of deserts rather than the average temperature in order to determine climate?
5. **Applying concepts** Explain the reason for the tremendous daily temperature ranges experienced by temperate deserts.
6. **Relating concepts** The specific heat of a substance is the amount of heat needed to raise 1 gram of the substance 1C°. Water has a relatively high specific heat. Use this information to explain why nearness to large bodies of water has a moderating effect on the temperatures of certain climate regions.

CONCEPT REVIEW: ESSAY

Discuss each of the following in a brief paragraph.

1. Explain how a large body of water such as an ocean can keep a nearby landmass cool in the summer and warm in the winter.
2. Describe how latitude, altitude, ocean and air currents, prevailing winds, and mountain ranges affect climate.

Weathering and Soil

15

CHAPTER SECTIONS

15–1 Weathering
15–2 Soil Formation
15–3 Soil Composition
15–4 Soil Types

CHAPTER OBJECTIVES

After completing this chapter, you will be able to

- **15–1** Distinguish between mechanical and chemical weathering.
- **15–2** Explain how soil is formed.
- **15–3** Identify the layers of mature soil.
- **15–3** Describe the factors that influence the speed of soil formation.
- **15–4** Classify the types of soil found in the United States.

If you have ever been to the Black Hills of South Dakota, you have probably visited Mount Rushmore. Carved into a high granite cliff of this mountain are the faces of four famous presidents—George Washington, Thomas Jefferson, Abraham Lincoln, and Theodore Roosevelt. Since their completion in 1941, these carvings have attracted thousands of visitors from all over the world.

Yet several years ago, this beautiful monument was almost ruined. After forty years, the granite rock was beginning to crumble. The presidents' faces were starting to wear away. Trees and grass were even sprouting from the head of George Washington! Worst of all, large pieces of the carved rock were falling off. Can you imagine what Lincoln would look like without his nose?

Luckily, workers for the National Park Service were able to save the monument before any serious damage was done. Using plaster and metal spikes, they were able to keep the presidents' faces from crumbling. But what had caused the damage? What had made hard, solid granite crumble and crack? As you read this chapter, you will learn the answer.

This National Park Service worker is repairing damage due to weathering on the Mount Rushmore National Memorial. Look a few meters below the worker to see where he has filled a crack in President Lincoln's nose with plaster.

15–1 Weathering

Section Objective

To compare the processes of mechanical and chemical weathering

The earth's surface is constantly undergoing a natural breaking-down process. The breaking down of rocks and other materials on the earth's surface is called **weathering.** Weathering is a slow, continuous process that affects all substances exposed to the atmosphere.

You have probably seen the effects of weathering if you ever noticed peeling paint on the side of a house. Or perhaps you have noticed changes on an old brick building. New bricks have a bright red color and sharp corners and edges. The bricks of an old building are darker in color. The corners and edges are rounded. Pieces of the bricks may have broken off.

Many effects of weathering are not noticeable for many years. But sometimes you can see the short-term effects of weathering. Have you ever left a bicycle or a pair of skates outdoors for several weeks? You may have noticed that rust forms on the exposed metal parts. Rust is a result of weathering.

But weathering does not affect only building materials and metal objects. Rocks on the earth's surface also undergo weathering. Large pieces often break off the rocks. Over a long period of time, the rocks crumble and decay. You can see the results of

Figure 15–1 *Rock fragments broken up by the process of weathering often pile up at the bases of mountains to form talus slopes.*

weathering at the base of a mountain or on a mountain slope. Pieces of broken rocks pile up in these areas. These piles of rock fragments are called **talus** (TAY-luhs) **slopes.**

Rocks on the earth's surface are broken down by two types of weathering. When the forces of weathering break rocks into smaller pieces but do not change the chemical makeup of the rocks, the process is called **mechanical weathering.** When the chemical makeup of the rocks is changed, the process is called **chemical weathering.**

Mechanical Weathering

During mechanical weathering, rocks are broken into different shapes and smaller pieces. At the beginning of the weathering process, typical rock fragments are sharp and angular. As weathering continues, they become smooth and rounded. There are several different agents, or causes, of mechanical weathering. But each process results in the breaking down of rocks.

TEMPERATURE Rocks can be broken apart by changes in temperature. During the day, rocks on the earth's surface are heated by the sun's rays. The outside of the rock heats up and begins to expand. But the inside of the rock remains cool and does not expand. When the air temperature drops at night, the outside of the rock cools and contracts.

The next day, the heat from the sun causes the outside of the rock to expand again. The cycle of heating and cooling continues. The repeated changes in temperature cause particles on the surface of the rock to crack or flake off. Often the pieces break off in curved sheets or slabs parallel to the rock's surface. This type of breaking off of rock is **exfoliation** (ehks-foh-lee-AY-shuhn). Other agents of mechanical weathering also cause exfoliation.

FROST ACTION Unlike most liquids, water expands when it freezes. The repeated freezing and melting of water is a common cause of mechanical weathering. This process of weathering is called **frost action.**

Frost action occurs when water seeps into a small opening or crack in a rock. When the temperature

Sharpen Your Skills

Expanding Water

1. Fill a clear glass or plastic container about three-fourths full of water. Mark the water level on the outside of the container with a piece of tape.

2. Place the water-filled container in the freezer of a refrigerator for at least six hours.

3. Remove the container and observe the level of the ice that has formed.

Explain your observations.

Figure 15–2 *This rock's surface is cracking off in small, curved sheets. This process is called exfoliation. Why do the weather conditions of deserts cause exfoliation?*

Figure 15–3 *A cast-iron container filled with water is placed in a beaker of dry ice and alcohol (top). As the water freezes and expands, a great amount of pressure is exerted on the walls of the container, causing it to burst (bottom). With the same tremendous pressure, freezing water breaks apart rocks.*

falls below 0°C, the freezing point of water, the water in the crack freezes and expands. The crack in the rock is made larger by the pressure of the expanding water. In time, the freezing and melting of the water cause the rock to break into pieces. The cracks and potholes you see in roads or cement driveways are caused by frost action.

ORGANIC ACTIVITY Plants and animals can cause mechanical weathering. Plant roots sometimes loosen rock material. A plant growing in a crack in a rock can make the crack larger as the plant's roots grow and spread out. This type of mechanical weathering is called **root-pry.** Root-pry is an organic activity, or an activity caused by living things. How do you think people cause mechanical weathering?

GRAVITY Gravity is another agent of mechanical weathering. Sometimes gravity pulls loosened rocks down mountain cliffs in a **landslide.** A landslide is a large movement of loose rocks and soil. As the rocks fall, they collide with each other and break into smaller pieces.

ABRASION Wind-blown sand causes mechanical weathering of rocks by **abrasion** (uh-BRAY-zhuhn). Abrasion is the wearing away of rocks by solid particles carried by wind, water, or other forces. In desert regions, the wind easily picks up and moves sand particles. Sand particles have sharp edges that scrape off small pieces of exposed rocks. Over a long period of time, the abrading sand can create unusual shapes in exposed rocks. See Figure 15–5.

Water also causes abrasion of rocks. Running water such as a river carries along loose rocks and other particles. The moving rocks and particles collide, scrape against one another, and eventually

Figure 15–4 *The growing roots of plants can increase the size of cracks in rocks and eventually break pieces off the rocks. What kind of weathering is this an example of?*

Figure 15–5 *These photographs show the results of mechanical weathering. Gravity causes landslides (left). What form of mechanical weathering carved out this natural sandstone bridge (right)?*

break. In addition, the moving rocks scrape the rocks in the riverbed. This action makes the riverbed rocks very smooth.

Chemical Weathering

During chemical weathering, changes occur in the mineral composition, or chemical makeup, of rocks. Minerals are solid substances found naturally in the earth. As chemical changes take place, minerals can be added to or removed from rocks. Or the minerals in rocks can be broken down into other substances in a process called **decomposition** (dee-kahm-puh-ZIHSH-uhn). Many substances react chemically with rocks to break them down.

WATER Most chemical weathering is caused by water. Water can dissolve most of the minerals that hold rocks together. Rocks that dissolve easily in water are said to be **soluble** (SAHL-yoo-buhl).

Water can also form acids when it mixes with certain gases in the atmosphere. These acids often speed up the decomposition of rocks. Water can also combine with a mineral to form a completely different mineral. When feldspar is dissolved in water, it forms clay.

OXIDATION Chemical weathering is also caused by **oxidation** (ahk-suh-DAY-shuhn). Oxidation is the process in which oxygen chemically combines with another substance. The result of oxidation is the

Figure 15–6 *Water has dissolved solid limestone, leaving a large, deep cavern. What characteristic of limestone is indicated by this?*

Figure 15–7 *Oxidation has turned these rock layers in the Valley of Fire, Nevada, dark red-brown. What happens during oxidation?*

formation of an entirely different substance. For example, iron in rocks combines with oxygen to form iron oxide, or rust. The color of some rocks is an indication that oxidation is occurring. If oxidation is taking place, the inner material will be a different color from the outer material. What color is iron rust?

CARBONATION When carbon dioxide dissolves in water, a weak acid called carbonic acid is formed. When carbonic acid reacts chemically with other substances, the process of **carbonation** takes place.

Carbonic acid is formed when carbon dioxide in the air dissolves in rain. This slightly acidic rain falls to the ground and sinks into the soil. The carbonic acid is able to dissolve the rocks on and beneath the earth's surface. Fortunately, carbonic acid is too weak to be harmful to plants and animals. But it does slowly wear away feldspars and limestone.

SULFURIC ACID In areas where there are a great number of factories, the air can become polluted by sulfurous gas. Sulfurous gas dissolves in rain water to form sulfuric acid. Rain containing sulfuric acid is called acid rain. Sulfuric acid is a much stronger acid than carbonic acid. Sulfuric acid corrodes, or

Sharpen Your Skills

Weathering in Action

1. Place a piece of steel wool outside your house in a location where it will be exposed to the air.

2. Place another piece of steel wool in a sheltered place inside your house.

3. Examine each piece daily for one month. Record your observations.

What changes do you observe? How are the pieces different from each other? What conditions do you think contributed to these differences?

wears away, rocks, metal, and other materials very quickly. How do you think sulfuric acid affects stone monuments and buildings?

PLANT ACIDS You read before that plants can be agents of mechanical weathering. Plants can also cause chemical weathering. Plants produce weak acids that dissolve minerals in rocks.

Mosses and lichens are plants that produce weak acids. These plants often grow on rocks. As they grow, the acids they produce seep into the rocks and dissolve some of the minerals. At some point, the rocks break into smaller pieces. This process is important in the formation of soil.

Figure 15–8 *Small groups of living things called lichens produce weak acids that slowly dissolve the minerals in rocks. What process does this contribute to?*

Rate of Weathering

The rate of weathering, or how fast weathering takes place, depends on several factors. One factor is the composition of the rocks. Two different types of rock in the same climate can weather very differently depending on the minerals that make up each rock type. If the minerals in a rock resist chemical weathering, the rock is called a **stable rock.**

The stability of a rock can differ depending on the climate in which that rock is found. Limestone,

Figure 15–9 *Granite is very stable in cool climates, as shown by these cliffs in Labrador, Canada (left). But this piece of granite in a hillside in Mexico (right) has been chemically weathered. What climatic conditions cause granite to weather easily?*

for example, weathers very little in a dry, warm climate. But in a wet climate, moisture can completely dissolve limestone.

Granite is very stable in cool, dry climates. But in tropical climates, granite crumbles easily. The abundant rainfall dissolves much of the mineral feldspar, which holds granite together. The feldspar becomes loose clay, which is too weak to keep the rock from breaking apart. The more moisture there is in an area, the more quickly rocks will weather.

Air pollution also speeds up the weathering process. The burning of fossil fuels such as oil and coal releases carbon dioxide and other gases into the air. These gases combine with water in the air to form acids. In cities that have highly polluted air, the rate of weathering is increased. You can see the effects of air pollution on buildings, statues, and monuments. For example, a stone structure called Cleopatra's Needle stood for 3500 years in an Egyptian desert with little change. But after it was moved to Central Park in New York City, the monument was badly weathered by air pollution and moisture in just a few years.

Figure 15–10 *Cleopatra's Needle stood in Egypt for centuries with little damage (top). But a short time after being moved to New York City, it had been badly weathered (bottom). What caused the damage?*

The amount of time a rock is exposed on the earth's surface also affects its rate of weathering. A very old rock that has not been exposed to the various forces of weathering can remain almost unchanged. But if a newly formed rock is immediately deposited on the earth's surface, it will begin to weather right away.

The amount of exposed surface area on a rock also affects its rate of weathering. As rocks are broken down into many small pieces, more rock surfaces are exposed and more weathering takes place. In rocks with many joints or cracks, various chemicals easily come in contact with the rock surfaces and break them down.

SECTION REVIEW

1. What is weathering?
2. What is the difference between mechanical weathering and chemical weathering?
3. Which agents of mechanical and chemical weathering have more impact on soil formation in cold, dry regions? In hot, humid regions? Explain.

15–2 Soil Formation

Section Objective

To describe how soil forms

The weathering of rocks on the earth's surface forms soil. Living organisms depend on soil directly or indirectly as a source of food. Soil supplies plants with minerals and water needed for growth. Animals eat plants and other animals to obtain the materials they need to live.

Soil is formed when rocks are continuously broken down by weathering. As rocks weather, they break into smaller pieces. These pieces are broken down into even smaller pieces to form soil.

Sometimes soil remains on top of its parent rock, or the rock from which it was formed. This soil is called **residual** (rih-ZIHJ-oo-uhl) **soil.** Residual soil has a composition similar to that of the parent rock it covers. Some soil is moved away from its parent rock by water, wind, glaciers, and waves. Soil that is moved from its place of origin is called **transported soil.** Transported soil can be very different from the layer of rock it covers. In either case, the layer of rock beneath the soil is called **bedrock.**

Living organisms help form soil. Some organisms produce acids that chemically break down rocks. Certain bacteria in the soil cause the decay of dead plants and animals. Decay is the breaking down of plants and animals into the substances they are made of. This decaying material is called **humus** (HYOO-muhs). Humus is a dark-colored material

Sharpen Your Skills

Humus

1. Obtain some topsoil from a forest or grassy area or from a gardener who uses compost to enrich the soil.

2. Carefully sort through the soil or compost. Using a magnifying glass, separate the small particles of soil from the particles of decaying plants and animals.

What type of soil particles are in your topsoil? What does the soil look like?

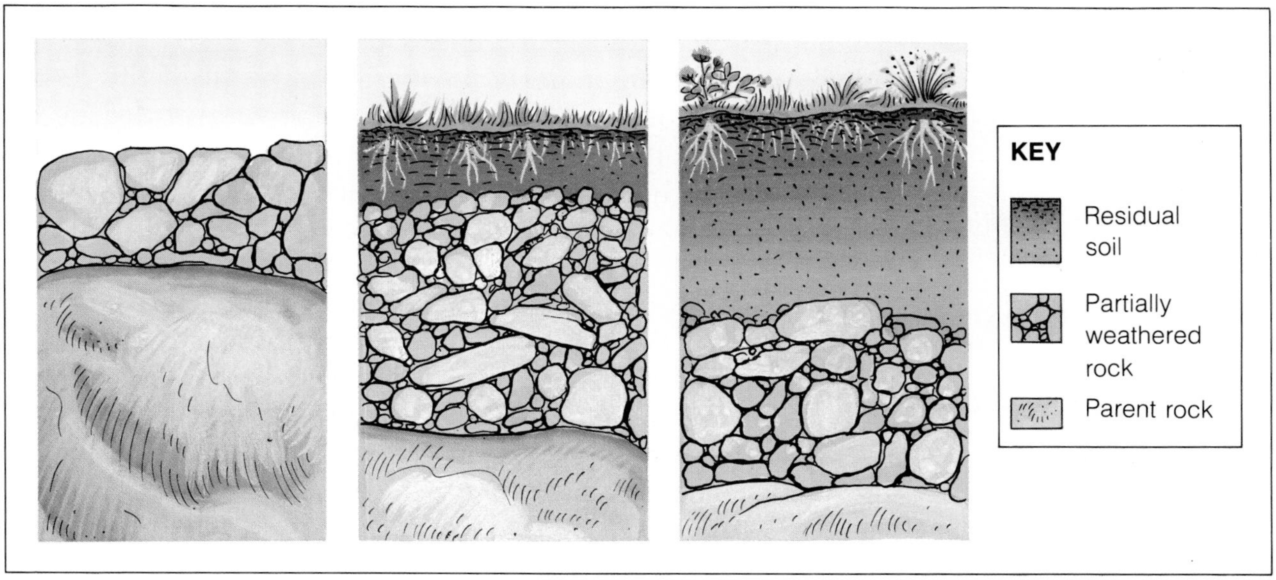

Figure 15–11 *Soil formation begins when solid parent rock is broken down into smaller pieces by weathering (left). As weathering continues, the rock is broken down further into soil particles (center). Under certain conditions, a thick layer of soil will develop above the parent rock (right).*

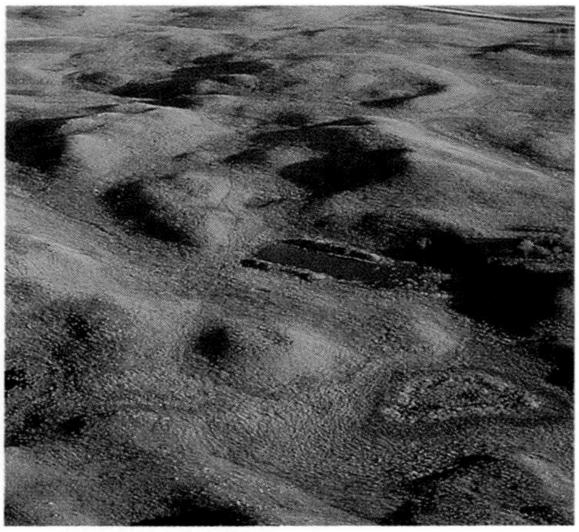

Figure 15–12 *Soil carried by glaciers is deposited in areas far from the soil's place of origin. Sometimes this soil forms hills. What would you call the soil found in these hills?*

important for the growth of plants. Some of the chemicals produced during decay speed up the breakdown of rocks into soil.

Living things such as moles, earthworms, ants, and beetles help break apart large pieces of soil as they burrow through the ground. The burrows enable water to move rapidly through the soil. The water speeds up weathering of the underlying rock.

SECTION REVIEW

1. How is soil formed?
2. What is the difference between residual soil and transported soil?
3. What is humus?

Section Objective

To identify soil layers

15–3 Soil Composition

Pieces of weathered rock and **organic material** are the two main ingredients of soil. Organic material is material that was once living or was formed by the activity of living organisms. Rock particles form more than 80 percent of soil. Air and water are also present in soil.

Clay and quartz are the most abundant minerals in soil. Because clay and quartz are very stable minerals, they exist in the greatest quantities. Potassium, phosphorus, and the nitrogen compounds called **nitrates** (NIGH-trayts) are other important minerals in soil.

Organic material in soil is the result of the decaying of dead plants and animals. As you learned earlier, this material is called humus. Humus is very rich in minerals that help plants grow.

Air and water fill the spaces between soil particles. These spaces are called **pore spaces.** Plants and animals use the water and air in these spaces, as well as the minerals dissolved in the water.

The composition of soil varies from place to place. The type of rock broken down by weathering

Figure 15–13 *The soil in the top photograph is low in organic material. How can you tell the soil in the bottom photograph is high in organic material?*

determines the kinds of minerals in the soil. For example, soil formed largely from a parent rock of limestone will be different from soil formed from a parent rock of sandstone.

The type of weathering that occurs affects the soil composition. Mechanical weathering produces soil with a composition similar to that of the rock being weathered. Chemical weathering produces soil with a composition different from that of the rock being weathered. Why?

Soil Texture

The type of weathering that occurs also affects soil **texture.** Texture refers to the size of individual soil particles. Soil particles can be large or small.

Both mechanical and chemical weathering first break rocks down into gravel. Gravel particles are between 2 and 64 millimeters in diameter. Both mechanical and chemical weathering then break gravel down into sand. Sand particles are less than 2 millimeters in diameter.

Silt is made of very small broken crystals of rock formed in the same way as sand. Silt particles are less than 1/16 of a millimeter in diameter. Clay is the only soil particle that is produced solely by chemical weathering. Clay particles are smaller than silt particles. They are the smallest particles in soil.

Soil Horizons

As soil forms, it develops separate soil layers called horizons (huh-RIGH-zuhns). Each soil **horizon** is different. Imagine making a vertical slice through these horizons. You would be able to see one horizon piled on top of another. Such a view is called a cross section. A cross section of the soil horizons is called a **soil profile.** A soil profile shows the different layers of the soil. A soil profile is shown in Figure 15–14 on page 396.

Soil that has developed three layers is called mature soil. It takes many thousands of years and the proper conditions for soil to develop three layers. Some soil contains only two layers. This soil is called immature soil. Immature soil has been more recently formed than mature soil.

Sharpen Your Skills

Rates of Weathering

1. Place an antacid tablet inside a folded piece of paper. Put on safety goggles. Carefully tap the tablet with a hammer until the tablet has broken into small pieces.

2. Place the broken tablet in a glass. Place an unbroken tablet in another glass.

3. At the same time, add 10 mL of water to both glasses. Observe both reactions until they are over. Record your observations.

What difference in the rate of reaction did you observe? What relationship can you identify between the amount of exposed surface area of the tablet and the rate of reaction? Make a hypothesis that relates this activity to the weathering process.

Sharpen Your Skills

Studying a Soil Profile

1. Using a shovel, dig down about 0.5 m and obtain a soil sample from your yard or neighborhood. Be sure not to disturb the soil sample or ground too much or you will not be able to see the different soil layers.

2. Observe the soil sample.

Answer the following questions:

a. How deep is the topsoil layer? What color is it?
b. How deep is the subsoil layer? What color is it?
c. How does the soil in the two layers differ?
d. Did you find the layer of weathered parent rock? If so, describe this layer.

The uppermost layer of mature soil is called the A horizon. The A horizon is a dark-colored soil layer in which much biological activity takes place. Bacteria, earthworms, beetles, and other organisms in this horizon constantly add to the soil through the process of decay. These organisms also break apart large pieces of soil as they burrow through the ground.

The soil in the A horizon is called **topsoil.** Topsoil is made mostly of humus and other organic materials. Humus supplies essential minerals for growing plants. Because humus is spongy, it stores water. It also contains many pore spaces through which both air and water can reach plant roots. Topsoil is the most fertile part of the soil. Plants grow well in nutrient-rich, A-horizon soil.

Water that soaks into the ground washes some minerals from the A horizon into the second layer of soil, or the B horizon. This process is called **leaching** (LEECH-ihng). The B horizon is just below the A horizon. In addition to leached-out minerals, the B horizon is made up of clay and some humus. The soil in the B horizon is called **subsoil.** Subsoil is formed very slowly. The B horizon may take more than 100,000 years to form! Why then do you think the removal of soil is of great concern to farmers?

The third layer of soil is called the C horizon. The C horizon consists of partly weathered rock. The C horizon extends down to the top of the un-

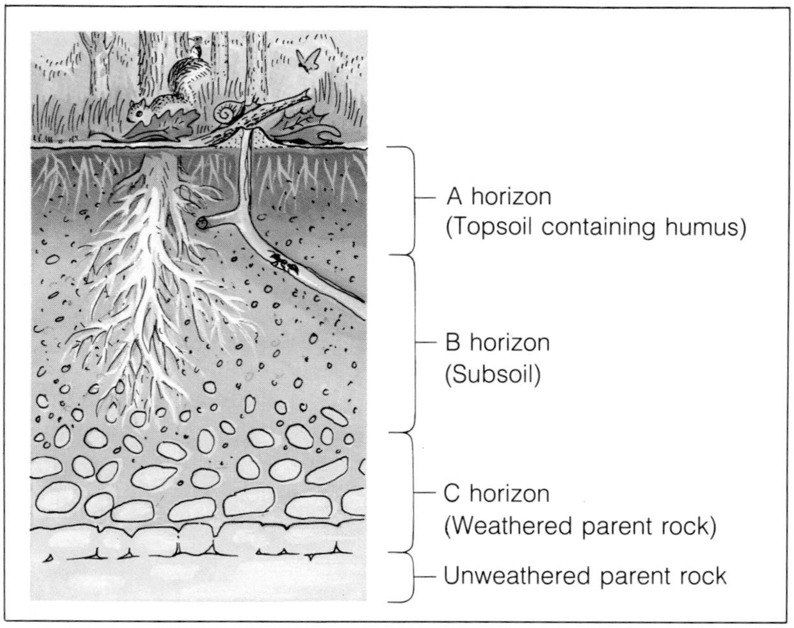

Figure 15–14 *Soil has visibly different layers, or horizons, as shown in the drawing (left) and the photograph (right). What soil horizons can you identify in the photograph?*

HELP WANTED: SOIL SCIENTIST To assist in farm planning. Bachelor's degree in geology or agronomy necessary. Outdoor and laboratory work involved.

People who study and classify soil are known as **soil scientists.** Soil scientists prepare maps of an area to show the soil types. They work with other scientists in studying the ability of different types of soil to produce certain crops, absorb pollutants, and support highways or large buildings.

Soil scientists take special courses in agronomy (uh-GRAHN-uh-mee). Agronomy is the science of crop production and soil management. Agronomists learn how soil behaves, how plants and soil interact, and how landscape features such as hills and rivers affect soil use.

To learn more about this challenging career, write to the American Society of Agronomy, 677 South Segoe Road, Madison, WI 53711.

weathered parent rock. The composition of the soil in the C horizon is similar to that of the parent rock.

Whether all three soil horizons develop depends on several factors. Time is one of the most important factors in soil formation. The longer a rock is exposed to the forces of weathering, the more it is broken down. Mature soil is formed if all three soil layers have had time to develop.

In some places, the upper layers of soil are removed, and the rocks below the soil are exposed. The weathering process then forms new soil from the exposed rocks. This recently formed soil is immature because there has not been enough time for all three soil layers to form. For example, soil in the northern regions where glacial erosion has taken place is immature soil. The glaciers that covered the area removed much of the soil from the top horizons. Since then, weathering has produced new soil.

Climate is another important factor in the formation of soil. In areas with heavy rainfall and warm temperatures, weathering takes place more rapidly. Organisms are more plentiful in the soil in these areas. They speed up the chemical and mechanical weathering of rocks. Heavy rainfall in tropical regions of the world washes much of the topsoil away. But because many plants and animals live in this climate, soil that is washed away is replaced quickly.

Figure 15–15 *Heavy rainfall can wash away loose topsoil. This can prevent all three soil horizons from forming. What type of soil would heavy rainfall produce?*

The type of rock in an area also affects soil formation. Some rocks do not weather as rapidly as others. Rocks that do not break down easily do not form soil rapidly. In some climates it takes a long time for granite to break down. So soil formation from granite in these climates is relatively slow. But sandstone breaks and crumbles into sand very quickly. Soil formation from the weathering of sandstone is rapid.

The surface features of the region also determine the speed at which soil is formed. On very steep slopes, rainwater drains rapidly. The rainwater does not have a chance to sink into the soil layers, so little weathering takes place.

SECTION REVIEW

1. What are the two most abundant minerals in soil?
2. What two factors affect soil composition?
3. Describe a typical soil profile.

Section Objective

To relate soil types and location

15–4 Soil Types

There are many different types of soil on the earth. The amount and type of soil formed varies from one region to another. In the United States, there are six major types of soil. As you have learned, soil type depends a great deal on the environment in which it is formed. **Geologists classify soil according to its composition and the region in which it formed.**

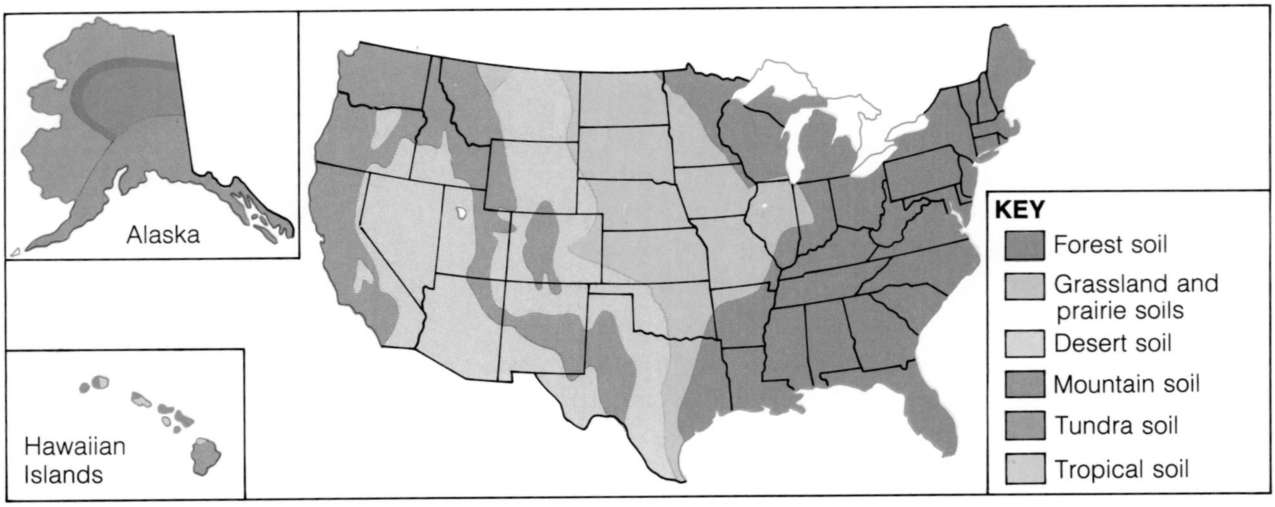

Figure 15–16 *The six soil types found in the United States are shown on this map. What is the soil type where you live?*

Figure 15–17 *The trees in this northeastern forest help to form topsoil. How?* Eric Gordon

Forest Soil

The eastern United States is covered with **forest soil.** In the Northeast, the forest soil is grayish brown in color. In the Southeast, the forest soil is reddish due to the presence of iron. Although forest soil forms under a cover of leaves and other plant remains, it contains very little humus. Heavy rainfall causes the leaching out of most of the minerals in the soil. The topsoil is very thin.

The southeastern forest soil is slightly more fertile than the northeastern forest soil. The warmer southern climate causes the organic matter to decay more quickly. So more minerals are able to enter the topsoil before being leached out.

Certain crops grow well in forest soil. Cranberries and blueberries are two of the crops that can be grown in this soil. But forest soil often needs to be fertilized before it can be farmed.

Grassland and Prairie Soils

The part of the United States from the Rocky Mountains to the eastern forest region is covered with **grassland** and **prairie soils.** Grassland and prairie soils are rich in humus and receive abundant rainfall. For these reasons, the grassland and prairie soil regions are very fertile and are excellent for growing crops.

Sharpen Your Skills

Farming Areas

Draw an outline map of the United States. Label each state. Make a key for your map, giving a symbol to each of the following types of farms in the United States:

- vegetable farm
- potato farm
- fruit/nut farm
- dairy farm
- cattle/sheep farm
- wheat farm

Find out where these farms are located in the United States and place their symbols on the map in the correct places. Using the soil map in your textbook and reference materials from the library, find out why each type of farm is suited to its location.

Figure 15–18 *Flat, grassy prairie soil regions, such as the one in this photograph, are used for grazing cows. What else might this land be used for?*

In grassland soil regions, wheat, barley, and rye are the major crops grown. The major crop grown in prairie soil is corn. The cornbelt of the United States is a prairie soil region. In addition to corn, other important crops, such as wheat and soybeans, are grown in prairie soil. Hogs and cattle are raised in this region as well.

Desert Soil

The dry regions of the western United States contain **desert soil.** Because water in these regions is limited, leaching does not occur. So desert soil contains a large quantity of minerals. But since water is not present, desert soil is not good for growing plants. Desert soil has little topsoil and few plants can grow in it.

Desert soil regions are used for raising sheep, goats, and cattle. Crops can only be grown in these regions if **irrigation** (ir-uh-GAY-shuhn) is used. Irrigation is the process of supplying land with water through artificial canals or sprinkler systems.

Mountain Soil

Figure 15–19 *Although desert regions are not ideal for plant growth, certain colorful flowers are able to bloom in thin desert topsoil. What must be done before this land can be used for farming?*

Soil on the slopes of mountains, such as those in the western United States, is called **mountain soil.** Mountain soil is a dry soil made of jagged pieces of rocks. It also contains very small amounts of clay and sand. Mountain soil often contains no topsoil. Most of the topsoil is washed down the mountain by rain or pulled down the mountain in landslides. So mountain soil, which is immature, consists mainly of weathered bedrock.

The higher mountain ranges are not used for growing crops. The soil in these regions is not very deep or fertile. But there are large deposits of metallic ores. Copper, silver, lead, and zinc can be found in the Rocky Mountains.

Tundra Soil

Only certain parts of the polar regions have soil. The soil in these regions is called **tundra soil.** The only place in the United States that has tundra soil is Alaska. Barren rock surfaces are common in tundra soil regions. Weathering of parent rock takes

Figure 15–20 *In arctic regions, thin tundra soil and cold temperatures allow only small plants to grow (left). In mountain regions, few plants are able to grow (right). Why?*

place very slowly in these regions. Tundra soil has peat on the surface and very limited subsoil. Peat is made of decayed plant fibers.

Small plants called lichens grow on the rocks and small trees in this area and provide food for the animals. Other plants do not grow well in this region because of the cold temperatures and thin soil. People who live in tundra soil regions must depend on animals for food.

Tropical Soil

Tropical soil is found in only one part of the United States—the rain forests of Hawaii. Tropical soil forms in very warm, humid climates.

The heat and excessive rain in the tropical forests cause plant and animal matter to decay rapidly. But this material does not form a thick layer of humus. The heavy rainfall leaches most minerals far down into the soil. And it also washes away most of the humus layer. Fortunately, the abundant plant and animal life quickly replaces the humus. The minerals needed to keep the rain forest growing are continuously replaced.

Figure 15–21 *Decay of the abundant plant and animal life of tropical forests continuously forms soil. Why, then, is the humus layer of tropical soil so thin?*

SECTION REVIEW

1. How do geologists classify soil types?
2. What are the six soil types found in the United States?

15 LABORATORY INVESTIGATION

The Effect of Chemical Weathering on Rocks

Problem

What types of rocks are affected by carbonated water—a form of carbonic acid?

Materials *(per group)*

2 fragments of each of the following rocks: limestone, marble, granite, sandstone
8 baby food jars
Carbonated water
Tap water
Masking tape

Procedure

1. Fill four baby food jars three-fourths full of carbonated water. Fill the remaining four baby food jars three-fourths full of tap water. Carefully place the jars on top of your desk.
2. Using masking tape, label the jars: limestone and carbonated water, limestone and tap water, marble and carbonated water, marble and tap water, granite and carbonated water, granite and tap water, sandstone and carbonated water, sandstone and tap water.
3. Place the appropriate rock fragment into each labeled jar.
4. Observe the effects of carbonated water and tap water on each rock fragment. Record your observations in a chart similar to the one on this page.
5. Continue to observe. After 20 minutes, record your observations again.
6. Let the jars stand overnight. Observe them the next day. Record any changes in the rock fragments.

Observations

1. Compare the effect of the carbonated water on each of the rock samples with the effect of the tap water.
2. Which samples show that a change has taken place in the rock?

Conclusions

1. What evidence supports the idea that a chemical change has occurred?
2. Relate elapsed time to the rate of chemical change.
3. How does carbonic acid affect rocks?

Rock	Carbonated Water			Tap Water		
	Initial	*20 min*	*24 hr*	*Initial*	*20 min*	*24 hr*
Limestone						
Marble						
Granite						
Sandstone						

CHAPTER REVIEW

SUMMARY

15–1 Weathering

- The earth's surface is constantly undergoing a natural breaking-down process called weathering.
- Mechanical weathering causes rocks to be broken into smaller pieces, but the chemical makeup of the rocks is not changed.
- The agents of mechanical weathering are temperature, frost action, organic activity, gravity, and abrasion.
- Chemical weathering causes a change in the mineral composition of rocks.
- Chemical weathering is caused by water, oxidation, carbonation, sulfuric acid, and plant acids.
- The rate of weathering depends on the composition of the rock, the amount of time the rock is exposed on the earth's surface, and the amount of exposed surface area on the rock.

15–2 Soil Formation

- Soil is formed when rocks are continuously broken down by weathering.
- Soil forms above a layer of solid rock called bedrock.
- Residual soil remains on top of its parent rock. Transported soil is moved from its place of origin.
- Humus is the material formed from the decay of plants and animals.

15–3 Soil Composition

- The two main ingredients of soil are pieces of weathered rock and organic material.
- Air and water fill the pore spaces between soil particles.
- The type of rock broken down by weathering determines the kinds of minerals in the soil.
- As soil forms, it develops separate layers, or horizons. A cross section of the soil horizons is called a soil profile.
- A typical soil profile has an A horizon, or topsoil, a B horizon, or subsoil, and a C horizon.

15–4 Soil Types

- Geologists classify soil according to its composition and the region in which it formed.
- The six major types of soil in the United States are forest, grassland and prairie, desert, mountain, tundra, and tropical.

VOCABULARY

Define each term in a complete sentence.

abrasion
bedrock
carbonation
chemical weathering
decomposition
desert soil
exfoliation
forest soil
frost action
grassland soil
horizon
humus
irrigation
landslide
leaching
mechanical weathering
mountain soil
nitrate
organic material
oxidation
pore space
prairie soil
residual soil
root-pry
soil profile
soluble
stable rock
subsoil
talus slope
texture
topsoil
transported soil
tropical soil
tundra soil
weathering

CONTENT REVIEW: MULTIPLE CHOICE

Choose the letter of the answer that best completes each sentence.

1. Piles of rock fragments at the base of a mountain or on a mountain slope are curved
a. talus slopes b. profiles c. landslides d. humus

2. The breaking off of rock pieces in curved sheets parallel to the rock's surface is
a. oxidation b. carbonation c. root-pry d. exfoliation

3. Rocks can be broken apart by
a. organic activity b. root-pry c. frost action d. all of these

4. The wearing away of rocks by solid particles carried by wind, water, and other forces is called
a. exfoliation b. abrasion c. oxidation d. gravity

5. Most chemical weathering is caused by
a. air pollution b. water c. sulfuric acid d. nitrates

6. If the minerals in a rock enable the rock to resist chemical weathering, the rock is described as
a. stable b. soluble c. organic d. residual

7. The solid rock layer beneath the soil is called
a. transported soil b. bedrock c. subsoil d. residual rock

8. The decayed parts of plants and animals in soil is called
a. humus b. topsoil c. residual soil d. mature soil

9. The size of individual soil particles is called soil
a. profile b. horizon c. texture d. porosity

10. Most of the northeastern and southeastern United States is covered with
a. prairie soil b. tundra soil c. desert soil d. forest soil

CONTENT REVIEW: COMPLETION

Fill in the word or words that best complete each sentence.

1. The breaking down of rocks and other materials on the earth's surface is called ________________.

2. The wearing away of rocks by the repeated freezing and melting of water is called ________________.

3. Mechanical weathering in which plant roots grow in cracks in a rock and loosen rock material is called ________________.

4. The chemical breakdown of minerals in rocks is called ________________.

5. A rock that dissolves easily in water is said to be ________________.

6. The process in which oxygen chemically combines with another substance is called ________________.

7. Weathering is helpful when it causes rocks to break down and form ________________.

8. Material that was once living or that was formed by the activity of living organisms is called ________________ material.

9. The process in which water washes minerals from one soil horizon to another is called ________________.

10. The process of supplying land with water through artificial canals or sprinkler systems is called ________________.

CONTENT REVIEW: TRUE OR FALSE

Determine whether each statement is true or false. If it is true, write "true." If it is false, change the underlined word or words to make the statement true.

1. When gravity pulls loosened rocks down mountain cliffs, a landslide results.
2. When weathering changes the chemical makeup of rocks, the process is called mechanical weathering.
3. A rock that dissolves easily in water is said to be stable.
4. Rain containing sulfuric acid is known as acid rain.
5. Air pollution slows down the weathering process.
6. Transported soil has a composition similar to that of the bedrock it covers.
7. Clay and quartz are the most abundant minerals in the soil.
8. The largest particles found in soil are silt.
9. The soil in the B horizon is called topsoil.
10. Soil is classified according to its composition and the region in which it formed.

CONCEPT REVIEW: SKILL BUILDING

Use the skills you have developed in the chapter to complete each activity.

1. **Analyzing data** In an experiment to measure soil's ability to hold water, particle size and amount of humus were tested. The data table below shows the results.

   Construct a graph that represents the relationship between the amount of water retained and the size of the soil particles. Your graph should have two lines. Label each line appropriately as either "Without Humus" or "With Humus."

   Based on your graph, describe a type of soil that would supply water for plant roots during a period of little rainfall.
2. **Applying concepts** Why would frost action not be a major cause of weathering in the polar regions?
3. **Making inferences** How would you determine whether a soil was formed by mechanical or chemical weathering?
4. **Making predictions** Predict what would happen if you rubbed a piece of granite with sandpaper. If you rubbed a piece of sandstone. What type of weathering is simulated in this activity?

	Small Particles		**Medium Particles**		**Large Particles**	
	With humus	*Without humus*	*With humus*	*Without humus*	*With humus*	*Without humus*
Water retained by soil	50.0 mL	20.8 mL	44.6 mL	13.6 mL	39.8 mL	10.2 mL

CONCEPT REVIEW: ESSAY

Discuss each of the following in a brief paragraph.

1. What is the difference between mechanical weathering and chemical weathering?
2. How is the weathering of rocks helpful to life on the earth?

Erosion and Deposition

16

CHAPTER SECTIONS

16–1 Changing the Earth's Surface
16–2 Gravity
16–3 Wind
16–4 Running Water
16–5 Glaciers
16–6 Waves

CHAPTER OBJECTIVES

After completing this chapter, you will be able to

16–1 Define erosion and deposition.

16–2 Describe the types of erosion caused by gravity.

16–3 Identify the effects of wind erosion and deposition.

16–4 Explain why running water is the major cause of erosion.

16–5 Distinguish among the different features of glacial deposition.

16–6 Describe the changes in the appearance of the earth's surface caused by waves.

To the people of the Huaylas Valley, the huge mass of ice and snow perched on the steep northwest face of Peru's highest peak was a familiar sight. Tending their flocks of sheep on the lower slopes or raising fruit, grain, and vegetables in the fertile soil along the Santa River, the people hardly took notice of the glacier. It had been there for as long as they could remember—creeping forward when fed by winter snows and shrinking back when warmed by summer temperatures. For this glacier, recently named Glacier 511 by Peruvian geologists, was one of the hundreds that dotted the Andes Mountains.

Then at 6:13 P.M. on January 10, 1962, Glacier 511 stirred and a great mass of ice suddenly lurched into motion. Why the sleeping glacier awoke, no one knew. But its movement spelled disaster for the people in the valley below.

The mass of ice that had broken loose from the glacier was about 182 meters long and nearly 1 kilometer wide. As it hurtled down the cliff, it picked up tons of rock material. It plowed up chunks of granite as big as houses. It swept up everything in its path: topsoil, trees, grazing sheep and llamas. Finally, it roared down on the inhabitants who had until then paid little attention to Glacier 511.

Within 8 minutes, the wall of ice, snow, rock, and mud had covered a distance of 16 kilometers and buried an estimated 4000 people from nine villages. It had demonstrated the awesome power of moving ice.

Glaciers, along with winds, waves, running water, and gravity, constantly reshape the earth's surface. In this chapter, you will learn about the harmful and helpful effects of these powerful forces of nature.

A glacier, similar to Glacier 511, sits peacefully above a village in the Huaylas Valley of Peru.

16–1 Changing the Earth's Surface

Section Objective

To identify the agents of erosion and relate erosion and deposition to the earth's changing surface

Millions of years ago, a large river flowed slowly across a broad, flat area in present-day Arizona. If you were to visit this area today, you would see a huge gorge called the Grand Canyon. The Grand Canyon is one of the seven natural wonders of the world. It was formed by one of the many natural processes that are constantly changing the surface of the earth.

The Grand Canyon was carved out of the earth by **erosion** (ih-ROH-zhuhn). Erosion is the process by which weathered rock and soil particles are moved from one place to another. In Chapter 15, you learned that weathering is the breaking down of rocks and other materials on the earth's surface. Erosion carries away the products of weathering.

Rock and soil particles carried away by erosion are deposited in other places. Over time, these materials build up to make new landforms. The process by which sediments are laid down in new locations is called **deposition** (dehp-uh-ZIHSH-uhn). Both erosion and deposition change the shape of the earth's surface. Erosion moves materials from place to place. Deposition builds new landforms. Weather-

Figure 16–1 *The fantastic rock formations of the Grand Canyon have been formed by erosion. For millions of years, the Colorado River has carved a huge gorge out of a once broad, flat area of the earth's surface.*

ing, erosion, and deposition form a cycle of forces that wear down and build up the earth's surface.

Erosion can be caused by gravity, wind, running water, glaciers, and waves. These are the five agents of erosion. An agent of erosion is a material or force that moves sediments from place to place.

SECTION REVIEW

1. What is erosion? How does it change the earth's surface?
2. What is deposition? How does it change the earth's surface?
3. List the five agents of erosion.

16–2 Gravity

Section Objective

To describe the types of mass wasting caused by gravity

Gravity pulls rocks and soil down slopes. The downhill movement of sediments caused by gravity is called **mass wasting.** Mass wasting can occur rapidly or slowly. In either case, sediments come to rest at the bottom of a slope in a formation called a talus slope.

One example of rapid mass wasting is a landslide. A landslide is the tumbling of soil, rocks, and boulders down a slope. A landslide can be caused by an earthquake, a volcanic eruption, or the weakening of supporting rocks as a result of heavy rain. Once a landslide begins, it can move millions of metric tons of rocks down a slope and cause tremendous damage.

A mudflow is another example of rapid mass wasting. A mudflow usually occurs after a heavy rain. The rain mixes with the soil to form mud. The mud begins to move downhill. As it does, it picks up more soil and becomes thicker. A mudflow can move almost anything in its path—including boulders and houses!

Sometimes a huge block of rock will slide rapidly down a slope. This type of mass wasting is called

Figure 16–2 *Heavy rains or earthquakes can cause a landslide by loosening rocks and soil along a steep slope (top). If weak layers of rock suddenly slip down a slope leaving a curved scar, slump occurs (bottom). What type of mass wasting is involved in landslides and slump?*

Figure 16–3 *Soil creep, the slowest downhill movement of soil particles, is often difficult to recognize. But tilted trees and telephone poles usually indicate soil creep is occurring.*

slump. Slump occurs when rock resistant to weathering lies on a layer of weak rock. The weak rock begins to slip down the slope, and the entire block of rock breaks off and slides downhill.

Earthflows and soil creep are two examples of slow mass wasting. An earthflow usually occurs after heavy rain. A mass of soil and plant life slowly moves down a slope. Soil creep is the slowest kind of mass wasting. Alternating periods of freezing and thawing, animal activity, or water movement disturb the soil particles. As the particles begin to move, gravity pulls them slowly downhill.

SECTION REVIEW

1. What is mass wasting?
2. What are two examples of rapid mass wasting?
3. What are two examples of slow mass wasting?

16–3 Wind

Section Objective

To identify the types of wind erosion and deposition

Wind is the most active agent of erosion in deserts, plowed fields, and on beaches. In these regions, loose material is exposed at the earth's surface. The material is picked up and carried by wind.

Sharpen Your Skills

The Dust Bowl

During the 1930s, a severe drought in the southwestern United States created the Dust Bowl. Using reference books in the library, find out about the Dust Bowl. Write a report in which you answer the following questions:

1. What states were located in the Dust Bowl?
2. What caused the Dust Bowl?
3. What effect did the dust have on the soil, crops, and farms in the area?
4. What measures have farmers in the area taken to prevent a new dust bowl from forming?

Types of Wind Erosion

Wind erodes the earth's surface in two ways. Wind removes loose material such as clay, silt, dust, and sand from the land. This type of wind erosion is called deflation (dih-FLAY-shuhn). Fine particles are carried many meters up in the air. Larger particles rise only a few centimeters.

As the wind blows, the larger particles roll or bounce along the ground. These particles slowly wear away exposed rocks. The particles often act like a sandblaster, cutting and polishing rocks. This type of wind erosion is called abrasion. The rock particles worn away by abrasion are carried away by the wind.

The amount of erosion caused by wind depends on the size of the particles being carried, the speed of the wind, and the length of time the wind blows.

Figure 16–4 *Wind erosion created these beautiful caves in Antelope Canyon, Arizona (top). An oasis, or fertile area within a desert, forms when wind erodes desert sand to a depth where water is present (bottom). What type of wind erosion forms an oasis?*

It also depends on the resistance of the rocks exposed to the wind.

In many desert regions, wind erosion forms wind caves by wearing away less resistant material. Sometimes wind erodes desert sand down to a depth where water is present. With water available, trees, shrubs, and grasses grow. A green, fertile area within a desert, called an oasis (oh-AY-suhs), forms.

Deposits by Wind

The amount of rock and soil particles carried by wind depends on the speed of the wind. The faster the wind blows, the more particles it can carry. The slower the wind blows, the fewer particles it can carry. As the speed of the wind decreases, the particles it can no longer carry are deposited.

DUNES In desert areas and along shorelines, windblown sand is often deposited near rocks and bushes. Wind blowing over these deposits is slowed down. More sand is deposited. The mounds of sand continue to grow and form **sand dunes.** A sand dune is a mound of sand deposited by wind.

Figure 16–5 *Sand dunes have many different shapes depending on location, amount of available sand, and wind direction and strength.*

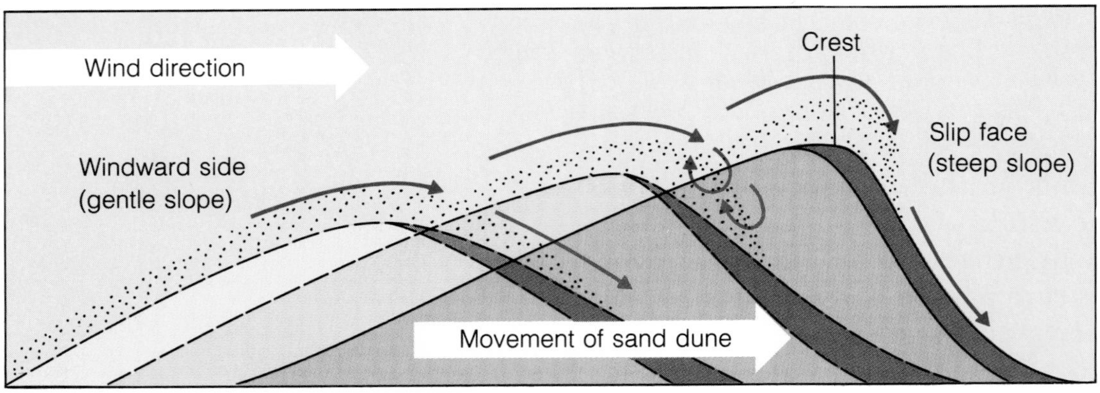

Figure 16–6 *A sand dune forms as material carried by the wind moves up the gentle slope, or windward side, of the dune and accumulates at the crest. Then this material moves down the steep slope, or slip face, of the dune and forms a series of layers. In this same way, a sand dune moves across the area where it forms. On what side of the dune does erosion take place? Deposition?*

Sand dunes vary in size. They also have many different shapes. Figure 16–6 shows the formation of a sand dune. The side of the dune facing the wind has a gentle slope. Sand is carried up the gentle slope, or windward side, to the crest, or top of the dune. At the crest, the sand is dropped by the wind. The sand slides down the other side. This side of the dune, the slip face, has a steep slope.

As the wind blows, sand dunes move across the areas where they form. They move in the direction that the wind is blowing. A sand dune moves by being eroded on one side and built up on the other side. Sometimes moving sand dunes cover buildings, farmlands, and trees.

LOESS Some very fine particles of sand and silt are not deposited in dunes. Instead, they are deposited by the wind many kilometers from where they were picked up. When many layers of fine sand and silt are deposited in the same area, **loess** (LOH-ehs) is formed. Loess deposits are very fertile.

Figure 16–7 *This loess deposit is a nearly vertical cliff of sand and silt. Does a loess deposit show any visible layers?*

Deposits of loess are light in color and may be many meters thick. Loess deposits are found near the northern and central parts of the Mississippi River valley. They are also found in northeast China. Large dust storms in the Gobi desert in Asia have formed loess deposits hundreds of meters thick.

A windbreak is often used to decrease wind erosion and aid in wind deposition. A windbreak is a barrier that causes the wind to slow down. When wind speed is decreased, the load carried by the wind is dropped. Fences are often used as windbreaks. So are plants. Many farmers surround their fields with bushes and trees to help stop wind erosion. Why are windbreaks important to farmers?

SECTION REVIEW

1. How are deflation and abrasion different?
2. What four factors determine the amount of erosion caused by wind?
3. What are two deposits caused by wind?
4. Why are windbreaks important?

16–4 Running Water

Section Objective

To describe running water as an agent of erosion

Running water is the major cause of erosion. From gently falling raindrops to rushing rivers, running water changes more of the earth's surface than any other agent of erosion.

Rivers, streams, and runoff are forms of running water. Runoff is water that flows over the earth's surface, usually after a rainfall or spring thaw. Runoff flows into streams and rivers.

Runoff and Erosion

When rain falls on the surface of the earth, three things can happen to the water. The rain can evaporate, it can sink into the ground, or it can flow over the land surface as runoff.

When water moves across the earth's surface as runoff, it picks up and carries particles of clay, sand, and gravel. Because of gravity, the water and sediments usually move downhill. As the water and sediments run downhill, they cut into the soil and form many tiny grooves called rills. As erosion continues, the rills become wider and deeper. They form gullies. Gullies act as channels for runoff. You may have seen gullies on slopes alongside highways. Where else might you see gullies caused by erosion?

The amount of runoff is affected by several factors. One factor is the amount of rainfall in an area. In areas with a high average rainfall, there is a lot of runoff. Runoff also increases during periods of heavy rain. When there is a great deal of runoff, there is a great deal of erosion.

The amount of runoff is also affected by the amount of plant growth in an area. Plant roots hold soil particles in place. The soil absorbs some of the water. The plant roots also absorb some of the

Figure 16–8 *This gorge in Taiwan was carved out of the earth's surface by the powerful force of running water.*

Sharpen Your Skills

Observing Local Erosion

After a heavy rain, take a walk around your school grounds or an area near your home. Answer the following questions:

1. Where is erosion taking place?
2. Why is erosion taking place?
3. What materials are being carried away?
4. Where are these materials being deposited?

water. Areas with little plant growth have greater runoff and greater erosion. Soil with little plant life can be easily washed away since there are few roots holding the soil in place.

The shape of the land also affects the amount of runoff. Areas that have steep slopes have the greatest amount of runoff. The water moves too fast to soak into the ground. As the water flows rapidly downhill, a great deal of erosion takes place. If land surfaces have adequate plant life and are properly cared for, little erosion will occur. Why is it important to control runoff?

Streams and Erosion

Gullies formed by runoff are actually tiny stream valleys. When runoff from several gullies merges, a larger stream is formed.

Streams are important agents of erosion because they carry large amounts of sediments. The soil particles and rock materials carried by a stream are called the stream's **load.** Large and fast-moving streams can carry large loads.

Sediments in a stream's load are transported in different ways. Large, heavy sediments are pushed or rolled downstream. Pebbles and boulders are moved in this way. Lighter sediments, such as silt or mud, are picked up and carried along by the force of the moving water. Still other sediments, such as salts, dissolve in the stream water.

Streams cause erosion by abrasion. Sediments carried by streams constantly collide with rocks, chipping away pieces and wearing down the rocks.

Sometimes the layers of rocks beneath a stream are eroded by abrasion. If the stream flows first over hard rock layers and then over soft rock layers, a waterfall will form. Abrasion wears away the soft rocks faster than the hard rocks. In time, the level of the stream flowing over the soft rocks is lower than the level of the stream flowing over the hard rocks. A waterfall results.

Figure 16–9 *As abrasion wears away underlying rock unevenly, a waterfall forms.*

Development of a River System

As you read, runoff forms rills. The rills deepen and widen to form gullies. Gullies then join to form streams. Finally, streams join to form rivers. Rivers

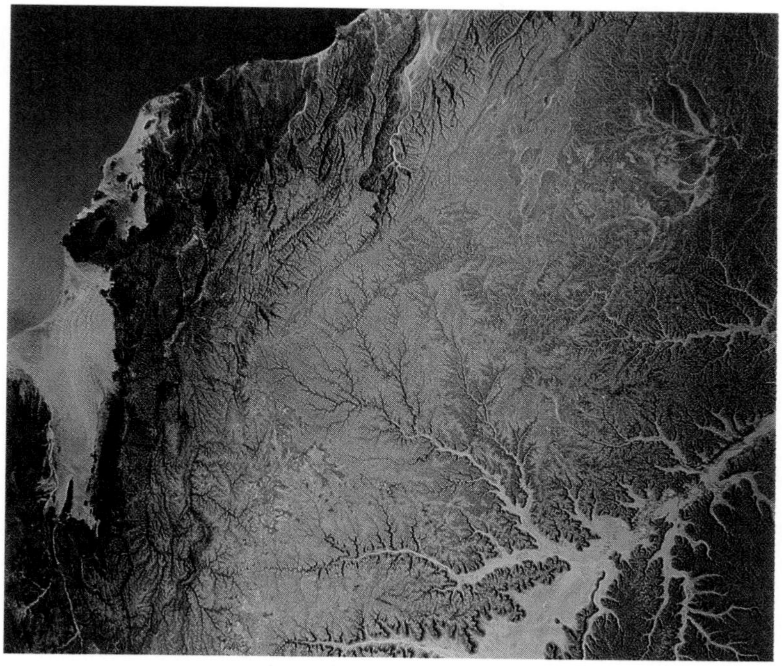

Figure 16–10 *The branching pattern of a drainage system can be seen in this aerial photograph. What does the branching system resemble?*

usually begin in mountains or hills. The downward pull of gravity gives them energy to cut away the land and form valleys. Rivers are important agents of erosion because they affect a large area.

The network of rills, gullies, and streams that forms a river is called a **drainage system.** You can compare the pattern of channels in a drainage system to the pattern of branches on a tree. The small twigs of a tree that grow from small branches are like the rills and gullies that join to form streams. The small branches are connected to larger branches just as the small streams flow into larger streams. These larger streams are called **tributaries** (TRIHB-yoo-tehr-eez). The tributaries flow into the main river just as the larger branches are joined to the trunk of the tree. The main river is like the tree trunk. In time, the main river empties into another river, a lake, or an ocean at a place called the mouth of the river.

The area drained by a main river and its channels is called a **drainage basin.** The land that separates one drainage basin from another is called a divide. One of the largest divides is the Continental Divide, located about 80 kilometers west of Denver, Colorado. The Continental Divide is a continuous line that runs north and south the length of North America. West of the divide, all water flows eventually to the Pacific Ocean. East of the divide, all water flows eventually to the Atlantic Ocean.

Sharpen Your Skills

Running Water and Erosion

1. After a heavy rain, collect a sample of runoff in a clear plastic or glass container.

2. Let the water stand for about 10 minutes.

3. Observe the bottom of the container for sediments carried by the runoff.

4. Collect and observe samples from several other areas.

Are there any differences in the samples? Was the runoff from one particular area carrying more sediments than the runoff from other areas? Explain your answer.

A divide starts off as a wide area. But as the drainage system of a river develops, the divide becomes narrower. Sometimes a drainage system will cut through its divide and steal runoff from another drainage basin.

A drainage system grows larger by deepening its channels, widening its valleys, and adding more rills and gullies to its system. The river grows larger and faster, and the river valley grows deeper and wider. In time, the river reaches a balance between the processes of erosion and deposition.

Life Cycle of a River

An **immature river,** or young river, is a river in an early stage of development. An immature river cuts a valley with steep sides in the earth's surface. The valley is typically V-shaped, and the river covers almost the entire valley floor. The waters of an immature river flow very rapidly over rocks, producing rapids. Waterfalls are also commonly found in immature rivers. These rivers erode the surrounding areas very rapidly. What size particles do you think an immature river is able to carry?

A river that has been developing for many thousands of years is called a **mature river.** Because of continued erosion, the rapids and waterfalls have largely disappeared. The river has also eroded

Figure 16–11 *The Yellowstone River is an example of an immature river (left). The Nenana River is an example of a mature river (right). How are these two rivers different?*

much of the valley floor. The valley walls are far from the river itself. The floor of the valley is broad and flat. The course of the river has also become curved and winding, forming loops called **meanders** (mee-AN-derz). The river has slowed down, so erosion has slowed down. What size particles do you think a mature river is able to carry?

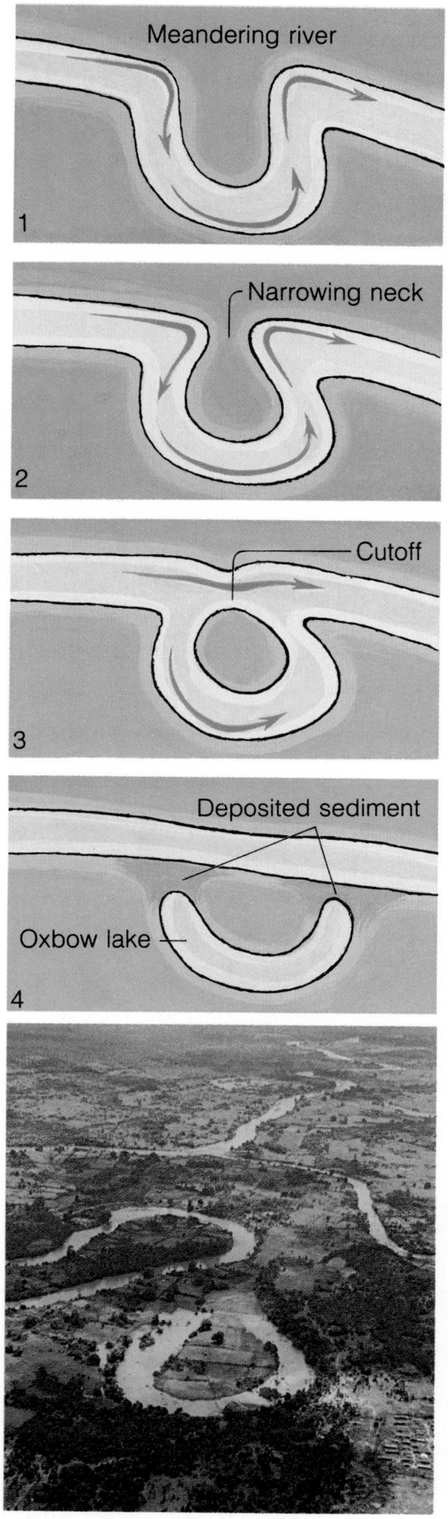

Figure 16–12 *An oxbow lake is often formed when a meander is cut off from the rest of the river. What type of river might have oxbow lakes along its course?*

Deposits by Rivers

A stream or river carries a large amount of sediments. In places where the stream or river slows down, the sediments are deposited. Some of the larger sediments settle on the riverbed. The riverbed is the bottom of the river channel. Some sediments are deposited along the riverbank, or the side of the river. These deposits constantly change surrounding land areas.

Sediments are usually deposited on a riverbank where a river bends, or curves. Rivers tend to erode material on the outside of the curve and deposit it on the inside. The outside of the curve receives the full impact of the current. The water on the inside of a river bend moves much more slowly.

OXBOW LAKES Sometimes the meanders of a river form large, U-shaped bends. Erosion and deposition along such bends can cut these bends off from the river. Deposited sediments dam up the ends of the meander. A small lake called an **oxbow lake** is formed. An oxbow lake is separated from the river. Figure 16–12 shows how oxbow lakes form.

ALLUVIAL FANS When a river leaves the mountains and runs out onto a plain, its speed decreases. Nearly all the sediments the river is carrying are dropped. They build up to form an **alluvial fan.** The sediments spread out from the river channel in a fanlike shape.

DELTAS Large amounts of sediments deposited at the mouth of a large river that flows into a lake or ocean form a **delta.** A delta forms because the river's speed decreases as it runs into the body of standing water. The river cannot carry as much material when it is moving slowly. So it deposits

CAREER

Soil Conservationist

HELP WANTED: SOIL CONSERVATIONIST To assist landscape designer. Bachelor's degree in geology, soil science, or environmental studies.

Each year, billions of tons of soil are lost from the land as a result of erosion. Efforts are being made to decrease this erosion by people known as **soil conservationists.**

Soil conservationists help farmers, ranchers, engineers, and others make the best use of their land without harming it. A soil conservationist may be asked to find the source of a farm's erosion problem and design a program to end it. A rancher may ask a soil conservationist how many cattle can safely graze on the ranch without destroying the grasses. Soil conservationists help design irrigation systems, build dams, and landscape recreational areas. They also provide information about types of soil pollution and methods of combating such pollution.

People who like to work outdoors might want to work in this field. To do so, they must go to college and study geology and agronomy. To learn more about this career, write to the Soil Conservation Service, United States Department of Agriculture, Washington, D.C. 20013.

much of the sediments. Sediments build up above the river's water level. What river delta is closest to where you live?

FLOOD PLAINS AND LEVEES On both sides of a mature river or stream, flat areas called **flood plains** form. After heavy rains or spring thaws, the river overflows its banks and covers the flood plain. Sedi-

Figure 16–13 *An alluvial fan forms when a river leaves the mountains and slows down as it runs out onto a plain (left). As a large river flows into a lake or ocean, its speed decreases and it deposits large amounts of sediments. These deposits form a delta (right).*

ments are deposited on the plain. Repeated flooding causes sediments to build up. Flood plains have fertile, rich soil. For example, the plains on either side of the Mississippi River are very fertile areas as a result of periodic flooding of the river. These areas are often used for farming.

Sediments deposited on a flood plain usually consist of fine particles. The larger particles, which settle first, are deposited along the sides of the river. These particles form a ridgelike deposit called a **levee** (LEHV-ee). The topographic map of Campti Quadrangle, Louisiana, on page 428 shows some of these depositional features.

SECTION REVIEW

1. How does running water cause erosion?
2. What factors affect the amount of runoff?
3. What is a drainage system? A drainage basin?
4. How are deltas and flood plains formed?

16–5 Glaciers

Section Objective

To describe glacial erosion and classify glaciers and glacial deposition

A **glacier** (GLAY-shuhr) is a large mass of moving ice and snow. Glaciers form where there are many large snowfalls and the temperatures remain very cold. Some glaciers form in high mountains where the snow that falls in the winter does not completely melt in the summer. The snow builds up over the years and gradually turns to ice. These glaciers move very slowly down the mountains through valleys. They are called valley glaciers.

Other glaciers form in the polar regions of the world. Some of these glaciers are very large sheets of ice called continental glaciers or icecaps. They often cover millions of square kilometers. See Figure 16–15 on page 420. What areas do you think have continental glaciers?

Figure 16–14 *A glacier is one of the most powerful agents of erosion, as this glacial mountain range in Mount McKinley Park, Alaska, shows. The large hollow circle in the foreground is a glacial feature known as a cirque.*

Glacial Ice and Erosion

A glacier is one of the most powerful agents of erosion. **Glacial ice erodes by abrasion and by plucking away at the rock beneath it.**

Figure 16–15 *Valley glaciers are long, narrow sheets of ice that move down steep mountain slopes (left). Continental glaciers are huge sheets of ice that cover vast areas of the earth's polar regions (right). What continent is covered almost entirely by a glacier?*

As a glacier moves through a valley, rocks, gravel, and silt are carried along and pushed in front of it. Gravel and silt carried by a glacier are called glacial debris. Other rocks and debris are frozen into the ice at the bottom of the glacier. Still more rocks and debris are loosened from the valley walls as the glacier scrapes against them.

A glacier may carry along large boulders as well as smaller particles of rocks. These make up the glacier's load. The load of a glacier helps wear down the land surface by grinding and polishing the rock it passes over. Erosion caused by glaciers is similar to erosion caused by streams and rivers. Glacial erosion changes V-shaped mountain valleys into U-shaped valleys.

During the Ice Age, huge icecaps covered a large part of North America. The Rocky Mountains, the mountains of New England, and many of the states in the Northeast and Midwest were at one time covered by glaciers. Glacial erosion caused many of the surface features that are present in these areas. For example, the Great Lakes were formed by glaciers.

Sharpen Your Skills

The Ice Age

Using reference books in the library, look up information about the Ice Age. Write a report about the Ice Age in which you answer the following questions:

1. When do scientists believe the Ice Age occurred?
2. How far south did the ice sheets extend into North America? What evidence exists to support this finding?
3. What do scientists think causes Ice Ages?

Include a map showing the area of North America covered by ice sheets during the Ice Age. Also show the areas of North America that today contain major glaciers.

Deposits by Glaciers

When the lower end of a glacier reaches a warm area, the ice at the front begins to melt. The glacier continues to move forward, but it may be melting so rapidly at the front that it appears to be moving

backward. Such a glacier is said to be retreating. As it retreats, the rocks and debris are deposited.

Rocks and debris deposited directly by a glacier are called **till.** Till is a mixture of material that varies in size from large boulders to very fine clay particles. Till is not sorted out by the action of running water. In other words, the material in till is not separated into layers according to its size.

Other glacial deposits are sorted out by running water from melting glaciers. The coarse and fine materials are separated into layers. Both sorted and unsorted materials are found in different features of the land formed by glaciers.

MORAINES When a glacier melts and retreats, it leaves behind till. The till forms a ridge called a **moraine.** There are different types of moraines. Till deposited at the front end of a glacier is called a terminal moraine. Till deposited along the sides of a glacier is called a lateral moraine.

Scientists can find out about glaciers that have melted by studying moraines. The rocks found in a moraine are evidence of where the glacier formed. Rocks can be carried great distances by glaciers. The position of a terminal moraine indicates how far the glacier advanced before retreating.

Sharpen Your Skills

Glacial Erosion

1. Cover a sheet of cardboard with a layer of clay 1 cm thick.

2. Rub some sand on top of the clay.

3. Slide an ice cube slowly along a path in the sand. Then hold the ice cube in one place and allow some of it to melt.

Describe the appearance of the sand after the ice cube has slid over it. What do you notice about the ice cube? What happened in the place where you held the cube? How does this activity relate to the erosion processes of glaciers?

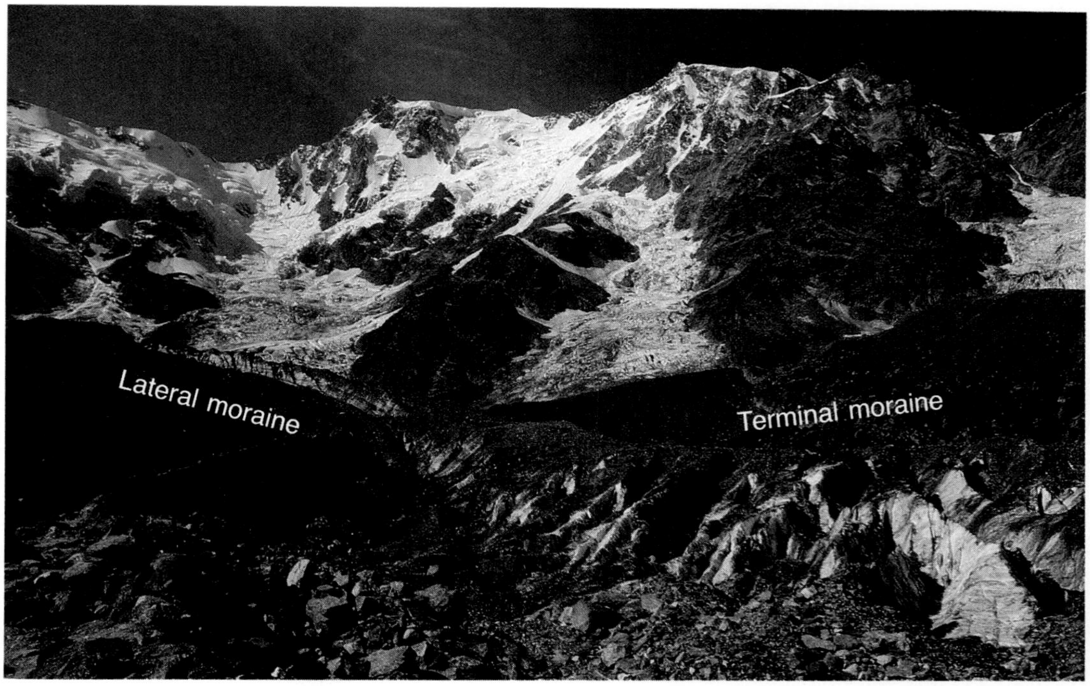

Figure 16–16 *Till left behind when a glacier melts and retreats forms ridges called moraines. Where is a lateral moraine located? A terminal moraine?*

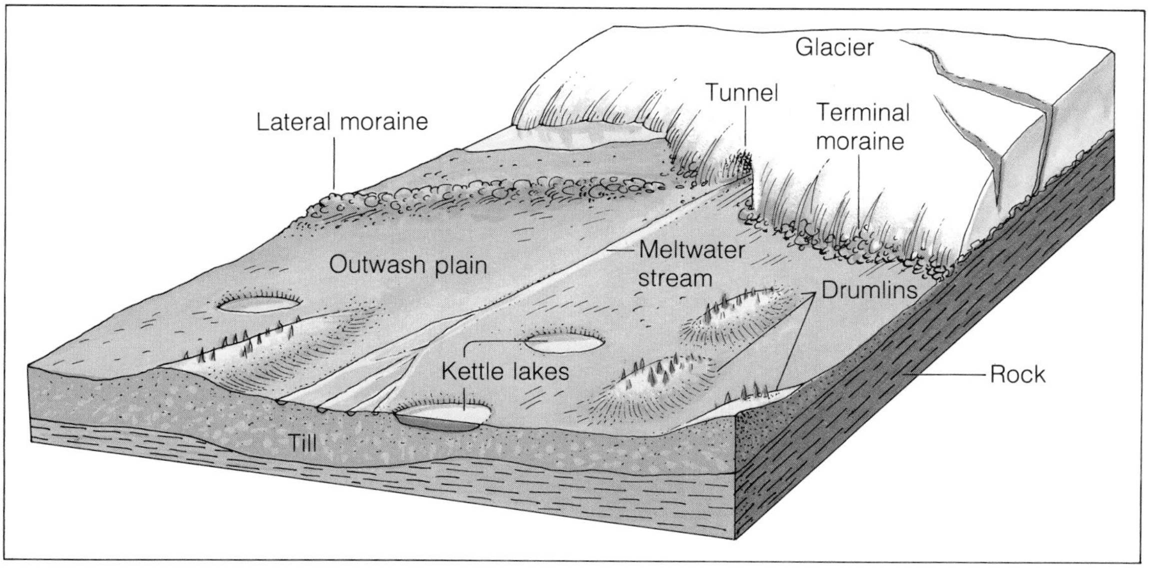

Figure 16–17 *The various land features formed by glacial deposits are shown in this diagram. What are some of these features?*

Figure 16–18 *Glacial deposits called drumlins can be seen in this photograph of Vermont farmland (top). Melting ice from a retreating glacier forms this meltwater stream in Kenai Fjords National Park, Alaska (bottom).*

DRUMLINS A **drumlin** is an oval-shaped mound of till. Its tip points in the direction that the glacier was moving. Scientists believe that drumlins are formed as deposits of till are rounded by the glacial ice.

MELTWATER DEPOSITS When valley glaciers stop advancing, melting ice forms streams that flow out from the glacier. These streams are called **meltwater** streams. The meltwater carries away sand and gravel. The sand and gravel sediments are deposited along the meltwater stream in long, trainlike deposits called valley trains. The meltwater may also form small lakes and ponds near the glacier. Many present-day rivers were originally meltwater streams.

Sediments deposited by rivers of glacial meltwater form areas called **outwash plains.** Outwash plains are fan-shaped and form in front of terminal moraines. Outwash plains are very fertile land areas. Today many farms can be found in outwash plains.

ICEBERG DEPOSITS Valley glaciers and continental glaciers sometimes reach the sea. When this happens, the glaciers form cliffs of ice and snow. Parts of the glacial ice break off and drift into the sea. These glacial parts are called **icebergs.** The continental glaciers of Greenland and Antarctica are the major sources of icebergs.

Icebergs may contain rocks and debris picked up from the land. As the icebergs melt, the rocks and debris are deposited on the ocean floor. These sediments are often found thousands of kilometers from their source.

GLACIAL LAKES Glaciers created many of the lakes in the United States. The Finger Lakes in New York, the Great Lakes, and many smaller lakes were formed by glaciers. Do you know of any other lakes formed by glaciers?

Glaciers can form lakes in two ways. Glacial till or deposits of sorted sediments from meltwater sometimes pile up in low-lying river channels and other areas. These deposits keep water from flowing away from the area. The land areas fill with water, and lakes are formed.

Sometimes huge blocks of glacial ice are left behind by a glacier. The ice blocks are surrounded by or covered with sediments deposited by the glacier. When the ice melts, it leaves a depression, or hole, in the ground. The depression fills with water and forms a lake. Lakes formed in this way are called **kettle lakes.** Kettle lakes are usually round and very deep. The topographic map of Holy Cross Quadrangle, Colorado, on page 429 shows some of these depositional features.

Figure 16–19 *An iceberg, such as this one in Drake's Passage, Antarctica, forms when chunks of glacial ice break off and drift into the sea (top). A kettle lake forms when a huge block of glacial ice, surrounded by or covered with sediments, melts and leaves a hole that fills with water (bottom).*

SECTION REVIEW

1. What is a glacier? How is it formed?
2. What is till? A moraine?
3. What are two meltwater deposits?
4. How are glacial lakes formed?

16–6 Waves

Section Objective

To relate wave action to erosion and deposition

If you have ever been to a beach at the ocean, you are probably familiar with waves. Waves are caused by winds, tides, and sometimes earthquakes. Waves can be very powerful. **The powerful force of waves constantly erodes and shapes the shoreline.** The shoreline is where a body of water meets the land.

Figure 16–20 *The powerful force of waves constantly erodes and shapes the shoreline.*

Waves and Erosion

Waves cause erosion in several ways. As waves reach shallow water near the ocean shore, they begin to break. As the breaking waves hit the shoreline, their force knocks fragments off existing rock formations. Waves also carry small rocks and sand. The force of the small rocks hitting other rocks on the shoreline chips fragments off. What kind of weathering is taking place in these two types of wave erosion?

Another way waves cause erosion is by forcing water into cracks in the rocks at the shoreline. The water causes pressure to build up in the cracks. The cracks become larger and the pressure breaks the rocks. Chemical action of salt water breaks down rocks. Some of the rocks dissolve in the salt water.

Erosion at the shoreline can occur at different rates. Various conditions cause these different rates. The size and force of the waves hitting the shoreline have an effect on the rate of erosion. Under normal conditions, waves may erode the shoreline at a rate of 1 to 1.5 meters per year. During storms, wave action is increased. Waves are larger and hit the shore with greater force. The rate of shoreline erosion may then increase to 25 meters in one day. The type of rock that makes up the shoreline also affects the rate of erosion. Some rocks do not erode as quickly as others. How might wave erosion differ along ocean shores and lake shores?

Figure 16–21 *Erosion at the shoreline, especially during storms, can cause extensive damage. What two characteristics of waves affect the rate of erosion?*

Figure 16–22 *This sea stack is the remains of a sea cliff, similar to the one in the background, that was eroded away by waves (left). A sea cave is a hollowed-out portion of a sea cliff (right).*

SEA CLIFFS AND TERRACES Wave erosion forms a variety of features along a shoreline. Erosion by waves sometimes produces steep faces of rock called **sea cliffs.** Over a long period of time, the bottom of a sea cliff may be slowly worn away by wave action. Overhanging rocks may break off the top of the cliff and fall into the sea. Waves will then grind the large rocks into sand and silt.

As the sea cliff continues to be eroded, the buildup of rocks, sand, and silt forms a flat platform at the base of the cliff. This flat platform is called a **terrace.** As waves move across the terrace, they are slowed down. They strike the cliff with less force. Terraces slow down erosion of sea cliffs.

SEA STACKS AND CAVES As waves erode a sea cliff, columns of resistant rock may be left standing. These columns of resistant rock are called **sea stacks.** Sometimes part of a sea cliff is made of less-resistant rock. When wave action erodes this rock, a cave is formed. A **sea cave** is a hollowed-out portion of a sea cliff.

Deposits by Waves

Waves carry large amounts of sand, rock particles, and pieces of shells. At some point, waves deposit the material they carry. Sand and other sediments carried away from one part of the shoreline

Sharpen Your Skills

Storm Action

If the rate of shoreline erosion during a storm is 25 meters per day, how many kilometers of shoreline would be eroded if an area had 50 days of storms per year?

by waves may be deposited elsewhere on the shoreline. The shape of the shoreline is always changing.

BEACHES Eroded rock particles deposited on the shoreline form beaches. Beaches may consist of fine sand or large pebbles. Some beach material comes directly from the erosion of nearby areas of the shoreline. Other beach materials can come from rivers and streams that carry sediments from inland areas to the sea. Waves transport the sediments from the mouths of rivers to different parts of the shoreline.

The type of material found on a beach varies according to its source. The color of the sand gives a clue to its origin. Beaches along the Atlantic coast have white sand. White sand usually consists of quartz material that originated in the eastern part of the United States. For example, most of the white sand on the Atlantic coast of Florida came from the erosion of the southern Appalachian Mountains. On Hawaii and other islands in the Pacific, some sand is black. The black sand comes from broken fragments of dark, volcanic rocks. Still other beaches may have deposits of shell fragments and coral skeletons.

SAND BARS AND SPITS Usually, waves do not come straight into the shore. They come in at an angle.

Sharpen Your Skills

What Causes Erosion and Deposition?

In a 300-word essay, describe how the processes of erosion and deposition occur. Use the following words in your essay.

continental glacier
valley glacier
terminal moraine
oxbow lake
sea stack
spits
loess
slipface

Figure 16–23 *The type of sand found on a beach varies according to its source. The color of the sand is a clue to its origin and composition. What might the sand found along the west coast of Australia be made of (left)? What is the likely origin of the black sand found on the island of Kauai (right)?*

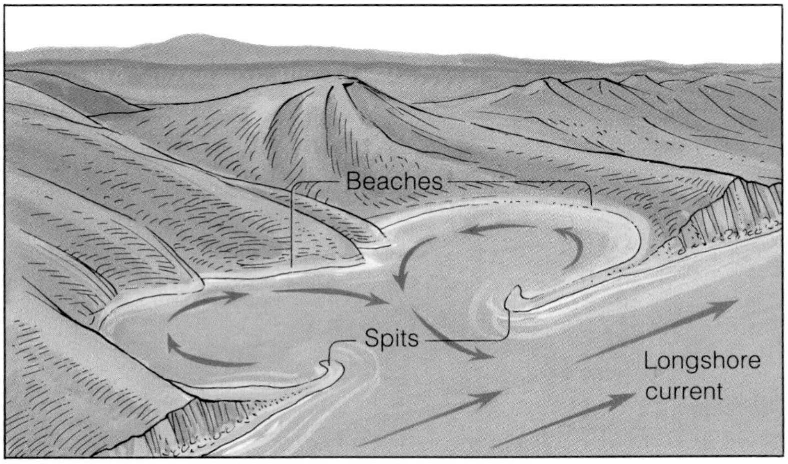

Figure 16–24 *Longshore currents slow down and deposit sand when shorelines curve or bend. What are these deposits called?*

The water is then turned so it runs parallel to the shoreline. The movement of water parallel to a shoreline is called a **longshore current.**

If the shoreline itself bends or curves, material carried by waves in a longshore current is deposited in open water. A long, underwater ridge of sand called a **sand bar** forms. If the sand bar is connected to the curving shoreline, it is called a **spit.**

Sometimes large sand bars are formed during the winter. During the winter, waves are large and carry more material away from the beaches. The material is deposited offshore. What do you think happens during the summer?

The Shape of a Shoreline

The shape of a shoreline often results from changes in the level of the sea. If the sea level drops, the resulting shoreline has many sea cliffs and terraces. The drop in sea level exposes new areas of shore to wave erosion, which forms many sea cliffs and terraces.

If the sea level rises, the resulting shoreline has many bays and harbors. The rise in sea level floods streams and small river valleys, forming bays and harbors.

SECTION REVIEW

1. How do waves cause erosion?
2. What is a sea cliff? A sea stack?
3. Why do different beaches have different colored sand?
4. How does a longshore current form sand bars and spits?

Sharpen Your Skills

Wave Erosion

1. Fill one end of a shallow pan with sand. Shape the sand into a slope.
2. Mark on the side of the pan where the edge of the sand slope ends.
3. Add 1 cm of water to the pan.
4. For a few minutes, make gentle waves with a piece of cardboard.

What changes do you observe in the shape of the sand slope? How does this activity relate to beach erosion?

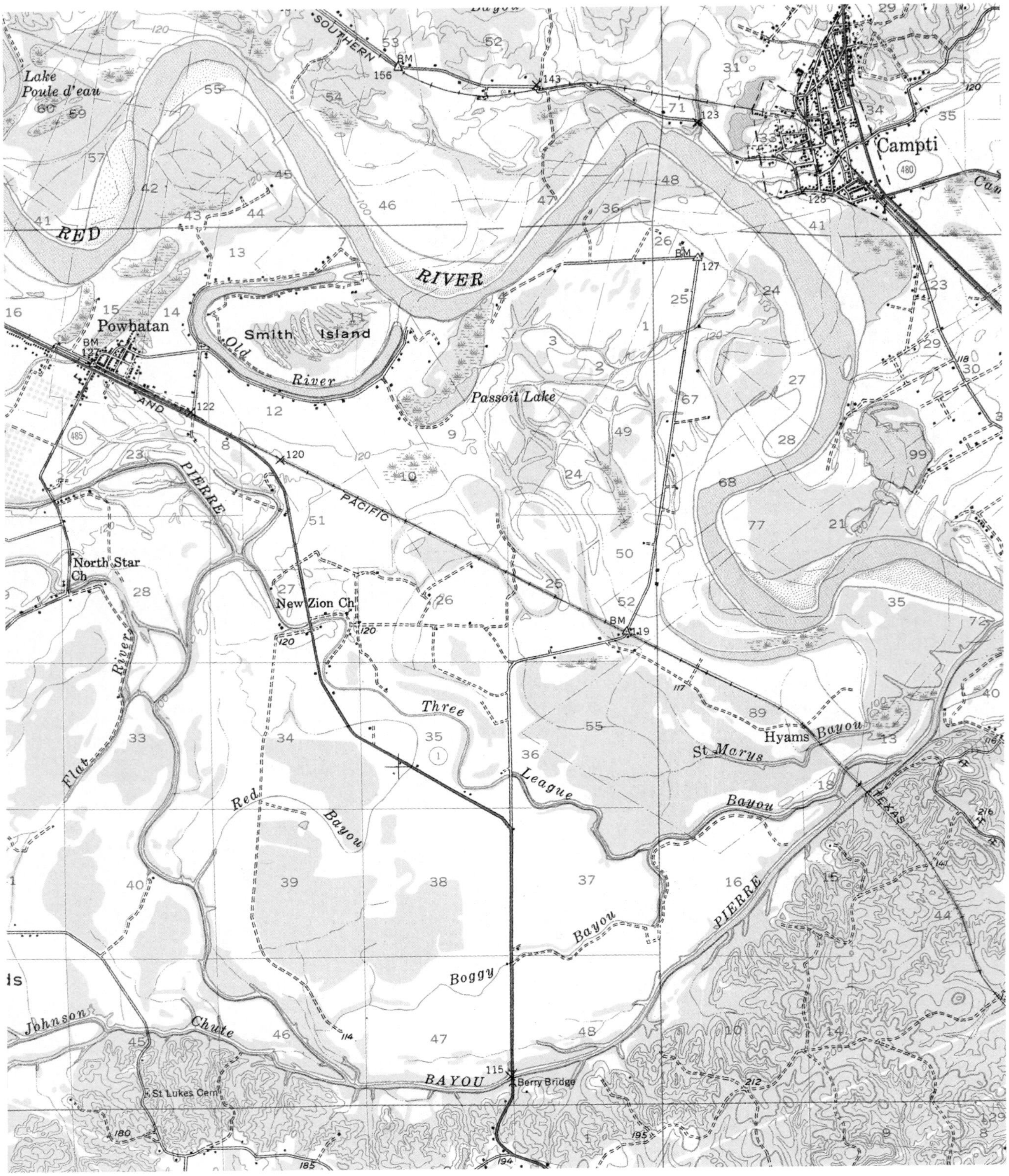

Sharpen Your Skills

Campti Quadrangle Topographic Map

Use Appendix F, Map Symbols.

1. What type of formation is Old River?
2. What are the loops in Red River called?
3. Is Red River an immature or mature river?
4. What land feature lies both west and north of Passoit Lake?
5. Where might you find a flood plain?

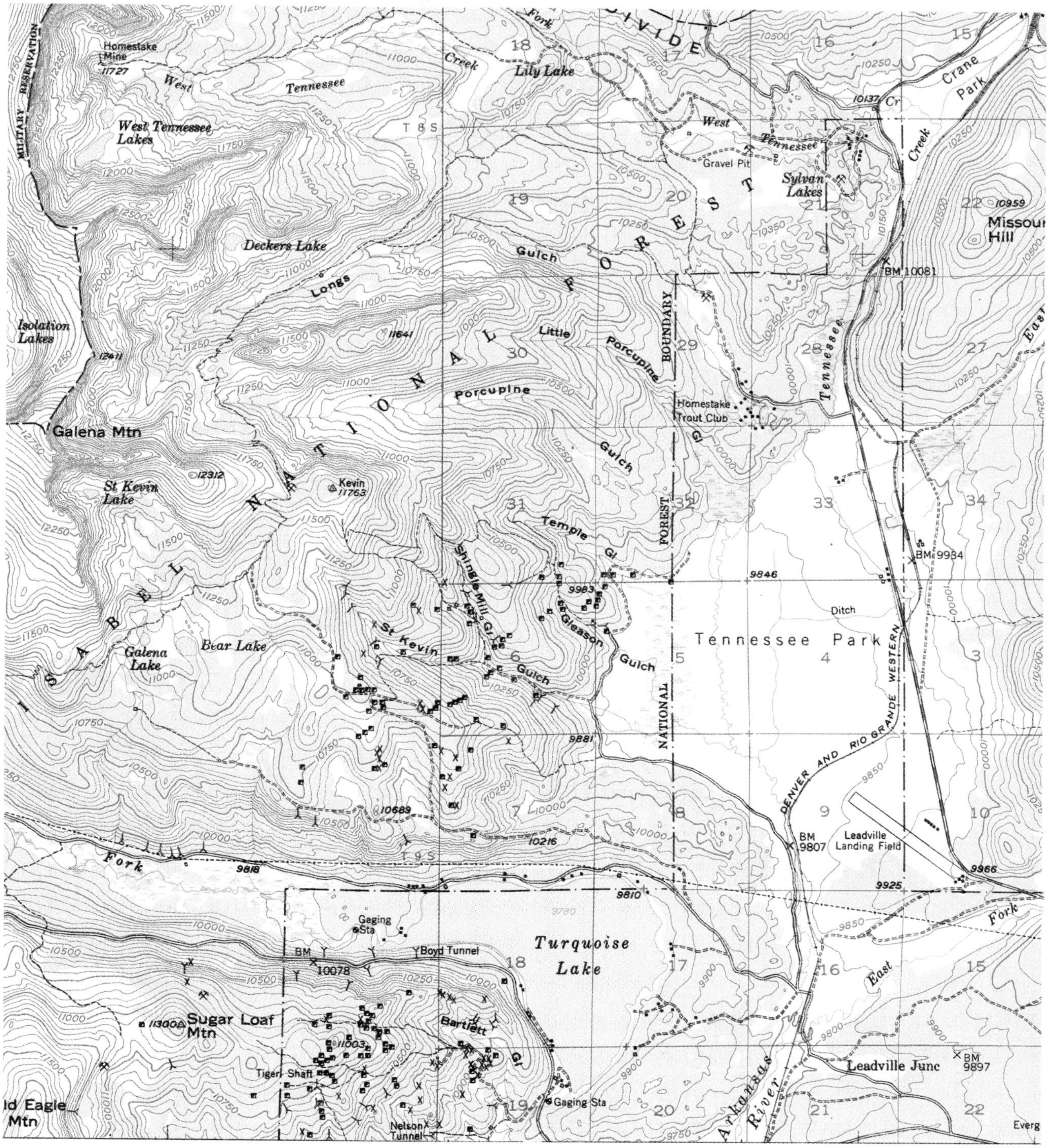

Sharpen Your Skills

Holy Cross Quadrangle Topographic Map

Many years ago, a glacier moved across part of this area from west to east.

1. What evidence supports this statement? Hint: Look for a glacial lake, a terminal moraine, and lateral moraines.

2. What is the name of the glacial lake?

3. With respect to the lake, in which direction is the terminal moraine located? The lateral moraines?

4. What features on the map suggest the presence of lateral moraines?

5. Where is the outwash plain?

16 LABORATORY INVESTIGATION

Observing Erosion and Deposition in a Model Stream

Problem

How is a stream's ability to erode and deposit earth material affected by a change in its flow?

Materials *(per group)*

Stream pan (2 cm × 50 cm × 8–10 cm)
2 25-cm lengths of rubber tubing (1 cm in diameter)
Sand
2 buckets
Support such as books
Food coloring or ink
Lab table
Screw clamp

Procedure

1. Set up a stream table similar to the one shown in the illustration.
2. Raise one end of the large pan slightly, so that the pan is at a very low angle to the table. To start the water flowing, siphon the water out of the bucket. Using the screw clamp, set the flow of water at a very low volume.
3. As the water runs to the end of the pan, observe and record changes that occur on the land surface, on the lake, and on the stream itself. Note any deposition features that may form. A drop of food coloring or ink can help reveal patterns of change.
4. Next change the slope of the stream, making it steeper by increasing the angle between the pan and the table. Observe and record the effects of this change.
5. Now increase the stream's volume by opening the screw clamp or by pouring more water down the stream table. Observe and record the effects of this change.

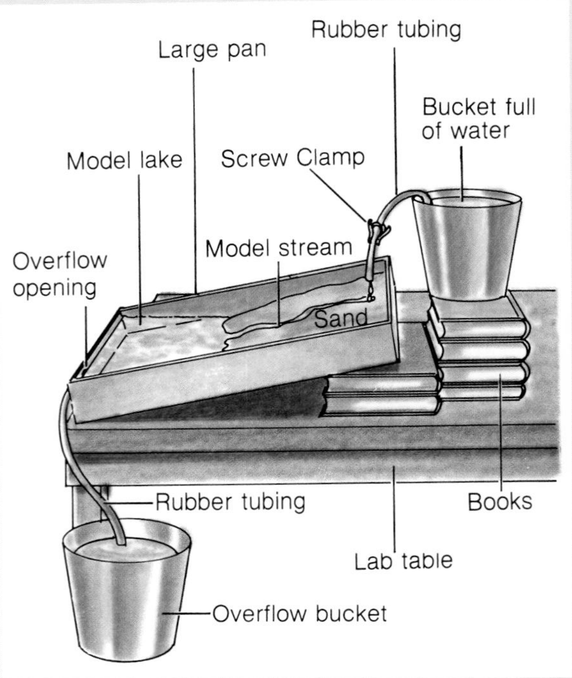

Observations

1. What, if any, deposition features formed?
2. What evidence of sideward erosion of the stream bed, undercutting of stream banks, and meandering did you observe?
3. What size particles were carried the farthest by the stream movement?
4. What changes in the stream occurred when you increased the steepness of the slope of your stream table? When you increased the volume of water?

Conclusions

1. What effect does an increase in stream velocity have on the processes of erosion and deposition?
2. What effects does an increase in stream volume have on the processes of erosion and deposition?
3. Why do you think old rivers meander?

CHAPTER REVIEW

SUMMARY

16–1 Changing the Earth's Surface

❑ Erosion is the process by which weathered rock and soil particles are moved from one place to another.

❑ Deposition is the process by which sediments are laid down in new locations.

❑ The five agents of erosion are gravity, wind, running water, glaciers, and waves.

16–2 Gravity

❑ The downhill movement of sediments caused by gravity is called mass wasting.

❑ Rapid mass wasting includes landslides, mudflows, and slump. Slow mass wasting includes earthflows and soil creep.

16–3 Wind

❑ Wind erodes by deflation and by abrasion.

❑ Sand dunes and loess are wind deposits.

16–4 Running Water

❑ Running water in the form of rivers, streams, and runoff is the major agent of erosion.

❑ The network of rills, gullies, and streams that forms a river is called a drainage system.

❑ The area drained by a main river and its branches is called a drainage basin.

❑ Deposits by rivers include oxbow lakes, alluvial fans, deltas, flood plains, and levees.

16–5 Glaciers

❑ A glacier is a large mass of moving ice and snow. Two types of glaciers are valley glaciers and continental glaciers.

❑ Rocks and debris deposited directly by a glacier are called till.

❑ Other glacial deposits include moraines, drumlins, meltwater streams, outwash plains, icebergs, and lakes.

16–6 Waves

❑ Waves erode and shape the shoreline.

❑ Wave erosion forms sea cliffs, terraces, sea stacks, and sea caves.

❑ The movement of water parallel to a shoreline is called a longshore current.

❑ Deposits by waves include beaches, sand bars, and spits.

VOCABULARY

Define each term in a complete sentence.

alluvial fan
delta
deposition
drainage basin
drainage system
drumlin
erosion
flood plain
glacier
iceberg
immature river
kettle lake
levee
load
loess
longshore current
mass wasting
mature river
meander
meltwater
moraine
outwash plain
oxbow lake
sand bar
sand dune
sea cave
sea cliff
sea stack
spit
terrace
till
tributary

CONTENT REVIEW: MULTIPLE CHOICE

Choose the letter of the answer that best completes each sentence.

1. The process by which sediments are laid down in new locations is called
a. erosion b. deposition c. abrasion d. mass wasting

2. Two examples of rapid mass wasting are
a. slump and soil creep b. landslides and earthflows
c. soil creep and earthflows d. landslides and slump

3. Layers of fine sand and silt deposited in the same area by wind are called
a. loess b. dunes c. terraces d. till

4. The network of rills, gullies, and streams that forms a river is called a
a. drainage basin b. tributary c. levee d. drainage system

5. Rich, fertile soil deposited on the sides of a river as it overflows forms flat areas called
a. terraces b. sand bars c. flood plains d. valley trains

6. A ridge of till deposited as a glacier melts and retreats is called a
a. moraine b. terrace c. levee d. flood plain

7. Glacial meltwater forms very fertile deposits of sediments called
a. flood plains b. outwash plains c. kettle lakes d. drumlins

8. Columns of resistant rock left as waves erode sea cliffs are called
a. spits b. sea stacks c. terraces d. sand bars

9. A sand bar connected to the curving shoreline is called a
a. terrace b. sea stack c. spit d. drumlin

10. A shoreline having many sea cliffs and terraces may indicate that the sea level has
a. dropped b. risen c. remained constant d. reversed direction

CONTENT REVIEW: COMPLETION

Fill in the word or words that best complete each sentence.

1. The process by which weathered rock and soil particles are moved from one place to another is called ________.

2. Wind removes clay, silt, dust, and sand from the land in a type of erosion called ________.

3. Water that flows over the earth's surface is called ________.

4. Soil and rock material carried by a stream are called the stream's ________.

5. When the course of a river becomes winding, loops called ________ form.

6. A large mass of moving ice and snow is called a (an) ________.

7. The place where a body of water meets the land is called a (an) ________.

8. Steep faces of rock that form along a shoreline because of wave erosion are called ________.

9. The movement of water parallel to a shoreline is called a (an) ________.

10. A long, underwater ridge of sand formed as waves deposit material in open water is called a (an) ________.

CONTENT REVIEW: TRUE OR FALSE

Determine whether each statement is true or false. If it is true, write "true." If it is false, change the underlined word or words to make the statement true.

1. The downhill movement of sediments caused by gravity is called mass wasting.
2. The most active agent of erosion in deserts and on beaches is waves.
3. When wind or water moves slowly, the amount of particles it can carry increases.
4. Areas with little plant growth have more erosion than areas with a lot of plant growth.
5. A river that cuts a V-shaped valley and has rapids and waterfalls is a mature river.
6. A large deposit of sediment formed at the mouth of a river is called a levee.
7. Rocks and debris deposited directly by a glacier are called till.
8. Parts of glacial ice that break off and drift into the sea are called drumlins.
9. During storms, the rate of erosion along a shoreline increases.
10. A shoreline with sea cliffs and terraces might indicate a rise in sea level.

CONCEPT REVIEW: SKILL BUILDING

Use the skills you have developed in the chapter to complete each activity.

1. **Sequencing events** The following steps are stages in the formation of a river system from the time rain falls to the earth to the time a steadily flowing river forms. The steps are not in order. Read the steps and then place them in the proper order.
   a. Runoff from several slopes collects in low places
   b. Rain falls to the earth's surface
   c. Water tumbles in broad sheets
   d. Branch gullies develop and then become tributaries
   e. A gully is formed
   f. A V-shaped valley with streams, waterfalls, and rapids forms
   g. Erosion lengthens the gullies
   h. The gully gets larger and collects more water
2. **Making diagrams** Use a diagram to illustrate how an immature and a mature river would look in an aerial photograph. How would each river look on a topographic map?
3. **Applying concepts** What are two ways in which people can cause erosion? Two ways in which they can prevent erosion?
4. **Making inferences** Why would a flood plain be characteristic of a mature river valley and not of an immature river valley?

CONCEPT REVIEW: ESSAY

Discuss each of the following in a brief paragraph.

1. Using glaciers as an example, explain how erosion of a land area usually involves more than one agent of erosion.
2. Explain how both erosion and deposition are involved in the formation of sand dunes.
3. What can scientists learn about glaciers by studying moraines?
4. Wind erosion in a desert area is usually harmful. In one instance, however, it can be helpful. Explain how wind erosion in a desert can be helpful.

Adventures in Science

JOANNE SIMPSON'S STORMY STRUGGLE

Joanne Simpson spent the year 1943 contributing to the American effort in World War II by teaching weather forecasting to air force personnel. At the same time, she was fighting a more personal battle. Simpson, who had graduated from the University of Chicago, wanted to return there to earn additional degrees in meteorology. Her efforts, however, were met with much opposition from professors at the University. They told Simpson that the idea of a woman meteorologist was a "lost cause." The concept of a female scientist, they claimed, was a "contradiction in terms," and "there was no point" in her trying to get an advanced degree. Yet, in 1949, the determined Simpson became the first American woman to receive a Ph.D. in meteorology.

Simpson's interest in meteorology began when she was a young girl. Her father was a journalist who wrote about aviation, and she sometimes went flying with him. During her teen years, Simpson spent summers as an assistant to the director of aviation for the state of Massachusetts. She also began to take flying lessons.

In 1940 Simpson enrolled at the University of Chicago. She was introduced to meteorology while training for her pilot's license. The ability to read and understand a weather map as well as knowledge of weather patterns and the atmosphere are important to flying. Simpson was so fascinated by the subject that she signed up for a course at the University.

After receiving her undergraduate degree and teaching military personnel for a year, Simpson decided to continue her studies in meteorology. At first none of the faculty at the University of Chicago would support her venture. But Simpson, a very determined young scientist, eventually won the support of Herbert Riehl. He agreed to supervise her research project, which involved the study of cumulus clouds—their interaction with the environment and their relationship to tropical waves.

Woods Hole, Massachusetts, a small town at the southwest tip of Cape Cod, provided an ideal natural environment for Simpson's research on cumulus clouds. Simpson studied at both Woods Hole and the University of Chicago before receiving her Ph.D. in meteorology in 1949.

Simpson's interesting and dynamic career has included teaching at several universities—among them, the University of California at Los Angeles and the University of Virginia. In 1979, she was invited to head the Severe Storms Branch of the Goddard Laboratory for Atmospheric Sciences. This laboratory is part of the National Aeronautics and Space Administration (NASA).

Dr. Simpson enjoys a challenge, so for her NASA is a perfect place to be. She continues to study the formation and development of cumulus clouds. And she is currently working on a new weather satellite that will provide accurate measurements of the rainfall in tropical ocean areas. The satellite, which is scheduled to be launched in 1994, should give meteorologists a better understanding of various changes in climate. These discoveries could enable scientists to make more accurate and longer range weather forecasts.

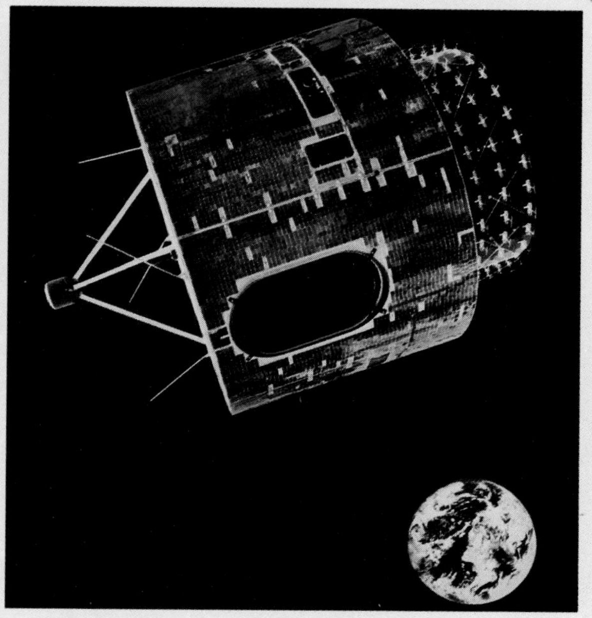

From information gathered by weather satellites, meteorologists like Joanne Simpson hope to learn more about various atmospheric conditions.

In the last 40 years, Simpson has published 115 scientific research papers, won numerous awards and honors, traveled across the globe, and served on many scientific councils and committees. The honors that have given her the greatest personal satisfaction are the Meisinger Award, given to her in 1962 for her work on cumulus clouds; NASA's Exceptional Scientific Achievement Medal; and the Carl-Gustav Rossby Research Medal, the American Meteorological Society's highest award. Simpson's courage and determination have earned her the respect of her colleagues and the public. She has truly paved the way for a generation of women meteorologists.

Issues in Science

Making the Desert Bloom

Is the Price Too High?

Start with plenty of sunlight and good soil. Add lots of water. What is the result? Some of the world's richest farmland located in the western and southwestern United States. Today, much of this area is green and golden with fruits, vegetables, grain, and cotton. But some people remember when this land was dry, dusty desert and arid scrubland. How was a desert transformed into fertile farmland?

Irrigation has made the difference. Canals and pipelines now bring the water from distant lakes and rivers to desert regions that were once dry and parched. Wells dug deep

In 1925 the Imperial Valley in California was dry and barren. Today the irrigation of desert areas provides good land for crops to grow.

into natural underground springs bring water to the surface. The water is then piped through fields and sprinkled on crops.

Some experts say that the price of growing crops in desert areas may be too high. Over the past 60 years, billions of dollars have been spent to bring water to desert areas. But the largest costs are not measured in money. Over time, irrigation causes serious problems.

One of the problems is the rapid depletion of general water reserves in order to provide water for irrigation. People are now using water faster than nature can replace it. Reservoirs and wells that once held large amounts of water are now running dry. Yet the demand for water increases.

The erosion of valuable topsoil as irrigation water runs off the land is another problem. Billions of tons of topsoil are washed from farmlands in the United States each year. Salts and toxic minerals from the water remain in the soil. These chemicals are harmful to plant growth. Eventually the amounts of salts and minerals increase to a level that kills plants. The soil becomes worthless for farming.

Water that runs off farmlands contains pesticides and fungicides as well as salts and minerals. This water then pollutes rivers, streams, lakes, marshes, and estuaries. Conservation groups warn that wildlife areas are frequently affected by this polluted runoff. In some wildlife areas, plants and animals have died because of poisonous agricultural chemicals in the water that runs off farmlands.

In many parts of the West and Southwest, farmers face a double-headed problem. The need for fresh water increases steadily, even as the supply of fresh water is depleted daily. The farmers know all too well that water shortages are likely. Yet without irrigation, farmers cannot use their land to grow crops.

Farmers, ranchers, and developers say that a solution to this problem involves the development of new irrigation projects. They need a larger supply of water or their land will again dry up and become a desert.

Some environmentalists say that desert areas should no longer be irrigated—even if that means losing farms and ranches. Without irrigation, they argue, the land will return to its natural desert state. Plants and animals that are adapted to living in the deserts will return.

A number of state and federal water experts say that such a drastic solution is not necessary. They point out that the amount of water used to irrigate farmland could be cut drastically. Various techniques for saving water have been suggested. One irrigation system would deliver water directly to the plant roots. This method would cut down on the amount of water lost through evaporation and by runoff. Another suggestion involves covering crops with plastic to prevent evaporation. Controlling sprinklers by computers is another possible method of water conservation—water would be supplied only when it is most needed. However, all of these methods are expensive and would greatly increase the cost of irrigation water.

Many choices will have to be made about the future of desert irrigation. Should it continue? If so, under what conditions? Obviously, making the desert bloom involves some thorny issues.

UNIT FIVE

The Changing Earth: Subsurface Activity

Pounded by the waters of the Pacific Ocean off the western coast of South America are islands called the Galápagos. Today the Galápagos are home to some of the most unusual animals and plants on the earth. But long ago, this stretch of ocean was unbroken by the islands. Nothing but fish, sea plants, and tiny organisms lived in the area. Then great changes took place in the land under the ocean. Volcanoes sprang up from the ocean floor. Tons of red-hot lava piled up and finally broke the water's surface. The Galápagos Islands had formed.

At first, the islands were gray-black chunks of barren rock—all that remained of the fiery lava. But at some point, the seed of a plant rode the wind from South America and landed in the folds of hardened lava. The seed may have been from a hardy cactus able to survive where there is little fresh water and scarce relief from the heat of the sun. Life had come to the Galápagos! Other forms of life would later make their home on islands created by changes in the earth.

CHAPTERS

These hardy cactuses thrive in the hardened folds of lava that have formed the Galápagos Islands.

Movement of the Earth's Crust

17

CHAPTER SECTIONS

17–1 Stress
17–2 Faulting and Folding
17–3 Plateaus and Domes
17–4 The Floating Crust

CHAPTER OBJECTIVES

After completing this chapter, you will be able to

17–1 Describe how the earth's crust is deformed by stress.

17–2 Identify the major types of faulting and folding.

17–3 Explain how plateaus and dome mountains are formed.

17–4 Define isostasy and explain its effect on the movement of the earth's crust.

Have you ever stood at the edge of a mountain and looked down into a valley far below? Did you know that millions of years ago the mountain and valley probably looked very different? The land may have been completely flat, without so much as a hill. Or possibly, the area was beneath an ocean. How could the mountain and valley have formed?

Geologists who study the earth's history have learned that the earth's surface is uplifted, pushed down, bent, and broken by forces beneath the surface. You probably have never seen a mountain rise out of the sea or become flat land. The movements are usually too small and slow to be noticed. But scientists know that the earth's surface is constantly changing. In fact, they believe that the earth looks very different today than it did billions of years ago.

For example, scientists believe that the Himalaya Mountains in Asia were once small hills. Today these mountains stand more than 9 kilometers above sea level. And they are rising still higher! What other areas do you suppose looked different billions of years ago?

These towering peaks in the Himalaya Mountains did not always exist. But over time, forces deep within the earth have pushed them up far above the surrounding land.

Section Objective

To relate stress to the deformation of the earth's crust

17–1 Stress

The Himalaya Mountains and all other mountains are made of thick layers of rocks. The ground beneath your school is also made of rocks. In fact, every part of the earth's surface is made of rocks. All the rocks at the earth's surface are part of the **crust,** or the outermost layer of the earth.

There are two major sections of the crust. One section is called **continental crust.** Continental crust makes up the earth's landmasses, such as the North American continent. In most places, it is about 32 kilometers thick. But under tall mountains, the continental crust can be up to 70 kilometers thick.

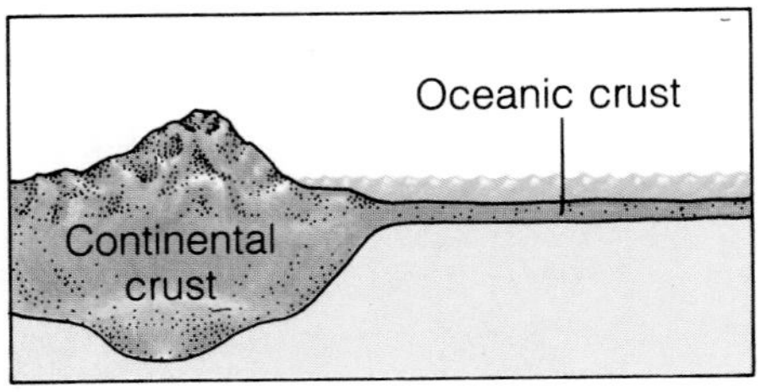

Figure 17–1 *The earth's crust consists of two sections. One section is continental crust. The other section is oceanic crust. Which section of crust is thicker?*

The other section of the crust is **oceanic crust.** Oceanic crust is found under the ocean floor. It is thinner than continental crust. Oceanic crust is usually about 8 kilometers thick.

Why are some parts of the crust thicker than others? How does the crust change its shape over time? Clearly, some force is at work pushing and pulling on the crust, causing changes on the surface and often well beneath the surface. This push-pull force is called **stress. As rocks undergo stress, they slowly change shape and volume.**

Sometimes stress causes a rock to become more compressed, or squeezed together. As particles in the rock move closer together, the rock becomes denser and smaller in volume. At other times, stress causes a rock to stretch out over a larger area. In this case, the volume of the rock increases, but its density decreases.

Figure 17–2 *These rocks have been bent, twisted, and broken by a very strong force. What is the force that can deform rocks so greatly?*

Stress can cause crustal rocks to move up or down or sideways. The movement causes crustal rocks to break, tilt, and fold. The breaking, tilting, and folding of rocks is called **deformation.**

SECTION REVIEW

1. What are the two major sections of the earth's crust?
2. What is stress? What can it do to rocks?
3. What is deformation?
4. Explain why a rock's density decreases as its volume increases. Does the rock's mass change?

17–2 Faulting and Folding

Section Objective

To describe the three main types of stress and relate them to faulting and folding

Rocks can be deformed by stress. But what types of stress cause the different kinds of deformation? **Scientists recognize three main types of stress: compression, tension, and shearing.** Crustal rocks may be squeezed together by a type of stress called **compression.** As crustal rocks are compressed, they are pushed both higher up and deeper down.

To understand this movement, imagine you are squeezing clay in your hand. As you squeeze the clay, some of it is pushed out the opening at the top of your hand. Some of it is pushed out the opening at the bottom.

Not only can crustal rocks be pushed together, they can also be pulled apart. The type of stress that pulls rocks apart is called **tension.** A rock under tension is stretched like a piece of warm taffy when it is pulled. The piece of taffy becomes thinner in the middle than at the ends.

A third type of stress is called **shearing.** Shearing pushes crustal rock in two opposite, horizontal directions. This causes the rock to twist or tear apart. During shearing, then, rocks are not compressed or stretched. They simply bend or break apart.

Figure 17–3 *Different types of stress deform rocks in different ways. The arrows show the direction in which the different types of stress act. Rocks can be pushed both higher up and deeper down by compression. Tension can pull rocks apart. Shearing pushes rocks horizontally in two opposite directions.*

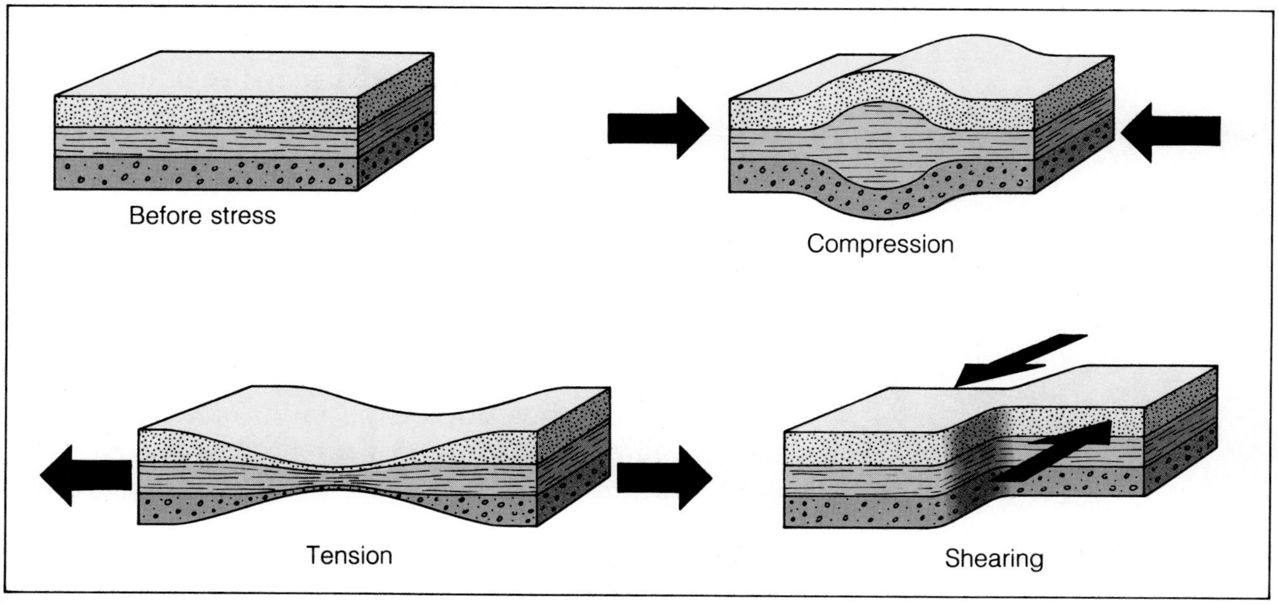

CAREER

Seismologist

HELP WANTED: SEISMOLOGIST For oil exploration company. Bachelor's degree in seismology or geophysics required. Some field experience helpful but will train.

Since the beginning of history, people have tried to explain earthquakes. Ancient civilizations believed that the earth was held up in space by some support. If the support moved, the earth shook. Some people believed this support was a giant catfish or tortoise.

Today our understanding of earthquakes is much more advanced. However, many questions still must be answered. The people who search for answers to these questions are called **seismologists,** or earthquake scientists.

Seismologists study the areas of the earth where earthquakes occur. They study how the earth's crust moves along faults. Seismologists interpret and analyze data collected by seismographs and other instruments.

Some seismologists specialize in related fields. For example, some help explore for oil and minerals. Others examine proposed construction sites to determine if buildings can safely be placed on the land.

People who plan to work in this field earn a degree in geophysics or seismology. You can learn more about this career by writing to the Seismological Society of America, 2620 Telegraph Avenue, Berkeley, California 94704.

Compression, tension, and shearing can change a rock's volume, its shape, or both. These stresses can also cause the rocks to fracture, or crack. If the rocks fracture along numerous flat surfaces, the cracks are called **joints.** Joints are parallel to each other. Some rocks have joints that form in more than one direction. Such rocks may break into blocks. The blocks form where the different sets of joints cross one another.

Figure 17–4 *These granite rocks have parallel sets of cracks called joints. What happens when different sets of joints cross one another?*

Faulting

Stress sometimes causes rocks to break. A break or crack along which rocks move is called a **fault.** The rocks on one side of the fault slide past the rocks on the other side of the fault. Movements along a fault can be up, down, or sideways. Earthquakes often occur along faults in the earth's crust. What are some other possible results of movements along a fault?

Figure 17–5 *The block of rocks to the left of this fault has moved down. The block of rocks to the right of the fault has moved up. The block on the left is called the hanging wall. What is the block on the right called?*

If you look at a cross section of faulted rocks, you will see two blocks of rock, one on top of the other. The block of rock above the fault is called the **hanging wall.** The block below the fault is called the **foot wall.**

Types of Faults

Stress can cause either the hanging wall or the foot wall to move up or down along a fault. If a stress due to tension is acting on a fault, the hanging wall will move down relative to the foot wall. If this occurs, the fault between the two blocks is called a **normal fault.** If a stress due to compression is acting on a fault, the hanging wall will move up relative to the foot wall. This type of fault is called a **reverse fault.**

A special type of reverse fault is a **thrust fault.** Thrust faults are formed when compression causes the hanging wall to slide over the foot wall. Thrust faults are special because they are almost horizontal. Regular reverse faults are almost vertical. Thrust faults usually carry rocks many kilometers from their original position. Rocks are usually severely bent at the same time thrust faulting occurs.

Older rocks are usually found under younger rocks. But during thrust faulting, older rocks are pushed up on top of younger rocks. The Lewis Overthrust Fault in Glacier National Park, Montana, is an example of a thrust fault. Here very old rocks have slid eastward more than 48 kilometers. They now rest on top of younger rocks.

Figure 17–6 *In these drawings, the red arrows show the direction in which stress acts on the rocks. Stress due to tension causes the hanging wall to move down relative to the foot wall, creating a normal fault (top). Stress due to compression can create a reverse fault (bottom). In this case, would the foot wall move up or down relative to the hanging wall?*

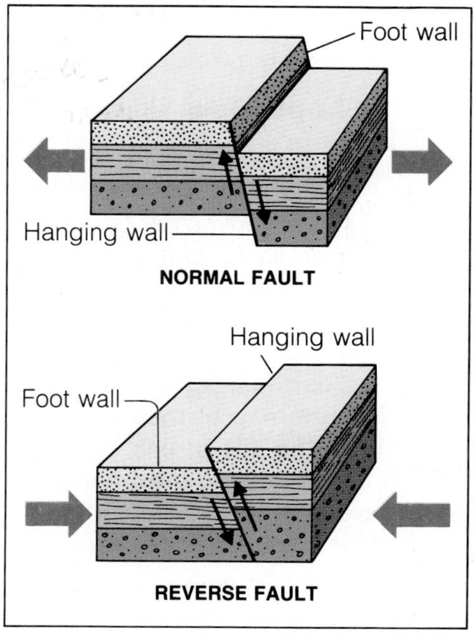

Figure 17–7 *This drawing of rock layers shows how older rocks are pushed on top of younger rocks along a thrust fault. The direction of the stress is shown by the red arrows. Regular reverse faults lie almost vertical. How are thrust faults different?*

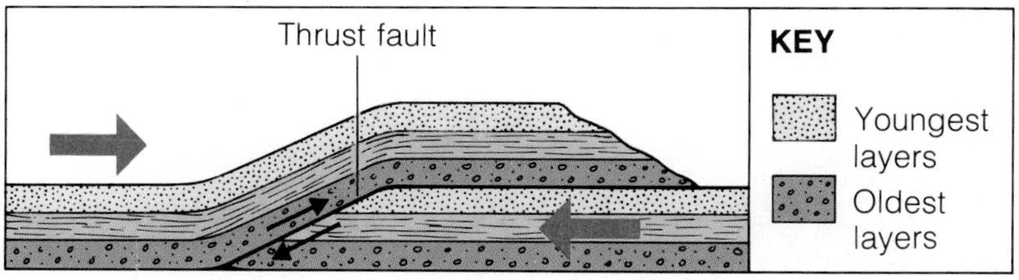

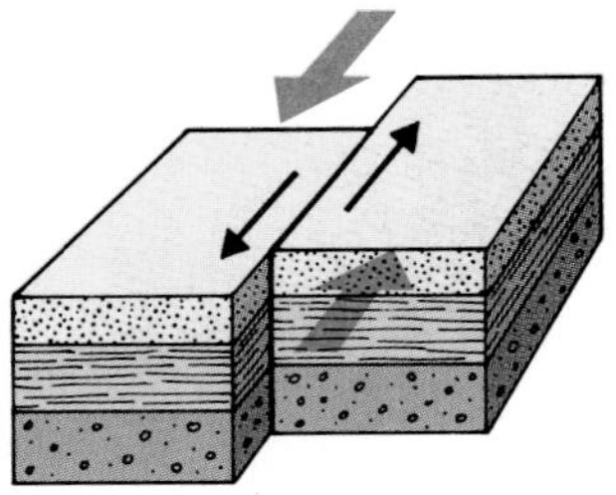

Figure 17–8 *This drawing shows a lateral fault along which shearing stress is acting. The red arrows show the direction of the stress. How do the two blocks move relative to each other?*

Stress does not cause blocks of crustal rock to move only up and down. A shearing stress will cause the blocks of rock to slide horizontally past each other. One block moves to the left or right in relation to the other block. The fault along which the blocks move horizontally past one another is called a **lateral fault.**

Faulted Mountains and Valleys

When there are many normal faults in one area, a series of mountains and valleys may form. Mountains formed by blocks of rock uplifted by normal faults are called **fault-block mountains.** A vast region in western North America called the Cordilleran Mountain region contains many fault-block mountains. The region extends from central Mexico to Oregon and Idaho. The region includes western Utah, all of Nevada, and eastern California.

Figure 17–9 *When a block of rocks between normal faults is pushed up (top), a fault-block mountain is formed. The Sierra Nevada Mountains in the western United States are fault-block mountains (bottom).*

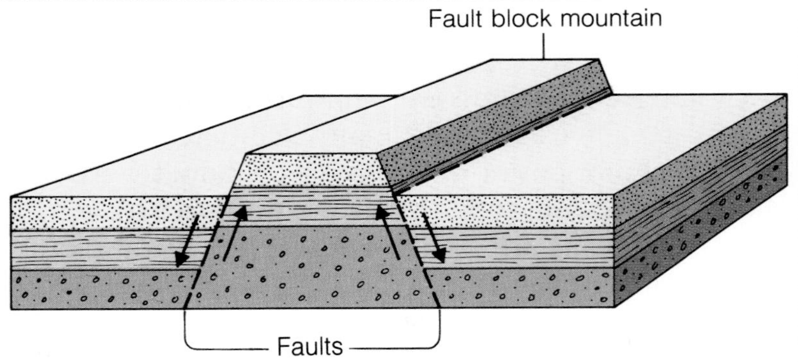

Sharpen Your Skills

The Earth's Changing Surface

1. During the next two months, collect newspaper clippings dealing with earthquakes, floods, volcanoes, and other "earth-changing" events.

2. On a map of the world, indicate the site of each event. Use a different-colored pencil for each category of event. Include a key with your map.

How did each event alter the earth's surface?

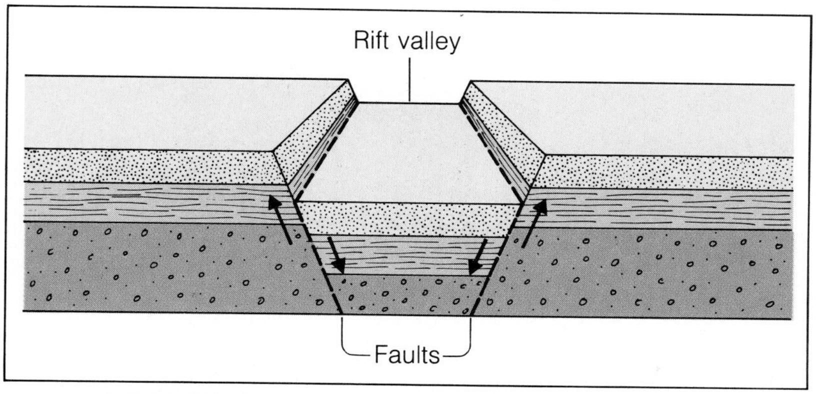

Figure 17–10 *Rift valleys form when a block of rocks between normal faults slips down (top). The photograph shows a rift valley called Death Valley, located in California (bottom). The low mountains in the background border along a normal fault. What type of stress would form a rift valley?*

Valleys also form when mountains form. Some valleys are formed when the block of land between two normal faults slides downward. Valleys created in this way are called **rift valleys.**

Death Valley in California is a rift valley. It is a long, narrow valley 87 meters below sea level. Scientists believe that the valley was formed by a series of small movements along two faults at either side of the valley. They estimate that the land along the eastern fault of Death Valley will move another 3 meters during the next 1000 years.

Folding

Sometimes when stress is applied to crustal rocks, the rocks bend but do not break. The rocks bend in much the same way as a carpet wrinkles as it is pushed across a floor. A bend in a rock is called a **fold.** An upward fold in rock is called an **anticline** (AN-tih-klighn). A downward fold in rock is called a **syncline** (SIHN-klighn). See Figure 17–11, page 448.

Folds vary in size. Some folds are so small that you would need a magnifying glass to see them

Sharpen Your Skills

Anticlines and Synclines

1. Flatten three pieces of different-colored modeling clay into thin, rectangular layers on a piece of waxed paper.

2. Place the flattened layers of clay on top of one another.

3. Place your hands at opposite ends of the clay rectangle. Slowly push the two ends together. This pressure should create folds in the clay similar to the anticlines and synclines created in rock layers.

In the earth, what forces might account for such folds in rock layers?

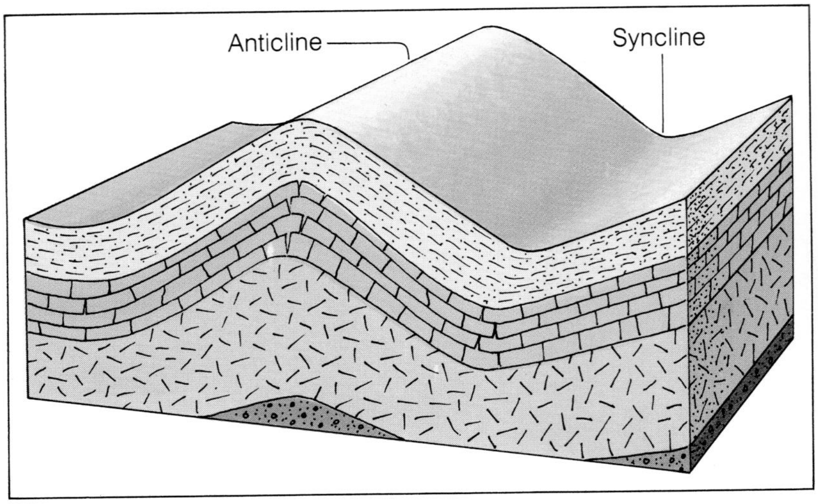

Figure 17–11 *Anticlines are upward folds in rocks, and synclines are downward folds in rocks, as can be seen in the drawing (left) and in the photograph of rock layers (right).*

clearly. Others are large enough to form mountains. Layered rocks with large folds often have smaller folds within the layers. The Appalachian Mountains in the eastern United States are made up of many anticlines and synclines. This folded mountain chain extends from Canada to the state of Alabama.

Even though an anticline is an upward fold, it is not always higher than the surrounding land. An anticline can be under hills, valleys, or flat areas. An anticline may be hidden because it may have been covered by sediments after the area was folded. Or the stress may not have been great enough to bring the fold to the earth's surface.

A number of factors determine whether rocks will fault or fold. One factor is temperature. If the rocks become extremely hot during compression, they are more likely to fold than to fault. Another factor is pressure. The greater the pressure applied to the rocks, the more likely they are to fold instead of fault.

Rock type also determines whether rocks will fault or fold. Some types of rocks are more **brittle** than others. This means that the rocks break easily when a force is applied. Sandstone is a brittle rock. Other rocks, such as rock salt, bend easily under stress. Rocks that bend easily are **ductile.** Ductile rocks are more likely to fold, while brittle rocks are more likely to fault.

How the force is applied to the rocks also determines whether the rocks will fault or fold. If the force is applied gradually, the rocks will usually fold. But if the force is applied suddenly, the rocks will usually fault.

Figure 17–12 *At the center of this photograph of a mountain in the Swiss Alps, you can see some large folds. If you look carefully at them, what else do you notice about the folds?*

SECTION REVIEW

1. Describe the three main types of stress.
2. Compare faulting and folding.
3. How could you identify a thrust fault on the face of a mountain?

17–3 Plateaus and Domes

Section Objective

To relate stress to the uplift of plateaus and domes

You have learned how faulting and folding have raised mountains high above the surrounding land. But mountains are not the only structures that are uplifted by the forces of the earth. **Plateaus and domes are two other structures formed by the gentle uplifting of an area.**

Plateaus

Large areas of the world are covered by layers of flat-topped rocks high above sea level. These structures are called **plateaus** (pla-TOHZ). Plateaus are often found near folded mountains.

Some of the same forces that cause the faulting and folding of mountains also form plateaus. Strong forces slowly push horizontally on an area, causing the uplift of a plateau. But unlike mountains plateaus are not faulted or folded. Instead, the raised rock layers remain flat.

Figure 17–13 *These low, gently sloping hills are part of the Appalachian Plateau. What kind of force may have uplifted the plateau?*

Sharpen Your Skills

A Geological Trip

Using information from the text, write a 300-word essay about an imaginary trip you are taking across the United States. Describe any important and dramatic geological formations you find along the way. In your essay, use the following vocabulary words.

plateau	fault-block mountain
dome mountain	rift valley
fault	fold
anticline	syncline
thrust fault	normal fault

The United States has two large plateaus that have been formed by horizontal forces. The Appalachian Plateau lies just west of the folded Appalachian Mountains. It covers much of New York, Pennsylvania, eastern Ohio, Kentucky, and Tennessee. The Appalachian Plateau was formed millions of years ago.

The Colorado Plateau is located west of the Rocky Mountains. It covers parts of New Mexico, western Colorado, eastern Utah, and northern Arizona. Most of the plateau is more than 1500 meters above sea level. The Colorado Plateau was formed much later than the Appalachian Plateau.

Plateaus can also be formed by a series of lava flows. Lava reaches the earth's surface through long cracks in the ground. Great floods of this hot molten lava periodically stream out of the cracks. The flowing lava spreads out over a large area and hardens in a sheet. The lava sometimes fills in valleys and covers hills. The flowing and spreading out of the lava is repeated over and over again. The hardened lava sheets pile up and form a raised plateau.

The Columbia Plateau, which covers parts of Oregon, Washington, and Idaho, is a lava plateau. Here lava built up a large, flat region covering almost 5 million square kilometers. The plateau is 1 to 2 kilometers thick.

Figure 17–14 *This is a spectacular view of the Grand Canyon and the Colorado Plateau. The Colorado River can be seen flowing through the canyon. How do you think the Grand Canyon was formed?*

Rivers often separate one large plateau into many smaller plateaus. Very often rivers cut deep valleys and canyons through plateaus. One of the most spectacular canyons formed by a river is the Grand Canyon in the Colorado Plateau.

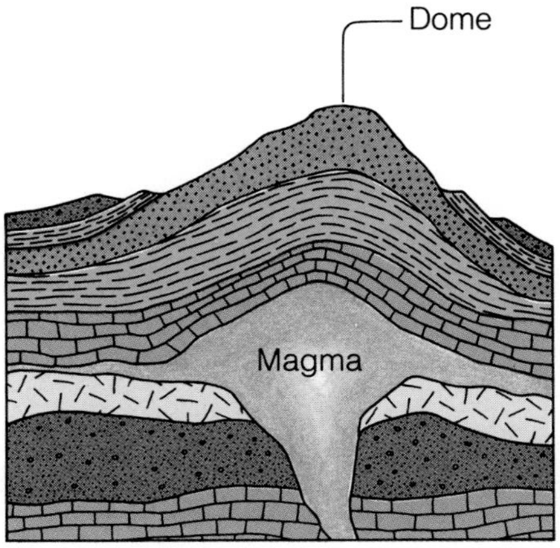

Figure 17–15 *An uplifted area called a dome is created when magma pushes up overlying rock layers without actually erupting onto the earth's surface. Often the upper layers of the dome are worn away.*

Domes

You know now that lava flows out onto the earth's surface to form plateaus. Sometimes, however, the hot molten rock does not reach the earth's surface. The molten rock found beneath the earth's surface is called **magma.**

An uplifted area can be formed by magma that works its way toward the earth's surface. Without actually erupting onto the surface, the magma pushes up overlying rock layers. At some point, the magma cools and forms hardened rock.

The uplifted area created by rising magma is called a **dome.** A dome is a raised area shaped roughly like the top half of a sphere. The outline of a dome is oval or circular. The rock layers over the hardened magma are warped upward to form the dome. But the rock layers of the surrounding area remain flat.

Domes that have been worn away in places form many separate peaks called **dome mountains.** The Black Hills of South Dakota and Wyoming are dome mountains. In this region, many layers of flat-lying

Figure 17–16 *The drawing of the Black Hills region of South Dakota shows the layers of rock that were pushed up by rising magma to form a dome. The rock layers have worn away to form the dome mountains in the center (right). The photograph of the same dome, shown in red, reveals the oval-shaped outline characteristic of many domes (left). Look at the photo. What may have worn away the dome into separate peaks?*

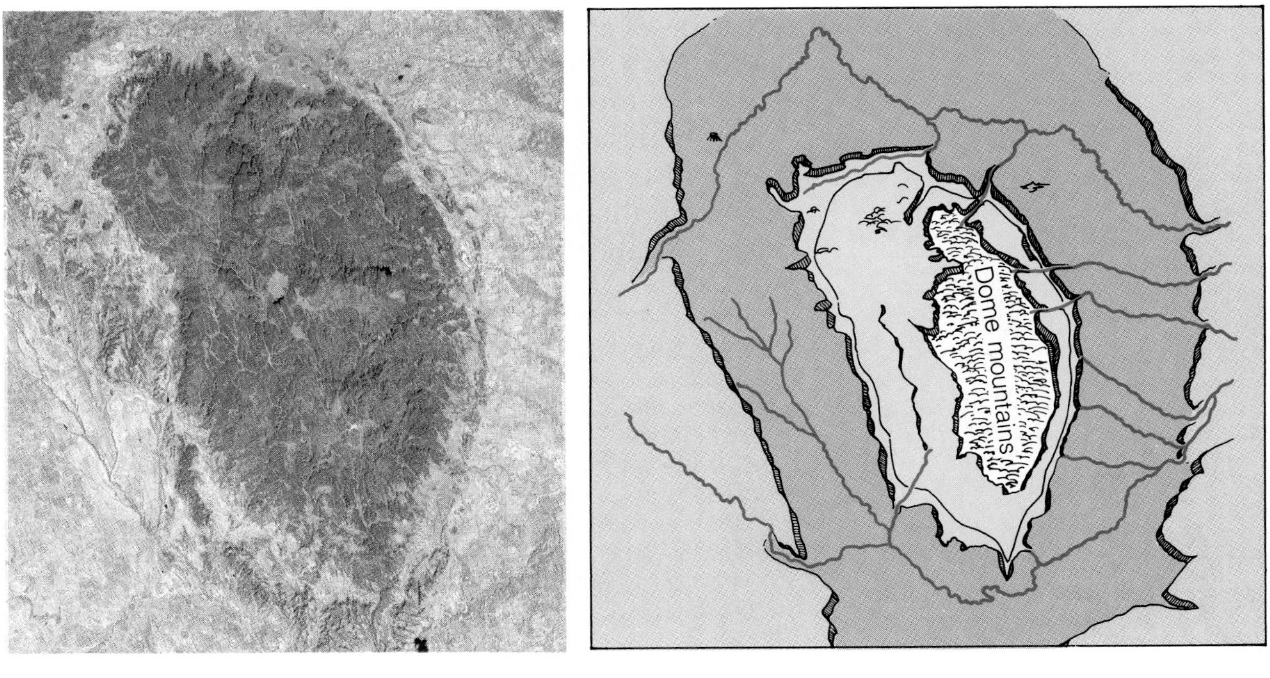

rocks were arched up. Over a long period of time, the rocks on top were worn away. The hardened magma that caused the uplifting was then exposed.

SECTION REVIEW

1. How are plateaus formed?
2. What is a dome mountain?
3. Do the streams around the dome mountains in Figure 17–16 flow away from or toward the dome? Explain your answer.

Section Objective

To describe the effects of isostasy on crustal movements

17–4 The Floating Crust

You have learned that the earth's crust can be deformed through faulting, folding, and uplifting. But deformation can also be caused by changes in the weight of the earth's crust. The changes create a stress on the earth's crust.

Beneath the earth's crust is the **mantle.** The mantle is the layer of the earth that extends from the bottom of the crust downward to the earth's core. The mantle rocks flow slowly, like hot, thick tar. **The solid crust floats on the mantle.** The crust floats because crustal rock is less dense than the mantle rock.

The floating crust exerts a downward force on the mantle. But the mantle also exerts a force. Its force is exerted upward on the crust. A balance exists between the downward force of the crust and the upward force of the mantle. The balancing of these two forces is called **isostasy** (igh-SAHS-tuh-see).

If material is added to an area of the crust, that area will float lower on the mantle. If material is removed, that area will float higher. So the crust is always balanced on the mantle.

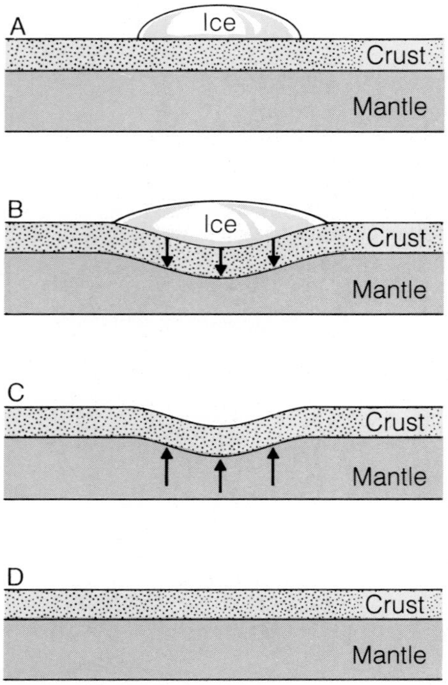

Figure 17–17 *These four drawings illustrate the effect that a heavy icecap has on an area's elevation. Drawing A shows an icecap forming on a flat area of crust. The added material increases the force with which the area of crust pushes down on the mantle. So that area sinks down lower (B). When the icecap melts, the downward force exerted by the crust is decreased (C). So the upward force exerted by the mantle causes the crust to slowly rise up again. Eventually a balance is reached between the upward force of the mantle and the downward force of the crust. And the crust no longer moves up or down (D). What process balances these two forces?*

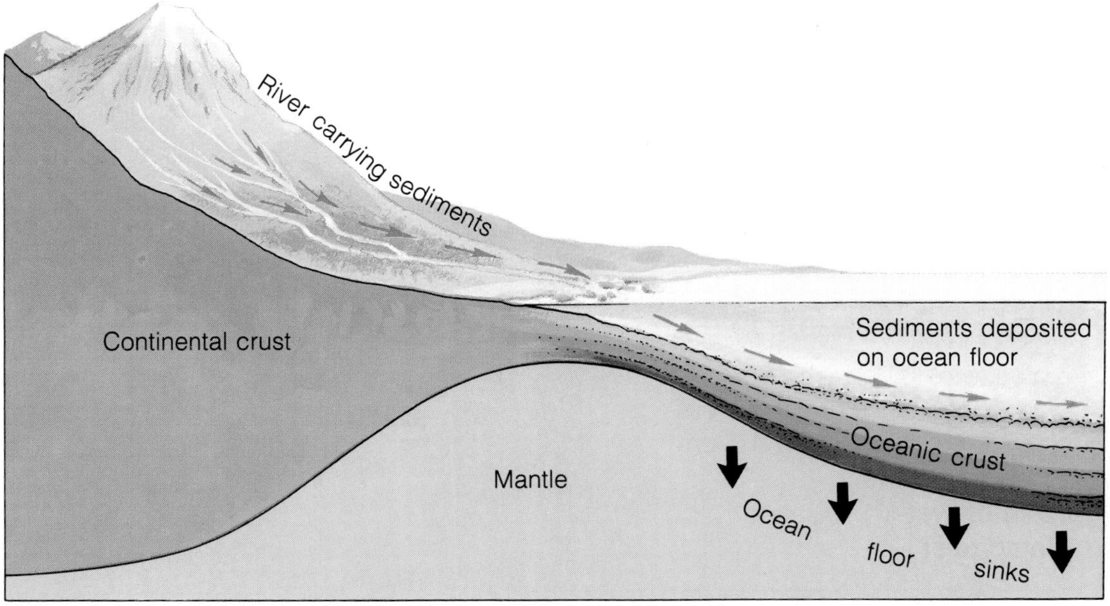

Figure 17–18 *Material is carried by rivers to the ocean where it is deposited on the ocean floor. You might think that eventually the ocean would be filled in with sediments. But this does not happen. Why?*

Isostasy explains why some low-lying regions, such as the Scandinavian countries, have slowly risen. Thousands of years ago, the Scandinavian countries were covered by tons of ice. As the ice melted, the area's crustal material was reduced. So the land began to float higher on the mantle. In fact, the land is still rising today. What do you think would happen to the elevation of Antarctica if the ice sheets covering most of the continent melted?

Crustal rock can also sink. Material carried by rivers is usually deposited where the river joins a larger body of water. As tons of sediment are deposited, there is more crustal material. So the crust slowly sinks.

The Mississippi River has dropped millions of tons of sediments into the Gulf of Mexico. As a result, the Gulf floor has sunk. But the water has not become any deeper. A balance is maintained between the sinking of the Gulf floor and the depositing of sediments.

SECTION REVIEW

1. Which are less dense, the crustal rocks or the mantle rocks?
2. What balances the downward force of the crust?
3. What happens when sediments are deposited on the ocean floor?

17 LABORATORY INVESTIGATION

Examining Isostasy

Problem

How does the earth's crust float on the earth's mantle?

Materials *(per group)*

2 blocks of wood—
  1: 10 cm × 10 cm × 2.5 cm
  2: 10 cm × 10 cm × 1.5 cm
25 metal washers
Basin of water
Metric ruler

Procedure

1. Label the larger block of wood "1" and the smaller block "2."
2. Float block 1 in the basin of water. Using a metric ruler, measure the amount of wood above the water's surface. Record your measurement in a data table like the one shown on this page.
3. Carefully place ten washers on the surface of block 1. Measure the amount of wood above the water's surface now. Record this information in your data table.
4. Continue adding washers two at a time. Carefully measure and record the amount of wood above the water's surface after each addition. Stop adding washers when the wood sinks or the washers spill into the basin of water.
5. Repeat steps 2 through 4 for block 2.

	Number of Washers	Amount Above Water
Block 1		
Block 2		

Observations

1. Are there any differences in the way the two blocks of wood float before the washers are added? After the washers are added?
2. Which block of wood is able to hold more washers before it sinks? Explain your answer.

Conclusions

1. How do the two blocks of wood resemble continental and oceanic crust? How does the water represent the earth's mantle?
2. If block 1 represents continental crust and block 2 represents oceanic crust, which crust is able to support the most weight?
3. How is the earth's crust able to stay balanced on the mantle?
4. How does this investigation illustrate isostasy?

CHAPTER REVIEW

SUMMARY

17–1 Stress

- The outermost layer of the earth and all the rocks at the earth's surface are part of the crust.
- The push-pull force called stress causes changes on the surface and often well beneath the surface of the earth.
- The breaking, tilting, and folding of rocks is called deformation.

17–2 Faulting and Folding

- Crustal rocks may be squeezed together by a type of stress called compression.
- The type of stress that pulls rocks apart is called tension.
- Shearing pushes on a block of crustal rock in two opposite directions.
- Compression, tension, and shearing can change a rock's volume, its shape, or both.
- The block of rock above a fault is called the hanging wall and the block of rock below a fault is called the foot wall.
- If a stress due to tension is acting on a fault, the hanging wall will move down relative to the foot wall.
- If a stress due to compression is acting on a fault, the hanging wall will move up relative to the foot wall.
- Thrust faults are almost horizontal.
- During thrust faulting older rocks are pushed up on top of younger rocks.
- A lateral fault is a fault along which the blocks move horizontally past one another.
- Mountains formed by blocks of rock uplifted by normal faults are called fault-block mountains.
- Valleys formed when the block of land between two normal faults slides downward are called rift valleys.
- When crustal rocks are bent, they are called folded rocks.
- If rocks become extremely hot during compression, they are more likely to fold than to fault.
- Ductile rocks are more likely to fold, while brittle rocks are more likely to fault.
- When the force applied to rocks is sudden the rocks will usually fault.

17–3 Plateaus and Domes

- Large areas of flat-topped rocks high above sea level are called plateaus.
- Plateaus are formed when horizontal forces slowly uplift a large area.
- Plateaus can also be formed from a series of lava flows.
- Rivers will often separate one large plateau into many smaller plateaus.
- An uplifted area called a dome can be formed by magma that works its way toward the earth's surface without actually erupting onto the surface.
- Domes that have been worn away in places form many separate peaks called dome mountains.

17–4 The Floating Crust

- Deformation of the crust can be caused by changes in the weight of the earth's crust.
- Mantle rocks flow very slowly, somewhat like hot, thick tar.
- The solid crust is always balanced on the mantle.
- If crustal material is removed from an area of the crust, that area will float higher on the mantle.
- If crustal material is added to an area of the crust, that area will sink lower on the mantle.

VOCABULARY

Define each term in a complete sentence.

anticline
brittle
compression
continental crust
crust
deformation
dome
dome mountain
ductile
fault
fault-block mountain
fold
foot wall
hanging wall
isostasy
joint
lateral fault
magma
mantle
normal fault
oceanic crust
plateau
reverse fault
rift valley
shearing
stress
syncline
tension
thrust fault

CONTENT REVIEW: MULTIPLE CHOICE

Choose the letter of the answer that best completes each sentence.

1. The breaking, tilting, and folding of rock is called
a. contraction b. compression c. deformation d. destruction

2. The type of stress that pulls rocks apart is called
a. shearing b. tension c. compression d. stretching

3. The block of rock above a fault is called the
a. fold b. syncline c. foot wall d. hanging wall

4. A fault formed when compression causes older crustal rock to slide up and over younger crustal rock is called a (an)
a. normal fault b. anticline c. syncline d. thrust fault

5. The fault along which the blocks move horizontally past one another is called a
a. lateral fault b. thrust fault c. reverse fault d. normal fault

6. Valleys that are formed when the block of land between two normal faults slides downward are called
a. horsts b. anticlines c. synclines d. rift valleys

7. An upward fold in a rock is called a (an)
a. normal fault b. anticline c. syncline d. thrust fault

8. Layers of flat-topped rocks high above sea level are called
a. mountains b. plateaus c. valleys d. rock flats

9. The mountains created when magma cools to form hardened rock are called
a. dome mountains b. fault-block mountains
c. plateaus d. none of these

10. The balancing of floating crustal rock on the denser mantle is called
a. floating b. syncline c. tension d. isostasy

CONTENT REVIEW: COMPLETION

Fill in the word or words that best complete each sentence.

1. The outermost layer of the earth that makes up the earth's landmasses is called the ______________.

2. ______________ is the push-pull force that causes changes on and beneath the earth's surface.

3. A break or crack in the earth's crust along which movement occurs is called a _______________.
4. When a stress due to tension is acting on a fault and the foot wall moves up relative to the hanging wall, it is called a (an) _______________.
5. When the block of land between two normal faults slides downward, a (an) _______________ is formed.
6. A bend in a crustal rock is called a (an) _______________.
7. Rocks that bend easily are _______________.
8. A (an) _______________ is created when magma pushes up overlying rock layers without actually erupting onto the earth's surface.
9. The layer of the earth that extends from the bottom of the crust downward to the earth's core is called the _______________.
10. If material is added to an area of the crust, that area will float _______________ on the mantle.

CONTENT REVIEW: TRUE OR FALSE

Determine whether each statement is true or false. If it is true, write "true." If it is false, change the underlined word or words to make the statement true.

1. The section of the earth's crust that makes up the earth's landmasses is called the <u>oceanic crust</u>.
2. Crustal rocks may be squeezed together by a type of stress called <u>contraction</u>.
3. <u>Tension</u> pushes on a block of crustal rock in two opposite directions.
4. Compression, tension, and shearing can change a rock's volume <u>but not its shape</u>.
5. Joints in a rock are <u>parallel</u> to each other.
6. Thrust faults are special because they lie almost <u>vertical</u>.
7. Mountains formed by blocks of rock uplifted by normal faults are called <u>plateaus</u>.
8. An upward fold in a rock is an <u>anticline</u>.
9. <u>Ductile</u> rocks are more likely to bend or fold, while brittle rocks are more likely to fault or break.
10. Crustal rock is <u>denser</u> than the mantle rock.

CONCEPT REVIEW: SKILL BUILDING

Use the skills you have developed in the chapter to complete each activity.

1. **Making comparisons** Draw a diagram that compares an anticline with a syncline.
2. **Making inferences** Coal miners dig their tunnels along faults. The miners named the blocks above and below the faults. They called one block the "hanging wall" and the other block the "foot wall." How do you think they came up with these names?
3. **Interpreting data** Geologists studying a rock formation have found that there are older rocks lying on top of younger rocks. How can you explain these findings?

CONCEPT REVIEW: ESSAY

Discuss each of the following in a brief paragraph.

1. How do faults affect the earth's surface?
2. Describe how the Colorado Plateau was formed.
3. How can lava form a plateau?
4. Compare the rising and sinking of a floating ship to the floating crust.

Earthquakes and Volcanoes

18

CHAPTER SECTIONS

18–1 Earthquakes

18–2 Formation of a Volcano

18–3 Volcano and Earthquake Zones

CHAPTER OBJECTIVES

After completing this chapter, you will be able to

18–1 Explain what happens during an earthquake.

18–1 Describe how earthquakes are detected.

18–2 Compare the different types of lava and volcanic particles.

18–2 Classify the three types of volcanoes.

18–3 Identify the locations of major zones of earthquake and volcanic activity.

On December 7, 1988, disaster struck! A devastating earthquake shook Soviet Armenia. As the ground heaved violently, large and small buildings trembled and then collapsed in ruins. Trees snapped like toothpicks. And bridges crashed to the ground below. The earthquake struck along a fault line that begins in eastern Turkey, goes through the Armenian city of Stepvanavan, and ends at Lake Sevan. The town of Spitak, with a population of 55,000 people, was completely leveled. The earthquake also caused havoc in the nearby town of Leninaken, the Armenian republic's second largest city.

The Armenian earthquake registered 6.9 on the Richter scale, which is not tremendously large. The damage, however, was severe. At least 45,000 people died and more than 500,000 Armenians were left homeless. Experts believe the damage was this severe—it was the worst earthquake in the history of the Soviet Union—because of poor building construction and a lack of planning for such a disaster.

Scientists estimate that more than 1 million earthquakes occur every year. Some are very small and cause little damage. Others are violent and cause severe damage. But in either case, earthquakes serve as reminders that the earth's crust is continually undergoing change.

Although the earth's crust is moving, you probably cannot detect most of the movements. They are slight and gradual. But sometimes the movements are sudden, dramatic, and destructive. In this chapter, you will learn what causes some movements of the earth's crust and how these movements are studied. You will also learn about two of the most sudden and violent movements: earthquakes and volcanoes.

The damage brought about by the 1988 earthquake in Armenia is a reminder of the awesome power of nature.

Section Objective

To describe the causes and characteristics of earthquakes

18–1 Earthquakes

An earthquake is the shaking and trembling that results from the sudden movement of part of the earth's crust. When you throw a pebble into a pond, waves move outward in all directions. In a similar manner, when rocks in the earth's crust break, earthquake waves travel through the earth in all directions. The ground shakes and trembles. During a severe earthquake, the ground can rise and fall like waves in the ocean. The motion of the ground causes buildings, trees, and telephone poles to sway and fall. Loud noises can sometimes be heard coming from the earth. What causes such sudden movements of the earth's crust?

The most common cause of earthquakes is faulting. As you learned in Chapter 17, a fault is a break in the earth's crust. During faulting, parts of the earth's crust are pushed together or pulled apart. Rocks break and slide past each other. Energy is released during this process. As the rocks move, they cause nearby rocks to move also. The rocks continue to move in this way until the energy is used up.

Figure 18–1 *When rocks in the earth's crust break, earthquake waves travel out in all directions. Their movement is similar to these waves, which form when water is disturbed. What is the shape of the waves that form?*

The San Andreas Fault in California is a very long fault that passes under the Gulf of California through the Great Valley and San Francisco. It continues under the Pacific Ocean off the coast of northern California. The fault is about 960 kilometers long and 32 kilometers deep. The land west of the San Andreas Fault is slowly moving north. The land east of the fault is moving south. But the rocks along the fault do not all move at the same time. Earthquakes occur in one area and then in another. In 1906, movement along the San Andreas Fault caused the famous San Francisco earthquake.

Earthquakes that occur on the ocean floor cause giant sea waves called **tsunamis** (tsoo-NAH-meez). These waves can travel at speeds of 700 to 800 kilometers per hour. As they approach the coast, tsunamis can be as high as 10 to 20 meters.

Figure 18–2 *This aerial view of the San Andreas Fault in California shows only a small portion of the 960-kilometer-long fault. Notice how the drainage patterns have been interrupted in the fault zone. The land east of the fault is moving south. In what direction is the land west of the fault moving?*

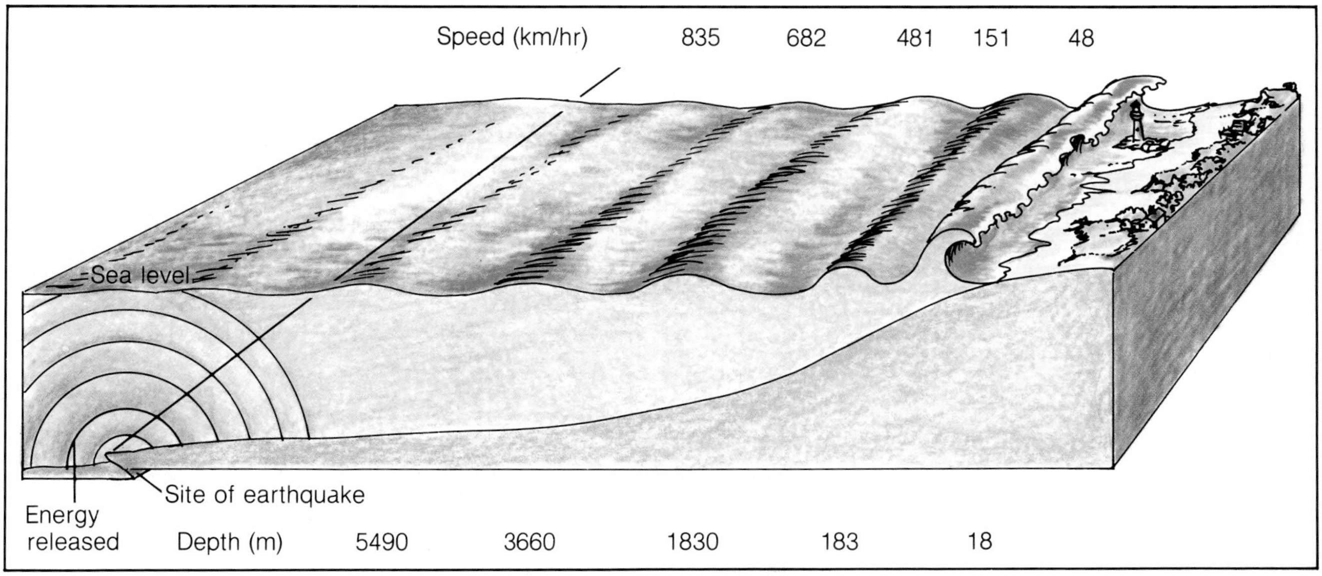

Figure 18–3 *Earthquakes that occur on the ocean floor cause giant sea waves called tsunamis. You can see that when tsunamis are out at sea, they are far apart, fast moving, and very low. What happens to these waves near shore?*

When they hit a coast, they destroy everything in their paths.

Seismic Waves

Some faults are deep inside the earth. Others are close to or at the earth's surface. Most faults occur between the surface and a depth of 74 kilometers.

The point beneath the earth's surface where the rocks break and move is called the **focus** (FOH-cuhs) of the earthquake. The focus is the underground point of origin of an earthquake. Directly above the focus, on the earth's surface, is the **epicenter** (EHP-uh-sehn-tuhr). Earthquake waves reach the epicenter first. The most violent shaking is found at the epicenter. See Figure 18–4, page 462.

Earthquake waves are known as **seismic** (SIGHZ-mihk) **waves.** Scientists have learned much about earthquakes and the interior of the earth by studying seismic waves. There are three main types of seismic waves. Each type of wave has a characteristic speed and manner of travel.

PRIMARY WAVES Seismic waves that travel the fastest are called **primary waves,** or **P waves.** P waves arrive at a given point before any other type of seismic wave. P waves travel through solids, liquids, and gases. They move through the earth at different speeds, depending on the density of the material. As they move deeper into the earth, where material is more dense, they speed up.

Sharpen Your Skills

Graphing a Tsunami

A tsunami far out to sea travels very quickly and carries a great deal of energy. However, out at sea, tsunami waves are quite low. As a tsunami approaches shore, its speed decreases drastically, but it still carries the same amount of energy. What effect does slowing down in speed have on the height of tsunami waves close to shore? Why are such waves so powerful?

Use the data from Figure 18–3 to make a graph plotting ocean depth against the speed of a tsunami. What general conclusions can you draw from your graph?

Figure 18–4 *This diagram shows the relationship between the epicenter and the focus of an earthquake. Where do the strongest seismic waves occur?*

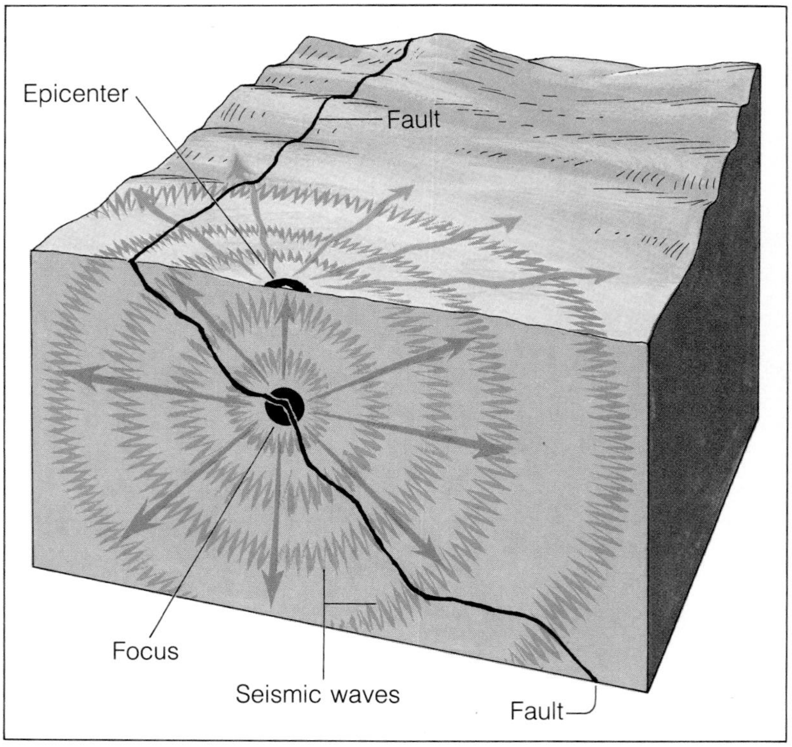

Figure 18–5 *P waves push together and pull apart rock particles in the direction of the wave movement. The slower S waves move rock particles from side to side at right angles to the wave movement. How do L waves move?*

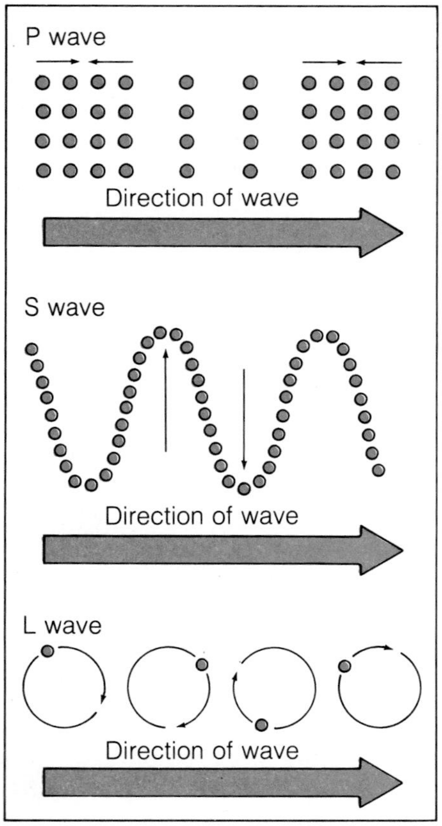

P waves are push-pull waves. They cause rock particles to move back and forth in the direction the waves are moving. As P waves travel, they push rock particles into the particles ahead of them and compress them. The rock particles then bounce back. They hit the particles behind them that are being pushed forward. The particles move back and forth as shown in Figure 18–5.

SECONDARY WAVES Seismic waves that do not travel through the earth as fast as P waves do are called **secondary waves,** or **S waves.** S waves arrive at a given point after P waves. S waves travel through solids but not through liquids and gases. Like P waves, S waves speed up when they pass through denser material.

Part of the earth's interior is molten, or a hot liquid. Because S waves do not travel through liquids, they are not always recorded at all locations during an earthquake. What happens to S waves when they reach the liquid part of the earth's interior?

S waves cause rock particles to move from side to side. The rock particles move at right angles to the direction of the waves. See Figure 18–5.

SURFACE WAVES The slowest seismic waves are called **surface waves,** or **L waves.** L waves arrive at a given point after primary and secondary waves. L waves travel from the focus directly upward to the epicenter. Then they move along the earth's surface the way waves travel in the ocean. Just as the surface of water rises and falls with each wave, the earth's surface moves up and down with each L wave that passes. L waves cause most of the damage during an earthquake because they bend and twist the earth's surface.

Detecting Seismic Waves: The Seismograph

A **seismograph** (SIGHZ-muh-grahf) is an instrument that detects and measures seismic waves. A seismograph consists of a weight attached to a spring or wire. Because the weight is not attached directly to the earth, it will remain nearly still even when the earth moves. A pen attached to the weight records any movement on a sheet of paper wound around a constantly rotating drum.

Because the pen is attached to the weight, it also remains nearly still when the earth moves. But the drum moves with the earth. When the earth moves, the pen records a wavy line on the paper. When the earth is still, the pen records a nearly straight line. What kind of line would be recorded during a violent earthquake?

Seismologists, scientists who study earthquakes, can determine the strength of an earthquake by studying the height of the wavy lines recorded on the paper. The seismograph's record of waves is called a **seismogram** (SIGHZ-muh-gram). The higher the wavy lines on the seismogram are, the stronger the earthquake is.

The strength of earthquakes is measured according to a scale called the **Richter scale.** The Richter scale measures how much energy an earthquake releases by assigning the earthquake a number from 1 to 10. The number indicates how strong the earthquake is. The more energy an earthquake releases, the stronger the earthquake is. Each number on the Richter scale represents an earthquake ten times stronger than an earthquake represented by the

Sharpen Your Skills

Making Waves

1. Strike the prongs of a tuning fork with a pencil and then place the ends of the prongs in a glass of water. What happens?

2. Tie a small piece of cork to a string. Hold the string in one hand so that the cork swings freely. Strike the prongs of the tuning fork and hold one prong against the cork. What happens?

Relate your observations to the movements of rocks inside the earth. How do the movements produce seismic waves?

Figure 18–6 *In a seismograph, a heavy weight attached to a wire holds a pen motionless while the support structure anchored in the earth moves with seismic waves. The difference in motion between the support structure and the motionless pen is recorded on a rotating drum. What is the record of seismic waves called?*

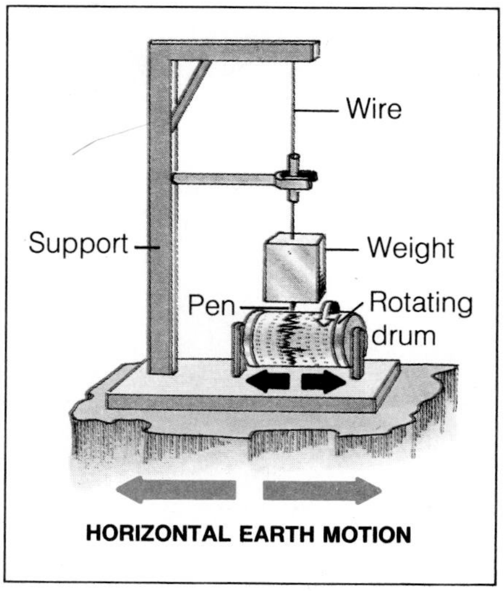

Figure 18–7 *An earthquake that occurred on the Kenai Peninsula in Alaska caused the compression and buckling of many railroad bridges. Where do you think this type of damage was greatest?*

preceding number. Any number above 6 indicates a very destructive earthquake.

The amount of damage caused by an earthquake depends on the earthquake's strength, the population of the area affected, the strength of buildings in the area, and the time at which the earthquake occurs. The 1906 San Francisco earthquake measured 8.3 on the Richter scale. Seven hundred people were killed. In 1923, an earthquake of similar strength occurred in Tokyo, Japan. More than 100,000 people were killed. Much of the earthquake damage was caused by fires. Why do you think more people were killed in the 1923 Tokyo earthquake than in the 1906 San Francisco earthquake?

Predicting Earthquakes

Scientists continue to study earthquakes in the hope of improving their ability to accurately predict them. For earthquake prediction to be useful, it must be reliable and complete. The information

Figure 18–8 *This Seismic Risk Map shows areas of the United States where earthquakes are likely to occur and the relative damage they are likely to cause. Where are earthquakes least likely to occur? To cause the most damage?*

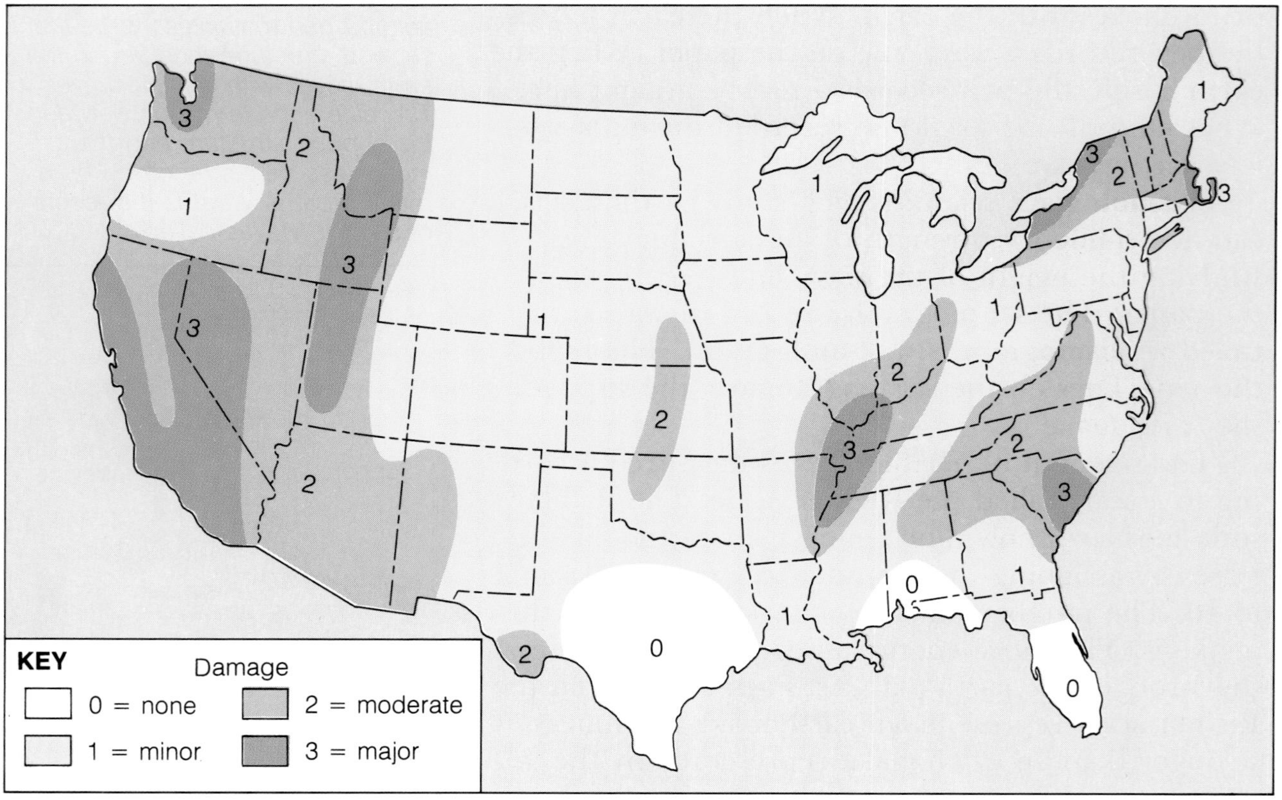

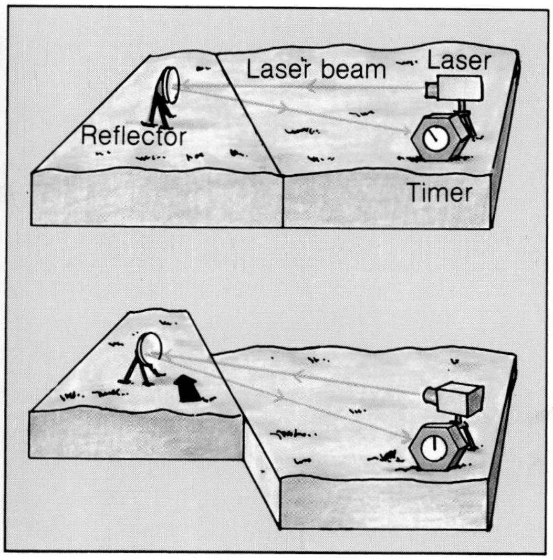

Figure 18–9 *A laser field station (left) sends out laser beams to accurately measure the movements of an earthquake. By measuring the time it takes for a laser beam to strike a reflector and bounce back (right), scientists can determine tiny shifts along a fault.*

must include where, when, and how strong the earthquake will be. If a strong earthquake is predicted, areas in danger can be evacuated. In 1975, the Chinese predicted an earthquake in their country so accurately that many thousands of lives were saved. Most of the people in three counties were evacuated before the earthquake struck.

If strong earthquakes could be predicted years in advance, people could better plan the growth of cities. Buildings could be reinforced to better withstand the shock from an earthquake. In San Francisco, attempts have already been made to build earthquake-proof buildings. How else might accurate earthquake prediction save lives?

Seismologists have found some warning signals that help predict earthquakes. Often there are changes in the speeds of P waves and S waves before a major earthquake. Sometimes slight changes in the tilt of the earth's surface can be detected. Land near a fault may rise or sink slightly. The water level in wells will often go up or down.

SECTION REVIEW

1. What is the most common cause of earthquakes?
2. What is the focus of an earthquake? The epicenter of an earthquake?
3. What are the three major types of seismic waves?
4. What is a seismograph?
5. How is the strength of an earthquake measured?

Sharpen Your Skills

The Seismograph

Contact the geology department of a college or university near your home. Find out whether they have a working seismograph. If not, locate the nearest seismograph station that has one.

Visit the school or station with the seismograph. Observe it at work. Ask someone there how to read the seismogram—the recording sheet on the rotating drum.

Write a report about your trip and present it to your class.

CAREER — *Volcanologist*

HELP WANTED: VOLCANOLOGIST Research position with the United States Geological Survey. Bachelor's degree in chemistry, geology, or physics required. Graduate work in geochemistry, geophysics, geology, or volcanology very helpful.

A volcano may be inactive for hundreds or even thousands of years. But as soon as it shows signs of activity, scientists from around the world rush to study it. These scientists are called **volcanologists.**

Volcanologists are interested in the origin of volcanoes, the kinds of materials they release, and the different shapes they develop. Volcanologists also study the distribution of volcanoes around the earth and the causes of volcanic eruptions.

After graduating from college, many volcanologists teach, do research, or work for government organizations. To learn more about this career, write to the American Geophysical Union, 2000 Florida Avenue, N W , Washington, DC 20009.

Section Objective

To relate types of volcanoes to types of volcanic eruptions

18–2 Formation of a Volcano

Deep within the earth, under tremendous pressure and temperature, rock exists as a hot liquid called **magma.** This molten rock is in pockets called magma chambers. Magma is constantly moving. It works its way toward the earth's surface through cracks in solid rock or by melting the solid rock.

When magma reaches the earth's surface, it is called **lava.** Lava can build up to form a cone-shaped mountain. The place where lava reaches the earth's surface is called a **volcano.**

Volcanic Eruptions

All volcanic eruptions are not alike. Some eruptions are quiet. Others are very violent. The opening from which lava erupts is called a **vent.** Volcanoes often have more than one vent. If there is more than one vent, lava will sometimes pour from the sides of the volcano as well as from the top.

Volcanoes are "windows" into the interior of the earth. By analyzing the mineral makeup of lava, geologists can determine the chemical composition

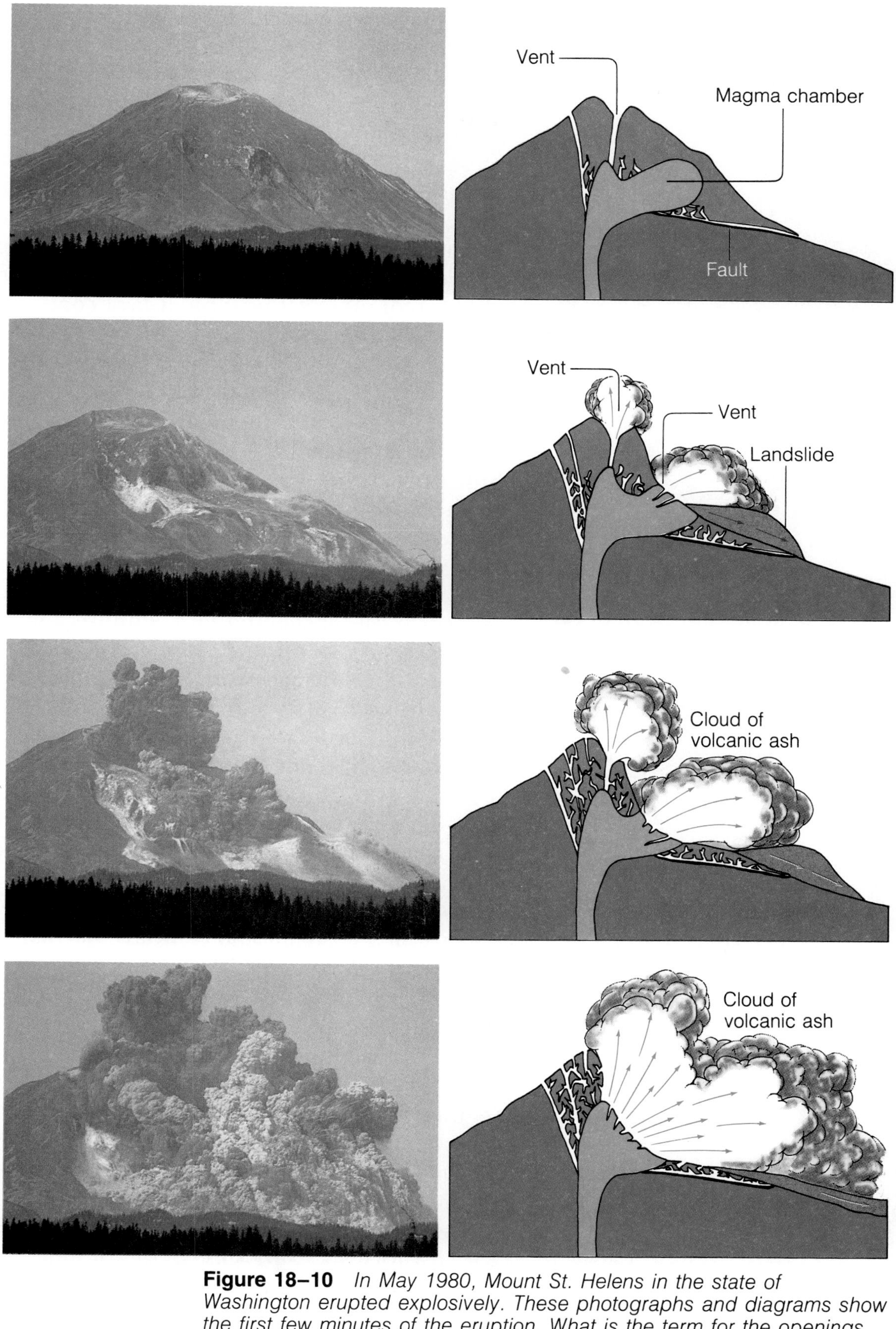

Figure 18–10 *In May 1980, Mount St. Helens in the state of Washington erupted explosively. These photographs and diagrams show the first few minutes of the eruption. What is the term for the openings from which lava erupts?*

Figure 18–11 *When very thin liquid lava cools, it often hardens with a wrinkled surface. This type of solid lava is called* pahoehoe *(pah-HOY-ay-HOY-ay), the Hawaiian term for "ropey" (top). Another type of solid lava, called* aa *(AH-ah), forms when the hardened crust of a lava flow breaks into jagged chunks as the liquid below flows on (bottom).*

of the magma from which the lava formed. There are four general types of lava.

One type of lava is dark colored and contains a lot of water. This lava is rich in the elements iron and magnesium. When this type of lava cools, igneous rocks such as basalt are formed.

Another type of lava is light colored and contains very little water. This lava, too, is rich in the elements iron and magnesium. But it also contains the chemical compound silica, which accounts for its lighter color. When this type of lava cools, it forms the igneous rock rhyolite, which resembles granite.

The third type of lava has a chemical composition similar to that of both the dark-colored type and the light-colored type. Different varieties of igneous rocks in the earth's crust, such as andesite, are formed from this type of lava.

The fourth type of lava contains large amounts of gases such as steam and carbon dioxide. When this lava hardens, it forms rocks with many holes in them. The holes are formed as gas bubbles are trapped in the hardening lava. Pumice and scoria are igneous rocks formed from this type of lava. Do you know an unusual property of pumice?

Because dark-colored lava is thin and runny, it tends to flow quietly. The islands of Hawaii and Iceland were formed by many quiet lava flows. Light-colored lava causes explosive eruptions. Because light-colored lava does not contain much water, it tends to harden in vents. Explosive eruptions are caused when lava in vents hardens into rocks. Steam and new lava build up under the rocks. When the pressure of the steam and new lava becomes great, a violent explosion occurs.

Many rock fragments are blown into the air during volcanic eruptions. The smallest particles are called **volcanic dust.** Volcanic dust is very fine, as tiny as grains of flour. Volcanic dust particles are less than 0.25 millimeters in diameter.

Rock particles more than 0.25 millimeters but less than 5 millimeters in diameter are called **volcanic ash.** Volcanic ash particles are the size of grains of rice. Volcanic ash falls to the earth's surface and forms small rocks. Both volcanic dust and volcanic ash can be carried away from a volcano by the wind. They can fall to the earth near the volcano or be carried completely around the world!

Larger rock particles are called **volcanic bombs.** Volcanic bombs are a few centimeters to several meters in diameter. Some bombs are the size of boulders and have masses of several metric tons. Small volcanic bombs about the size of golf balls are called **cinders.** When volcanic bombs are hurled out of a volcano, they are molten. They harden as they travel through the air.

Types of Volcanoes

Different types of volcanic eruptions form different types of volcanoes. Some volcanoes are built from quiet flows of thin, runny lava that spread over a broad area. Other volcanoes are formed from violent eruptions. Some volcanoes are formed from a combination of quiet flows of lava and violent eruptions.

CINDER CONES Volcanoes made mostly of cinders and other rock particles that have been blown into the air are called **cinder cones.** Cinder cones form from explosive eruptions. Because the material in cinder cones is loosely arranged, the cones are not very high. But they do have a fairly narrow base and steep sides. Paricutin in Mexico is a cinder cone.

Sharpen Your Skills

Volcano Models

1. Using the diagrams in Figure 18–12, make a papier-mâché model of a cross section of one of the three types of volcanoes.
2. On your model, label the structures of each volcano.

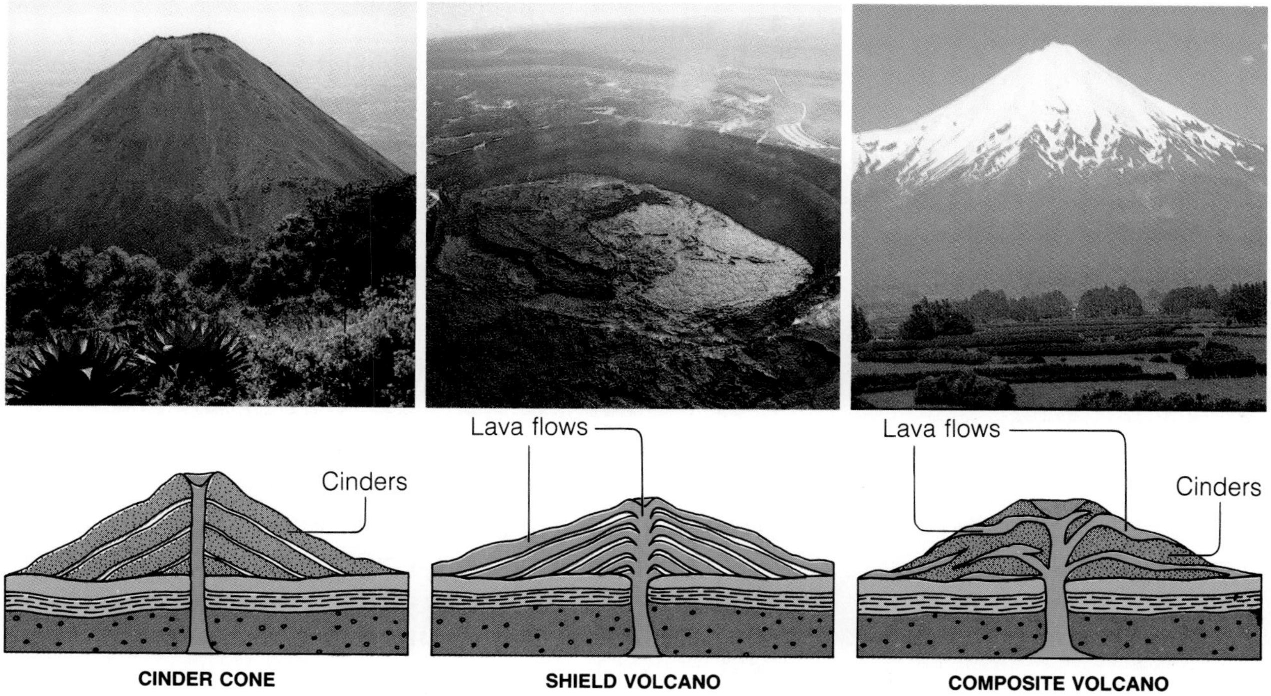

Figure 18–12 *An example of each of the three types of volcanoes is shown in these photographs. The diagrams show how each type forms. Izalco in El Salvador is a cinder cone (left). Kilauea in Hawaii is a shield volcano (center). Mount Egmont in New Zealand is a composite volcano (right).*

Figure 18–13 *At the top of a volcanic cone, there is often a depression called a crater. Here you see the crater of Mount Vesuvius in Italy (top). Sometimes a crater becomes very large, forming a caldera. This caldera in El Salvador has filled with water and formed a lake (bottom).*

SHIELD VOLCANOES Volcanoes composed of quiet lava flows are called **shield volcanoes.** The lava flows over a large area because it is runny. After several quiet eruptions, a gently sloping, dome-shaped mountain is formed. The largest shield volcano is Mauna Loa in the Hawaiian Islands. Mauna Loa rises from the bottom of the Pacific Ocean to 4 kilometers above sea level.

COMPOSITE VOLCANOES Volcanoes built up of alternating layers of rock particles and lava are called **composite volcanoes.** During the formation of a composite volcano, a violent eruption first occurs, hurling volcanic bombs, cinders, and ash out of the vent. Then a quiet eruption occurs, producing a lava flow that covers the rock particles. After many alternating eruptions, a large cone-shaped mountain forms. The most famous composite volcanoes are Mount Vesuvius in Italy and Mount Etna in Sicily.

At the top of a volcanic cone, there is often a funnel-shaped pit or depression. This pit is called a **crater.** If a crater becomes very large as a result of the collapse of its walls, it is called a **caldera.** A caldera may also form when the top of a volcano collapses or explodes.

SECTION REVIEW

1. What is the difference between magma and lava?
2. What is a volcano?
3. List the different particles blown from a volcano in order of increasing size.
4. What are the three types of volcanoes? How are they formed?

18–3 Volcano and Earthquake Zones

Section Objective

To identify volcano and earthquake zones

Volcanic eruptions and earthquakes often occur in the same areas of the world. Sometimes volcanic eruptions set off earthquakes. Although the two events need not occur together, there is a relationship between their occurrences. **Most major earthquakes and volcanic eruptions occur in three zones of the world.** Scientists believe that there is a great

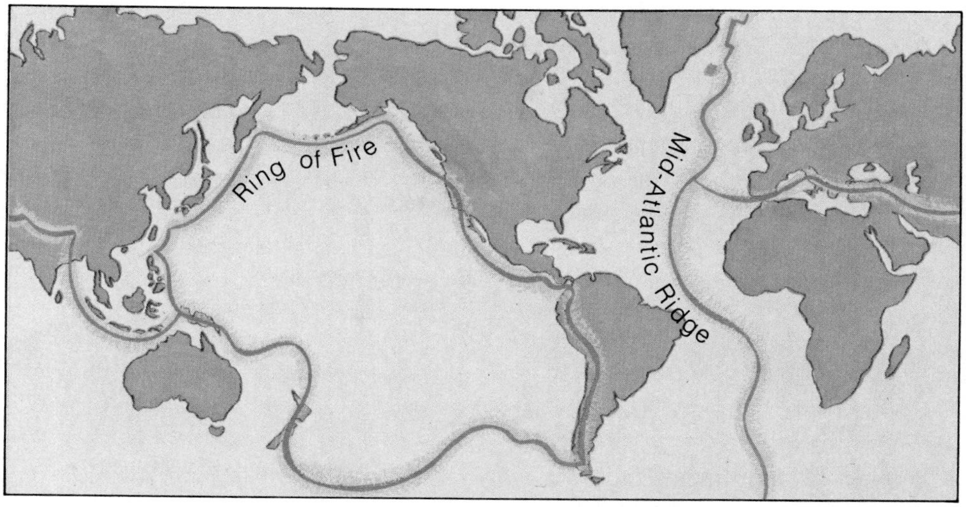

Figure 18–14 *This map shows the Ring of Fire, a zone of earthquake and volcano activity that surrounds the Pacific Ocean. What is the name of the zone of volcanic mountains under the Atlantic Ocean?*

deal of movement and activity in the earth's crust in these zones.

One major earthquake and volcano zone extends nearly all the way around the edge of the Pacific Ocean. This zone goes through New Zealand, the Philippines, Japan, Alaska, and along the western coasts of North and South America. The San Andreas Fault is part of this zone. This zone of the Pacific Ocean is often called the **Ring of Fire.**

A second major earthquake and volcano zone is found near the Mediterranean Sea. The zone extends across Asia into India. Many countries in the zone, including Italy, Greece, and Turkey, have violent earthquakes. Many volcanic eruptions have also occurred in this zone.

The third major earthquake and volcano zone extends from Iceland to the middle of the Atlantic Ocean. Under the ocean, there is a long ridge of volcanic mountains called the Mid-Atlantic Ridge. Scientists believe that the volcano and earthquake activity are due to the formation of new parts of the earth's crust along the ridge. Volcanic islands in the Atlantic Ocean, such as Iceland, are part of the Mid-Atlantic Ridge.

Sharpen Your Skills

Volcano in Motion

1. On 8 to 10 unlined note cards, draw each successive step in the movement of magma up and out of a volcano. Use Figures 18–10 and 18–12 as guides, and use your imagination.

2. Number each note card in sequence as you draw it.

3. Tape the cards together along the top.

Hold the cards at the taped end and flip from card 1 to the last card.

SECTION REVIEW

1. What is the Ring of Fire?
2. What do scientists believe causes so many earthquakes in the middle of the Atlantic Ocean?
3. Would a volcanic eruption be likely on the east coast of the United States? Explain.

18 LABORATORY INVESTIGATION

Locating Patterns of Earthquake and Volcano Distribution

Problem

What is the pattern of earthquake and volcano distribution worldwide?

Materials *(per student)*

World map showing latitude and longitude
4 pencils of different colors

Procedure

1. Using the information in the table on earthquakes, plot the location of each earthquake. With a colored pencil, label each earthquake with the letter E in a circle.
2. Using the information in the table on volcanoes, plot the location of each volcano. With another pencil, label each volcano with the letter V in a circle.
3. With another pencil, lightly shade the areas in which earthquakes are found.
4. With another pencil, lightly shade the areas in which volcanoes are found.

Observations

1. Are earthquakes scattered randomly over the surface of the earth or are they concentrated in definite zones?
2. Are volcanoes scattered randomly or concentrated in definite zones?
3. Are most earthquakes and volcanoes located near the edges or near the center of continents?
4. Are there any active volcanoes located near your home? Has an earthquake occurred near your home?

Conclusions

1. Describe any patterns you observe in the distribution of earthquakes and volcanoes.
2. What relationship exists between the locations of earthquakes and of volcanoes?

EARTHQUAKES

Longitude	Latitude
120°W	40°N
110°E	5°S
77°W	4°S
88°E	23°N
121°E	14°S
34°E	7°N
74°W	44°N
70°W	30°S
10°E	45°N
85°W	13°N
125°E	23°N
30°E	35°N
140°E	35°N
12°E	46°N
75°E	28°N
150°W	61°N
68°W	47°S

VOLCANOES

Longitude	Latitude
150°W	60°N
70°W	35°S
120°W	45°N
61°W	15°N
105°W	20°N
75°W	0°
122°W	40°N
30°E	40°N
60°E	30°N
160°E	55°N
37°E	3°S
145°E	40°N
120°E	10°S
14°E	41°N
105°E	5°S
35°E	15°N
70°W	30°S

CHAPTER REVIEW

SUMMARY

18–1 Earthquakes

❑ An earthquake is the shaking and trembling that results from the sudden movement of part of the earth's crust.

❑ The most common cause of earthquakes is faulting.

❑ Giant sea waves called tsunamis are caused by earthquakes on the ocean floor.

❑ The underground point of origin of an earthquake is called the focus.

❑ Directly above the focus, on the earth's surface, is the epicenter.

❑ Earthquake waves are called seismic waves. There are three types of seismic waves: primary, secondary, and surface waves.

❑ Seismic waves are detected and measured by a seismograph.

❑ The strength of an earthquake is measured according to the Richter scale.

❑ Accurate earthquake prediction is a goal of seismologists.

18–2 Formation of a Volcano

❑ Hot liquid rock in the earth's interior is called magma.

❑ Magma that reaches the earth's surface is called lava.

❑ The place where lava reaches the earth's surface is called a volcano.

❑ The opening from which lava erupts is called a vent.

❑ The mineral makeup of lava provides a clue to the chemical composition of magma inside the earth.

❑ Many rock fragments of varying sizes are blown into the air during volcanic eruptions. They include volcanic dust, volcanic ash, volcanic bombs, and cinders.

❑ Different types of volcanic eruptions form different types of volcanoes. These include cinder cones, shield volcanoes, and composite volcanoes.

18–3 Volcano and Earthquake Zones

❑ Most major earthquakes and volcanic eruptions occur in parts of the world where there is a great deal of movement and activity in the earth's crust.

❑ There are three major earthquake and volcano zones in the world where a great deal of movement in the earth's crust occurs.

VOCABULARY

Define each term in a complete sentence.

caldera
cinder
cinder cone
composite volcano
crater
epicenter
focus
lava
L wave
magma
primary wave
P wave
Richter scale
Ring of Fire
secondary wave
seismic wave
seismogram
seismograph
seismologist
shield volcano
surface wave
S wave
tsunami
vent
volcanic ash
volcanic bomb
volcanic dust
volcano

CONTENT REVIEW: MULTIPLE CHOICE

Choose the letter of the answer that best completes each sentence.

1. The most common cause of earthquakes is
a. tsunamis b. faulting c. seismic waves d. magma

2. Giant sea waves caused by earthquakes on the ocean floor are called
a. volcanoes b. faults c. seismograms d. tsunamis

3. The underground point of origin of an earthquake is called the
a. focus b. epicenter c. magma d. lava

4. The most violent shaking during an earthquake occurs at the
a. Ring of Fire b. epicenter c. focus d. vent

5. The fastest seismic waves are called
a. S waves b. L waves c. V waves d. P waves

6. The seismic waves that cause most of the damage during an earthquake are called
a. S waves b. L waves c. V waves d. P waves

7. The instrument that detects and measures earthquake waves is called a
a. seismograph b. seismogram c. voltmeter d. barometer

8. The scale used to measure the strength of an earthquake is called the
a. focus scale b. seismic scale c. Richter scale d. San scale

9. Hot liquid rock in the earth's interior is called
a. lava b. magma c. ash d. basalt

10. The largest rock fragments blown into the air during a volcanic eruption are called
a. volcanic ash b. volcanic dust
c. volcanic cinders d. volcanic bombs

CONTENT REVIEW: COMPLETION

Fill in the word or words that best complete each sentence.

1. The shaking and trembling that results from the sudden movement of part of the earth's crust commonly caused by a fault is called a (an) ______________.

2. Earthquake waves reach the earth's surface at the ______________ first.

3. Earthquake waves are called ______________ waves.

4. The instrument that measures earthquake waves is called a (an) ______________.

5. The most violent earthquake would be assigned the number ______________ on the Richter scale.

6. Magma that reaches the earth's surface is called ______________.

7. Dark-colored lava rich in iron and magnesium cools to form igneous rocks such as ______________.

8. The smallest rock particles blown into the air during volcanic eruptions are called ______________.

9. Volcanoes that are made of alternating layers of rock particles and lava are called ______________ volcanoes.

10. A very large crater at the top of a volcanic cone is called a (an) ______________.

CONTENT REVIEW: TRUE OR FALSE

Determine whether each statement is true or false. If it is true, write "true." If it is false, change the underlined word or words to make the statement true.

1. The most common cause of earthquakes is folding.
2. Earthquakes on the ocean floor cause giant sea waves called tsunamis.
3. The point beneath the earth's surface where the rocks break and move is called the epicenter.
4. Surface waves travel the fastest.
5. Secondary waves travel through solids but not through liquids.
6. Any number above 6 on the Richter scale indicates a very destructive earthquake.
7. The opening from which lava erupts is called a fault.
8. Small volcanic bombs are called craters.
9. Volcanoes composed of quiet lava flows are called shield volcanoes.
10. A funnel-shaped pit at the top of a volcanic cone is called a vent.

CONCEPT REVIEW: SKILL BUILDING

Use the skills you have developed in the chapter to complete each activity.

1. Relating concepts In 1883, the island of Krakatoa, located northwest of Australia between Java and Sumatra, was destroyed by a volcanic eruption. Volcanic dust circled the globe for several years before settling out of the atmosphere onto the earth's surface. The temperature of the earth's atmosphere was lower for several years after the eruption. Explain why this was so.

2. Sequencing events The Richter scale measures the energy of an earthquake but not the amount of damage done. The Mercalli scale, created in 1902 by the Italian seismologist Giuseppe Mercalli, is often used to describe the amount of damage done by an earthquake. Listed below are 10 of the 12 steps in the Mercalli scale. Read each step and then put the steps in order of increasing damage.

Cracks appear in the ground. All buildings are damaged.
Objects are thrown into the air. Damage is total.
Earthquake is felt by only a few people near the epicenter.
Windows and fragile objects are broken.
Earthquake is felt in buildings but only on upper levels. Automobiles sway.
People escape from buildings as bricks and concrete break and collapse.
All buildings are destroyed. Rails are bent.
Ground is cracked. Landslides occur. Rivers overflow.
Few buildings are left standing. Bridges and underground pipes are destroyed.
Broad cracks appear in the ground. Earth slumps.

CONCEPT REVIEW: ESSAY

Discuss each of the following in a brief paragraph.

1. Compare the shape and method of formation of cinder cones, shield volcanoes, and composite volcanoes.

2. Explain why L waves are more destructive than P and S waves.

Plate Tectonics 19

CHAPTER SECTIONS

CHAPTER OBJECTIVES

After completing this chapter, you will be able to

19–1 Describe the theory of continental drift.

19–1 Relate fossil and rock evidence to continental drift.

19–2 Explain ocean-floor spreading.

19–3 Identify the major lithospheric plates.

19–3 Describe the three types of plate boundaries.

19–3 Discuss the reasons for lithospheric plate motion.

19–3 Distinguish between the different kinds of plate collisions.

Have you ever looked at a globe or world map and noticed that the earth's landmasses look like pieces of a giant jigsaw puzzle? For example, South America and Africa look like pieces that might fit together. The Arabian Peninsula and the northeast coast of Africa also might fit together. According to many scientists, about 280 million years ago all of the earth's land was connected. One great ocean surrounded the land. Then, about 80 million years later, the land started to split apart, and the Atlantic Ocean began to form.

Scientists have been studying the earth's landmasses for many years. But they were not able to study the ocean floors as carefully until the 1950s and 1960s. Data from these recent studies of the ocean floors and their history support the theory that all the land on the earth was once connected. If this theory sounds strange to you, you are not alone. For years, many scientists rejected it as impossible. But today scientists have found much evidence to support the theory. In this chapter, you will learn more about this evidence and about the giant jigsaw puzzle, Earth.

This photograph taken from space shows that the Arabian Peninsula (top) and northeastern Africa (bottom) look as if they are two pieces of a giant jigsaw puzzle that could easily fit together.

19–1 The Theory of Continental Drift

Section Objective

To describe evidence in support of continental drift

In the early 1900s, the German scientist Alfred Wegener became interested in the way the outlines of the continents, or large landmasses, seemed to fit together. He also noted that certain rock structures on opposite sides of the Atlantic Ocean were similar.

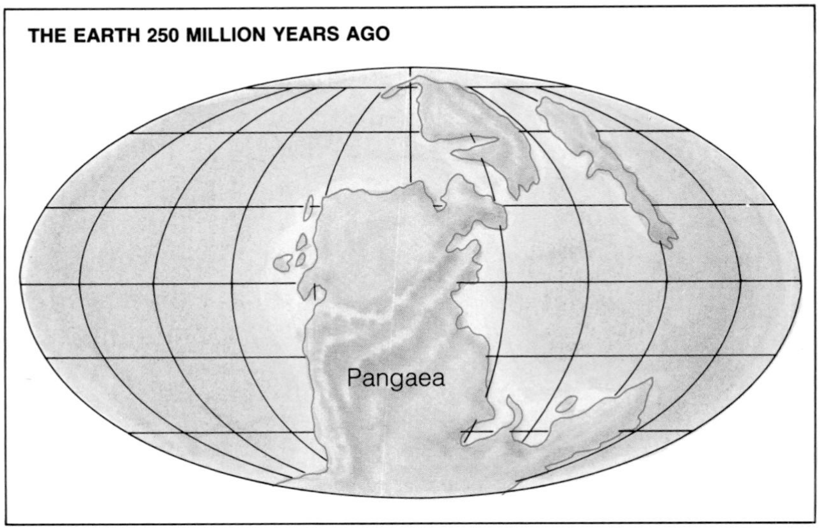

Figure 19–1 *This shows what the earth may have looked like 250 million years ago. A famous scientist proposed that at one time all the continents were part of one large landmass called Pangaea. Who was this scientist?*

Wegener developed a theory to explain these observations. **Alfred Wegener proposed that at one time the earth had one giant landmass that split apart to form today's continents.** He called the landmass **Pangaea** (pan-JEE-uh). Wegener suggested that parts of Pangaea "drifted" to their present positions. For this reason, Wegener called his idea the **theory of continental drift.**

At first, many scientists did not accept Wegener's theory of continental drift. They could not understand how the continents could have moved. In fact, it took more than 50 years and some very important discoveries before Wegener's theory was finally accepted by most scientists.

Figure 19–2 *This fossil leaf found in southwestern Australia came from an extinct fern called* Glossopteris. *Many fossils of this fern have been found in Australia, South Africa, and India. Their presence on three continents suggests that the continents were once connected.*

Evidence From Fossils

Scientists have used evidence from **fossils** to support Wegener's theory of continental drift. Fossils are remains or traces of plant or animal life, usually preserved in rocks and sediments.

Many years ago, fossils of the extinct, or no longer living, plant ***Glossopteris*** (glahs-SAHP-tuh-ruhs) were found in South Africa, Australia, and India. *Glossopteris* was a seed fern that grew about 250 million years ago. Most scientists agree that the seeds of these plants were too large to have been carried by winds over the ocean to the different continents. How then did the ferns develop on such widely separated continents? Scientists believe that at one time these plants grew on a single landmass that later split apart.

Fossils of the extinct animal ***Mesosaurus*** (meh-soh-SAWR-uhs) have also been used as evidence. *Mesosaurus* was a reptile that swam in freshwater ponds, lakes, and rivers. Its fossils have been found in both South America and Africa. If these animals were able to survive only in shallow fresh water, they could not have swum thousands of kilometers

Figure 19–3 *Scientists have found the same fossils on widely separated continents. What might this indicate?*

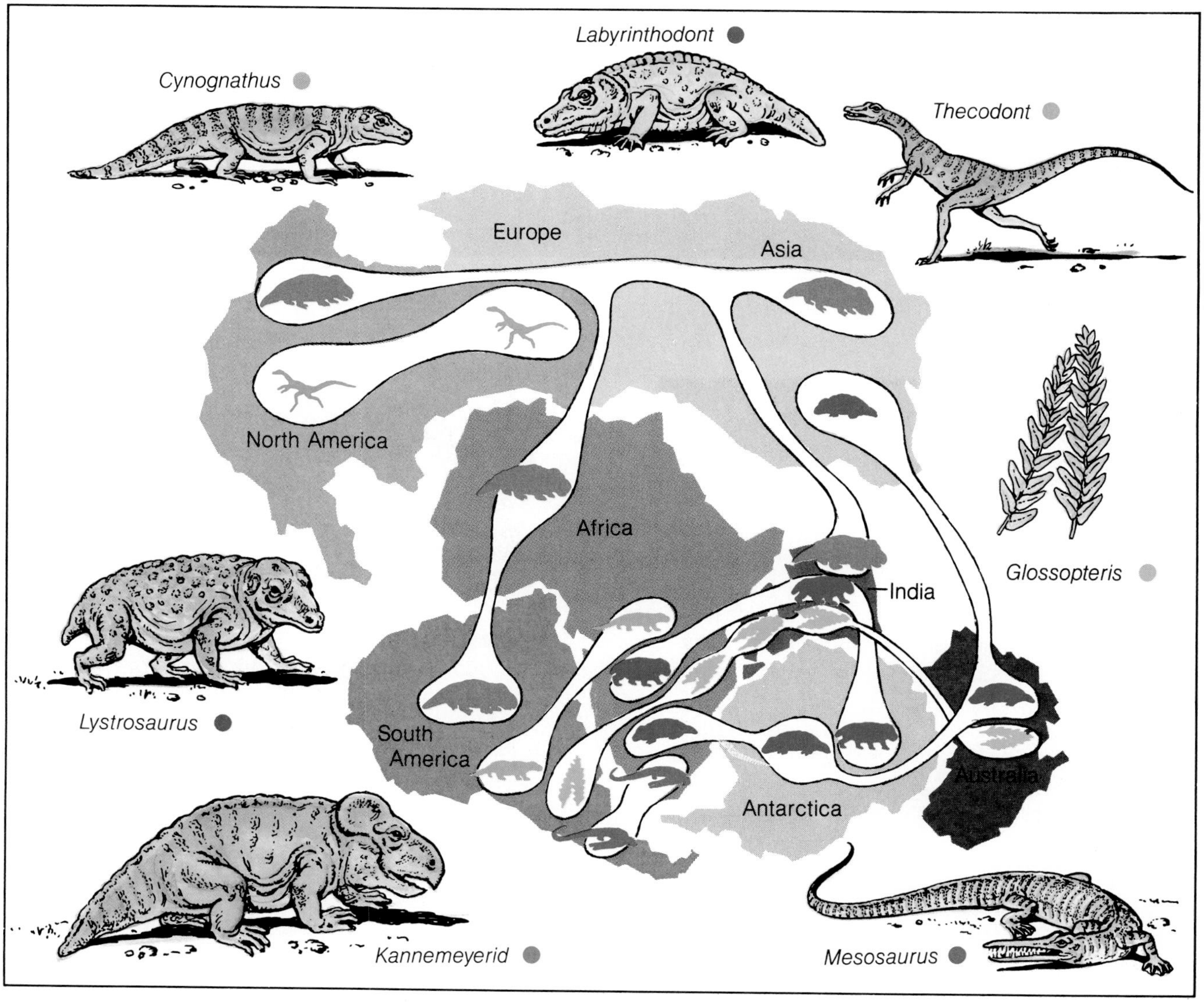

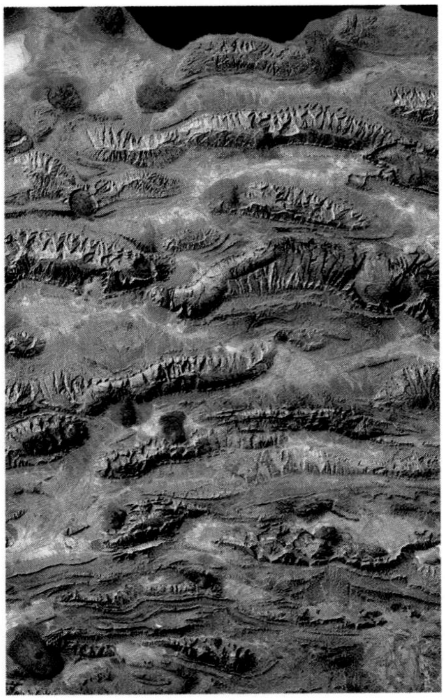

Figure 19–4 *Folded mountain ranges similar to this one are found in western Africa and eastern South America. If Africa and South America are "pieced" together, the two mountain ranges line up.*

across the salty Atlantic Ocean. How then did they develop on unconnected continents so far away from each other? Scientists believe that the animals swam in the freshwater ponds, lakes, and rivers of one landmass. When the landmass separated, some of the animals were left on each part.

Over the years, many more fossil "links" between the continents were found. This evidence has led most scientists to believe that continental drift took place. Figure 19–3 on page 479 shows several other examples of fossil evidence of continental drift.

Evidence From Rocks

Fossils are not the only evidence scientists have used to support the theory of continental drift. Rock structures such as the Cape Mountains of South Africa have also provided useful evidence. Scientists know that the Cape Mountains are folded mountains. Folded mountains are formed from rocks in the earth's crust that have been crumpled by forces within the earth. The Cape Mountains end suddenly at the Atlantic Ocean. Across the ocean, near Buenos Aires, Argentina, are mountains made of folded rocks of the same age and type. If South

CAREER — *Geophysicist*

HELP WANTED: GEOPHYSICIST To work in geology department at major university. PhD and research experience necessary. Some teaching involved.

The earth has changed greatly during its existence, and it will continue to change. Scientists who study the processes that change and shape the earth are called **geophysicists.** Geophysicists study the earth's surface, interior, oceans, and atmosphere.

There are many different kinds of specialists in this branch of earth science. Geodesists measure and study the size and shape of the earth. Geomagneticians measure and study changes in the earth's magnetic field. Exploration geophysicists study the structure of rocks far beneath the earth's surface and use their knowledge to locate oil and mineral deposits.

Geophysicists use highly complex instruments such as magnetometers and gravimeters. They conduct tests from ships, airplanes, and satellites. They use computers to store and analyze data.

People who work in this field attend college and gain a good understanding of geology, physics, chemistry, mathematics, and engineering. To learn more about this field, write to the American Geophysical Union, 2000 Florida Ave., NW, Washington, DC 20009.

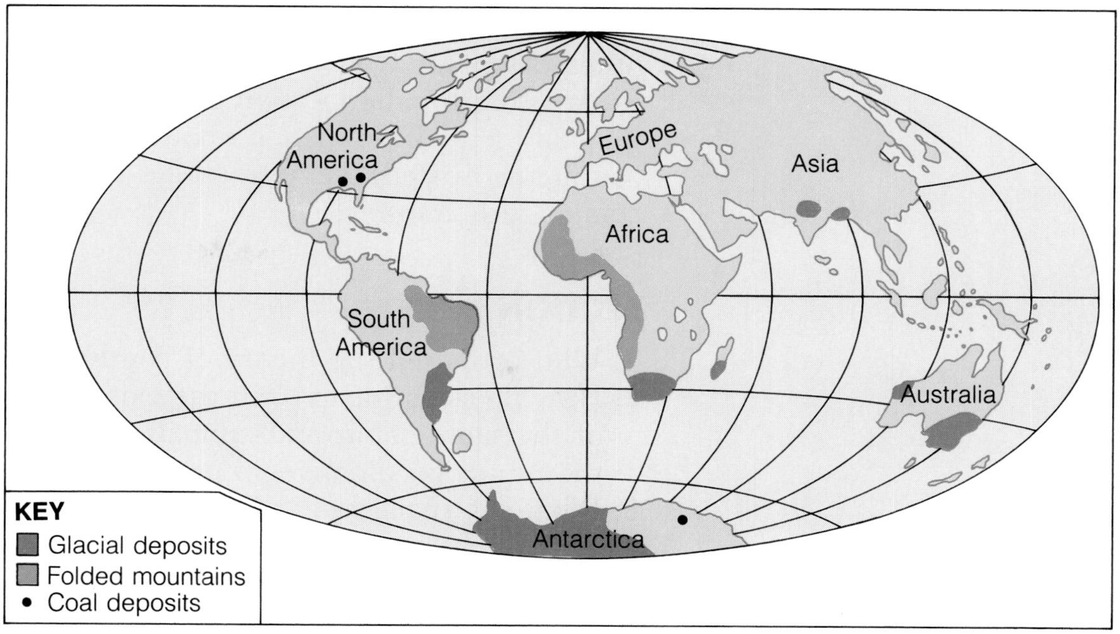

Figure 19–5 *This map shows the folded mountain ranges and coal and glacial deposits believed to have formed when the continents were part of one landmass. Look carefully and try to imagine how the continents would fit together. Would the mountains and deposits of each continent line up?*

America and Africa were "pieced" together, the two mountain ranges would line up. So scientists have concluded that the mountains were probably once part of the same belt. The mountain belt broke in two when the continents separated.

Rock deposits left behind by glaciers have also been used as evidence to support the theory of continental drift. Many glacial deposits are found in South America, Africa, India, Australia, and Antarctica. The similarity of these deposits indicates that they were deposited by the same ice sheet. The direction of glacial flow appears to have been the same on Africa as on South America.

Also, although glaciers usually form close to the poles, many ancient glacial deposits have been found in areas with very warm climates. From this evidence, scientists have concluded that these areas were once part of a giant landmass located near the South Pole.

Deposits of salts, coal, and limestone derived from coral reefs have provided further rock evidence of continental drift. Today most salts form in areas between 10° and 35° north and south of the equator. But salt deposits hundreds of millions of years old have been found as far north as Michigan.

Coal forms in warm, swampy climates. Yet large coal deposits have been discovered in Antarctica. And limestone deposits from coral reefs, which form in tropical climates, have been found in western Texas, the northern central United States, and

Sharpen Your Skills

Continental Drift

Make a trip to the library to do research about earth scientists who have discovered evidence that supports the theory of continental drift. Use indexes to magazines and periodicals to find recent articles that may be helpful. Look up and write a report about one of the scientists listed below:

David Harwood
Bruce Heezen
John H. Mercer
Sara L. Samson
Peter N. Webb
Dr. J. Tuzo Wilson

other places far from the equator. The most likely explanation for the location of these deposits is that the continents have drifted about the earth. As the continents drifted, they sometimes passed from one climate into another.

SECTION REVIEW

1. Who proposed the theory of continental drift?
2. How do scientists explain the existence of fossils of the same plants and animals on continents thousands of kilometers apart?
3. What two main types of evidence support the theory of continental drift?

Section Objective

To relate ocean-floor spreading to continental drift

19–2 Ocean-Floor Spreading

In spite of all the evidence from fossils and rocks, some scientists still refused to accept the theory of continental drift. They were waiting for the answer to a very important question: How could the continents plow through hard, solid ocean floor?

Until recently, there was no acceptable answer to this question. Then, during the 1950s and 1960s, new techniques and instruments enabled scientists to make better observations of the ocean floor. An answer to their question was at last provided.

Figure 19–6 *This illustration shows the underwater mountains called the midocean ridge. The deep crack running through the center is called a rift valley. Hot lava erupts through the rift valley. What happens to the lava?*

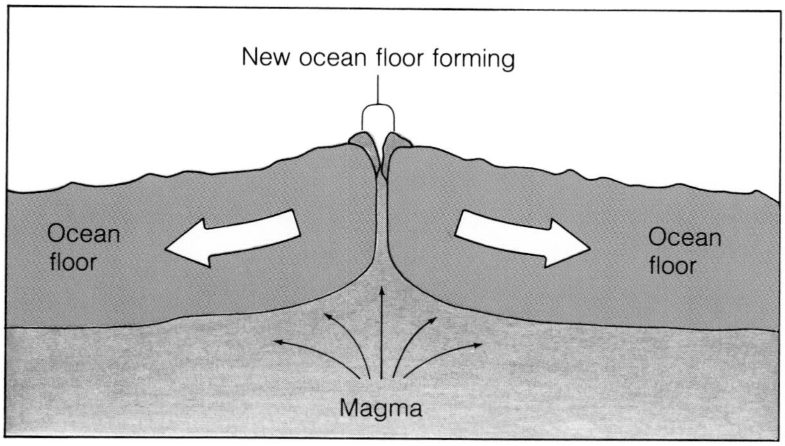

Figure 19–7 *Magma from beneath the earth's crust erupts as lava onto the ocean floor. The lava hardens to form new ocean floor. The old ocean floor is pushed away to both sides of the midocean ridge. What is this entire process called?*

New mapping techniques gave scientists a much clearer picture of the ocean floor. They discovered a large system of underwater mountains that have a deep crack, called a **rift valley,** running through their center. These underwater mountains, called **midocean ridges,** can be found in all of the oceans. The midocean ridges form the single largest mountain chain in the world. The chain is approximately 80,000 kilometers long and 3 kilometers high. What is the name of the ridge in the Atlantic Ocean?

Scientists discovered that a great deal of volcanic and earthquake activity occurs at the midocean ridges. Lava erupts from the rift valley that runs the length of a ridge. When the lava wells up and hardens, the ocean floor is pushed away on either side of the ridge. The hardened lava forms new ocean floor. This process is called **ocean-floor spreading.** So the ocean floor scientists once *thought* was solid and immovable actually can move! **Ocean-floor spreading helps explain how continents drift.**

New deep-sea drilling machines also provided evidence to support the idea of ocean-floor spreading. Rock samples from the ocean floor indicate that rocks next to a midocean ridge are younger than rocks farther away. The youngest rocks are in the center of the ridge. As the ocean floor spreads, the older rocks move farther away from the ridge.

Magnetic stripes in ocean-floor rocks further convinced scientists of ocean-floor spreading. Scientists know that some minerals have magnetic properties and are affected by the earth's magnetism. In molten rock, the magnetic mineral particles line up in the direction of the earth's magnetic poles. When the molten rock hardens, a permanent record of the

Figure 19–8 *The island of Iceland was formed where the midocean ridge rose above the ocean's surface. Here you can see the deep crack running through the center of the exposed midocean ridge. What is this crack called?*

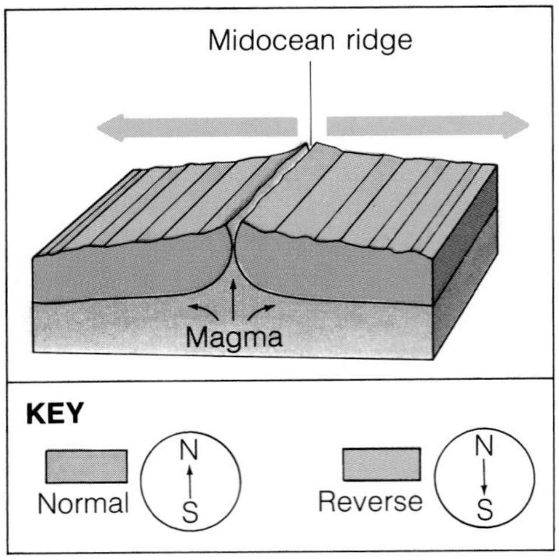

Figure 19–9 *Ocean-floor rocks closer to the midocean ridge are younger than the rocks farther away. Reversals of the earth's magnetic poles are recorded in magnetic stripes all along the ocean floor. The pattern of normal and reverse stripes is identical on both sides of the midocean ridge. What is indicated by the ocean-floor rocks' age and the magnetic stripe pattern?*

earth's magnetism remains in the rocks. Scientists discovered that the history of the earth's magnetism is recorded in magnetic stripes in the rocks. Although these stripes cannot be seen, they can be detected by special instruments. What, scientists wondered, caused these stripes to form?

When scientists studied the magnetic stripes, they made a surprising discovery. The earth's magnetic poles reverse themselves from time to time. In other words, the magnetic north and south poles change places. Studies show that during the past 3.5 million years, the magnetic poles have reversed themselves nine times.

But the scientists were in for an even bigger surprise. They discovered that the pattern of magnetic stripes is identical on both sides of a midocean ridge. In other words, the pattern of magnetic stripes on one side of a ridge matches the pattern on the other side! The obvious conclusion was that as magma hardens into rock at a midocean ridge, half of the rocks move in one direction and the other half move in the other direction. The pattern of magnetic stripes provides clear evidence of ocean-floor spreading. See Figure 19–9.

You might think that as a result of ocean-floor spreading, the earth's surface should be getting larger. But this is not so. How do scientists explain why the earth's crust remains the same size?

From ocean-floor mapping, scientists know of another undersea feature. Deep, V-shaped valleys called **trenches** lie along the bottom of the oceans. The trenches are the deepest part of the oceans. They are found close to the continents or near strings of islands such as Alaska's Aleutian

Figure 19–10 *This illustration shows how the crust moves during ocean-floor spreading. New ocean floor is created at the midocean ridge. What happens to the ocean floor at the trench?*

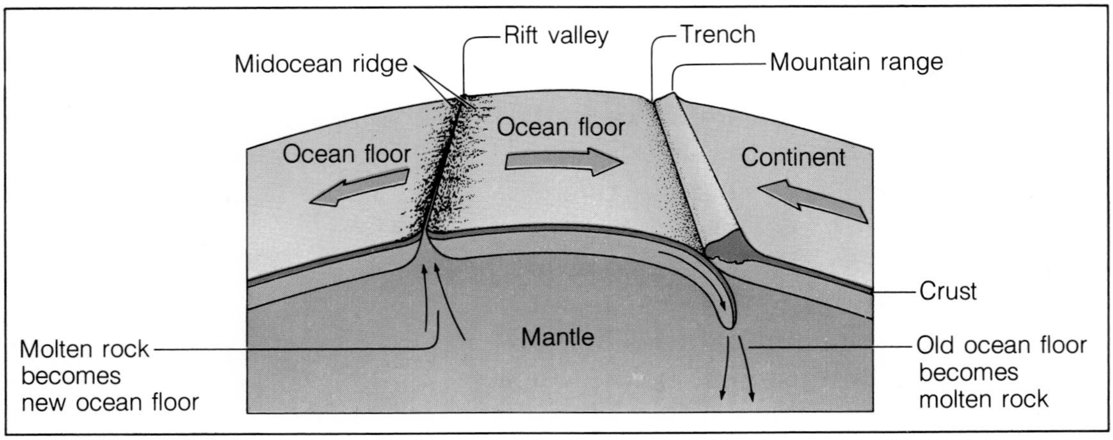

Islands. The Pacific Ocean has many trenches around its edges.

Scientists made another surprising discovery. The oldest rocks on land are almost 4 billion years old. But the oldest rocks on the ocean floor are only 200 million years old! How can the ocean floor be so much younger than the continents?

As you learned earlier, older ocean floor is pushed away from the midocean ridges as new ocean floor is formed. Scientists believe that the older ocean floor is then pushed down deep into the earth along the trenches. The process of the ocean floor plunging back into the interior of the earth is called **subduction** (suhb-DUHK-shuhn).

When the rocks are pushed deep enough, they are melted by the heat of the earth. Some of the molten rock will rise up through the crust and produce volcanoes. But most of the molten rock will become part of the mantle. So as new rocks are formed along the midocean ridges, older rocks are subducted into the trenches. One process balances the other. The earth's crust remains the same size.

SECTION REVIEW

1. What process helps explain how continents drift?
2. Where are the youngest rocks on the ocean floor found?
3. What did the identical normal and reverse magnetic stripes on both sides of a midocean ridge indicate to scientists?

19–3 The Theory of Plate Tectonics

Section Objective

To relate plate motion to various features of the earth

The branch of earth science that deals with the movements that shape the earth's crust is called **tectonics** (tehk-TAHN-ihks). The **theory of plate tectonics** is a new theory that combines the ideas of continental drift and ocean-floor spreading. **The theory of plate tectonics helps to explain the formation of the earth's crust and its movements, collisions, and destruction.** It also helps to explain the origins of volcanoes, earthquakes, and mountains.

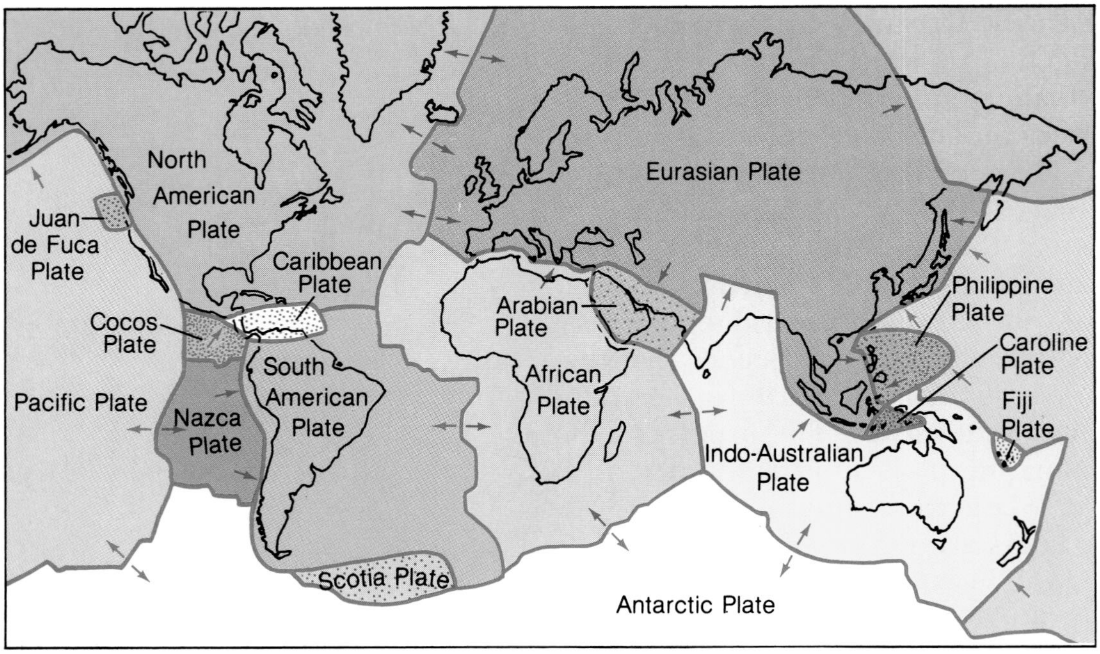

Figure 19–11 *This map shows the various plates of the lithosphere on which the continents and oceans move. Which plate is most of the United States on?*

Lithospheric Plates

Most scientists believe that the topmost solid part of the earth, called the **lithosphere** (LIHTH-uh-sfir), is made of a number of plates. The plates contain a thin layer of crust above a thick layer of cool, rigid rocks. Plates usually contain both oceanic and continental crust. The outlines of the plates are shown in Figure 19–11.

There are seven major lithospheric plates. The major plates are named after their surface features. The Pacific plate is the largest plate. It covers one-fifth of the earth's surface. The other major plates are the North American, South American, Eurasian, African, Indo–Australian, and Antarctic plates.

There are also several smaller plates, such as the Caribbean and Arabian plates. The Arabian plate includes the Arabian Peninsula, the Red Sea, and the Persian Gulf. The Caribbean plate lies between North America and South America.

The edges of the continents are not always the boundaries of plates. For example, the eastern edge of North America and the western edge of Europe are not plate boundaries. These continents are on plates that extend into the Atlantic Ocean. The plates include parts of the ocean floor. In fact, most plate boundaries are on the ocean floor.

Sharpen Your Skills

Pangaea

1. Using a globe and paper, trace the shape of each continent and Madagascar. Also trace the shape of India and the Saudi Peninsula.

2. Cut out each piece, leaving Asia and Europe as one.

3. Disconnect India and the Saudi Peninsula from Asia.

4. Piece together the continents as they may have looked before the breakup of Pangaea. Use the directions of plate motion shown in Figure 19–11 as a guide.

5. Attach your reconstruction of Pangaea to a sheet of paper. Compare your version with those of your classmates.

Plate Boundaries

There are three types of plate boundaries. The first type is the midocean ridges. Hot liquid rock from the mantle rises to the surface through the rift valleys of midocean ridges. The plates move apart to either side of the rift valleys. Because the plates move apart at the midocean ridges, the ridges are called **divergent** (digh-VER-juhnt) **boundaries.** These boundaries are also called **constructive boundaries** because new material is added to the plates there.

The second type of plate boundary is the trenches. The lithosphere is pushed down into the earth along a trench. One plate is being pushed under another. Because the plates come together at the trenches, the trenches are called **convergent** (kuhn-VER-juhnt) **boundaries.** These boundaries are also called **destructive boundaries** because plate material is being subducted.

The collision of plates at convergent boundaries causes tremendous pressure and friction. Severe earthquakes often result. As plate material melts in the earth's mantle, some of it surges upward to produce volcanoes. The Ring of Fire, a line of volcanoes circling the edge of the Pacific plate, outlines the major ocean trenches in that area of the world.

The third type of plate boundary is transform faults. A fault is a deep crack or break in the earth's

Sharpen Your Skills

Traveling Cities

Los Angeles, on the Pacific plate, is slowly moving northwest. San Francisco, on the North American plate, is slowly moving southeast. These two cities are moving toward each other at a rate of about 5 cm per year. About 11 million years from now, the two cities will be next to each other. How many meters does each city have to travel before they meet?

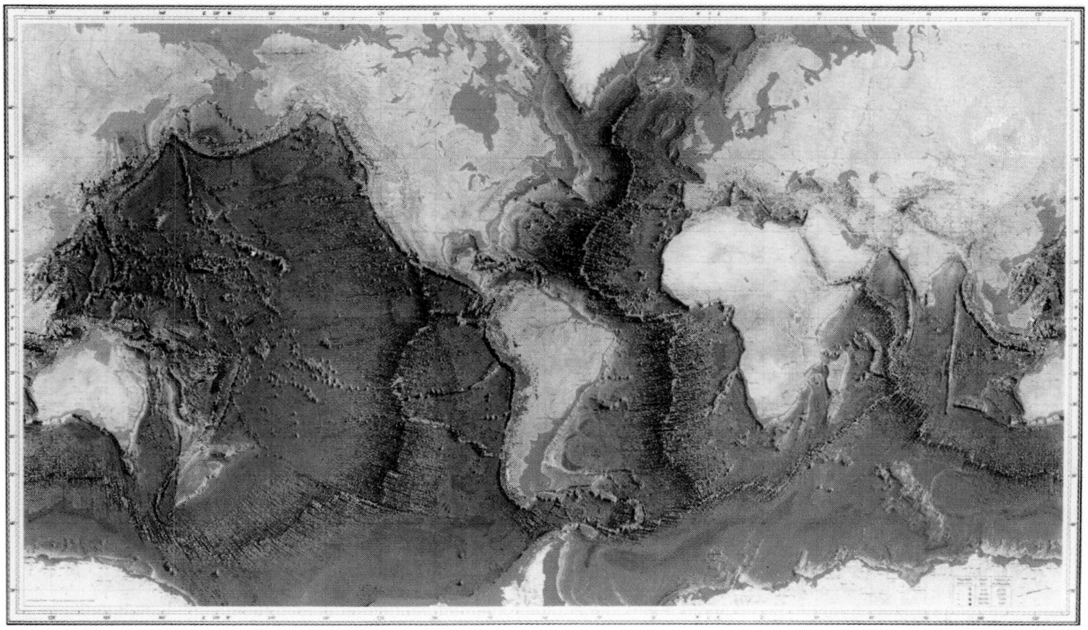

Figure 19–12 *The red areas on this map indicate major volcanic and earthquake sites. These sites also outline the midocean ridges and trenches of the earth. Notice the circle of red surrounding the Pacific Ocean. This is a very active volcanic and earthquake area called the Ring of Fire. What other large area appears to have a great deal of volcanic and earthquake activity?*

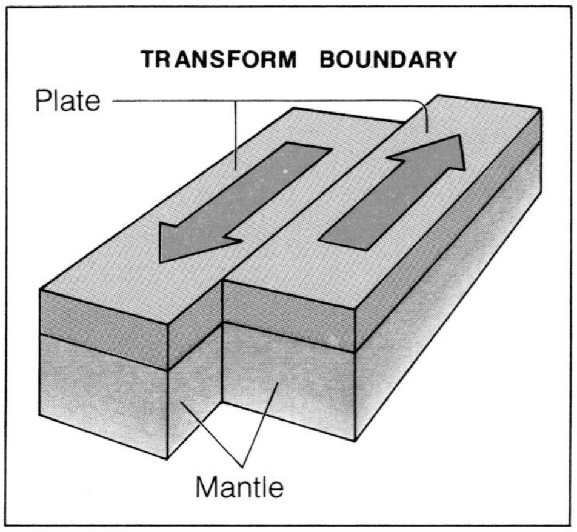

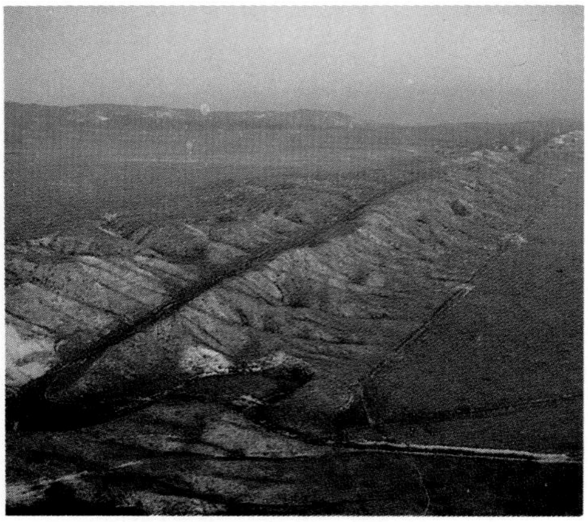

Figure 19–13 *At a transform boundary (top), one plate slides horizontally past another plate. The San Andreas Fault in California (bottom) is an example of a transform boundary.*

crust along which movement has occurred. Transform faults are called **transform boundaries.** These boundaries are usually found at right angles to the midocean ridges. At a transform boundary, two plates grind and slide past one another. Many times, earthquakes occur along transform boundaries. An example of a transform boundary is the San Andreas Fault in California. The Pacific plate, on the west, is grinding slowly northwest, while the North American plate is sliding southeast. Today San Francisco is farther north than Los Angeles. But someday Los Angeles, which is on the northward-moving Pacific plate, will be farther north than San Francisco, which is on the North American plate.

Plate Motion

Scientists are not sure exactly what makes the plates move. They have searched a long time to find the source of the forces that can move continents. They now think large **convection currents** within the earth move the plates.

A convection current is the movement of material caused by differences in temperature. Mantle material close to the earth's core is very hot. Mantle material farther from the core, near the lithosphere, is cooler. The cooler material sinks down toward the earth's core. The hot material is then pushed up to replace the cooler material. As the cooler material nears the core, it becomes hot and rises once again. The rising and sinking cycle repeats over and over. Scientists believe that this circular motion carries the plates of the lithosphere along with it, thus causing the continents to move.

The earth's crust consists of oceanic crust and continental crust. All of the lithospheric plates contain oceanic crust. Oceanic crust is made of dense igneous rocks such as basalt. Most plates also contain continental crust. The thicker continental crust is made of less dense igneous rocks such as granite. The Pacific plate is the only major plate that does not contain continental crust. The other major plates contain both oceanic and continental crust.

When an oceanic plate collides with a continental plate at a trench, the less dense continental plate rides over the denser oceanic plate. The oceanic

Sharpen Your Skills

Plate Tectonics

1. Fill a cooking pan with water. Place the pan on a heat source. Add several drops of food coloring to the water. Observe the convection currents created.

2. Place several balsa wood blocks in the center of the heated water. What happens to the blocks?

Relate this activity to the theory of plate tectonics.

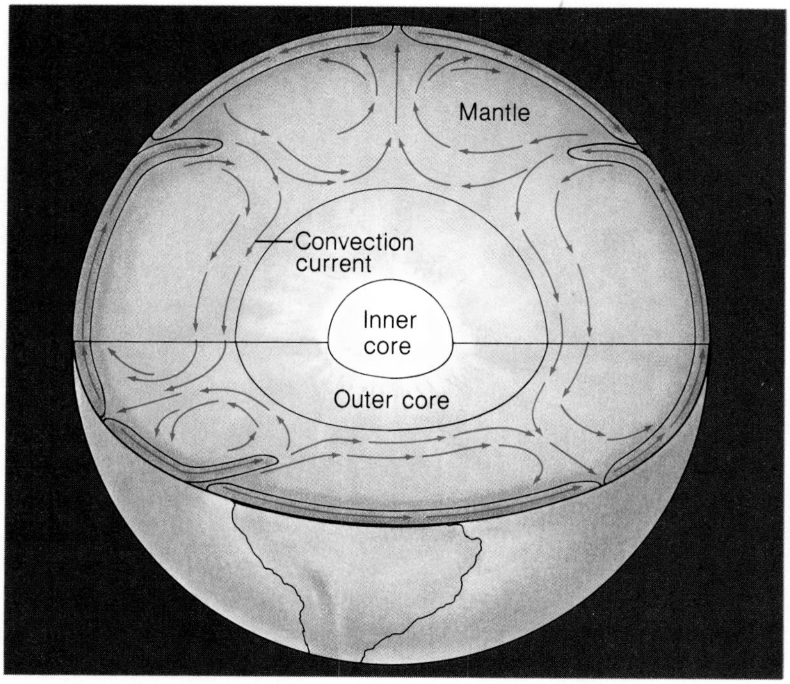

Figure 19–14 *Scientists believe that the movement of the continents is caused by rising and sinking currents of molten rock in the mantle. These circular currents, called convection currents, carry along the plates of the lithosphere, causing the continents to move.*

plate is forced down, or subducted, into the trench. The continental crust on the continental plate is pushed up and folded by the subducting plate, the oceanic plate. Melting rocks from the oceanic plate rise and erupt as volcanoes on the continent. The Andes Mountains of South America were formed in this way. They have many active volcanoes.

When two continental plates collide, neither plate is pushed down into the lower mantle. This is because the density of the two plates is nearly the same. Instead the edges of the continents buckle upward to form large mountain ranges. The Himalaya Mountains probably formed when the plate carrying India collided with the Eurasian plate. What mountain ranges in the United States may have been formed by the collision of plates?

When two oceanic plates collide, one oceanic plate is subducted under the other, forming a deep trench. The crust of the plate going into the trench melts. Molten rock then rises up and breaks through the surface. As a result, a string of volcanoes erupts on the ocean floor along the trench. In time, this string of undersea volcanoes may rise above the ocean's surface as a string of islands. Because the islands usually appear in a curved line, they are called **island arcs.** The Aleutian Islands of Alaska form an island arc.

Sharpen Your Skills

Prefixes

Knowing the meaning of a prefix can often help you remember the meaning of a word. Using a dictionary, find the meaning of the prefixes *con-, di-, pan-, sub-,* and *trans-*. Relate what you have learned about the prefixes to the definition of the following vocabulary words:

convection current
constructive boundary
Pangaea
divergent boundary
subduction
transform boundary

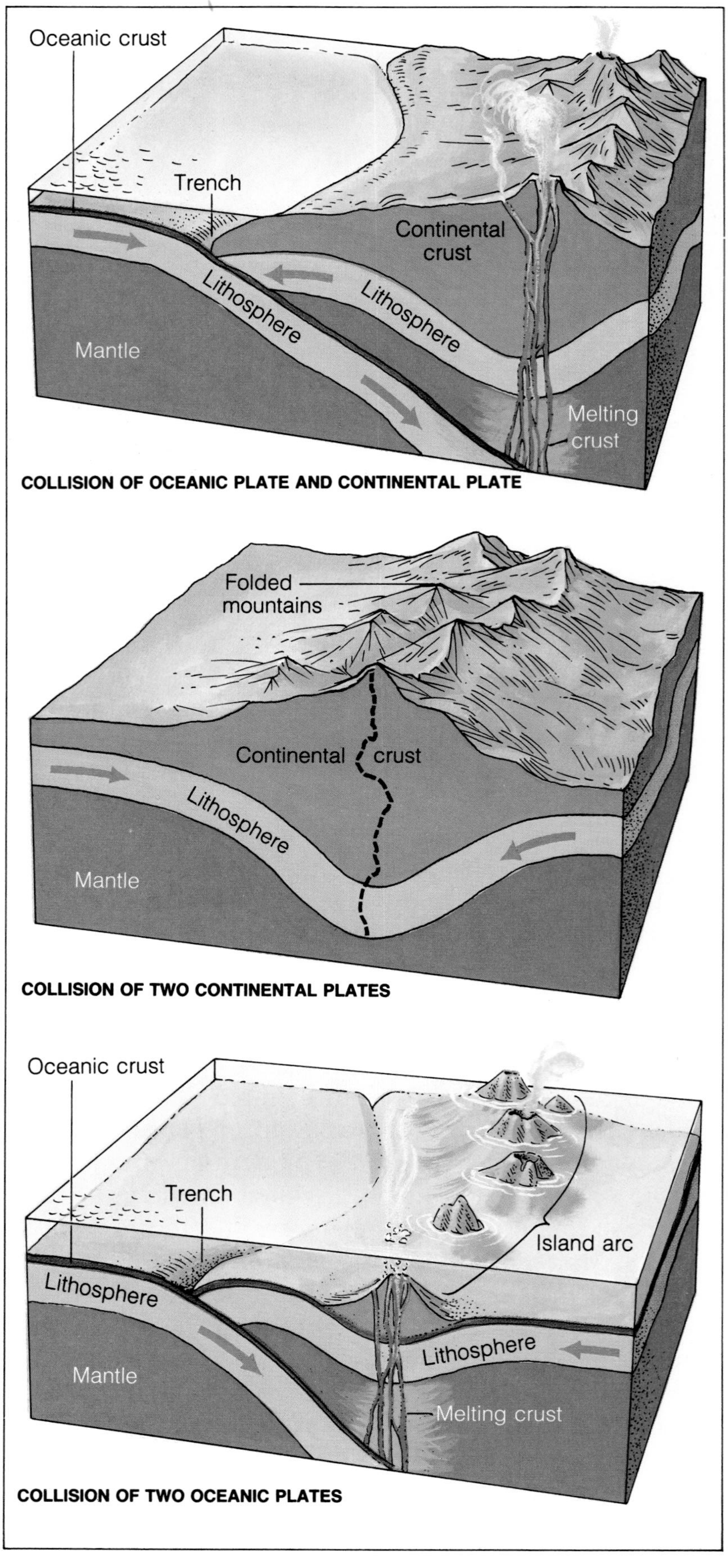

Figure 19–15 *These illustrations show the three kinds of plate collision. When an oceanic and continental plate collide (top), the oceanic plate is pushed under the continental plate. The material of the oceanic crust, melted by the intense heat of the mantle, rises and erupts as volcanoes on the continent. When two continental plates collide (center), the edges of the continents are pushed together and upward to form large mountain ranges. When two oceanic plates collide (bottom), one plate is pushed under the other. The melting ocean crust rises and erupts on the ocean floor forming an island arc.*

As you have learned, the plates carry different types of crust. But there are still other differences among the plates. The plates move at different speeds and in different directions. And the speed and direction of each plate's motion can change. At times, plates join together to form one plate. At other times, one plate breaks apart into two separate plates. In fact, some geologists believe that the North American plate is beginning to divide at the Basin and Range Province in southwestern United States. Scientists also believe that entire plates may be subducted into a trench and completely disappear!

Figure 19–16 *These illustrations show a plate splitting in two. Magma from the mantle rises. It heats and weakens an area of a continental plate (top). The area cracks and sections slip down to form a rift valley (top center). Lava erupts through the cracks, splitting the plate and continent. Ocean-floor spreading widens the gap between the split continent. Ocean water fills the gap (bottom center). Over millions of years, much oceanic crust is added (bottom).*

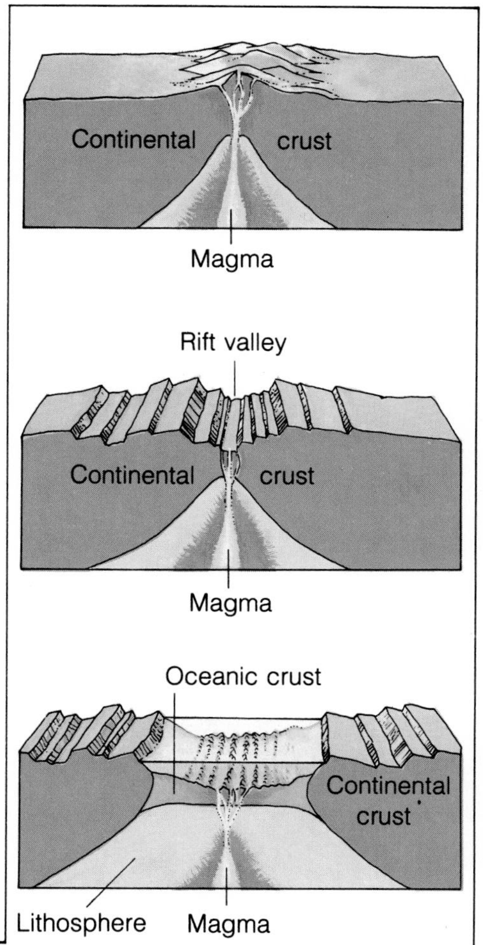

Past and Future Drifting

Since Wegener first proposed his theory of continental drift, a more complete theory has been developed. But this new theory is based on Wegener's original idea of a large landmass splitting into smaller continents that drifted apart.

According to current ideas about continental drift, almost 510 million years ago the world's landmasses existed as many different fragments. Millions of years later, these fragments joined together to form one large continent, Pangaea. One enormous ocean, Panthalassa, surrounded the continent.

About 200 million years ago, Pangaea broke into two large continents, Gondwanaland and Laurasia. Gondwanaland split into three parts. One part consisted of South America and Africa. Another part consisted of Antarctica and Australia. The third part was India, which had broken away from Africa. India drifted north and collided with Asia. South America and Africa separated. Laurasia, the other continent, split apart to form North America and

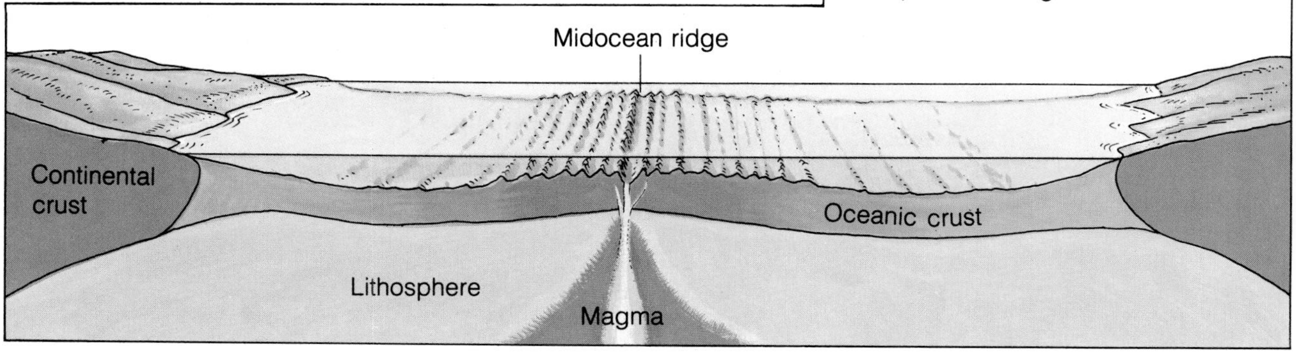

Figure 19–17 *Over millions of years, the continents' shapes and positions have changed greatly. These illustrations show how the earth may have looked 250 million years ago (top), 135 million years ago (top center), 100 million years ago (bottom center), and 45 million years ago (bottom).*

THE EARTH 250 MILLION YEARS AGO

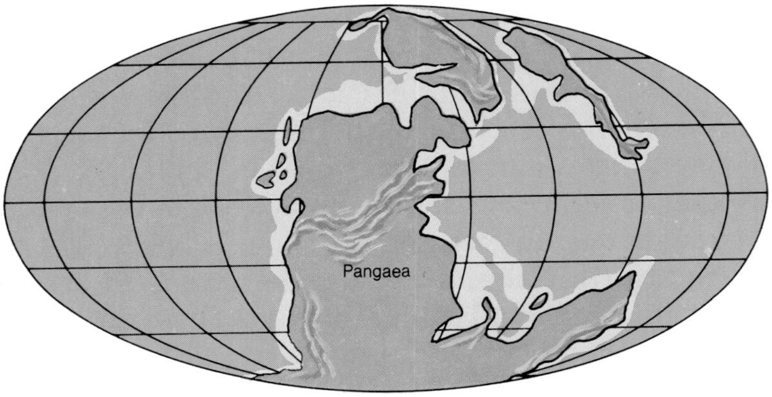

THE EARTH 135 MILLION YEARS AGO

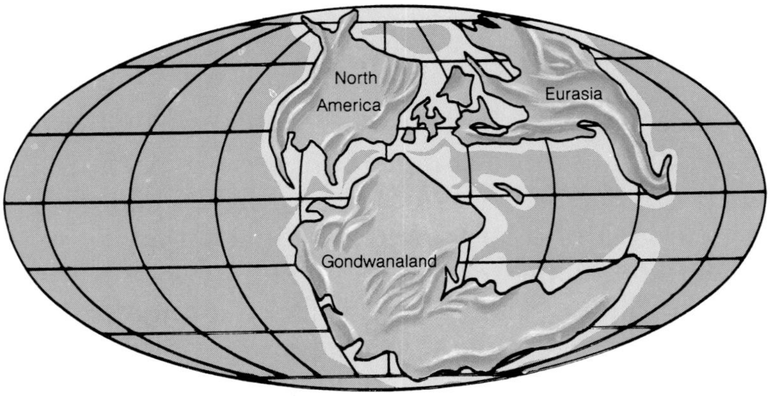

THE EARTH 100 MILLION YEARS AGO

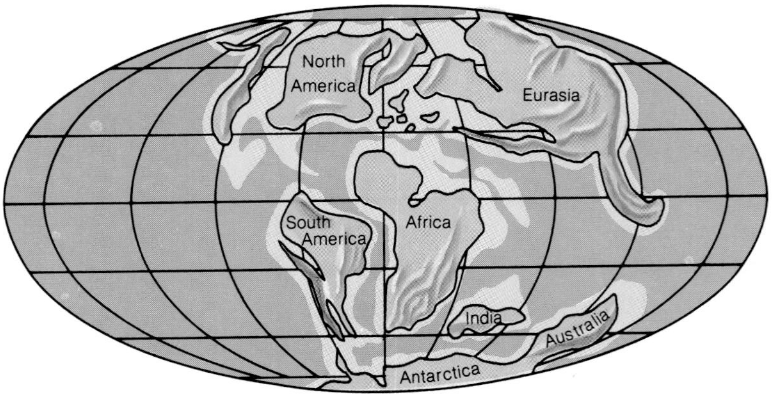

THE EARTH 45 MILLION YEARS AGO

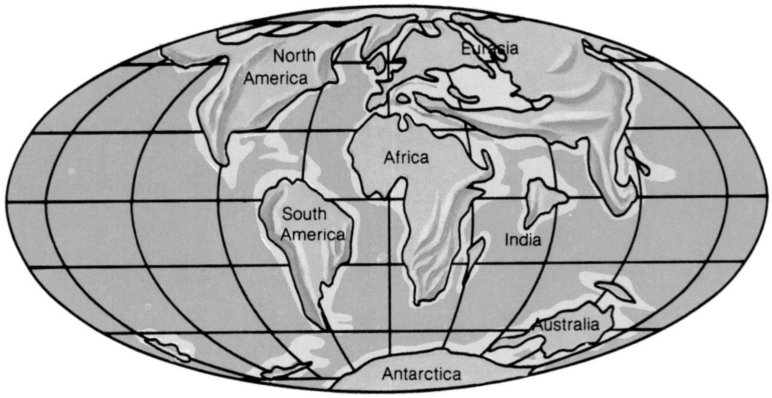

Eurasia. Australia broke away from Antarctica and drifted northeast to its present position.

Scientists believe that the continents are drifting today at a rate of about 1 to 5 centimeters per year. At this rate, in 50 million years the South Atlantic Ocean and the Indian Ocean will become larger. The Pacific Ocean will become smaller. Australia will continue to drift north and collide with Asia. Africa will also drift north, causing the Mediterranean Sea to disappear. What do you think the "jigsaw-puzzle" earth will look like then?

THE EARTH AT PRESENT

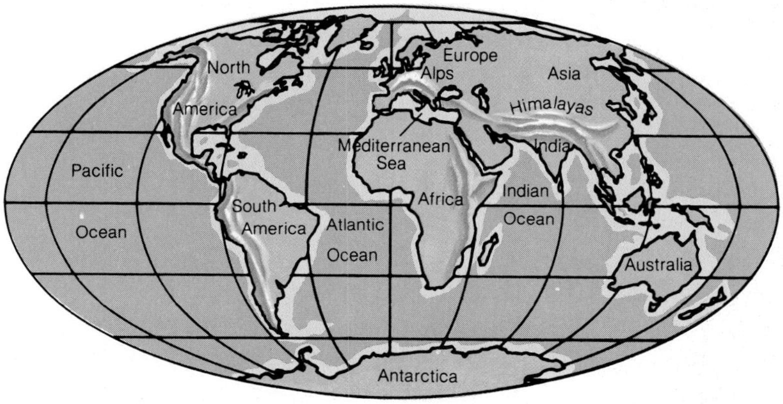

THE EARTH IN 100 MILLION YEARS

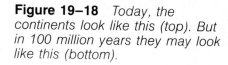

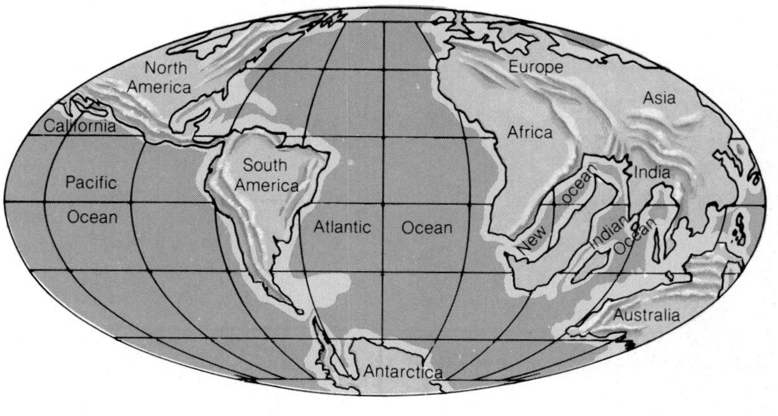

Figure 19–18 *Today, the continents look like this (top). But in 100 million years they may look like this (bottom).*

SECTION REVIEW

1. Name the seven major lithospheric plates.
2. What is another name for divergent boundaries? For convergent boundaries?
3. Where are convergent boundaries found? Where are divergent boundaries found?
4. Explain the origins of volcanoes, earthquakes, and mountains as they relate to plate tectonics.

Sharpen Your Skills

A Jigsaw Puzzle

An important vocabulary term in this chapter is "continental drift." Using Figures 19–17 and 19–18 as references, write a 200-word essay about the present-day continents as pieces of a gigantic jigsaw puzzle. Be sure to explain the following names in your essay: Pangaea, Laurasia, and Gondwanaland. Also discuss some of the specific plants and animals that give supporting evidence for the movement of the jigsaw pieces. Mention on which present-day continents these fossils have been found.

19 LABORATORY INVESTIGATION

Mapping Lithospheric Plates

Problem

How are the locations of the earth's volcanoes, earthquakes, and mountain ranges related to the locations of the lithospheric plates?

Materials *(per student)*

Colored pencils (black, red, brown, green)
Paper

Procedure

1. With the black pencil, trace the outline of the world map on this page onto the paper.
2. Using the map on page 487 as a guide, draw the Ring of Fire on the world map with a red pencil. Also draw the other earthquake and volcano zones.
3. Using reference maps in this chapter and other chapters, shade in the general boundaries of the world's mountain ranges with a brown pencil. Be sure to include the Himalaya Mountains, Alps, Andes Mountains, and Rocky Mountains.
4. Using the maps in this chapter as guides, draw in with a green pencil the boundaries of the seven lithospheric plates as well as the boundaries of the Arabian and Caribbean plates. Label each plate.

Observations

1. What is the relationship of the Ring of Fire to the Pacific plate?
2. Where are the most earthquakes, volcanoes, and mountains located in relation to the lithospheric plates?

Conclusions

From the map you have made and the information in this chapter, how can you explain the apparent relationships between the lithospheric plates and the occurrence of earthquakes, volcanoes, and mountain ranges?

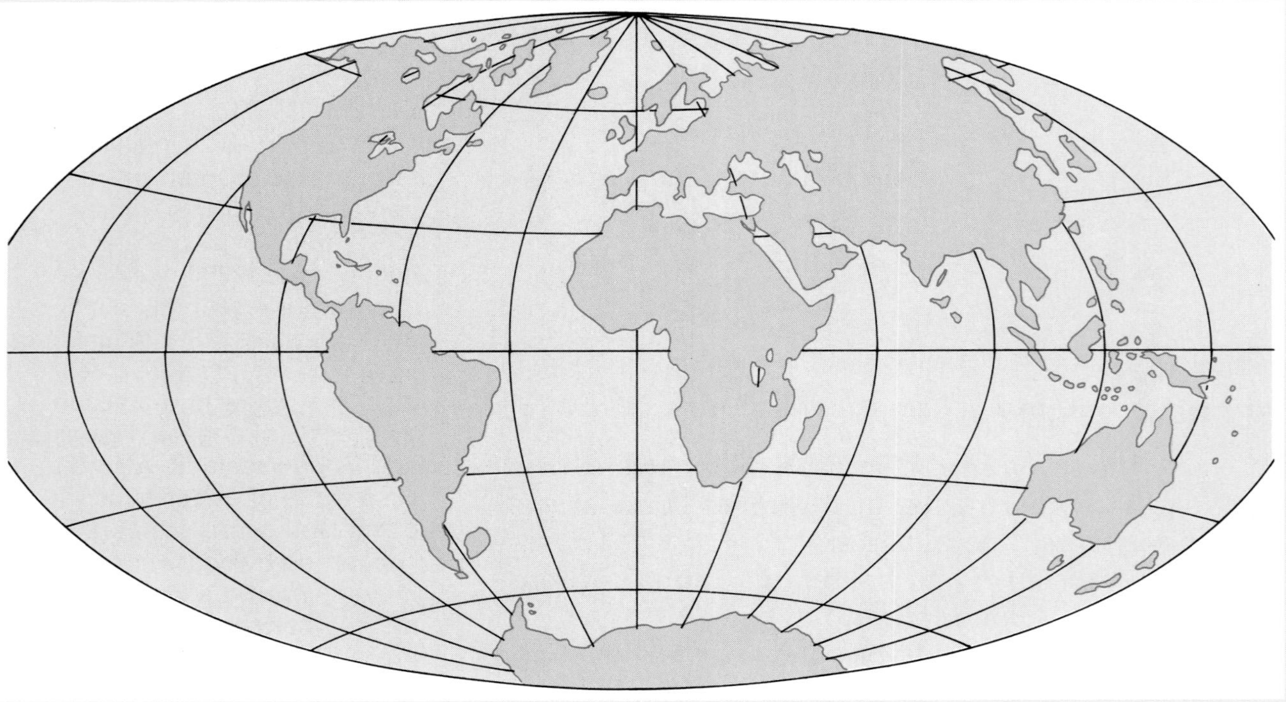

CHAPTER REVIEW

SUMMARY

19–1 The Theory of Continental Drift

❑ The theory of continental drift states that all the continents were once part of one giant landmass, Pangaea. The landmass split apart, and the continents drifted to their present positions.

❑ Fossils of the same types of plants and animals have been discovered on widely separated continents.

❑ The fossils are evidence that ancient animals and plants developed on a single landmass that later split apart.

❑ Various rock deposits have been found in locations far from the type of climate in which the deposits normally form.

❑ The rock deposits support the theory of continental drift. As the continents drifted, they passed from one climate to another.

19–2 Ocean-Floor Spreading

❑ Lava rises to the surface through a rift valley in the center of a midocean ridge.

❑ When the lava hardens, it pushes the ocean floor away from both sides of the ridge, causing the ocean floor to spread.

❑ Ocean-floor spreading may explain how the continents have drifted.

❑ Ocean floor is destroyed in the trenches.

❑ Both the ages of the ocean-floor rocks and the magnetic stripes on the ocean floor support the idea of ocean-floor spreading.

19–3 The Theory of Plate Tectonics

❑ The theory of plate tectonics helps to explain the formation of the earth's crust and its movements, collisions, and destruction.

❑ The lithosphere is made of a number of plates that contain both oceanic and continental crust.

❑ Because the plates move apart at the midocean ridges, the ridges are called divergent boundaries. Because the plates come together at the trenches, the trenches are called convergent boundaries.

❑ Along a transform fault, called a transform boundary, two plates grind past each other.

❑ Scientists believe that convection currents within the earth cause the plates to move.

❑ When a continental plate collides with an oceanic plate, the oceanic plate is subducted. The collision creates high mountains and volcanic activity.

❑ When two continental plates collide, neither is subducted. Instead the edges of the continents buckle upward to form large mountains.

❑ When two oceanic plates collide, one oceanic plate is subducted under the other. A string of volcanoes erupts along the trench.

VOCABULARY

Define each term in a complete sentence.

constructive boundary
convection current
convergent boundary
destructive boundary
divergent boundary
fossil
Glossopteris
island arc
lithosphere
Mesosaurus
midocean ridge
ocean-floor spreading
Pangaea
rift valley
subduction
tectonics
theory of continental drift
theory of plate tectonics
transform boundary
trench

CONTENT REVIEW: MULTIPLE CHOICE

Choose the letter of the answer that best completes each sentence.

1. Scientists have been convinced of continental drift by fossils of a plant called
a. *Lystrosaurus* b. *Mesosaurus* c. *Glossopteris* d. *Thecodont*

2. Evidence that supports the theory of continental drift has been provided by
a. coal deposits b. the North and South poles
c. convection currents d. ocean currents

3. A deep crack that runs through the center of a midocean ridge is called a
a. trench b. tectonic plate c. rift valley d. river valley

4. The movement of the ocean floor on either side of a midocean ridge is called
a. rift valleys b. ocean-floor spreading
c. trenches d. midocean ridges

5. The process of the ocean floor plunging back into the earth's interior is called
a. subduction b. earthquakes c. volcanoes d. convection

6. The theory used to explain the formation of the earth's crust and its movements, collision, and destruction is called the theory of
a. continental drift b. plate tectonics
c. transform boundaries d. magnetic stripes

7. The largest lithospheric plate is the
a. Cocos plate b. North American plate
c. Eurasian plate d. Pacific plate

8. Plate boundaries usually found at right angles to the midocean ridges are called
a. divergent boundaries b. transform boundaries
c. rifts d. ocean plates

9. The collision of two oceanic plates creates
a. mountain belts b. rift valleys
c. convection currents d. island arcs

10. According to current ideas, South America was originally connected to
a. Eurasia b. India c. Australia d. Africa

CONTENT REVIEW: COMPLETION

Fill in the word or words that best complete each sentence.

1. Wegener proposed that all of the continents were once part of one large landmass called ______.

2. Glaciers form near the ______.

3. Volcanic underwater mountains called ______ can be found in all of the oceans.

4. The history of the earth's magnetism is recorded in ______ in the rocks on the ocean floor.

5. Deep, V-shaped valleys at the bottom of the ocean are called ______.

6. The ______ is made of a number of plates.

7. The pressure and friction created by plate collision cause ________.

8. Two plates grind past one another at a (an) ________ boundary.

9. Scientists think that large ________ currents within the earth move the lithospheric plates.

10. The Aleutian Islands are an example of a (an) ________.

CONTENT REVIEW: TRUE OR FALSE

Determine whether each statement is true or false. If it is true, write "true." If it is false, change the underlined word or words to make the statement true.

1. Mesosaurus is an extinct reptile that swam in fresh water.
2. Mountains formed by the crumpling of rocks in the earth's crust are known as volcanic mountains.
3. Glacial deposits have been found in Africa.
4. The youngest ocean-floor rocks are found at the midocean ridges.
5. Ocean floor is subducted at transform boundaries.
6. The oldest rocks on the ocean floor are 4 billion years old.
7. Tectonics deals with the movements that shape the earth's crust.
8. The Arabian plate lies between North America and South America.
9. Conduction currents may be the cause of plate movement.
10. Pangaea broke into two large continents, Panthalassa and Gondwanaland.

CONCEPT REVIEW: SKILL BUILDING

Use the skills you have developed in the chapter to complete each activity.

1. **Analyzing data** The two imaginary continents each have three rock sections. The arrows show the magnetic field direction that existed when each section formed. The rock's ages are shown in billions of years. Reptile fossils are found in sections A, B, and Z. Fish fossils in sections C and X.

   On a piece of paper, trace all the information given in the figure. Cut out both continents. Then follow the instructions and answer the questions.

   a. Try to fit the two continents together. Do they fit more than one way? Choose the better fit. Explain what evidence you used to make your choice.

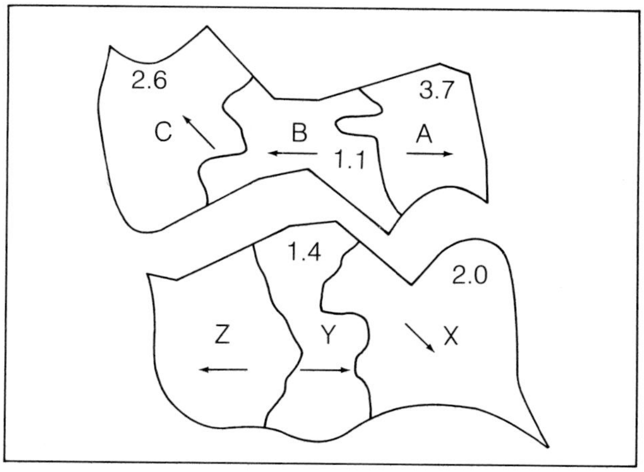

   b. What is a close estimate of the age of the rocks in section Z?

CONCEPT REVIEW: ESSAY

Discuss each of the following in a brief paragraph.

1. What evidence supports the theory of continental drift?
2. How might convection currents in the earth cause the continents to drift?

Adventures in Science

Robert Smith Explores the HOT SPOTS of Yellowstone Park

Imagine working in a laboratory consisting of boiling mud pots, bubbling hot pools, beautiful canyons, and spectacular geysers shooting hot water several meters into the air! For scientist Robert Smith it's not imagination—it's his outdoor research lab. Majestic Yellowstone National Park in Wyoming is home to Smith's geological experiments.

Robert Smith, who was born and raised near Yellowstone National Park, has been attracted to this area since he was a child. He is still amazed by the dynamic features of the park. His fascination with Yellowstone led him to study geophysics. Geophysics is the study of the natural features and processes of the earth. It includes the study of oceans, volcanoes, earthquakes, and weather. Geophysics also involves the study of the movement of large portions of the earth's crust, which is Smith's specialty.

To Robert Smith, the beauty of Yellowstone Park goes deeper than the spectacular sights that make this park famous. Beneath the park's surface, Smith sees beauty in what he and other scientists believe are hot spots. Hot spots are places in the earth's crust where columns of melted rock, or magma, have burned through. Hot spots are areas of considerable geologic activity.

Smith believes that Yellowstone National Park sits over a hot spot. He bases this conclusion on the fact that parts of the park are 60 times hotter than the rest of the continent! It is no wonder that Yellowstone has boiling-hot mud pots and steaming geysers.

Smith also believes that the area around Yellowstone was formed in much the following way. During the past two million years, three tremendous volcanic eruptions occurred in the Yellowstone region. The eruptions melted right through the Rocky Mountains, creating a plateau, or large flat area high in the mountains. Yellowstone Park sits on this plateau. The intense heat of the eruptions "cooked" the rock, turning it yellow. This is how Yellowstone got its name.

The third and last major volcanic eruption caused the surface of the plateau to sink several hundred meters. The crater left

From this photograph, you can understand Robert Smith's fascination with Yellowstone National Park.

Boiling-hot mud pots are evidence of hot spots and incredible volcanic forces beneath Yellowstone National Park.

by the eruption is 75 kilometers long and 45 kilometers wide. It is so large that Smith and his fellow geologists have only recently been able to trace the outline of its rim. These scientists were amazed to discover that most of Yellowstone Park lies inside this volcanic crater.

Within this crater there are two swollen areas, called domes. Smith's team uses advanced laser technology to measure movements of the earth's surface in the area between the domes. They have found that the area rises more than 14 millimeters per year. The movement may indicate that the magma chambers beneath the park are refilling with hot magma. If this is true, a fourth volcanic eruption may occur in a few million years or so.

Smith also studies the Yellowstone region for seismic waves, which are vibrations in the earth. "In 1985 alone," says Smith, "several thousand shocks were recorded in the Yellowstone area." Smith uses the data he collects to create computer models of the geology of the region. The models help him determine the depth of the hot spot. According to his estimates, the magma extends 5 to 10 kilometers beneath the park.

The geysers, boiling pools, and mud pots provide evidence of the hot spots and incredible volcanic forces beneath Yellowstone.

Smith believes that Yellowstone is just one stepping stone on a hot spot "trail." The North American plate moves southwest at a rate of 4.5 centimeters per year. In the last 18 million years, the hot spot that is now under Yellowstone has melted through the continent many times and in many locations within the states of Idaho and Wyoming.

"In a sense," Smith says, "there have been many Yellowstones. Eighteen million years ago a tourist in search of geysers and boiling mud pools would have gone to look near Boise, Idaho; fifteen million years ago, around Twin Falls [Idaho]; and ten million years ago, around Pocatello [Idaho]." And if the North American plate continues to move in its current direction, tens of millions of years from now Dr. Smith's spectacular outdoor laboratory may be somewhere near Cook City, Montana!

Issues in Science

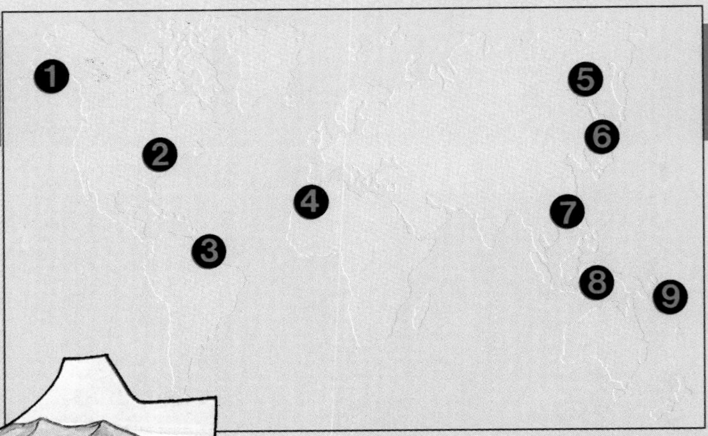

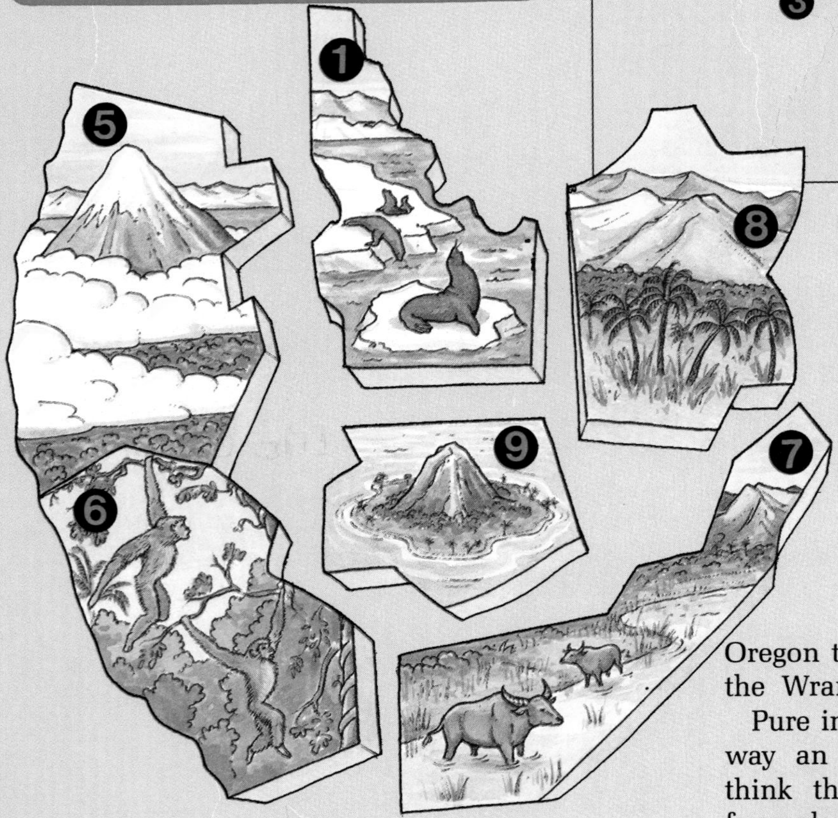

Terranes in the United States originated in other parts of the world. The corresponding numbers on the world map show their origins.

Imagine floating high above the earth and watching the past 600 million years flash by you in about ten minutes. You would witness the earth in what might best be described as utter chaos!

As you watch, a huge landmass that includes Africa rams into North America and glues Florida and Georgia into place. Then a chunk of Georgia breaks loose and slides up the east coast to become part of Connecticut and Newfoundland. A wedge of land slips out from between Texas and Alabama and collides with Mexico to become the Yucatan Peninsula. Soon after, a continent splits apart, scattering its pieces from China to California. Next a block of Guatemala travels a grueling 2600 kilometers, bumps into Los Angeles, and gets smeared onto the coast of California. Finally, a slab of land rises out of the Pacific Ocean near the equator and ends up strewn from Oregon to Alaska, with some of it forming the Wrangell Mountains of Alaska.

Pure imagination? Not exactly. This is the way an increasing number of geologists think that parts of the continents were formed. They have proposed a new theory to explain the formation of the world's landmasses.

The new theory is called the theory of accretion. According to the theory of accretion, small fragments of land, called terranes, join with large continental landmasses. The terranes, which can be as large as the state of Maine or as small as a football field, originate in different parts of the world. The process by which numerous and widely scattered terranes move and then join to continents is called accretion, which explains the name of this theory.

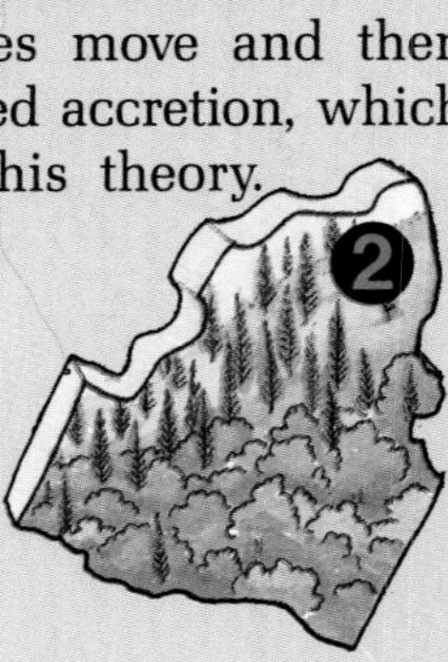

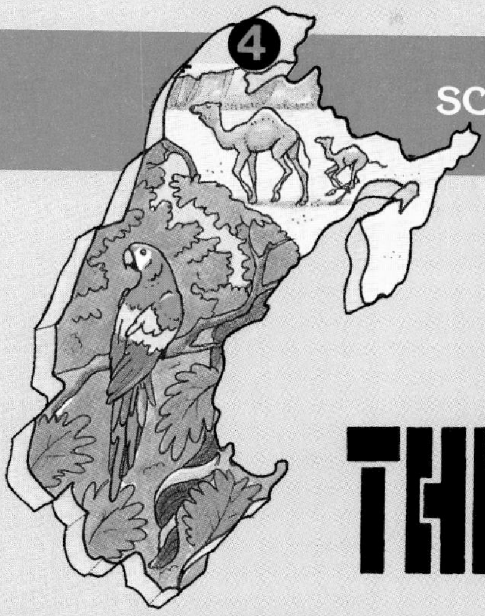

THE GLOBAL JIGSAW PUZZLE

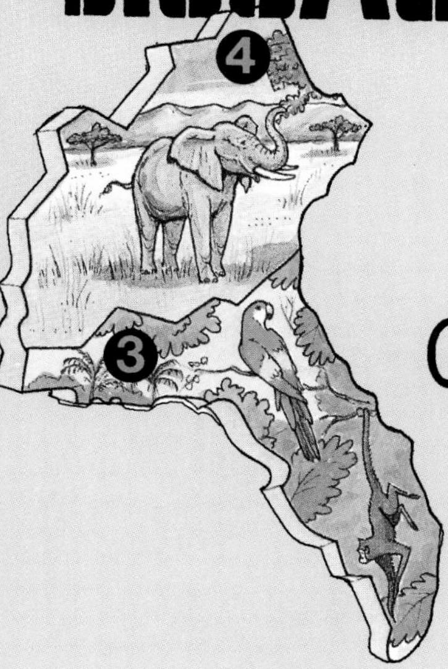

TRACING THE ORIGIN OF CONTINENTS

Many geologists tend to think differently. They believe that a limited number of large masses of the earth's crust, called plates, move slowly about the globe. This theory, called plate tectonics, has been accepted by most geologists since the early 1940s. According to the theory of plate tectonics, continents are parts of large thin plates on the earth's crust. These plates ride on top of the mantle in much the same way a conveyor belt moves on rollers.

However, Dave Howell of the United States Geologic Survey is one of many geologists who believes in the accretion theory. And he has evidence to support his belief—evidence that can be found worldwide. For example, Howell has found rocks in Alaska that were formed during the same period of time but that have very different mineral compositions. These rocks were found lying next to each other. Howell thinks the rocks originally came from different places on the globe and could not have been part of the same plate.

More evidence for the accretion theory is provided by fossils found in the Wrangell Mountains of Alaska. These fossils could have been made only by animals that lived in an ancient tropical sea. So the rock comprising the Wrangell Mountains apparently formed from sediments that came from a sea near the equator. Somehow that rock made its way north from the equator to the region of Alaska.

Elizabeth Miller, a Stanford University geologist, thinks Howell and other scientists are jumping to conclusions in their excitement about finding something new. Although she does not oppose considering the new idea, she believes that all the available information should be carefully examined before the theory of accretion is accepted. She cautions against applying the theory to all parts of the world just because it seems to explain the formation of Alaska.

New ideas such as the accretion theory are interesting, but they must be carefully examined before they are accepted as legitimate explanations. There is still a great deal of the earth's past to uncover. Frequently the evidence that scientists discover has several possible interpretations. Have all the continents formed according to the theory of plate tectonics? Or have portions of some continents been formed as terranes collided with the continents, as explained by the theory of accretion? If so, will the theory of plate tectonics have to be modified? The history of the earth, and possibly its future, ride on an answer.

UNIT SIX

History of the Earth

A gentle breeze sent ripples across the glistening surface of the shallow pond. The ground shook slightly as a giant ground sloth lumbered out of the nearby woods. Dipping its head toward the water, the sloth drank deeply. Suddenly the sloth raised its head and stood very still, trying to detect a whisper of danger from the trees.

Hearing nothing, the sloth bent its head toward the water again. At just that moment, a saber-toothed cat leaped from the woods. With claws bared and teeth flashing, the cat flew through the air toward its startled prey. With the giant cat on its back, the sloth plunged into the pond. Its feet splashed through the water but did not find solid rock. Instead a gooey tar seemed to grab the animal, pulling it further and further down.

In a matter of minutes, both animals were trapped in the tar. They remained there for thousands of years. In the early 1900s, scientists discovered their remains and pieced together a picture of the area in which the sloth and the cat had made their home. Today this place is the site of Los Angeles, California.

CHAPTERS

In just seconds, the giant ground sloth and saber-toothed cat became the remains that scientists would discover thousands of years later.

Fossils and the Past

20

CHAPTER SECTIONS

CHAPTER OBJECTIVES

After completing this chapter, you will be able to

20–1 Identify some of the ways in which fossils are formed.

20–2 Describe how fossils are useful in understanding the earth's past.

20–3 Explain how the relative ages of rock layers and features of the earth can be determined.

Imagine, for a moment, that you have hiked to the top of a very tall mountain. Exhausted, you sit down on some rocks to rest. As you observe the rocks upon which you are sitting, you notice something very strange. Imbedded in the rocks are what seem to be seashells. After a closer look, you are sure they are seashells! But if they are seashells, why are they on top of a mountain so far from the sea?

You are confused by the shells, so you take some samples back to show your teacher. Your teacher suggests that you go to the library to find out what kind of shells they are. But after reading every book on shells, you discover that the shells are not from any sea creature living today. They are the shells of a sea creature that died off more than 75 million years ago. Now you are even more confused.

You are not alone in your confusion. For centuries, people have wondered about the presence of strange shells in areas far from where they are normally found. "How can seashells end up atop tall mountains?" people asked. But today scientists have explanations for such mysteries. And when you have read this chapter, so will you.

This limestone rock contains many fossils of shells and various sea organisms that lived on the earth about 400 million years ago.

Section Objective

To describe the ways in which fossils form

20–1 Formation of Fossils

There are many different kinds of **fossils** in rocks and other material. **A fossil is the remains or evidence of a living thing.** A fossil can be the bone of an organism. Or a fossil can be a print of a shell in a rock. A fossil can even be a burrow or tunnel left by a worm. The most common fossils are bones, shells, pollen grains, and seeds.

Most fossils are incomplete because usually only the hard parts of a plant or animal become fossils. In many cases, the soft flesh of dead organisms was eaten by animals before the fossils formed. The soft tissues of dead plants and animals also tend to **decay** before fossils can form. Decay is the breakdown of dead organisms into the substances from which they were made.

Scientists believe that there were many ancient forms of life that left no fossils at all. In fact, the chances of any plant or animal leaving a fossil are slight. To form most fossils, organisms usually have to be buried in **sediments** (SEHD-uh-muhnts) soon after they die. Sediments are small pieces of rocks, shells, and other material that were broken down over time. Quick burial in sediments prevents ani-

Figure 20–1 *In this photograph, a young man is uncovering fossil woolly mammoth bones in Hot Springs, South Dakota. Are animal bones a common or rare type of fossil?*

Figure 20–2 *Fossils are usually found in sedimentary rocks. Because lower sedimentary rock layers are older than upper sedimentary rock layers, scientists can determine the sequence of changes in life forms on the earth.*

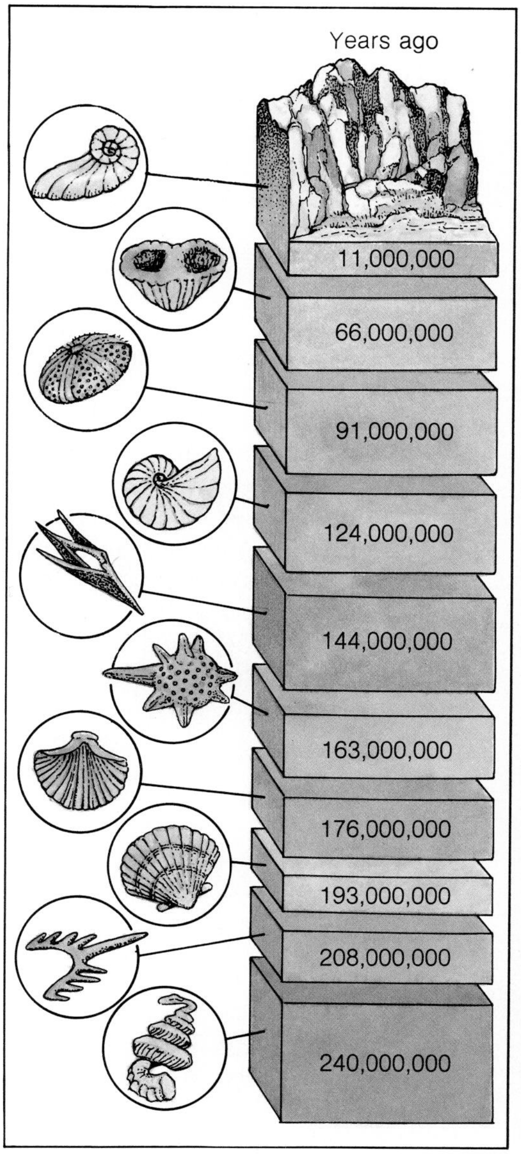

mals from eating the dead organisms. It also slows down or stops decay.

Plants and animals that lived in or near water were preserved more often than other organisms. Sediments in the form of mud and sand could easily bury plants and animals that died in the water or along the sides of a river or other body of water. When the sediments slowly hardened and changed to **sedimentary** (sehd-uh-MEHN-tuhr-ee) **rocks,** the organisms were trapped in the rocks. Sedimentary rocks are formed from layers of sediments. Most fossils are found in sedimentary rocks.

Fossils are almost never found in **igneous** (IHG-nee-uhs) **rocks.** Igneous rocks are formed by the cooling and hardening of hot molten rock, or magma. Most magma is found deep within the earth, where no living things exist. Sometimes the magma flows onto the earth's surface as lava. Living things caught in lava are usually burned up. There is nothing left of the living things to form fossils when the lava cools to form rock.

Fossils are rarely found in **metamorphic** (meht-uh-MOR-fihk) **rocks.** Metamorphic rocks are formed when sedimentary or igneous rocks are changed by heat, pressure, and chemical reaction. If there are fossils in a rock and the rock undergoes these changes, the fossils are usually destroyed or damaged by the forces changing the rock.

Molds, Casts, and Imprints

Two types of fossils are formed when an animal or plant is buried in sediments that harden into rock. If the soft parts of the organism decay and the hard parts are dissolved by chemicals, an empty space will be left in the rock. The empty space, called a **mold,** has the same shape as the organism.

Many fossils are formed when molds fill with minerals. Minerals are solid substances that occur naturally in the earth. The minerals harden to form a **cast,** or filled-in mold, in the same shape as the original organism.

Figure 20–3 *The exact shapes of fossils, such as this seashell from a mountaintop in California, are preserved as casts and molds. A mold is an empty space left in a rock when an organism buried in the rock dissolves. What is a cast?*

CAREER — *Geochronologist*

HELP WANTED: GEOCHRONOLOGIST
For two-year assignment studying fossil dig in East Africa. PhD and field experience necessary. All expenses paid.

Many exciting events have occurred on the earth since it was formed. Scientists are aware of these events because of certain clues left in the earth. For example, on a mountain scientists have found sandstone that was formed beneath an ocean. Elsewhere, they have found bones of huge reptiles that lived long ago.

Geochronologists are scientists concerned with the history of the earth. They determine the ages of rocks and landforms. They determine the sequence of events that took place on the earth before written records. They also develop theories about the history of continents, oceans, and mountain ranges. Geochronologists study geology, paleontology, and related subjects.

To learn more about this career, write to the American Geological Institute, 4220 King Street, Alexandria, Virginia 22302.

Sometimes a fossil is formed before the sediments harden into rock. Thin objects such as leaves and feathers leave **imprints,** or impressions, in soft sediments such as mud. When the sediments harden into rock, the imprints are preserved as fossils.

Figure 20–4 *These fish died 50 million years ago, leaving an imprint of the larger fish trying to swallow the smaller fish. What other thin objects might leave imprints?*

Figure 20–5 *These are just a few of the thousands of pieces of petrified wood in the Petrified Forest National Park in Arizona. The colorful petrified wood was formed when the original wood was replaced by minerals. How else can organisms become petrified?*

Petrification

Some fossil remains of organisms have turned to stone, or become **petrified** (PEHT-ruh-fighd). An organism becomes petrified when minerals gradually replace the original substances of the plant or animal. Plants and animals also become petrified when minerals fill in the air spaces of bones or shells and harden.

The process of petrification usually takes place very slowly. The minerals show many of the details of the original plant or animal. But the petrified fossil may take on the color of the minerals that replaced the plant or animal remains. Thousands of colorful petrified logs can be seen in the Petrified Forest National Park in Arizona.

Preservation of Entire Organisms

It is very rare for both the soft and hard parts of an animal or a plant to be preserved. However, some entire organisms have been preserved. Decay of these organisms was stopped completely. Entire organisms can be preserved in three ways.

FREEZING You probably know that freezing substances helps preserve them. Freezing prevents substances from decaying.

Sharpen Your Skills

Preservation in Ice

1. Place fresh fruit, such as apple slices, strawberries, and blueberries, in an open plastic container. Completely cover the fruit with water. Put the container in a freezer.

2. Put the same amount of fresh fruit in another open container. Place it somewhere where it will not be disturbed.

3. After three days, observe the fruit in both containers.

What differences do you see between the frozen and nonfrozen fruit? Discuss the reason freezing slows the decay of food.

Figure 20–6 *This drawing shows woolly mammoths in the cold, icy climate in which they lived. Taking the climate into consideration, how do you think some woolly mammoths were preserved?*

Some species of animals that once lived on the earth have died out, or become **extinct.** Some extinct animals have been preserved by freezing. Several extinct elephantlike animals called woolly mammoths have been discovered frozen in large blocks of ice. The woolly mammoths and another extinct animal called the furry rhinoceros have also been preserved in the loose frozen soil of arctic regions.

AMBER When the resin from certain evergreen trees hardens, it forms a hard substance called **amber.** Flies and other insects are sometimes trapped in the sticky resin that flows from these trees. When the resin hardens, the insects are preserved in the amber. Insects found trapped in amber are usually perfectly preserved.

TAR PITS **Tar pits** are found in some areas of southern California. Tar pits are large pools of tar. These tar pits contain the fossil remains of many different animals. The animals were trapped in the sticky tar pits when they went to drink the water that often covered the pits. Other animals came to feed on the trapped animals and were also trapped in the tar. Eventually the trapped animals sank to the bottom of the tar pits. Bison, camels, giant ground sloths, wolves, vultures, and saber-toothed cats are some of the animals found as fossils in the tar pits.

Most of the fossils recovered from the tar pits are bones. The flesh of most of the trapped animals had either decayed or been eaten before they could be preserved. But whole furry rhinoceroses have been found in tar pits in Poland.

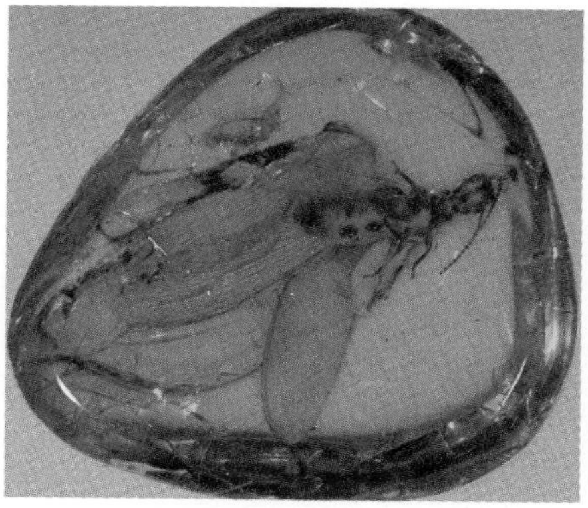

Figure 20–7 *Many insects trapped in amber, or hardened tree resin, are perfectly preserved. Even the delicate parts of this flylike insect—including its wings, legs, and antennae—have been preserved.*

Trace Fossils

Not all fossils are made from the remains of a once-living organism. Some fossils are only the marks or evidence of the activities of an organism. These fossils are called **trace fossils.** The clearly visible dinosaur footprints in many rocks are trace fossils. Tracks, trails, and burrows are also trace fossils.

Figure 20–8 *Dinosaur footprints are an example of trace fossils. Trace fossils help scientists determine what an extinct organism looked like. The drawing is based on the dinosaur footprint in the photograph.*

SECTION REVIEW

1. What is a fossil?
2. How are organisms preserved as fossils?
3. Do molds and casts represent the remains of organisms or evidence of those organisms? Explain.

20–2 Interpreting Fossils

Section Objective

To relate fossil evidence to the earth's history

Scientists can learn much about the earth's past from fossils. **Fossils indicate that many different life forms have existed at different times throughout the earth's history.** In fact, some scientists believe that for every type of organism living today, there are at least 100 types of organisms that have become extinct. There are thousands of fossils of different extinct plants and animals.

The most dramatic example of extinct organisms is the dinosaurs. The word *dinosaur* means "terrible lizard" in Greek. Scientists estimate that between 65 million and 200 million years ago hundreds of different types of dinosaurs roamed the earth. But not a single dinosaur lives today.

Figure 20–9 *Trilobites were small shelled animals that lived in the ocean between 600 and 230 million years ago. If a trilobite was found in a rock layer, what would scientists be able to tell about that layer?*

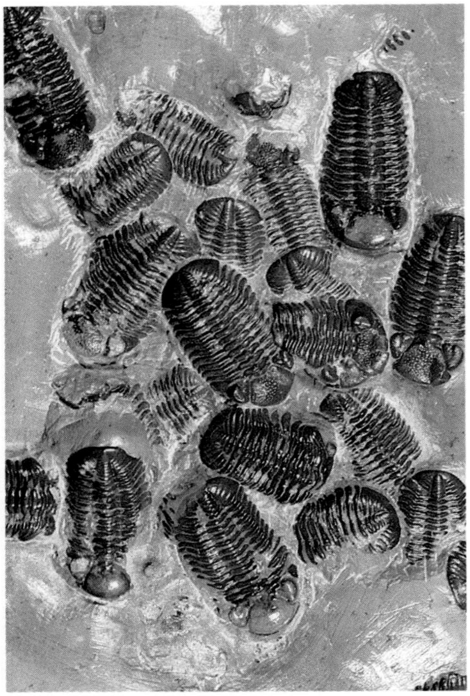

Many other animals, such as saber-toothed cats, woolly mammoths, and giant sloths, lived once but are now extinct. Trilobites (TRIGH-luh-bights) existed for 300 million years in great numbers before becoming extinct. From trilobite fossils, scientists have discovered that many different types of trilobites existed during these 300 million years.

When fossils are arranged according to age, they show that living things have changed, or evolved, over time. For instance, there is fossil evidence of ancient animals that resemble present-day horses. The fossils seem to show changes in the form and size of horses from ancient times to the present.

Fossils also indicate how the earth's surface has changed over time. For example, if scientists find fossils of sea organisms in rocks high above sea level, they can assume that the land was once covered by ocean.

Fossils also give scientists clues to the earth's past climate, or long-term weather conditions. For example, fossils of coral have been found in arctic re-

Figure 20–10 *Fossils of an alligatorlike reptile have been found as far north as Canada. But today alligators live only in warm climates. What do the fossils indicate about the past climate of Canada?*

gions. Coral is an animal that lives only in warm ocean areas today. Scientists assume that ancient coral also lived only in warm ocean areas. But the presence of coral fossils in arctic regions indicates that the climate in these regions was once warmer than it is today.

Scientists have found many other examples of plant and animal fossils that indicate climate changes in a region. Fossils of alligators similar to alligators found in Florida today have been found as far north as Canada. What kind of climate might have existed in the past in Canada where the fossils of alligators are found?

Fossils also tell scientists about the appearance and activities of extinct animals. From fossils of footprints, bones, and teeth, scientists construct models of extinct animals. They can even tell how big or heavy the animals were. Fossils of teeth give clues about the kind of food the animals ate. How might the shape of a tooth help scientists determine if an animal ate plants or animals?

Figure 20–11 *Fossils tell scientists a great deal about the appearance and activities of extinct animals. This fossil tooth is from an extinct flesh-eating shark. What characteristics of the tooth indicate that the animal was a flesh-eater?*

SECTION REVIEW

1. How are scientists able to tell that living things have changed over time?
2. What are some extinct organisms?
3. What does the presence of fossil coral in arctic regions indicate?

Section Objective

To describe methods of determining the relative ages of rocks and fossils

20–3 Relative Ages

Sediments are usually deposited in horizontal layers. As these layers build up, the sediments are pressed together and harden into sedimentary rock. The **law of superposition** states that in undisturbed sedimentary rocks each layer is older than the one above it and younger than the one below it. Why? Each layer of sediments is deposited at a different time. Layers on the bottom are deposited first. Layers on the top are deposited later. So the lower layers are older than the upper layers.

The law of superposition is based on the idea that sediments have been deposited in the same way throughout the earth's history. This idea was first proposed by James Hutton, a Scottish scientist, in the late eighteenth century. He called his idea the **principle of uniformitarianism.** The principle of uniformitarianism states that the processes that act on the earth's surface today are the same as the processes that have acted on the earth's surface in the past. These processes include weathering, erosion, and deposition. Weathering is the breaking down of rocks into sediments. Erosion is the carrying away of sediments. Deposition is the laying down of sediments.

Scientists use the law of superposition to determine whether a layer of rocks or a fossil is older

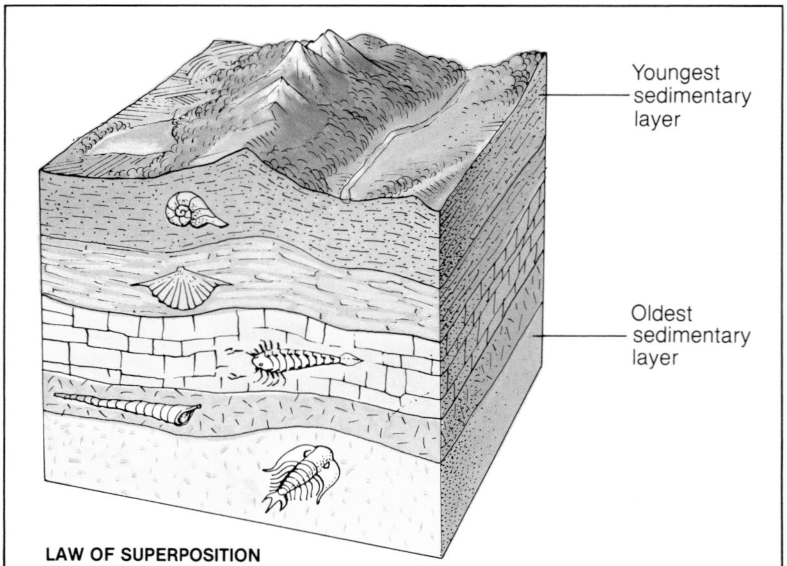

Figure 20–12 *This drawing illustrates the law of superposition. This law states that younger sedimentary layers and their fossils usually are found on top of older sedimentary layers. How does this law help scientists determine whether a fossil is older than another fossil in a rock layer above it or below it?*

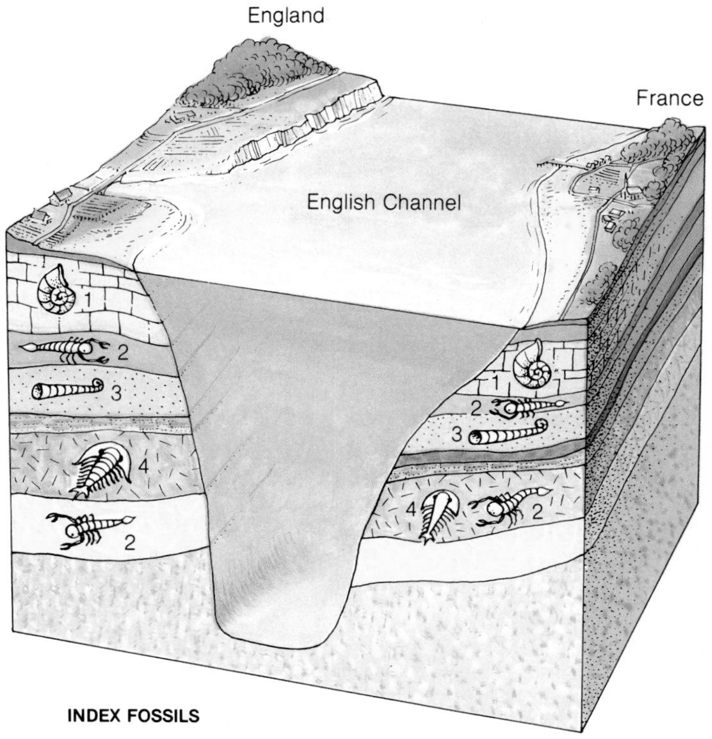

Figure 20–13 *Index fossils are fossils of organisms that lived during only one short period of time. This illustration shows the rock layers on both sides of the English Channel. Even though the rock layers are separated by about 30 kilometers, there are three kinds of index fossils (Fossils 1, 3, and 4) that are found on both the English side and the French side of the channel. So scientists concluded that the English rock layers with the same index fossils as the French rock layers were the same age. Why could fossil 2 not be used to determine the relative age of the English and French rock layers?*

or younger than another layer of rocks or fossil. That is, the **relative age** of a rock layer or fossil is determined through the law of superposition. The relative age of anything is its age compared to the age of something else. Relative age is not the same as **absolute age.** Absolute age is a measure of how many years ago an event occurred or an organism lived. Using the relative ages of fossils and rock layers, scientists can place geological events in order of their occurrence. Scientists use several kinds of evidence to determine a rock layer's relative age.

Index Fossils

One kind of evidence scientists use to determine the relative age of rocks is **index fossils.** Index fossils are fossils of organisms that lived during only one short period of time. Scientists believe that index fossils of the same type of organism are all nearly the same age. So a layer of rock with an index fossil in it is close in age to another layer of rock with the same type of index fossil in it. Even though the rock layers may be in different regions

Sharpen Your Skills

Animal Footprints

1. Spread some mud in a low, flat-bottomed pan. Make sure the mud is not too wet and runny. Smooth the surface of the mud.

2. Have your pet or a neighbor's pet walk across the mud. Let the mud dry naturally so that it hardens and the footprints are permanent.

3. Bring your footprints to school. Exchange your set of footprints for the set of another student.

Examine the footprints and predict what type of animal made them. Explain how you arrived at your answer. How is this activity similar to the way scientists determine what organism left the fossils they have found?

of the world, the index fossils indicate that the layers are close in age. Why would the fossil of an organism that lived through several periods of time not be a good index fossil?

Unconformities

Sedimentary rock layers may be disturbed by forces within the earth. The rock layers may be folded, bent, and twisted. Sometimes older, deeply buried layers of rock are uplifted to the earth's surface. At the surface, the exposed rocks are weathered and eroded. Sediments are then deposited on top of the eroded surface of the older rocks. The deposited sediments harden to form new horizontal sedimentary rock layers. The old eroded surface beneath the newer rock layers is an **unconformity** (uhn-kuhn-FOR-muh-tee). Tilted sedimentary rock layers covered by younger horizontal sedimentary rock layers is an example of an unconformity.

There is a wide gap in the ages of the rock layers above and below an unconformity. There is also a wide gap in the ages of the fossils in these rock layers. By studying unconformities, scientists can tell where and when the earth's crust has undergone changes such as tilting, uplift, and erosion.

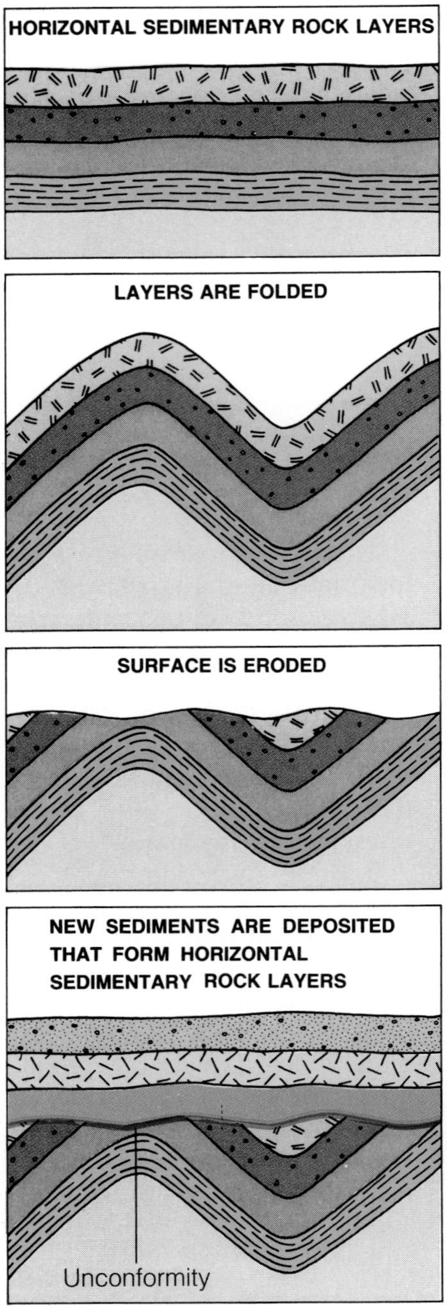

Figure 20–14 *This unconformity (below) is in Helwith Bridge, England. Some unconformities begin when sedimentary rock layers are deposited horizontally (top left). Forces within the earth fold and tilt the rock layers (top center). In time, the layers are worn down to an almost flat surface (bottom center). More sediments are deposited horizontally. These sediments harden into rock. The eroded surface (bottom left) marks the unconformity between the new rock layers and the old folded and tilted rock layers.*

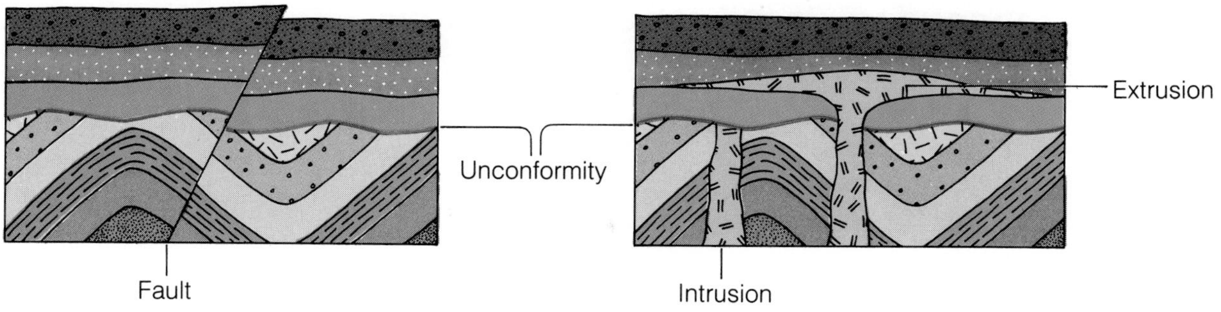

Figure 20–15 *Faults, extrusions, and intrusions are used to determine relative age. On the left, a fault cuts through an unconformity. So the fault is younger than the rocks and unconformity through which it cuts. On the right, an extrusion cuts through an unconformity but lies below some layers of rock. The extrusion, then, is younger than the unconformity and rock layers below it and older than the rock layers above it. An intrusion is also shown. Is it older or younger than the unconformity?*

Faults, Intrusions, and Extrusions

During movements of the earth's crust, rocks may break or crack. A break or crack along which rocks move is called a fault. The rock layers on one side of a fault may have shifted up or down relative to the rock layers on the other side of the fault.

Because faults can only occur after rock layers are formed, rock layers are always older than the faults they contain. The relative age of a fault can be determined from the relative age of the sedimentary layer that it cuts across. Scientists can determine the forces that have changed the earth's surface by examining the faults in rock layers.

The relative ages of igneous rock formations can also be determined. Magma often forces its way into layers of rocks. The magma hardens in the rock layers and forms an **intrusion** (ihn-TROO-zhuhn). An intrusion is younger than the sedimentary rock layers it passes through. Sometimes magma reaches the surface of the earth as lava and hardens. Igneous rock that forms on the earth's surface is called an **extrusion** (ihk-STROO-zhuhn). Extrusions are younger than the rock layers beneath them. What do extrusions tell scientists about the earth's past?

SECTION REVIEW

1. How does the law of superposition date fossils?
2. Do index fossils give absolute or relative ages?
3. Can an index fossil occur above and below an unconformity? Explain your answer.

Sharpen Your Skills

Local Geology

Contact someone in your community who is familiar with the local geology. Interview him or her about the geology in your area. Write a short report about your interview. Include the following information about your area:

- major rock types
- relative ages of the different rock layers
- important rock features
- ages of these features
- organisms that inhabited the area in the past
- good spots for fossil collecting or viewing

20 LABORATORY INVESTIGATION

Observing Fossil Molds and Casts

Problem

What fossil evidence can be obtained from molds and casts?

Materials *(per group)*

Small, empty milk carton
Plaster of Paris
Water
Petroleum jelly
Stirring rod or spoon
3 small objects

Procedure

1. Open the top of the empty milk container completely. Grease the inside of the container with petroleum jelly.
2. Mix the plaster of Paris, following the directions on the package. Pour the mixture into the milk container so that the container is half full.
3. Rub a coat of petroleum jelly over the objects you are going to use.
4. When the plaster of Paris begins to harden, gently press the objects into the plaster so that they are not entirely covered. After the mixture has hardened, carefully remove the objects. You should be able to see the imprints of your objects.
5. Coat the entire surface of the hardened plaster of Paris with petroleum jelly.
6. Mix more plaster of Paris. Pour it on top of the hardened plaster of Paris so that it fills the container. After the plaster hardens, tear the milk carton away from the plaster block. Gently pull the two layers of plaster apart. You now have a cast and a mold of the objects.
7. Exchange your molds and casts for those of another group. Number each cast and mold set from 1 to 3. In a chart like the one shown, record the number of each set. Record your prediction of what object made each cast and mold.
8. Get the original objects from the other group and see if your predictions were correct. Record what the actual object is in your chart.

Number	Predicted Object	Actual Object

Observations

1. What are the similarities and differences between the casts and molds?
2. What are the similarities and differences between the casts and the original objects they were made from?

Conclusions

1. Compare the formation of a plaster mold with the formation of a fossil mold.
2. Compare the way you predicted what the unknown object was with the way a scientist predicts what object left a fossil cast or mold.

CHAPTER REVIEW

SUMMARY

20–1 Formation of Fossils

❑ Most fossils are incomplete because usually only the hard parts of organisms are preserved.

❑ Most fossils are formed when organisms are buried in sediments that slowly harden into sedimentary rocks.

❑ Fossils can be molds, casts, imprints, or petrified plant and animal remains.

❑ Entire organisms can be preserved in ice blocks, frozen soil, amber, and tar pits.

❑ Trace fossils are the marks or evidence of the activities of organisms.

20–2 Interpreting Fossils

❑ Fossils indicate that many different life forms have existed at different times.

❑ When fossils are arranged according to age, they show that living things have changed over time.

❑ Fossils indicate how the earth's surface has changed. Clues to the earth's past climate can be gained from fossils. Scientists learn about the appearance and activities of extinct animals from their fossils.

20–3 Relative Ages

❑ The law of superposition states that in undisturbed sedimentary rocks each layer is older than the one above it and younger than the one below it.

❑ The principle of uniformitarianism states that the processes that act on the earth's surface today are the same processes that have acted on the earth's surface in the past.

❑ The law of superposition can be used to determine the relative age of a rock layer or fossil.

❑ If a layer of rock in one area contains the same index fossil as a layer in another area, the two layers are probably very close in age.

❑ By studying unconformities, scientists can tell where and when the earth's crust has undergone changes such as uplifting, tilting, and erosion.

❑ An intrusion is younger than the sedimentary rock layers it passes through.

❑ An extrusion is younger than the rock layers beneath it.

VOCABULARY

Define each term in a complete sentence.

absolute age
amber
cast
decay
extinct
extrusion
fossil
igneous rock
imprint
index fossil
intrusion
law of superposition
metamorphic rock
mold
petrified
principle of uniformitarianism
relative age
sediment
sedimentary rock
tar pit
trace fossil
unconformity

CONTENT REVIEW: MULTIPLE CHOICE

Choose the letter of the answer that best completes each sentence.

1. Rock formed by the cooling and hardening of magma is called
a. sedimentary b. metamorphic c. igneous d. tar

2. A type of extinct animal whose fossils have been preserved in large blocks of ice is called
a. *Glossopteris* b. amber
c. woolly mammoth d. saber-toothed cat

3. Fossils of giant ground sloths have been found in
a. frozen arctic soil b. pools of water c. amber d. tar pits

4. Fossils resulting from the activities of organisms are called
a. imprints b. fossil molds
c. petrified fossils d. trace fossils

5. A type of fossil that gives clues to the earth's past climate is
a. coral reefs b. teeth c. ice blocks d. none of these

6. Sediments are usually deposited into layers that are
a. vertical b. horizontal c. curved d. igneous intrusions

7. The principle that states that each layer of sedimentary rock is older than the layer above it is the
a. principle of uniformitarianism b. law of superposition
c. law of geochronology d. law of geology

8. A measure of how many years ago an event occurred or an organism lived is
a. absolute age b. relative age c. decay time d. rock time

9. A break or crack in rocks along which the rocks move is called a (an)
a. fault b. unconformity c. intrusion d. igneous extrusion

10. Igneous rock that forms on the earth's surface is called a (an)
a. fault b. trace fossil c. extrusion d. petrified fossil

CONTENT REVIEW: COMPLETION

Fill in the word or words that best complete each sentence.

1. Remains or evidence of plant or animal life are called ________________.

2. Most fossils are found in ________________ rocks.

3. A filled mold that has the same shape as the original organism is called a (an) ________________.

4. The hardened resin of certain evergreen trees is called ________________.

5. The word ________________ means "terrible lizard" in Greek.

6. ________________ existed for 300 million years before becoming extinct.

7. The ________________ states that the processes that act on the earth's surface today are the same processes that have acted on the earth's surface in the past.

8. Sediments are carried away through the process of ________________.

9. An eroded rock surface that is buried by new rock layers is called a (an) ________________.

10. Rock that forms when magma forces its way into rock layers and hardens is called a (an) ________________.

CONTENT REVIEW: TRUE OR FALSE

Determine whether each statement is true or false. If it is true, write "true." If it is false, change the underlined word or words to make the statement true.

1. The soft parts of plants and animals usually become fossils.
2. An empty space called a cast is left in a rock when a buried organism dissolves.
3. Saber-toothed cats are sometimes preserved in amber.
4. Footprints of extinct dinosaurs are examples of trace fossils.
5. Some scientists believe that for every type of animal living today, there are at least 1000 animals that have become extinct.
6. Fossils of alligators have been found as far north as Canada.
7. Sediments are usually deposited in vertical layers.
8. Erosion is the laying down of sediments.
9. The measure of how many years ago an event occurred or an animal lived is called its relative age.
10. Faults are always younger than the rock layers they cut through.

CONCEPT REVIEW: SKILL BUILDING

Use the skills you have developed in the chapter to complete each activity.

1. **Applying concepts** Suppose you are a scientist who finds some fossils while looking at a cross section of rock in an area. One layer of rock has fossils of the extinct woolly mammoth. In a layer of rock below this, you discover the fossils of an extinct alligator. What can you determine about how the climate of this area has changed over time?
2. **Analyzing diagrams** Use the figure to answer the following questions.
   1. Which letter marks the unconformity?
   2. According to the way in which layers D, E, F, and G lie, what might have happened in the past?
   3. List the events that occurred from oldest to youngest. Include the order in which each layer was deposited and when the fault, extrusion, intrusion, and unconformity were formed. Explain why you chose this order.

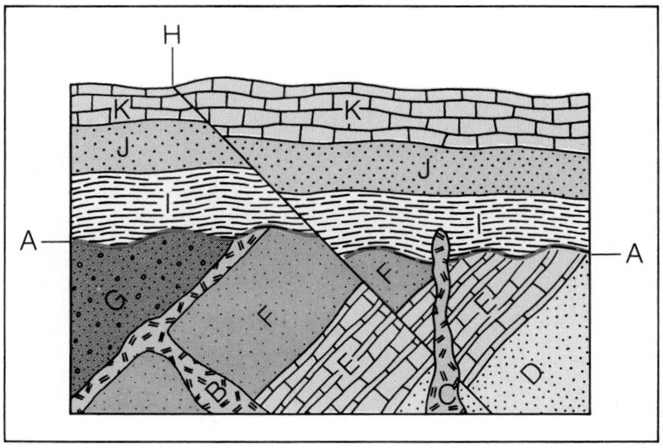

CONCEPT REVIEW: ESSAY

Discuss each of the following in a brief paragraph.

1. Why are most fossils found in sedimentary rocks rather than in igneous or metamorphic rocks?
2. What do fossils indicate to scientists about the earth's history?

Change and Geologic Time

21

CHAPTER SECTIONS

21–1 Measuring Geologic Time
21–2 Divisions of Geologic Time
21–3 Geologic Eras

CHAPTER OBJECTIVES

After completing this chapter, you will be able to

21–1 Describe the methods scientists use to date the age of rocks.
21–2 Name the four geologic eras.
21–2 Distinguish between organic and inorganic changes.
21–3 Identify the major life forms and geologic events that occurred in each of the geologic eras.

The time: 65 million years ago. The place: the earth. A fiery object suddenly shoots across the sky. Large dinosaurs and smaller mammals roaming the earth in search of food panic and run for cover. The fiery ball hits the earth, causing a tremendous explosion. Because the object is so gigantic, its impact sets fire to the vegetation not only where it hits but also on continents hundreds of kilometers away. As the worldwide firestorm burns, it uses up much of the oxygen in the air and poisons the air with carbon monoxide. The fire also creates a huge cloud of soot around the earth. The cloud blocks the sunlight for months and sends the temperatures in the once-tropical regions plunging. In this environment, plants wither and grazing animals starve. Predators that feed on the grazing animals become extinct.

These terrible events were recently proposed by scientists after they accidentally discovered soot in some ancient clay sediments in Denmark, Spain, and New Zealand. The soot is the first direct evidence that fire may have swept the world 65 million years ago. This evidence has been used to support the asteroid-impact hypothesis. According to this hypothesis, a large asteroid struck the earth 65 million years ago. The impact of the asteroid caused the mass extinction of some forms of life, including the dinosaurs.

There is evidence to support the idea that an asteroid or large meteorite struck the earth 65 million years ago. This caused continent-wide firestorms that may have led to the extinction of the dinosaurs.

21–1 Measuring Geologic Time

Section Objective

To describe the methods used to measure geologic time

Geologic time is the very long period of time the earth has existed. **Scientists measure geologic time by applying the law of superposition and the concept of radioactive half-life.** These methods along with other observations provide an outline of the earth's history. In this outline, past events are placed in the order in which scientists believe they occurred.

Law of Superposition

According to the law of superposition, older rocks are found under younger rocks. But the law of superposition only provides the relative age of rocks. It can be used only to determine which rocks and objects in them are older than other rocks and objects in them. It cannot be used to find the absolute, or exact, age of a rock.

Rate of Sedimentation

In the past, scientists used the concept of rate of sedimentation to measure geologic time. By measuring the thickness of sediment layers, scientists estimated how long it took each layer to be deposited.

Figure 21–1 *Layers of sedimentary rocks, such as in the Grand Canyon, are stacked in order of their age. Where would you find the oldest rocks in this photograph?*

The rate of sedimentation, however, is not an accurate method of measuring geologic time. Many factors affect the rate of sedimentation. For example, the size of a river affects the amount of sediments it can carry and deposit. Large rivers carry more sediments than small rivers. So when a large river slows down, it deposits more sediments than a small river would. The speed of a river also affects the amount of sediments the river can carry. Fast-moving rivers carry more sediments and, therefore, can deposit more sediments than slow-moving rivers.

Radioactive Decay

The discovery of **radioactive elements** in 1896 led to the development of an accurate method of determining the absolute age of rocks and fossils. An atom of a radioactive element has an unstable nucleus that breaks down, or decays. During radioactive decay, particles and energy called radiation are released by atoms of the radioactive element.

As some radioactive elements decay, they form **decay elements.** A decay element is the stable element into which a radioactive element breaks down. The breakdown of a radioactive element into a decay element occurs at a constant rate.

HALF-LIFE The **half-life** of a radioactive element is the amount of time it takes for one-half of the atoms of a sample of the radioactive element to decay. For example, if you begin with 1 kilogram of a radioactive element, half of the kilogram will decay during one half-life. Half of the remaining element will decay during another half-life. At this point, one-quarter of the radioactive element remains. Figure 21–2 on page 526 illustrates the breakdown of an element with a half-life of 1 billion years. The half-lives of radioactive elements are not all the same. Some elements take longer to decay.

RADIOACTIVE DATING If certain radioactive elements are present in a rock or fossil, scientists can find the absolute age of the rock or fossil. For example, suppose a rock contains a radioactive element that has a half-life of 1 million years. If tests show that the rock contains equal amounts of the radioactive element and its decay element, the rock

Sharpen Your Skills

Half-Life

1. Suppose a radioactive element has a half-life of 30 days. How much of a 4-g sample will be unchanged after 90 days?

2. Suppose a radioactive element has a half-life of 10,000 years. How much of the original element will be left after 20,000 years?

is about 1 million years old. Since the proportion of radioactive element to decay element is equal, the element has gone through only one half-life. Scientists use the proportion of radioactive element to decay element to determine how many half-lives have occurred. If the rock contains three times as much decay element as radioactive element, how many half-lives have occurred? How old is the rock?

Many different radioactive elements are used to date rocks and fossils. Figure 21–3 lists some radioactive elements and their half-lives. One radioactive element used to date the remains of living things is carbon-14. Carbon-14 is present in all living things. It can be used to date fossils such as wood, bones, and shells that were formed within the last 50,000 years. It is difficult to measure the amount of carbon-14 in a substance more than 50,000 years old because almost all of the carbon-14 will have decayed into nitrogen. Nitrogen is the decay element of carbon-14.

Sharpen Your Skills

Discovery of Radioactivity

Using reference materials in the library, find out about the discovery of radioactivity and radioactive dating. Write a report about radioactive dating. In your report, include the contributions of Antoine Henri Becquerel and Marie and Pierre Curie.

Figure 21–2 *The rate of decay of a radioactive element is measured by its half-life. How much of the radioactive element remains after 2 billion years?*

DECAY OF A RADIOACTIVE ELEMENT WITH A HALF-LIFE OF 1 BILLION YEARS

Time	Amount of Radioactive Element	Amount of Decay Element
4 billion years ago, when rock became solid	1 kg (1)	0 kg (0)
3 billion years ago	0.5 kg (½)	0.5 kg (½)
2 billion years ago	0.25 kg (¼)	0.75 kg (¾)
1 billion years ago	0.125 kg (1/8)	0.875 kg (7/8)
Present	0.0625 kg (1/16)	0.9375 kg (15/16)

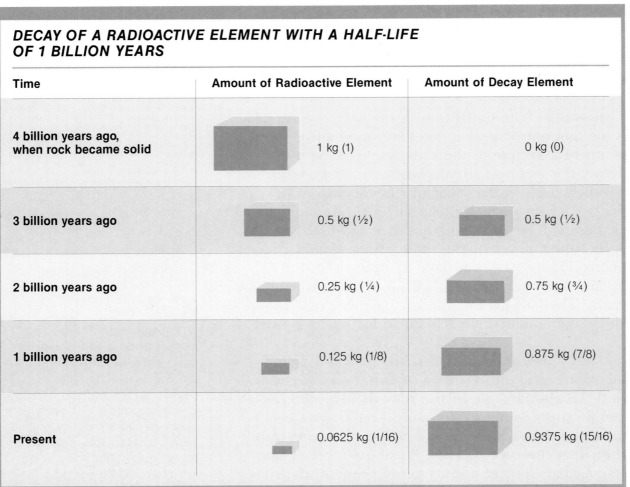

HALF-LIVES OF ELEMENTS USED TO FIND THE AGE OF ROCKS AND FOSSILS

Element	Half-life	Used to Find Age of:
Rubidium-87	50.00 billion years	Very old rocks
Thorium-232	13.90 billion years	Very old rocks
Uranium-238	4.51 billion years	Old rocks and fossils in them
Potassium-40	1.30 billion years	Old rocks and fossils in them
Uranium-235	713 million years	Old rocks and fossils in them
Carbon-14	5770 years	Fossils (usually no older than about 50,000 years)

Figure 21–3 *Each radioactive element has a different half-life. These elements are used to measure the age of different rocks. What is the half-life of the element uranium-238?*

Another radioactive element used for dating is uranium-238. Uranium-238 has a half-life of 4.51 billion years. This makes it very useful in dating rocks formed many millions of years ago. Uranium-238 decays into lead. Why would uranium-238 not be used to date rocks that formed 10,000 years ago?

AGE OF THE EARTH Scientists use radioactive dating to help determine the age of rocks. By finding the age of rocks, scientists can estimate the age of the earth. Scientists have found some rocks in South Africa that are more than 4 billion years old. These are the oldest rocks found on the earth so far.

Radioactive dating of moon rocks brought back by the Apollo missions shows them to be 4.0 to 4.6 billion years old. The oldest rocks brought back from the moon are more than 0.5 billion years older than the oldest known earth rocks. Scientists have evidence that the earth and moon may have formed at about the same time. So from the age of rocks on the earth and moon, scientists believe that the earth is about 4.6 billion years old.

SECTION REVIEW

1. What three methods have scientists used to measure geologic time?
2. What happens during radioactive decay?
3. Explain why carbon-14 would be used to date a piece of wood but not a piece of granite.

Sharpen Your Skills

Detecting Radiation

A Geiger counter is an instrument that detects and counts the amount of radioactivity given off by an object. The counter clicks as it detects the radioactivity.

1. Place a piece of uranium ore next to a Geiger counter.

2. Hold the piece of uranium ore about 1 m away from the counter. *Note:* A watch or clock with a luminous dial containing radium may be used instead of a piece of uranium ore.

Why does the rate of clicking decrease when the radioactive object is farther away from the Geiger counter?

21–2 Divisions of Geologic Time

Section Objective

To identify the divisions of the geologic time scale

Scientists have set up a geologic time scale to record events in the history of the earth. They have divided geologic time into units based on fossil records of extinct organisms and evidence based on the law of superposition.

The largest divisions of the geologic time scale are called **eras.** There are four geologic eras. The **Precambrian** (pree-KAM-bree-uhn) **Era** is the earliest time period. Scientists know very little about the Precambrian Era because so few fossils from this era have been found. Many scientists disagree about the events that occurred during this era. They also disagree about the life forms that may have existed. Why do you suppose few fossils from the Precambrian Era have been found?

Figure 21–4 *Many unusual animals lived long ago, such as plant-eating* Brontosaurus *(bottom) and the meat-eating saber-toothed cat (top).*

The **Paleozoic** (pay-lee-uh-ZOH-ihk) **Era** follows the Precambrian Era. It began about 570 million years ago. The **Mesozoic** (mehs-uh-ZOH-ihk) **Era** follows the Paleozoic Era. The Mesozoic Era began about 225 million years ago. The current era is the **Cenozoic** (see-nuh-ZOH-ihk) **Era.** It began about 65 million years ago. Scientists do not know when the Cenozoic Era will end and a new era will begin. The changes scientists use to mark the ending and beginning of eras are very gradual. The passage from one era to another may take millions of years.

Except for the Precambrian Era, each era is divided into smaller divisions called **periods.** Periods

of the Cenozoic Era are divided into smaller divisions called **epochs** (EHP-uhks).

The division of geologic time into eras, periods, and epochs is based on changes that occurred on the earth. Some of the changes were **organic.** Organic changes are changes in living things due to evolution. For example, the extinction of **trilobites** marks the end of the Paleozoic Era. Trilobites were animals that had jointed legs like those of modern insects or lobsters. The extinction of trilobites is one change that separates the Paleozoic Era from the Mesozoic Era.

Other changes on the earth were **inorganic.** Inorganic changes do not involve living things. They are changes in the surface and climate of the earth. For example, the melting of a worldwide icecap is one change that separates the Precambrian Era from the Paleozoic Era. Episodes of mountain building also separate time periods.

Figure 21–5 *The division of geologic time into eras, periods, and epochs is based on changes that occurred on the earth. The extinction of marine animals, such as the clamlike brachiopods, marks the end of the Paleozoic Era. Is this an example of organic or inorganic change?*

SECTION REVIEW

1. What is the geologic time scale?
2. What are the names of the four geologic eras?
3. What is the geologic time scale based on?

21–3 Geologic Eras

Section Objective

To compare the characteristics of the earth's four geologic eras

The earth's four geologic eras were of different lengths. The Precambrian Era was the longest geologic era. Scientists believe that it lasted about 4 billion years. The Precambrian Era accounts for about 87 percent of the 4.6 billion years of the earth's history. The Paleozoic Era lasted about 345 million years, while the Mesozoic Era lasted about 160 million years. The Cenozoic Era has lasted for only 65 million years.

Precambrian Era

The Precambrian Era includes all of the events from the formation of the earth to the beginning of the Paleozoic Era. Scientists have evidence that most Precambrian rocks have been changed or destroyed

Figure 21–6 *Many volcanic eruptions occurred during the Precambrian Era. How long did the Precambrian Era last?*

by crustal movements, volcanic activity, and long periods of weathering and erosion. But an area of Precambrian rocks is found on each continent, or large landmass. These areas of Precambrian rocks are called shields. Large areas of Precambrian rocks are exposed in Canada, Greenland, and South Africa. Rocks in these areas are nearly 4 billion years old. How do you suppose these rocks were dated?

Many scientists believe that there were different periods of mountain building and volcanic activity during the Precambrian Era. There were also large glaciers spreading across vast areas of land. Scientists believe that the continents changed shape often during this era.

Scientists have found very few fossils from the Precambrian Era. But they have found some fossils of simple marine, or ocean, organisms. These fossils include mostly small, soft-tissued organisms such as jellyfish and primitive worms. Fossils of bacteria, algae, and fungi have also been found.

Paleozoic Era

Figure 21–7 *The fossil starfish in this photograph is one of the many different kinds of invertebrates that lived during the Devonian Period. What are invertebrates?*

During the Paleozoic Era, many changes took place on the earth's surface. Fossils of many different kinds of plants and animals have been found.

The most common life forms early in this era were **invertebrates** (ihn-VER-tuh-brayts). Invertebrates are animals without backbones. Marine invertebrates called trilobites were numerous early in the Paleozoic Era. Marine animals called **brachiopods** (BRAYK-ee-uh-pahds) also lived during this era. Brachiopods looked like clams. They were more abundant than trilobites.

Fossils of **vertebrates** (VER-tuh-brayts), or animals with backbones, have also been found in Paleozoic rocks. For example, scientists have found many fossils of fish in rocks of the Devonian Period, one of the periods of the Paleozoic Era. The Devonian Period is also known as the Age of Fish. Also numerous during this era were **amphibians** (am-FIHB-ee-uhns). Amphibians are animals that live part of their life in water and part on land. Reptiles were also present. What parts of the animals of this era were most often found as fossils?

Figure 21–8 *Amphibians such as* Eryops *lived part of their life in water and part on land. What are the names of some present-day amphibians?*

There were many plants during the Paleozoic Era. Large tree ferns and other land plants grew very well in the warm swampy areas that existed during this era. Scientists believe that the remains of these plants formed the huge coal deposits in the United States and other parts of the world.

CAREER

Museum Technician

HELP WANTED: MUSEUM TECHNICIAN Work with curator and designer to renovate exhibit of fossil vertebrates. Some college work in biology or paleontology helpful. On-the-job training.

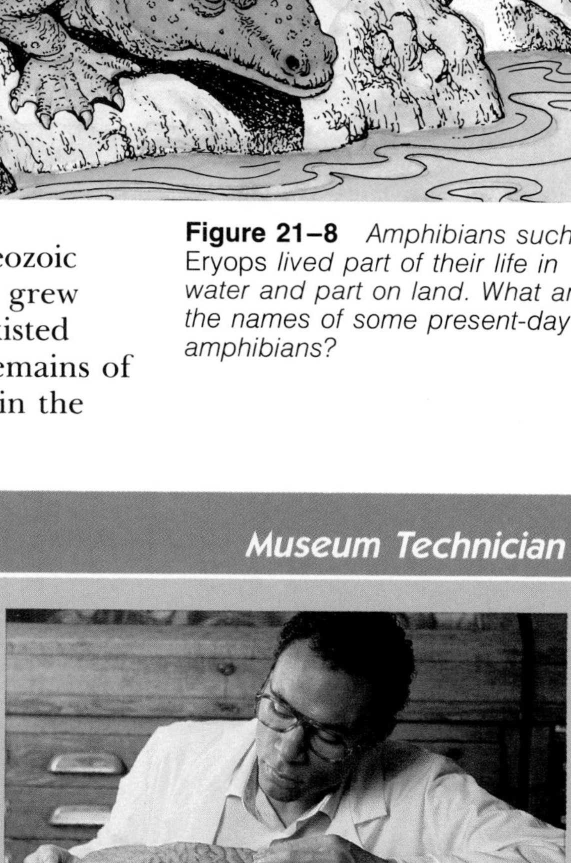

People who prepare museum collections and exhibits are called **museum technicians.** They clean and preserve animal and plant specimens and carefully mount and arrange them in glass cases. When an exhibit is replaced, technicians carefully remove and store the old specimens.

Museum technicians work with fossils that have been recently discovered. They restore the skeletal parts of fossil organisms, using clay, plaster, and other materials. Sometimes they construct copies of entire fossil skeletons. Museum technicians require special skills in doing detailed work. So on-the-job training is important. College training is helpful in advancing to higher positions. Employment positions are also available in the natural history departments of colleges and universities.

For further career information, write to American Association of Museums, 1055 Thomas Jefferson St., NW, Washington, DC 20007.

Figure 21–9 *This is one of the oldest fossils of a complete flower ever found (top). It is an 80-million-year-old relative of the rose. An artist's idea of what this flower may have looked like when alive is also shown (bottom).*

From fossils and other evidence, many scientists have concluded that the continents were much closer together during the early Paleozoic Era than they are today. By the end of the Paleozoic Era, the continents had moved together to form a giant landmass called Pangaea. Some of the world's major mountain ranges, such as the Urals in Asia and the Appalachians in North America, formed when the continents collided in the Paleozoic Era.

Mesozoic Era

The Mesozoic Era is divided into three periods. The oldest period is called the Triassic (trigh-AS-ihk) Period. The middle period is called the Jurassic (joo-RAS-ihk) Period. The youngest period is called the Cretaceous (krih-TAY-shuhs) Period.

Scientists believe that Pangaea began to break apart during the Mesozoic Era. The expansion of the ocean floor along midocean ridges caused the continents to gradually spread apart. Midocean ridges are chains of underwater volcanic mountains. Scientists believe that the continents are still moving apart today.

As Pangaea broke apart, there were many earthquakes and volcanic eruptions. Many mountains were formed at this time. The Appalachian Mountains were leveled by erosion during the early part of the Mesozoic Era. Then they were uplifted again late in the era. The Sierra Nevada and Rocky Mountains were formed during the late stages of the Mesozoic Era.

During the Mesozoic Era, shallow inland seas covered North America several times. By the end of the Cretaceous Period, more of the continent was covered by oceans than at any other time. What fossil evidence would support this?

During the Triassic and Jurassic periods, giant mosses and tree ferns were the most common forms of plants. Palmlike seed plants called **cycads** (SIGH-kads) covered large areas of land. Cone-bearing plants, called **conifers** (KAHN-uh-fuhrs), such as pine, cedar, spruce, and cypress were common. During the Cretaceous Period, oak, maple, elm, birch, and beech trees were plentiful.

During the Mesozoic Era, reptiles were the dominant life form. The Mesozoic Era is known as the Age of Reptiles. Many dinosaurs roamed the earth. Dinosaurs were large reptiles. The word *dinosaur* means "terrible lizard." Large marine reptiles were also abundant.

One of the best-known dinosaurs is *Brontosaurus* (brahn-tuh-SOR-uhs), or "thunder lizard." *Brontosaurus* was 4.5 meters high at the shoulder and 21 meters long. It had a mass of about 27 tons.

Another type of dinosaur was *Tyrannosaurus* (tigh-ran-uh-SOR-uhs) *rex.* It roamed the earth over 70 million years ago, long after *Brontosaurus* lived. *Tyrannosaurus rex* means "king tyrant lizard." It was the largest, most powerful flesh-eating dinosaur. It walked upright on two strong hind legs. It stood over 3 meters high and grew to a length of about 12 meters .

There were many other flesh-eating dinosaurs during the Mesozoic Era. There were also plant-eating dinosaurs. *Stegosaurus* (stehg-uh-SOR-uhs) was a plant-eating dinosaur. What other dinosaurs can you name?

In the oceans, there were giant turtles and other reptiles, such as ichthyosaurs (IHK-thee-uh-sors). Ichthyosaurs were fishlike in form. They were 5 to 7 meters long and had flippers and large, sharp teeth.

Scientists have found fossil evidence of flying animals in rocks from the Mesozoic Era. Pterodactyls (ter-uh-DAK-tuhls) were flying reptiles. They had wings made of thin pieces of skin attached to their front legs and body. They had a long, thin beak

Figure 21–10 *This present-day cycad resembles its palmlike ancestors of the Triassic and Jurassic periods. What other plants were common then?*

Figure 21–11 Archaeopteryx *was a flying animal that lived during the Mesozoic Era. Was* Archaeopteryx *a bird or reptile?*

Sharpen Your Skills

Terrible Lizards

Using reference materials in the library, look up information about the following dinosaurs:

Brachiosaurus
Triceratops
Ankylosaurus
Plesiosaurus

Write a report that includes a description of each dinosaur and its habitat.

filled with sharp, curved teeth. Another winged animal was *Archaeopteryx* (ahr-kee-AHP-tuhr-ihks). It had wings with feathers. *Archaeopteryx* was an ancient bird. Modern birds may have evolved from *Archaeopteryx*.

By the end of the Mesozoic Era, dinosaurs were extinct. Scientists have many theories to explain why dinosaurs became extinct. One theory is that a huge asteroid or comet hit the earth with such force that dust or soot in the air blocked out sunlight. The blocking of sunlight may have resulted in worldwide freezing temperatures. Warmblooded mammals were better able to survive this sudden temperature change than were the dinosaurs.

Another theory to explain the extinction of dinosaurs is that gradual changes occurred in the physical environment. The widespread tropical climate of the Mesozoic Era was slowly replaced by temperate and cold climates. Large plant-eating dinosaurs could not adapt fast enough to the resulting changes in plant growth. How do you suppose flesh-eating dinosaurs were affected when plant-eating dinosaurs died off?

Cenozoic Era

The Cenozoic Era is the era you live in. It is divided into two periods. The Tertiary Period began 65 million years ago. The Quaternary Period began 1.8 million years ago. Scientists often call the Cenozoic Era the Age of Mammals because mammals are the dominant life form. Mammals such as horses, bison, and deer characterize this era. Fossils of apes have been found in rocks dating from earlier in this era. Many large animals, such as mammoths, roamed the earth then.

From fossil evidence and rock records, scientists have concluded that the highest plateaus and mountain ranges of the world were uplifted during the Cenozoic Era. During this era, there has been a general drying and cooling of the earth. As a result, there is more variety in climate now than at any time in the past.

There were at least four ice ages during the Cenozoic Era. During one of these ice ages, an ice sheet 2400 to 3000 meters thick developed. This ice sheet reached from the Arctic to as far south as the

Figure 21–12 Uintatherium, *which lived in the Cenozoic Era, was an odd-looking animal that had the legs of an elephant, the tail of a lion, and the head and ears of a rhinoceros.*

Missouri and Ohio rivers in North America. In Europe and Asia, ice sheets covered most of the Soviet Union and extended into Germany. Antarctica and Greenland are still covered by the remnants of the last ice age.

Ice ages are brought on by a general cooling of the earth's air. The times between ice ages are called **interglacials** (ihn-ter-GLAY-shulz). During interglacials, glaciers melt and the ocean level rises. The earth may be in an interglacial today. Evidence shows that the ocean level is rising.

The earliest humanlike fossils scientists have found date from the late Pliocene Epoch. Humanlike fossil skulls have been found on several continents. One of the most important finds of humanlike fossils has been in East Africa. Many primitive stone tools have been found in western Europe as well as in Africa.

Figure 21–13 *During the Cenozoic Era, there were at least four ice ages. An ice sheet such as this one developed and covered large landmasses during one of these ice ages. What are the times between ice ages called?*

SECTION REVIEW

1. Describe the Precambrian Era.
2. What are the most common animals in each of the following eras: Paleozoic, Mesozoic, Cenozoic?
3. Explain why it is difficult to determine the geologic era to which an area of metamorphic rock belonged.

GEOLOGIC HISTORY OF THE EARTH

Era	Precambrian	Paleozoic			
Began (millions of years ago)	4600	570			
Ended (millions of years ago)	570	225			
Length (millions of years)	4030	345			
Period	None	Cambrian	Ordovician	Silurian	Devonian
Began (millions of years ago)	4600	570	500	430	395
Ended (millions of years ago)	570	500	430	395	345
Length (millions of years)	4030	70	70	35	50
	Earth's history begins; seas form; mountains begin to grow; oxygen builds up in atmosphere; first life forms in sea; as time passes, bacteria, algae, jellyfish, corals, and clams develop	Shallow seas cover parts of continents; many trilobites, brachiopods, sponges, and other sea-living invertebrates are present	Many volcanoes and mountains form; North America is flooded; first fish (jawless) appear; invertebrates flourish in the sea	Caledonian Mountains of Scandinavia rise; coral reefs form; first land plants, air-breathing animals, and jawed fish develop	Acadian Mountains of New York rise; erosion of mountains deposits much sediment in seas; first forests grow in swampy areas; first amphibians, sharks, and insects develop

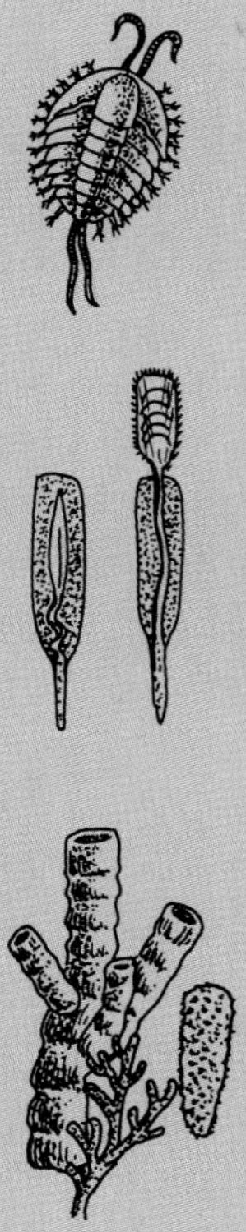

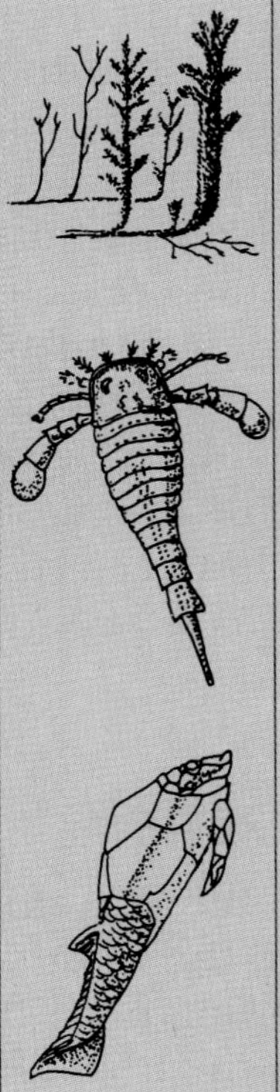

Figure 21–14 *In this chart of the geologic history of the earth, you can see when each geologic era began and ended. When did modern humans first appear on the earth?*

*In North America, the Carboniferous Period is often subdivided into the		**Mesozoic**			**Cenozoic**	
		225			65	
Mississippian Period (345-310 million years ago) and the		65			The present	
Pennsylvanian Period (310-280 million years ago).		160			65	
Carboniferous *	Permian	Triassic	Jurassic	Cretaceous	Tertiary	Quaternary
345	280	225	190	136	65	1.8
280	225	190	136	65	1.8	The present
65	55	35	54	71	63.2	1.8
Appalachian Mountains of North America form; ice covers large areas of the earth; swamps cover lowlands; first mosses, reptiles, and winged insects; great coal-forming forests form; seed-bearing ferns grow	Ural Mountains of Russia rise; first cone-bearing plants appear; ferns, fish, amphibians, and reptiles flourish; many sea-living invertebrates, including trilobites, die out	Palisades of New Jersey and Caucasus Mountains of Russia form; first dinosaurs and first mammals appear; modern corals, modern fish, and modern insect types develop	The Rocky Mountains rise; volcanoes of North American West are active; first birds appear; palms and cone-bearing trees flourish; largest dinosaurs thrive; primitive mammals develop	First flowering plants appear; placental mammals develop; dinosaurs die out, as do many sea-living reptiles	Andes, Alps, and Himalayan Mountains rise; first horses, primates, and humanlike creatures develop; flowering plants thrive; mammals take on present-day features	Ice covers large parts of North America and Europe; Great Lakes form as ice melts; first modern human beings appear; woolly mammoths die out; civilization begins

21 LABORATORY INVESTIGATION

Constructing a Geologic Time Line

Problem

What can be interpreted from a time line that plots, to scale, a series of dates from the earth's past?

Materials *(per student)*

Meterstick
5 m adding-machine tape
Pencil

Procedure

1. For this procedure, the scale is 1 mm = 1 million yrs, or 1 m = 1 billion yrs.
2. Stretch out the adding-machine tape. Using the meterstick, draw a continuous straight line down the middle of the tape. This line represents your time line. Draw a straight line across the tape at one end. Label this line "The present."
3. From the line labeled "The present," draw five more lines, each exactly 1 m apart. Label the first of these lines "1 billion years ago." Label the second line "2 billion years ago," and so on. The fifth line, then, will be labeled "5 billion years ago."
4. Draw a line 600 mm from the line labeled "4 billion years ago." Label this line "4.6 billion years ago." On this line, write "Earth's beginning?"
5. Plot each event in the table on the tape. Label both the number of years ago and the event. Add other important events you can think of.

Observations

1. Which time period is the longest? The shortest?
2. In which era did dinosaurs exist or begin to exist? In which era did mammals exist or begin to exist?
3. Which lived on the earth the longer time, dinosaurs or mammals?

Conclusions

1. How many years does 1 cm represent on this scale?
2. Why is there a question mark in the label "Earth's beginning?"?
3. Did you have difficulty plotting any of the events on the list? If so, why?

INFERRED AGES OF EVENTS IN YEARS BEFORE PRESENT

Event Label	Number of Years Ago
First mammals and dinosaurs	200 million
Beginning of Carboniferous Period	345 million
Oldest fungi	1.7 billion
Beginning of Jurassic Period	190 million
Beginning of Devonian Period	395 million
Last Ice Age	10,000
Beginning of Cretaceous Period	136 million
Beginning of Paleozoic Era (first abundant fossils)	570 million
Oldest rocks known	4.2 billion
Beginning of Quaternary Period	1.8 million
Oldest carbon from plants	3.6 billion
Beginning of Ordovician Period	500 million
First birds	160 million
Beginning of Cenozoic Era	65 million
First humanlike creatures	2 million
Beginning of Silurian Period	430 million
First reptiles	290 million
Beginning of Mesozoic Era	225 million
Humans begin to make tools	500,000
Beginning of Permian Period	280 million

CHAPTER REVIEW

SUMMARY

21–1 Measuring Geologic Time

❑ To measure geologic time, scientists have used the law of superposition. This law states that older rocks are generally found under younger rocks.

❑ In the past, scientists used the rate of sedimentation to measure geologic time.

❑ As some radioactive elements decay, they form decay elements. The breakdown of a radioactive element into a decay element occurs at a constant rate.

❑ The half-life of a radioactive element is the amount of time it takes for one-half of the atoms of a sample of the radioactive element to decay.

❑ Today scientists use radioactive dating to determine the absolute age of rocks and fossils.

❑ Using this method of radioactive dating, scientists have concluded that the earth is about 4.6 billion years old.

21–2 Divisions of Geologic Time

❑ Scientists have divided the geological time scale into four eras: Precambrian, Paleozoic, Mesozoic, and Cenozoic.

❑ The Precambrian Era began about 4.6 billion years ago. It was followed by the Paleozoic Era, which began about 570 million years ago. This era was followed by the Mesozoic Era, which began about 225 million years ago. The current era is the Cenozoic Era, which began about 65 million years ago.

❑ The eras are divided into periods. The periods are divided into epochs.

❑ During the course of geologic time on earth, many changes have occurred. Some changes were organic, or changes in living things. Other changes were inorganic, or changes that do not involve living things.

21–3 Geologic Eras

❑ The Precambrian Era is the earliest time period. During this era, jellyfish, worms, bacteria, algae, and fungi first appeared.

❑ The Precambrian Era was an era of mountain building and volcanic activity.

❑ During the Paleozoic Era, marine animals and plants appeared. Also numerous during this era were fish, amphibians, and reptiles.

❑ Scientists have concluded that the continents were much closer together during the early Paleozoic Era than today. By the end of the era, the continents moved to form a giant landmass called Pangaea.

❑ The Mesozoic Era is divided into the Triassic, Jurassic, and Cretaceous periods. During this era, mammals, dinosaurs, and birds evolved.

❑ The Cenozoic Era includes the Tertiary and Quaternary periods. It is called the Age of Mammals because mammals are the dominant life form.

VOCABULARY

Define each term in a complete sentence.

amphibian
brachiopod
Cenozoic Era
conifer
cycad
decay element
epoch
era
geologic time
half-life
inorganic
interglacial
invertebrate
Mesozoic Era
organic
Paleozoic Era
period
Precambrian Era
radioactive element
trilobite
vertebrate

CONTENT REVIEW: MULTIPLE CHOICE

Choose the letter of the answer that best completes each sentence.

1. According to the law of superposition, older rocks are generally found
a. above younger rocks b. next to younger rocks
c. under younger rocks d. scattered among younger rocks

2. The breaking apart of the nuclei of radioactive atoms is called radioactive
a. decay b. half-life c. superposition d. period

3. Scientists estimate the earth's age to be about
a. 46,000 years b. 460,000 years
c. 4.6 million years d. 4.6 billion years

4. The era that includes the formation of the earth is called the
a. Precambrian Era b. Cenozoic Era
c. Mesozoic Era d. Paleozoic Era

5. The Cenozoic Era began about
a. 4.6 billion years ago b. 570 million years ago
c. 65 million years ago d. 225 million years ago

6. Ancient clamlike invertebrates are called
a. trilobites b. cycads c. conifers d. brachiopods

7. Cycads are
a. cone-bearing plants b. ferns
c. fungi d. palmlike seed plants

8. The era known as the Age of Reptiles is called the
a. Precambrian Era b. Cenozoic Era
c. Mesozoic Era d. Paleozoic Era

9. Pterodactyls were flying
a. birds b. reptiles c. mammals d. fish

10. The current era is called the
a. Precambrian Era b. Cenozoic Era
c. Mesozoic Era d. Paleozoic Era

CONTENT REVIEW: COMPLETION

Fill in the word or words that best complete each sentence.

1. The long period of time the earth has existed is called ________.

2. The time it takes one-half of the atoms of a radioactive element to decay is called the element's ________.

3. The largest divisions of geologic time are called ________.

4. Eras are divided into smaller divisions called ________.

5. Animals without backbones are called ________.

6. Cycads and conifers first appeared during the ________ Era.

7. *Dinosaur* means ________.

8. *Archaeopteryx* was an ancient winged ________.

9. The era known as the Age of Mammals is called the ________ Era.

10. The times between ice ages are called ________.

CONTENT REVIEW: TRUE OR FALSE

Determine whether each statement is true or false. If it is true, write "true." If it is false, change the underlined word or words to make the statement true.

1. The breaking up of the atomic nucleus of a radioactive element is called radioactive decay.
2. Uranium-238 has a half-life of 10,000 years.
3. Scientists have estimated that the age of the earth is 4.6 million years.
4. The Paleozoic Era began about 65 million years ago.
5. Periods are divided into eras.
6. Extinct animals that have jointed legs like those of modern insects and lobsters are called trilobites.
7. The period known as the Age of Fish is called the Devonian Period.
8. Pangaea was an ancient landmass.
9. The Triassic, Jurassic, and Cretaceous periods are divisions of the Mesozoic Era.
10. Humanlike fossils have been found in East Africa.

CONCEPT REVIEW: SKILL BUILDING

Use the skills you have developed in the chapter to complete each activity.

1. **Making charts** Make a chart of the geologic eras and the life forms characteristic of each era. Include when each era began and ended.
2. **Sequencing events** List five events in your life in the order they happened. Have a friend or classmate list five events in his or her life in the order they happened. Now try to list all ten events in the order they happened.

   What difficulties did you have in deciding whether a certain event occurred before or after other events? How long did it take each event to occur? Give the time span between each event. How has this activity helped you understand the difficulty scientists had in developing a time scale without radioactive dating?
3. **Relating concepts** Why do you think present-day clams are so similar to clam fossils 500 million years old?
4. **Making calculations** A radioactive element has a half-life of 500 million years. After 1.5 billion years, how many half-lives have passed? How many kilograms of a 5-kg sample would be left at this time? If the half-life were 3 billion years?
5. **Developing a theory** Explain why an animal that reproduces every year would have a better chance of surviving a change in its environment than an animal that reproduces only once or twice in ten years.
6. **Relating concepts** Explain why rocks that account for the first 600,000 years of the earth's existence have never been found on the earth.

CONCEPT REVIEW: ESSAY

Discuss each of the following in a brief paragraph.

1. How are radioactive elements used to determine the age of rocks and fossils?
2. Describe some of the geologic changes that took place during the Paleozoic Era.
3. Why was the rate of sedimentation a poor method of measuring geologic time?
4. What conditions may have led to the extinction of the dinosaurs?

SCIENCE GAZETTE

Adventures in Science

Sara Bisel Uncovers the Past with ANCIENT BONES

You probably know a bone when you see one. And you might even be able to tell the difference between a chicken bone and a steak bone. But if you saw a pile of bones you probably couldn't tell much more about them. Dr. Sara Bisel is different. She studies bones to reveal a story within the bones—a story of ancient times. Dr. Bisel is an anthropologist, a person who studies the physical characteristics and cultures of people who lived in the past. She has studied chemistry, nutrition, and art. All of these fields help her in her work with bones.

Today, Sara Bisel works in Italy. There she studies the remains of a great disaster that occurred almost two thousand years ago. On August 24, A.D. 79, Mount Vesuvius, a volcano in Southern Italy, erupted. For many people living near the volcano this day was their last.

Herculaneum, a busy port city on the Bay of Naples, was located at the base of the volcano. The people of Herculaneum fished in the surrounding waters. They stored their fishing boats in stone huts on the beach. In one of the stone huts Sara Bisel made her most important discovery—not boats, but the remains of people who perished during the eruption of Mount Vesuvius. Although these remains are now only silent witnesses to a dreadful event, they tell a story to Sara Bisel.

"Who says dead men don't talk?" Dr. Bisel asks. "These bones will have a lot to say about who these people were and how they lived." For Dr. Bisel uncovers more than bones in her work. She tries to bring the lives of ancient people into focus.

In 1982 Dr. Bisel began to reconstruct the lives of people who hid in the boat shed during the eruption of Mount Vesuvius. That eruption was followed by an avalanche that buried the dead under thirty meters of lava and mud. This volcanic covering sealed the bones from the air. The mud hardened and preserved the skeletons.

Near the boat shed, Dr. Bisel found the remains of a woman she calls Portia. In examining Portia's badly crushed skull, Dr. Bisel concluded that Portia fell from a great height during the eruption. By measuring one of Portia's leg bones, Dr. Bisel was able to determine Portia's height. The condition of the bones also told Dr. Bisel about the kind of life Portia lived. For example, Dr. Bisel analyzed Portia's bones with special chemical tests. These tests could tell if Portia was well nourished and if she had any diseases. The shape and texture of the bones could tell what Portia did for a living. Ridges and rough spots on the arm bones indicated to Dr. Bisel the way in which Portia used her arm muscles. "I think she was a weaver."

Sara Bisel works very carefully, loosening the fragile bones from their stony resting place. If the bones are treated roughly, they can break as easily as eggshells. She washes each bone and dips it into a liquid plastic solution to preserve it. Next she stores the bones in special yellow plastic boxes. To date, Dr. Bisel has collected the bones of 48 men, 38 women, and 25 children.

Putting the pieces of a skull together requires some artistic skills as well as scientific knowledge. Sara Bisel is an expert at working out these complex, three-dimensional puzzles. "Just look at her profile and that delicate nose," Dr. Bisel exclaimed excitedly about Portia's reconstructed skull. "In your mind's eye, spread a little flesh over these bones. She was lovely!"

In one family, Dr. Bisel found four men, three women, and five children. One of the children was very young, only about seven months old the day of the eruption. Because the baby wore jewelry, Dr. Bisel thinks this family was wealthy.

Dr. Bisel, who works six days a week at her interesting job, truly enjoys her work. She takes great delight in reconstructing the skeletons and listening to the stories they silently tell.

"Who says dead men don't talk?" From bones such as these Dr. Bisel is reconstructing the lives of people buried during the eruption of Mt. Vesuvius in A.D. 79.

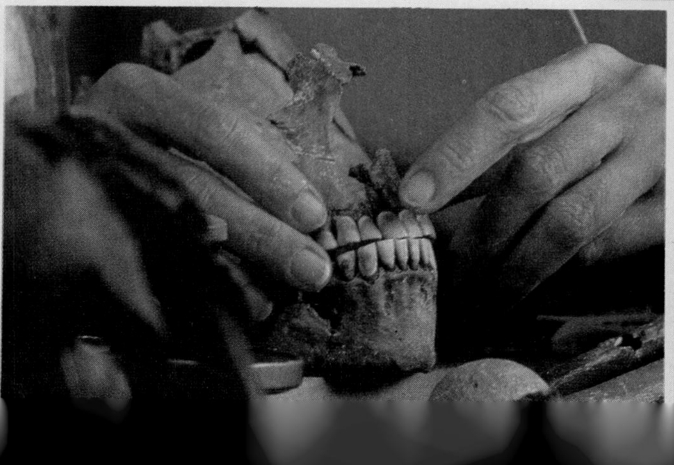

From Rulers to Ruins: WHAT KILLED THE DINOSAURS?

Issues in Science

Sixty-five million years ago, dinosaurs—giant reptiles that ruled the earth for more than 165 million years—may have spent their last days on the earth. Imagine what one of those days might have been like. . . . A baby *Stegosaurus* is running for its life through a tropical forest. The *Stegosaurus* is pursued by *Tyrannosaurus,* king of the flesh-eating dinosaurs. Nearby, a *Triceratops* watches the chase while munching on tropical bushes. Suddenly, a dark shadow moves across the land. The shadow grows larger as a huge rock, the size of a mountain, blocks the sun.

The huge rock is hurtling toward the earth. When it strikes, a deafening boom and tremendous earthquake shake the land. White-hot rocks are thrown for kilometers in every direction. The collision causes forest fires that rage across the earth. At the same time, dust particles fill the sky. The dust particles combine with smoke and ash from forest fires to block the sun for several months or longer.

Without sunlight, the earth soon becomes much colder. Plants that need the sun to produce food begin to die off. Plant-eating dinosaurs, without a source of food, also begin to die off. In time, even the flesh-eating dinosaurs die because they can no longer feed on smaller dinosaurs. But it is not just the dinosaurs that are dying. Almost 96 percent of all plant and animal species are killed during this time period!

It is a proven fact that a mass extinction of living things occurred about 65 million years ago. But was this extinction caused

by an object from outer space? Luis Alvarez and his son Walter believe it was. Their theory, called the asteroid-impact theory, suggests that a large asteroid struck the earth and began the chain of events you have read.

The Alvarez team has evidence to support their theory. They have studied layers of clay formed during the time of the dinosaur extinction. In the clay they found high levels of an element called iridium. Iridium is rare on the earth. Yet the Alvarez team found levels of iridium almost 160 times greater than normal in this clay layer. Where did the iridium come from?

Luis Alvarez believes that asteroids from outer space are the source. Scientists know that asteroids often contain high levels of iridium. According to the asteroid-impact theory, the iridium was deposited in the clay when an asteroid struck the earth.

Although the evidence of iridium in the clay seems convincing, not all scientists agree with the theory. They believe that iridium deep within the earth can be carried to the surface during volcanic eruptions. These scientists believe that the high levels of iridium in the clay can be accounted for without looking to outer space.

If the asteroid-impact theory is incorrect, what other occurrence might have caused the extinction of the dinosaurs? Another theory of dinosaur extinction proposes that a major climate change caused the animals' downfall. Many scientists think it is likely that the climate on the earth cooled dramatically around this time. The cooler climate might have killed off many plants, which in turn would have led to the death of the dinosaurs.

Still other scientists explain the dinosaur extinction in terms of the large-scale development of small furry mammals. How could small mammals kill off huge dinosaurs? The answer lies in dinosaur eggs. If the small mammals—which were probably smarter and faster than the dinosaurs—fed on dinosaur eggs, then in time fewer dinosaurs would be born. Over the course of time, the dinosaurs would have become extinct as older dinosaurs died and there were no new ones to take their place.

Did an object from outer space kill off the dinosaurs? Was it a change in climate or a worldwide epidemic that destroyed the largest land creatures ever to walk on the earth? Could it have been tiny furry mammals that spelled doom for the dinosaurs? Or perhaps a combination of all these factors brought about dinosaur extinction. What do you think?

UNIT SEVEN

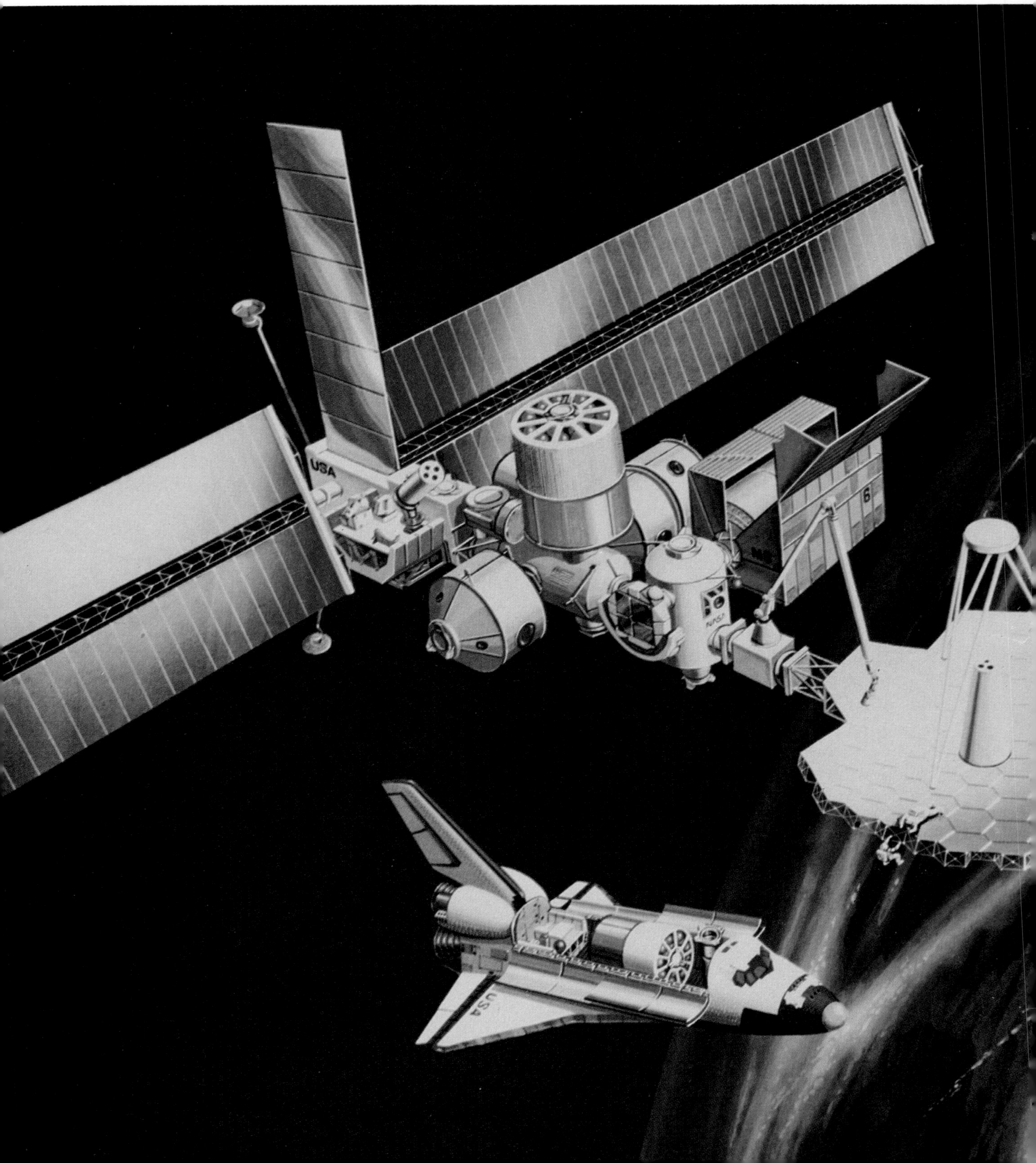

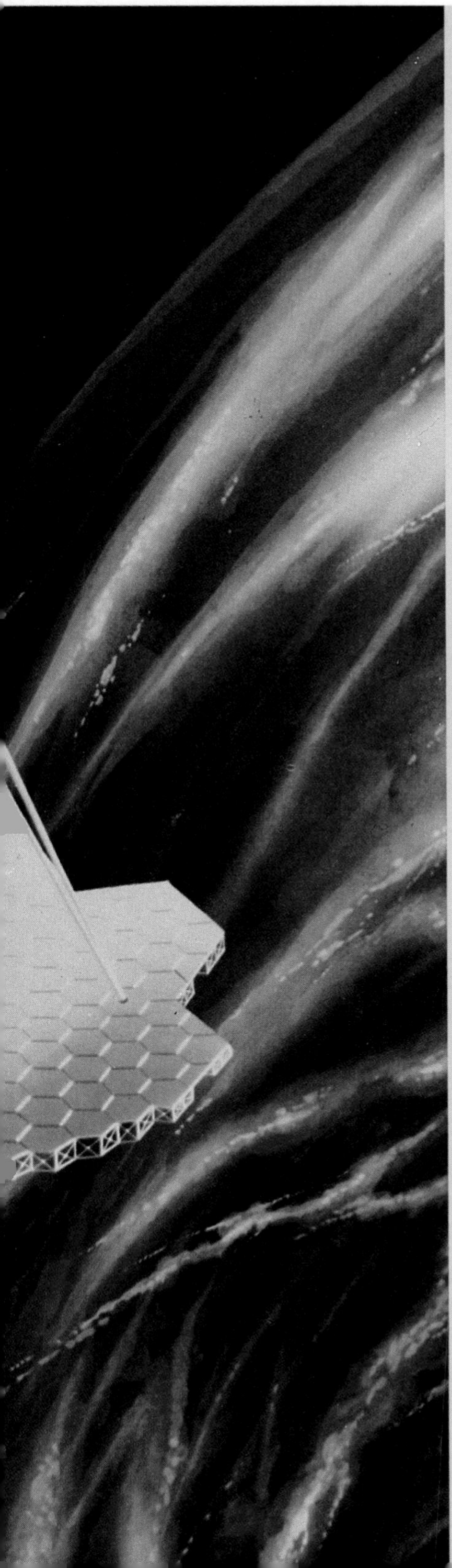

New Directions in Earth Science

People have visited the dusty surface of the moon. They have roared into space aboard the Space Shuttle. They have spent weeks sailing high above the earth in space laboratories. But as yet, they have not built a permanent home beyond the planet Earth.

If all goes as planned, the first permanent space station will be launched into Earth-orbit sometime in the 1990s. The space station will have separate "buildings" for scientific laboratories, space factories, living quarters, and power plants. Here the earth's resources will be turned into new and unusual materials that may change the way people live. With the launching of the space station, boundaries will be extended hundreds or thousands of kilometers into space.

CHAPTERS

This artist's concept of a space station shows a modular platform of rotating pallets, or arms, that will hold space science and applications payloads. Airlocks join the three modules, which will house space travelers. At the lower center, the Space Shuttle hovers near a large antenna platform.

The Earth's Natural Resources 22

CHAPTER SECTIONS

CHAPTER OBJECTIVES

After completing this chapter, you will be able to

22–1 Compare renewable and nonrenewable resources.
22–1 Define conservation.
22–2 Describe how land becomes polluted and how it can be conserved.
22–3 Discuss water pollution and water conservation.
22–4 Compare metallic and nonmetallic minerals.
22–5 Describe the formation and uses of fossil fuels.
22–6 Describe various alternative sources of energy.

On March 16, 1978, a storm raged off the coast of Brittany, France. By the next day, the storm was over. But it was a storm people would remember for the rest of their lives.

During the stormy evening of March 16, the oil tanker *Amoco Cadiz* crashed into jagged rocks near the coastline and broke apart. As it sank, millions of tons of oil gushed into the water.

People awoke the next morning to find that gooey oil had already begun to blacken the coastline. Dead plants, sea creatures, and sea birds dotted the shore. The crashing of the *Amoco Cadiz* had become an environmental disaster.

Immediately experts rushed to the scene. Every modern method of cleaning oil spills was tried. None were successful. In the end, it took millions of dollars and enormous effort to clean the oil from the coast.

The crashing of the *Amoco Cadiz* was a terrible tragedy. But some good did come of it. It taught people a valuable lesson. Parts of our environment can be damaged, even destroyed, overnight. But correcting that damage may take months, even years, to accomplish. Sometimes environmental damage can never be corrected. The earth's resources, such as oil, can be a great help to people when used wisely. When used or handled unwisely, the same resources can cause great harm to the earth and its inhabitants.

Millions of tons of oil escaped into the sea from the Amoco Cadiz *tanker.*

Section Objective

To compare renewable and nonrenewable resources

22–1 Natural Resources

The earth is like a giant storehouse of useful materials. Materials removed from the earth and used by people are called **natural resources.** Natural resources are the riches of the earth. They provide a bounty of materials that improve our lives.

Scientists divide the earth's natural resources into two groups. One group is the **renewable resources.** Renewable resources can be replaced by nature. Water is a renewable resource because it is constantly replaced by rain. Wood is a renewable resource because forests can be replanted. Soil, too, is a renewable resource because new soil is formed on the earth every day.

The other group of natural resources is the **nonrenewable resources.** These resources cannot be replaced by nature. Fuels such as coal and oil are nonrenewable resources. Once they are gone, they cannot be replaced. Minerals such as copper and iron are also nonrenewable resources. They are not replaced by nature.

Today many people are concerned about conserving our natural resources. **Conservation** is the wise use of natural resources so that they will not be used up too soon, or used in a way that will damage the environment. Most people realize that nonrenewable resources must be conserved, for they cannot be replaced. But conservation of renewable resources is also important. Water, for example, is renewable. But in many parts of the world there are water shortages. People in these parts of the world must conserve water to survive.

Figure 22–1 *To conserve trees, people plant new trees (left) to replace mature trees that have been cut down (right). What kind of resource are trees?*

SECTION REVIEW

1. Name at least two renewable resources.
2. Name at least two nonrenewable resources.
3. Are people and wildlife natural resources? Explain your answer.

22–2 Land and Soil Resources

Section Objective

To identify methods of conserving land

Land and soil are renewable resources. They are, however, often difficult to replace. Although they are renewable, it may take nature anywhere from a few decades to several million years to replace land and soil that have been lost.

One-third of the earth's surface is covered by land. This land amounts to about 32 billion acres. But only a portion of the land can be used for farming or living. Most mountain regions are too rocky. Deserts do not have enough water for crops. Snow-covered areas cannot be farmed.

Land Use

Land is needed for building cities and towns to house the increasing population. Land is needed for industry and for farming, too. These needs must be carefully weighed and balanced. If too much land is used for cities, there may not be enough for farms. But both are important.

An increasing population requires an increase in food production. The earth's farmland must be used to its fullest potential. New and improved crop varieties must be developed. Better growing methods must be developed to make existing farms more productive. And land that is now unusable must be made fertile. One way to do this is **irrigation** (eer-uh-GAY-shuhn). Irrigation is the watering of dry regions. As a result of irrigation, desert regions have been made suitable for farming.

Farmland is also needed for raising animals. Pigs, sheep, chickens, and cows are renewable resources. But they must be fed. And an enormous amount of farmland is used to grow food for them. For example, it takes over ten kilograms of grain to produce one kilogram of beef in a steer.

Figure 22–2 *What percentage of the earth's land is used for farming?*

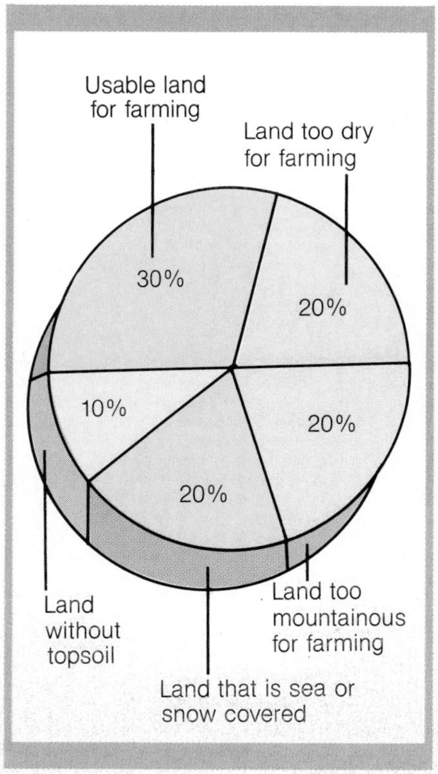

Land Pollution

Take a moment to look around your neighborhood or school grounds. Both areas probably have cans, bottles, paper, and plastic materials scattered on the ground. These discarded materials are called **litter.** People produce litter. And much of the litter people discard is thrown away without regard to the environment.

But litter is not the only kind of land pollution people produce. Every day nearly 3.6 kilograms of garbage per person is thrown away. Garbage is unavoidable, but there are ways to reduce the wasted resources in garbage. One way is to save those parts of the garbage that can be used again, such as bottles and cans. These items can be brought to recycling plants. At a recycling plant, certain kinds of garbage are processed to be used again.

A great deal of land pollution is caused by industry. Industrial chemical wastes and other wastes are often buried under the land. But if they are not buried properly, wastes can leak out of their containers and severely damage the environment. Sometimes the wastes leak into the water supply. This can contaminate the water so that it cannot be used for drinking or washing without expensive cleanup measures.

Figure 22–3 *This litter, which was illegally dumped, can seriously damage the environment.*

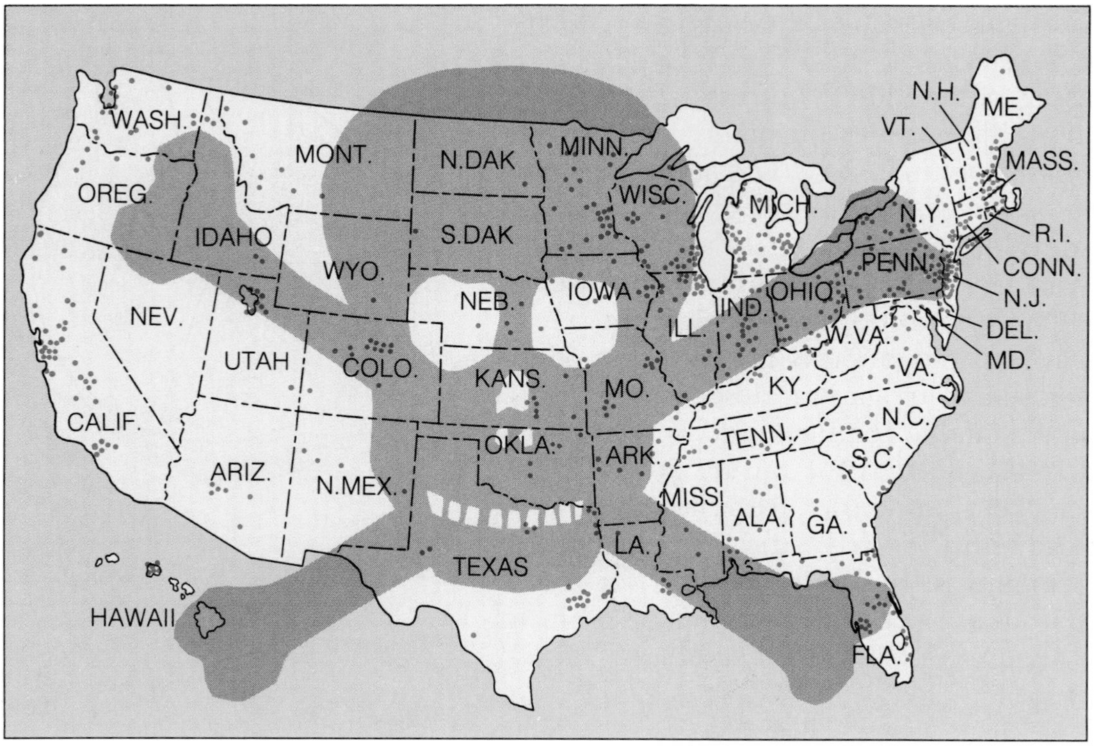

Figure 22–4 *This chart shows some of the most hazardous waste sites in the United States. Where are the sites in your state?*

Land and Soil Conservation

To protect land as a resource, conservation measures must be taken. If the land is to be preserved, its use must be planned carefully. Some land areas, for example, are best for growing trees. Other land areas can grow only grasses for feeding farm animals. Different land areas are best suited for different purposes. Areas that can produce the best crops should become farmland. Recreational areas should be built so as to preserve farmlands and forests. Cities, towns, and factories should be built in areas where the least harm will be done to the environment. What do you think would happen if cities were built without planning?

Even farming must be a planned activity. Crops use up **nutrients** (NOO-tree-uhnts) in the soil. Nutrients are chemical substances necessary for plant growth. To put nutrients back into the soil, farmers add fertilizers to the soil. Certain crops naturally put back nutrients that others remove. For example, legumes such as peanuts put nitrogen back into the soil. So farmers alternate crops on the same land each year. They may plant nitrogen-using crops one year and nitrogen-producing crops the next. This method of farming is called **crop rotation.** Crop rotation keeps soil nutrients from being used up.

The removal of topsoil by water or wind can be controlled by several methods. Topsoil is the fertile top layer of soil. One method is called **terracing.** Terracing is plowing a slope into a series of level

Sharpen Your Skills

Growing Plants With Nutrients

1. Obtain two plants that have recently sprouted in potting soil. Make sure each plant is the same species and has grown to about the same height.

2. Add some fertilizer to one of the pots. Do not add fertilizer to the other pot. Follow all directions on the fertilizer container.

3. Record the height of the plant in each pot every three days. Put your data in a data table.

Did the fertilizer affect plant growth? If so, in what observable ways? What was the purpose of the plant to which no fertilizer was added? Were there any hidden factors that may have affected the results of this investigation? If so, what were they and how could they be eliminated?

Figure 22–5 *To prevent soil erosion due to water running down the sides of this hill in Bali, the hill has been plowed into a series of level steps. What is this method of plowing called?*

Figure 22–6 *In Nepal, a country northeast of India, many trees have been stripped from a mountainside to obtain much needed firewood. But in doing so, the people have speeded up the erosion of the mountain soil.*

steps for planting. Another method is called **contour farming.** Contour farming involves plowing the land across the face of a slope. Both terracing and contour farming are used on slopes to slow down the runoff of water after heavy rains or when snow melts on the mountain's peak. Both methods help prevent the water from rushing downhill and carrying away valuable soil.

The carrying off of soil by water or wind is called **erosion.** Terracing and contour farming help prevent water erosion. To prevent erosion due to wind, farmers often plant **windbreaks.** Windbreaks are rows of trees planted between fields of crops. The trees break the wind and help prevent soil from being blown away.

In many areas, wind erosion is prevented by grasses. Many grasses have deep root systems that help retain the soil. But if farmers allow animals to overgraze a particular area, the soil may soon be blown away. The prevention of overgrazing is an important part of land and soil conservation.

Land and Soil Reclamation

Sometimes valuable land resources must be disturbed to get at valuable resources beneath the land. Coal just beneath the surface of the land is often mined. But to mine this coal, the land must be dug up. This does not mean that the land must be destroyed forever. The land can still be reclaimed, or restored to its original condition.

Figure 22–7 *Mining of coal just beneath the land's surface can destroy the land (left). But the land can be reclaimed and returned to its natural beauty (right). What is this kind of coal mining called?*

Land reclamation involves several steps. First the valuable topsoil is removed and stored. Then the less valuable land under the topsoil is stripped away. This is called strip mining. The coal, now exposed, is mined and shipped to coal processing plants. During this procedure, water in the area is carefully monitored to make sure it does not become polluted. After all the coal is mined, the topsoil is put back in place. The final step in land reclamation is seeding and planting the land.

SECTION REVIEW

1. What is the term for the watering of dry regions?
2. Describe two methods that help prevent soil erosion due to water runoff.
3. Describe two methods that help prevent wind erosion of soil.
4. Predict how an increase in population will affect land use.

22–3 Water as a Resource

Section Objective

To relate freshwater supplies to people's needs

In the United States, billions of liters of water are used daily. **Even though water is a renewable resource, there is a limited amount of fresh water.** Most of the earth's water is in the oceans. Ocean water cannot be used for drinking, irrigation, or industrial processes because it is too salty.

Figure 22–8 *A portion of this desert in Nevada can now support plant life because of irrigation.*

Uses of Water

Each person drinks about 1.5 liters of water per day. People also use water for other things, such as bathing, cooking, and cleaning. It has been estimated that each person in the United States uses more than 400 liters of water daily! Based on this figure, what would be the total amount of water used by your class in one year?

In the United States, industry uses more than 10 billion liters of water every day. It takes more than 375 billion liters of water per day to irrigate farmland in the southern and western United States. Where do you think this water comes from?

The earth's fresh water and ocean water are also important food sources. Fish provide a good source of food for the earth's population. What other foods come from the earth's waters?

Sharpen Your Skills

Phosphates and Plant Growth

Design an experiment to test the effect of phosphates on plant growth in a model lake. Make sure your experiment has a control. State your variables clearly. Describe the results you expect to obtain based on the information in your textbook. What hidden factors might cause your actual results to be different from your expected results?

Water Pollution

In order to have enough usable water in the future, **pollutants,** or harmful and unwanted substances, must be kept out of the water. Polluted water cannot be used for drinking, swimming, or bathing. Pollution also destroys many organisms that live in water.

Water can be polluted in many ways. Industrial chemicals and raw sewage are sometimes dumped into streams and rivers. These pollutants can make people ill and even cause death. In lakes, pollutants such as phosphates used in some detergents cause uncontrolled growth of some green plants. These plants may use up the oxygen in the water, which would cause many fish to die.

Water Purification and Conservation

Water for drinking and bathing must be purified. Water **purification** (PYOOR-uh-fih-kay-shuhn) is the process by which water is cleaned so that it is usable. Water purification takes place in special plants. The water is filtered to remove particles. Then it is chemically treated to kill bacteria and other dangerous organisms.

Cities have treatment plants to purify drinking water. Large industries may have their own treatment plants to clean wastewater before it is released

Figure 22–9 *This pipe is dumping raw sewage into a river. Can this water ever be used for drinking purposes again?*

into lakes and streams. What kinds of wastes might be found in water from industrial plants?

At the present time, many cities are having trouble purifying enough water for all the people that live in the area. One way to help the situation is to prevent as much water pollution as possible. Preventing water pollution, both from industry and from sewage, is extremely important. Scientists are beginning to discover that even small amounts of some pollutants can cause health problems.

Water conservation is also very important. Recent water shortages have made people realize that water is not limitless. People can help conserve water in many ways. One obvious way is to make sure that faucets in homes do not leak. In what other ways can people help conserve water?

Figure 22–10 *A severe drought in Africa has led to the death of many animals. Notice how the land has become cracked because of the lack of water.*

A New Source of Fresh Water

A large supply of fresh water can be made available by **desalination** (dee-sal-uh-NAY-shuhn) of ocean water. Desalination is a process by which salt is removed from water. Some cities in the United States, such as Key West, Florida, and Freeport, Texas, have already built desalination plants. The desalination plants supply these cities with over 20 million liters of fresh water daily.

SECTION REVIEW

1. About how much water does each person in the United States use daily?
2. How can phosphates, which promote plant growth, kill all the fish in a lake?
3. Describe an experiment that could be used to remove salt from ocean water. Include a control.

22–4 Mineral Resources

Section Objective

To identify common metallic and nonmetallic minerals

A **mineral** is a natural chemical substance found in soil or rocks. Today minerals are used to make a variety of products. **Minerals are nonrenewable resources.** Why do you think minerals are considered nonrenewable resources?

SOME NONMETALLIC MINERALS

Mineral	Use
Asbestos	Insulation
Limestone	Cement
Quartz	Watches
Sulfur	Chemicals
Halite	Salt
Potash	Fertilizer
Clay	Brick

Figure 22–11 *This chart shows some of the uses of nonmetallic minerals or rocks containing nonmetallic minerals. Which of these minerals are used in or around your home?*

Ores

To obtain a useful mineral, the mineral must be mined. Rock deposits that contain minerals that can be mined at a profit are called **ores.** Ores are found all over the earth. Do you know of any ores that are mined in your state?

Some ores contain metals such as iron, aluminum, and copper. Such ores are called metallic ores. Nonmetallic ores are also important resources. Nonmetallic ores contain nonmetallic minerals such as quartz, limestone, and sulfur.

The earth's crust is a storehouse of mineral riches. Iron is the most widely used metal found in metallic ores. Other substances can be added to iron to produce steel. Chromium, for example, is added to iron in the steelmaking process. Chromium provides resistance to rusting. Other metal resources include copper, which is used in electric wires, and aluminum, which is used in cans. Gold and silver, used in jewelry, are also found in metallic ores. What other metals do you use in your daily life?

Mining an ore is only the first step in using a mineral. To remove the mineral from the ore, wastes in the ore are extracted. A purified mineral remains. Then the mineral is processed so that it can be sent to manufacturing plants in a usable form. Finally, at the manufacturing plant, the mineral is used to make the final product. It is important to point out that each of these steps can add pollutants to the land and water. So measures must be taken to prevent pollution.

Sharpen Your Skills

From the Earth

Many of the items you use every day are made from minerals and other resources of the earth. For the next 24 hours, record the items you use that are made from minerals. Using reference materials, determine which minerals may soon be scarce and which appear to be plentiful.

Conservation of Minerals

The minerals in the earth's crust have been formed over millions, even billions, of years. The crust, as well as the oceans, contains only a limited amount of the minerals used today. Mining of minerals cannot continue at its present rate or people will run out of these minerals. To preserve these minerals, conservation measures must be taken.

One way of conserving minerals is to find other resources to take their place. A great deal of steel is used in car engines. Today scientists are working to replace metal engines with plastic engines. If plastics

Figure 22–12 *By recycling scrap metal, the earth's supply of minerals will last longer. What is the main metal used in cars?*

and other products can take the place of some minerals, supplies of these minerals will last longer.

Another way of conserving minerals is through recycling. You have probably seen dumps where old cars are rusting away where they sit. Recycling the metal in these old cars, and in any other old metallic objects, can help preserve mineral supplies.

SECTION REVIEW

1. Name three metals obtained from metallic ores.
2. Name three nonmetals obtained from nonmetallic ores.

22–5 Fossil Fuel Resources

Section Objective

To describe the uses and problems of fossil fuels

The energy your family uses to light, heat, and cool your home and to run your car comes from **fossil fuels.** Fossil fuels are products of decayed plants and animals that are preserved in the earth's crust. The remains of these organisms were chemically changed over millions of years. Why are fossil fuels nonrenewable?

Fossil fuels contain hydrogen and carbon. They are called **hydrocarbons.** When hydrocarbons burn, they give off light and heat.

Liquid fossil fuel is called **petroleum,** or oil. Petroleum is found in areas that geologists believe

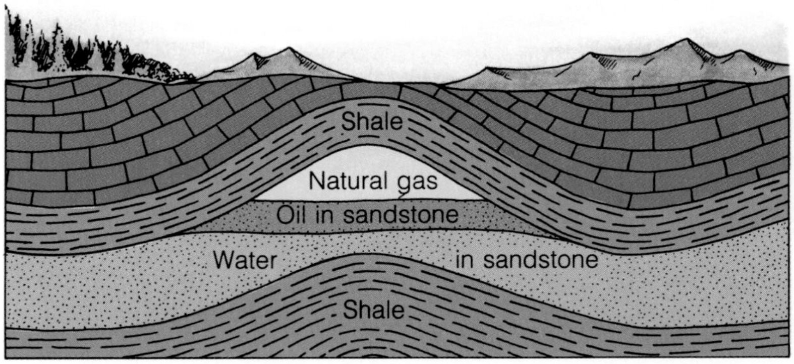

Figure 22–13 *Petroleum and natural gas are often found in the same deposit. Why is the natural gas usually found above the petroleum?*

were once covered by oceans. Geologists think that petroleum was formed from partly decayed sea plants and animals. These plants and animals were covered by **sediments** that built up on the ocean floor. Sediments are rock and mineral particles. As the sediments piled up, they changed into rock. Pressure, bacteria, and heat changed the plant and animal remains into oil. The oil droplets seeped through pores and cracks in the rock. In time, underground pools of oil formed. Oil pools can usually be found in sandstone or shale. Shale is a rock made of hardened clay. See Figure 22–13.

Another type of fossil fuel is natural gas. Natural gas is usually found with petroleum. Since it is less dense than petroleum, it is usually on top of the oil pool. The most abundant natural gas is **methane.** Methane is used in heating systems and in gas stoves.

Figure 22–14 *The four types of coal are shown in this photograph. Going counterclockwise from the top left, they are peat, lignite, bituminous, and anthracite. Which is the hardest type of coal?*

Coal is a solid fossil fuel. There are four types of coal. Each type represents a stage in the formation of coal. And each type can be used for fuel. The first type is **peat,** a soft substance made up of decayed plant fibers. The second type is **lignite** (LIHG-night), which is produced by the pressure of sediments deposited on top of peat. Lignite, or brown coal, is soft and has a woody texture. Continued pressure on lignite turns it into **bituminous** (bigh-TOO-muh-nuhs) coal, the third type of coal. Bituminous coal is found deep within the earth. Bituminous coal is dark brown or black and is called soft coal. It is the most abundant type of coal. Very high pressure produces the final type of coal, **anthracite** (AN-thruh-sight). Anthracite is very hard and brittle. It is almost pure carbon. Very few deposits of anthracite coal are found in the United States.

Uses of Fossil Fuels

Coal, petroleum, and natural gas are the main sources of energy for industry, transportation, and homes. Industry is a major consumer of fossil fuels. The automobile is another very large consumer of fossil fuels.

The **crude oil** brought up from beneath the earth's surface is a mixture of many hydrocarbons. Crude oil is used to make many products you use every day, including gasoline for automobiles. Crude oil must be refined before it can be used. Then it is used to make heating oil for homes, kerosene for lamps, waxes for candles, asphalt for roads, and **petrochemicals.** Petrochemicals are useful chemicals derived from petroleum. Some of these chemicals are used to make plastics, fabrics, medicine, and building materials. What other petroleum products do you know of?

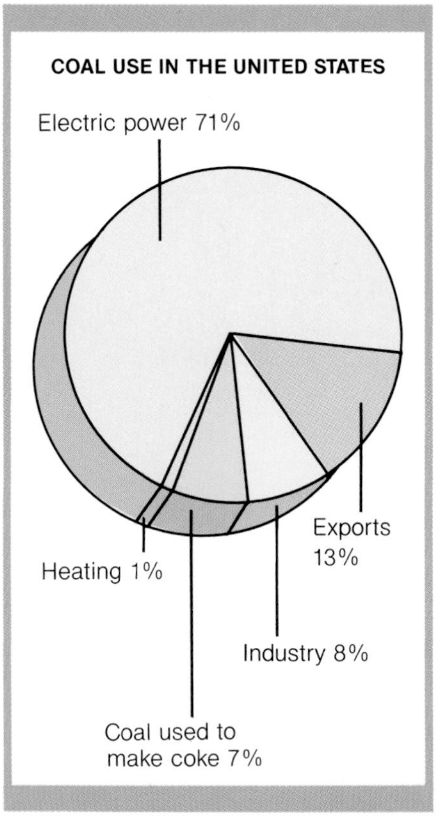

Figure 22–15 *This chart shows the various uses of coal in the United States. What is most of the coal used for?*

Fossil Fuel Shortages

Since 1900, energy use in the United States has increased ten times. Today the United States uses nearly 30 percent of all the fossil fuel energy produced in the world.

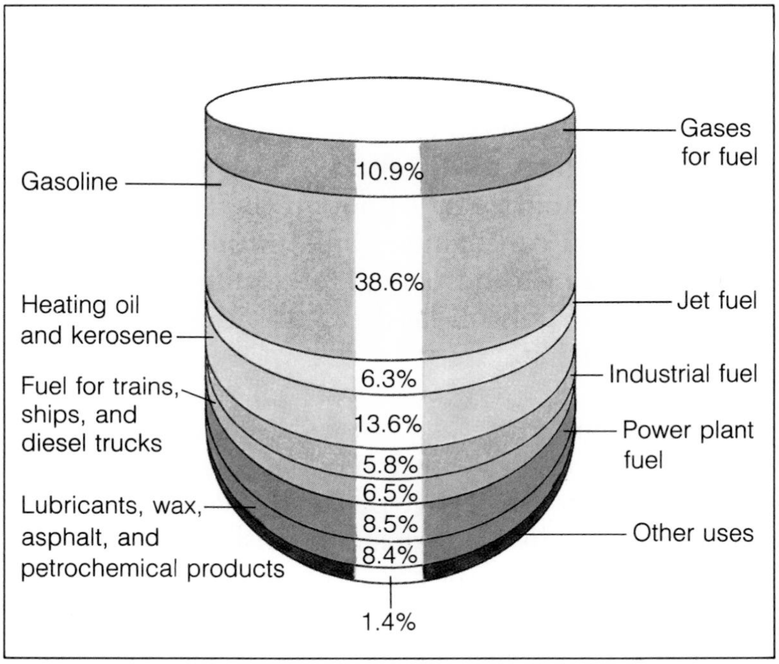

Figure 22–16 *A wide variety of products can be derived from petroleum when it is refined. What percentage of the refined petroleum is used to produce petrochemicals?*

Petroleum and gas reserves in the earth are limited. Reserves are the unused fossil fuel deposits left in the earth. At the present rate of use, the United States may run out of fossil fuels by the year 2060. By the year 2080, the world may run out. How do you think this will affect living conditions in the United States?

In the United States, coal is more abundant than oil and natural gas. At the present rate of use, the coal will last another 300 to 500 years. But more coal is used for energy production every year. It may become the main fossil fuel resource by the year 2000. In that case, reserves of coal will run out much sooner.

Geologists are hard at work finding new sources of fossil fuels. But conservation of present fuel resources is the best way to help provide energy for the future. Alternate energy sources are also being developed. Some of these are discussed in the next section. What ways can you think of to conserve fossil fuels?

Figure 22–17 *Factory smokestacks and car exhausts produce emissions that pollute the air. What causes these polluting emissions?*

Fossil Fuels and Air Pollution

You probably already know that air pollution is a very serious problem. It is particularly serious in industrialized nations that burn large quantities of fossil fuels. Burning fossil fuels release a variety of pollutants into the atmosphere. The most common air pollutants are gases such as sulfur oxides, nitrogen oxides, ammonia, and carbon dioxide. What other pollutants are found in the air?

Some of the gases released by burning fossil fuels combine with water vapor and form weak acids. When these acids fall to the earth in rain, the rain is called **acid rain.** Although the acid in acid rain is weak, it can damage buildings. Acid rain that falls into lakes can destroy plant and animal life. Acid rain that falls on land can also destroy many forms of plant life.

Pollutants that build up in the air because of the burning of fossil fuels can also damage people's health. Air pollution can irritate the eyes and cause respiratory, or breathing, problems. People who suffer from lung diseases must stay inside when air pollution levels become too high.

CAREER

Mine Inspector

HELP WANTED: MINE INSPECTOR If you are concerned with mine safety and have worked in a mine, the U.S. government may have the job for you. Call the telephone number below to make a date for an examination.

The mining industry supplies the coal, ores, building materials, and raw materials necessary to make many products. The mining industry plays an important part in the utilization of the earth's resources.

Mine inspectors work in coal mines, metal mines, or quarries. Some mine inspectors are employed by mining companies. Other inspectors may work for the federal government or state governments.

Mine inspectors examine mines to be sure that health and safety regulations are being followed. They test the air quality to be sure that it is safe. Mine inspectors may also check the structure of mines. They prepare reports of their findings. Sometimes mine inspectors teach classes in safety and first aid to miners.

To learn more about the requirements of a career as a mine inspector, write to the National Coal Association, Education Division, 1130 17th Street, NW, Washington, DC 20036.

Air pollution is made worse by a **temperature inversion** (ihn-VER-shuhn). Normally, cooler air is at higher altitudes than warmer air. During an inversion, a layer of warm air sits on top of the cooler air. The warm air traps pollutants near the ground. The trapped pollutants form a dangerous mixture of smoke and fog called **smog.**

The Federal Clean Air Act gave the Environmental Protection Agency (EPA) the authority to control air pollution. The EPA sets limits on the amount of pollutants that can be released into the air. When these limits are exceeded, industry is ordered to stop burning fuel for a while. Automobile use may also be limited.

Current laws require automobile manufacturers to control gas emissions from car exhausts. Local and state pollution laws often prohibit the burning of garbage and leaves. These measures help in controlling air pollution.

Many industries and cities spend billions of dollars to improve the quality of the air. Although the cost of improving the quality of the air is high, clean air means a healthy environment for everyone,

Figure 22–18 *During a temperature inversion, cool air containing pollutants becomes trapped under a layer of warm air.*

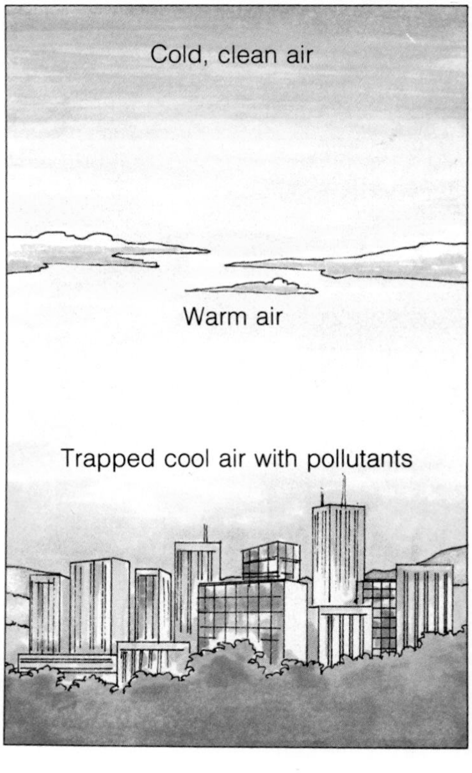

now and in the future. What can you do to help stop air pollution?

SECTION REVIEW

1. What are the two main elements in fossil fuels?
2. Name the four types of coal.
3. Name three materials that are derived from petrochemicals.

Section Objective

To identify new sources of energy

22–6 Replacing Fossil Fuels

No matter how much conservation of fossil fuels takes place, sooner or later the earth will run out of these nonrenewable resources. But people cannot live without energy sources. **Scientists are hard at work developing ways to replace fossil fuels and provide enough energy for everyone.** Whenever possible, they look for energy sources that will not pollute the environment. The best new sources of energy will be renewable, so they will not run out in the future.

Figure 22–19 *Water in the solar panel (top) is heated by the sun. The heat is then transferred at the heat exchanger and used to provide hot water and warmth (bottom).*

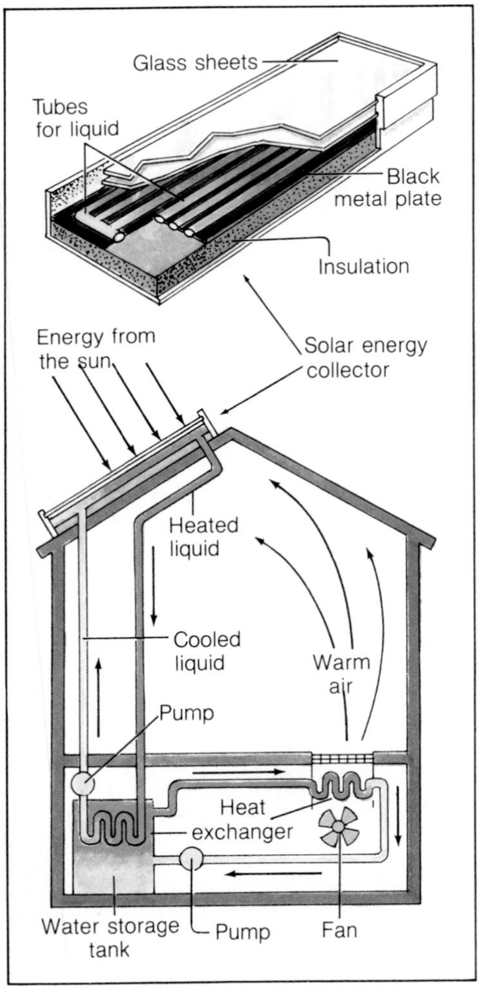

Solar Energy

One possible alternate energy source is **solar energy.** Solar energy is energy from the sun. It is nonpolluting and almost unlimited. Solar heating of buildings can reduce the amount of fossil fuels used. Large solar collectors located on the roofs of buildings can convert the sun's energy into heat to warm the building and provide hot water.

Solar collectors consist of blackened aluminum tubes that have water circulating in them. The tubes are covered with glass to reduce heat loss. The sun heats the water as it moves through the tubes. The heated water can be used both for home heating and for hot water.

Another way of using solar energy is through the **solar cell.** Solar cells transform light energy directly into electricity. But these cells are expensive and produce only small amounts of electricity. Improvements in solar cells should make them more efficient and economical.

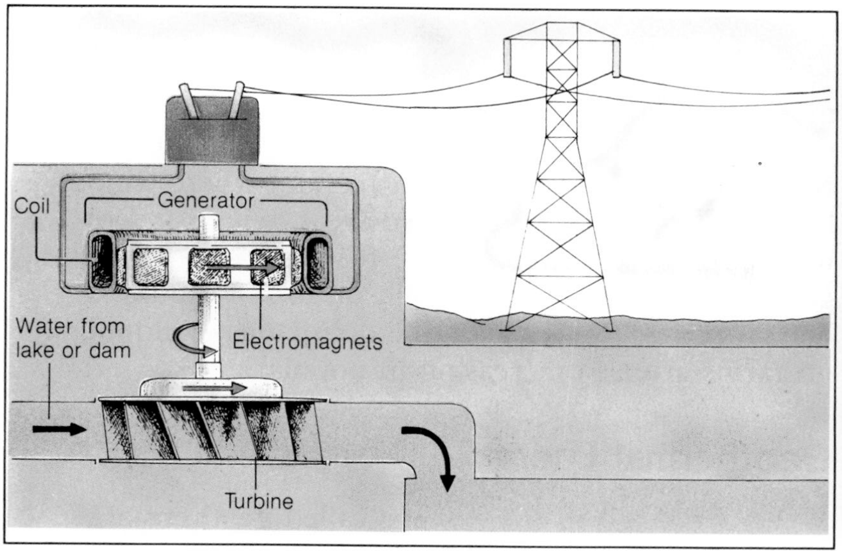

Figure 22–20 *In a hydroelectric plant (left), the energy of moving water powers turbines and generators (right) that provide electric energy.*

Water and Wind as Energy Sources

At the present time, falling or flowing water is used to produce one-fourth of the world's electricity. Dams built across rivers can hold back millions of tons of water. Some of this water is channeled through a hydroelectric plant. In the plant, the moving water spins a turbine in an electrical generator. The spinning turbine produces electricity. In this way, the mechanical energy of moving water is converted into electricity.

The construction of new hydroelectric plants will certainly help limit our need for fossil fuels such as coal, which is often burned to produce electric power. But such plants do cause problems. The water trapped behind a dam may flood large areas of land that are used for farming or other purposes. So building a hydroelectric plant involves a trade-off. The trade-off is the need for energy versus the environmental damage such a plant may cause.

There is another way to use moving water to produce electricity. Each day the waters of the oceans rise and fall with the tides. In some coastal areas, the difference between high and low tide can be as much as 15 meters. If a power plant is built at the mouth of a bay or river, the moving water due to tides can be used to spin a turbine. The turbine, then, produces electricity. Tidal power is too limited to be a major source of energy. But tidal power may help replace the burning of some fossil fuels.

Sharpen Your Skills

Using Electricity

1. On a Monday morning, read the electric meter in your home before going to school. The next morning read the meter again.

2. Subtract the first day's reading from the second day's reading to determine the number of kilowatt-hours of electricity used in one day.

3. Call your local power company to find out the cost per kilowatt-hour. Multiply the number of kilowatt-hours by this cost. The answer is the cost of the electricity for one day.

4. Record your electric use for one week and determine the cost. What is the cost for one month? One year?

Figure 22–21 *At Altamont Pass in California, thousands of windmills are used to generate electricity.*

Just as moving water can spin a turbine, so can moving air, or wind. Today windmills that can generate electricity are being built all over the world. Naturally such windmills must be built where winds blow fairly constantly. In these areas, scientists look to wind power to help replace fossil fuels. Windmill generators are even being built on top of tall buildings to provide energy for the occupants. Windmills on farms are also increasing in popularity.

Geothermal Energy

Heat created in the earth is called **geothermal energy.** Rocks within the earth are heated by geothermal energy. Water comes in contact with the heated rocks and becomes steam. The steam and hot water are released at the earth's surface through hot springs and geysers. A geyser is a hot spring that shoots steam and hot water into the air.

Geothermal energy is tapped by drilling wells into underground sources of hot water and steam. The steam is fed into electric generating plants. Several plants around the world are now producing electricity from geothermal energy. In Iceland, almost 80 percent of the homes get their heat and hot water directly from hot springs and geysers. Is geothermal energy renewable or nonrenewable?

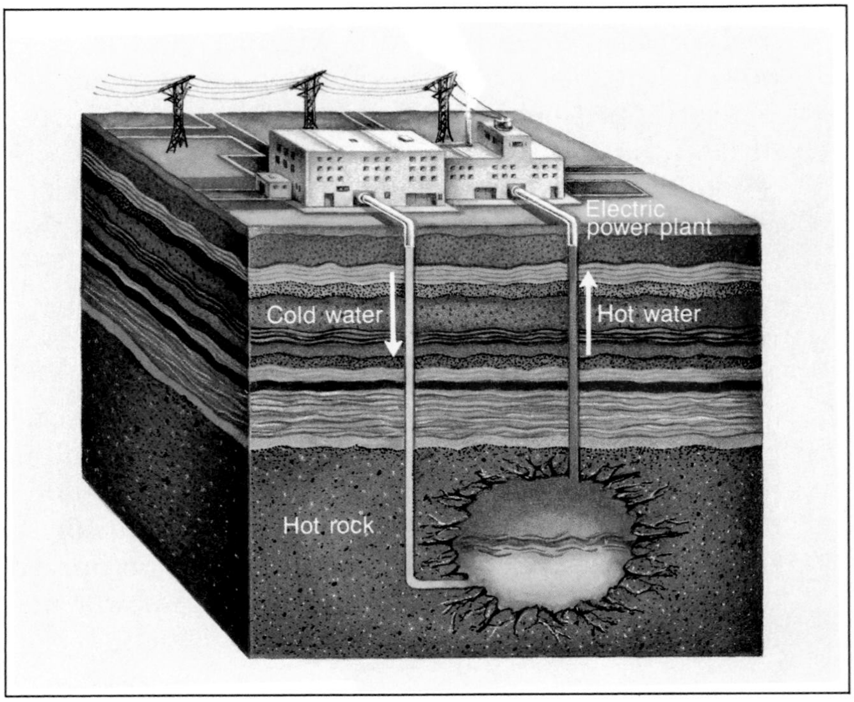

Figure 22–22 *In this power plant, cold water is pumped into the earth, where it becomes hot. The heated water is then sent back to a power plant where it is used to generate electricity. What is heat created within the earth called?*

Nuclear Energy

Another source of energy that may help replace fossil fuels is nuclear energy. Vast amounts of energy can be released when the nucleus of an atom is split. In a nuclear power plant, atoms of uranium are split in a nuclear reactor. This process is called **nuclear fission.** When the nucleus is split, the heat given off can be used to convert water to steam. The steam is then sent through a turbine and electric energy is produced.

There are many problems with nuclear fission that must be solved before it can replace other energy sources. One problem is that radioactive wastes are produced during the fission process. These wastes give off radiation, which is deadly to all forms of life. To date, no safe way of storing nuclear wastes has been discovered. Yet more and more nuclear wastes are being stockpiled. If a way to store nuclear wastes is not found, then the future of nuclear energy is in serious doubt.

Another danger of nuclear power is that radiation may be released if there is an accident at a nuclear power plant. Such accidents have already occurred, but the amount of radioactive material sent into the environment has not as yet caused great damage in the United States. But such accidents have caused people to reconsider the need for nuclear power plants.

Yet another problem with nuclear energy is that it has not turned out to be an inexpensive source of energy. The costs of building nuclear plants have risen tremendously. Because of the costs of the plants and the dangers of radiation, very few new nuclear power plants are being planned today in the United States. But if these problems are solved, nuclear power could become an extremely important source of energy.

Figure 22–23 *In a nuclear power plant, radioactive uranium fuel rods give off energy that produces a blue glow in the water.*

Sharpen Your Skills

Chernobyl

In 1986, the most serious nuclear accident to date occurred at the Chernobyl nuclear power plant in the Soviet Ukraine. Using reference materials in the library, write a report on the cause of the Chernobyl disaster, its short-term effects, and its potential long-term effects. Describe its impact on the future of nuclear power.

SECTION REVIEW

1. Why is solar energy a renewable resource?
2. What form of energy is produced when moving water or air spins a turbine?
3. Can geothermal energy be used on a worldwide basis? Explain your answer.

22 LABORATORY INVESTIGATION

Comparing the Decomposition of Different Types of Litter in a Landfill

Problem

A great amount of litter and garbage is buried under soil in landfills every day. How does the rate of decomposition differ for different substances in a model landfill?

Materials *(per group)*

4-L glass jar with a lid
Topsoil (enough to fill the jar one-third to one-half full)
Water
Litter (orange peels, bits of paper, old gloves, scrap metal, etc.)
Glass-marking pencil

Procedure

1. Cover the bottom of the glass jar with a layer of soil.
2. Place one-third of the litter in the jar. Make sure the litter is close to the sides of the jar.
3. With the glass-marking pencil, circle on the outside of the jar the location of each item of litter.

4. Add another layer of soil on top of the litter.
5. Place another one-third of the litter in the jar near the sides. Mark the location of each item of litter with the glass-marking pencil.
6. Add another layer of soil on top of the litter.
7. Place the last of the litter in the jar near the sides. Mark the location of each item of litter with the glass-marking pencil.
8. Cover the litter with a final layer of soil. Add water to the jar until all the soil is slightly moist. Cover the jar with its lid.
9. Observe your landfill every week for one month. Predict whether or not each item of litter in the jar will decompose.

Observations

1. Describe each item of litter in the landfill after one day, one week, two weeks, and one month. Place your observations in a data table.
2. Which items of litter decompose fastest? Which items of litter decompose more slowly? Which items do not decompose at all?

Conclusions

1. Compare the kinds of litter and their decomposition rates. Can you see any pattern to the litter that decomposes as compared to the litter that does not decompose?
2. Based on your observations, what recommendations would you make to a town that was considering building a landfill?
3. Suppose the soil, jar, water, and litter had been sterilized before the investigation. Would the results have been the same? Explain your answer.

CHAPTER REVIEW

SUMMARY

22–1 Natural Resources

❑ Materials removed from the earth and used by people are called natural resources.

❑ Conservation is the wise use of natural resources so that they will not be used up too soon, or used in a way that will damage the environment.

22–2 Land and Soil Resources

❑ Although land is renewable, it may take nature from decades to millions of years to replace land that has been lost.

❑ Crop rotation, terracing, contour farming, and windbreaks can help prevent soil erosion.

22–3 Water as a Resource

❑ Although water is renewable, there is a limited amount of fresh water.

❑ Pollutants can make available water supplies unsuitable for human use.

22–4 Mineral Resources

❑ A mineral is a natural chemical substance found in soil or rocks.

❑ Minerals are a nonrenewable resource.

❑ Recycling is one way people can help conserve minerals.

22–5 Fossil Fuel Resources

❑ Liquid fossil fuel is called petroleum.

❑ Natural gas is often found near petroleum deposits.

❑ Coal is a solid fossil fuel. The four types of coal are peat, lignite, bituminous, and anthracite.

❑ The burning of fossil fuels adds a variety of pollutants to the atmosphere.

22–6 Replacing Fossil Fuels

❑ One possible energy source is solar energy.

❑ Wind and water can be used to spin turbines and produce electricity.

❑ Geothermal energy is a potential alternate source of energy.

❑ The energy within the atom can be released in a controlled manner through nuclear fission. Nuclear fission involves the splitting of an atom in a nuclear power plant.

VOCABULARY

Define each term in a complete sentence.

acid rain
anthracite
bituminous
conservation
contour farming
crop rotation
crude oil
desalination
erosion
fossil fuel
geothermal energy
hydrocarbon
irrigation
lignite
litter
methane
mineral
natural resource
nonrenewable resource
nuclear fission
nutrient
ore
peat
petrochemical
petroleum
pollutant
purification
renewable resource
sediment
smog
solar cell
solar energy
temperature inversion
terracing
windbreak

CONTENT REVIEW: MULTIPLE CHOICE

Choose the letter of the answer that best completes each sentence.

1. Which of these is not a nonrenewable resource?
a. copper b. coal c. soil d. iron

2. The surface area of land on the earth is about
a. 13 million acres b. 32 million acres
c. 320 million acres d. 32 billion acres

3. Plowing the land across the face of a slope is called
a. terracing b. contour farming
c. crop rotation d. strip plowing

4. The process by which salt is removed from ocean water is
a. purification b. detoxification
c. desalination d. sewage treatment

5. A natural chemical substance found in soil or rocks is called a (an)
a. ore b. mineral c. petrochemical d. natural resource

6. Which of these is a metallic mineral?
a. sulfur b. copper c. quartz d. limestone

7. Liquid fossil fuel is called
a. petrochemicals b. coal c. methane d. petroleum

8. The first stage in the formation of coal is
a. peat b. anthracite c. lignite d. none of these

9. Energy from the sun is called
a. geothermal energy b. solar energy
c. nuclear energy d. nonrenewable

10. The process of splitting the atom to release energy is called
a. geothermal energy b. refining petroleum
c. atomic energy d. nuclear fission

CONTENT REVIEW: COMPLETION

Fill in the word or words that best complete each sentence.

1. Useful materials found in or on the earth are called ________.

2. Resources that can be replaced by nature are called ________.

3. ________ is the wise use of natural resources.

4. The watering of dry regions is called ________.

5. To replace soil nutrients, farmers add ________ to the soil.

6. ________ is the carrying off of soil by wind or water.

7. ________ are unwanted or dangerous substances in air, land, or water.

8. The most widely used mineral found in ores is ________.

9. Hydrocarbons contain ________ and ________.

10. A dangerous mixture of smoke and fog is called ________.

CONTENT REVIEW: TRUE OR FALSE

Determine whether each statement is true or false. If it is true, write "true." If it is false, change the underlined word or words to make the statement true.

1. Renewable resources cannot be replaced once they are used up.
2. Crops use up nutrients in the soil.
3. Crop rotation involves planting crops in a series of plowed steps on a slope.
4. To prevent erosion due to wind, farmers often plant windbreaks.
5. Grasses have shallow root systems that help hold down soil.
6. Most water on earth is fresh water.
7. Rock deposits that contain minerals which can be mined at a profit are called ores.
8. Bituminous is the hardest form of coal.
9. To generate electricity, wind or water is used to spin a turbine.
10. Heat within the earth is called nuclear energy.

CONCEPT REVIEW: SKILL BUILDING

Use the skills you have developed in the chapter to complete each activity.

1. **Interpreting graphs** From A.D. 650 to A.D. 1650 the earth's population doubled from 250 million to 500 million. This doubling of the earth's population took 1000 years. But now the earth's population doubles every 33 years. The population of the earth in 1986 was about 4.5 billion. Determine the population of the earth using these figures for the years A.D. 2019, A.D. 2052, and A.D. 2085. Graph your results. How many times greater will the earth's population be in 100 years? Relate this population increase to our need to conserve natural resources.
2. **Making calculations** The population of the United States is approximately 215 million people. For each person, approximately 35 kilograms of fossil fuels are consumed every day. How much fuel is used every day in the United States? Every month? Every year?
3. **Developing a model** Plan a "new town" to replace the town you live in. Consider the placement of industries, shopping malls, parks and recreational facilities, housing developments, farms, and road systems. What would you do in your "new town" to control pollution?

CONCEPT REVIEW: ESSAY

Discuss each of the following in a brief paragraph.

1. Many states, such as Texas, Louisiana, and Alabama, depend upon oil and natural gas reserves for much of their state's income. What do you think might happen if the oil and gas reserves were depleted? In your essay, consider alternative measures to extend the usability and life of current oil and gas wells.
2. Why does the decreasing supply of nonrenewable natural resources pose a difficult problem for conservationists?
3. How does land and water pollution endanger wildlife? How does it affect people?
4. In what ways does an increase in population affect land as a resource?

Earth Science and Technology 23

CHAPTER SECTIONS

23–1 Technology and the Ocean

23–2 Space Technology

CHAPTER OBJECTIVES

After completing this chapter, you will be able to

23–1 Describe the different techniques used to explore the ocean.

23–1 Explain the benefits of mining and farming the ocean.

23–2 Discuss the uses of various types of artificial satellites.

23–2 Explain how the Space Shuttle and laboratories in space are used by scientists and by industry.

23–2 Identify several spinoffs of space technology.

It was April 1985. Onboard the Space Shuttle, the astronauts prepared to launch the *Leasat 3* communications satellite. Despite hopes for a successful mission, things did not go as planned. Although the satellite was released from the shuttle, its engines did not fire up. The satellite was unable to rocket into its intended orbit some 35,000 kilometers above the earth.

The failure to launch *Leasat 3* was a big disappointment to scientists at the National Aeronautics and Space Administration, or NASA. But few of the scientists were willing to give up the project. So in September 1985, when the Space Shuttle *Discovery* was launched, two scientists, James D. van Hoften and William F. Fisher, attempted a daring rescue of the faulty satellite. First they retrieved the satellite with the shuttle's robot arm. Once the satellite was positioned in the shuttle's cargo bay, they began the repair job.

To fix the satellite, van Hoften and Fisher had to replace a defective timing device. The astronauts completed the repair in two days. All that remained to be done was the release of the 5 meter × 5 meter cylindrical satellite. "I'm going to give it a heck of a push," reported van Hoften to mission control at the Johnson Space Center in Houston, Texas. The push worked! The satellite was soon clear of the shuttle. The crew of the *Discovery* had just completed "the most successful salvage mission in the history of the space program."

The rescue of *Leasat 3* is a good example of how technology is used by modern earth scientists. In this chapter, you will read more about space technology successes, as well as how technology is also used to study the earth's oceans.

Astronaut William F. Fisher repairs the Leasat 3 *communications satellite.*

23–1 Technology and the Ocean

Section Objective

To relate technology to ocean exploration

The study of the ocean is called **oceanography.** Oceanography includes the study of the physical characteristics, the chemical composition, the life forms, and the natural resources of the ocean.

Today scientists have a wide variety of technological tools to help them study the ocean and use its resources. For example, satellites orbiting the earth provide information about the temperature and chemical composition of the ocean. Satellites also track waves and currents. They map the ocean floor and coastlines. They record the movements of life forms in the ocean.

Let's look at some of the ways technology has aided scientists in learning more about the ocean. In the process, you will also learn about some of the future advances ocean technology may bring to the world.

Figure 23–1 *This satellite map, taken by the Seasat satellite, shows average sea and land surface temperatures all over the world. What was the temperature on this day where you live?*

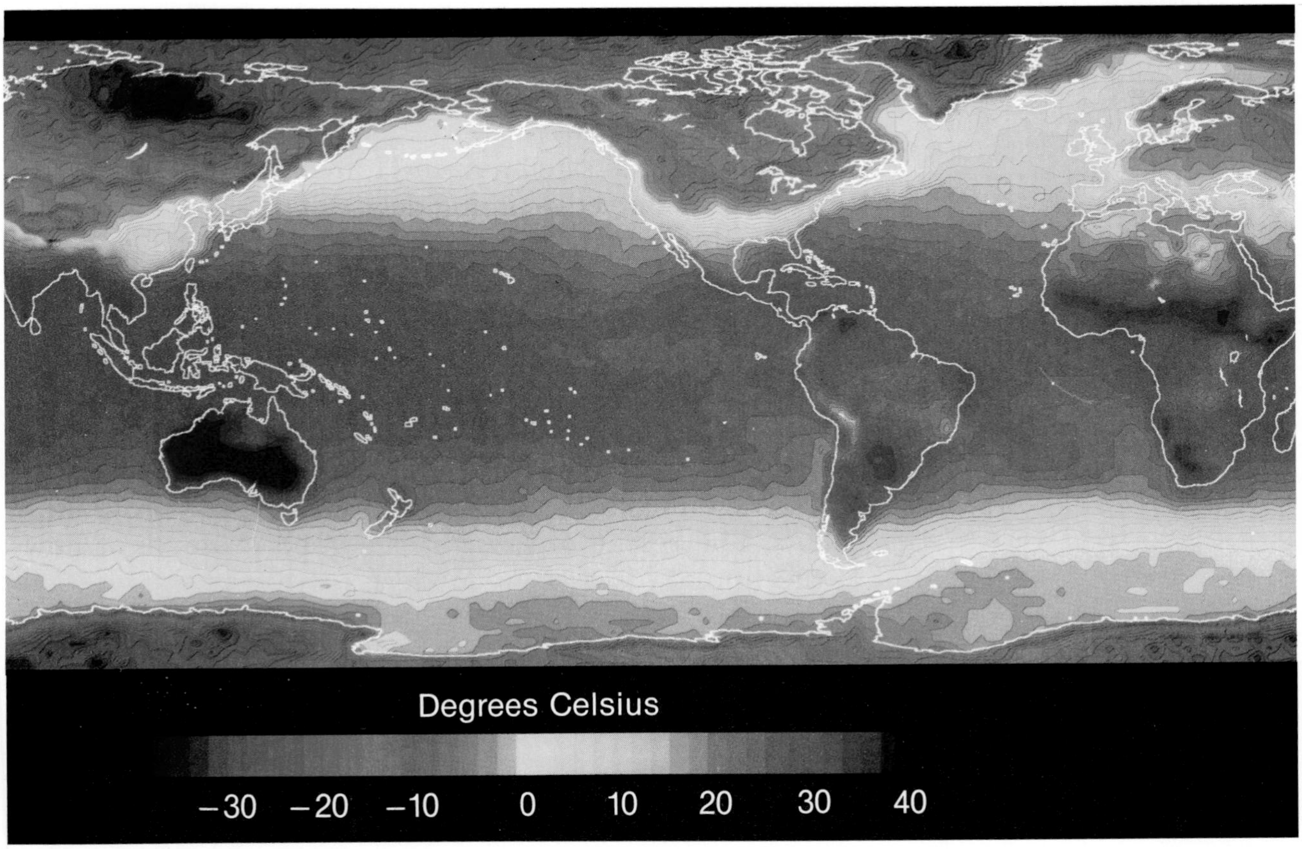

Mapping the Ocean Floor

A detailed map of the ocean floor has many uses. Navigators on ships use information about the depth of the ocean to avoid areas that are too shallow. Submarine captains need precise data about the ocean floor to steer safely through underwater mountain ranges and past volcanoes. Oceanographers use such maps to study the patterns of deep-ocean currents. Geologists, too, use ocean maps to better understand the forces involved in the formation of new ocean floor. As you can see, detailed maps of the ocean floor are very important. But just how do scientists make such maps? Do they need to travel to the ocean floor directly?

To map the ocean floor, **sonar** is used. *Sonar* stands for sound navigation and ranging. Sonar is an echo-sounding instrument used to measure the depth of the ocean at various places. First a sound wave is sent from a ship toward the ocean floor. The sound wave is reflected off the ocean floor back to the ship. Scientists know how fast sound travels in water. So they can determine the depth of the ocean floor from the amount of time it takes for the sound wave to leave the ship and return. Computers then translate the sonar information into a map of the ocean floor.

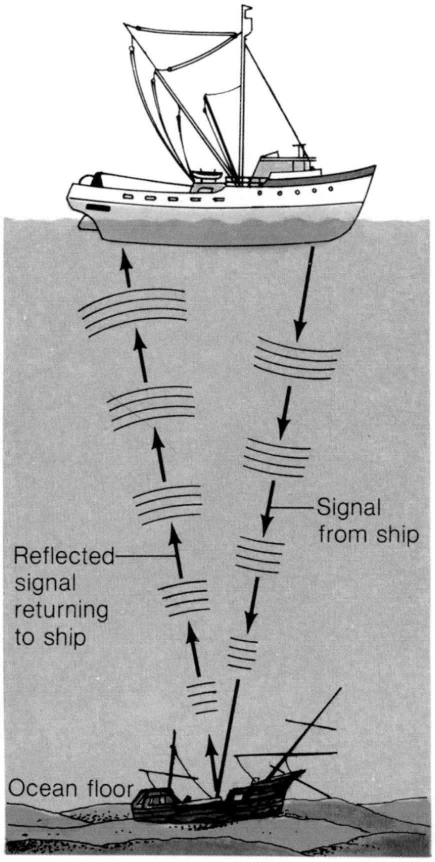

Figure 23–2 *Scientists on board a surface vessel time how long it takes for a sound wave to strike the ocean floor and reflect back to the ship. In this way they can determine the exact depth of the ocean at this particular spot. What is this depth charting process called?*

Exploring the Ocean

Scientists use research vessels called **submersibles** to explore the ocean. Some submersibles carry scientific instruments and cameras. Other submersibles carry people as well.

One kind of submersible is called a **bathysphere** (BATH-uh-sfir). A bathysphere is a small, sphere-shaped diving vessel. It is lowered into the water by a steel cable from a ship. Because it remains attached to the ship, the bathysphere has limited movement.

The **bathyscaph** (BATH-uh-skaf) is a more useful submersible. It is a self-propelled submarine observatory that can move about in the ocean to explore different areas. Bathyscaphs have reached depths of more than 10,000 meters while exploring some of the deepest parts of the ocean.

Figure 23–3 *The* Alvin *has discovered unusual sea creatures living near ocean vents. What type of submersible is* Alvin?

Figure 23–4 *These tube worms were among the unusual creatures* Alvin *discovered near ocean vents.*

The bathyscaph *Alvin* has made over 1600 dives. Some of *Alvin's* discoveries have helped scientists learn more about life on the ocean floor. During one dive, scientists aboard *Alvin* found several communities of unusual ocean life near vents, or natural chimneys, in the ocean floor. The vents discharge poisonous hydrogen sulfide into the water. Water temperatures near the vents reach up to 350°C. The combination of high temperatures and deadly hydrogen sulfide should make the existence of any life forms near the vents impossible. But as the scientists discovered, giant tube worms, clams, mussels, and other strange life forms make their homes near the vents. These life forms exist without any sunlight. Some scientists suggest that conditions near the vents may be similar to conditions on distant planets. So the discoveries made by *Alvin* may well help astronomers study the possibility of life on distant worlds.

In September 1985, another submersible made a remarkable discovery. This submersible is a robot craft that can be guided along the ocean floor from

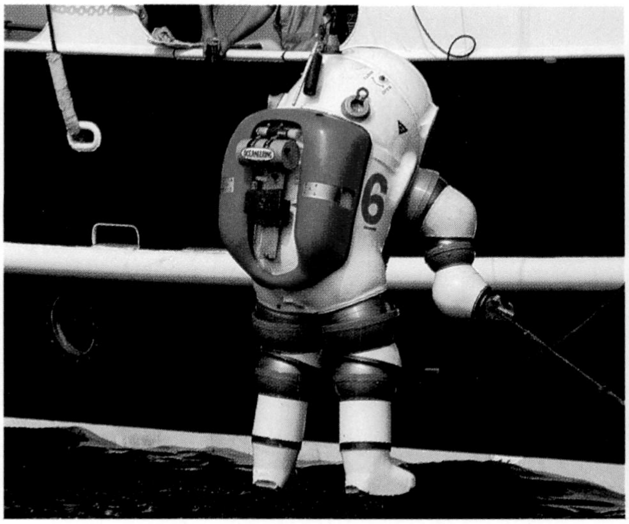

Figure 23–5 *A scientist inside* Jim, *a one-person submersible, is about to explore the ocean (left). This photograph of the long-lost* Titanic *was taken by a robot submersible, which can be guided from the ocean surface (right).*

a ship on the ocean surface. The robot craft discovered the remains of the famous steamship *Titanic.* The ship was lying on the ocean floor in very deep water off the coast of Newfoundland, Canada. In 1912, on its maiden voyage, the *Titanic* had struck an iceberg and sunk.

Yet another kind of submersible has been nicknamed *Jim. Jim* is a one-person vehicle about 2 meters tall. Inside *Jim,* a scientist can descend to depths of more than 600 meters. *Jim* has an amazing ability to move underwater. It can pick up objects from the ocean floor and even climb a ladder. The use of submersibles like *Jim* promises to open up new frontiers in the exploration of the ocean.

Mining the Ocean

In Chapter 22, you learned about the earth's dwindling supply of natural resources. One source of natural resources that has barely been tapped is the ocean floor. The ocean floor is like a treasure chest of important resources. Vast oil fields, for example, lie beneath the ocean floor. Some of the oil fields that lie under shallow water have already been tapped. But some oil lies under the ocean in deeper places. And as yet, there is no way to drill for oil trapped at such depths.

Large deposits of minerals have also been discovered on and beneath the ocean floor. These minerals contain manganese, tungsten, vanadium, nickel, cobalt, tin, titanium, silver, platinum, and gold.

Sharpen Your Skills

An Underwater Habitat

Using reference materials from the library, find information on how people can live and work underwater for long periods of time. Write a short report on underwater habitats. Make sure you discuss Jacques-Yves Cousteau's ocean-floor habitat called *Conshelf Three.* This structure supported six men for 22 days at a depth of about 100 meters. Also answer these questions in your report:

1. What are some of the problems that must be resolved when living and working underwater for long periods of time?

2. What might be some beneficial results of living and working under the ocean?

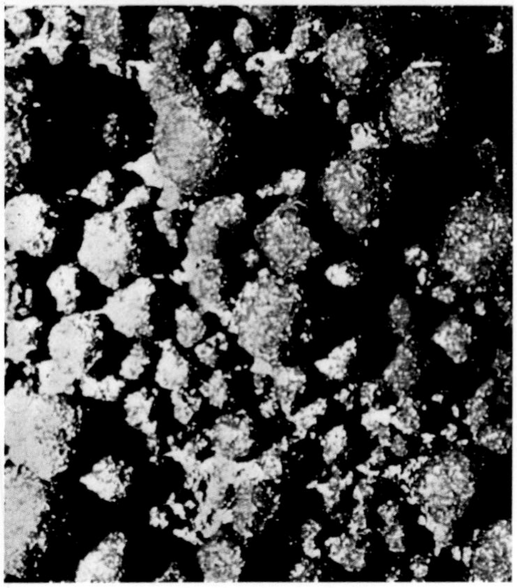

Figure 23–6 *This oil rig is drilling for oil in the shallow waters of the Gulf of Mexico (top). These lumps of the mineral manganese are lying on the ocean floor (bottom). What are these lumps of minerals called?*

Some of these minerals are deep beneath the ocean floor and have to be mined. So scientists are hard at work developing technology that will allow them to mine the ocean floor.

But some of the ocean's minerals are lying right on the surface of the ocean floor. Trillions of tons of mineral riches are simply waiting to be scooped up. These minerals are usually found in potato-sized lumps called **nodules.** A number of American companies have designed equipment to gather these nodules. One craft, a tractorlike robot, will soon roam the ocean floor scooping up nodules. The craft will crush the nodules and pipe the minerals to the surface.

Farming the Ocean

The ocean is more than a treasure chest of mineral riches. It is a huge storehouse of plants and animals that can be used for food and by industry. It is also a place where plants and animals can be grown by people. This "farming" of plants and animals is called **aquaculture.** Today aquaculture provides about 6 percent of the world's yearly fish catch. In the future, aquaculture may be the most important new source of food on the earth.

Some scientists predict that large areas of the ocean may one day be enclosed by nets or fences. Fish will be raised in herds in these special farms. The fish will provide food for many countries on the earth. At the same time, this method of fish farming will keep other parts of the ocean from being overfished. So the people of the world will obtain more food, but the ocean will not be depleted of its supply of fish.

Another food from the ocean that may have great future use is plankton. Plankton are mostly microscopic plants and animals that float on or near the ocean's surface. One type of plankton is krill.

Sharpen Your Skills

Food From the Ocean

1. Visit a major supermarket and make a list of the different kinds of seafood available.

2. Determine which products you now eat. Which products are canned, frozen, or fresh. Organize your information in a chart.

3. Add a column in the chart in which you predict seafoods that you may find in the near future.

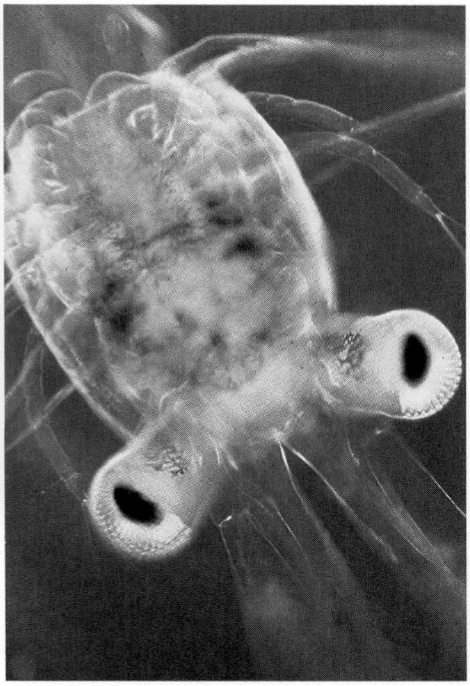

Figure 23–7 *The pens in this ocean fish farm contain salmon, an excellent food fish (left). Shrimplike creatures like this may one day provide food for fish in ocean fish farms (right). What term is used for "farming" the ocean?*

Krill are tiny shrimplike creatures that are the main diet of the largest animal on the earth, the blue whale. Some scientists believe that krill could be harvested for human food needs.

Ocean plants such as algae are already being farmed. Algae produce a jellylike substance called algin. Industry uses algin in products such as ice cream. Algae farms will also be used to produce the food for fish in fish farms.

SECTION REVIEW

1. How is sonar used to map the ocean floor?
2. Why are bathyscaphs more useful than bathyspheres?
3. Name four minerals that may one day be mined from the ocean floor. What are some of their uses?

23–2 Space Technology

Section Objective

To identify practical applications of space technology

On October 4, 1957, a Soviet rocket launched *Sputnik 1* into orbit around the earth. *Sputnik 1* was the world's first artificial satellite. It marked the beginning of the space age.

Artificial satellites and other products of space technology have improved the lives of people. Such devices have also given scientists new

Figure 23–8 *The satellite* Leasat 2 *beams telephone and radio messages from one place on the earth to another. What type of satellite is* Leasat 2?

Sharpen Your Skills

Escape Velocity

In order for a rocket to carry a satellite into space, the rocket must reach a speed that allows it to escape the earth's gravitational pull. This speed is called escape velocity.

The chart below shows the escape velocities from the earth and from several other objects in space. Determine how many times greater (+) or less (−) the escape velocities of the other objects are as compared to that of the earth.

What can you infer about their relative masses based on their escape velocities?

Object	Escape Velocity (km/sec)
Earth	11.2
Moon	2.3
Sun	616.0
Venus	10.3
Mars	5.0
Jupiter	63.4

technological tools to explore the universe. Since *Sputnik 1,* more than 1000 satellites have been put in orbit around the earth.

Artificial Satellites

A satellite is any object that revolves around a larger object in space. The moon, for example, is a natural satellite of the earth. The earth is actually a natural satellite of the sun. Artificial satellites are satellites built by people.

There are several different types of artificial satellites orbiting the earth. Each of these types has a specific function.

COMMUNICATIONS SATELLITES Many of the satellites orbiting the earth are **communications satellites.** Communications satellites beam television programs, radio messages, telephone conversations, and other kinds of information all over the world. You can think of a communications satellite as a relay station in space. The satellite receives a signal from an earth station. The satellite then transmits the signal back to another earth station on the other side of the world. In this way, information is quickly transmitted from one place to another.

Communications satellites are often placed in **geosynchronous** (jee-oh-SIHNG-kruh-nuhs) **orbit.** A geosynchronous orbit is one in which the satellite moves at a speed that exactly matches the earth's rate of rotation. As a result, the satellite stays in one place above a certain point on the earth's surface. Three such satellites placed equal distances apart at about 35,000 kilometers above the earth can relay signals to any place on the earth.

WEATHER SATELLITES Artificial satellites have greatly improved our ability to track weather patterns and forecast weather conditions all over the world. **Weather satellites** take pictures of weather patterns all around the world. By studying and charting weather patterns, scientists can predict the weather with greater accuracy than ever before. Such predictions are particularly important when dangerous storms such as hurricanes are being tracked. Today with the use of weather satellites, scientists can bet-

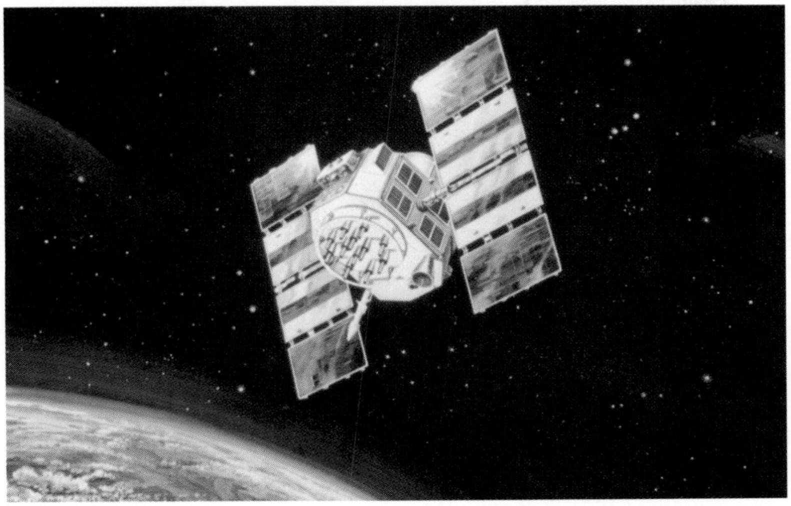

Figure 23–9 *The Navstar satellite helps boats at sea determine their exact location. What type of satellite is the Navstar?*

ter predict when and where a hurricane will strike. Such information gives people time to protect themselves and their property and often saves lives.

NAVIGATION SATELLITES Another type of artificial satellite is **navigation satellites.** Navigation satellites send precise, continuous signals to ships and planes. Using information from navigation satellites, pilots and sailors can determine their exact location within seconds. This information is especially useful during storms when other kinds of navigation equipment may not provide accurate information.

SCIENTIFIC SATELLITES Many types of **scientific satellites** orbit the earth. Some are used to prepare detailed maps, especially in remote areas. Satellites are often the only instruments through which detailed maps can be made of areas that are hard to get to. A satellite can map large areas, detailing rivers, streams, and mountain ranges. Or it can map smaller areas, providing a view of city streets.

Other scientific satellites scan the earth for signs of undiscovered natural resources. Satellites can detect mineral deposits beneath the earth's surface. Or they may search for signs of oil and gas deposits.

In 1985, a scientific radar satellite made an astonishing discovery. It discovered the remains of dried up river beds in the Sahara Desert. Scientists later discovered that these ancient rivers once supported an entire community of people. Today similar satellites are searching for remains of ancient civilizations that may have been buried long ago.

Figure 23–10 *A scientific satellite took this infrared photograph of Galveston Bay on the Gulf Coast of Texas. The satellite is charting the flow of sediments, located in the pale-blue areas, which stream off the land and are carried away by the Gulf Stream current.*

HELP WANTED: ASTRONAUT If you are interested in adventure and exploration, apply for a job as a crew member for the Space Shuttle. Scientific or engineering background or experience as a pilot required.

Sally Ride was the first woman **astronaut** from the United States. Like all the astronauts, Sally Ride worked long and hard to achieve her place in the space program. Astronauts must endure difficult training periods with complex equipment. For example, they must practice moving about in a spaceship environment. They do this by performing daily activities during periods of weightlessness. They become used to working in space suits, and they practice approaching and landing in a special aircraft.

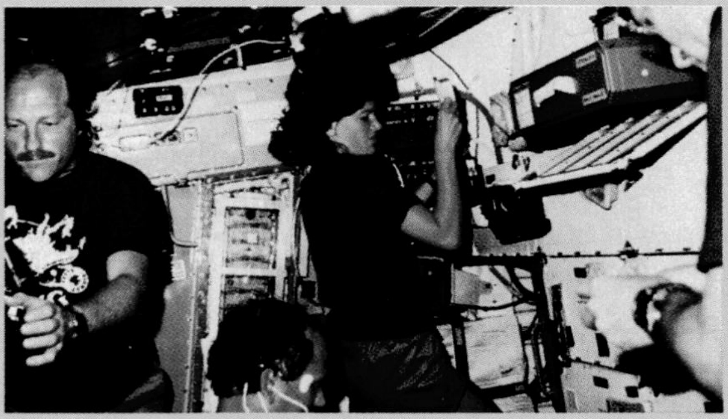

Men and women who keep physically fit, who enjoy flying, who have a keen interest in space, and who have superior academic qualifications in the sciences can make effective astronauts. If becoming an astronaut interests you, write to the Johnson Space Center, National Aeronautics and Space Administration, Houston, TX 77058.

Laboratories in Space

In 1973, the United States placed Skylab into orbit. Skylab was a space station designed to perform experiments in space. Astronauts aboard rockets could dock with Skylab and enter its laboratory. Later these astronauts could return to the earth with their data. Skylab was the United States' first scientific laboratory in space.

Figure 23–11 *The Space Shuttle is carried into space by rockets. How does it return to the earth?*

Today the Space Shuttle has taken the place of Skylab. The Space Shuttle is a ship carried into space by rockets. But unlike any space vehicle ever built, the Space Shuttle can return from space and be used again. The Space Shuttle returns to the earth like a glider.

One of the most important functions of the Space Shuttle is to place artificial satellites into orbit. In addition, the Space Shuttle also has a built-in laboratory. The laboratory can be fitted with different types of scientific equipment, depending on the kinds of experiments being run.

Using the Space Shuttle laboratory, scientists are able to perform many experiments that cannot be done on the earth. For example, telescopes aboard the Space Shuttle can study the planets and stars without the interference of the earth's atmosphere.

Figure 23–12 *The first satellite released by the Space Shuttle was this communications satellite. It remains over the same spot on the earth at all times. What type of orbit is the satellite in?*

Industry will also find the Space Shuttle laboratory very valuable. For example, in the absence of gravity in space, perfect crystals can be grown. Such crystals have many practical uses back on the earth.

The ultimate laboratories in space will be large-scale space stations. These stations, built with parts ferried into space by the Space Shuttle, will eventually house many scientists and workers. Scientists believe that the first orbital space station may well lead to the building of large self-sufficient settlements in space. Fueled by almost unlimited solar energy and supplied with raw materials from meteoroids, asteroids, moons, and planets, such a settlement could serve as a supply source for the "old world," Planet Earth. It could also serve as a jumping-off point for exploration of new worlds beyond the solar system.

Figure 23–13 *Astronauts on board the Space Shuttle practice techniques that will be used to build large space stations (right). Here you see an artist's idea of what a space station may look like (left).*

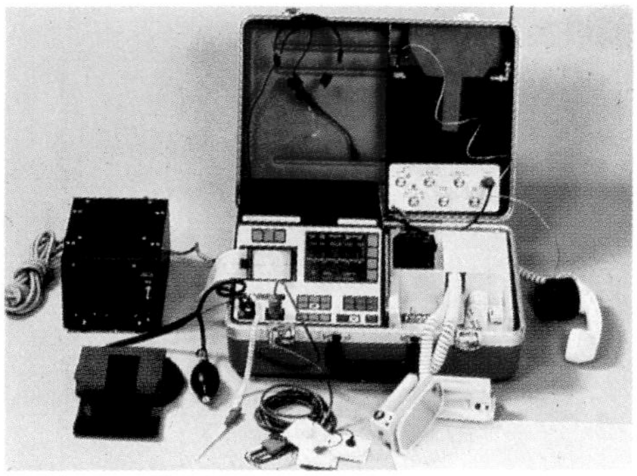

Figure 23–14 *This emergency medical kit, called the Portable Medical Status and Treatment System (PMSTS), uses technology developed to monitor astronauts in space. The kit has already saved many lives on the earth—one of the many benefits of space technology.*

Space Technology Spinoffs

Although most of the major discoveries of the United States space program have been made far from the earth, many of them have very down-to-earth, practical applications. For example, from the space program has come a device that keeps marathon runners from overheating during a race. The dome of a football stadium in which players and spectators are protected from the weather is an application of the space program. And portable instrument packages that can help save the lives of heart attack or accident victims is still another application of space technology.

Because these devices owe their existence to the exploration of space, they are called space technology spinoffs. They have been "spun off" the space program.

An astronaut exposed to sunlight in space runs the risk of overheating. To reduce the possibility of overheating, space scientists developed various devices to be fitted into space suits. One of these devices is a gel packet that can draw excess heat away from various parts of the body. These gel packets are now used by marathon runners to absorb excess heat from their forehead, neck, and wrists.

Figure 23–15 *In Alexandria, Virginia, firefighters now use special gear that employs lightweight fire-resistant materials. This gear uses materials first developed for astronaut space suits.*

Figure 23–16 *The roof of the Silverdome in Detroit, Michigan, is made of a lightweight fabric first developed for use by astronauts in space.*

In 1967, NASA scientists and engineers were hunting for a fabric for space suits. The fabric had to be strong enough to withstand the extreme temperature variations found in space yet easy to weave. Soon after the fabric was invented and used for space suits, it was used to roof a department store in California, an aquatic entertainment center in Florida, and a football stadium in Michigan.

To determine how astronauts would react to the environment of space, scientists designed automatic monitoring devices that relayed to the earth an astronaut's blood pressure, heart rate, and other vital statistics. Such devices are now used by paramedics when they answer emergency calls. These devices provide rapid and accurate information about a patient's condition.

SECTION REVIEW

1. Name four kinds of artificial satellites and describe the benefits of each.
2. How does Skylab differ from the Space Shuttle?
3. Explain the phrase, "The space program is a down-to-earth success."

23 LABORATORY INVESTIGATION

Constructing a Balloon Rocket

Problem

How can a balloon rocket be used to illustrate Newton's third law of motion?

Materials (*per group*)

Balloon
Masking tape
Scissors
9 m of string
Drinking straw
Meterstick

Procedure

1. Cut the drinking straw in half. Pull the string through one of the halves.
2. Blow up the balloon and hold the end so that the air does not escape. Note: Do not tie the end of the balloon.
3. Have someone tape the drinking straw with the string pulled through it to the side of the balloon as shown in the illustration. Do not let go of the balloon.
4. Have two students pull the string tight between them.
5. Move the balloon along the string to one end of the string. Release the balloon and observe its flight toward the other end of the string.
6. Make a data table similar to the one on this page. Record in the data table the distance the balloon flew.
7. Repeat the flight of the balloon four more times. Record in your data table the distances the balloon travels.

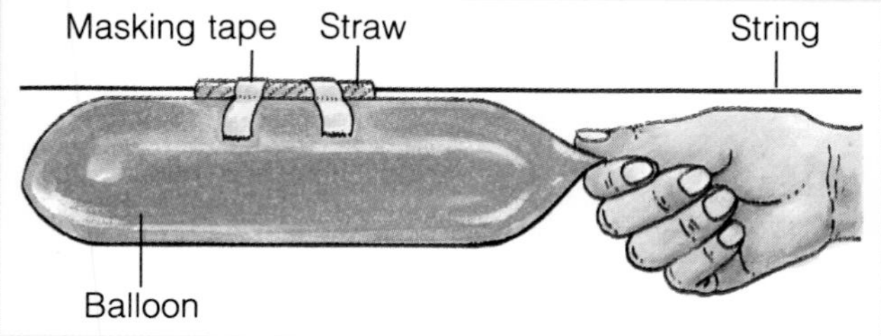

Observations

1. What was the longest flight of your balloon rocket? The shortest flight?
2. What was the average distance reached by your balloon rocket?

Flight	Distance (*m*)
1	
2	
3	
4	
5	

Conclusions

1. During the seventeenth century, Sir Isaac Newton proposed the third law of motion. The law states that every action produces an equal and opposite reaction. Using the third law of motion, explain what caused the movement of the balloon.
2. Compare your balloon rocket to the way a real rocket works.
3. Suppose your classmates obtained different results for the distance their balloons traveled. What variables may have caused the differences in their results?

CHAPTER REVIEW

SUMMARY

23–1 Technology and the Ocean

- Oceanography includes the study of the physical characteristics, the chemical composition, the life forms, and the natural resources of the ocean.
- Sonar is an echo-sounding instrument used to measure the depth of the ocean at various places.
- Submersibles are research vessels that explore the earth's ocean.
- A bathysphere is a diving vessel lowered by a steel cable from a ship. A bathyscaph is a self-propelled submarine observatory.
- The bathyscaph *Alvin* discovered unusual sea communities living near vents in the ocean floor.
- The ocean floor is a treasure house of minerals such as manganese, tungsten, vanadium, nickel, titanium, silver, platinum, and gold.
- Some minerals are found resting on the ocean floor in potato-sized lumps called nodules.
- Aquaculture is the "farming" of ocean plants and animals.

23–2 Space Technology

- The earth is now ringed by artificial satellites.
- Communications satellites transmit television programs, radio messages, and telephone conversations all over the world.
- Communications satellites are often placed in geosynchronous orbit. A geosynchronous orbit is one in which the satellite moves at a speed that exactly matches the earth's rate of rotation.
- Weather satellites have greatly improved our ability to predict the weather.
- Navigation satellites provide sailors and pilots with signals that help them determine their exact location within seconds.
- Scientific satellites are used to prepare maps and to search for deposits of fossil fuels and mineral resources.
- The first laboratory sent into space by the United States was Skylab.
- The Space Shuttle is carried into orbit by a rocket but returns to the earth like a glider.
- The Space Shuttle is now used to place artificial satellites into orbit.
- In the future, large-scale space stations may house many scientists and workers. Long-term experiments will be run on such space stations.
- Many practical products now used on the earth were first used in one form or another in space.

VOCABULARY

Define each term in a complete sentence.

aquaculture
bathyscaph
bathysphere
communications satellite
geosynchronous orbit
navigation satellite
nodule
oceanography
scientific satellite
sonar
submersible
weather satellite

CONTENT REVIEW: MULTIPLE CHOICE

Choose the letter of the answer that best completes each sentence.

1. Oceanography includes the study of the ocean's
a. chemical composition b. life forms
c. natural resources d. all of these

2. An echo-sounding instrument used to make a map of the ocean floor is
a. radar b. mapping satellite c. sonar d. submersible

3. A self-propelled submarine observatory is a
a. bathysphere b. "Jim" c. underwater boat d. bathyscaph

4. Submersibles have dived as deep as
a. 5000 meters b. 10,000 meters
c. 20,000 meters d. 10,000 kilometers

5. Potato-sized mineral lumps found on the ocean floor are called
a. globules b. gold nuggets c. titanium clumps d. nodules

6. The "farming" of ocean plants and animals is called
a. fish farms b. aquaculture c. krill farms d. algae farms

7. Television programs are relayed through space by
a. the Space Shuttle b. scientific satellites
c. mapping satellites d. communications satellites

8. Sailors can determine their exact location using signals from
a. radar satellites b. communications satellites
c. navigation satellites d. Skylab

9. Scientific satellites search for
a. oil and gas b. mineral deposits
c. ancient civilizations d. all of these

10. The United States' first attempt to place a laboratory in space was
a. the Space Shuttle b. a space colony c. Skylab d. *Sputnik*

CONTENT REVIEW: COMPLETION

Fill in the word or words that best complete each sentence.

1. The Space Shuttle was used to repair the ______________ satellite.

2. Sound waves from sonar equipment strike the ocean floor and ______________ back to a ship on the surface.

3. ______________ is the term for any research vessel that goes underwater to explore the ocean depths.

4. A (An) ______________ is a diving vessel lowered into the ocean by steel cables.

5. *Alvin* found unusual underwater communities near ______________ in the ocean floor.

6. Vast deposits of the fossil fuels ______________ and ______________ may be located beneath the ocean floor.

7. Microscopic plants and animals that live in the ocean are called ______________.

8. A (An) ______________ is any object that revolves around a larger object in space.

9. Hurricanes are tracked through the use of ______________ satellites.

10. The ______________ is a vehicle that rockets into space and returns to the earth like a glider.

CONTENT REVIEW: TRUE OR FALSE

Determine whether each statement is true or false. If it is true, write "true." If it is false, change the underlined word or words to make the statement true.

1. A bathysphere is capable of only limited movement.
2. Aquaculture means farming the ocean.
3. Tiny shrimplike creatures are called algae.
4. The moon is a satellite of the earth.
5. A geosynchronous orbit is one in which a satellite moves at a speed that is exactly one-half the earth's rate of rotation.
6. Weather satellites are often placed in geosynchronous orbit.
7. Detailed maps can be obtained through the use of navigation satellites.
8. The Space Shuttle is the first space vehicle that can return to the earth and be used again.
9. Perfect nodules can be grown in space due to the lack of gravity.
10. Experiments in space could be run for years at a time on the Space Shuttle.

CONCEPT REVIEW: SKILL BUILDING

Use the skills you have developed in the chapter to complete each activity.

1. **Making calculations** The speed of sound in water at a temperature of 25°C is about 1500 meters per second. Assuming the water temperature is a constant 25°C, determine the depth of the water if a sound wave takes 4 seconds to travel from a ship to the ocean floor and back to the ship. What is the depth if the sound wave takes 3 seconds to make the round trip? 6 seconds? 10 seconds? Record your answers in a data table.
2. **Interpreting maps** Using the photograph on page 574, determine the approximate average temperature at the following locations: central Texas, southern Florida, central Australia, and the southern tip of Greenland.
3. **Making graphs** You are a technician on a research ship. Your job is to use sonar to map the ocean floor. Your ship is moving at 10 km/hr from west to east. Taking a measurement once an hour, you collect the following data.

   Using the data and graph paper, draw a profile of the sea floor over which you have sailed. Identify a ridge, a trench, and a continental shelf.

Hour	Sonar Round Trip *(sec)*	Hour	Sonar Round Trip *(sec)*
0	9	7	10
1	9	8	8
2	8	9	2
3	7	10	1
4	6	11	0.5
5	12	12	0.5
6	11.5	13	0.5

Note: Sound travels through sea water at about 1500 m/sec.

CONCEPT REVIEW: ESSAY

Discuss each of the following in a brief paragraph.

1. What are some advantages of using the ocean as a source of food and minerals? Some disadvantages?
2. Some think the space program is a waste of money. What do you think? Explain.
3. Describe what you think it might be like to live in an underwater city. Do the same for a space station.

SCIENCE GAZETTE

Adventures in Science

Robert Ballard... AND THE SEARCH FOR THE TITANIC

She was billed as the largest, most luxurious, and most technologically advanced passenger ship of her day. But even more important was the proud claim of her builders that their masterpiece was unsinkable. So when the ocean liner *Titanic* set out on her maiden voyage from England to New York in April 1912, no one could possibly have foreseen the events of the night of April 15. On that fateful night, the *Titanic* hit an iceberg in the North Atlantic Ocean. Three hours later, the "unsinkable" ship and many of her 1522 passengers had plunged to the bottom of the ocean floor. There the ship remained beneath three kilometers of water—unseen and untouched until September 1, 1985. On that historic day, Robert Ballard and a team of French and American oceanographers found the first piece of wreckage from the *Titanic*.

Robert Ballard, a senior scientist at Woods Hole Oceanographic Institution, is part explorer, part geologist, and part engineer. One of his most important projects was the creation of a vessel that could descend into the underwater depths to locate and photograph objects on the ocean floor.

When Ballard began his research, the Woods Hole Oceanographic Institution already had *Alvin*, a submersible that could explore the ocean bottom. *Alvin* could carry people deep beneath the ocean surface and could collect ocean-floor material with a mechanical arm. According to Ballard, a trip in *Alvin* was like a voyage to the moon. He describes the journey as a trek into a freezing pitch-black "inner-space."

Ballard designed a new submersible, which he named the Argo-Jason. The Argo-Jason can be sent undersea without a crew. It is controlled by a mother ship that remains at the water's surface. The Argo is a long cage equipped with special lights, complex sonar devices, and computer-enhanced underwater cameras. These cameras can take perfect pictures of the underwater world and then send the images to a video screen on the mother ship.

The Argo can also scan sections of the ocean floor. When it detects something of interest, it sends Jason out to investigate. Jason is a smaller robot attached to the Argo by a long "leash." Equipped with mechanical arms, Jason's duty is to collect samples from places along the ocean floor that cannot be reached by the Argo.

Ballard was pleased with the creation of the Argo-Jason, but many other scientists did not believe that his invention would be able to collect ocean-floor samples effectively. So Ballard had to think of a way to prove that the Argo-Jason could indeed work. Thus was born Ballard's search for the *Titanic,* using the Argo-Jason.

Ballard had always been fascinated by the sunken luxury liner. He considered himself an expert on the details of the incident. "I read just about every book or document ever published about the disaster," says Ballard. But even Ballard admitted that the search for the *Titanic* would be difficult. "From the historical data, the best we could do was to reduce the likely site to an area of no less than 388 square kilometers. And when you consider the depth (of the ocean), you'd have to admit that locating the ship makes finding a needle in a haystack seem trivial."

The Argo-Jason made the difference. Within several days, and after a couple of malfunctions, the Argo began scanning the ocean bottom with its cameras. Less than a week later, the Argo found the *Titanic,* and its cameras focused on the ship's boilers. During the next few days, the Argo took hundreds of photographs of the *Titanic.* Dr. Ballard was amazed with the results. Although the ship had been lying 3.2 kilometers below the ocean surface for 73 years, many objects were perfectly preserved.

Dr. Ballard had succeeded twice: he had discovered the resting place of the *Titanic* and he had proved that the submersible Argo-Jason did work. Ballard still had one more wish, however. He wanted to see the *Titanic* with his own eyes. Ten months after the discovery, Dr. Ballard went down to the wreck in the *Alvin.* He carefully examined the inside and outside of the great ship in an attempt to figure out what had gone wrong on that terrible day in 1912. But Ballard, who has asked Congress to declare the *Titanic* an international memorial and protect its burial site, would not touch anything or bring any souvenirs back to the surface. "The quest for the *Titanic* is over," he said. "May she now rest in peace."

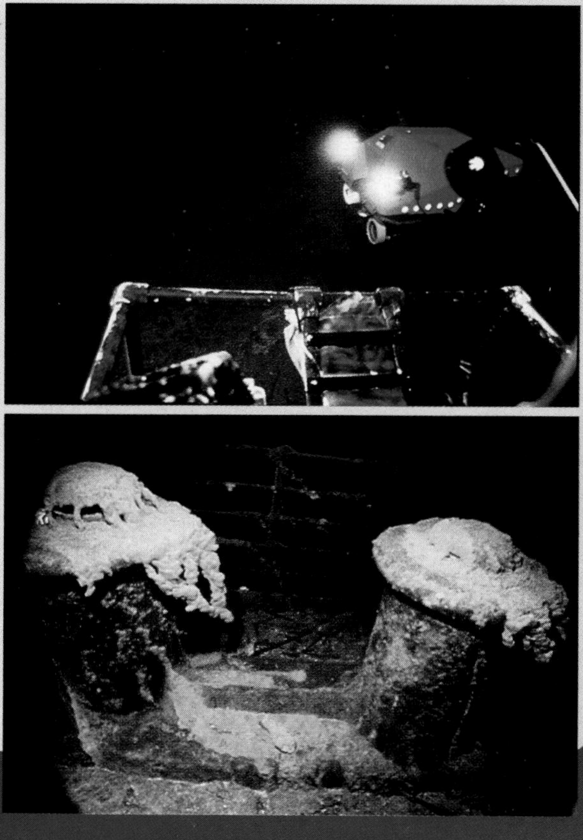

Cameras on board the Jason photographed the *Titanic* lying on the ocean floor under 4000 meters of water.

Issues in Science

ACID RAIN

What Can Be Done?

High in the Adirondack Mountains of northern New York State, a crystal blue lake shimmers in the sun. Cradled by green slopes, the lake once held huge trout, which drew anglers from all over the country. But now the lake has no fish. Why? For years the lake has been pelted by polluted rain that is almost as acidic as vinegar. Unable to survive the high acid content of the water, the fish died.

The tragedy of acid rain has struck not just this one lake in the Adirondacks. At least 180 trout ponds and lakes in these mountains no longer support fish. What is more, acid rain is not limited to the Adirondacks.

Acid rain has fallen from coast to coast. This has led conservation groups such as the National Wildlife Federation to issue warnings about acid rain's danger to the environment. "Acid rain is a growing threat," says the federation. The wildlife federation estimates that "acid rain may be slowly poisoning 100,000 miles of streams and 20,000 lakes" across the United States, mostly in the eastern half of the country. Acid rain also kills trees and other plant life. Even worse, acid rain may be affecting our drinking water and posing serious health hazards.

The problem begins with the burning of coal, oil, and natural gas. When these and

▲ The effects of acid rain can be seen in the discoloration and erosion of this stone statue.

RAIN

other fossil fuels are burned, they release nitrogen oxides and sulfur oxides into the air. Large smokestacks of factories spew out these dangerous gases. The gases react with water vapor in clouds to form droplets of nitric acid and sulfuric acid. The acid droplets are captured by rain or snowflakes. At some point, this rain or snow falls to the earth as the precipitation known as acid rain.

The chemicals that cause acid rain can also enter the atmosphere naturally from volcanoes and forest fires. And they can also come from automobile engine exhaust.

Acid in the air can travel hundreds or thousands of kilometers from its source. The acid rain that is polluting the Adirondack lakes may in fact have originated in the midwest or south. Canadian officials are now claiming that acid rain from American industries is polluting their lakes. They are demanding that the United States government do something about it.

But many scientists who have studied the problem say that tracing acid rain to its source is still difficult. And proving that an industrial plant in one area of the nation is responsible for the pollution that is killing fish in a lake in Canada is practically impossible. Perhaps arguing about the location of the source of acid rain is not as important as determining the cause and developing a solution.

The effects of acid rain depend on the location of an area. Not all areas are affected in the same way. In some regions acid rain is highly destructive while in other regions it is not. But as the demands for energy in our highly industrial society continue, more fossil fuels will be burned. And more acid rain will be produced. Finding a solution is vital.

The National Academy of Sciences suggests that industry reduce by 12 million tons the amount of chemical pollutants being released into the air. One way to do this is to install "scrubbers" in smokestacks. The scrubbers clean emissions before they rise into the air. Another solution is to use low-sulfur coal, although it is expensive.

One of the most promising solutions to the acid rain problem is to develop alternate energy sources. Such sources include solar energy, geothermal energy, wind and tidal energy, and nuclear energy. This solution, too, will be expensive. Someone will have to pay for solving the acid rain problem. Should it be industry? But would industry pass on the cost to consumers? Should the government—that is, the taxpayers—pay the bill?

Industry and government scientists disagree on who should pay for cleaning up the air. With the problem of acid rain becoming more critical, however, almost everyone agrees that now is the time for action.

Many pollutants are found in the air. This photograph shows a drop of acid rain.

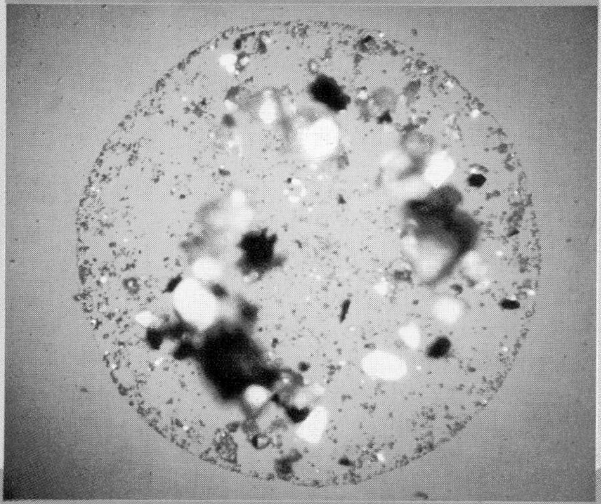

For Further Reading

If you have an interest in a specific area of Earth Science or simply want to know more about the topics you are studying, one of the following books may open the door to an exciting learning adventure.

Chapter 1: Exploring Earth Science

Freeman, Ira, and Mae Freeman. *Your Wonderful World of Science.* New York: Random House.

Kohn, Bernice. *The Scientific Method.* Englewood Cliffs, NJ: Prentice-Hall.

Ruchlis, Hy. *Discovering Scientific Method.* New York: Harper & Row.

Chapter 2: Stars and Galaxies

Bova, Ben. *In Quest of Quasars.* New York: Crowell-Collier Press.

Lauber, Patricia. *Look-It-Up Book of Stars and Planets.* New York: Random House.

Zim, Herbert. *Stars.* New York: Golden Press.

Chapter 3: The Solar System

Branley, Franklyn M. *The Sun: Star Number One.* New York: Thomas Y. Crowell.

Ley, Willie. *Gas Giants: The Largest Planets.* New York: McGraw-Hill.

Nourse, Alan E. *Nine Planets.* New York: Harper & Row.

Chapter 4: The Earth and Moon

Branley, Franklyn M. *The Earth: Planet Number Three.* New York: Thomas Y. Crowell.

Gamow, George. *The Moon.* New York: Abelard-Schuman.

Rublowsky, Jack. *Is Anybody Out There?* New York: Walker.

Chapter 5: The Nature of Matter

Asimov, Isaac. *Building Blocks of the Universe.* New York: Abelard-Schuman.

Asimov, Isaac. *Inside the Atom,* rev. 3rd ed. New York: Abelard-Schuman.

Snell, Cornelia T., and Foster D. Snell. *Chemistry Made Easy.* New York: Chemical Publishing Co.

Chapter 6: Minerals

Gilbert, Miriam. *The Science Hobby Book of Rocks and Minerals.* Minneapolis: Lerner.

Keene, Melvin. *The Beginner's Story of Minerals and Rocks.* New York: Harper & Row.

Sootin, Harry, and Laura Sootin. *The Young Experimenter's Workbook: Treasures of the Earth.* New York: Norton.

Chapter 7: Rocks

Gallant, Ray A., and Christopher J. Schuberth. *Discovering Rocks and Minerals: A Nature and Science Guide to Their Collection and Identification.* New York: Natural History Press.

Shepherd, Walter. *Wealth From the Ground.* New York: John Day.

Simon, Seymour. *The Rock-Hound's Book.* New York: Penguin.

Chapter 8: The Earth's Interior

Adler, Irving, and Ruth Adler. *The Earth's Crust.* New York: John Day.

Matthews, William H. *Introducing the Earth.* New York: Dodd, Mead.

Shepherd, Walter. *Geophysics.* New York: Putnam.

Chapter 9: The Earth's Landmasses

Bauer, Ernst. *Wonders of the Earth.* New York: Franklin Watts.

Jacobs, Lou, Jr. *The Shapes of Our Land.* New York: Putnam.

Ruchlis, Hy. *Your Changing Earth.* New York: Harvey House.

Chapter 10: The Earth's Fresh Water

Davis, Delwyn. *Fresh Water: The Precious Resource.* New York: Natural History Press.

Lavine, Sigmund, and Mart Casey. *Water Since the World Began.* New York: Dodd, Mead.

Meyer, Jerome. *Water at Work.* New York: World.

Chapter 11: The Earth's Oceans

Engel, Leonard. *The Sea.* New York: Time-Life.

Limburg, Peter, and James B. Sweeney. *102 Questions and Answers About the Sea.* New York: Julian Messner.

Scott, Frances, and Walter Scott. *Exploring Ocean Frontiers: A Background on Who Owns the Seas.* New York: Parents Magazine.

Chapter 12: The Earth's Atmosphere

Brewer, A. C., and Nell Garland. *Exploring and Understanding Air.* Westchester, IL: Benefic Press.

Chandler, T. J. *The Air Around Us: Man Looks at His Atmosphere.* New York: Natural History Press.

Simon, Seymour. *Projects with Air.* New York: Franklin Watts.

Chapter 13: Weather

Bova, Ben. *Man Changes the Weather.* Reading, MA: Addison-Wesley.

Milgrom, Harry. *Understanding Weather,* rev. ed. New York: Thomas Y. Crowell.

Weiss, Malcolm E. *Storms – From the Inside Out.* New York: Julian Messner.

Chapter 14: Climate

Bramwell, Martyn. *Glaciers and Ice Caps.* New York: Watts.

Lydolph, Paul E. *The Climate of the Earth.* Totowa, NJ: Rowman & Allanheld.

Pringle, L. *Frost Hollows and Other Microclimates.* New York: Morrow.

Chapter 15: Weathering and Soil

Adams, George F., and Jerome Wyckoff. *Landforms.* New York: Golden Press.

Shimer, John A. *The Changing Earth: An Introduction to Geology.* New York: Barnes & Noble.

Wyckoff, Jerome. *The Story of Geology.* New York: Golden Press.

Chapter 16: Erosion and Deposition

Collins, Henry Hill, Jr. *The Wonders of Geology.* New York: Putnam.

Marcus, Rebecca. *The First Book of Glaciers.* New York: Franklin Watts.

Riedman, Sarah R. *Water for People.* New York: Abelard-Schuman.

Chapter 17: Movement of the Earth's Crust

Clayton, Keith. *The Crust of the Earth: The Story of Geology.* New York: Natural History Press.

Ladyman, Phyllis. *Inside the Earth.* New York: William R. Scott.

Matthews, William H., III. *The Story of the Earth.* New York: Harvey House.

Chapter 18: Earthquakes and Volcanoes

Brown, Billye Walker, and Walter R. Brown. *Historical Catastrophes: Earthquakes.* Reading, MA: Addison-Wesley.

May, Julian. *Why the Earth Quakes.* New York: Holiday House.

Nixon, Hershell H., and Joan Lowery Nixon. *Volcanoes: Nature's Fireworks.* New York: Dodd, Mead.

Chapter 19: Plate Tectonics

Anderson, Alan H. *The Drifting Continents.* New York: Putnam.

Asimov, Isaac. *How Did We Find Out About Earthquakes?* New York: Walker.

Golden, Frederick. *The Moving Continents.* New York: Scribner's.

Chapter 20: Fossils and the Past

Holden, Raymond. *Famous Fossil Finds.* New York: Dodd, Mead.

Keen, Martin L. *Hunting Fossils.* New York: Julian Messner.

Matthews, William H. *Wonders of Fossils.* New York: Dodd, Mead.

Chapter 21: Change and Geologic Time

McGowen, Tom. *Album of Dinosaurs.* New York: Rand McNally.

Moore, Ruth. *The Earth We Live On.* New York: Knopf.

Poole, Lynn, and Gray Poole. *Carbon-14 and Other Methods That Date the Past.* New York: McGraw-Hill.

Chapter 22: The Earth's Natural Resources

Adler, Irving. *Petroleum: Gas, Oil, and Asphalt.* New York: John Day.

Atkinson, Brooks. *This Bright Land: A Personal View.* Garden City, NY: Doubleday.

Shuttlesworth, Dorothy, and Lee Ann Williams. *Disappearing Energy: Can We End the Crisis?* Garden City, NY: Doubleday.

Chapter 23: Earth Science and Technology

Fields, A. *Satellites.* New York: Franklin Watts.

Voss, Gilbert L. *Oceanography.* New York: Golden Press.

The metric system of measurement is used by scientists throughout the world. It is based on units of ten. Each unit is ten times larger or ten times smaller than the next unit. The most commonly used units of the metric system are given below. After you have finished reading about the metric system, try to put it to use. How tall are you in metrics? What is your mass? What is your normal body temperature in degrees Celsius?

COMMONLY USED METRIC UNITS

Length The distance from one point to another

meter (m)	1 meter = 1000 millimeters (mm)
(a meter is slightly longer than a yard)	1 meter = 100 centimeters (cm)
	1000 meters = 1 kilometer (km)

Volume The amount of space an object takes up

liter (L)	1 liter = 1000 milliliters (mL)
(a liter is slightly larger than a quart)	

Mass The amount of matter in an object

gram (g)	1000 grams = 1 kilogram (kg)
(a gram has a mass equal to about one paper clip)	

Temperature The measure of hotness or coldness

degrees Celsius (°C)	0°C = freezing point of water
	100°C = boiling point of water

METRIC-ENGLISH EQUIVALENTS

2.54 centimeters (cm) = 1 inch (in)
1 meter (m) = 39.37 inches (in)
1 kilometer (km) = 0.62 miles (mi)
1 liter (L) = 1.06 quarts (qt)
250 milliliters (mL) = 1 cup (c)
1 kilogram (kg) = 2.2 pounds (lb)
28.3 grams (g) = 1 ounce (oz)
C° = 5/9 × (F° − 32)

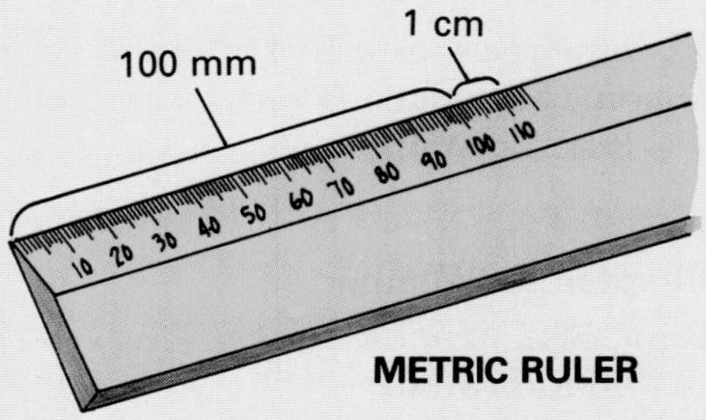

METRIC RULER

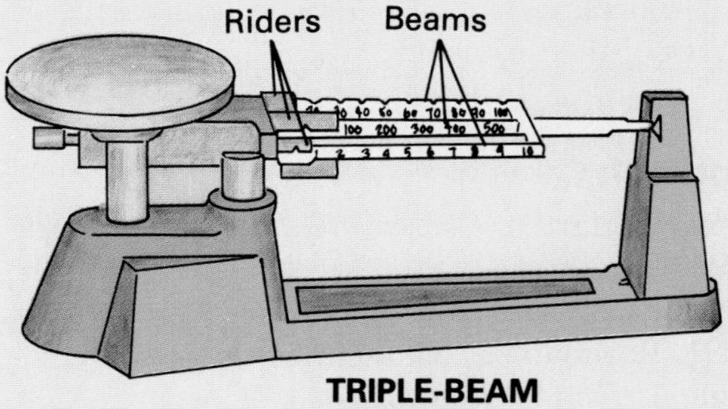

TRIPLE-BEAM BALANCE

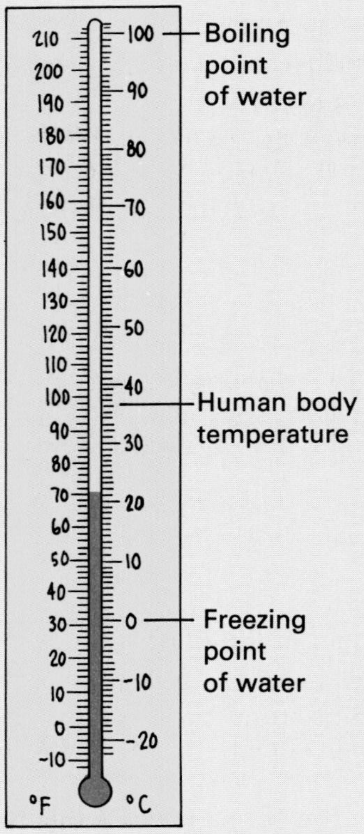

THERMOMETER

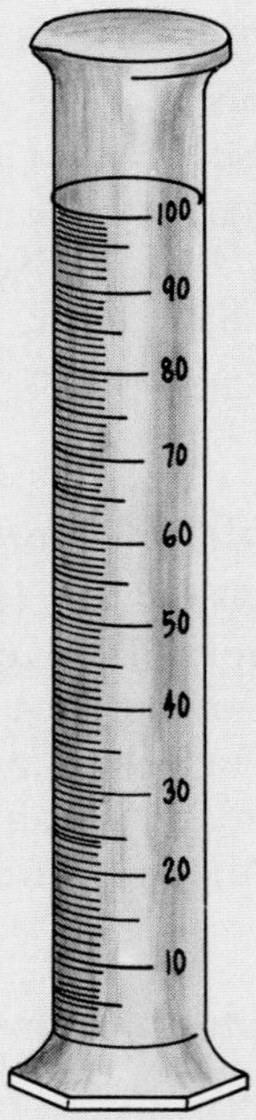

GRADUATED CYLINDER

The laboratory balance is an important tool in scientific investigations. You can use the balance to determine the mass of materials that you study or experiment with in the laboratory.

Different kinds of balances are used in the laboratory. One kind of balance is the double-pan balance. Another kind of balance is the triple-beam balance. The balance that you may use in your science class is probably similar to one of the balances illustrated in this appendix. To use the balance properly, you should learn the name, function, and location of each part of the balance you are using. What kind of balance do you have in your science class?

The Double-Pan Balance

The double-pan balance shown in this appendix has two beams. Some double-pan balances have only one beam. The beams are calibrated, or marked, in grams. The upper beam is divided into 10 major units of one gram each. Each of these units is further divided into units of 1/10 of a gram. The lower beam is divided into 20 units, and each unit is equal to 10 grams. The lower beam can be used to find the masses of objects up to 200 grams. Each beam has a rider that is moved to the right along the beam. The rider indicates the number of grams needed to balance the object in the left pan. What is the total mass the balance can measure?

Before you begin using the balance, you should be sure that the pans are empty and both riders are pointing to zero. The balance should be on a flat, level surface. The pointer should be at the zero point. If your pointer does not read zero, slowly turn the adjustment knob so that the pointer does read zero.

The following procedure can be used to find the mass of an object with a double-pan balance:

1. Place the object whose mass is to be determined on the left pan.

2. Move the rider on the lower beam to the 10-gram notch.

3. If the pointer moves to the right of the zero point on the scale, the object has a mass less than 10 grams. Return the rider on the lower beam to zero. Slowly move the rider on the upper beam until the pointer is at zero. The reading on the beam is the mass of the object.

DOUBLE-PAN BALANCE

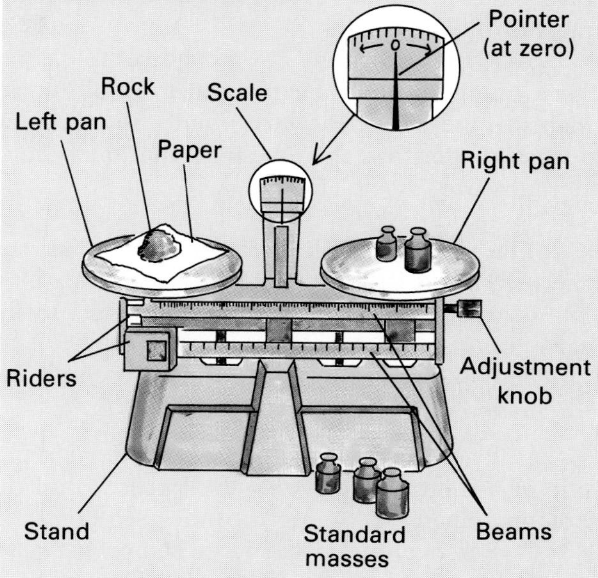

Parts of a Double-Pan Balance and Their Functions

Pointer Indicator used to determine when the mass being measured is balanced by the riders or masses of the balance

Scale Series of marks along which the pointer moves

Zero Point Center line of the scale to which the pointer moves when the mass being measured is balanced by the riders or masses of the balance

Adjustment Knob Knob used to set the balance at the zero point when the riders are all on zero and no masses are on either pan

Left Pan Platform on which an object whose mass is to be determined is placed

Right Pan Platform on which standard masses are placed

Beams Horizontal strips of metal on which marks, or graduations, appear that indicate grams or parts of grams

Riders Devices that are moved along the beams and used to balance the object being measured and to determine its mass

Stand Support for the balance

4. If the pointer did not move to the right of the zero, move the rider on the lower beam notch by notch until the pointer does move to the right. Move the rider back one notch. Then move the rider on the upper beam until the pointer is at zero. The sum of the readings on both beams is the mass of the object.

5. If the two riders are moved completely to the right side of the beams and the pointer remains to the left of the zero point, the object has a mass greater than the total mass that the balance can measure.

The total mass that most double-pan balances can measure is 210 grams. If an object has a mass greater than 210 grams, return the riders to the zero point.

The following procedure can be used to find the mass of an object greater than 210 grams:

1. Place the standard masses on the right pan one at a time, starting with the largest, until the pointer remains to the right of the zero point.

2. Remove one of the large standard masses and replace it with a smaller one. Continue replacing the standard masses with smaller ones until the pointer remains to the left of the zero point. When the pointer remains to the left of the zero point, the mass of the object on the left pan is greater than the total mass of the standard masses on the right pan.

3. Move the rider on the lower beam and then the rider on the upper beam until the pointer stops at the zero point on the scale. The mass of the object is equal to the sum of the readings on the beams plus the mass of the standard masses.

The Triple-Beam Balance

The triple-beam balance is a single-pan balance with three beams calibrated in grams. The front, or 100-gram, beam is divided into 10 units of 10 grams each. The middle, or 500-gram, beam is divided into 5 units of 100 grams each. The back, or 10-gram, beam is divided into 10 major units of 1 gram each. Each of these units is further divided into units of 1/10 of a gram. What is the largest mass you could find with a triple-beam balance?

The following procedure can be used to find the mass of an object with a triple-beam balance:

1. Place the object on the pan.

2. Move the rider on the middle beam notch by notch until the horizontal pointer drops below zero. Move the rider back one notch.

3. Move the rider on the front beam notch by notch until the pointer again drops below zero. Move the rider back one notch.

4. Slowly slide the rider along the back beam until the pointer stops at the zero point.

5. The mass of the object is equal to the sum of the readings on the three beams.

TRIPLE-BEAM BALANCE

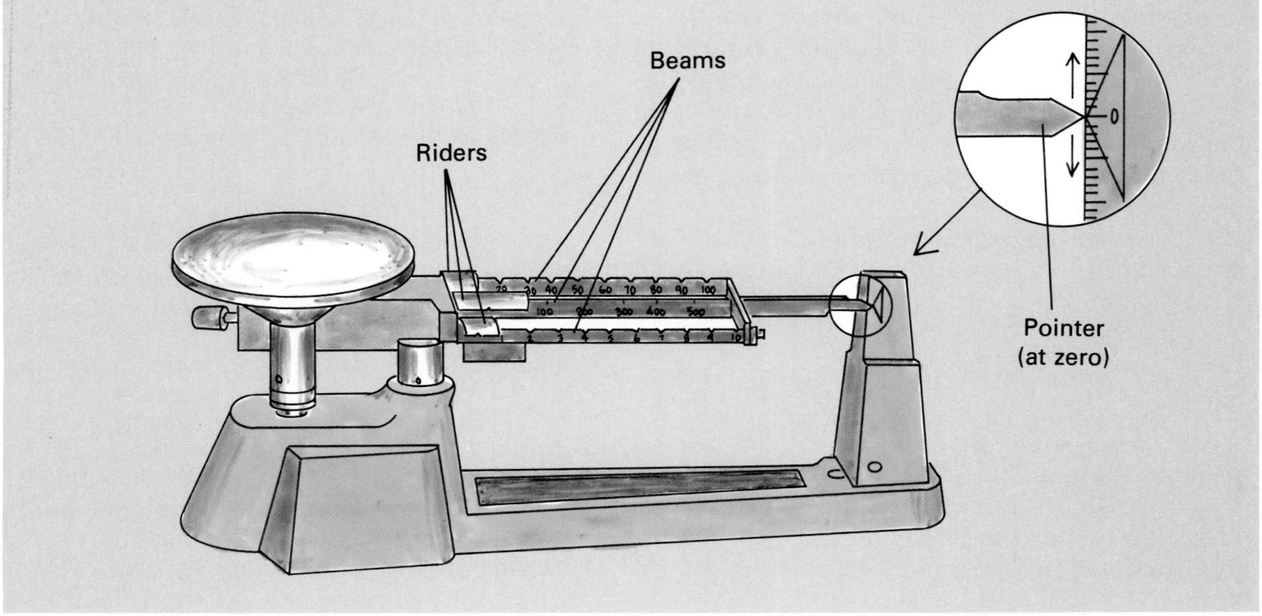

One of the first things a scientist learns is that working in the laboratory can be an exciting experience. But the laboratory can also be quite dangerous if proper safety rules are not followed at all times. To prepare yourself for a safe year in the laboratory, read over the following safety rules. Then read them a second time. Make sure you understand each rule. If you do not, ask your teacher to explain any rules you are unsure of.

Dress Code

1. Many materials in the laboratory can cause eye injury. To protect yourself from possible injury, wear safety goggles whenever you are working with chemicals, burners, or any substance that might get into your eyes. Never wear contact lenses in the laboratory.
2. Wear laboratory aprons or coats whenever you are working with chemicals or heated substances.
3. Tie back long hair to keep your hair away from any chemicals, burners and candles, or other laboratory equipment.
4. Remove or tie back any article of clothing or jewelry that can hang down and touch chemicals and flames before working in the laboratory.

General Safety Rules

5. Read all directions for an experiment several times. Follow the directions exactly as they are written. If you are in doubt about any part of the experiment, ask your teacher for assistance.
6. Never perform activities that are not authorized by your teacher. Obtain permission before "experimenting" on your own.
7. Never handle any equipment unless you have specific permission.
8. Take extreme care not to spill any material in the laboratory. If spills occur, ask your teacher immediately about the proper clean-up procedure. Never simply pour chemicals or other substances into the sink or trash container.
9. Never eat in the laboratory. Wash your hands before and after each experiment.

First Aid

10. Report all accidents, no matter how minor, to your teacher immediately.
11. Learn what to do in case of specific accidents such as getting acid in your eyes or on your skin. (Rinse acids on your body with lots of water.)
12. Become aware of the location of the first-aid kit. But your teacher should administer any required first aid due to injury. Or your teacher may send you to the school nurse or call a physician.
13. Know where and how to report an accident or fire. Find out the location of the fire extinguisher, phone, and fire alarm. Keep a list of important phone numbers such as the fire department and school nurse near the phone. Report any fires to your teacher at once.

Heating and Fire Safety

14. Again, never use a heat source such as a candle or burner without wearing safety goggles.
15. Never heat a chemical you are not instructed to heat. A chemical that is harmless when cool can be dangerous when heated.
16. Maintain a clean work area and keep all materials away from flames.
17. Never reach across a flame.
18. Make sure you know how to light a Bunsen burner. (Your teacher will demonstrate the proper procedure for lighting a burner.) If the flame leaps out of a burner toward you, turn the gas off immediately. Do not touch the burner. It may be hot. And never leave a lighted burner unattended!
19. Point a test tube or bottle that is being heated away from you and others. Chemicals can splash or boil out of a heated test tube.
20. Never heat a liquid in a closed container. The expanding gases produced may blow the container apart, injuring you or others.
21. Never pick up a container that has been heated without first holding the back of your hand near it. If you can feel the heat on the back of your hand, the container may be too hot to handle. Use a clamp or tongs when handling hot containers.

Using Chemicals Safely

22. Never mix chemicals for the "fun of it." You might produce a dangerous, possibly explosive substance.
23. Never touch, taste, or smell a chemical that you do not know for a fact is harmless. Many chemicals are poisonous. If you are instructed to note the fumes in an experiment, gently wave your

hand over the opening of a container and direct the fumes toward your nose. Do not inhale the fumes directly from the container.

24. Use only those chemicals needed in the activity. Keep all lids closed when a chemical is not being used. Notify your teacher whenever chemicals are spilled.

25. Dispose of all chemicals as instructed by your teacher. To avoid contamination, never return chemicals to their original containers.

26. Be extra careful when working with acids or bases. Pour such chemicals over the sink, not over your work bench.

27. When diluting an acid, pour the acid into water. Never pour water into the acid.

28. Rinse any acids off your skin or clothing with water. Immediately notify your teacher of any acid spill.

Using Glassware Safely

29. Never force glass tubing into a rubber stopper. A turning motion and lubricant will be helpful when inserting glass tubing into rubber stoppers or rubber tubing. Your teacher will demonstrate the proper way to insert glass tubing.

30. Never heat glassware that is not thoroughly dry. Use a wire or asbestos screen to protect glassware from any flame.

31. Keep in mind that hot glassware will not appear hot. Never pick up glassware without first checking to see if it is hot.

32. If you are instructed to cut glass tubing, fire-polish the ends immediately to remove sharp edges.

33. Never use broken or chipped glassware. If glassware breaks, notify your teacher and dispose of the glassware in the proper trash container.

34. Never eat or drink from laboratory glassware. Thoroughly clean glassware before putting it away.

Using Sharp Instruments

35. Handle scalpels or razor blades with extreme care. Never cut material toward you; cut away from you.

36. Notify your teacher immediately if you are cut in the laboratory.

End-of-Experiment Rules

37. When an experiment is completed, clean up your work area and return all equipment to its proper place.

38. Wash your hands after every experiment.

39. Turn off all candles and burners before leaving the laboratory. Check that the gas line leading to the burner is off as well.

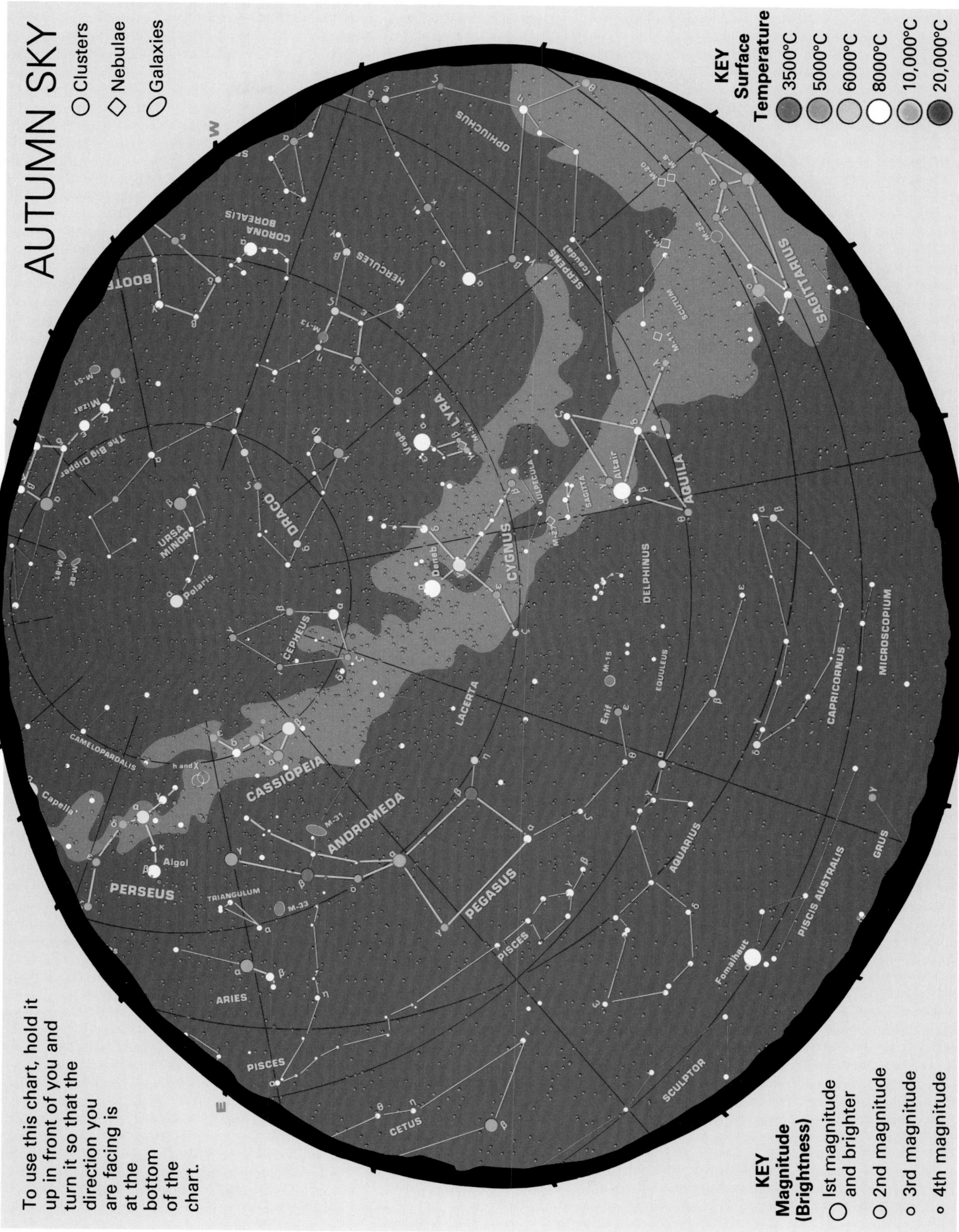

AUTUMN SKY
Clusters
Nebulae
Galaxies
KEY
Surface Temperature
3500°C
5000°C
6000°C
8000°C
10,000°C
20,000°C
To use this chart, hold it up in front of you and turn it so that the direction you are facing is at the bottom of the chart.
KEY
Magnitude (Brightness)
1st magnitude and brighter
2nd magnitude
3rd magnitude
4th magnitude
N
S
E
W
OPHIUCHUS
CORONA BOREALIS
HERCULES
SERPENS (cauda)
SCUTUM
SAGITTARIUS
LYRA
Vega
The Big Dipper
Mizar
M-51
URSA MINOR
Polaris
DRACO
CYGNUS
Deneb
VULPECULA
SAGITTA
Altair
AQUILA
DELPHINUS
CEPHEUS
CAMELOPARDALIS
Capella
CASSIOPEIA
h and χ
LACERTA
M-15
EQUULEUS
Enif
CAPRICORNUS
MICROSCOPIUM
ANDROMEDA
M-31
PERSEUS
Algol
TRIANGULUM
M-33
PEGASUS
AQUARIUS
PISCIS AUSTRALIS
GRUS
Fomalhaut
PISCES
ARIES
SCULPTOR
CETUS
M-8
M-20
M-17
M-22
M-11
M-13
M-27
M-81
M-82

WINTER SKY

○ Clusters

◇ Nebulae

⬭ Galaxies

To use this chart, hold it up infront of you and turn it so that the direction you are facing is at the bottom of the chart.

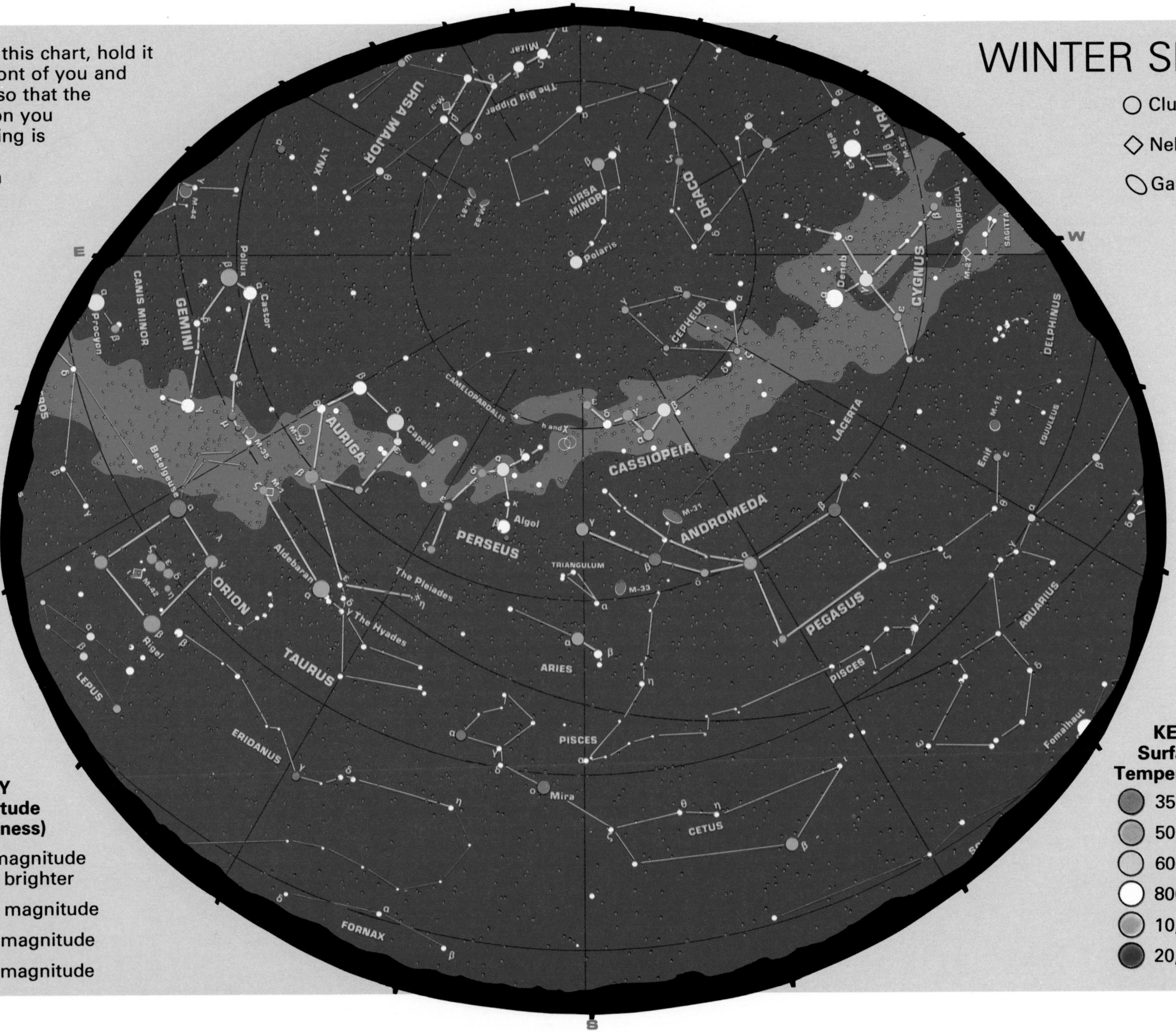

KEY
Magnitude (Brightness)

- Ist magnitude and brighter
- 2nd magnitude
- 3rd magnitude
- 4th magnitude

KEY
Surface Temperature

- 3500°C
- 5000°C
- 6000°C
- 8000°C
- 10,000°C
- 20,000°C

SPRING SKY

To use this chart, hold it up in front of you and turn it so that the direction you are facing is at the bottom of the chart.

○ Clusters

◇ Nebulae

⬯ Galaxies

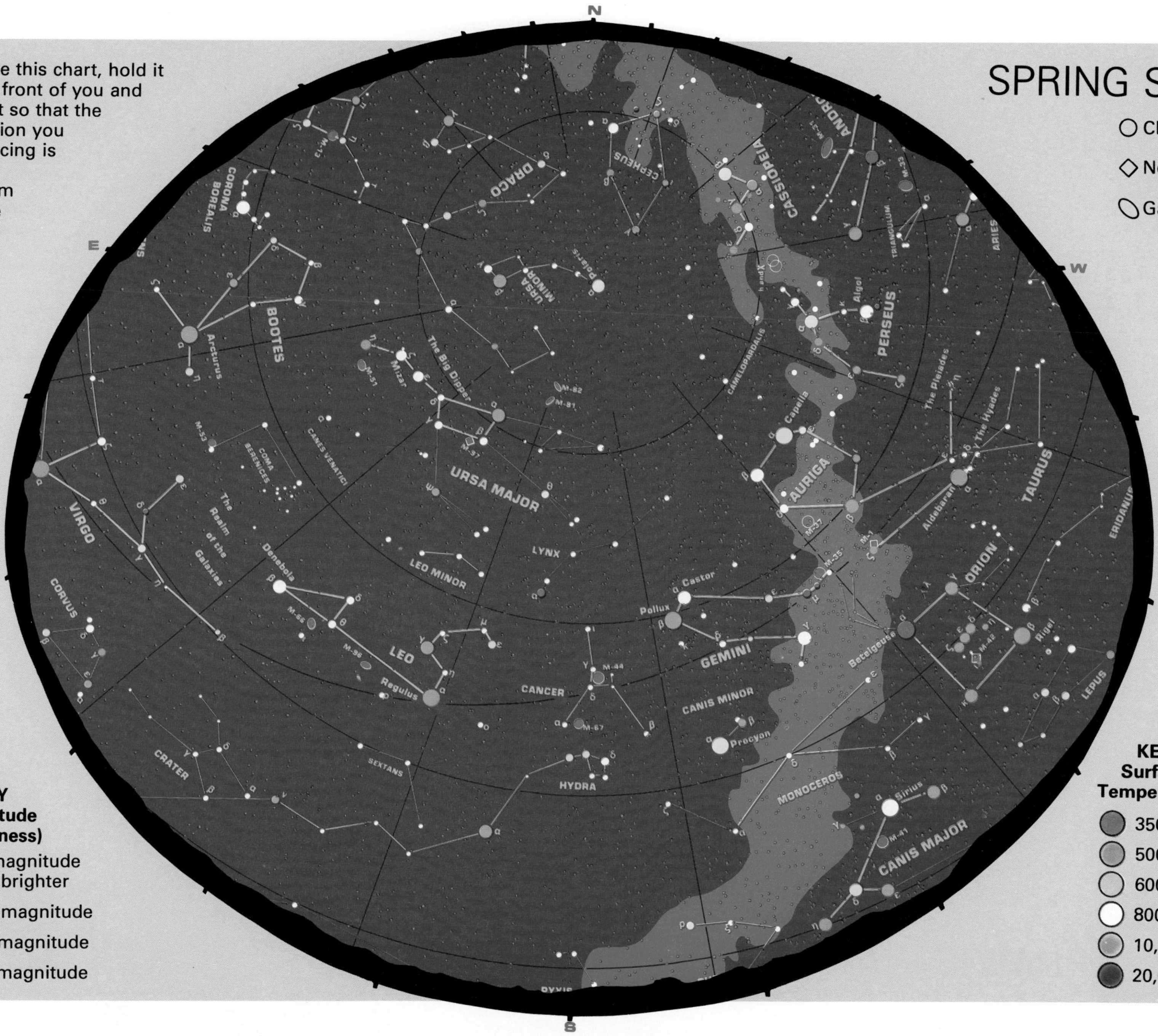

KEY
Magnitude (Brightness)

- Ist magnitude and brighter
- 2nd magnitude
- 3rd magnitude
- 4th magnitude

KEY
Surface Temperature

- 3500°C
- 5000°C
- 6000°C
- 8000°C
- 10,000°C
- 20,000°C

SUMMER SKY

To use this chart, hold it up in front of you and turn it so that the direction you are facing is at the bottom of the chart.

○ Clusters
◇ Nebulae
⬯ Galaxies

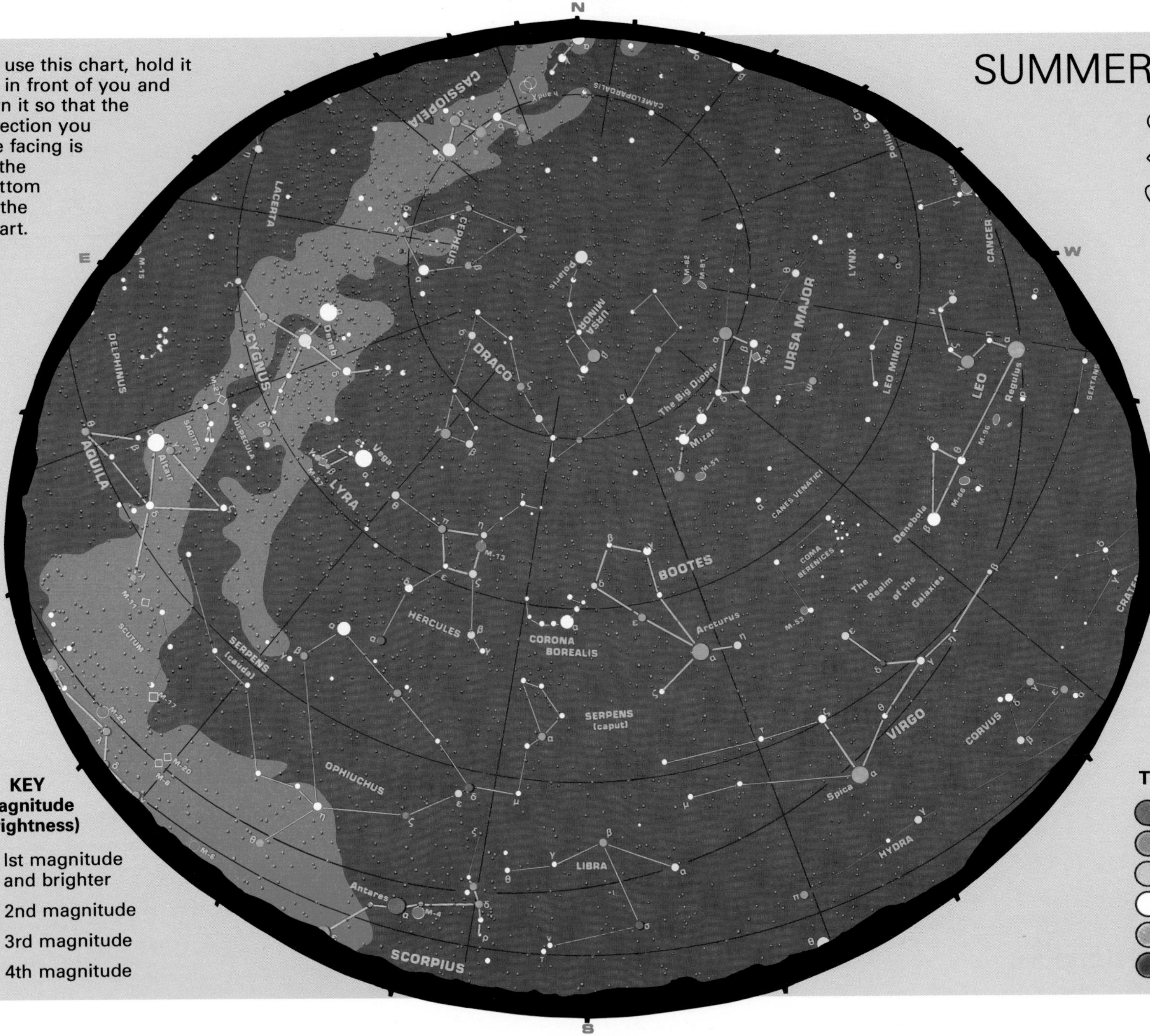

KEY
Magnitude (Brightness)

- ○ Ist magnitude and brighter
- ○ 2nd magnitude
- ∘ 3rd magnitude
- ∘ 4th magnitude

KEY
Surface Temperature

- 3500°C
- 5000°C
- 6000°C
- 8000°C
- 10,000°C
- 20,000°C

GROUP 1

Metallic Luster, Mostly Dark Colored

Hardness	Specific Gravity	Luster/ Color	Streak	Cleavage	Other Properties/ Remarks	Chemical Formula	Mineral
6–6.5	5.02	Metallic; brass, yellow	Greenish, brownish black	Uneven	Harder than chalcopyrite and pyrrhotite; called "fool's gold" but harder than gold	FeS_2	**Pyrite**
5–6	5.18	Metallic; iron black	Black	Partly octahedral	Very magnetic; important iron ore; known as "lodestone"	Fe_3O_4	**Magnetite**
5.5–6.5	5.26	Metallic; reddish brown to black	Light to dark red	Uneven	Most important ore of iron; known as "red ocher"	Fe_2O_3	**Hematite**
4	4.6	Metallic; brownish bronze	Black	Uneven	Less hard than pyrite; slight magnetism	FeS	**Pyrrhotite**
3.5–4	3.9–4.1	Resinous; brown to black	White, yellow, or brown	Dodecahedral	Important zinc ore; known as "ruby zinc"	ZnS	**Sphalerite**
3.5–4	4.1–4.3	Metallic; brass, yellow	Greenish black	Uneven	Ore of copper; softer than pyrite; also known as "fool's gold"	$CuFeS_2$	**Chalcopyrite**
3	5.06–5.08	Metallic; bronze but turns to purple and black	Gray black	Uneven	Important ore of copper; known as "peacock ore" because of purple color when exposed to air for a time	Cu_5FeS_4	**Bornite**
2.5–3	8.5–9	Metallic; copper red to black	Copper red	Fracture	Can be pounded into various shapes and drawn into wires; used in making electrical wires, coins, pipes	Cu	**Copper**
2.5–3	19.3	Metallic; gold	Yellow	Fracture	Does not tarnish; used in jewelry, coins, dental fillings	Au	**Gold**
2.5	10–12	Metallic; silver white tarnishes to black	Silver to light gray	Fracture	Can be pounded into various shapes and drawn into wires; used in jewelry, coins, electrical wire	Ag	**Silver**
2.5	7.4–7.6	Metallic; lead gray	Lead gray	Cubic	Main ore of lead; used in shields against radiation, plumbing	PbS	**Galena**
1–2	2.3	Metallic; black to gray	Black	Basal cleavage (scales)	Feels greasy; very soft; used as pencil "lead" and as a lubricant	C	**Graphite**

GROUP 2
Nonmetallic Luster, Mostly Dark Colored

Hardness	Specific Gravity	Luster/ Color	Streak	Cleavage	Other Properties/ Remarks	Chemical Formula	Mineral
9	4.02	Brilliant to glassy; usually brown	White	Hexagonal	Very hard; used as an abrasive; as gems, called "ruby" (red), "sapphire" (blue)	Al_2O_3	**Corundum**
6.5–7.5	3.5–4.3	Glassy to resinous; red-brown	White, light brown	Dodecahedral	Mainly used in jewelry and as an abrasive	$Mg_3Al_2Si_3O_{12}$	**Garnet**
6.5–7	3.27–3.37	Glassy; olive green	White	Imperfect	Found in volcanic rocks; sometimes used as a gem	Mg_2SiO_4	**Olivine**
5–6	3.2–3.4	Glassy; dark green to black	Greenish gray	Perfect prism	Found in volcanic rocks	$Ca\ (Mg, Fe)(SiO_3)_2(Al, Fe)_2O_3$	**Augite**
5–6	3.2	Glassy, silky; dark green, brown, black	Gray to white	Long prism	Found in igneous and metamorphic rocks	Complex substance containing Fe, Mg, Si, O, and other elements	**Hornblende**
5	3.15–3.2	Glassy; green, brown, red	White	Hexagonal	Sometimes used as a gem	$Ca_5(PO_4)_3F$	**Apatite**
3.5–4	3.77	Glassy to dull; intense blue	Pale blue	Fibrous	Ore of copper; used as a gem	$Cu_3(Co_3)_2(OH)_2$	**Azurite**
2.5–3	2.8–3.2	Pearly glassy; black, brown, dark green	White to light brown	Thin sheets	One of the micas; sometimes used as a lubricant	Complex substance containing Fe, Mg, Si, O, and other elements	**Biotite**
2.5	2.2–2.65	Greasy, waxy, silky; green	White	Parallel fibers	Once used in insulation but found to be cancer causing; used in fireproofing; is a form of "asbestos"	$Mg_3Si_2O_5(OH)_4$	**Serpentine**
1–5.5	3.6–4	Glassy; dark brown to black	Yellow-brown	Varies	Ore of iron; also known as "yellow ocher," a pigment; a mixture, which is not strictly a mineral	Mixture of hydrous iron oxides	**Limonite**
1–3	2–3	Dull to earthy; brown, yellow, grey, white	Colorless to gray	Uneven fracture	Ore of aluminum; smells like clay when wet; a mixture, which is not strictly a mineral	Mixture of hydrous aluminum oxides	**Bauxite**

GROUP 3
Nonmetallic Luster, Mostly Light Colored

Hardness	Specific Gravity	Luster/ Color	Streak	Cleavage	Other Properties/ Remarks	Chemical Formula	Mineral
10	3.5	Brilliant, greasy; colorless, pale yellow, red, orange, green, blue, black	Colorless	Octahedral	Hardest known substance; used in jewelry, as an abrasive, in cutting instruments	C	**Diamond**
8	3.4–3.6	Glassy; straw yellow, pink, bluish, greenish	Colorless or white	Prismatic	Valuable gem	$Al_2SiO_4(F,OH)_2$	**Topaz**
7.5–8	2.65	Glassy, greasy; colorless, white, any color when not pure	Colorless, white	Hexagonal	Many varieties are gems (amethyst, cat's-eye, bloodstone, agate, jasper, onyx); used in making glass	SiO_2	**Quartz**
6	2.55–2.75	Glassy; colorless, white, various colors	Colorless, white	In two planes at or near 90°	Most common mineral found in igneous rocks	$(K,Na,Ca)\ (AlSi_3O_8)$	**Feldspar**
4	3.18	Glassy; light green, yellow, bluish green, other colors	Colorless	Octahedral	Some types fluoresce (glow when exposed to ultraviolet light); used in making steel	CaF_2	**Fluorite**
3.5–4	2.85	Glassy or pearly; pink, white, gray, green, brown, black	Colorless	Conchoidal fracture	Used in making concrete and cement, type of limestone	$CaMg(CO_3)_2$	**Dolomite**
1.5–2.5	2.07	Resinous; yellow	White	Conchoidal fracture	Used in making many medicines, in producing of sulfuric acid, and in vulcanizing rubber	S	**Sulfur**
1	2.7–2.8	Pearly to greasy; gray, white, greenish	White	Uneven fracture	Very soft; used in talcum powder; found mostly in metamorphic rocks; also called "soapstone"	$Mg_3(OH)_2Si_4O_{10}$	**Talc**

Boundaries

- National
- State or territorial
- County or equivalent
- Civil township or equivalent
- Incorporated-city or equivalent
- Park, reservation, or monument
- Small park

Roads and related features

- Primary highway
- Secondary highway
- Light duty road
- Unimproved road
- Trail
- Dual highway
- Dual highway with median strip
- Bridge
- Tunnel

Buildings and related features

- Dwelling or place of employment: small; large
- School; church
- Barn, warehouse, etc.: small; large
- Airport
- Campground; picnic area
- Cemetery: small; large

Railroads and related features

- Standard gauge single track; station
- Standard gauge multiple track

Contours

- Intermediate
- Index
- Supplementary
- Depression
- Cut; fill

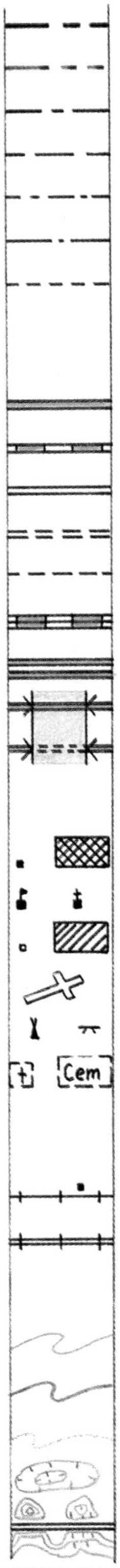

Surface features

- Levee
- Sand or mud areas, dunes, or shifting sand
- Gravel beach or glacial moraine

Vegetation

- Woods
- Scrub
- Orchard
- Vineyard

Marine shoreline

- Approximate mean high water
- Indefinite or unsurveyed

Coastal features

- Foreshore flat
- Rock or coral reef
- Rock bare or awash
- Breakwater, pier, jetty, or wharf
- Seawall

Rivers, lakes, and canals

- Perennial stream
- Perennial river
- Small falls; small rapids
- Large falls; large rapids
- Dry lake
- Narrow wash
- Wide wash
- Water well; spring or seep

Submerged areas and bogs

- Marsh or swamp
- Submerged marsh or swamp
- Wooded marsh or swamp
- Land subject to inundation

Elevations

- Spot and elevation

Appendix G

Weather Map Symbols

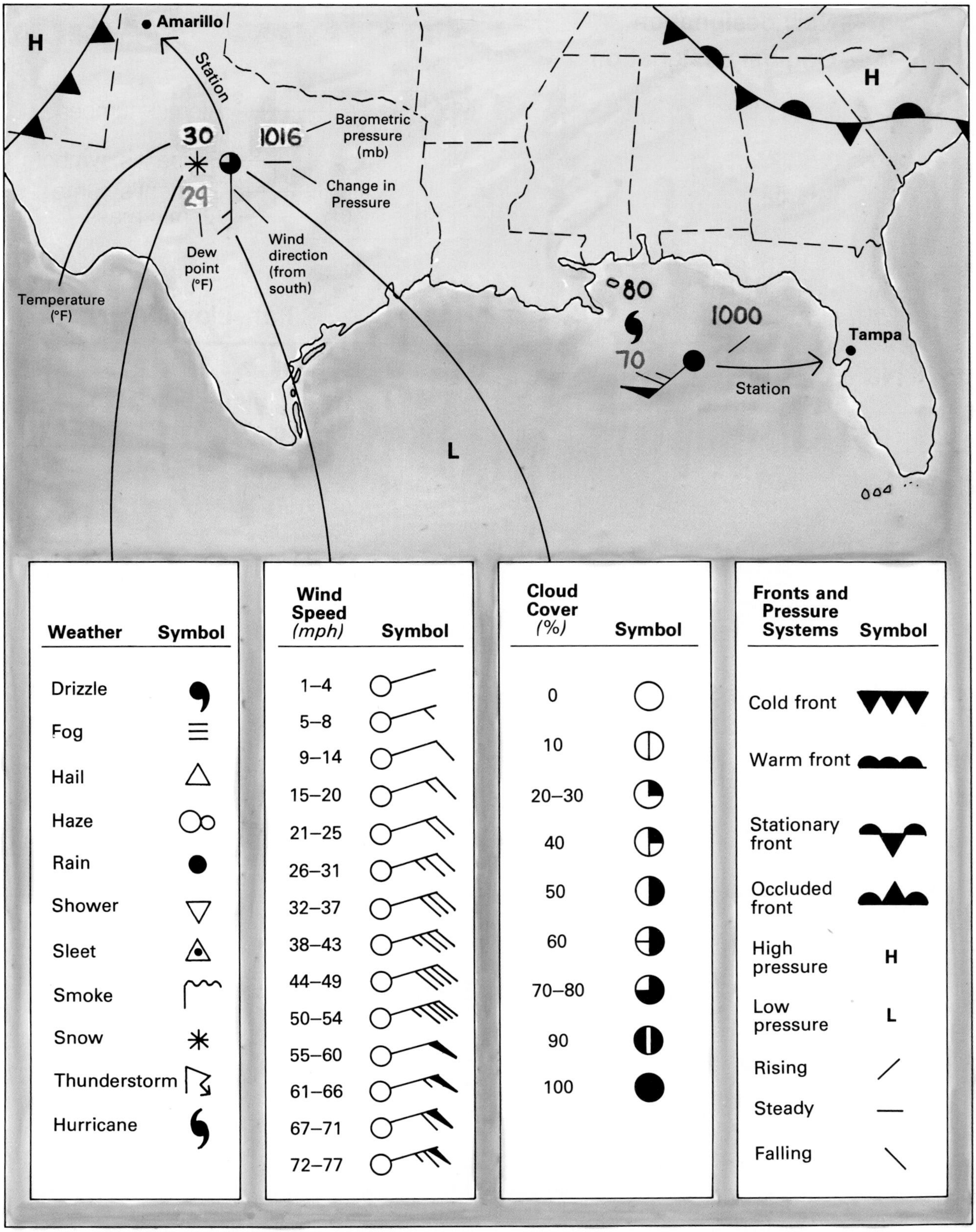

Appendix H

PERIODIC TABLE

1 —**New designation**
IA —**Original designation**

Key

6	Atomic number
C	Element's symbol
Carbon	Element's name
12.011	Atomic mass

Transition Metals (groups 3–9)

Period	1 IA	2 IIA	3 IIIB	4 IVB	5 VB	6 VIB	7 VIIB	8 VIIIB	9 VIIIB
1	1 **H** Hydrogen 1.00794								
2	3 **Li** Lithium 6.941	4 **Be** Beryllium 9.0122							
3	11 **Na** Sodium 22.990	12 **Mg** Magnesium 24.305							
4	19 **K** Potassium 39.098	20 **Ca** Calcium 40.08	21 **Sc** Scandium 44.956	22 **Ti** Titanium 47.88	23 **V** Vanadium 50.94	24 **Cr** Chromium 51.996	25 **Mn** Manganese 54.938	26 **Fe** Iron 55.847	27 **Co** Cobalt 58.9332
5	37 **Rb** Rubidium 85.468	38 **Sr** Strontium 87.62	39 **Y** Yttrium 88.9059	40 **Zr** Zirconium 91.224	41 **Nb** Niobium 92.91	42 **Mo** Molybdenum 95.94	43 **Tc** Technetium (98)	44 **Ru** Ruthenium 101.07	45 **Rh** Rhodium 102.906
6	55 **Cs** Cesium 132.91	56 **Ba** Barium 137.33	**57 to 71**	72 **Hf** Hafnium 178.49	73 **Ta** Tantalum 180.95	74 **W** Tungsten 183.85	75 **Re** Rhenium 186.207	76 **Os** Osmium 190.2	77 **Ir** Iridium 192.22
7	87 **Fr** Francium (223)	88 **Ra** Radium 226.025	**89 to 103**	104 **Unq** Unnilquadium (261)	105 **Unp** Unnilpentium (262)	106 **Unh** Unnilhexium (263)	107 **Uns** Unnilseptium (262)	108 **Uno** Unniloctium (265)	109 **Une** Unnilennium (266)

The new Group designations are those assigned by IUPAC in 1984.

Rare-Earth Elements

Series						
Lanthanoid Series	57 **La** Lanthanum 138.906	58 **Ce** Cerium 140.12	59 **Pr** Praseodymium 140.908	60 **Nd** Neodymium 144.24	61 **Pm** Promethium (145)	62 **Sm** Samarium 150.36
Actinoid Series	89 **Ac** Actinium 227.028	90 **Th** Thorium 232.038	91 **Pa** Protactinium 231.036	92 **U** Uranium 238.029	93 **Np** Neptunium 237.048	94 **Pu** Plutonium (244)

OF THE ELEMENTS

C	Solid
Br	Liquid
H	Gas

Nonmetals

10	11 IB	12 IIB	13 IIIA	14 IVA	15 VA	16 VIA	17 VIIA	18 VIIIA
								2 **He** Helium 4.003
			5 **B** Boron 10.81	6 **C** Carbon 12.011	7 **N** Nitrogen 14.007	8 **O** Oxygen 15.999	9 **F** Fluorine 18.998	10 **Ne** Neon 20.179
			13 **Al** Aluminum 26.98	14 **Si** Silicon 28.086	15 **P** Phosphorus 30.974	16 **S** Sulfur 32.06	17 **Cl** Chlorine 35.453	18 **Ar** Argon 39.948
28 **Ni** Nickel 58.69	29 **Cu** Copper 63.546	30 **Zn** Zinc 65.39	31 **Ga** Gallium 69.72	32 **Ge** Germanium 72.59	33 **As** Arsenic 74.922	34 **Se** Selenium 78.96	35 **Br** Bromine 79.904	36 **Kr** Krypton 83.80
46 **Pd** Palladium 106.42	47 **Ag** Silver 107.868	48 **Cd** Cadmium 112.41	49 **In** Indium 114.82	50 **Sn** Tin 118.71	51 **Sb** Antimony 121.75	52 **Te** Tellurium 127.60	53 **I** Iodine 126.905	54 **Xe** Xenon 131.29
78 **Pt** Platinum 195.08	79 **Au** Gold 196.967	80 **Hg** Mercury 200.59	81 **Tl** Thallium 204.383	82 **Pb** Lead 207.2	83 **Bi** Bismuth 208.98	84 **Po** Polonium (209)	85 **At** Astatine (210)	86 **Rn** Radon (222)

The symbols shown here for elements 104-109 are being used temporarily until names for these elements can be agreed upon.

Metals

Mass numbers in parentheses are those of the most stable or common isotope.

63 **Eu** Europium 151.96	64 **Gd** Gadolinium 157.25	65 **Tb** Terbium 158.925	66 **Dy** Dysprosium 162.50	67 **Ho** Holmium 164.93	68 **Er** Erbium 167.26	69 **Tm** Thulium 168.934	70 **Yb** Ytterbium 173.04	71 **Lu** Lutetium 174.967
95 **Am** Americium (243)	96 **Cm** Curium (247)	97 **Bk** Berkelium (247)	98 **Cf** Californium (251)	99 **Es** Einsteinium (252)	100 **Fm** Fermium (257)	101 **Md** Mendelevium (258)	102 **No** Nobelium (259)	103 **Lr** Lawrencium (260)

Glossary

Pronunciation Key

When difficult names or terms first appear in the text, they are respelled to aid pronunciation. A syllable in SMALL CAPITAL LETTERS receives the most stress. The key below lists the letters used for respelling. It includes examples of words using each sound and shows how the words would be respelled.

Symbol	Example	Respelling
a	hat	(hat)
ay	pay, late	(pay), (layt)
ah	star, hot	(stahr), (haht)
ai	air, dare	(air), (dair)
aw	law, all	(law), (awl)
eh	met	(meht)
ee	bee, eat	(bee), (eet)
er	learn, sir, fir	(lern), (ser), (fer)
ih	fit	(fiht)
igh	mile, sigh	(mighl), (sigh)
ir	ear	(ir)
oh	no	(noh)
oi	soil, boy	(soil), (boi)
oo	root, rule	(root), (rool)
or	born, door	(born), (dor)
ow	plow, out	(plow), (owt)

Symbol	Example	Respelling
u	put, book	(put), (buk)
uh	fun	(fuhn)
yoo	few, use	(fyoo), (yooz)
ch	chill, reach	(chihl), (reech)
g	go, dig	(goh), (dihg)
j	jet, gently, bridge	(jeht), (JEHNT lee), (brihj)
k	kite, cup	(kight), (kuhp)
ks	mix	(mihks)
kw	quick	(kwihk)
ng	bring	(brihng)
s	say, cent	(say), (sehnt)
sh	she, crash	(shee), (krash)
th	three	(three)
y	yet, onion	(yeht), (UHN yuhn)
z	zip, always	(zihp), (AWL wayz)
zh	treasure	(TREH zher)

abrasion (uh-BRAY-zhuhn): wearing away of rocks by solid particles carried by wind, water, or other forces

absolute age: measure of how many years ago an event occurred or an organism lived

absolute magnitude: actual amount of light a star gives off

abyssal (uh-BIHS-uhl) **plain:** large, flat area on the ocean floor

abyssal zone: open-ocean zone that extends from about 2000 meters down to about 6000 meters

acid rain: rain containing nitric acid and sulfuric acid droplets

air mass: large body of air that has the same temperature and humidity throughout

air pressure: pressure exerted on the earth by gravity pulling the air toward the earth's surface

alluvial fan: sediments spread out from a river channel in a fanlike shape

amber: hardened resin from evergreen trees

ammonia: poisonous gas made of nitrogen and hydrogen

amphibian (am-FIHB-ee-uhn): animal that lives part of its life in water and part on land

anthracite (AN-thruh-sight): hard, brittle coal that is almost pure carbon

anticline (AN-tih-klighn): upward fold in a rock

anticyclone: high-pressure area containing cold, dry air

apogee (AP-uh-jee): point of the moon's orbit farthest from the earth

apparent magnitude: measure of a star's brightness as it appears from the earth

aquaculture: commercial raising of ocean plants and animals

aquifer (AK-wuh-fuhr): layer of rock or sediment that allows water to pass through easily

artesian (ahr-TEE-zhuhn) **well:** well from which water flows on its own without pumping

asteroid: small clumps of matter floating in space

asteroid belt: region of space between Mars and Jupiter where asteroids are found
astronomy (uh-STRAHN-uh-mee): study of the position, composition, size, and other characteristics of the planets, stars, and other objects in space
atmosphere (AT-muhs-fir): envelope of gases surrounding the earth
atoll: ring of coral reefs that surrounds an island that has sunk beneath the waves
atom: basic building block of matter
atomic number: number of protons in the nucleus of an atom of a substance
autumnal equinox: first day of autumn
axis: imaginary vertical line through the center of a body around which the body rotates or spins

background radiation: energy left from the big bang that is spread evenly throughout the universe
barometer: instrument that measures air pressure
barrier reef: type of coral reef that is separated from the shore by a lagoon
batholith (BATH-uh-lihth): huge, irregularly shaped intrusion that extends deep into the earth's crust
bathyal (BATH-ee-uhl) **zone:** open-ocean zone that extends from a continental slope down about 2000 meters
bathyscaph (BATH-uh-skaf): self-propelled submarine observatory
bathysphere (BATH-uh-sfir): small, sphere-shaped diving vessel used for underwater research
bedrock: the layer of rock beneath the soil
benthos (BEHN-thahs): organisms that live only on the ocean floor
big bang theory: theory that states that the universe was formed by the explosion of very dense and hot matter compacted into a small area
binary star: pair of stars that revolve around each other
bituminous (bigh-TOO-muh-nuhs): dark brown or black coal found deep within the earth; called soft coal
black hole: core of a supermassive star after a supernova
blue shift: shift toward the blue end of the spectrum of a star moving toward the earth
brachiopod (BRAYK-ee-uh-pahd): clamlike marine animal that lived during the Paleozoic Era
brittle: easily broken

caldera: very large crater resulting from the collapse of its walls
carbonation: process in which carbonic acid reacts chemically with another substance
cast: fossil in which the space left in a rock by a dissolved organism has filled, showing its outward shape
cavern (KAV-uhrn): cave
Celsius (SEHL-see-uhs): temperature scale in which there are 100 degrees between freezing and boiling temperatures of water
cementation (see-mehn-TAY-shuhn): process by which sediments are cemented together by minerals dissolved in water to form sedimentary rock
Cenozoic (see-nuh-ZOH-ihk) **Era:** current period of geologic time that began about 65 million years ago
cepheid (SEHF-ee-ihd) **variable:** pulsating variable star; star that varies in brightness and size
chemical change: change in a substance that produces a new substance with new and different properties
chemical property: property of matter that describes how a substance changes into a new substance
chemical weathering: weathering process in which the chemical makeup of the rocks is changed
chromosphere (KROH-muh-sfir): middle layer of the sun's atmosphere
cinder: small volcanic bomb about the size of a golf ball
cinder cone: volcano made mostly of cinders and other rock particles that have been blown into the air
cirrus cloud: feathery, fibrous cloud that forms at a very high altitude
cleavage: breaking of a mineral along smooth, definite surfaces
climate: the general conditions of temperature and precipitation for an area
coastal plain: low, flat area along the coast
cold front: type of front that forms when a mass of cold air meets and replaces a mass of warm air
coma: cloud of dust and gas surrounding the nucleus of a comet
comet: object made of ice, dust, and gas that travels through space
communications satellite: artificial satellite that beams television programs, radio messages, telephone conversations, and other information all over the world
compaction (kuhm-PAK-shuhn): process by which layers of sediments are pressed together to form sedimentary rocks
composite volcano: volcano built up of alternating layers of rock particles and lava
compound: any combination of two or more different kinds of atoms
compression: type of stress that squeezes rocks together
condensation (kahn-duhn-SAY-shuhn): process by which vapor changes back into a liquid
conduction: direct transfer of heat from one substance to another

conifer (KAHN-uh-fuhr): cone-bearing plant, such as pine, cedar, spruce, or cypress

conservation: wise use of natural resources so that they will not be used up too soon or used in a way that will damage the environment

constellation (kahn-stuh-LAY-shuhn): group of stars that form a pattern

constructive boundary: type of plate boundary where new material is added to the plates

contact metamorphism: type of metamorphism that occurs when rocks are heated by contact with magma or lava

continent: large land area that measures millions of square kilometers and rises a considerable distance above sea level

continental climate: climate found in areas located within a large landmass

continental crust: section of the earth's crust that makes up the earth's landmasses

continental glacier: polar ice sheets that cover millions of square kilometers of the earth's surface

continental margin: area where the underwater edge of a continent meets the ocean floor

continental polar: cold, dry air mass that forms over northern Canada

continental rise: area that separates a continental slope from the ocean floor

continental shelf: relatively flat part of a continental margin covered by shallow ocean water

continental slope: part of a continental margin where the ocean floor plunges steeply 4 to 5 kilometers to the ocean floor

continental tropical: dry, hot air mass that forms over Mexico in the summer

contour farming: plowing land across the face of a slope to prevent soil erosion

contour interval: difference in elevation from one contour line to the next

contour line: line that passes through all points on a map that have the same elevation

control: experiment done in exactly the same way as another experiment but without the variable

convection (kuhn-VEHK-shuhn): transfer of heat in a fluid

convection current: movement of a fluid caused by the unequal heating of the fluid

convergent (kuhn-VER-juhnt) **boundary:** type of plate boundary where the plates come together, such as a trench

coral reef: limestone structure built from the shells of animals that surrounds an island

core: center of the sun

Coriolis effect: apparent shift in the path of any fluid or object moving above the surface of the earth due to the rotation of the earth

corona (kuh-ROH-nuh): outermost layer of the sun's atmosphere

crater: funnel-shaped pit at the top of a volcanic core

crest: highest point of a wave

crevasse (krih-VAS): crack on the surface of a glacier

crop rotation: method of farming in which alternate crops are grown on the same land each year

crude oil: fossil fuel made of a mixture of many hydrocarbons that must be refined before it can be used

crust: thin outermost layer of the earth

crystal: solid formed from a repeating pattern of atoms

cumulonimbus cloud: large cloud that produces thunderstorms

cumulus cloud: puffy cloud with a flat bottom that forms at an altitude of 2.4 to 13.5 kilometers

cycad (SIGH-kad): palmlike seed plant that lived during the Triassic and Jurassic periods

cyclone: area of low pressure containing rising warm air

data: recorded observations and measurements

decay: breakdown of dead organisms into the substances from which they were made

decay element: stable element into which a radioactive element breaks down

decomposition (dee-kahm-puh-ZIHSH-uhn): process in which minerals in a rock are broken down into other substances

deep current: ocean current caused mainly by differences in water density deep beneath the ocean surface

deep zone: area of very cold water that extends from the bottom of the thermocline to depths of 4000 meters or more

deformation: breaking, bending, tilting, and folding of rocks

delta: large amounts of sediments deposited at the mouth of a large river that flows into a lake or an ocean

density: amount of matter in a given amount of a substance, or mass per unit volume

deposition (dehp-uh-ZIHSH-uhn): process by which sediments are laid down in new locations

desalination (dee-sal-uh-NAY-shuhn): process by which salt is removed from water

desert climate: climate that receives the lowest amount of precipitation of any climate region in the United States

desert soil: soil found in dry regions that contains a large quantity of minerals

destructive boundary: type of plate boundary where plate material is subducted

dew point: temperature at which water vapor condenses

dike: narrow, flat formation of igneous rock formed in vertical cracks in the existing rocks

divergent (digh-VER-juhnt) **boundary:** type of plate boundary where the plates move apart, such as a midocean ridge

dome: raised area shaped roughly like the top half of a sphere created by rising magma

dome mountain: dome that has been worn away in places to form many separate peaks

Doppler effect: apparent change in the wavelengths of light that occurs when an object is moving toward or away from the earth

drainage basin: area drained by a main river and its channels

drainage system: network of rills, gullies, and streams that forms a river

drumlin: oval-shaped mound of till

ductile: easily bent

ductility (duhk-TIHL-uh-tee): ability of a substance to be pulled into thin strands without breaking

eclipse (ee-KLIHPS): total or partial blocking out of the sun or moon

eclipsing binary: binary star system in which one star blocks out the light from the companion star

electron: negatively charged subatomic particle

electron cloud: space in an atom in which electrons are likely to be found

element: substance that cannot be separated into simpler substances by ordinary chemical means

elevation: height above sea level

elliptical (ih-LIHP-tih-kuhl) **galaxy:** type of galaxy that can vary in shape from nearly spherical to a flat disk

elliptical orbit: oval or egg-shaped orbit

El Niño: a warm water current that flows from west to east across the Pacific Ocean near the equator and down the west coast of South America; strikes with little warning every two to seven years and brings with it dramatic changes in world climate

energy level: most likely place within an electron cloud in which an electron can be found

epicenter (EHP-uh-sehn-tuhr): point directly above the focus of an earthquake on the earth's surface

epoch (EHP-uhk): division of geologic time that is smaller than a period

equal-area projection: representation of the curved surface of the earth on a flat piece of paper, in which distance is accurate and size and shape are distorted

equator: imaginary line around the earth that divides the earth into hemispheres; parallel halfway between the North and South poles

equinox (EE-kwuh-naks): date on which day and night are of equal length

era: largest division of geologic time

erosion (ih-ROH-zhuhn): process by which weathered rock and soil particles are moved from one place to another

evaporation (ih-vap-uh-RAY-shuhn): process in which the heat energy of the sun causes the water on the earth's surface to change into a vapor

evaporite (ih-VAP-uh-right): sedimentary rock formed when water evaporates and leaves behind mineral deposits

exfoliation (ehks-fohl-lee-AY-shuhn): breaking off of pieces of rocks that are parallel to the rock's surface

exosphere (EHK-suh-sfir): upper thermosphere

extinct: no longer in existence

extrusion (ihk-STROO-zhuhn): igneous rock formation that forms on the earth's surface

extrusive (ihk-STROOS-ihv) **rock:** igneous rock formed from lava at the earth's surface

fault: break or crack along which rocks move

fault-block mountain: mountain formed by a block of rock uplifted by a normal fault

flood plain: flat area on both sides of a mature river or stream where the river overflows its banks

focus (FOH-kuhs): point beneath the earth's surface where the rocks break and move during an earthquake

fold: bend in a rock

foliated (FOH-lee-ay-tuhd): texture of some metamorphic rocks in which mineral crystals are arranged in parallel bands along which the rocks tend to break

foot wall: block of rock below a fault

forest soil: soil that forms under a cover of leaves and other plant remains and contains very little humus

fossil: remains or evidence of a living thing

fossil fuel: product of decayed plants and animals that is preserved in the earth

fracture: breaking of a mineral along rough, jagged surface

fringing reef: type of coral reef that touches the shoreline of a volcanic island

front: boundary between air masses

frost action: mechanical weathering process caused by the repeated freezing and melting of water

full moon: phase of the moon when the entire lighted side of the moon is visible

galaxy: huge collection of stars

gas: phase of matter that has neither a definite shape nor a definite volume

gem: mineral that is rare, beautiful, and durable

geologic time: very long period of time the earth has existed

geology (jee-AHL-uh-jee): study of the earth's origin, history, and structure

geosynchronous orbit: orbit in which a satellite moves at a speed that exactly matches the earth's rate of rotation
geothermal energy: heat created within the earth
giant star: star with a diameter 10 to 100 times that of the sun
glacier (GLAY-shuhr): large mass of moving ice and snow
globe: spherical model of the earth
globular (GLAHB-yuh-luhr) **cluster:** group of stars in a spherical shape
Glossopteris (glahs-AHP-tuh-ruhs): extinct seed fern that grew about 250 million years ago
grassland soil: very rich, fertile soil that is excellent for growing crops
gravity: force of attraction between objects
greenhouse effect: heat-trapping process, in which heat energy is trapped by the earth's atmosphere and cannot return to space
groundwater: water that remains in the ground
guyot (gee-OH): flat-topped seamount

half-life: amount of time it takes for one-half of the atoms of a sample of a radioactive element to decay
hanging wall: block or rock above a fault
hardness: ability of a mineral to resist being scratched
hard water: water containing large amounts of dissolved minerals
hemisphere: northern or southern half of the earth
Hertzsprung-Russell (H-R) diagram: chart of the relationship between the absolute magnitude and the surface temperature of stars
highlands: mountains of the moon
high tide: bulge in the ocean on the side of the earth facing the moon and on the opposite side
horizon (huh-RIGH-zuhn): soil layer
humus (HYOO-muhs): dark-colored organic material in the soil
hydrocarbon: compound formed from hydrogen and carbon
hydrosphere: part of the earth's surface covered by water
hypothesis: proposed solution to a scientific problem

ice age: periods throughout history when much of the earth's surface has been covered with enormous sheets of ice
iceberg: large chunk of ice that falls off a continental glacier and drifts into the ocean
igneous (IHG-nee-uhs) **rock:** rock formed by the cooling and hardening of hot liquid rock
immature river: river in an early stage of development
impermeable: unable to be passed through by a substance
imprint: fossil formed when a thin object leaves an impression in soft mud, which hardens
index fossil: fossil of an organism that lived for only a short period of time that scientists use to determine the relative age of a rock
inner core: solid, innermost layer of the earth
inorganic: composed of material that is not and was never living
interglacial (ihn-ter-GLAY-shuhl): time between ice ages
interior plain: low, flat area found inland on a continent
international date line: imaginary line located along the 180th meridian at which the date is adjusted, being one day later west of the line than east of it; the starting point for a day on the earth
intertidal zone: area between the low- and high-tide lines
intrusion: irregular formation of intrusive rock formed by magma beneath the earth's crust
intrusive (ihn-TROO-sihv) **rock:** igneous rock formed deep within the earth
invertebrate (ihn-VER-tuh-brayt): animal without a backbone
ion: electrically charged atom that has either lost or gained electrons
ionosphere (igh-AHN-uh-sfir): lower thermosphere, which extends from an altitude of 80 kilometers to 550 kilometers
irregular galaxy: type of galaxy with no definite shape
irrigation (ir-uh-GAY-shuhn): process of supplying land with water through artificial canals or sprinkler systems
island: small landmass completely surrounded by water
island arc: string of underwater volcanoes that has risen above the ocean's surface in a curved line
isobar (IGH-suh-bahr): line on a weather map connecting locations that have the same barometric pressure
isostasy (igh-SAHS-tuh-see): balance between the downward force of the crust and the upward force of the mantle
isotherm (IGH-suh-therm): line on a weather map connecting locations that have the same temperature
isotope (IGH-suh-tohp): atom of a substance with the same number of protons but a different number of neutrons as another atom of the same substance

jet stream: very strong eastward winds that blow horizontally around the earth in the lower stratosphere

joint: crack in the crustal rock

kettle lake: lake formed when a large block of glacial ice melted, leaving a depression in the ground

kilogram: basic unit of mass in the metric system

laccolith (LAK-uh-lihth): domelike intrusion that pushes overlying rocks into an arch and has a flat floor

land breeze: flow of air from the land to the sea

landscape: physical features of the earth's surface found in an area

landslide: large downhill movement of loose rocks and soil caused by gravity

lateral fault: fault along which the blocks of rock move horizontally past one another

latitude: measure of distance north or south of the equator

lava: magma that reaches the earth's surface

lava plateau (pla-TOH): layers of lava that build up on a flat area on the earth's surface

law: generalization that describes behavior in nature

law of inertia: Newton's law that states that an object's motion will not change unless that object is acted on by an outside force

law of superposition: law that states that in undisturbed sedimentary rocks each layer is older than the one above it and younger than the one below it

leaching (LEECH-ihng): process in which water washes minerals from the A horizon into the B horizon

leeward side: the side of a mountain that faces away from the wind

legend: key that explains what symbols on a map represent

levee (LEHV-ee): ridgelike deposit of sediments on a flood plain

light-year: distance light travels in one year

lignite (LIHG-night): soft, brown coal with a woody texture

liquid: state of matter that has a definite volume but not a definite shape

liter: basic unit of volume in the metric system

lithosphere (LIHTH-uh-sfir): topmost solid part of the earth

litter: discarded materials

load: soil particles and rock materials carried by a stream

loess (LOH-ehs): many layers of fine sand and silt deposited by wind in an area

longitude: measure of the distance east or west of the prime meridian

longshore current: movement of water parallel to a shoreline

low tide: lowest level of the ocean that occurs between the two high tides

lunar: referring to the moon

lunar eclipse: blocking out of the moon when the moon passes through the earth's shadow

luster: way a mineral reflects light from its surface

L wave: surface wave

magma: hot liquid rock beneath the earth's surface

magnetosphere (mag-NEET-uh-sfir): magnetic field of the earth

magnitude (MAG-nuh-tood): measure of a star's brightness

main-sequence star: star located in an area that runs from the upper left corner to the lower right corner of the Hertzsprung-Russell diagram

major glaciation: major ice age

malleability (mal-ee-uh-BIHL-uh-tee): ability of a substance to be hammered into thin sheets without breaking

mantle: layer of the earth that extends from the bottom of the crust to the earth's core

map: drawing of the earth or part of the earth on a flat surface

maria (MAR-ee-uh): dark, broad, smooth lowland area on the moon

marine climate: climate in areas near an ocean having more precipitation and more moderate temperatures than inland areas

marine west coast climate: rainy climate, with cool winters and only slightly warmer summers

maritime polar: air mass that forms over the Pacific Ocean and brings cool air in the summer and heavy snow in the winter

maritime tropical: warm, moist air mass that forms over the ocean near the equator

mass: amount of matter in an object

mass number: total number of protons and neutrons in an atom

mass wasting: downhill movement of sediments caused by gravity

matter: anything that has mass and takes up space

mature river: river that has been developing for thousands of years

meander (mee-AN-der): loop in a river

mechanical weathering: weathering process in which rocks are broken down into small pieces without changing their chemical makeup

Mediterranean climate: climate with cool wet winters and only slightly warmer but dry summers

meltwater: stream of water formed by the melting of ice as a valley glacier moves

Mercator projection: representation of the curved surface of the earth on a flat piece of paper, in which direction and shape are accurate but size and distance are distorted

meridian (muh-RIHD-ee-uhn): line on a map or globe between the points that represent the geographic North and South poles of the earth

Mesosaurus (meh-soh-SAWR-uhs): extinct reptile that swam in freshwater ponds, lakes, and rivers

mesosphere (MEHS-uh-sfir): layer of the atmosphere that extends from the stratopause to an altitude of about 80 kilometers

Mesozoic (mehs-uh-ZOH-ihk) **Era:** period of geologic time that began about 225 million years ago and ended about 65 million years ago

metal: element that is shiny, able to conduct heat and electricity, malleable, and ductile

metamorphic (meht-uh-MOR-fihk) **rock:** rock formed when sedimentary or igneous rocks are changed by heat, pressure, or chemical reaction

metamorphism (meht-uh-MOR-fihz-uhm): changing of one type of rock into another as a result of tremendous heat, great pressure, or chemical reactions

meteor (MEET-ee-uhr): streak of light made of hot gases produced by a burning meteoroid in the earth's atmosphere

meteorite: meteoroid that strikes the earth's surface

meteoroid (MEET-ee-uh-roid): solid, rocklike object that may strike the earth's atmosphere

meteorologist (meet-ee-uh-RAHL-uh-jihst): scientist who studies the weather

meteorology (mee-tee-uh-RAHL-uh-jee): study of the earth's atmosphere, weather, and climate

meter: basic unit of length in the metric system

methane: poisonous gas made of hydrogen and carbon

metric system: common system of measurement

microclimate: very localized climate

midocean ridge: large system of underwater mountains

Milky Way Galaxy: galaxy in which the earth's solar system is located

mineral: naturally occurring substance formed in the earth

mixture: two or more substances physically combined

Moho: boundary between the earth's outermost layer and the mantle

moist continental climate: climate with very cold winters and very hot summers

moist subtropical climate: climate with cool mild winters and hot moist summers

mold: fossil formed in a rock by a dissolved organism that leaves an empty space, showing its outward shape

molecule (MAHL-uh-kyool): smallest part of any substance that still has all the properties of that substance

monsoon (mahn-SOON): major seasonal land and sea breeze

moraine: ridge of till left behind by a retreating glacier

mountain: natural landform that reaches high elevations

mountain belt: group of mountain ranges and mountain systems

mountain range: roughly parallel series of mountains that have the same general shape and structure

mountain soil: soil found on the slopes of mountain ranges that contains very small amounts of clay and sand and often no topsoil

mountain system: group of mountain ranges in one area

natural resource: material removed from the earth and used by people

navigation satellite: artificial satellite that sends information to pilots and sailors to help them determine their exact location within seconds

neap tide: lower high tide than normal that occurs during the first- and last-quarter phases of the moon

nebula (NEHB-yuh-luh): gas and dust cloud

nebular theory: theory that states that the solar system began as a huge cloud of dust and gas called a nebula

nekton (NEHK-tahn): forms of ocean life that swim

neritic (nuh-RIHT-ihk) **zone:** ocean area that extends from the low-tide line to the end of a continental shelf

neutron: subatomic particle with no electric charge

neutron star: smallest type of star that results from the supernova of a massive star

new moon: phase of the moon when it is not visible in the sky

nitrate (NIGH-trayt): nitrogen compound

nodule: potato-sized lump of mineral on the ocean floor

nonmetal: mineral that is not shiny, malleable, or ductile and is a poor conductor of heat and electricity

nonrenewable resource: natural resource that cannot be replaced by nature

normal fault: fault formed when the hanging wall moves down relative to the foot wall

nova: star that suddenly greatly increases in brightness and soon after slowly becomes dimmer

nuclear fission: process in which atoms of uranium are split in a nuclear reactor

nuclear fusion: process in which hydrogen atoms are fused to form helium atoms

nucleus (NOO-klee-uhs): center of an atom

nutrient (NOO-tree-uhnt): chemical substance necessary for plant growth

occluded front: type of front that occurs when a cold front overtakes a warm front, pushes it upward, and meets cool air
ocean-floor spreading: process in which the ocean floor on either side of a rift valley is pushed away by lava that erupts from the rift valley and forms new ocean floor
oceanic crust: section of the earth's crust under the ocean floor
oceanographer (oh-shuh-NAHG-ruh-fuhr): scientist who studies the ocean
oceanography (oh-shun-NAHG-ruh-fee): study of the earth's oceans, including their physical features, life forms, and natural resources
open cluster: large, loosely organized group of stars
orbit: path an object in space takes while traveling around another object
ore: rock deposit that contains minerals that can be mined at a profit
organic: composed of material that is or was living
organic material: material that was once living or was formed by the activity of living organisms
outer core: liquid layer of the earth surrounding the inner core
outwash plain: sediments deposited by rivers of glacial meltwater in a fan-shaped area in front of a terminal moraine
oxbow lake: small lake formed when a bend in a river is cut off from the river
oxidation (ahk-suh-DAY-shuhn): process in which oxygen chemically combines with another substance
ozone: molecule made of three atoms of oxygen

Paleozoic (pay-lee-uh-ZOH-ihk) **Era:** period of geologic time that began about 570 million years ago and ended about 225 million years ago
Pangaea (pan-JEE-uh): one large landmass of which all the continents were once a part, according to the theory of continental drift
parallax (PAR-uh-laks): apparent change in the position of a star in the sky due to the change in the earth's position as it moves around the sun
parallel: line from east to west across a map or globe
peat: soft substance made of decayed plant fibers; softest type of coal
penumbra (pih-NUHM-bruh): outer area of a shadow cast by one object in space onto another object in space in which the light is only partly blocked
perigee (PEHR-uh-jee): point of the moon's orbit closest to the earth
period: division of geologic time that is smaller than an era but larger than an epoch
period of revolution: time it takes a planet to make one orbit around the sun
period of rotation: time it takes for a planet to turn once on its axis
permeable (PER-mee-uh-buhl): able to be passed through by a substance
petrified (PEHT-ruh-fighd): having turned to stone
petrochemical: useful chemical derived from petroleum
petroleum: liquid fossil fuel; oil
petrologist (pih-TRAHL-uh-jihst): scientist who studies rocks and their mineral composition
photosphere: innermost layer of the sun's atmosphere
physical change: change in a substance that does not produce a new kind of substance
physical property: property of a substance that can be determined without changing the substance into a new kind of substance
plain: flat land area not far above sea level
plankton (PLANGK-tuhn): small organisms that float at or near the ocean's surface
plasma: very high energy phase of matter
plasticity (plas-TIHS-uh-tee): ability of a solid to flow
plateau (pla-TOH): broad, flat area of land that rises more than 600 meters above sea level
Polaris (poh-LAR-ihs): North Star
polarity (poh-LAR-uh-tee): property of a molecule with oppositely charged ends
polar zone: climate zone in each hemisphere that extends from the pole to about 60° latitude
pollutant: harmful or unwanted substance
pore space: space between soil particles
porphyry (POR-fuhr-ee): igneous rock whose cooling rate has changed and thus has two or more different-sized crystals
prairie soil: very rich, fertile soil that is excellent for growing crops
Precambrian (pree-KAM-bree-uhn) **Era:** earliest time period in geologic time
precipitation (prih-sihp-uh-TAY-shuhn): process in which water returns to the earth in the form of rain, snow, sleet, or hail
prevailing wind: wind that blows more often from one direction than from any other direction
primary wave: fastest type of seismic wave, which can travel through solids, liquids, and gases
prime meridian: meridian that runs through Greenwich, England, at 0° longitude
principle of uniformitarianism: principle that states that the processes that act on the earth's surface today are the same as the processes that have acted on the earth's surface in the past
prism: piece of glass that bends light so that it forms a spectrum
projection: a representation of a three-dimensional object on a flat surface
prominence (PRAHM-uh-nuhns): solar storm in the form of huge bright arches or loops of gas

proton: positively charged subatomic particle
protoplanet: early stage of a planet
protostar: new star
protosun: newborn sun
pulsar: neutron star that gives off pulses of radio waves
purification (PYOOR-uh-fih-kay-shuhn): process by which water is cleaned so that it is usable
P wave: primary wave

quasar (KWAY-zahr): quasi-stellar radio source; starlike object that gives off radio waves

radiant energy: energy from the sun
radiation: transfer of heat energy in the form of waves
radioactive element: element whose atoms have an unstable nucleus, which decays
red shift: shift toward the red end of the spectrum of a star moving away from the earth
reflecting telescope: optical telescope in which a series of mirrors gather light from the stars
refracting telescope: optical telescope in which a series of lenses are used to focus and magnify light from the stars
regional metamorphism: type of metamorphism that occurs over large areas when rocks buried deep within the earth are changed by increases in temperature and pressure
relative age: age of anything compared to the age of something else
relative humidity: percentage of moisture the air holds relative to the amount it can hold at a particular temperature
relief: difference in elevations within a landscape region
renewable resource: natural resource that can be replaced by nature
reservoir (REHZ-uhr-vwahr): artificial lake where fresh water is stored
residual (rih-ZIHJ-oo-uhl) **soil:** soil that remains on top of its parent rock
retrograde motion: rotation of a planet on its axis from east to west, which is the reverse motion of most planets
reverse fault: fault formed when the hanging wall moves up relative to the foot wall
Richter scale: measure of the amount of energy an earthquake releases
rift valley: valley formed when the block of land between two normal faults slides downward; deep crack in an underwater mountain system
rille: long valley on the moon
Ring of Fire: major earthquake and volcano zone that extends nearly all the way around the edge of the Pacific Ocean
rock cycle: continuous changing of rocks from one type to another
root-pry: mechanical weathering process caused by plant roots growing in a crack in a rock

salinity (suh-LIHN-uh-tee): amount of dissolved salts in ocean water
sand bar: long underwater ridge of sand
sand dune: mound of sand deposited by wind
satellite: natural or artificial object in space orbiting another object in space; moon
scale: comparison of a distance on a map or globe to actual distance on the earth's surface
scientific method: basic steps used by scientists in solving problems and uncovering facts
scientific satellite: artificial satellite that sends valuable scientific data to scientists
sea breeze: flow of air from the sea to the land
sea cave: hollowed-out portion of a sea cliff
sea cliff: steep face of rock produced by wave erosion
seamount: underwater mountain that rises more than 1000 meters above the surrounding ocean floor
sea stack: column of resistant rock left standing after waves have eroded a sea cliff
secondary wave: type of seismic wave that can travel through solids but not through liquids and gases
sediment (SEHD-uh-muhnt): small pieces of rocks, shells, or the remains of plants and animals that have been carried along and deposited by wind, water, or ice
sedimentary (sehd-uh-MEHN-tuhr-ee) **rock:** rock formed from sediments that have been pressed and cemented together
seismic (SIGHZ-mihk) **wave:** shock wave produced by an earthquake
seismogram (SIGHZ-muh-gram): seismograph's record of seismic waves
seismograph (SIGHZ-muh-graf): instrument that detects and measures seismic waves
seismologist: scientist who studies earthquakes
shearing: type of stress that causes a rock to twist or tear apart by pushing on the rock in two opposite directions
shield: large area of very old rock exposed at the surface
shield volcano: gently sloping, dome-shaped volcano composed almost entirely of quiet lava flows
sill: sheetlike mass of igneous rock
smog: thick cloud of pollutants
soft water: water that does not contain many minerals
soil profile: cross section of soil horizons
solar cell: device that transforms light energy directly into electricity; also called a photovoltaic cell

solar eclipse: eclipse of the sun that occurs when the moon is directly between the sun and the earth

solar energy: energy obtained from the sun

solar flare: solar storm in the form of bursts of light on the sun's surface

solar system: earth and other eight planets that travel around the sun

solar wind: continuous stream of high-energy particles released from the corona of the sun into space

solid: phase of matter that has a definite shape and volume

soluble (SAHL-yoo-buhl): able to be dissolved in water

solution: mixture on the molecular level of two or more substances

solvent (SAHL-vuhnt): substance in which another substance dissolves

sonar: sound navigation and ranging; echo-sounding instrument used to measure depth underwater

specific gravity: ratio of the mass of a substance to the mass of an equal volume of water

spectroscope: instrument that breaks up the light from a star into its characteristic colors

spectrum: band of colors formed when light passes through a prism

spiral galaxy: type of galaxy that is made of a thick mass of material and flattened arms that spiral around the center

spit: sand bar, or long underwater ridge, connected to the curving shoreline

spring tide: higher high tide that occurs during the full- and new-moon phases

stable rock: rock that has the ability to resist chemical weathering

stalactite (stuh-LAK-tight): iciclelike deposit hanging from the ceiling of a cavern, usually made of limestone

stalagmite (stuh-LAG-might): iciclelike deposit built up on the floor of a cavern, usually made of limestone

stationary front: type of front that forms when a mass of warm air meets a mass of cold air and no movement occurs

steppe climate: climate that receives only slightly more precipitation than does the desert climate

stock: intrusion similar to a batholith that has an exposed area of less than 100 square kilometers

strata (STRAYT-uh): layers of sedimentary rocks

stratopause (STRAT-uh-pawz): zone in the stratosphere in which the temperature is at its highest

stratosphere (STRAT-uh-sfir): layer of the atmosphere that extends from the tropopause to an altitude of about 50 kilometers

stratus cloud: gray, smooth cloud that forms at an altitude of about 2.5 kilometers

streak: color of the powder left by a mineral when it is rubbed against a hard, rough surface

stress: push-pull force

subduction (suhb-DUHK-shuhn): process in which the ocean floor plunges back into the interior of the earth through a trench

submarine canyon: deep V-shaped valley cut in hard rock through the continental shelf or slope

submersible: underwater research vessel

subsoil: soil in the B horizon made mostly of clay and some humus

summer solstice (SAHL-stihs): time of year when the Northern Hemisphere has its longest day and the Southern Hemisphere has its shortest day

sunspot: storm in the lower atmosphere of the sun that appears as dark spots on the sun's surface

supergiant star: star with a diameter up to 1000 times that of the sun

supernova: tremendous explosion in which a star breaks apart, releasing energy

surface current: ocean current caused mainly by wind patterns

surface runoff: water entering a river or stream after a heavy rain or during a spring thaw of snow or ice

surface wave: slowest type of seismic wave

surface zone: area in the ocean where water is mixed by waves and currents

S wave: secondary wave

syncline (SIHN-klighn): downward fold in a rock

talus (TAY-luhs) **slope:** pile of rock fragments at the base of a mountain or on a mountain slope

tar pit: large pool of tar

tectonics (tehk-TAHN-ihks): branch of earth science that deals with the movements that shape the earth's crust

temperate zone: climate zone in each hemisphere that extends from about 30° to 60° latitude

temperature inversion (ihn-VER-zhuhn): atmospheric condition in which a layer of cool air containing pollutants is trapped under a layer of warm air

tension: type of stress that pulls rocks apart

terrace: flat platform formed at the base of a sea cliff as the sea cliff erodes

terracing: making a slope into a series of level steps for planting to prevent soil erosion

texture: size of individual soil particles

theory: most logical explanation for events that happen in nature

theory of continental drift: theory that says that all of the present-day continents were joined together in one large landmass, which split apart, and the continents drifted to their present positions

theory of plate tectonics: theory that combines the ideas of continental drift and ocean-floor spreading to explain the formation of the earth's crust and its movements
thermocline (THER-muh-klighn): area of rapid temperature change in the ocean
thermosphere (THER-muh-sfir): outermost layer of the atmosphere where the air is very thin
thrust fault: fault formed when compression causes the hanging wall to slide over the foot wall
tide: rise and fall of the oceans caused by the moon's gravitational pull on the earth
till: rocks and debris deposited directly by a glacier
time zone: longitudinal belt of the earth in which all areas have the same local time
topographic map: map that shows the different shapes and sizes of a land surface
topography (tuh-PAHG-ruh-fee): shape of the earth's surface
topsoil: soil in the A horizon that is made mostly of humus and other organic materials
total eclipse: total blocking out of the moon when the moon passes through the umbra of the earth's shadow
trace fossil: mark or evidence of the activities of an organism
transform boundary: transform fault where two plates grind and slide past one another
transported soil: soil that is moved from its place of origin
trench: deep V-shaped valley along the ocean floor
tributary (TRIHB-yoo-tehr-ee): large stream that joins rills and gullies to the main river
trilobite: insect- or lobsterlike animal with jointed legs whose extinction marks the end of the Paleozoic Era
tropical soil: soil in warm, humid climates formed from the rapid decay of plants and animals
tropical zone: climate zone in each hemisphere that extends from about 30° latitude to the equator
tropopause (TRAHP-uh-pawz): zone in the atmosphere that divides the troposphere from the stratosphere
troposphere (TRAHP-uh-sfir): lowest layer of the earth's atmosphere
trough (TRAWF): lowest point of a wave
tsunami (tsoo-NAH-mee): giant ocean wave caused by an earthquake
tundra soil: soil found in the polar regions that has peat on the surface and very limited subsoil
turbidity (ter-BIHD-uh-tee) **current:** flow of water down the continental slope that is very dense because of the sediments it carries

umbra (UHM-bruh): inner area of a shadow cast by one object in space onto another object in space in which the light is completely blocked out
unconformity (uhn-kuhn-FOR-muh-tee): eroded rock surface, pushed up from deeper within the earth, that is much older than the new rock layers above it
unfoliated: texture of some metamorphic rocks in which crystals are not arranged in bands and do not break in layers
upwelling: rising of deep cold currents to the ocean surface

valley glacier: long, narrow glacier that moves downhill between the steep sides of a mountain valley
Van Allen radiation belt: band of high radiation around the earth that captures particles given off by the sun
variable: factor being tested in an experiment
variable star: star with a brightness that varies
vent: opening in a volcano from which lava erupts
vernal equinox: first day of spring
vertebrate (VER-tuh-brayt): animal with a backbone
volcanic ash: rock particles more than 0.25 millimeters but less than 5 millimeters in diameter that are blown into the air during volcanic eruptions
volcanic bomb: rock particle from a few centimeters to several meters in diameter that is blown into the air during volcanic eruptions
volcanic dust: very fine particles of rock fragments that are blown into the air during volcanic eruptions
volcano: place where lava reaches the earth's surface
volume: amount of space an object takes up
waning-crescent (KREHS-uhnt): phase of the moon between one-half and new moon when the lighted area of the moon appears to grow smaller
waning-gibbous (GIHB-uhs): phase of the moon between full and one-half when the lighted area of the moon appears to grow smaller
warm front: type of front that forms when a mass of warm air overtakes a mass of cold air and moves over it
water cycle: continuous movement of water from the oceans and freshwater sources to the air and land and then back to the oceans
watershed: land area in which runoff drains into a river or a system of rivers and streams
water table: level below which the ground is saturated
wavelength: horizontal distance between two consecutive crests or troughs

waxing-crescent: phase of the moon between the new moon and one-half moon when the lighted area of the moon appears to grow larger

waxing-gibbous: phase of the moon between one-half and full when the lighted area of the moon appears to grow larger

weathering: breaking down of rocks and other materials on the earth's surface

weather satellite: satellite that takes pictures of weather patterns all around the world

weight: measure of the gravitational attraction between objects

white dwarf: small, very dense star

wind: movement of air

windbreak: rows of trees planted between fields of crops to prevent wind erosion of soil

windward side: the side of a mountain that faces toward the wind

winter solstice: time of year when the Northern Hemisphere has its shortest day and the Southern Hemisphere has its longest day

zone of aeration (ehr-AY-shuhn): underground region in which the pore spaces are filled mostly with air

zone of saturation (sach-uh-RAY-shuhn): underground region in which all the pore spaces are filled with water

Index

Photograph Credits

i Ed Cooper; **ii** David Muench/David Muench Photograph; **v** NASA; **vi** top: E.R. Degginger; bottom: Michael and Barbara Reed/Earth Scenes; **vii** John Bowden/*Discover* magazine; **viii** C.C. Lockwood/Bruce Coleman; **2** NASA; **4** Pete Turner; **6** Zig Leszczynski/Earth Scenes; **8** Laura Riley/Bruce Coleman; **13** left: Ken Sakamota/Black Star; top right: E.R. Degginger; bottom right: DPI; **16** Ken Karp; **18** NASA; **19** top: Stan Osolinski/The Stock Market; bottom: Angelo Giampiccolo/FPG; **20** Ken Karp; **21** top right top: Hale Observatories; top right bottom: Gary Ladd/Photo Researchers; bottom left: Hans Uehrenberg/Hansen Planetarium; bottom right: NASA; **23** left: Shorty Wilcox/Wilcox Collection; right: National Astronomy and Ionosphere Center; **24** top left: Rodney Jones; right: Rodney Jones; bottom: Ken Karp; **30** NASA; **32** Dennis de Cicco/Peter Arnold; **33** Hale Observatory; **36** Center for Astrophysics; **38** top left: Lick Observatory; bottom left: U.S. Naval Observatory; right: NASA; **39** Kitt Peak Observatory/Aura Inc.; **40** Lund Observatory; **41** left: Hale Observatories; right; NASA; **42** top: R.B. Minton; bottom: Lick Observatory; **46** Ken Karp; **51** NASA; **52** NASA; **53** Lick Observatory; **55** Lick Observatory; **57** NASA; **62** NASA; **67** NASA; **68** NASA; **72** Joel Gordon/DPI; **73** NASA; **76** left: NASA; right: NASA; **77** JPL/CIT/NASA; **78** NASA; **79** NASA;**80** NASA; **81** top: NASA; center: NASA; bottom: NASA; **82** NASA; **83** top: NASA; bottom: NASA; **87** Breck P. Kent/Earth Scenes; **89** top: Kitt Peak National Observatory/Aura, Inc.; bottom: British Museum; **97** top: David Sumner/The Stock Market; bottom: Steve Vidler/Leo deWys: **98** NASA; **101** top: J. Alex Langley/DPI; bottom: Melinda Berge/Photographers Aspen; **102** William E. Ferguson; **104** top: NASA; center: NASA; bottom: NASA; **105** top: Dodge/DPI; bottom: Robert Comport/Earth Scenes; **106** top: NASA; bottom: NASA; **108** Lick Observatory; **111** top: A. Kalnik/Photo Researchers; bottom: D. Zirinsky/Photo Researchers; **116** AP/Wide World Photos: **117** Vera A. Lentz/Visions; **118** NASA; **119** NASA; **120** E.R. Degginger; **122** Spencer Swanger/Tom Stack & Assoc.; **124** Wendell Metzen/Bruce Coleman; **125** top: Patricia Agre/Photo Researchers; bottom: Barbara Docktor/Leo deWys; **126** left: Ron Sefton/DPI; right: Ken Karp; **127** J. Alex Langley/DPI; **128** top left: Lenore Weber/Taurus Photos; top center: E.R. Degginger; top right: Ian R. Gilbert/DPI; bottom: NASA; **129** Ken Kay/DPI; **130** Dan McCoy/Rainbow; **132** left: Clay Kelton/Peter Arnold; right: Norman O. Tomalin/Bruce Coleman; **136** Paul Shainbroom/Photo Researchers; **137** left: Tom McHugh/Photo Researchers; center: Herbert Lanks/Monkmeyer Press; right: R. Dias/H. Armstrong Roberts; **139** left: Robert D. Rubic/DPI; right: Tom Myers/DPI; **144** Fred Ward/Black Star; **146** top: E.R. Degginger; center: E.R. Degginger; bottom: Stephanie Ferguson/William E. Ferguson; **147** top left: Breck P. Kent/Earth Scenes; top right: Breck P. Kent/Earth Scenes; top right bottom:Jane Burton/Bruce Coleman; bottom top: Dave Spier/Tom Stack; bottom bottom: John Gerard/DPI; **148** top left: Breck P. Kent/Earth Scenes; top right: G.R. Roberts; bottom: Charles R. Belinky/Photo Researchers; **150** left: E.R. Degginger; top right: E.R. Degginger; bottom right: Karen Tompkins/Tom Stack; **151** top left: E.R. Degginger; top right: Breck P. Kent; top right bottom: Runk/Schoenberger/Grant Heilman; bottom: Brian Parker/Tom Stack; **152** top left: Breck P. Kent; top center: E.R. Degginger; top right: Breck P. Kent; left center: E.R. Degginger; left bottom: Breck P. Kent/Earth Scenes; **154** left: Ken Karp; right: Ken Karp; **155** Steve Vicler/Leo deWys; **156** courtesy of Carolina biological Supply Company; **157** left: Breck P. Kent/Earth Scenes; center: Breck P. Kent; right: John Cancalosi/Tom Stack; **158** top to bottom: Charles R. Belinky/Photo Researchers; Breck P. Kent; Breck P. Kent, Breck P. Kent; Breck P. Kent/Earth Scenes; **160** left: E.R. Degginger; right: Arthur Levine/Leo deWys; **161** top to bottom: Breck P. Kent/Earth Scenes; Breck P. Kent; E.R. Degginger; Breck P. Kent; E.R. Degginger; E.R. Degginger; E.R. Degginger; **166** Frank Sleksandowicz/Int'l Stock Photo, Ltd.; **168** top: John Gerlach/Tom Stack; left: Breck P. Kent; right: Phil Degginger; **170** top: E.R. Degginger; left: Tom Bean/Tom Stack; right: E.R. Degginger; **171** top: Stephanie F. Ferguson/William E. Ferguson; left: Monty Monsees/DPI; right: Milton Rand/Tom Stack; **172** top left: Lynn M. Stone/Earth Scenes; top center: E.R. Degginger; top right: E.R. Degginger/Earth Scenes; bottom left: E.R. Degginger; bottom center: Runk/Schoenberger/Grant Heilman; bottom right: Breck P. Kent/Earth Scenes; **173** top left: Al Merrill/Breck P. Kent; top right: William E. Ferguson; bottom top: E.R. Degginger; bottom bottom: G.R. Roberts; **175** G.R. Roberts; **176** left: Rathbone/Monkmeyer Press; right: Tom Bean/DRK Photo; **177** G.R. Roberts; **178** Brian Parker/Tom Stack; **179** Breck P. Kent/Earth Scenes; **180** top: Len Rue, Jr./DPI; bottom: Phil Degginger; **181** Lynn Stone/Earth Scenes; **182** John Gerlach/Tom Stack; **183** left: Nadine Gradona/Tom Stack; center: John Shelton, right: Bob McKeever/Tom Stack; **185** left and right: Hubbard Scientific; **186** top left and right: Hubbard Scientific; bottom left and right: Hubbard Scientific; **188** Ken Karp; **192** left: Michael Elias; right: Jack Edmond/MIT/Courtesy Woods Hole Oceanographic Institution; **193** left: Jack Donnelly/Courtesy Woods Hole Oceanographic Institution; right: Courtesy of Colleen Cavanaugh; **196** Michael and Barbara Reed/Earth Scenes; **198** Henry T. Kaiser/Leo deWys; **200** National Geophysical Data Center; **204** left: E.R. Degginger/Earth Scenes; right: Woods Hole Oceanographic Institution; **207** Yoram Kahana/Peter Arnold; **208** Ken Karp; **212** The Granger Collection; **215** top: David C. Fritts/Earth Scenes; bottom: David C. Rentz/Bruce Coleman; **217** John Lemker/Earth Scenes; **218** R. Ingo Riepl/Earth Scenes; **219** Larry V. Smith/DPI; **220** top: Robert M. Frank/DPI; bottom: S. Vidler/Leo deWys; **225** NASA; **226** Gunnar/Bruce Coleman; **231** United States Geological Survey; **232** United States Geological Survey; **233** United States Geological Survey; **238** Stone Flower Studio/DPI; **240** left: John Lemker/Earth Scenes; right: NASA; **243** George Dodge/DPI; **244** left: Charlie Ott/DPI; right: Betty Groskin/Monkmeyer Press; **245** John Eastcott/Yva Momatiuk/DRK Photo; **246** Gary W. Griffin/Earth Scenes; **248** Paul Stephanus/DPI; **249** left: Monty Monsees/DPI; right: Charlie Ott/DPI; **250** DPI; **254** Runk/Schoenberger/Grant Heilman; **255** Fiona Sunquist/Tom Stack; **257** Michael Baytoff/Black Star; **262** Bruce Robinson; **266** Leverett Bradley/DPI; **267** Robert Ballard/Woods Hole Oceanographic Institution; **268** Steve Solum/Bruce Coleman; **269** F.G. Love; **272** David L. Shogren/Tom Stack; **273** Nicholas Devore/DPI; **275** "Carte Du Fond Des Oceans" by Tanugy de Remur/© Hachette-Guides Bleus; **276** bottom top: Nicholas deVore/Bruce Coleman; bottom bottom: Adam Woolfitt/Woodfin Camp; **277** Kim Taylor/Bruce Coleman; **278** top left: R. Sefton/DPI; top right: Ron and Valerie Taylor/Bruce Coleman; bottom top: R. Sefton/DPI; bottom bottom: Joy R. Wilson/DPI; **280** C.C. Lockwood/Bruce Coleman; **283** Tony Arruza/Bruce Coleman; **288** S.J. Krasemann/Peter Arnold; **294** DPI; **296** NASA; **297** top left: NASA; top right: George Gerster/Photo Researchers; bottom: Thomas Nebbia/DPI; **299** Wayne Lankinen; **302** top top: Dennis Maisel/DPI; top bottom: R. Ingo Riepl/Earth Scenes; bottom left to right: Roger J. Cheng; **303** Keith Gunnar/Bruce Coleman; **304** top: Gerald A. Corsi/Tom Stack; bottom: Barry Runk/Grant Heilman; **305** left: John McGrail/Wheeler Pictures; right: Ted Jones/DPI; **306** Roger H. Cheng/SUNY; **309** NASA; **311** NASA; **316** top: Anita Brosius; **316–317** William Haxby/Lamont-Doherty Geological Observatory; **318** Fred Ward/Black Star; **319** Jeffrey D. Smith/Woodfin Camp; **320** John Bowden/*Discover* magazine; **322** Bill Bachman/Photo Researchers; **324** left: E.R. Degginger; right: Ray Mathis/The Stock Market; **330** Runk/Schoenberger/Grant Heilman; **331** Sharon Green/The Stock Market; **335** Stephen J. Krasemann/DRK Photo; **336** left: Herman J. Kokojan/Black Star; right: David W. Hamilton/The Image Bank; **337** NASA; **338** top: Gene Moore; bottom left: J. Alex Langley/DPI; bottom right: Stephen J. Krasemann/DRK Photo; **341** top left to right: G.R. Roberts; Dr. E.R. Degginger; Grant Heilman; **342** John Running/Black Star; **343** Runk/Schoenberger/Grant Heilman; **344** NOAA/NESDIS; **345** top: NOAA/NESDIS; bottom: NOAA/NESDIS; **346** Yvonne Freund/Earth Scenes; **347** NOAA; **348** left: DPI; right: Everett C. Johnson/Leo deWys; **349** Jack McConnell/DPI; **354** John Colwell/Grant Heilman; **355** Jim Brandenburg/Woodfin Camp; **362** left: Don Smetzer/Click/Chicago; right: Naideau/The Stock Market; **363** top: D. Fishman/Click/Chicago; bottom: Jadwiga Lopez/Click/Chicago; **365** Geoff Juckes/The Stock Market; **368** left: David C. Fritts/Earth Scenes; right: Arthur Gloor/Earth Scenes; **369** top: Zig Leszczynski/Earth Scenes; bottom: Dr. E.R. Degginger; **372** left: Jack Wilburn/Earth Scenes; right: David M. Dennis/Tom Stack & Assoc.; **373** Robert Frerck/Woodfin Camp; **374** Zig Leszczynski/Earth Scenes; **375** John Gerlach/Tom Stack & Assoc.; **377** Brent Petersen/The Stock Market; **379** Craig Aurness/Woodfin Camp; **384** National Park Service; **386** Norman R. Thompson/Taurus Photos; **387** G.R. Roberts; **388** top: Ken Kay/Time Life Books, Inc.; center: Ken Kay/Time Life Books, Inc.; bottom: Tom Stack; **389** left: Phil Farnes/Photo Researchers; right: Richard W. Tolbert/DPI; bottom: Jirak/Monkmeyer Press; **390** Charlie Ott/DPI; **391** top: Grant Heilman; bottom left: John Eastcott/Yva Momatiuk/DRK Photo; bottom right: John S. Shelton; **392** top: Townsend, P. Dickinson/Photo Researchers; bottom: Townsend, P. Dickinson/Photo Researchers; **394** top: John S. Shelton; center: USDA; bottom: USDA; **396** USDA; **397** top: Walter Dawn; bottom: Carolina Biological Supply Company; **399** E.R. Degginger/Earth Scenes; **400** top: Luray Parker/USDA Forest Service Photo; bottom: Richard W. Tolbert/DPI; **401** left: Joel W. Rogers/Earth Images; right: Johnston/DPI; bottom: William E. Ferguson; **406** Chester Christian/Alpha; **408** Cameron Davidson/Bruce Coleman; **409** top: G.R. Roberts; bottom: Gary Milburn/Tom Stack; **410** G.R. Roberts; **411** top top: Spencer Swanger/Tom Stack; top bottom: Bob Smith/Int'l Stock Photo, Ltd.; bottom left: L.L. T. Rhodes/Taurus Photos; bottom right: Anthony Bannister/Earth Scenes; **412** G.R. Roberts; **413** Judith Aronson/Peter Arnold; **414** Roz Joseph/Omni Photo Comm.; **415** NASA; **416** left: N. Haynes/Monkmeyer Press; right: Charlie Ott/DPI; **417** Hubbard Scientific; **418** top: Tim McCabe/Soil Conservation Service/USDA; bottom left: Mike Andrews/Earth Scenes; bottom right: C.C. Lockwood/Earth Scenes; **419** Breck P. Kent/Earth Scenes; **420** left: The Stone Flower Studio/DPI; right: DPI; **421** Helmut Gritscher/Peter Arnold; **422** top: E.R. Degginger; bottom: V.J. Cioffi; **423** top: S. Chester/Tom Stack; bottom: Michael P. Gadomski/Bruce Coleman; **424** top: Richard W. Tolbert/DPI; bottom: Lynn M. Stone/Earth Scenes; **425** left: DPI; right: E.R. Degginger; **426** left: Jan Taylor/Bruce Coleman; right: Werney Stoy/Camera/DPI; **428** United States Geological Survey; **429** United States Geological Survey; **434** left: Joanne Simpson; right: David W. Hamilton/The Image Bank; **435** NASA; **436** center: San Diego Historical Society/Ticor Collection; **436–437** Ken Nahoun/The Stock Market; **438** C.C. Lockwood/Bruce Coleman; **440** Steven C. Kaufman/Peter Arnold; **442** Breck P. Kent/Earth Scenes; **444** top: Doug Wechsler/Earth Scenes; bottom: G.R. Roberts; **445** William E. Ferguson; **446** Hubbard Scientific; **447** Charlie Ott/DPI; **448** top: G.R.Roberts; bottom: G.R. Roberts; **449** Jay Lurie/Bruce Coleman; **450** Tom Till/Int'l Stock Photo, Ltd.; **451** USGS/EROS; **458** Peter Turnley/Black Star; **460** top: James H. Karales/Peter Arnold; bottom: William Felger/Grant Heilman; **464** EROS Data Center; **465** Chuck O'Rear/West Light; **466** J.C. Ratte/USGS; **467** top to bottom: Gary Rosenquist/Earth Images; **468** top: Stephanie S. Ferguson/William E. Ferguson; bottom: William E. Ferguson; **469** left: Jerry Frank/DPI; center: Thomas Nebbia/Woodfin Camp; right: G.R. Roberts; **470** top: Antonio Ernazza/Leo deWys; bottom: Yoram Kahana/Peter Arnold; **476** USGS/EROS; **478** J. Fennel/Bruce Coleman; **480** top: NASA/Grant Heilman; bottom: Kinne/Photo Researchers; **483** John S. Shelton; **487** Marie Tharp-Rebecca/M. Espinosa; **488** Craig Aurness/West Light; **498** top: J. Bapis; **498–499** M.P.L. Fogden/Bruce Coleman; **499** top left: C.C. Lockwood/Bruce Coleman; top right: M.P.L. Fogden/Bruce Coleman; **504** Breck P. Kent; **506** Breck P. Kent; **507** William E. Ferguson; **508** top: Ann Hagen Griffiths OPC; bottom: Ed Gerken/courtesy of Black Hills Institute of Geological Research Inc.; **509** Alan Pitcairn/Grant Heilman; **511** top: E.R. Degginger; bottom: Sullivan and Rogers/Bruce Coleman; **512** Breck P. Kent; **513** top: Bruce Coleman; bottom: Breck P. Kent; **516** G.R. Roberts; **524** John Eastcott/Leo deWys; **529** Fred Bavendam/Peter Arnold; **530** top: Vanderbes/Leo deWys; bottom: Breck P. Kent; **531** Ken Karp; **532** Nature; **533** John Cancalon/Tom Stack; **535** James David Brandt/Earth Scenes; **542** inset: Joe McNally/*Discover* magazine 10/84, Time Inc.; **543** Joe McNally/*Discover* magazine 10/84, Time Inc.; **544** Terry Husebye/*Discover* magazine 3/87, Time Inc.; **546** NASA; **548** Martin Rogers/Woodfin Camp; **550** left: Erich Hartmann/Magnum Photo; right: Milton Rand/Tom Stack; **552** Michael Patrick/Picture Group; **553** Mike Yashita/Woodfin Camp; **554** left: Steven C. Kaufman/Peter Arnold; right: Walley McNamee/Woodfin Camp; **555** Mike Andrews/Earth Scenes; **556** Tom Stack; **557** Victor Englebert/Photo Researchers; **559** Tom Stack; **560** Breck P. Kent/Earth Scenes; **562** top: Everett C. Johnson/Leo deWys; bottom: Ruth Black/Monkmeyer Press; **563** John Running; **565** G.R. Roberts; **566** Dan McKoy/Rainbow; **567** Los Alamos National Laboratory; **568** Rodney Jones; **572** NASA; **574** JPL; **576** J. Frederick Grassie; **577** left: Bob Evans/Peter Arnold; right: W.H.O.I.; **578** top: Ron Sherman/Bruce Coleman; bottom: Dr. Bruce Heezan/Lamont-Doherty/Scripps Institution of Oceanography; **579** left: Terry Domico/Earth Images; right: David Denning/Earth Images; **580** NASA; **581** top: NASA; bottom: NASA; **582** top: NASA; bottom: NASA; **583** top: NASA; bottom left: NASA; bottom right: NASA; **584** top: NASA; bottom: NASA; **585** D.E. Cox/Alpha; **590** Woods Hole Oceanographic Institution; **591** top: Sygma; bottom: Woods Hole Institution/Sygma; **592** Ted Spiegel/Black Star; **593** Roger J. Cheng/Atmospheric Sciences Research Center/State University of New York, Albany; **601–604** Artwork used with permission of *Astronomy* magazine, Kalmbach Publishing Co., Milwaukee, Wisconsin. Text illustrations by Lee Ames & Zak Ltd. with special acknowledgement to David Christensen.